Indo-Portuguese Diplomacy During the 16th and the 17th Centuries (1500-1663)

Afzal Ahmad

Originals
Delhi

First Published 2008

ISBN 978-81-8454-079-6

Published by
Originals
(an imprint of Low Price Publications)
A-6, Nimri Commercial Centre,
Near Ashok Vihar Phase-IV,
Delhi-110052
Phones: 27302453
e-mail: info@Lppindia.com
website: www.Lppindia.com

Printed at
D K Fine Art Press P Ltd.
Delhi-110052

PRINTED IN INDIA

Foreword

The arrival of the Portuguese in the Indian Ocean has usually been seen as one of the great turning points of history – the beginning of the period when first Western Europe and then the United States imposed their economic and political dominance on the world by force of arms. The instrument of this supremacy was, first and foremost, the armed warship of which the Portuguese *naus* were the earliest and in some ways the most impressive examples. The story of the foundation of the first European empire in the East has been endlessly and repetitively repeated, the exploits of Vasco da Gama, Cabral, Almeida and Albuquerque being told and retold as the centenaries of the Discoveries and the *Estado da India* come and go. In contrast the way the *Estado da India* grew and evolved during the sixteenth and seventeenth centuries is much less widely known.

There are difficulties in giving a coherent account of the *Estado da India* since it was a state like none other in history – indeed there is no consensus among historians on what terminology can be used to describe it. The *Estado da India* was originally conceived as sovereignty over the sea. The sea was claimed to be the domain of the king of Portugal, giving him the right to levy customs dues on goods entering and leaving his dominions, to issue passports and permits to travel, and to enforce royal monopolies and embargos. Initially this 'state' had little or no territory and depended on treaties made with friendly or coerced rulers. At the same time the king of Portugal claimed jurisdiction over all Christians east of the Tordesillas line by virtue of the papal Bulls which granted ecclesiastical privileges to the Order of Christ of which he was governor. This royal patronage over the Church (the *padroado real*) enabled the king of Portugal to make church appointments, collect church taxes, authorise church Councils and exercise jurisdiction over matters which fell within the remit of the ecclesiastical courts. Such wide ranging claims, not rooted in any territorial sovereignty, opened the way for subsequent European claims that the power of the state was in some way attached to the body of the subject and could be exercised wherever the subject might be.

Meanwhile historical debate focused on the economic impact of the Portuguese - some seeing the beginning of a new world economic order, others in contradiction stating that the economic activities of the Portuguese were small compared with the total volumes of eastern trade and their economic impact proportionally insignificant.

Although the Jesuit missions to the Mughal courts have always attracted a certain interest, there has been no detailed examination of Portugal's relations with the states of southern India in the years following the foundation of the *Estado da India.* This is a story dominated by the rise of Mughal power in the north and the decline and disintegration of the empire of Vijayanagara in the south. These seismic shifts in the power structures of India offered numerous opportunities to the Portuguese to expand their commercial interests and to increase their military and territorial control. As first Gujerat and then Bijapur were threatened by Mughal power, the Portuguese offered military aid in return for extensive territorial concessions in the *Provincia do Norte* and around Goa. With the decline of the power of Vijayanagara after the battle of Talikota in 1565, the Portuguese acquired control of the Kanara ports of Honovar, Mangalor and Barcelor which secured their supplies of rice and pepper. In Malabar Portuguese influence depended on the compliance of the smaller states like Cochin and Cranganor who depended on Portuguese support for protection against Calicut. Towards the end of the sixteenth century the Portuguese position was enormously strengthened when the ruler of Calicut fell out with the Kunjalis, the admirals who controlled the warships that protected Calicut. Together Calicut and the Portuguese were able to defeat and severely weaken Kunjali seapower.

However, just as Portugal appeared to have strengthened its military and commercial position along the whole western coast of India, the arrival of the Dutch and the English threatened to erode this carefully constructed political, military and commercial edifice. This was not immediately fatal for the Portuguese who were not finally driven from their strongholds in Malabar and

Kanara until the 1660s and continued to hold the *Provincia do Norte* and the Goan territories. However, the new power relations in the Indian Ocean forced the Portuguese to rethink their political relations with the Indians states and to adopt a more active and more sophisticated diplomacy.

Afzal Ahmad's book examines in detail the consequences for the *Estado da India* of the arrival of the northern Europeans. His book gives an account of the treaties and negotiations that led eventually to the loss of Kanara and Malabar but it also examines the cultural background to the diplomacy of the period. Indian diplomacy, like that of contemporary Europe, was highly ritualised. The protocols to be observed by ambassadors, which included elaborate court ceremonial and the giving of presents were all of great significance if diplomatic negotiations were to run smoothly. Effective diplomacy also needed to be backed by a steady flow of information and the book also examines the work of the agents and spies who provided the *Estado da India* with intelligence. There are surprises in this story, which serve to emphasise the extent to which this was a pre-nationalist era. Frequently the Portuguese employed professional Indian interpreters and negotiators while Portuguese priests and merchants might be employed as agents of the Indian rulers.

Two factors, in particular, tended to weaken Portuguese diplomacy. The tenure of viceroys was only three years and this was seldom long enough for serious diplomatic relations to be negotiated and stabilised. Viceroys frequently claimed not to be bound by agreements made by their predecessors. The semi-independent activity of the church could also undermine Portuguese diplomatic efforts. On the one hand missionaries could be a permanent presence in the Indians states, providing useful intelligence and personnel to act as interpreters or diplomats. On the other hand the missionary zeal of the ecclesiastical establishment might, and frequently did, lead to behaviour which outraged Hindu and Muslim sentiment and got in the way of smooth diplomatic relations.

This book takes us into relatively uncharted historical waters. It largely leaves to one side the European dimension of the struggle between the Portuguese and the Dutch and English companies and tries to see the *Estado da India* in its Indian context.

Malyn Newitt (King's College, University of London), 2007

Preface

The idea of working on this subject had come up over a decade ago when I started teaching diplomatic history of Portugal and noticed that there was a great dearth of work not only on Portuguese diplomatic relations with various states of Europe but there was hardly any attempt to study the Portuguese diplomatic relations with Asian empires, especially with the Indian, with which they had almost five hundred years of political, economical and social interactions. Although a few works could be counted on Portuguese Chinese diplomacy, written in Portuguese, which many researchers have repeatedly reproduced. Nevertheless, it appears, almost impossible even to imagine how historians and social scientists of the whole world who have dedicated more than three decades in researching variable subjects, recently, but none directly focussed on Indo-Portuguese diplomacy and the way this society evolved. On the contrary, most of the historians have been quite seriously involved in some unproductive debates on which they have not, so far, reached or appears that they will ever reach to any possible conclusion. The reason of not working on the topic in question may not, possibly, be ever unearthed. But I can assure one thing that it was certainly not due to the lack of documentation.

On the other hand, besides requirement of an elaborate work on Indo-Portuguese diplomacy, there have been some questions, directly related to the Indo-European history, which remained for long to be answered. We noticed that there are a number of misinterpretations by historians of this part of history, for over half a century, and especially, during the recent past. It could be considered, most possibly, due to the lack of proper knowledge which has overshadowed the socio-political society of India. Historians, whether intentionally or not, have made the people of India believe that it was due to the treachery of a Muslim *Subahdar*,

Mir Jafar, who betrayed his sovereign overlord, Siraj-ud-Daulah, in favour of English East India Company that India lost her Freedom. The history of Mir Jafar's deceitful alliance with the English against Siraj-uda-Daulah is quite known and taught in all the schools and at the levels in a way that has mined the Hindu Muslim sound relations and has caused much damages to the socio-political integrity of the country altogether. Nevertheless, it is to remind readers that the story of loss of India's freedom doesn't start with the devious act of Mir Jafar nor during his period. But, before indulging in this complicated discussion, I must make it clear that my intention here is not to accuse or remove the charge from any Indian ruler, whether he was Muslim or Hindu. On the contrary, the main objective, among others, of the present study is to clarify and shed some light over some part of Indo-European history of which, so far, very little is known.

Although, the present work may not exercise any influence on the mentality of those who do not tend to new findings but an attempt is being made to bring to light the history of the early Indo-European political and cultural interactions which was started through the exchanges of diplomacies, between the Portuguese and the rulers of South India since the late fifteenth century. In this regard, the area of study is confined to South Indian states of Malabar, the present Kerala state, keeping in mind that it was in this region that the foundation of European contacts, especially with Portugal was laid in the early sixteenth century and that was, later, expanded to the other areas of India. Portugal was soon joined by other European nations, such as Netherlands, England and France, in their quest for extra-European expansions.

In history, in general terms we don't have, at least I don't find any right to either blame or judge the way rulers in past, whether he was an Indian or of a foreign origin, ruled his territories, commanded his armies or whatever political blunders have done that might have turned out to be beneficial for one and disastrous for others. We can only analyse the facts and provide justifiable conclusions, in the light of available sources, although it may not be suitable to everyone's likings.

A few decades before, Pandit Sunderlal wrote a book, *How India Lost her Freedom,* explaining in a very elaborate manner how India's freedom was bartered by a few deceivers in 1757. The leader of this group although was Mir Jafar, he was accompanied by his favourite courtiers like Nund Kumar and Amin Chand. The destiny of India's freedom was put to stake on the day of the battle of Plassey, which took place between the British and Indian combined soldiers and the army of Siraj-ud-Daulah, in 1757.[1] The treachery of Mir Jaffar and companions had done its duty and not until 1947, the people of India would breathe the same air as they used to, before 1757. Although Mir Jafar had realised his folly soon after the war and had no strength left in his legs to step over even to the *Gaddi* of Nawab Siraj-ud-Daulah, without the help of Lord Clive. But it was too late to remedy the blunder he had done. Though Mir Jafar's treachery is always taught all over in the history books that has eclipsed almost all the Indian socio-political minds for decades, but the heroic acts of Siraj-ud-Daulah and Mir Madan are almost overlooked and have been hardly ever valued.

Even though the present work can hardly be considered as response to what Pandit Sunderlal and other historians have written, but it certainly mean to clarify that if we want to date the foundation of the loss of India's freedom, it is certainly the year 1498 when the king of Cochin, Gangadhara, a vassal of the kingdom of Calicut, invited and gave shelter to Vasco da Gama, who was fleeing from the wrath of the Zamorin, and not exactly 1757.

The king of Cochin, who in return of alliance with the Portuguese against his own sovereign overlord, the Zamorin of Calicut, dreamt of becoming a powerful ruler, with the help of the modern navy of Vasco da Gama. Although, the relation between these two grown stronger as the years passed but the king of Cochin could never became a powerful ruler, instead, a puppet in the hands of the Portuguese for over a century and a half. On the other hand, this act of the King of Cochin and the other neighbouring rulers such as the king of Cannanore, Cranganore and Quilon, helped in diminishing the resisting power of Zamorin who was, almost on regular basis, kept busy in wars either against the king of Cochin, Cranganore or the Portuguese themselves, in one or the other ways.

Then onwards, the King of Cochin and his successors started receiving a gold crown and instructions for his administrative and social welfare from the king of Portugal, a thing never happened in the history of India. The King's support to Vasco da Gama, against the Zamorin, who often rose against the Portuguese authority in the sea and on the land, was breakthrough of the independence of India. The Zamorin fought, almost a century and a half battle, sometimes in alliances with the other Indian states, such as the sultans of Bijapur, Ahmadnagar, Gujarat and even the

Egyptian rulers, and sometimes, alone, depending up on the circumstances.

All these rulers, the king of Cannanore, Cranganore and Quilon though remained Portuguese vassals and weakened the Zamorins position, were not free now either to take political, social or religious decisions without the consents of the Portuguese which they had enjoyed for centuries under the sovereignty of the Zamorins.

Although allied, the Portuguese availed all kinds of tactics to keep these rulers weak, so that neither they could become powerful enough to defy their authority nor weaker enough to be engulfed by the Zamorin. Many often the Portuguese even allied with the Zamorin in order to keep these rulers to their senses. Many times several rulers were helped one against the other so that they would keep themselves exhausted with the wars and would have no chance to fight against the Portuguese. Many other states than that of South India were brought to their political orbit to serve their political requirements during the course of time. When these rulers understood the Portuguese tactics, it was only too late to take any proper action until the arrival of the Dutch and the English in the Indian Ocean. It was during the period of the Portuguese governance that the policy of "divide and rule" had been introduced. The English had only followed this policy, later, in all over India.

In brief, one could say that the rulers of Cochin, Cranganore, Cannanor and Quilon are to be nominated as precursors of those who sowed the seed of the loss of India's freedom and the policy of "divide and rule" was only modernized about two and a half centuries later by the English in India.

Most of these questions have been enhanced in the later parts of this work.

Afzal Ahmad
Lisbon, 2007

1 Pandit Sunderlal, *How India Lost her Freedom,* Popular Prakashan, Bombay, 1970, pp. 35-40; Besides this author there are hundreds of book that narrate the story of Mir Jafar and Lord Clive's alliance.

Contents

Maps

Plates

Acknowledgements

I wish to place on record the unflinching help I received from my supervisor, Prof. Malyn D.D. Newitt. He was a constant source of inspiration to me. His love, care and affection and overall criticism of my work throughout the period of this research, made it possible to bring it to this shape. He has not only been simply a supervisor, but has gone beyond the limit of it to the point of editing and correcting minor errors to make this work up to date, which was supposed to be done by me. I find no adequate words to express my heartfelt and profound gratitude.

Dr. Rudy Bauss spared almost a week from his very tight teaching schedule to go through this work and made valuable comments and suggestions. Apart from this, he has been a source of inspiration and encouragement throughout the period of this research. It is difficult to express my gratitude to him.

Although at a long distance, Prof. K.S. Mathew's support in sending me some very useful bibliography and occasional clarifications on various subjects, over telephone, had been much too helpfull. I extend my respectful thanks to him.

The material for this work was primarily collected from the *Arquivo Nacional da Torre do Tombo*, Lisbon, *Arquivo Histórico Ultramarino*, Lisbon; *Filmoteca Ultramarina Portuguesa*, Lisboa, which contains most of the documents from the Goa Historical Archives on microfilm. I wish to thank all the Directors and staff members who rendered their help during my research.

My gratitude is also due to all the Librarians and staff members of the *Biblioteca Nacional, Biblioteca da Ajuda, Biblioteca da Sociedade de Geografia de Lisboa, Biblioteca da Universidade de Clássica de Lisboa,* and *Biblioteca João Paulo II of the Universidade Católica, Lisboa,* the Maughan Library, King's College, Central Library, University of London, who have been a great help for the present study. I extend my indebtedness to the respective Directors and Library staff of these institutions for their help.

Afzal Ahmad

Chapter 1

A Survey of the Published Works on Portuguese Commercial Expansion and Diplomatic Relations

In India, history books at the school have little to say about the Portuguese except that long ago Vasco da Gama came from Portugal and that Albuquerque was an important governor in Goa. Needless to say, however, that a lot more has been written in Portuguese about the discoveries and the heroic expansion of Portugal and, after the middle of the twentieth century, a substantial amount has also appeared in English. This has focussed on the Portuguese in Asia in general and in India in particular, studying their commercial and administrative activities and the propagation of Christianity. Though some of these writings have made comments about Portuguese diplomatic relations with the Indian states, these have been confined to a few sweeping remarks which give no specific idea of Portuguese diplomacy or the Indian diplomatic system. Though there are some studies directly related to Portuguese diplomacy, they are very limited and it is for this reason that a study of Portuguese diplomatic relations with the Indian states would be a worthwhile contribution to the history of India.

This chapter has been divided into two parts. In the first, I would like to give a brief description of some selected works, which for over a century have contributed to enriching our knowledge about the Portuguese socio-economic and diplomatic history. In the second part, I have selected some of the most important and recent studies pertaining to the Indo-Portuguese history, which have expressed contradictory views and have been the subject of wide ranging discussions among historians. I have tried to show where my present work stands in relation to this historiography.

Some Important Publications on Portuguese Overseas History

Research into Portuguese overseas expansion has been cyclical, at least from the middle of the nineteenth century.[1] Whenever a centenary of the period of the Discoveries or the Restoration approached, scholars accelerated their researches into the documents pertaining to the period. This trend first became apparent during 1840s, when Portugal was celebrating the second centenary of the Restoration. A group of researchers, which included the Visconde de Santarém[2] and Júlio Firmino Judice Biker[3] in Portugal, and J.H. da Cunha Rivara[4] in Goa, decided to undertake the difficult job of collecting and publishing the scattered documents relating to the diplomatic contacts of Portugal with European countries as well as with the states of Asia. These sources still continue to be the fundamental starting point for anyone wishing to research Portugal's diplomatic history.

Subsequently a number of scholarly journals have focused on Indo-Portuguese history. In 1875, the *Sociedade de Geografia de Lisboa,* came into existence and started its quarterly journal, *Boletim da Sociedade de Geografia de Lisboa.*[5] Later, in 1926, *Instituto Vasco da Gama,* at Panjim, Goa, started the *Boletim do Instituto Vasco da Gama;* which continued to publish research papers until 1961, when Goa was seized by Indian forces. A year later, the same *Instituto* was named *Instituto Meneses Bragança,* and the journal was renamed the *Boletim do Instituto de Bragança,* and continued its regular publications. These journals served historians for over a century by publishing valuable research articles and documents. The series of *O Oriente Portuguêz*[6] was published in Macau from 1892 and, in 1904, it appeared in Goa with the same name, the two editions continuing simultaneously. Although a lot of archival work has been done in producing Indo-Portuguese general history but there was very little attempt to use it to tell the story of Portugal's diplomatic relations with the Indian states or the *Reis Vizinhos,* as the Portuguese termed them.

Significant research activity resumed around 1928, after a gap of almost thirty years, and continued till the early 1940s, during which time some important work on Portuguese colonial history appeared and some publications,[7] which had been left incomplete after the celebration of the four hundred years since the Portuguese discovery of the route to India, were finished. The rate of publication slowed down somewhat during 1950-1960, after which it gathered pace again, stimulated in part by the celebrations marking the quincentenary of the death of Henry 'the Navigator' in 1960.

The systematic collection and publication of archival material was resumed under the guidance of António da Silva Rego, a Catholic priest, who set out to catalogue and microfilm, most of the Portuguese documents in libraries around the world and to bring them to Portugal. The initiation of this gigantic work took place on the eve of the 1940s. The work of microfilming was very carefully done and was for a long time kept in a centre known as the *Filmoteca Ultramarina Portuguesa,* at the *Junta da Investigação Cientifica Tropical, Lisboa.* Besides this, Silva Rego also took up the heavy burden of publishing the *Gavetas da Torre do Tombo,* and *Documentos Remettidos da Índia.*[8] Although this enterprise had been planned with a view to showing the grandeur of the Portuguese achievement, it constituted one of the most important and useful bodies of work undertaken during the Salazar regime and one for which researchers will always remain grateful.

After 1970, a new period of research started. Historians from different parts of the world, especially from India and Portugal, joined together to organize seminars, which became well known as the "International Seminar on Indo-Portuguese History".[9] These started in 1978 in Goa and took place every two years, changing their venue from Goa to Lisbon, Macau, Cochin and the Azores. The last seminar of this series took place in 2006. This organisation had as its objective to study the Portuguese 'age of discoveries' and its economic impact in Asia as well as in the continents of America and Africa.

The *Fundação Calouste Gulbenkian* (Lisbon), *Instituto de Língua* and *Cultura Portuguesa,*[10] *Fundação Oriente,* and the *Comissão Nacional para a Comemoração dos Descobrimentos Portugueses*[11] sponsored numerous researchers from all over the world. The Comissão provided the financial support to start various periodical publications such as *Mare Liberum,* and *Oceanos* in Portugal. It also published papers from conferences, most of which were organised by this institution itself. Since a great many documents have been published and most of the archives have been catalogued, researchers now find it easier to pursue their investigations. However there are still important documents, and even whole series, that have not been published and it remains imperative for students to work in the archives.

Keeping this institutional framework in mind, the following pages will review the work done so far, both in Portuguese and in English, to reconstruct the history of Portuguese diplomatic relations with the states of the south-western coast of India in the seventeenth century up to 1663[12] and its significance in shaping the Indian statecraft and diplomacy.

Reference

1 See appendix I-A, on the early works and the sources used in this work.

2 Visconde de Santarém, (also reffered in various publication as 2º Visco de Santarém as well as Visconde de Borges de Castro) Luiz Augusto Rebello da Silva e José da Silva Mendes Leal, *Quadro Elementar das Relações Políticas e Diplomáticas de Portugal com as Diversas Potências do Mundo desde o Princípio da Monarchias Portuguezas até aos nossos dias.* 18 vols., Paris, & Lisboa, 1842-1876 (This series belong to the ANTT); Santarém, *Visconde de, Collecção dos Tratados Convenções, Contratos e Actos Públicos Celebrados entre a Coroa de Portugal e as mais Potencias, desde 1640 até ao presente,* 8 vols., Lisboa, 1856-1858; Santarém, Visconde de, and Júlio Firmino Judice Biker, *Supplemento à Collecção dos Tratados, Convenções, Contratos e Actos Públicos Celebrados entre a Coroa de Portugal e as mais Potências, desde 1640.* 22 vols., Lisboa, 1872-1879.

3 J.F.J Biker (ed) *Collecção de tratados e concertos de pazes que o Estado da Índia Portuguesa fez com os reis e senhores em que teve relações nas partes da Ásia e África Oriental desde o princípio da conquista até ao fim do Século XVIII, tomos* 1-14, Lisboa, 1881-1887: Biker's Edition of *Collecção de Tratatos e Concertos ...* are mostly based on the *Archivo Português Oriental* of Cunha Rivara, which is based on *O Cronista de Tissuary,* collection and these are based on the documents *Livros das Pazes* and *Livros grande das Pazes* which is not catalogued in any of the published catalogues either by Boxer, or Pissurlenkar, though Pissurlenkar mentions that they have been published in the *Boletim Oficial de Estado da Índia.*

4 J.H. da Cunha Rivara, (ed.) *Arquivo Português Oriental,* 6 vols. in 9 parts, Nova Goa, 1857-1876. Hereafter it is only referred as *APO-CR.*

5 *Boletim da Sociedade de Geografia de Lisboa,* Imprensa Nacional, 1882, and continued then after.

6 *O Oriente portuguez: semanario dedicado aos interesses portuguezes da China e Oceania,* Adm. A. V. da Silva, Macau, 1892; *O Oriente portuguez: revista da Comissão Archeologica da Índia portugueza.* Imprensa Nacional.

7 Like that of *Documentos Remettidos da Índia, Cartas de Affonso de Albuquerque,* and many more.

8 It was initiated by Bulhão Pato in the late nineteenth century.

9 This name was used when this seminar took place in any part of India (Goa, Cochin), and it was named as *Seminário Internacional de História Indo-Portuguesa.*

10 Former ICALP, which is now known as *Instituto Camões.*

11 Hereafter it is mentioned as (CNCDP). This institution has been closed in 2002.

12 Although in a few cases, (like Bijapur and Kanara) some overlapping is found until 1670 that is only to mention the aftermath of the situation rather than dealings of diplomacy with those states.

Part I

a) General works on the diplomatic history of Portugal and Indo-Portuguese Socio-Economic History during the sixteenth and seventeenth centuries

During the twentieth century, a number of authors have studied Portuguese diplomatic relations with the states of Europe.[13] Scholars such as Carlos Hermenegildo de Sousa,[14] Edgar Prestage,[15] José Calvet de Magalhães,[16] Pedro Soares Martinez,[17] Luís Soares de Oliveira,[18] and Jorge Borges de Macedo,[19] among others, have tried to reconstruct the history of the general diplomatic relations of Portugal during the period from the seventeenth to the nineteenth centuries. Some of these authors, to whom reference will be made in the following pages, have concentrated on the period following 1640, the reestablishment of independence after sixty years of Spanish rule. However, with the exception of a few writers like Carlos Hermenegildo de Sousa, Eduardo Brazão and Pedro Soares Martinez, no scholar tried to include the texts of the terms of even the most important treaties, such as those which saw the recognition of Portuguese independence by the English and the Dutch through the embassies sent by the King D. João IV to these countries. In some cases, these diplomatic historians have not bothered to cite even a single document.

There are afew works that have tried to focus on the chronological history of Portugal's diplomatic relations with the countries of Europe. One such study is Pedro Soares Martinez's, *História Diplomática de Portugal,* which is a textbook for the general reader. This is probably the only book available that analyses the reasons for the failures of Portuguese diplomacy in Europe during the seventeenth and the eighteenth centuries. The drawback of this work, from the point of view of the historian of the *Estado da Índia,* is that it has dedicated only two paragraphs to the centuries-old Portuguese diplomatic relations with the Indian states, though it provides a valuable bibliography of Portuguese diplomatic relations over the centuries. Jorge Borges de Macedo's *História*

Diplomática Portuguesa, is a semi-chronological, politico-diplomatic history of Portugal, and is a collection of lectures delivered by the author at the Portuguese Air Force Academy. It is typical of the patriotic history writing of the time and is seriously lacking in any analysis of the documents used. There are hardly any footnotes and there is no bibliography. It appears that it is a serial edition of the journal, *Nação e Defesa.* In this book also it is very unusual to find references to Portuguese diplomatic relations with any oriental kingdom or any state with which the Portuguese had established contacts outside Europe. It is a book for general reading and for the improvement of knowledge about Portuguese international relations with the European states with which the Portuguese maintained "cordial marriage relations". A third publication, *Breve História Diplomática de Portugal* by José Calvet de Magalhães, is also a summary of the history of the diplomatic relations of Portugal with European Countries.

Eduardo Brazão,[20] a Portuguese career diplomat, discovered a keen interest in the field of the diplomatic history of Portugal as early as 1932, and left numerous studies of Portuguese diplomatic relationships with the European nations, especially for the period that followed the Restoration. He had realised the lack of research in this area and was well acquainted with the documents already published. His are serious research works based on the original treaties that were signed in the seventeenth and the eighteenth centuries. However, a researcher who wants to find out about the period before 1640 will have to look elsewhere. In the same list one could also put Carlos Hermengildo de Sousa, who studied Portuguese diplomatic relations with England from the early medieval period until the third decade of the twentieth century. Chief credit for all these works on Portuguese diplomatic relations might be given to António Ferrão who, in 1928,[21] in his *Os Estudos de história diplomática em Portugal,* had pointed out the lack of studies relating to the history of Portuguese diplomatic relations and had stressed the need for more research based on the collections of documents compiled and edited by Visconde de Santarém and Júlio F. J. Biker which were already available to researchers.[22]

Through these entire documentary editions one is aware of the fundamental lack of any historical interpretation. This may have something to do with the political turmoil of the Republic and the early days of the *Estado Novo.* The only exception, scarcely relevant to this study, was Edgar Prestage's, *Primeira Embaixada de El-Rei*

D. João IV: A Embaixada de Tristão de Mendonça Furtado à Holanda em 1641 published in 1920.

A acção diplomática dos portugueses nos séculos XV e XVI, destinada à realização de descobertas e conquistas by Francisco da Costa Lobo appeared in 1937. This work is almost entirely based on the documents published by Santarém in his *Quadro Elementar,* already mentioned earlier. It has been divided into three parts, the second providing a summary of the treaties and diplomatic relations concluded between 1500 and 1580 with the Asian states. Costa Lobo provides a justification for Portuguese actions which, he says, has been ignored by other Europeans and Asians. According to him the Portuguese discoveries had given Portugal and her people the exclusive right of governing and monopolising the areas under their control, a theory which had been contested by most of the moderate historians. Nevertheless, even historians of present generation, except for a few exceptions, share the same ideology. After this publication, historians in Portugal concentrated mostly on the history of the Portuguese discoveries themselves[23] and on national propaganda, which was encouraged by Salazar's dictatorial government. No one could write anything except what was in the interest of the nation or approved by the regime.

Among the Portuguese historians whose contributions are the most highly regarded in the field of economic history over the last half a century, are J. Lúcio de Azevedo and Vitorino Magalhães Godinho. Azevedo's work *Épocas de Portugal Económico*[24] is considered among the most valuable and informative works and the precursor of all subsequent works by Indo-Portuguese historians on Portuguese commercial expansion. It was the first work of its kind to be published in a very turbulent period when Portugal was experiencing a political crisis almost annually. Azevedo focused on the economic situation of Portugal on the eve of the great discoveries and on the sixteenth century, although he looked at later periods as well. He pinpointed the way that Portuguese commerce was handled, and identified the German and Italian financiers who played a key role in maintaining it. Until this time, most work had been devoted either to the voyages of discovery themselves or simply to the publication of documents. This book was the forerunner of all the interpretative works that appeared later on the socio-economic history of Portuguese colonial expansion and became a guide for other scholars towards the end of the twentieth century.[25]

Lúcio de Azevedo was followed in the 1960s by some renowned historians, among whom Vitorino Magalhães Godinho comes first. In the first edition of his, *Os Descobrimentos e a Economia Mundial*, (though probably by mistake as he corrected it in later editions), he had miscalculated the volume of pepper which was transported from Goa to Portugal in 1611-1620, basing his calculation on a manuscript belonging to the *Arquivo Histórico Ultramarino* and the Goa Archives.[26] However, this does not, in any way, minimize the book's scientific or academic value. He has analysed in depth the economic aspects of Portuguese expansion, including the investments, the money economy, coinage, the origins of merchandise and the mechanisms of African and Asian trade. Though he has studied Portuguese trading activities thoroughly, he has focussed on a very few commodities, especially spices, leaving aside textiles and food-grains which brought great profits to both the Portuguese and the Asian traders. Although in more than a hundred publications he has dealt with Portuguese trade and commerce in Africa and Asia from the fifteenth to the early seventeenth centuries, he has largely ignored important issues like the diplomatic relations of the Portuguese with the states he so frequently mentions.

Geneviève Bouchon, a French historian, focused her researches on the Portuguese establishments on the south-western coast of India.[27] She looked at Portuguese relations with the powerful local merchant class, which reacted against Portuguese violence and their control of the sea. Her best-known study is *Regents of the Sea*, an account of the Mamalis of Cannanore, a business family of Arab-Indian origin, which was established in Cannanore and enjoyed the protection of its rulers. Through this study, Bouchon has argued that the Portuguese strategy of creating divisions between the Muslims merchants and the Hindu kings, based on their religious differences, was a mistake and that the Portuguese failed in their efforts to mount a 'Crusade' in the Indian Ocean. She has also published studies of Vasco da Gama and Afonso de Albuquerque and their role in the foundation of the Portuguese empire in the early sixteenth century.

In 1971, F. D. Lach began publishing his *Asia in the Making of Europe*.[28] Lach's work is widely read and stresses that European expansion contributed more to the growth of the European economy than it did to the Asian. Among many other topics, he examines the role of the merchant bankers, such as Rott, Rovellesca and the family of Ximenes de Aragão, who participated in the Portuguese Asian trade in the sixteenth century and places it in its proper context. There is no other work in English or Portuguese, which examines on such a broad scale the commercial and cultural relations between Europe and Asia. He is also one of the first writers to stress that the cultural and economic impact of the Discoveries was a two way process with Europe being influenced as much as Asia by the new contacts – a point totally ignored by earlier Eurocentric historians who had assumed that Asia in general, and India in particular, gained more from the European presence than Europe gained from them.

In contrast to the approach adopted by Lach, Baillie Diffie and George Winius[29] viewed the Portuguese essentially as empire builders and conquerors. *The Foundation of the Portuguese Empire* is a chronological history of Portuguese expansion to the year 1580. Winius has a good number of other works to his credit, among them a critical study of Portuguese Ceylon, entitled *The Fatal History of Portuguese Ceylon.* This book goes deeply into the problems of the rule of the Portuguese in Ceylon, its importance in their Asian empire and their conflict with the Dutch. In other works he has covered the turbulent period of the Portuguese in seventeenth century Asia - *The Merchant-warrior Pacified: the VOC (the Dutch East India Company) and its changing Political Economy in India,* and *The black legend of Portuguese India.* These help to fill a gap in the study of Portuguese imperial history in the seventeenth century and include an examination of Portuguese-Dutch rivalries. The book on the "Black Legend," based on Diogo do Couto's *O Soldado Prático,* looks especially at the corruption that engulfed the Portuguese administration and contributed to brining about its fall.

Anthony Disney published his *Twilight of the Pepper Empire* in 1978, focusing on the Portuguese pepper trade during the first four decades of the seventeenth century. His major contribution is to describe the Portuguese East India Company, which started in 1628[30] and collapsed in 1633[31] due to jealousy and non-cooperation from the Portuguese authorities in India as well as opposition from the Inquisition and the nobility in Portugal.[32] However, according to Disney, the fall of the Portuguese East India Company was a low point, after which the Portuguese trade ceased to exist, which is certainly not true. Disney has mostly considered the Portuguese pepper trade from the areas of Malabar and Kanara but he is, nevertheless, after Magalhães Godinho, the first author who tried to study not only the movement of pepper to the Portuguese ships but also the intermediaries and the cultivators from whom the pepper was bought, the means of transportation and the prices paid. Until the publication of this book, most of the knowledge about seventeenth century Portuguese trade was derived from the work of Magalhães Godinho,[33] which was quite inaccessible to the majority of the English reading public.

Teotonio de Souza completed his *Medieval Goa* in 1979, studying the society and economy of Goa in the seventeenth century. This book also largely ignored the diplomatic relations of Portuguese Goa with the surrounding states. Souza himself later pointed out, in one of his numerous articles, the lack of research in this area.[34]

In 1982 Artur Teodoro de Matos published *Estado da Índia nos anos de 1581-1588: Estrutura Administrativa e económica, alguns elementos para o seu estudo.* This book (which in one place makes use of a manuscript without mentioning its origin) describes some important economic and administrative aspects of the *Estado da Índia* in the late sixteenth century.[35] Teodoro de Matos's other contribution of considerable importance to Indo-Portuguese history appeared in 2001, when he edited the *Diário de Conde de Sarzedas.* Although, the first half of this diary had already been published by Pissurlenkar in volume III of *Assentos do Conselho do Estado,* it provided first hand knowledge about the economic and political situation in which the Conde de Sarzedas found the *Estado da Índia* when he reached Goa in 1654. This diary provides details of the meetings he had with ambassadors of different states and has been of especial help in reconstructing Portuguese diplomatic relations with Bijapur and the Kanara states in the middle of the seventeenth century.

In 1985, I defended a doctoral thesis at the University of Baroda, India, on Indo-Portuguese Trade in the Seventeenth Century.[36] This present work is aimed to fill the gap, left by almost all previous scholars, by analysing the nature and variety of the merchandise traded by the Portuguese. In this work it is argued that, when the merchants found it difficult to trade in pepper and cinnamon, which had been declared to be the "commodities of royal monopoly", they started carrying large quantities of textiles, which so far had not been ever noticed by the economic historians, and when, due to the Dutch and English attacks on their ships, this became too risky, they started trading in diamonds. Of course a major part of these were smuggled as they did not want to pay any customs. Portuguese relations with the English and the Dutch, and their rivalries over the Indian merchant goods, especially spices, as well as its impact over the increase in the prices of the Indian merchandises have been dealt in their proper perspective. The English and the Dutch shares in the overall Asian trade also resulted in perturbing the Portuguese commercial relations with the local merchants who now preferred dealing with the Dutch and the English than the Portuguese who paid rather arbitrary prices. This work starts with the foundation of the East India Companies of the English (1601) and the Dutch (1602) and goes up till 1663, when the Portuguese lost their major strongholds in Malabar, including Cochin.

One of the major objectives of this work has been to show the finances and the expenditure of the *Estado da Índia* – how much was received from Portugal under various heads and how much was derived from the treasury of Goa, which enabled the empire to survive during the difficult years until 1663. In this work specific mentions have been made to show that, amidst all round reduction in the volume of Portuguese spice trade, there was, strangely, a considerable rise in the volumes of rice and saltpetre. At the same time it has also been noticed that these two specific items were bought to supply the Portuguese men and soldiers in the war affected colonies. This was an extra expenditure on their difficult economy rather than it provided any income to the Portuguese state, which is wrongly assumed by some historians, without providing any justification why or even bothering to analyse who bought and consumed. However, this study too, presented commercial features of the Portuguese presence in India as main theme of discussion rather than the diplomacy. In 1990, I published with K. S. Mathew *The Emergence of Cochin in the Pre-Industrial Era* which is the publication of a bound manuscript from the Ajuda Library in Lisbon. It covers the history of Cochin under the Portuguese including the diplomatic and socio-economic aspects during the sixteenth and the early parts of the seventeenth centuries.

About the same time, 1985-86, appeared the work of K.N. Chaudhuri, *Trade and Civilisation in the Indian Ocean: an Economic History from the rise of Islam to 1750*, which placed his own research in a much wider perspective. In his earlier work, *The Trading World of Asia and the English East India Company, 1660-1760*, he had focused on the role of the English East India Company from the time of its acquisition of Bombay. However, Chaudhuri became caught up in the current of the Portuguese discovery celebrations and changed his direction towards Portuguese expansion and trade and its role in the formation of the world economy. In *The Trading World of Asia*, he mostly used published sources, to study the economic and trading network of the Portuguese and the difficulties they faced after the arrival of the English and the Dutch when ideological rivalry, combined with the armed conflict, gave the impression that the European companies were a revolutionary force in Asia. Chaudhuri's involvement in the work of the Discoveries Commission took him to Florence and resulted in the five volumes of the *História da Expansão Portuguesa,* which he edited with Francisco Bethencourt in 2000, covering a vast area from Brazil to East Asia. Extensive as it was, this work also largely ignored the subject of Portuguese diplomacy with the states of Asia.

During the period when the work of Chaudhuri and Bethencourt was in preparation, an International Seminar was hosted by the Calouste Gulbenkian Foundation in Paris in 1998, and resulted in the publication of numerous papers under the title, *Vasco da Gama e a Índia*. In the papers by António Vasconcelos de Saldanha and Luís Adão de Fonseca among others there is an attempt to focus on Portuguese diplomacy. According to these authors, diplomacy was mostly dominated by the Portuguese, who were the conquerors, in contrast to the Asian merchants and rulers who were unwilling to allow the Portuguese to control Asian commerce and have been described, in a way, as ignorant. However, despite the extreme point of view which these authors have tried to present, this collection remains a useful compendium of the latest research.

In 1998 Jeyaseela Stephen published some research on the socio-economic aspects of the South-East Indian coast.[37] He argued that the Portuguese exercised considerable influence on the pearl fisheries of the coast of Coromandel during the sixteenth and the seventeenth century, though his work concentrates mostly on private trade. As Stephen says in his book, in order to face the "commercial rivalry and religious antagonism of the Muslim population, the Portuguese had to rely on their naval power".[38] In other words, he too, followed the trends of the Portuguese historians while justifying the Portuguese atrocities. Though he refers to the Portuguese diplomatic relations with the Nayakas of Jinji and the Vijaynagar Empire, there is little detail regarding the procedures they followed in their diplomacy. Somehow, he tried to add a little more details to Sanjay's *Improvising Empire*.

Dutch relations with the states of Malabar are the subject of work by Poonen.[39] He provides exhaustive information about Malabar's small princely states, like Calicut, Cochin and Cannanore, which tried to increase their political as well as their economic power with the help of the Dutch. Naturally the kings of Malabar were, by that time, anxious to get rid of the Portuguese who had proved neither good friends nor satisfactory commercial partners. The Dutch treaties with the Malabar states, starting with the Zamorin of Calicut at the beginning of the seventeenth century, and including the kings of Cannanore, Proccad and even the king of Cochin, had been a cause of much concern to the Portuguese. Poonen has explained that the reasons why the Dutch wanted to keep such a tight hold over these states was because they were petty rulers who had no power of their own to resist any strong forces, especially those of the Portuguese. On the other hand the Dutch did not have the same chance to exercise their power over the Mughals or the Sultans of Bijapur.

One of the major drawbacks of Poonen's work is that he has, probably deliberately, avoided discussing Portuguese-Dutch diplomatic relations.[40] He makes no mention at all as to whether the Dutch or the Portuguese ever tried to reach a diplomatic solution to their problems although, after the independence of Portugal from Spanish rule in 1640, the Portuguese authorities in Goa sent a number of embassies to the Dutch commanders at Batavia, their Asian capital.

Recently Glenn J. Ames has published a research paper on "The Salssette Campaign of 1658-1659: Issues of War and Peace in Bijapuri-Portuguese Relations during the mid-17th Century" a rare example of a historian looking at the diplomatic relations of the Portuguese with their Indian neighbours. This paper has provided a brief description of the war 1658-59 that took place between the Bijapur and Portuguese armies. Most of the article consists of a description of the Portuguese Bijapuri relations over 170 years to which the author has dedicated almost twelve of the seventeen pages. He has followed almost the same line as other historians in describing Portuguese relations with the Bijapuri state; 'the Bijapuris were at fault for invading the poor Portuguese settlements without any reason and whenever they wanted.' An example of this is his account of Abdul Hakim, the general of the Bijapuri kingdom, who marched with his army of almost eight thousand soldiers through the Portuguese Goan territories, as if he was on a military exercise and turned back after killing some Portuguese soldiers and capturing their commander. He withdrew because he knew that there was Portuguese reinforcement on the way from Onor.[41] Ames does not explain why an army commander would enter into a sovereign territory without any reason at a time when his own Sultan had sent ambassadors to the court of Ikkeri to make representations on behalf of the Portuguese?[42] Among the reason he has presented is that, the Sultan of Bijapur allowed the Dutch to establish factories at Karwar, Rajapur and Vingurla, (in fact the Dutch had already been given permission to settle at Vengurla in 1638 and later at Karwar) and in return the VOC promised to support the Sultan with their navy against the Portuguese provided he attacked Goa. Therefore, according to him the Sultan was encouraged by the Dutch emissary to attack Goa because of the Portuguese involvement with the Shivappa Nayaka of Ikkeri. In fact this is what is believed by the pro-Portuguese historians without searching for more reasons. (Here one should remember that all the Portuguese fortresses in the territories of Kanara had already been lost to the Nayaka by 1656.)[43] Therefore, the present article of Ames is another repetitive and confusing work. He has mixed the reason of one war that took place in 1654, with the other on 1659.

The Portuguese phase in Kerala history has been covered by several standard works like *History of Kerala* by K.P. Padmanabha Menon, *Medieval Kerala* by P. K. S. Raja, *A Survey of Kerala History* by A. Sreedhara Menon. These works deal with the Portuguese period in a very superficial way without making a critical study of the Portuguese sources or focussing on any long term impact of the Portuguese presence.

Besides all these works, there has been quite a substantial amount of research devoted to the socio-economic history of south India. One could include the works of Sinappa Arasaratnam,[44] M. O. Koshy[45] K.K. Kusuman,[46] and many others which provide ample information regarding the commercial relations of coastal south India, but do not add anything to our knowledge of diplomacy and statecraft. However, the work of Burton Stein[47] covers almost three centuries of the political and economic history of the Vijayanagar Empire, in particular analysing the political and economic structure of this "Hindu Empire", especially its internal and foreign trade and who the merchants were. This Empire stood as a strong barrier against the "Muslim Imperialism" of the Bahmani Empire[48] for almost a century and a half until its disintegration in 1565 after which most of its governors, although still nominally accepting the allegiance of the Emperors of Vijayanagar, became independent. Although this book does not deal specifically with the political or diplomatic relations with the Portuguese, it does focus on the internal political situation of this Empire which helps one understand the political environment in which the Portuguese had to interact with the states that surrounded this Empire.

In the same line, although not directly related, one could also include the work of C.A. Bayly, *Empire and Information*[49], which deals with an altogether different theme so far very little touched by researchers, the 'information and spying network' of the British Empire builders of the eighteenth and the nineteenth centuries in northern India which, undoubtedly, helped them succeed in their goals. Bayly describes how they created and made use of an extensive intelligence services to obtain all sorts of information, ranging from political and economic issues to the socio-religious disorder in the decaying Mughal Empire. Through this study one also comes to understand the socio-political structure of the later Mughal state.[50] Although this work is concerned with a period and a part of India beyond the area and period of the present study, it is important in raising hypothetical questions about the nature of the information network that the Portuguese had developed during the sixteenth and the seventeenth centuries in India.

So far as northern India under the Mughals is concerned, although strictly beyond the area of this study, the recent work edited by Muzaffar Alam and Sanjay Subrahmanyam is most informative.[51] One of the articles in this book describes in detail the court ceremonial under the Mughal Emperor Jahangir when Sir Thomas Roe visited during 1615-1619. Among other recent works one could mention is, *Os Firangis na Chancelaria Mogol* by Jorge Flores and António Vasconcelos de Saldanha, in which some of the documents have been translated from Portuguese to English. This work examines the diplomatic aspects of Portuguese-Mughal relations. However, a close examination suggests that a substantial part of the information has already been provided in detail by Sir Edward Maclagan, and Fr. Pierre du Jarric.[52]

References

13 Such as, Isabel Cluny, *D. Luís da Cunha e a ideia de diplomacia em Portugal* Lisboa, 1996; Maria do Carmo Jasmins Dias Farinha, *Os documentos dos Negócios Estrangeiros na Torre do Tombo*, Arquivo Nacional da Torre do Tombo, Lisboa, 1990; João de Deus Ramos, *História das Relações Diplomáticas entre Portugal e a China*, (1721-1725), Instituto Cultural de Macau, 1991; Maria Manuela R. C. Mendonça, *As Relações Externas de Portugal nos finais da Idade Média*, Edições Colibri, Lisboa 1994; Manuel Gonçalves Martins, *O novo imperialismo e os direitos de Portugal: elementos de diplomacia portuguesa e política internaciona*, Braga: Associação Académica da Universidade do Minho, 1985; Humberto Baquero, Moreno, *O papel da diplomacia portuguesa no Tratado de Tordesilhas*, Porto: [Faculdade de Letras], 1995. Sep. de *Revista da Faculdade de Letras*, 2ª Série, vol. XII, Porto, 1995; Eduardo Augusto Vera-Cruz Pinto - *Comparar a diplomacia portuguesa no séc. XIV com a diplomacia do séc. XV* /, Lisboa, 1984.

14 Carlos Hermenegildo de Sousa, *A Aliança Anglo-Portuguesa, depositária*: Livraria Portugália, Lisboa, 1939.

15 Edgar Prestage, *Primeira Embaixada de El-Rei D. João IV: A Embaixada de Tristão de Mendonça Furtado à Holanda em 1641*, Coimbra, Imprensa da Universidade, 1920.

16 José Calvet de Magalhães, *Breve História Diplomática de Portugal, Bertrand*, Lisboa, 1990; Magalhães, *A Diplomacia Pura*, Bertrand Editora, Lisboa, 1995; Magalhães, 'A Acção diplomática no pensamento dos diplomatas portugueses dos séculos XVII e XVIII', in *A Diplomacia na História de Portugal*, Academia Portuguesa da História, Lisboa, MCMXC, pp. 15-27.

17 Pedro Soares Martinez, *História Diplomática de Portugal*, Verbo, Lisboa, 1992.

18 Luís Soares de Oliveira, *História diplomática: o período europeu 1580-1917*, P.F.Pedro Ferreira, Lisboa, 1994.

19 Jorge Borges de Macedo, *História diplomática Portuguesa*: constantes e linhas de força, Rev. Nação e Defesa, Lisboa, 1987.

20 (Also written as Brasão) Eduardo Brazão, *História diplomática de Portugal*, com um prefácio de Moses Bensabat Amzalak., Livr. Rodrigues, Lisboa, 1932; *A participação portuguesa nas conferências pacifistas da Haia*, Tip. da Casa Portuguesa, Lisboa, 1936; *A Restauração: relações diplomáticas de Portugal de 1640 a 1668*, Bertrand, Lisboa, 1939; *Apontamentos para a história das relações diplomáticas de Portugal com a China 1516-1753*, Ag. Geral das Colónias, Lisboa, 1949; *The Anglo-Portuguese Alliance*, London: Sylvan Press, 1957; *A Diplomacia portuguesa nos séculos XVII e XVIII*, (1640-1700), vol. I, Ed. Resistência, SARL, 1979.

21 António Ferrão, *Os estudos de história diplomática em Portugal e as publicações da Academia das Ciências sobre tal especialidade, o corpo diplomático português e o quadro elementar das relações políticas...* Coimbra, 1928. Sep. *Boletim segunda classe da Academia das Ciências de Lisboa.*

22 It is important to notice that a considerable number of the documents published by Santarém in volumes one to seven were subsequently reproduced by Biker in his *Supplemento* series, which starts with volume eight. Researchers need to be aware of this when they use either of the collections and should be especially careful how they refer to the documents as the page numbers are completely different from one to the other although the titles and documents are the same.

23 Damião Peres, *História dos Descobrimentos Portugueses,* Porto, 1943; António Galvão, *Tratado dos Descobrimentos,* Liv. Civil., Porto, 1944, among others.

24 J. Lúcio de Azevedo, *Épocas de Portugal económico: esboços de história,* Lisboa, 1928. Among his earlier and other important works, *Historia dos Cristãos novos portugueses,* Livraria Clássica Editora, Lisboa, 1922, could also be included.

25 For Example Vitorino Magalhães Godinho, *Os descobrimentos e a economia Mundial,* 2 vols., Lisboa, 1963-65; A.R. Disney, *Twilight of the Pepper Empire- Portuguese Trade in South-West India in the Early Seventeenth Century,* Harvard, 1978; K.S. Mathew, *The Portuguese Trade with India in the Sixteenth Century,* New Delhi, 1983, and Afzal Ahmad, *The Indo-Portuguese Trade in the Seventeenth century on the Western Coast of India (1600-1663),* Gyan Publishing House, New Delhi, 1991, have followed the pattern and broadened the dimension of Azevedo's work.

26 AHU, *Índia,* Cx. 9, doc. 177; *LMG,* N° 13-A, fls. 164-179: In fact these documents are copies of the same report prepared by the escrivão of the *Conselho da Fazenda* in 1627, and a copy was sent to the *Casa da Índia.* The other copy remained in Goa and has been compiled in the codex of *Livros das Monções.*

27 Geneviève Bouchon, *Mamale de Cananor: un adversaire de l'Inde portugaise: 1507-1528.* Libr. Droz, Genéve, 1975. Its English translation is *'Regent of the Sea', Cannanore's Response to Portuguese Expansion,* 1507-1528, Oxford, 1988; *Caderno dos ofiçiaes da India da carreguaçam das naos que vieram o anno de 1518,* bcxbiij (introd., éd.) Paris, 1977; *Bengal and Pagu at the begining of sixteenth century according to an anonymous Portuguese narrative*: IICTCEH e Cartografia Antiga, Lisboa 1985;- *L'Asie du Sud à l'époque des grandes découverts,* Variorum Reprints, London, 1987; *A French traveller in Portuguese India 1601-1610: François Pyrard de Laval.* Lisboa, 1989. - Sep. Stvdia, 49; *Afonso de Albuquerque: leão dos mares da Ásia,* (trad. Isabel de Faria e Albuquerque). Quetzal, Lisboa 2000. It's original in French was published in 1992; *Portugal e o Oriente: 1° ciclo de conferências,* Fundação Oriente, Quetzal, Lisboa,

1994; *Vasco da Gama,* (trad. Ana Santos Silva), Terramar, Lisboa, 1998; *Inde découverte, Inde retrouvée: 1498-1630: études d'histoire Indo-Portugaise,* Fundação Calouste Gulbenkian, Lisboa 1999; *Voyage de Pyrard de Laval aux Indes orientales, 1601-1611,* (préf., établissement du texte et notes Xavier de Castro), Chandeigne-Libr. Portugaise, Paris 1998.

28 F. D Lach, *Asia in the Making of Europe,* 3 vols., in two parts each, Chicago, 1971.

29 Baillie Diffie, & G. D Winius, *Foundation of the Portuguese Empire, 1450-1580.* Vol. 1: Europe and the world in the age of expansion. 1977: This book has been translated into Portuguese and published in Lisbon, 1989:For other works by Winius, see bibliography in the end.

30 Disney, *Twilight of the Pepper Empire* pp. 109-113; More exhaustive information about the dealings of the *Companhia do Comércio Portuguêz,* could be obtained from the codex at *Arq. Simancas, Sec. Provinciales,* Cód. 1526 and *Sir Joseph Bart Lynch* collection, at King's College, London.

31 *LMG,* cod. 19-A, fols. 252-256, 270-274: *Carta Régia para o Vice-rei da Índia o Conde de Linhares,* 4 de Fevereiro de 1634.

32 Disney, *Twilight of the Pepper Empire,* pp. 114-125.

33 His work had first appeared in French (1969) and later in Portuguese (1969-1971). Therefore, all those do not dominate either of these languages, could hardly have access to the knowledge he has provided.

34 Teotonio R. De Souza, 'Embassies and Surrogates: Case-Study of a Malacca Embassy to Siam in 1595', in the *Indica,* Journal of the Heras Institute of Indian History and Culture- (Separata) no. 49, pp. 39-45, Bombay, 1989.

35 Portuguese colonial dominance is commonly known as *Estado da Índia.* From the early 1500 until 1854 it geographically covered the area between Mozambique till Macau. It means that a Viceroy or Governor General of *Estado da Índia,* had under his jurisdiction the mentioned area. In 1854 Macau was detached. Then onwards, the area covered by the *Estado da Índia* was between the Western Coast of India till the East Timor.

36 This thesis was published in 1991 under the title, *Indo-Portuguese Trade in Seventeenth Century (1600-1663),* Gian Publishing House, New Delhi.

37 S. Jeyaseela Stephen- *Portuguese in the Tamil Coast: Historical Explorations in Commerce and Culture (1507-1749),* Navajothi: Navajothi Publishing House, 1998.

38 Stephen, *Portuguese in the Tamil Coast,* see his Introduction.

39 T.I. Poonen, *A Survey of the Rise of the Dutch Power in Malabar, 1603-78.* St. Joseph's Industrial School Press, Trichinopoly, 1948; One can't miss numerous articles and books by Boxer on this subject too.

40 Most of the treaties signed between the Dutch and the Malabar states have been translated from the original Dutch and Malaylam by Poonen. See pages 25-31 in Poonen, *A Survey of the Rise of the Dutch* ...,

41 Glenn J. Ames, "The Salssette Campaign of 1658-1659: Issues of War and Peace in Bijapuri-Portuguese Relations during the mid-17th Century" in *The Portuguese, Indian Ocean and European Bridgeheads: Festschrift in Honour of Prof. K.S. Mathew* edited by Pius Malekandathil and Jamal Mohammed, Tellicherry, 2001, pp. 223-40.

42 *Ibid.*

43 For details, see chapter 4 on *Portuguese Kanara Relation* in this work.

44 *Maritime India in the Seventeenth Century. Maritime India in the Seventeenth Century,* Oxford University Press, New Delhi, 1994.

45 M. O. Koshy, *The Dutch Power in Kerala,* Mittal Publications, New Delhi, 1989.

46 K.K. Kusuman, *A History of Trade and Commerce in Tavancore,* Mittal Publications, Delhi, 1987.

47 Burton Stein, *Vijayangara, - The New Cambridge History of India,* Cambridge University Press, Cambridge, 2005.

48 When the Tughlaque Dynasty fell apart, its governors in South India declared themselves, independent and founded their own dynasties. The Bahmany kingdom, during period of Muhammad Shah Bahmanee (1482-1518), faced the same fate. On the ruins of this empire, emerged five new kingdoms. The governor of Bijapur, Yusuf Adil Shah, founded the dynasty of Bijapur with the title of *Adil [Khan]Shah*; Malik Ahmad [Nizam-ul-Mulk], the Governor of Daulatabad founded the dynasty of *Nizam Shahi* with his capital at Ahmadnagar and bore the title of Nizam Shah; the governor of Berar, Imad-ul-Mulk, founded the dynasty *Imad Shahi* at Berar; and the governor of Golconda, Qutb-ul-Mulk founded his dynasty under *Qutb Shahi* and finally Amir Barid founded the dynasty at Bider and assumed the title of *Barid Shah*. Thus, in Bijapur, the Sultans used the title of *Adil Shah*, in Berar *Imad Shah*, Ahmadnagar *Nizam Shah*, in Bider *Barid Shah* and finally in Golconda, *Qutb-Shah*. All these Sultans and their followers used their respective titles till they were subjugated by the Mughal Empire in the seventeenth century. Muhammad Qasim Ferishta has provided a brief but elucidative history of all these dynasties. See *Tarikh-i-Ferishta*, English Translation by Briggs, first three volumes; D.C. Varma, *History of Bijapur,* Kumar Brothers, New Delhi, 1974, pp. 1-8; J.D.E.Gribble, *History of the Deccan,* 2 Vols. Mittal Publications, New Delhi, 1990, vol. I, pp. 128-134.

49 C.A. Bayly, *Empire and Information: Intelligence Gathering and Social Communication in India,* 1780-1870, Cambridge University Press, 1996.

50 This terminology is used to express the period after the death of Auranzeb in 1707.

51 Muzaffar Alam and Sanjay Subrahmanyam (edited), *The Mughal State 1526-1750*, Oxford University Press, New Delhi, (3rd ed.) 2003.

52 Fr. Pierre Du Jarric, (Edited Sir E. Denison Ross and Eileen Power) *Akbar and the Jesuits: An Account of the Jesuit Missions to the Court of Akbar by Father Pierre du Jarric, (reprinted)*, George Routledge & Sons, Ltd. London, 1926, (Reprinted) by D.K. Publishers, New Delhi, 1999.

b) Works on the Portuguese Diplomatic Relations in Asia

i) Works on Portuguese Diplomatic relations with the States of Asia other than India

Ronald Bishop Smith tried to fill some gaps in the history of Portuguese diplomatic relations with the Asian states and published four volumes between 1968 and 1970.[53] These volumes, though they provide some information about Portuguese political and diplomatic relations with Asian states in the early sixteenth century, are mere translations into English of the Portuguese already printed sources. He does not give any background history nor does he analyse the circumstances that led to the diplomatic exchanges. Though he himself has listed the bibliography he has consulted, he does not introduce any new documentation.

In 1989 Teotonio de Souza wrote an article, 'Embassies and Surrogates: Case-Study of a Malacca Embassy to Siam in 1595' for the Heras Intitute Journal, *Indica,* about a merchant, Jacques de Couttre, a Flemish jewel trader, who served the Portuguese as a soldier and a merchant and who acted as ambassador to various neighbouring kingdoms in the service of the Malaccan authorities. He was eventually arrested by the Inquisition and sent to Lisbon in 1623. Souza has made use of the account of Couttre in writing this article, in which, incidentally, he refers to the lack of works on Portuguese diplomatic relations with the Indian States, as mentioned earlier.[54]

Charles Boxer's study *Francisco Vieira de Figueiredo, a Portuguese merchant-adventurer in South East Asia* (1624-1667),[55] illustrates the key diplomatic role played by the merchant Figueiredo in safeguarding Portuguese trade and commerce in the Lesser Sunda Islands after the loss of Malacca. Other recent works on diplomacy include N. R. Farooqi, *Mughal Ottoman Relations,*[56] *and State and Diplomacy under Tipu Sultan, (Documents and Essays)* by Irfan Habib. These works deal mostly with the seventeenth and the eighteenth centuries and provide details of the protocols and instructions for the ambassadors exchanged between the different states. Although they deal with a region beyond the interest of the present study, they provide exhaustive details of the manner in which the diplomacy was conducted in these kingdoms.

ii) Works on the Portuguese Diplomatic Relations with the India States

There are very few works on Indo-Portuguese diplomacy, which have concentrated on the limited area of the western coast of India. Among such works, Pissurlenkar's, *Agentes da Diplomacia Portugesa na Índia: Hindus, Muçulmanos, Judeus e Pareses,*[57] is directly related to the diplomatic relations of the Portuguese with the Indian states. He has categorised the Indian diplomats of various religions who served the *Estado da Índia,* as messengers and ambassadors to the courts of numerous Indian States, of which Hindus were overwhelmingly in the majority. This work published selected documents, covering a period starting in 1546 and ending in 1811. This work, among other shortcomings,[58] lacks any analysis of the situation under which treaties and diplomatic ties were established. Pissurlenkar's *The Portuguese and the Marathas,* as mentioned earlier, is another contribution to Indo-Portuguese diplomatic history, which examines the nuances of the history of the seventeenth and eighteenth centuries in south-western India.

M. A. Nayeem published his thesis, *External Relations of the Bijapur Kingdom (1489-1686)* in 1974, based mostly on Persian, English and Portuguese sources. This work is probably the only one of its kind, which has studied in detail the diplomatic relations of the Bijapuri kingdom with its neighbouring empires as well as with the Portuguese. However, the passages describing relations with the Portuguese amount to little more than occasional references to military and diplomatic encounters. There is another problem relating to the references to Biker's work. Nayeem has given the name of Biker but has given the title of the editions as "*Monções*". This is clearly a mistake and researchers, while making use of his work, should be careful about this aspect.

An unpublished doctoral thesis, *O Estado Português da Índia: da Rendição de Ormuz a Perda de Cochin, 1622-1663* by Maria Manuela Sobral Blanco, submitted at the *Faculdade de Letras de Universidade de Lisboa* in 1992, deals with the final phase of Portuguese rule in Cochin and shows how the breaking of the caravan routes, caused by the loss of Hormuz, led to the downfall of the Portuguese commercial and political establishment. She has provided a volume full of documents as appendices, which deal with all aspects of the subject except diplomacy. The author has dedicated only about a dozen pages to the diplomatic relations of the Portuguese with the states of Malabar, without much analysis. And whatever analysis Manuela has provided is quite biased and it appears quite clearly that she maintain the mentality of the Portuguese who lived in the sixteenth century and those followed during the regime of Salazar. The problem with this work can be illustrated when she confuses the embassy of 1631 with the presents sent to the Sultan of Bijapur in 1638. In many respects this work appears like a traditional history full of the glory of the heroic past of a nation.

In 1991 Jorge Manuel Costa da Silva Flores submitted a dissertation[59] for his M. Phil. degree in which he concentrated on the Portuguese on the Coromandel Coast and their commercial relations with Ceylon. The political aspect of the history of Ceylon, which permitted the Portuguese to establish themselves there, is considered specifically and the work covers a period earlier than that studied by authors like George Winius[60] and Richard Chandra da Silva[61] who focused on the downfall of the Portuguese in Ceylon. So far as diplomacy is concerned this work does not go beyond a few references and notes.

Reference

53 Ronald Bishop Smith, *The First Age of the Portuguese Embassies, Navigations and Peregrinations to the Kingdoms and Islands of Southeast Asia (1509-1521)*, Bethesda: Decatur Press, 1968; Smith, *The first Age of the Portuguese Embassies, Navigations and Peregrinations to the Ancient Kingdoms of Cambay and Bengal (1500-1521)*,1969; *The First Age of the Portuguese Embassies, Navigations and Peregrinations to Persia (1507-1524)*, 1970.

54 *Souza*, 'Embassies and Surrogates: ... p. 39.

55 C.R. Boxer, *Francisco Vieira de Figueiredo: a Portuguese Merchant-Adventurer in South East Asia, 1624-1667*, Martinus Nijhoff, Gravenhage, 1967.

56 N.R. Farooqi, *Moghal Ottoman Relations*, Idarah-i Adabiyat-i Delhi, Delhi, 1989: Dr. Farooqui has provided us with a profoundly analytical work on the diplomatic systems of two powerful empires; see Also see Irfan Habib, (edited) *State and Diplomacy under Tipu Sultan,(Documents and Essays)* Tulika, New Delhi, 2001. Although this book deals mostly about the eighteenth century, but it does provide a good details of protocols and instructions for the ambassadors exchanged between the different states.

57 Panduronga S. S. Pissurlencar, *Agentes da diplomacia portuguesa na Índia...op.cit.*.

58 For example, he left out all the diplomats and emissaries who were of Portuguese origin and other Indian ambassadors like Manguji Sinai and his family who followed. But at the same time one could

understand that this work is simply a collection of documents from the Goa Archives.

59 Jorge Manuel Costa da Silva Flores *Os portugueses e o mar de 1498-1543: Trato, diplomacia e guerra*, Lisboa, (unpublished masters dessertation), 1991.

60 George Davison Winius, *The Fatal History of Portuguese Ceylon: Transition to Dutch Rule*, 1638-1658, Harvard, 1971; See also his 'The Shadow Empire of Goa in the Bay of Bengal' in *Itinerario*, Vol. VII, 1983, pp. 83- 100.

61 Chandra Richard de Silva, *The Portuguese in Ceylon, 1617-1638*, Colombo, 1972.

Part II

Analysis of Issues raised in some Recent Studies

During the course of the present research it has become clear that there are a few recent works which have tried to give a new approach to Indo-Portuguese historiography using original manuscripts in Portuguese and in other languages, while the majority of authors have contented themselves with using published material and basing their conclusions on the work of others. The themes which still seem to preoccupy historians are the following: What motivated the Portuguese to embark on the voyages to India? Whether the Portuguese established any "Empire" in Asia? Can it be said that the arrival of the Portuguese brought a "Commercial Revolution" to Asia? There are some historians who have tried to minimise the impact of the Portuguese on Asia in general and on the Indian mode of commerce in particular. Some Portuguese historians still seek to justify the Portuguese use of force in establishing diplomatic and commercial relations with the Indian states as their lawful right based on the Papal Bulls. Others have tried to explain how the Portuguese survived as an imperial power during the sixteenth and the seventeenth centuries and why they ultimately failed. If on the one hand, some Portuguese historians have blamed the Dutch and the English for the decline and fall of the Portuguese "Empire", on the other, Dutch historians have emphasised, in a way defending the name of their nation that it was the administrative and commercial corruption that weakened Portuguese military and commercial strength and was really responsible for the Portuguese decline. Therefore, the Dutch had nothing to do with the Portuguese. Historians with a Eurocentric perspective tend to ignore almost completely the role of Indian merchants and rulers as well as the diplomacy, which, from the time of the arrival of Vasco da Gama, ultimately decided the Portuguese success and failure in the Indian sub-continent.

The discussion that follows, therefore, is only marginally concerned with diplomatic questions, which are the subject of the resent work. Instead it deals with the wide range of controversial socio-economic and administrative aspects of Indo-Portuguese history that have caused so much argument among historians, and seeks to show where the study of diplomacy fits in the general field of Luso-Indian historiography.

a) Views on the Portuguese Commercial Revolution

Until the last quarter of the twentieth century, history writing in Portugal was largely focussed in one direction, to study the glory of the "Portuguese Empire". The Portuguese dictator, António de Oliveira Salazar, used all his efforts to make sure, through his department of propaganda, that the whole world knew the "glory" of the Portuguese past. He idealised the greatness of Portugal and its history in such a way that it could be compared to the British Empire and its importance in the world. However, many of the works produced during his regime were in Portuguese and remained out of reach of non-Portuguese readers. Nevertheless, there were historians outside Portugal, especially in India and Britain, who tried to study the Portuguese past from a different perspective. During the period of British rule the history of the Portuguese presence in India was hardly known to anyone outside academic circles, for there were hardly any book, besides the works of Danvers[62] and Whiteway,[63] available for English readers. In Goa, still under the Portuguese regime, Pissurlenkar who, however, wrote mostly in Portuguese and later some of his works were translated into English, could be considered as the most important. Sir Jadunath Sarkar, a renowned Indian historian, referring to one of Pissurlenkar's papers based on Portuguese sources, wrote, "You are doing capital work in filling up, with your researches, a corner of Indian history in which you are sole emperor".[64] Pissurlenkar was followed by C.R. Boxer who began writing about Portuguese activities in the East in the late 1920s. It was probably Boxer's works that motivated K. M. Panikkar to study Portuguese imperial history from the Indian point of view at almost the same period. It was Panikkar who developed the idea of the 'Vasco da Gama epoch' in Asian history that brought about the ideia of a 'Commercial Revolution' during the Portuguese period.[65] This prompted some European historians to contest Panikkar's views. Among such historians, one can mention J.C. Van Leur (in fact a sociologist) who published in 1953 his revised thesis with some sharp comments that were directed against the views of Panikkar.[66]

Among the historians, mainly Dutch historians were to be found on one side of the debate while English and Indian historians tended to support Panikkar. These historians questioned whether the Portuguese commercial activities could be called a "commercial revolution" and whether they introduced any change in the existing patterns of commerce. In 1955 Van Leur wrote, that "the Portuguese colonial regime, then, did not introduce a single new economic element into the commerce of southern Asia,"[67] which was certainly contrary to the opinion of Panikkar.[68] Van Leur wrote these lines at a time when the Portuguese approach towards the history writing was confined in the circle of nationalism, as also mentioned above. Since the early 1960s, many historians from different parts of the world took up Van Leur and Panikkar's views and there followed an unconclusive long debate.

Though Panikkars' works have been long out of print and, in certain aspects outdated, one should not minimise their importance as among the leading works of the time which still provide much useful information. In particular, it was Panikkar who started all the debates that have taken place since then. No doubt his works are not presented in the scholarly way that would be expected today, but they remained the centre of attention for many modern historians, even though some of these fail to admit it. Though he has not given references in a very accurate manner for some important events of the Portuguese period, one finds from reading the Portuguese chronicles of the sixteenth and the seventeenth centuries that what he says is based on the original Portuguese sources.

When Panikkar and Van Leur wrote, there were hardly any detailed studies available of Portuguese official or private trade or of the way they tried to conduct diplomacy except the books of Danvers, Whiteway and, J. Lúcio de Azevedo. Magalhães Godinho's work, which would provide extensive detail about the Portuguese commercial adventures in Asia, was yet to be conceived. When they did appear, they were not available to English readers for it was first published in French and later in Portuguese. This means that the opinions, of both Panikkar and Van Leur were rather premature and were not based on the documents and information which were made public much later.[69]

A more radical opinion was expressed by Nambiar.[70] He viewed the Portuguese in the Indian seas as intruders, who based their right to attack and destroy Indian shipping on a few Papal Bulls. He rejected the Portuguese view that the Kunjali Marakkars were "*piratas*" (pirates), pointing out that they were the admirals of the navy of the Zamorin of Calicut and, therefore, had every right to defend the interests of their sovereign. Nilakanta Sastri, a well-known historian of South India, has also reduced the importance of the Portuguese presence in the East to almost nothing.[71] According to him the Portuguese did not bring any change either in the political or in the economic field, contrary to the views of Panikkar.

Van Leur was soon to be bitterly criticised by Meilink-Roelofsz for his lack of a thorough consultation of the available sources in Portuguese and more generally for his thesis, taking into consideration two aspects in particular: his acceptance that the Asian economy was based on the "peddling trade" and the fact that Portuguese naval supremacy was based on "technical superiority"[72] which caused a kind of revolution in the commercial organisation of Asia. As Meilink-Roelofsz truly points out, "whatever its defects, during the period of expansion, Portuguese commercial traffic was organised on a higher level than its Asian counterpart. Adequate proof of this is provided by the centralization of Portuguese Asian trade in one port of assembly and despatch, which was governed, moreover, by a highly organized bureaucracy...even if this organisation did not always work efficiently in practice."[73] In the light of the Portuguese commercial organisation and technical superiority, Meilink-Roelofsz has justified her claim that the changes that occurred to the commercial system in Asia, and the new commercial patterns and trade routes that were opened in order to escape the Portuguese controls, were revolutionary.[74] She is quite critical of the opinion of Van Leur who, in her words, "is unwilling to see the emergence of a new element until the period of Dutch expansion set in."[75] The work of Meilink-Roelofsz has been a constant inspiration and incentive for historians over many decades, even though some have not adequately recognised its importance or even mentioned it properly. On the contrary, M.N. Pearson and K.S. Mathew, for example, have fully accepted the views of Meilink-Roelofsz.

On the other hand, F.C. Lane[76] and a couple of years later, Niels Steensgaard[77] favourably accepted Van Leur's view. While the efforts of Portuguese scholars to prove the grandeur of the Portuguese discoveries and their great impact all over the world were multiplied during the Salazar's regime, these two authors were trying, with some determination, to minimise it.

Lane, in his *Venice and History,* argued that the Portuguese did not cause a 'Commercial Revolution' as had been claimed by

Panikkar and Meilink-Roelofsz. According to him the Portuguese could never satisfy the demand of the European market, as the Venetian merchants had done. Above all he claimed that, in spite of the large quantity of spices that the Portuguese carried via the Cape of Good Hope, the old caravan trade had recovered by the middle of the sixteenth century so that the new route had little long-term effect on the Italian business class.[78] He almost totally neglected the Portuguese system of *Cartaz* in imposing taxes on Asian merchant ships and commodities, which was fundamental to the operation of the *Estado da Índia*. What revolution he expected, is also a matter of discussion. If he meant that the Portuguese were unable to break the Muslim monopoly and that the old trade routes to Europe (an issue discussed later by Steensgaard) had been reopened after the middle of the sixteenth century, this is true, but it is not enough to ignore the whole of the Portuguese activities and their aggressive presence. Then there is the question, for whom was this a revolution? If it was for the Indian merchants, it was hardly any revolution in terms of the volume of commodities that they used to trade.[79] However, there clearly was a revolution in the field of commercial policy. The fact that the Portuguese tried to insert themselves into Asian trade and economy by force and the Asian traders resisted this, was altogether a new situation. It may even have constituted a revolution. However, Lane was making his comparisons of the Portuguese operation with the commercial turnover that took place during the period of British supremacy, which became fully effective from the middle of the eighteenth century and was followed by the industrial revolution, could easily be considered as far beyond the period.

Boxer on the other hand, instead of criticising the views of Panikkar, has suggested that, "this period [1500-1949] may be defined as an age of maritime power, of authority based on the control of the seas by the European nations alone; at any rate down to the emergence of America and Japan as major naval powers at the end of the nineteenth century."[80] I would agree with this simple and reasonable conclusion, although he too has avoided admitting that major changes took place in the commercial organisation of Asia enforced by the Portuguese presence.

Boxer had started his life-long adventures in the field of history as early as in the year 1928,[81] and, while on a military mission in the East, devoted his time to collecting manuscripts.[82] His work relating to diplomacy is focused on the South-East Asian states and his study of the embassy of Gonçalo Pereira to Japan and the life of Francisco Vieira de Figueiredo are major contributions to the field of diplomatic relations. Boxer also wrote about the vicissitudes of Anglo-Portuguese and the Portuguese-Dutch relations but among his most significant works on India were the essays which were published as *Portuguese India in the Mid-seventeenth century.*[83] This book, a collection of three lectures, which were delivered at the University of Bombay, looks at a period which was very critical for the Portuguese not only in Europe but all over Asial. Boxer has clearly explained the military and political position faced by the Portuguese during the period that followed the restoration of Portugal's independence. Among the reasons he gives for the Portuguese failure to maintain outright naval supremacy in Asia are their occupation of so many ports and settlements in Asia and the continuous confrontation not only with their Dutch and English rivals but also with their Asian enemies with whom they never wanted to share any of their commercial or political activities. Moreover, the king of Portugal, D. João IV, did not have the same enthusiasm for his Asian colonial dominions that had marked the dynasty of Aviz and was even apparent during the Hapsburg period. He preferred Brazil to India and referred to it as his "milch cow".[84] This leads to the conclusion that India was deliberately abandoned, a view already presented by Poonen in 1948,[85] and the Portuguese who lived there, or who were sent to govern the *Estado da Índia,* had to organise on their own without much support. In this collection of articles, Boxer has described the voyage of Vasco da Gama in 1498 as a "pioneer". Naturally he meant that it was a pioneer voyage for Europeans, and especially for the Portuguese, since India had already been in regular contact with more than half of the world.

On the other hand, Niels Steensgaard, while accepting the views of Van Leur and contradicting what Meilink-Roelofsz had written, tried to justify his position by saying that "the destructive effects of the discovery of the sea route to Asia upon the traditional intercontinental trade routes were not felt until after the elapse of an entire century".[86] This conclusion seems to be rather vague as it does not explain for whom this was "destructive"? However, the Portuguese commercial and military organisation, were, no doubt, very destructive for the Asian economy from the outset, and not after the arrival of the Dutch. A good part of the income of Asian rulers was derived from taxing merchant shipping. This was now taken by Portugal to be used to maintain their establishments in Asia. At the same time Asian shipping suffered severe losses through the confiscation of merchants' goods and this had the effect of reducing the income of the state to which they belonged. After the arrival of the English and the Dutch, a considerable number of Indian merchants started dealing directly with them and this boosted their economy contrary to what had been suggested by Steensgaard. This situation gave the business class a stronger bargaining position. Steensgaard appears to be speaking only of the 'peddler' economy of the caravan routes of Arabia. This suffered initially but recovered after the middle of the sixteenth century, as Lane has pointed out. For Steensgaard the destructive effect is what happened in the eighteenth century as a result of British commercial policy. This is a completely different issue, which does not concern this work, neither in space nor in time.

Steensgaard's work provides excellent detail on the sources he has used, though he admitted that there was still a dearth of sources to illustrate the full extent of Portuguese trading activities.[87] His main intention was to prove that the caravan trade only ended after the arrival of the English and the Dutch and not during the time of Portuguese dominance, for the Dutch and English only came to control the Gulf route after the fall of Hormuz towards the middle of the seventeenth century. In reality the Portuguese had never controlled Arabian commerce but had only been able sporadically to intercept it. As many historians have pointed out corruption among the administrative personnel was responsible for that as the Portuguese were more interested in pocketing the sumptuous profits of their private trade than looking after the interests of the state. Steensgaard is aware that the end of the caravan route was not the only thing that changed during the British dominance in Asia. The heavy ships and guns that the Portuguese carried during the sixteenth and seventeenth centuries were used also in the eighteenth century during the British period. Above all the British had far more success in controlling the mode of production in India than the Portuguese could ever possibly do in the sixteenth or the seventeenth centuries and concentrated mainly in buying and selling what were produced there for centuries. The Portuguese had only started to exploit the Asian system and were not able to manipulate it as the British were later to do.

Later Pearson elaborated on the views of Van Leur, Steensgaard and Lane by explaining the whole commercial and political network that the Portuguese had created in Asia and the way they tried, "although weakly", to control the Asian commerce with their war fleets.[88] Pearson examined the Portuguese economic and political relations with the traders and the Sultans of Gujarat. He asserted that "...peaceful competition was never the Portuguese aim."[89] They did not try to solve their political problems through diplomatic means, rather they insisted on fighting over all the issues which could have been solved in other ways. Because the Portuguese believed more in the superiority of their firearms than in diplomacy, they continued as long as they could to harass and dominate the merchant class. In brief, Pearson does not accept the legality of the Portuguese *Cartaz* system. On the other hand, he says that "the Portuguese in the sixteenth century had more impact on India than did the Dutch and British in the seventeenth century" for "during their first century in India, the northern Europeans simply merged into an existing commercial framework as two more groups of foreign merchants[90]..., for India had always been hospitable to foreigners come to trade.[91] The Portuguese, however, were not like this. They had no intention of trading peacefully alongside the dominant Muslim merchants in the Indian Ocean."[92] These themes were further developed in his *Coastal Western India* and his volume in the *New Cambridge History of India*.[93]

Among modern historians Sanjay Subrahmanyam has left no one untouched by his criticism, though most of his writings have been based, quite substantially, on published works. He has challenged all the views presented so far by both Indian and European historians. However, after reading his books one becomes more confused and finds it difficult to understand what he really accepts and rejects. Subrahmanyam's work has ranged widely over the whole of Asia but he has had comparatively little to say about coastal western India and the states of Ahmadnagar, Bijapur, Malabar and Kanara, though his book on Vasco da Gama's origin and achievements caused an outcry when he touched the sentiments of the Portuguese who have often idolised da Gama as a great discoverer and hero.

Subrahmanyam, although initially an economist, turned his attentions to Indo-Portuguese history in the early 1990s. His interest in the socio-economic history of the Portuguese in India grew stronger with the passage of time and made him a good critic of the history of the region. He has to his credit many well-received books,[94] besides numerous research papers. He focuses on the local trade networks of the *casados,* which contributed to maintaining the Portuguese empire, and especially on the Portuguese commercial establishments in the Bay of Bengal, an area not usually touched by historians. However, he has not discussed how the rulers of the Indian states tried to deal with the problems caused by the presence of the Portuguese.

Subrahmanyam's view of the political relations of the Portuguese with the merchants and rulers of both the western and the eastern coasts of India was one of "contained conflict",[95] a view later followed closely by António Vasconcelos de Saldanha.[96] But was it really a contained conflict or is this simply a way of avoiding the complexity of the issues that divided the Portuguese and the rulers of India? In this regard he could possibly have referred it to as 'contained friendship'! Subrahmanyam follows closely some of the Portuguese historians, such as Luís Filipe Thomaz, suggesting that the Portuguese presence and their commercial activities had had little impact on the Asian commercial system and society before the middle of the sixteenth century. In this he is close to the views of Steensgaard, though he does say that Indian cultivators adjusted the volume of their production as the demand kept increasing after the arrival of the Europeans, including the Portuguese. This was clearly a change in the Indian economy, even if it was on a minor scale. The volume of trade did increase but more importantly it brought a major change to the existing mentality of the Asian merchants and rulers. However, if a broader change was noticed in the pattern of Asian commerce in the seventeenth century, it was due to the increase in demand by the Dutch and the English Companies. Other trade routes from the northern hemisphere to the eastern archipelagos were also opened, avoiding the Cape of Good Hope. Therefore, sixteenth century commerce adjusted to the new conditions brought by the Portuguese, which included the factor of maritime power.

Although Subrahmanyam agrees with many of the Pearson's viewpoints, he has by and large omitted to acknowledge his works. As for the views put forward by Van Leur and Steensgaard, he has reformulated these in a more intellectual way. He agrees with both Van Leur and Steensgaard that the Portuguese did not introduce a single new aspect to the already existing economic patterns, either in the commodities traded or the trading practices. He further quoted Schama[97] that the "Dutch in their trade of the period were never too keen on the notion of improving efficiency through competitions, but preferred instead to use legislation, state power, and force to promote trade".[98] This view had already been presented much earlier in 1976 by Michael Pearson, though in different words.[99] It is also necessary to recall that all the business communities from Gujarat to the extreme south of India, though they failed to expel the Portuguese, never allowed them any peace and did not allow them to introduce any changes into the existing pattern of commerce. In this point at least I agree with Subrahmanyam, but the same point had been noticed by Nambiar and others much earlier. According to Pearson and others, including Subrahmanyam, the Dutch and the English tried to observe and respect Indian custom by approaching rulers for permission to trade and settle, thereby giving continuity to what had been in practice before the arrival of the Portuguese in the late fifteenth century. It was Portuguese stubbornness, which made them ignore the changing situation and led them to believe that they could continue with their *Cartaz* system at gunpoint.

Subrahmanyam's view on the Portuguese presence and their control of the Indian Ocean by imposing *Cartazes* and confiscating ships which did not possess them is rather confusing. Take for example his refusal to accept the view of Panikkar, who described the year 1498 as the beginning of the 'Vasco da Gama Epoch' and Sanjay' comment that "...it would be far more acceptable to state that 1500 marks a sharp break in historiography and that this is in large measure on account of the new sources for the writing of Asian history that make themselves available from the early sixteenth century on."[100] What Panikkar had actually written is as follows: "The four hundred fifty years which began with the arrival of Vasco da Gama in Calicut (in 1498), and ended with the withdrawal of British forces from India in 1947 and of the European navies from China in 1949, constitute a clearly marked epoch of history."[101] This clearly indicates that the period between the arrival of Vasco da Gama in India and the end of British rule constituted a distinct era that changed the course of history not only of Asia but the whole world.[102] It was certainly a period when two completely different civilisations came into contact.[103] It is true, as Subrahmanyam has suggested that a period of new documentation and new historiography began. But why limit this to history writing only when the whole socio-economic mentality of the leading merchant class and the rulers of India were forced to accept to the new circumstances based on the "system of *Cartazes*".

Subrahmanyam's work has principally covered the Bay of Bengal from Chittagong south to Ceylon to which he has dedicated a whole book.[104] This means that the information, which he provides about Western India is less focussed and less securely based in the documentation. Moreover he sometimes compares one incident of the early sixteenth century with one that happened in the last quarter of the 1700 in a way that is confusing. After all, even the Portuguese had changed over a period of two hundred years!

Subrahmanyam does not consider that the Portuguese were ever able to sustain a monopoly based on the *Cartaz* system,[105] and it is true that, because of corruption, the system had many loopholes, but the fact remains that both the merchants and the rulers of India feared the Portuguese warships and, although their commercial monopoly may not have been very effective, when it came to diplomacy, the Portuguese were able to exercise full control of the sea so that the kings of coastal India, fearing that would lose ships and men, were prepared to ask for *Cartazes*. Here the Portuguese continued to exercise considerable influence until the middle of the 1650s. In Subrahmanyam's view it was Indian resistance that prevented the Portuguese from changing their commercial practices, but it is clear that the Portuguese as well as the Indians, could, under the circumstances, influence each other. We can't ignore tha fact that the Indian merchants and rulers adopted the Portuguese fighting and diplomatic tactices.

To make a brief, overall summary, it can be concluded that before the arrival of the Portuguese, the Asian business class was free to trade in whatever commodities and to whatever countries and ports it wished. Merchants paid customs duties to the ruler of the country where they unloaded their merchandise and in return they were respected and protected by the authorities of that country. But, after the arrival of the Portuguese, they were not free to do what they used to do before. Earlier they only feared the sea-pirates, now they feared the Portuguese as well who forced them to go to a port controlled by them to pay duties even if they had no intention of selling their ware at that port. If those merchants did not obey, their merchandises would be confiscated and in most cases their ships were burnt. According to Portuguese authors, this was Portuguese rule, but in the eyes of an Asian, and especially in eyes of an Indian historian, it was piracy. Contrary to what many historians have written, this Portuguese practice brought a tremendous change to the trading pattern of the Asian merchants, both in the way that commodities had to be handled and in the scale of production. In addition, the control of quality had to be changed to meet the demands of the Portuguese buyers. Moreover, there were other restrictions imposed by the Portuguese on the circulation of certain merchandise, persons, arms and ammunition on the ships. Although fear for the safety of their ships obliged Asian merchants to comply with the Portuguese rules, many powerful merchants challenged the Portuguese authorities and travelled without paying dues. When corruption among the Portuguese administrative bodies became common, many more ships could travel than before.

The point I am trying to make here is that the Indian traders, under the Portuguese regime, had to pay double taxes, to the Portuguese first and the port authorities later where they sold their goods. Therefore, even if this did not constitute a 'commercial revolution', it cannot be ignored that some serious changes were brought about by Portuguese commercial policies and practices. If historians like Van Leur or Steensgaard would analyse the period in this way, they would realise how right K.M. Panikkar was in his judgment.

b) Views on the Portuguese "Empire"

There have been many other questions raised by the recent historians during their ongoing debates.Amongh that one could find the question of "Portuguese Empire". Some historians asserted that there was a "Portuguese Empire", while the thers have denied altogher its existence. In the following paragraphs, this question I have tried to analyse, in detail, keeping in view the viewpoints of other historians.

Dom Manuel's assumption of the title of the "Lord of Navigation, Conquest and trade pf Ethiopia, Arabia, Persia and India" (*"Senhor da Navegação, Conquista e commercio da Ethiopia, Arabia, Persia e Índia"*)[106] has been accepted by the Portuguese and those who followed them but its exact meaning has been challenged by many historians. Whether the *Estado da Índia* was an empire in the sense that Britain later had an empire in Asia has been much debated, particularly since the time of Salazar. From the very beginning Panikkar rejected this view as has been mentioned above and, later he was joined in this by Boxer. Luís Filipe Thomaz, among the last generation of the Salazar's regime, too, had viewed, though in a more moderate way, the Portuguese as empire builders and set out his views in *De Malaca a Pegu: viagens de um Feitor Português,* covering an area so far little known to scholars.[107] In this work he published three manuscripts with an introduction, concentrating on the major Portuguese strongholds as well as the commercial centres in Southeast Asia with which the Portuguese maintained trading relations. He has focussed on the geographical dimension of the Portuguese Empire in the East and the problem it posed for the governing bodies, as most of the areas they controlled were scattered around the world. According to him, "The Portuguese Empire in the sixteenth century was the biggest and the smallest 'empire' that Asia knew - biggest because it extended from the Red Sea to Japan, from Cambay to the Moluccas, at the same time the smallest, because it was hardly of the size of even the smallest district of China."[108] Although this book fills a gap in our knowledge about Portuguese commercial activities in the East, and the way Portuguese maintained their "Empire", it does not give any idea about the diplomacy that the Portuguese pursued with the rulers of this area.

Most historians like George Winius,[109] Luíz Filipe Thomaz, Artur Teodoro de Matos, Maria Manuela Sobral Blanco, Luís Adão de Fonseca and António Vasconcelo de Saldanha, believe that the Portuguese were displaced by their Protestant rivals, the English and the Dutch and that the Dutch were responsible for the downfall of the "Portuguese Empire". In one of their articles Winius and Blussé,[110] have maintained that the Dutch tried initially to take part in Asian trade on an amicable basis, but when the Portuguese left them no other choice they had to use force. Van Veen has also made the Portuguese responsible for the Dutch violence against their territory and shipping and considers the fall of the "Portuguese Empire" was due to their own folly. While, authors like Damião Peres,[111] Shirodkar,[112] Maria Manuela Sobral Blanco,[113] Luís Adão de Fonseca,[114] among others[115] consider that the root of the trouble between the Dutch and the Portuguese was due to the former being Catholic and the latter Protestant. Portuguese historians have tried to show that the Dutch had no right to be in Asia or to trade in Asian merchandise, whereas Dutch historians have not only tried to justify their presence but have maintained that the Portuguese were already in decline with corruption deep-seated in all their administrative and commercial establishments.

Subrahmanyam has emphasised the involvement of the Indian rulers in the downfall of the "Portuguese Empire". There is no doubt that it was the Indian rulers who initially tried to make the

Portuguese understand that there was a way by which they could all live in harmony and when they sensed that it was no use and the time was right, they gave the final blow. Nevertheless, in destroying Portuguese power on the Indian Coast, they were always assisted by a foreign hand, that of the Dutch. In this work I express the view that, on the contrary, the Indian rulers were, through their internal disputes, responsible for the survival of the "Portuguese Empire" and for prolonging its existence.

Om Prakash has recently tried to contribute to these debates with his work *Portuguese in India.* This is almost entirely based on a few already published works such as those of Danvers and Whiteway. With these volumes Om Prakash entered into the international debate on whether there was a "Portuguese Empire" or whether the Portuguese presence could better be called "Portuguese Power".[116] All these questions had already been raised and discussed by Panikkar, the only difference being that these volumes are newly published and readers can have easy access to them while the work of Panikkar has never been reprinted.

Om Prakash argues, as did Panikkar, that the Portuguese, by having a few coastal areas like Goa, Bassein, Daman and Diu under their political control, and a few small kingdoms like Cochin, Cranganore and Quilon as vassals, did not rule over more than a few square miles on the south-western coast of India. This cannot be called an "Empire". On the other hand he has also challenged the European historians who constantly refer to "Portuguese Power" just because they possessed some powerful warships which they used against the Asian rulers who, with the exception of the Zamorin, did not have any. As he points out, even with their powerful navy the Portuguese could not break the sea power of the Zamorin. After the fall of the Kunjalis, which was masterminded by the Zamorin himself, the Zamorin continued his fight against the Portuguese with the "support" of the Dutch. By this argument Om Prakash has tried to clear up the myth around Portuguese power.

In chapter thirteen of his second volume, he has discussed another issue questioning the use of the term "Portuguese India" since the Portuguese only possessed a few pockets of land here and there along the wide coastline of India which did not amount to five percent of the total. He has also questioned why, since they had the city of Macau in China, they did not refer to the State of China?[117] However, this is all very repetitive and contributes little new to the discussion. Among the earlier works of Om Prakash, one can also include his publication of one full chapter in *The New Cambridge History of India,*[118] focusing mainly on economic aspects of the Portuguese in India during the 1500-1640. This work was entirely based, for its analysis of economic data, on earlier published works and therefore adds little or no new information.

After going through the works of most of the important historians who took part in these theoretical debates, justifying their own views and contradicting the views of others, it seems that nothing conclusive can be proved. This must raise a question about whether it is really so important to waste time on such debates, especially about the question whether there was any "commercial revolution" due to the presence of the Portuguese, or if there was a "Portuguese Empire"! It appears that instead of creating a scholarly curiosity such questions became matters of prestige among the historians. Instead of producing some qualitative and unbiased research and bringing this before a new generation, they have been wasting their scholarly genius on issues which can never be answered precisely.

At the same time that these historians have been indulging in these disputes, there has been a tremendous failure to research some of the very important issues, such as the diplomatic relations of the Portuguese with the states of the south-west coast of India, which became an urgent requirement for the Portuguese to modernise in the seventeenth century. The commercial rivalry that started between them and the Dutch and the English was seriously accompanied by the diplomacy and the Portuguese by trying to adjust their position exhausted their resources and failed. Therefore, an effort has been made in the present work to study the role of diplomacy in keeping up of the "Portuguese Empire" or "naval hegemony" in India in the seventeenth century.

c) Causes of the decline of the Estado da Índia

James C. Boyajian, an accountant by profession, got interested in Portuguese commercial history towards the end of the 1980s and made use of his professional knowledge to examine one of the themes, which was then largely untouched. His first book[119] analysed the network of the Portuguese bankers in overseas commerce and he studied the role of the citizens of Lisbon and the New Christians, and the methods by which they raised their capital and managed their investments. Before this work little more than the names of the Portuguese financiers, who were actively participating in Asian commerce, were known. Boyajian is one of the authors who took up the challenge of looking into the vast and disorganised Lisbon Inquisition, notarial and financial archives which provided him with most of the evidence needed to reconstruct the activities of the great families of bankers, such as Thomás de Sampaio, Angel, Caldeira, Coronel, Frias de Salazar, Gomes d'Elvas, Mendes, Rodrigues d'Évora, Rodrigues Solis, Ximenes d'Aragão and their enterprises.

Boyajian continued this subject in another book, *Portuguese Trade in Asia under the Hapsburgs, 1580-1640,*[120] which came out in 1993. In this book he argued that the crown trade was diminishing during the Hapsburg period in contrast to the private trade of the New Christians, who were the principal investors in Portuguese overseas trade and had been deprived of their rights and any opportunities for profitable investment in the country of their origin. Boyajian even denies that any Portuguese trade was lost due to the commercial intervention of the Dutch and the English. According to him it was the Dutch blockade that inflicted most damage. These two books of Boyajian are very important and unravel many of the secrets of the Portuguese commercial activities throughout the world.

R.J. Barendse's *The Arabian Seas 1640-1700,*[121] deals with the commercial history of the Persian Gulf and the Indian Ocean during a period of 160 years, following almost the same path as did Niels Steensgaard, but it says little about the diplomatic relations between the Portuguese and the Asian states.

Ernst Van Veen[122] has also inquired if the Dutch presence in any way caused or accelerated the downfall of the Portuguese and whether the decay of the "Portuguese Empire" was not rather due to the corruption and lack of coordination among the *Estado da Índia's* officials. In other words he has enquired whether, in fact, the Portuguese Empire died a natural death. He has pointed out that "during the major part of this period the Portuguese *Estado da Índia* and the Portuguese private merchants hardly suffered from the Dutch presence in Asia. Still at least according to the Portuguese sources, there was 'something terribly rotten in the *Estado da India*'".[123] This study contrary to the others discussed earlier, has analysed the Portuguese-Dutch relations with a different perspective and has tried to show that the Dutch contributed relatively little to the fall of the "Portuguese Asian Empire". He has pointed to the weak economic situation of the Portuguese and their fractured diplomatic relations with the neighbouring states, which also contributed heavily to the decay of the Portuguese in Asia.

Although the issue of the Dutch responsibility for the decline of the Portuguese will be discussed in more detail later, a few lines are needed at this point. There is no doubt that the Portuguese sources and correspondence speak about the very fragile Portuguese economic situation, the corruption that had overtaken the administration of the *Estado da Índia* and the fact that their relations with the neighbouring states were based on mistrust on both the sides. The appearance of the Dutch in this scenario further weakened the Portuguese bargaining power during their diplomatic exchanges. By attacking Portuguese shipping and their commercial posts, the Dutch further weakened the Portuguese position. Even so the Portuguese were able to resist on many fronts until the decade between 1652 and 1663 when the Indian rulers played at least as big a part as the Dutch in bringing about the downfall of the Portuguese in Kanara and Malabar.

Van Veen has asserted that, "In the first forty years of its existence the VOC was far from the effective business organization or war machine that many writers have made it out to be."[124] He has even accused, in a delicate way, some of the historians of the twentieth century of being biased against the Dutch in relation to the Portuguese. He writes, "the writings of well-known authors on Portuguese expansion, who can hardly be accused of national bias, such a Charles Boxer, A.R. Disney, Jonathan Israel, A.J.R. Russell-Wood and George Winius, betray something of their own background, experiences and the time in which they wrote".[125]

There is no doubt that the Portuguese-oriented historians have exaggerated the involvement of the Dutch. On several occasions historians, as well as Portuguese official correspondence of the time, have mentioned that the Bijapuri sultans, the Nayaka of Ikkeri, the Zamorin of Calicut, and their ambassadors provoked such and such a war under the influence from the VOC officers. However, they do not give any detail of any incident or say if Dutch soldiers or officers were ever present with the Indian armies. A kind of Dutch phobia had been created in the seventeenth century, which is undoubtedly reflected in the work of some recent historians. On several occasions in this work I have questioned why there is no document or any name of the Dutch personnel mentioned when it is asserted that the Dutch were allied with the

Indian kings. However, this does not mean that the Dutch presence in the Indian Ocean was negative or that they did not harass Portuguese shipping, or if there was no direct war, that their presence was not felt.

Van Veen has asserted that the Mughal expansion towards South India was one of the causes of the Portuguese failure to maintain their "Empire". Up to a point this is true, but Mughal expansion provided the Portuguese with positive rather than negative opportunities for maintaining their power and prolonging their stay in India, as most of the threatened states of the *Deccan,* as have been found in sources, approachig the Portuguese Viceroys, every off and on, for help and they in exchange were able to demand the expulsion of the Dutch from their territories. Had it not been for the Mughal expansion southwards, the Portuguese would have been taken over by either the Nayakas of Ikkeri or by the Sultans of Bijapur and Ahmadnagar in alliance with the Dutch much earlier.

The main thrust of Van Veen's book is to look at the way the Portuguese tried to finance their operations and how, in the decade of the 1630s, this became increasingly problematic. Although this book largely ignores Portuguese diplomacy with the Indian States, Van Veen has given his opinion very clearly. "To begin with there was no "Portuguese Empire".[126] And "the Dutch 'threat' in terms of the numbers of ships sent to Asia, was not directed against the *Estado da India.*"[127]

After seeing all the enthusiasm with which the Portuguese discovery of the sea-route to India has been celebrated, and the incalculable amount of money that has been spent on publications, seminars and conferences in which numerous researchers from all over the world have reflected on Portuguese socio-economic relations with the states where 'spices were grown', one may wonder why few have found it worthwhile to study Portuguese diplomatic relations with the Indian states with which they were so anxious to maintain contact. Still, although a large number of the documents dealing with the diplomacy and treaties signed between the Portuguese and the Indian states have been published, most scholars have preferred to concern themselves with the diplomatic relations of China and Japan,[128] with whom, when compared with the Indian kingdoms, the Portuguese had fewer contacts over any substantial period of time.

After analysing the work done so far, it is clear that a thorough study of the diplomatic relations of the Portuguese with the south-western coastal states is essential because, without this, a part of the history of Portugal and India will remain hidden. The present work meant, therefore, to analyse, avoiding any biased view, whatsoever, the diplomatic relations of the Portuguese with the Indian States, covering the area from Goa to Malabar in the seventeenth century, keeping in view several nuances of the Indian history of that period. This study will be based on primary sources in Portuguese and English, collected from European and Indian archives and libraries. The Historical Archives of Goa, the *Arquivo Nacional da Torre do Tombo*, Lisbon, *Arquivo Histórico Ultramarino*, Lisbon and *Filmoteca Ultramarina Portuguesa*, Lisbon are among several repositories known for their documents relating to the Portuguese diplomatic relations with the Indian states, where research has been carried out to complete the study.[129] The Dutch and French sources consulted are in English translations.

Reference

62 F. C. Danvers, *The Portuguese in India*, 2 vols, London, 1894.

63 R.S. Whiteway, *The Rise of Portuguese Power in India*, (2nd ed.), New Delhi, 1979.

64 Quoted from B. S. Shastry, *Studies in Indo-Portuguese History*, IBH Prakashana, Bangalore, 1981, pp. 9-10.

65 K. M. Panikkar, *Malabar and the Portuguese*, Bombay: D. B. Taraporevala Sons & C°, 1929; *India and the Indian Ocean*. 2nd imp. London: George Allen & Unwin, 1946; *Asia and Western Dominance- A Survey of the Vasco da Gama Epoch of Asian History*, 1498-1945, London, 1953; *A History of Kerala 1498-1801*, Annamalainagar, 1960.

66 J. C. Van Leur, *Indonesian Trade and Society: essays in Asian social and Economic History*, The Hague. W. Van Hoeve, 1955.

67 Quoted from Sanjay Subrahmanyam, *The Portuguese Empire in Asia*, p. 272.

68 Panikkar, *Asia and Western Dominance: A Survey of the Vasco da Gama Epoch of Asian History*.

69 Meilink-Roelofsz, *Asian trade and European influence in the Indonesian Archipelago between 1500 and about 1630*, The Hague, 1962, pp. 2-12.

70 O.K.Nambiar, *The Kunjalis: Admirals of Calicut*, Delhi, 1963.

71 K.A Nilakanta Sastri, *A History of South India from Prehistoric Times to the Fall of Vijayanagar*, Oxford University Press, Delhi, 1966.

72 Meilink-Roelofsz, *Asian Trade and European Influence...*, pp. 2-12

73 *Ibid.*, pp. 9-10.

74 *Ibid.*

75 *Ibid*, p. 10.

76 F.C.Lane, 'Venice and History, The Mediterranean spice trade: Its revival in the sixteenth century' in *American Historical Review*, XLV, 1940, pp. 549-566.

77 Niels Steensgaard, *Carracks, Caravans and Companies: The Structural Crisis in the European-Asian Trade in the 17th Century*, Copenhagen, 1973.

78 Lane, 'Venice and History..., pp. 549-566.

79 Disney has given a tentative detail of the pepper production in the South India, *Twilight of the Pepper Empire- Portuguese Trade in South-West India in the Early Seventeenth Century* Harvard, 1978. See pages 51-52, of his Portuguese version, *A Decadência do Império da Pimenta*, edições 70, Lisboa, 1981.

80 Boxer, *The Portuguese Seaborne Empire*, 1415-1825, London, 1969, P. 39

81 Boxer, *Portugueses e holandeses*. Sep. de *Arqueologia e História*, 1928, no. 6

82 Boxer, Nuno Álvares Botelho e a sua armada de alto bordo (1624-1625): relação contemporânea, inédita, na Biblioteca Nacional de Lisboa (publ. e anot. por C. R. Boxer), Porto, 1928; A Portuguese Embassy to Japan (1644-1647) (translated by C. R. Boxer), Kegan Paul, Trench, Trübner, London 1928: European Rivalry in the Indian seas: 1600-1700, 1928, Sep. The Mariner's Mirror, 1928, vol. 14, Jan., nº 1.

83 Boxer, *Portuguese India in the Mid-seventeenth century*, Oxford Univ. Press, New Delhi, 1980.

84 *Ibid*. p. 4.

85 T.I. Poonen, *A Survey of the Rise of the Dutch Power in Malabar: 1603-78*, p. 5.

86 Steensgaard, *Carracks, Caravans and Companies...*, p. 9.

87 *Ibid*, pp. 12-15. (Although a large number of sixteenth and seventeenth century documents are said to have perished during the earthquake of 1755, much contemporary information can be found in the diaries and documents left by the Italian and German merchants in the sixteenth century. K.S. Mathew and Joan-Pau Rubíes have made good use of many such documents.)

88 M.N. *Pearson, Merchants and Rulers in Gujarat: The Response to the Portuguese in the Sixteenth Century*, New Delhi, 1976, (Passim).

89 *Ibid*, p. 54.

90 This opinion Sanjay Subrahmanyam has also accepted in his *The Portuguese Empire in Asia, 1500-1700: a Political and Economic History*, Longman, London, 1993, p. 273, but he doesn't mention if he followed the points of view of Pearson anywhere in this work.

91 This had already been expressed by an Arabian traveller, Abdul Razzak, in the mid fifteenth century, see Mathew, (edited) *Indian Ocean and Cultural Interaction (A.D. 1400-1800)*, Pondicherry University, 1996..., pp. XVI.

92 Pearson, *Merchants and Rulers in Gujarat*, p.1.

93 His other contribution to Portuguese studies could be name as following: M. N. Pearson and Blair B. Kling, (edited) *The Age of Partnership: Europeans in Asia before dominion* by Honolulu : University Press of Hawaii , 1979; Pearson, M. N. (Michael Naylor), *Coastal Western India : Studies from the Portuguese Records*, Concept, New Delhi,1981; Pearson, *The Portuguese in India*, Cambridge University Press, 1987; Ashin Das Gupta and M.N. Pearson (edited by), *India and the Indian Ocean 1500-1800*, Calcutta, Oxford University Press, 1987; Pearson, 'Indigenous Dominance in Colonial Economy- The Goa Rendas 1600-1670' in *Mare Luso-indicum*, Geneva, Librarie Droz, 1973, pp. 61-73.

94 Sanjay Subrahmanyam, *The Political Economy of Commerce, Southern India 1500-1650*, Cambridge University Press, 1990; (edited) *Merchants, Markets and the State in Early Modern India*. Oxford University Press, Delhi, 1990; *Improvising Empire: Portuguese Trade and Settlement in the Bay of Bengal 1500-1700*, Oxford University Press, Delhi, 1990; (edited) *Merchant Networks in the Early Modern World*, Aldershot; Brookfield, Great Britain, 1996; *The Career and Legend of Vasco da Gama*: Cambridge University Press, 1997. .

95 Sanjay Subrahmanyam, *The Political Economy of Commerce*, pp. 282-284.

96 António Vasconcelos de Saldanha, 'Os Portugueses no Oriente. Um Exercício de Poder: Paz, Tratados e Conflito Contido', in *Vasco da Gama*, FCG, Lisboa, 1999, vol. I, p. 335.

97 Simon Schama, *The Embarrassment of riches: an interpretation of Dutch culture in the golden age*, pp. 339-43: Quoted from Sanjay, *The Portuguese Empire in Asia, 1500-1700*...pp. 272-273.

98 Sanjay, *Political Economy of Commerce*, pp. 273.

99 Pearson, *Merchants and Rulers in Gujarat...*, p. 1.

100 Sanjay, *Political Economy of Commerce*, p. 1.

101 Panikkar, *Asia and Western Dominance*, pp. 11-15.

102 One should be reminded of the fact that recently in 1998 when Portugal planned to celebrate 500 years of the discovery of the Sea-Route to India by Vasco da Gama, not only India but many countries of the world repudiated the idea of celebration and the title had to be changed to as "The Seas".

103 Panikkar, *Asia and Western Dominance* (Passim).

104 Sanjay Subrahmanyam, *Improvising Empire: Portuguese Trade and Settlement in the Bay of Bengal 1500-1700*.

105 Sanjay Subrahmanyam, *The Portuguese Empire in Asia, 1500-1700...*pp. 108-109.

106 João de Barros, *Da Ásia..., Década* I, parte II, pp. 11-19.

107 Luís Filipe Thomaz, *De Malaca a Pegu: viagens de um Feitor Português*, Lisboa, 1966.

108 *Ibid*, p. 11-12.

109 Bailey and Winius, *Foundation of the Portuguese Empire*, 1415-1580: vol. I, *Europe and the world in the age of expansion*, Oxford, 1977, pp. 427-29; O.C. Kail, *The Dutch in India*, New Delhi, 1981.

110 George D. Winius, & Leonard Blussé, "The Origin and Rhythm of Dutch Aggression against the *Estado da Índia" in Indo-Portuguese History: Old Issues, New Questions*, (Edited Teotonio R. D'Souza), Concept, New Delhi, 1985, pp. 73-83.

111 Damião Peres, *História dos Descobrimentos Portugueses*, Porto, 1943; António Galvão, *Tratado dos Descobrimentos dos Descobrimentos*, Liv. Civil., Porto, 1944, among others.

112 P.P. Shirodkar, «Dutch-Portuguese Relations in the East», in *Stvdia*, vol. 48, pp. 123-144,

113 Manuela Sobral Blanco, *O Estado Português da Índia: da rendição de Ormuz a Perda de Cochin, 1622-1663*, (unpublished thesis) Universidade de Lisboa (1992).

114 Luís Adão da Fonseca, 'O significado Político em Portugal das Primeiras Viagens à Índia de Vasco da Gama,' in *Vasco da Gama*, vol. I, pp. 69-100.

115 Y. R. Bruijn, F. J. Gaastra, J. Schoffer, *Dutch-Asiatic Shipping in the 17th and 18th centuries*, , Martinus Nijhoff, The Hague 1987, pp. 2-8, the Dutch already had the intentions of trading with the East as they were aware of the Portuguese commercial profits.

116 Om Prakash, (ed.) *Portuguese in India*, 2 vols., Anmol Publications Pvt. Ltd, New Delhi, 2002, vol. 2, pp. 132-148.

117 *Ibid*. see chapter 13, pp. 166-230.

118 Om Prakash, 'European Commercial Enterprise in pre-colonial India: The Portuguese in India, 1500-1640,' in *The New Cambridge History of India*, part. II, Cambridge University Press, 1998. pp. 23-71; There is a little mistake in this work, though it bears no historical consequence. On page 55, it reads D. Miguel de Noronha, Fourth Count of Linhares, which should be the *third* Count of Linhares.

119 James C. Boyajian, *Portuguese Bankers at the Court of Spain, 1626-1650*, New Jersey, 1983.

120 Boyajian, *Portuguese Trade in Asia under the Hapsburgs, 1580-1640*, John Hopkins, 1993.

121 R.J. Barendse, *The Arabian Seas 1640-1700*, Leiden, 1998.

122 Earnst Van Veen, *An inquiry into the Portuguese decline in Asia 1580-1645: Decay or Defeat?: Studies in Overseas History/*1, University of Leiden, The Netherlands, 2000.

123 *Ibid*, p. 3.

124 *Ibid*. p. 8.

125 *Ibid*. p. 4.

126 *Ibid*. p. 227.

127 *Ibid*. p. 232.

128 João de Deus Ramos, *História das Relações Diplomáticas entre Portugal e a China*, (1721-1725), Instituto Cultural de Macau, 1991.; -*Estudos Luso-Orientais* (Séculos XIII-XIX) *Subsídios para a História Portuguesa*, volume 28; Eduardo Brazão, *The Embassy of Manuel de Saldanha to China in 1667-1670*, (*Notes on Sino-Portuguse Diplomatic Relations*); -*Apontamentos para a história das relações diplomáticas de Portugal com a China 1516-1753, A Embaixada de Tomé Pires*, 1516-1524 (?); *A Embixada de Manuel de Saldanha (1667-1670);-A Embaixada de Alexandre Metelo de Sousa e Meneses, 1725-1728;* John E. Wills, Jr., *Embassies and Illusions, (Dutch and Portuguese Envoys to K'ang-his, 1666-1687*); Boxer, *The Embassy of Captain Gonçalo de Sequeira de Souza to Japan in 1644-7.*

129 See Appendix I-A, and bibliography for the specific series of the documents used in this work.

Chapter 2

An Overview of the Indo-Portuguese Diplomatic System

Part I

The Portuguese

Before beginning the discussion of Portuguese diplomatic relations with the Indians states, it is necessary, briefly, to understand the real motivation that took the Portuguese to the Asian continent. It has sometimes been claimed that the Portuguese intended to propagate Christianity[130] and to find spices, for if they had been motivated by the desire for territorial expansion, it is not clear why they had to travel to such a far-off continent. Although it is true that from the middle years of the sixteenth century their missionaries tried to spread Christianity wherever they could, they only had limited success and they never had sufficient military forces to establish or expand their territorial possessions in the East. Nor did they have sufficient wealth to invest in peaceful commercial activity on a large scale. According to F.C. Lane, 'the Portuguese could never satisfy the demand of the European market, as did the Venetian merchants'.[131] The question then arises, what did they really want to accomplish with all their voyages to the East? What one must conclude is that they wanted to trade in Asian merchandise through the application of military power. They expanded their territorial bases and propagated Christianity only when the opportunity arose.

Although generally the Portuguese employed any means they could to achieve their goals, they were forced from time to time to resort to diplomacy to resolve the difficulties in which they found themselves in the course of their wars. Usually they underestimated the Asian rulers, and from their very first encounters with them, their arrogant attitude showed a total disregard for local diplomatic and political practice. They created their own law of the sea, the *'Mare Clausvm'*, completely disregarding the centuries old custom, which recognised the freedom of the seas and of commerce.[132] Later, Dutch and English theorists were to frame these ideas into a new doctrine of *'Mare Liberum'* to counter the claims of the Portuguese.

Nevertheless, in a short space of time, in the sixteenth century, the Portuguese created a network of vassal states from Africa to the Moluccas, which enabled them to achieve extensive, although weak, control over maritime trade in Indian and South-East Asian waters. In Africa the Portuguese had little difficulty overcoming the resistance of the small city-states of the seaboard. However, in Asia they encountered organised commercial networks and powerful kingdoms. To justify their presence and affect their control of the commercial shipping of the non-vassal kingdoms, the Portuguese, backed as they supposed by the papal Bulls, implemented the system of *Cartazes*, which brought them into conflict with the merchants and rulers of this region, thus initiating a period of naval warfare in the Indian Ocean.

In order to create tributary states, they used all the means at hand; exploiting local rivalries between sovereigns and their vassals, applying the policy of divide and rule and trying to make use of the religious differences between the Muslim and the Hindu states. When their plans for expansion stalled, they were forced to develop diplomatic strategies. However, in analysing the whole Portuguese commercial and diplomatic structure in Asia, it is clear that, whether they were dealing with vassal states or rival kingdoms, they always looked after their own economic interests above all others, ignoring the local social and religious values and commercial practices and paying no attention to the conventions that governed relations between states.

The religious policy adopted by the Portuguese in India was largely influenced by the crusading mentality that had been dominant in Portuguese ruling circles since the twelfth century and which they continued to demonstrate in the wars they waged against the Muslim (Moorish) states of North Africa.[133] As Manuel de Faria e Sousa, a seventeenth century historian, made very clear, "The most important instruction that the portuguese carried was that, firstly they should try to preach the Gospel[134] but if this didn't work, they were free to use force".[135]

In the course of time it became evident that their intention was to create a large Christian Asian population that would be favourable to their interests, especially in the field of commerce. In order to spread Christianity they established churches near their coastal settlements and sought to convert the local population through missionary work. In addition to that, from the time of Albuquerque, a system of inter-caste marriage was instituted which established ties with the rich and influential merchant families from which the Portuguese could get both good dowries and commercial contacts among the merchant classes of India. This practice was also intended to increase the Euro-Asian population in India, and efforts were always made to convert to Christianity those who contracted marriages with the Portuguese and their descendants.

It is with this historical realities bearing in mind or at least this is what emerges from the pages of contemporary documents that the diplomatic relations between the Portuguese and the States of South-Western India have been stuied in the following pages. But before entering into the subject directly, it is here found indispensable to focus, although in brief, on the diplomatical system that the Portuguese as well as the Indian states were accustomed to before they actually came into physical conacts.

a) The Origin and Practice of Diplomacy

The Webster English Dictionary defines diplomacy as "the art and practice of conducting negotiations between nations for the attainment of mutually satisfactory terms; adroitness or artfulness in securing advantages without arousing hostility; address or tact in conduct of affairs".[136] The Short Oxford English Dictionary defines it as, "the management of international relations by negotiation; the method by which these relations are adjusted and managed by ambassadors and envoys".[137] José Calvet de Magalhães, whose detailed analysis of diplomacy throughout the ages was published in 1995, describes diplomacy as a pacific instrument of external relations or foreign policy, while its violent instrument is war.[138]

The word *diplomacy* is derived from the Greek word *diplomã* (a folded paper). In ancient Greece, a diploma was a document certifying the completion of a course of study, typically folded in two. During the Roman period, the word *diploma* was used to describe official travel documents, such as passports and passes for imperial roads. Later, the meaning was extended to cover other official documents such as treaties with foreign tribes. The word was adopted, in the 1700s, by the French who called the body of officials attached to foreign legations the *corps diplomatique*. Edmund Burke first introduced the word 'diplomacy' into English in 1796, deriving it from the French word *diplomatie*.

The ancient Chinese preferred avoiding contacts or relations with neighbouring empires. However, records have been found that describe the protocol and rules to be followed in diplomatic dealings whenever they took place.[139] The Hindus in India also recognized the importance of diplomacy earlier than 400 years B.C. A political treatise by Kautilya, written around 300 BC, includes a chapter about envoys that outlines their responsibilities, including transmitting the points of view of their rulers, preserving treaties, defending their countries' positions and gathering information.[140]

By the fifth century BC, the Greeks had developed a system of continuous diplomatic relations. A good deal of what is known about diplomacy in ancient Greece comes from histories recorded by Thucydides, which include an account of a diplomatic conference that took place in Sparta in 432 BC.[141] This conference included "modern" concepts such as making speeches, debating, proposing motions and voting. It is also clear that the idea of diplomatic immunity had already taken root, allowing representatives from city-states with antagonistic relationships to take part in these conferences. The famous orator Demosthenes acted as an ambassador for Greece on several occasions.[142]

The Romans followed the Greek system of diplomacy[143] but their contribution was not to its practice but to its theory, stressing the importance of adhering to agreements and treaties. In the dark ages and in feudal Europe there was little in the way of an established system of dialogue between states. However the Italian cities, more than any other society at the time, remained outside the feudal system and, during the thirteenth and fourteenth centuries, the diplomatist-statesman began to appear as a result of both the common interests and the rivalries between the city-states.[144]

During the ancient and medieval periods, diplomatic missions were usually of a temporary nature, although in some cases they had to remain in being for a longer time in order to achieve their goal. Before the fifteenth century permanent diplomatic missions were unknown in Europe but, as the need to contact other states increased among the Italians, the cities resorted to maintaining permanent missions and this practice became rapidly institutionalised. The practice of appointing resident ambassadors to a foreign land is attributed to Giangaleazo Visconti of Milan who kept an ambassador for more than seven years (between May 1425 and July 1432) at the court of Sigismundo, the King of Hungary and Holy Roman Emperor. From 1448 the states of Venice and Florence also started exchanging resident ambassadors. In 1457-8 the kingdom of Naples appointed resident ambassadors in Venice and Milan.[145]

Though the popes had started receiving resident ambassadors from the Italian states, they themselves adopted this practice much later, during the pontificates of Leo X (1513-1521) and Clement VII (1523-1534).[146] From Italy the system of resident ambassadors passed to the rest of Europe. The first Portuguese permanent mission was sent to Rome in 1512, the position being filled by Dr. João de Faria for a period of three years. In 1521 Spain and Portugal exchanged ambassadors and by 1522 a permanent mission had also been set up in France. These Portuguese missions were operational till 1580, the year when Portugal lost its independence to Spain.

b) Diplomatic Practice in Portugal

In Portugal, the term *embaixador* has been found in a document belonging to the period of D. Fernando, dated 25th of July 1382, and there is a document setting out the duties of an ambassador dated 1436 during the reign of D. Duarte.[147] During the reign of D. Fernando terms such as *embaixador, mensageiro* and *procurador* were used to refer to the emissaries of the monarchs.[148] The Portuguese may have begun to use the word *embaixador* because of the influence of papal correspondence. Thus in the Bull *Saudemus et Exultamus* of Pope Benedict XII, dated 30 April 1341, the bishop of Évora, Lopo Fernandes, and Lourenço Gomes de Abreu, are referred to as *ambaxiatores et nuntii tui.*[149]

During the sixteenth century the Portuguese Crown developed its diplomatic practice. When a diplomatic mission was organised, it was the King, through his councillors,[150] who decided who would be the best ambassador, keeping in view the objective of the mission. It was also the King who gave the written instructions, or sent them on later if the ambassador had already gone to his destination. Ambassadors were supposed to follow their instructions closely. Sometimes, if necessary, the ambassadors could take the liberty of signing a treaty, going beyond what was instructed, provided they were given the power to do so. When the King of Portugal received the ambassador of a particular country, definite protocols were to be observed which depended on the nature and the origin of the mission, the status of the ambassador and the type of embassy. Only ambassadors of a very high status could contact the King directly, the rest had to approach him through the Secretary of the State, who served as intermediary. So far as the less important representatives were concerned, they were not allowed to contact the King. They could only communicate with him through diplomats of a higher category. In general ambassadors of higher status were given more privileges and more power to make decisions than the representatives of a lesser category. The same pattern was followed when sending an ambassador to other countries. A diplomat from the high nobility or aristocracy would be sent if a mission was of great importance. In some cases this proved to be very prejudicial when a diplomat from the high nobility, with less capacity for negotiation, was sent on a very important mission.

In the sixteenth century, this difference of status created rival groups of diplomats and a competition to obtain the better posts in countries like England, France and Austria. As Portugal continued to increase in importance among the states of Europe during the sixteenth century, its diplomatic activity gained in significance and complexity. Nevertheless, even as late as the seventeenth century, Portugal did not possess an organised or specialised institution for the selection and training of personnel for diplomatic service.

The important tasks of nominating diplomats and providing them with instructions were generally discharged by the King with the help of the Secretary of the State in collaboration with the *Conselho do Estado*. It was this body that, in practice, decided the payments and position of a diplomat in foreign courts. The fact that there was no fixed salary or expenses for diplomats, remained a cause of much dissatisfaction and intrigue, especially when one ambassador received an amount higher than another who was posted to discharge the same job in a country of similar status.[151] There was another drawback to the system by which they were paid. On leaving Lisbon on a diplomatic mission, most of the diplomats were given a part of their salaries in money as expenses, while the rest they had to obtain through the sale of goods, such as salt, sugar, pepper and cloves, which were in great demand in other parts of Europe.[152] In some cases ambassadors had to borrow money for their survival from Portuguese businessmen settled in the country to which they were accredited. However, such a system sometimes left the diplomats in an extremely difficult situation.

c) Organisation of Portuguese Diplomatic Missions in India

The lack of proper organisation behind diplomatic missions had a profound impact on the establishment of Portugal's relationships with the Indian states from the early sixteenth century. In the *Estado da Índia,* it was the Viceroy or the *Governador Geral,* with the consent of the *Conselho do Estado,* who decided the appropriate person for a mission to a neighbouring state as well as the kind of reception that was to be given to a visiting ambassador. Even when a letter arrived from a governor of a Portuguese fortress or town relating to a military emergency, or if a letter was received by the provincial governors from a neighbouring King who was interested in sending an ambassador to the Portuguese Viceroy, the *Conselho do Estado* was called to deliberate on the matter. The same process was followed when letters of instruction had to be issued to an ambassador to an Indian state to guide him in his discussions on relevant matters during his mission.

The membership of the *Conselho do Estado* was not fixed. It depended on which officers and *fidalgos* were present at the time of the meeting. However, the Viceroy or the *Governador Geral,* the archbishop, the captain of the city of Goa, the *Vedor da Fazenda,* the Chancellor of the city, the *desembargador,* the judges of the High Court of Goa, and any visiting officer from any part of the *Estado da Índia,* or from Portugal (the *Reino*), could be called to assist the meeting and give their opinion.[153] The final decisions were taken only with the consent of the majority but, if it was a serious matter, the Viceroy or the *Governador Geral* could suggest the decision and it had to be accepted. In brief, this *Conselho do Estado* was a body of officers whose function was to assist the Viceroy in taking decisions on civil or military affairs, including diplomacy with the neighbouring states.[154]

In their relations with the Indian states during the sixteenth century, the Portuguese hardly ever bothered to prepare an embassy or concern themselves with the status of the ambassador to be sent. Their preoccupation was solely with the results that were obtained. A Portuguese ambassador only had to possess the capacity to handle the affairs of state with dignity and honour. Although, an ambassador could be from any strata of Portuguese society, from a businessman to a *fidalgo* and from a captain to a priest, the classes on which the viceroys mostly had to depend were the resident missionaries and later on businessmen with influence in the official circles of the country to which embassies were sent. Boxer's study of Francisco Vieira de Figueiredo,[155] and of the activities of Lopo Sarmento de Carvalho[156] demonstrate, the importance of merchants in conducting diplomacy. Another such study by George D. Winius throws some light on the merchants' involvement in diplomacy.[157] He describes how Jacques de Couttre, a jewel merchant in the East, often served as a Portuguese ambassador in the neighbouring kingdoms.[158]

By the seventeenth century, the Portuguese administration was almost a monopoly of the military *fidalgos*.[159] Noble origin had become the most important quality required for any post, whether administrative or diplomatic. Boxer has called it a "mania for *fidalguia*" – a belief that only persons from high society were fit to hold certain posts.[160] However, in the case of the *Estado da Índia,* Portuguese diplomacy, more often had to depend on other personnel and there are numerous cases of the diplomatic groundwork for the Portuguese being done by missionaries.

d) The Role of Missionary in the Indo-Portuguese Diplomacy

Although from the beginning of the sixteenth century there had always been secular Catholic priests, and later Jesuits, resident in most of the neighbouring states who, from time to time, mediated between the Portuguese and the states with which the Portuguese had entered into conflict, the first permanent diplomatic missions started only in 1576 at the suggestion of the Sultan of Bijapur. He proposed to the Portuguese Viceroy in Goa that both sides should keep ambassadors at the other's court in order to avoid conflict and maintain friendly relations.[161] In the south Indian states too, there is no reference whatsoever to resident ambassadors until the arrival of the Portuguese and their Jesuit missionaries who exercised their function both as missionaries and as envoys, quite often, remained for long periods. In contrast, the Portuguese maintained direct contact with the rulers of the vassal kingdoms of Cochin, Cannanore, and Cranganore through their state governors, captains of the fortresses or the factors in their factories.

More will be said later in this chapter about the role of missionaries as ambassadors and spies, so the question inevitably arises why the Portuguese made use of the services of missionary priests as diplomats, and why the Indians, as will be seen later, preferred to receive them rather than Portuguese officials as ambassadors? There was usually at least one priest with every diplomatic mission. The explanation is likely to have been as follows. Firstly, the priests were the most educated and articulate of all the Portuguese in the East and possessed skills very different from those demonstrated by men like Vasco da Gama and Álvares Cabral. This factor alone would have been sufficient for the members of the Council to have nominated them for positions as ambassadors. Secondly, the Portuguese were aware of the conservative Indian mentality, which was typified by the Brahmins.[162] They assumed that, as Hindus were accustomed to the presence of religious persons and used to being governed by the laws of the temple, their priests would be more readily accepted. Thirdly, the missionary priests had learned the local languages and this made it easier for them to circulate in Indian society and communicate with people of all classes, muchin the same way as did the Brahmin priest. At the same time it made the task of gathering information much easier as they had access to almost all the classes of Indian society.

The role of the missionaries in Indo-Portuguese diplomacy was extremely important in maintaining and prolonging Portuguese dominance in Asia, in general, and in India, in particular. The missionary priests, whether they belonged to the Jesuit, Dominican or Franciscan Orders, performed two different roles, one as ambassadors serving the Portuguese *Estado da Índia* and the other as agents for the religious Orders to which they belonged. They always gave priority to spreading the faith rather than to pursuing political objectives. They tended to assume that, if they were successful in bringing the Indian rulers to the Christian faith, their political problems would be solved without any trouble.[163]

After the arrival of Francisco Xavier in 1542, the Jesuits came to dominate the Christian missions in India. The Jesuits were highly respected in all the Indian courts and could discharge diplomatic missions with more success than the Portuguese officials. Jesuits at the Mughal court, like Fr. Rudolfo Aquaviva[164] and Fr. António Monserrate; Father Gonçalo Martins and António Botelho at the court of Bijapuri sultan; Fr. Simão Graça and Fr. Pimentel at the court of the Chinese emperors are examples of the churchmen who were employed in the service of the Portuguese *Estado da Índia* and who, from time to time, led the embassies or served as messengers of peace on the western coast of India. Priests were also employed by the local rulers as the representatives of the Indian states to the Portuguese court at Goa. Between 1613 and 1615, for example, Portuguese-Mughal relations became difficult because the Portuguese had seized a large ship belonging to the Mughals, as a result of the latter's support for the English. The Mughal governor cut off all relations with the Portuguese, confiscating all the goods belonging to the Church and to Christians throughout his domain. The Jesuit priest, Father Jeronymo Xavier, was sent by the Mughals to Goa to discuss the terms of peace.[165] During the same period, Father João de Cruz, one of the prisoners of war, conducted the diplomacy between the Portuguese and the Mughal concerning the Portuguese expulsion from Hoogly. As a result Shah Jahan issued a Farman releasing all prisoners and returning all booty captured during the war.[166] Similarly, two Jesuit priests, as mentioned above, António Botelho and Gonçalo Martins, were sent to the court of the Sultan of Bijapur to mediate between the Portuguese authorities and the Sultan in 1654.[167] In fact António Botelho, at the request of the Adil Shah, became a permanent resident at the court of Bijapur. In addition, it was through the efforts of these two priests that Dom Manuel Lobo da Silveira, the Portuguese military commander, was freed from the prison of the Bijapuri Sultan. Moreover, when trouble arose between the Portuguese and the Bijapuri kingdom, the Sultan asked the Portuguese Viceroy specifically to send Gonçalo Martins to deal with the matter. Gonçalo Martins was not only a priest, but also a moneylender and a businessman who had been on various diplomatic missions to the court of the Nayakas of Ikkeri.

The role of Jesuits did not stop there. In 1659, Pero (or Pedro) da Costa de Brito S.J., was found mediating at the court of Shivappa Nayaka, along with Ramogy Sinai Kothari, son of Santuji Sinai, over the question of the lost fortresses of Mangalore, Bareclore and Onor.[168] These were not isolated cases for on several occasions in sixteenth century Christian priests from various Orders were employed to mediate between states or to resolve some intricate social questions.

When priests were sent by the *Estado da Índia* on diplomatic missions, they carried precise instructions concerning the matters to be discussed in the name of the state, whereas it was the superior of the Order who provided instructions for promoting religious activities when their mission was religious only. Many Jesuits carried out commercial activities to meet their expenses, whereas other priests were more dependent on being financed by their Order. When on purely religious missions to the courts the priests had to seek permission to carry on preaching and to make conversions. It was only during time of war that the authorities of the *Estado da Índia* had to worry about their safety.

The religious missions, contrary to the political ones, were not concerned about the nature of the reception that they were given, which officials were present and what gifts they carried for the king. There are no records to show whether the missions ever experienced problems over the lack of protocol from any court. The success of these missions always depended on the benevolence of the kings and Sultans, who never expected to get anything in return from those missionaries. The only conditions were that the missionaries would not apply or employ force to convert any one from any sect or creed. However, the missionaries in the field were supposed to remain in touch with their superiors, who were mostly in Goa, on a regular basis. Much of the correspondence of the various Jesuit priests has been published and constitutes a very rich source.[169]

On the other hand, the political diplomacy carried out by the same missionaries had to benefit both sides. It had to attain specific objectives and to be of mutual benefit. It had to make sure that treaties were signed and their conditions carried out. These diplomatic missions were supposed to bring lasting peace between states, whereas the religious missions were more dependent on the goodwill of the people who wanted to accept the Christian Gospel.

When such missionaries had religious intentions and visited any court they were given a less formal reception than if they came as ambassadors. They were not burdened by official diplomatic protocols as were diplomats representing their state on political missions, whether they were clergy or professional diplomats. An example of this can be seen at the Mughal court where Akbar invited the Jesuits from Goa to discuss religious issues and met with them as though he was meeting someone from his circle of friends. He was quite often seen walking with his hands on the shoulders of Fathers Aquaviva, Monserrate and Pierre du Jarric and talking to them as if he had known them for a long time. He allowed them to teach his sons Portuguese and Christian doctrine, which had not previously been seen in Mughal history.[170] Whereas in the normal day to day life of the court no body would dare even to go close to a Mughal Emperor without his permission. The same relationship can be seen when the Sultan of Bijapur asked the Portuguese authorities at Goa especially to send Fr. Martins to discuss diplomatic or religious affairs. This was unusual as in the political diplomacy no one commands or requests that an ambassador of his or her choice should be sent.

e) Mouros de Mecca - Mouros da Terra

While the Indian rulers, especially the Muslims, apparently held the Portuguese religious and non-religious authorities in high regard, the Portuguese considered them to be little more than infidels and unworthy of their status. The Portuguese generally referred to all the Muslim merchants and rulers with only one name, *mouros*, whether they were the rulers of Bijapur, Ahmadnagar or the Mughal Empire, or businessmen like Ali Raja and the Marakkars. In this study I have generally used only one term 'Muslim' in order to reduce the confusion that some historians have created by defining separately the Arab Muslims, calling them *mouros da Mecca* and the Muslims of Asia who they call *mouros da terra* (Muslims of the land or native Muslims).[171] According to such historians, the Portuguese considered the former more their enemy than the latter. Most writers, however, have termed the first group *paradesi* (foreign) Muslims.[172] It is necessary to examine the difference that Sanjay Subrahmanyam, quoting Geneviève Bouchon,[173] claims existed between the *mouros da terra* and *mouros de Mecca.* According to him, "...the Portuguese now carefully distinguished between the *mouros da terra* ('native Moors') and the *mouros de Meca* ('Moors from Mecca' - which is to say the Middle East); they saw the latter rather than the former as their principal adversaries."[174]

The early encounters of the Portuguese with the Arabian merchants on the Malabar Coast, especially the Karimi merchants from Egypt and some others from Arabia, who were the dominant traders among Asian business communities, made them realise that they would have tough competition if they wanted to transact business in those regions.[175] However, similar commercial rivalry also existed between the foreign Muslims, and the local Muslims.

Subrahmanyam took the example of the early Portuguese and Arab encounters which were based on some serious misunderstandings created by the interpreter and fear to loosing their commercial outposts and, which became more complicated when the Portuguese, instead of competing with them commercially, tried to eliminate them by force. On the other hand, the Portuguese found no other way except to side, occasionally, with the local merchants, such as *Mopilahs* and *Marakkars*,[176] the most prominent merchants classes of the Indian Ocean region, for the their initial pepper contracts. These Muslim merchants of coastal south India did not hesitate to have commercial dealings with the Portuguese irrespective of the fact that the latter were Christiansas long as they paid for the goods they sold.[177]

So far as the Muslims from the Arabian peninsula are concerned, after the two naval battles (1507-1509) and especially after the assassination of the Zamorin by his own nephew with the help of the Portuguese in 1513,[178] most of the merchants, terrified by what had happened and noting the absence of the support which they had enjoyed for centuries, tried to keep away from that zone and left the local business class to take care of the commerce with the Portuguese. Portuguese relations with the local Muslims remained relatively cooperative until the governorship of Albuquerque, after which the governors and viceroys started to control the ships and merchandises of even these Muslims. This marked the beginning of hostilities and wars that continued for over a century. Even before this period, when the Portuguese lacked supplies, they would plunder the ships of the local Muslims. Therefore, it is clear that the distinction made by Subrahmanyam was never made by the Portuguese. A clearer picture of the relationship of the Portuguese with local Muslims and with Arabs is given by Pius Malekandathil who is of the opinion that 'since the early sixteenth century, as the Portuguese wanted to put a check on or even to destroy completely the commercial activities of the *paradesi* or foreign Muslims, the local Muslim communities such as those from the Marakkar origin took maximum benefit of this situation and joined hands with the Portuguese.'[179] Nevertheless, when the Portuguese started to enforce their *Cartaz* system over these merchants too, they challenged the Portuguese attitude. Two things came up, that they organised their forces against the Portuguese and fled to Calicut where they turned the captains of the Zamorins navy. On the other hand the Portuguese earned a long term resistance and called them 'pirates,' who systematically attacked the Portuguese and their commercial interest.[180] Joan-Pau Rubiès explains the motives and attitude of the Portuguese in the following way, "...the initial reaction of the Portuguese in India was to identify the Hindus with Christians, whom they had been led optimistically to expect there and to regard the Muslim communities involved in oceanic trade as natural enemies, whom they could and should legitimately fight".[181]

In practice the Portuguese tried to control every ship no matter to whom it belonged and no matter what it was carrying, and to force it to pay taxes. There are no documents from the Portuguese king, or the authorities of *Estado da Índia,* which suggested treating the *'mouros da Mecca'* differently from the *'mouros da terra'*. They treated both alike while looting and burning their merchant ships, especially after 1513.

Boxer had already pointed out that. "The Portuguese habit of describing all the Muslims they met from Morocco to Mindanao as 'Moors' (*Mouros*) tends to obscure the fact that when they reached the Indian Ocean the Arabs no longer dominated the seaborne trade of Monsoon Asia from Ormuz to Canton, as they had done much earlier."[182] Rather than employing the terms mentioned by Subrahmanyam and Bouchon, the Portuguese frequently refer in contemporary documents to the Turks, Rumes and Habshees, as their most inveterate enemies in the early sixteenth century as these were fighting races. All the *Cartazes* which were issued by the Portuguese, not only in the sixteenth but also in the seventeenth centuries and later, used the same formula, 'that the ship so and so, among the prohibited items is not allowed to either carry or bring any *rumes, turcos, abexins.'*[183] No mention is made either of *Mouros da Terra* or *Mouros de Mecca.*

There is no doubt the Portuguese wanted to eliminate the most powerful merchants of Arab origin, who had their 'trade monopoly' throughout Asia. However, in the Southeast Asian coastal regions, it was the Gujarati and Malabari Muslims, who dominated the local trade.[184] Reference is made to the family of Ali Raja, which constituted the oldest Muslim commercial network, and which was of mixed Arab and Indian origin, tracing its ancestry back to the seventh century. They were the leading business magnates of Cannanore and from the time of their first arrival the Portuguese not only traded with them but fought them as well.[185] The same applies to the Marakkars, or Kunjali Marakkar family, originally from the area of the present Tamil Nadu and later settled at Cochin and later left for Ponnani in the dominion of the Zamorin when the Portuguese started to interfere with their commercial activities. These two most important families with which the Portuguese had commercial relations and with which they fought over and over again were *mouros da terra* and not *mouros de Mecca.*[186]

It was the Marakkar family that the Portuguese resented most and they were *mouros da terra*.[187]

Michael Pearson has given more information on the merchants who operated in the Indian Ocean and what areas, routes and commodities they traded. He particularly mentions that Muslims originating from Arabia, Persia, Turkey and from India, from Gujarat to Malabar, all participated equally in Indian Ocean commerce. On certain routes it was the Arab merchants who predominated. This domination was based on the volume of their trade and investments rather than on adopting violent measures to prohibit others from trading in certain commodities or going to particular areas as was done by the Portuguese.[188] Pearson is silent on the question of whether the Portuguese distinguished between the *Mouros da Terra* and *Mouros da Mecca*. His are among the most reliable works which assess the role of Muslim merchants in sustaining the Portuguese economy and in ensuring their survival during the seventeenth century through the taxes they paid on their own official and unofficial trade, especially when other sources of finance for the *Estado da Índia* were insufficient to maintain the wars against the Dutch and the struggle with the Indian neighbouring states.

In the end, one is tempted to ask a simple question - would Portuguese conduct have been different if they had encountered another business community than the Muslim? The sources suggest that the answer would be in the negative. The Portuguese had no intention of allowing any ships belonging to *Vaniyas*, or Jains or Muslim merchants from Gujarat, Ahmadnagar, Bijapur or any part of Asia if they did not carry a *Cartaz*. They would not even allow businessmen from the communities of Syrian Christians and they tried to intercept and control the Dutch and the English ships, which were trading without their consent. As it is known, this attitude and policy wihtout sufficinet economic and miltiary resources, turned out to be fatal for their own survival.

Therefore, in conclusion, one can assert that for the Portuguese the whole Muslim merchant or ruling class, whether they were *Mouros da terra* or *Mouros de Mecca,* were alike, especially after the second decade of the sixteenth century. They made no distinction in the terminology they used, either in correspondences or in direct dealings.

Reference

[130] Many historians refer it to propagate Christianity. *"Vimos buscar cristãos e especiarias,"* see Álvaro Velho, (notas e anexos por A. Fontoura da Costa), *Roteiro da primeira viagem de Vasco da Gama,* Agência Geral do Ultramar, Lisboa 1960, p. 36.

[131] Lane, *Venice and History*, pp. 549-566.

[132] *The Laws of Manu*, pp. 278-302.

[133] Joan-Pau Rubiès, *Travel and Ethnology in the Renaissance: South India through European Eyes, 1250-1625*, Cambridge University Press, 2002, p. 165; For an exhaustive detail about the Moors, see a complete section dedicated in this chapter.

[134] Here this mean dicatating terms or na imposed conversation.

[135] Faria e Sousa, *A Ásia Portuguesa*, 6 vols., Livraria Civilização, Porto, 1947, vol. I, p. 129: Faria e Sousa's work is based mostly on Fernão Lopes de Castenheda, João de Barros *Da Ásia de João de Barros,* & Diogo de Couto's *Décadas.*

[136] *Webster's Third New International Dictionary*, G&C, Meriam Co, USA, 1966, p. 638.

[137] A Short *Oxford English Dictionary*, vol. I, Oxford, 1947, p. 514.

[138] José Calvet de Magalhães, *A Diplomacia Pura,* pp. 15-30; Joel Serrão (dirigido por), *Dicionário de História de Portugal,* volume 1/ A-D, pp. 823-827.

[139] *Ibid.*

[140] His work is known as *The Kautilyas Arthashástra,* (ed.) R. P. Kangle, University of Bombay, 1965, (or the Economics of Kautilya/ the science of polity), and his full name was Vishnugupta Kautilya who is also known as Chanakya. He was the Prime Minister of Chandra Gupta Maurya.

[141] Thucidides, *History of the Peloponnesian War,* William Benton, Chicago, 1952, vol. I, pp. 57-79, 121-23.

[142] Magalhães, *A Diplomacia Pura...,* pp. 40-41.

[143] Harold Nicolson, *Diplomacy,* Oxford University Press, 1969, p. 9.

[144] *Ibid*, pp. 6-29.

[145] Garrett Mattingly, *Renaissance Diplomacy*, Penguin Books, Baltimore, 1964, pp. 55-87.

[146] Magalhães, *A Diplomacia Pura,* pp. 58-59.

[147] João Martins da Silva Marques, *Descobrimentos Portugueses: Documentos para a sua História.* (Publicada e prefaciada por) vol. I, (1147-1460) INIC., Lisboa, 1987. (Edição Facsimilada da 1ª Edição de Instituo de Alta Cultura, 1944). pp. 349, 372, 418.

148 Fernão Lopes, *Crónica do Senhor Rei Dom Fernando Nono Rei destes Regnos,* Civilização Editora, Porto, 1966, pp. 9-10, 25, 83, 139-141, 159, 177, 187, 215, 314.

149 Silva Marques, *Descobrimentos Portugueses,* vol. I, p. 66.

150 See collection in ANTT entitled, *Secretaria de Estado / Ministério dos Negócios Estrangeiros.*

151 Pedro Cardim, 'Embaixadores e Representantes diplomáticos da Coroa Portuguesa no século XVII', in *Cultura: Revista de História e Teoria das Ideias,* (II Série) nº 15, Universidade Nova de Lisboa, 2000, p. 57.

152 *Ibid.*, pp. 75-76.

153 See the whole series of the *Conselho do Estado* (Published by Pissrulenkar) for the procedure to be followed in order to take decisions by the members of the same *Counselho do Estado.*

154 M.N. Pearson, *Merchants and Rulers of Gujarat...,* New Delhi, 1976, pp. 3-34; In a more recent work Luiz Filipe F. Reis Thomaz, 'A questao de pimenta em meados do século XVI' in, Artur Teodoro de Matos, & Luís Filipe F. Reis Thomaz. (dir.) *A Carreira da Índia e as Rotas dos Estreitos: actas* do VIII Seminário Internacional de História Indo-Portuguesa, Angra do Heroísmo, 1998, pp. 37-44, has explained how the *Conselho do Estado* functioned in the sixteenth century. There is a specific case regarding the purchase of pepper on which the *Conselho do Estado* during the time of the Portuguese Viceroy, D. João de Castro had met to take decision. A full report on how each Councillor gave his opinion for the purchase of pepper has been brought to light in this article.

155 Boxer, *Francisco Vieira de Figueiredo....* (Passim)

156 Boxer, *Breve Relação da vida e feitos de Lopo e Inácio Sarmento de Carvalho...* (Passim)

157 Winius, 'Jewels and Jewel Traders in Portuguese Asia', a Seminar paper presented in the IV International Seminar on Indo-Portuguese History, (ISIPH/4) 1985, Junta de Investigação Ciêntífica Tropical (*JICT*), Lisboa.1985 A similar study appeared, in 1989, by Teotonio R. De Souza, 'Embassies and Surrogates, op.cit.

158 Winius, '*Jewels and Jewel Traders in Portuguese Asia*' in ISIPH/4.

159 Boxer, *Portuguese India in the Mid-Seventeenth Century,* p. 6; Also see the article of Pedro Cardim, 'Embaixadores e Representantes diplomáticos da Coroa Portuguesa no século XVII', in *Cultura: Revista de História e Teoria das Ideias,* (II Série) nº 15, pp. 47-86,

160 Boxer, *Portuguese India in the Mid-Seventeenth Century,* p. 6.

161 *Contrato das pazes feitas com o Idalxá por seu Embaixador Zaerbeque, que veio do Reino, governando este estao António Moniz Barreto, no anno de 1576,* Biker, (ed.) *Collecção de tratados e concertos de pazes...,* tomo I, pp.170-176; *APO-CR,* fascículo, 5, doc. 742.

162 See section on, Indian diplomatic origin, for more details.

163 See for example the Jesuit missions under Fr. Rudolfo Aquaviva at the court of Mughal Emperor Akbar and his efforts to convert the later to Christianity, failing which he wrote a very sad letter to his superior. Most of correspondences could be seen in Sir Edward Maclagan, *Os Jesuitas e o Grão Mogol,* Livraria Civilização-Editora, Porto, 1946.

164 *Ibid.*, pp. 30-32.

165 Maclagan, *Os Jesuitas e o Grão Mogol...*, pp. 97-99; Biker (ed) *Collecção de tratados ...*, tomo 1, pp. 189-192.

166 J.J.A. Campos, *History of the Portuguese in Bengal,* Delhi, 1979, pp. 142-44.

167 Artur Teodoro de Matos, (edited), *Diário do Conde de Sarzedas, Vice-rey do Estado da Índia (1655-1656),* Lisboa, 2001, see footnotes on the page 82.

168 Pissurlenkar, *Agentes da Diplomacia Portuguesa na Índia...*, pp. 50-54.

169 Details of these publications and the archives where they can be consulted are given in the section, "Information and spying services".

170 For an exhaustive account of Jesuits activities and their relations with the Mughal Emperors, see the following works; Maclagan, *Os Jesuitas e o Grão Mogol*; Fr. Pierre Du Jarric, *Akbar and the Jesuits: An Account of the Jesuit Missions to the Court of Akbar by Father Pierre du Jarrics,* George Routledge & Sons, Ltd. London, 1926, (Reprinted) by D.K. Publishers, New Delhi, 1999.; Father António Monsserate, *The Commentary of Father Monsserate, S.J., on his Journey to the Court of Akbar,* (First published in 1922) reprinted by Asian Educationsal Services, New Delhi, 1992.

171 Such as, Geneviève Bouchon and Sanjay Subrahmanyam.

172 This word *Pradesi* is an indo-persian word and now very well integrated in the north Indian languages, such as in Hindi and Urdu. Subrahmanyam has generally used it in most of his studies and has been followed by, Jayaseela Stephen, *Portuguese in the Tamil Coast: Historical Explorations in Commerce and Culture (1507-1749),* and recently Fr. Pius M.C. Malekandathil, "From Merchant Capitalists to Corsairs: The Response of the Muslim Merchants of Malabar to the Portuguese Commercial Expansion (1498-1600)," in *Portuguese Studies Review,* volume 12, no. 1, Winter-Spring, 2004-2005, pp. 75-96, has used it frequently. But it is necessary to point out that this is totally a modern term used in the northern India and is never mentioned in either the Portuguese or the local languages of south India. These authors have used this term only to make their studies seem more exotic. It was not part of the official terminology of the age.

173 Subrahmanyam, *The Portuguese Empire in Asia, 1500-1700...*, p. 56.

174 *Ibid.*

175 Boxer, *Portuguese Seaborne Empire*, pp. 45-46;

176 About the origin of Mopilahs and Marakkars, see a recent work of Fr. Pius, already cited above beside the prominent work of Mme Geneviève Bouchon, *Mamale de Cananor: un adversaire de l'Inde portugaise: 1507-1528*, its English translation is *Regent of the Sea, Cannanore's Response to Portuguese Expansion.* ,

177 Pius Malekandathil, "From Merchant Capitalists to Corsairs: pp. 75-96.

178 *Cartas de Affonso de Albuquerque*, tomo, I, pp. 152-53. *For more detailed view of the Portuguese Zamorin relation during the early years of the sixteenth century, see chapter two in Mathew, Portuguese Trade with India...op.cit.*

179 *Ibid.*

180 Ibid. pp. 80-88.

181 Joan-Pau Rubiès, *Travel and Ethnology in the Renaissance..., 1250 1625*, p. 165.

182 *Ibid.*, p. 44.

183 See a specimen copy of a *Cartaz* in Apendix, II-A & B .

184 Pearson, *Merchants and Rulers...* (op.cit)

185 Geneviève Bouchon, *Afonso de Albuquerque: leão dos mares da Ásia*, trad. Isabel de Faria e Albuquerque, Quetzal, Lisboa, 2000.

186 Subrahmanyam, *The Portuguese Empire in Asia, 1500-1700*, p. 56

187 Pius, "From Merchant Capitalists to Corsairs: The Response of the Muslim Merchants of Malabar to the Portuguese Commercial Expansion (1498-1600)," pp. 75-96.

188 Pearson, *Merchants and Rulers..*, pp. 7-18.

16.

Boxer, Portuguese Seaborne Empire, pp. 60-61.

About the original [illegible]

[illegible] [illegible] [illegible] [illegible] [illegible] [illegible] pp. [illegible]

[illegible] [illegible] [illegible] [illegible] [illegible] [illegible] [illegible]

Ibid., pp. 80-85.

[illegible] [illegible] [illegible] [illegible] [illegible]

Ibid., p. 41.

[illegible] [illegible] [illegible] [illegible] [illegible]

[illegible] [illegible] [illegible]

[illegible] [illegible] [illegible] [illegible] [illegible]

[illegible] [illegible] [illegible], Lisboa, 2400.

[illegible] [illegible] [illegible] [illegible]

[illegible] [illegible] [illegible] [illegible] [illegible] [illegible] [illegible] of the Portuguese [illegible] Experience (1498-1630), pp. [illegible]

[illegible] [illegible] [illegible], p. [illegible]

Part II

Indian States

a) The Origin of Indian State Craft and Diplomacy through the Ages

"In the happiness of his subjects lays the king's happiness, in their welfare his welfare. He shall not consider as good only that which pleases him but treat as beneficial to him whatever pleases his subjects" –

Kautilya

Although in each chapter, the political structure of the different states has been provided, in the following passages an attempt has been made to provide, an overview of the Indian polity and diplomatic system that persisted, which the Portuguese testified after their arrival.

Indian Polity through the ages

The origin of Indian political thought lies further in the past than the composition of the treatise of *The Laws of Manu* and the *Arthashastra* of Chanakya, but it is in these two, and especially since the time of Chanakya, that the Indian political system finds its foundation. *Manav Dharm Shastra* or *The Laws of Manu,* based on traditions and scriptures, the *Vedas,*[189] are still important in the present Indian civil code and justice. This book was one of the most important handbooks to be consulted in all the matters concerning the law of the country, covering the civil and criminal codes, from small disputes to international diplomacy, religious and non-religious affairs, marriages and adultery and so on. It is considered one of the sacred books of Hindu society. The Indian penal code and social laws are still based on it, though, naturally, taking into account the present Indian social structure.

Arthashastra[190] was written or compiled by the 'king maker' Chanakya who is also known as Kautilya or Vishnugupta, during the early years of the Mauriyan Empire, between the 4th century B.C and 150 A.D. However, authorship of this treatise has been variously disputed due to its internal stylistic variations and it has been argued by analysts that it could have had a collective authorship. *Arthshastra* explores the needs of statecraft in the

Mauryan Empire during Chandragupta Maurya's reign (322-298 B.C.). It argues for a benevolent autocracy managing an efficient and stable economy. It discusses political and economic ethics and, most important of all, the duties and obligations of a king. Many of the topics discussed remained current in Indian political philosophy up to the late eighteenth century and, after India gained its independence, the ideas set out in this treatise were widely accepted, alongside concepts deriving from the periods of Muslim and British rule.

According to the *Arthashashtra*, the supreme head, the symbol and expression of the state, was the king. Kingship required exceptional qualities. Every part of the day and night was apportioned into suitable periods for the ruler's various, administrative duties: hearing of public and confidential reports and consultation with the ministerial council, treasury, and army heads. The intervals for rest, sleep, meals, entertainment, or the pleasures of the harem were severely restricted. Far from 'wallowing in oriental luxury', the *Arthashastra* monarch was the hardest-worked person in his realm. Not every king could stand the pace, particularly as the most detailed precautions had to be taken at all times against poison and the assassin's knife. The king had to possess his own army instead of depending on the armies of the nobles and he was to march at the head of his army whenever it was needed. Spies and secret agents of various kinds were to be maintained. Peace missions were to be carried out by the supreme *Brahaman.*

The scope of *Arthashastra* is, however, far wider than the statecraft of the ruler. It emphasises the extreme importance of *Dharma* and knowledge, and it offers an outline of the entire legal and bureaucratic framework for administering a kingdom, with a wealth of descriptive cultural detail on topics such as mineralogy, mining and metals, agriculture, animal husbandry and medicine. Although he wrote in a period of absolute rule by emperors, Chanakya also focuses on issues of welfare (for instance, the redistribution of wealth during a famine) and the collective ethics that hold a society together.

This remained the most important political treatise until the arrival of the Muslims from Central Asia at the end of the twelfth century. Until this time, the Indian political system was a Hindu system almost totally under the control of the Brahmins. They followed the strict rules suggested by all the *Vedas* and no ruler would dared violate or ignore the decree of a court Brahmin.

Initially the Muslim rulers followed a very strict Islamic code, especially during the period 1206-1526 but, as time passed, they became accustomed to the Indian mentality and realised the difficulties they would face if they continued to follow their way of government. Even though the Muslim conquerors, initially, disregarded Hinduism, they had to change their way of dealing when they realised the importance of religion within Indian society. The Muslims had no choice but to adapt to the new society and to change their governing system so that it could be accepted by all, even if with some reservation. Various aspects of the Indian political system were maintained and some more added which were suitable to both the Hindu and the Muslim population. Though Muslims do not practise the idolatry, they had to respect Hindu ideas and it was here that they understood the importance of the Brahmins from whom many Muslim scholars learnt not only the system of government but also astronomy and astrology. The presence of a Brahmin was highly esteemed and many Muslim rulers appointed a Brahmin or a highly respected elderly person from Hindu society as a minister to advise, especially, related with their Hindu subjects. Muslim rulers also appointed senior ministers, army generals and ambassadors from Hindu society.

This period in India is known Sultanate Period when the Sultans of Delhi used to received the insignia of royalty from the Caliphs of Baghdad. It was during this period that the Bahmani Empire emerged and gave way on its downfall, to the five kingdoms of southern India - Ahmadnagar, Golconda, Berar, Bijapur and Bider. However, with the expansion of Muslim rule in India, Hindu rule did not disappear completely, in South India. There were many Hindu dominated states, among them Vijayanagar and all the Malabar states of coastal Western India. Hindu resistance to Muslim expansion continued. When both groups became used to the presence of one another, they liberalised their policies towards their subjects. Whether Hindu or Muslim, they created civil codes which protected each community.

With the arrival of the Mughal Emperor, Babar, in the north, who replaced the last of the Lodi dynasty in 1526, the image of the Muslim rulers started to change. Mughals were more liberal minded and avoided any type of influence from the Caliphs. From the beginning they followed a policy of mutual understanding keeping in mind who their subjects were. They employed Raajputs and Brahmins in the high offices of state and, as well as relying on

Hindu soldiers, appointed most of the army generals from the Rajput class. They married Hindu women and followed the Hindu agrarian and land revenue systems by employing the most qualified persons in the state departments.

Although the system of caste in the northern Indian states played a very important role, it was in the southern Indian kingdoms that it dominated in almost all the walks of life even after the occupation of several states in south India by Muslim rulers during the fifteenth and the seventeenth centuries. For example, there was always a Brahmin sitting next to the Zamorin in his court to advise him and to check that he observed everything that was holy. The importance of the court Brahmins during the sixteenth and the seventeenth centuries was such that even a ruler like the Zamorin of Calicut considered prestigious by sitting next to the Chief Brahmin of the state to have supper with him.[191] Most of the state representatives sent to other states on diplomatic missions were Court Brahmins. In Kanara, too, things were the same as in Malabar. Most of the ambassadors from the court of Ikkeri were from the Sinai family and they all were Brahmins.

It is difficult to write in general terms about the Indian polity, especially when it involves many different kingdoms with different political orientations and religious beliefs. In the opinion of some present-day religiously oriented historians[192] and theologians, the Emperors of Vijayanagar were the 'saviours and protectors' of the *Hindu Dharma,*[193] while the Muslim rulers of Bijapur, were the 'destroyers of the idolaters'. The Zamorins, although Hindu Nayar rulers of Calicut, were by and large, the 'protectors of Muslims', even though, due to this, they became the perpetual enemies of the Portuguese. In reality, the historical sources make it clear that the rulers of Vijayanagar were never the 'protectors' of *Hindu Dharma,* nor were the Sultans of Bijapur the 'destroyers of the idolaters' nor the Zamorins protectors of Muslims as a whole. Each ruler employed different kinds of terminology as per his interests and played the cards of politics according to the circumstances. Some tried to paint the pages of history with Hindu and some with Muslim colours, while others posed as secularists. In brief one could also say that all the rulers, whether Hindu or Muslim, governed according to the best of the interest of his subject and state, irrespective of their religious origins. Nevertheless, one can not altogether ignore the differences and prejudices that existed between Muslims and the Hindu rulers and their respective subjects, but the same existed between Hindu rulers and the Muslim rulers. Therefore, one could only analyse these factors in the light of human nature and not in terms of their religious origins, even though it appears quite often.

Sometimes the Hindu rulers would unite to destroy a Muslim neighbour, on other occasions they allied with the same ruler to destroy another who might be Hindu or Muslim. Nevertheless, there were occasions when these rulers were governed by their religious sentiments, either forced by the clerics or because they themselves wanted to achieve some political objectives by being seen as the 'saviours' of one religion or the other. Modern understanding of these political relations depends on who the historians are, how they have created the images of the past and what sources they have used to defend their ideologies. But if we notice with attention then we understand that the only picture clearly emerges out of the pages of history, regarding the role of Hindu or Muslim rulers is that they all wanted to become the most powerful using the religion as shield and all of them knew it quite well. This is why we do not find, at any time, either Hindu or Muslim rulers ever united to create any specific empire. Occasional alliances could only be considered as exceptions.

b) The Origins of Indian Diplomatic Practice

Since time immemorial, Indian *Rishis*[194] and *Munis,*[195] were highly respected in society and played a vital role in solving disputes between people and even states. They were also known as messengers of peace. They belonged to the Brahmin caste and were, therefore, supreme in the social structure. They were learned in both, worldly and spiritual matters. They were also well versed in religious affairs and were accustomed to advise even the rulers of the country to make them understand their duties and responsibilities. It was considered that they were in possession of some supernatural or divine powers. Since everyone respected them they were ideal for carrying out diplomatic missions. In ancient India, when kingdoms had begun to be established, it was they who used to perform all the coronation ceremonies and to bless the kings. A post of Head Priest was created in the Hindu kingdoms to advise the king on political, religious and social affairs. He was known, by various names such as *Sabha Pandit,*[196] *Raaj Guru,*[197] *Maharaaj,*[198] *Jagat Guru*[199] and so on. In most cases his decisions were considered final. No king would dare to challenge his verdict or opinion. It was something like having a Pope in each state.

In the *Varnasharam* or caste system of the Hindus, a Brahmin is at the top of the social formation. He is symbolised as being the Head (in its literal meaning), where the brain of the body is located and he is therefore the most important part of the body. Though Brahmins never governed[200] or took part directly in political affairs, their presence was not only regarded as necessary but to have their blessings was considered as a good omen. Since these *Sabha Pandits* had a profound knowledge of Astronomy, they were also predictors of the future and fortune tellers of the king as well as the empire who used to forecast the success or failure of military campaigns. Most of the itineraries of the kings as well as day to day affairs of the court were also referred to them for their predictions. These Brahmins also used to forecast the suitability of a bride or a groom before a marriage actually took place. In short, a Hindu king was almost totally dependent on the Court priests. Since it was believed that they would not cheat or mislead anyone, their presence in diplomacy was regarded with much respect, not only by the kingdom which they represented, but also by the state where they were going as mediators.

It was customary for such an emissary to be received by an official of the state before he reached the capital and it is from this that originated the custom of receiving emissaries and ambassadors at the frontier as was practised at later periods by states such as Bijapur, Vijayanagar and the Mughal Empires.

Brahmins and later scholars in the sciences, theological as well as humanistic, were the main persons who represented the states to discuss peace. The following lines from the *Laws of Manu* reveal the importance of ambassadors in the Hindu scripture and society: "(66)- For the ambassador alone makes [kings'] allies and separates allies; the ambassador transacts that business by which [kings] are disunited or not".[201]

This is supposed to have happened even during the epic war, *Mahabharata,* between *Kauravas* and *Pandavas,* at Kurukshetra, near Delhi. Lord Krishna, friend and mentor of both the families and highly respected, tried to mediate and advise them, in all the possible manners, to not to go to war. He was able to enter the war camps of the rival groups without any hesitation anytime he thought it was necessary. Even though he was not successful in his efforts, he was always received with the maximum respect. It was through such orientation and profound understanding that the Indian diplomatic system had its foundation. The importance of the messengers of peace became deeply understood by all the Indian rulers.

c) Panchayat System or the system of Counselling

The tradition of mediation to resolve disputes is deeply rooted in the Indian society, so that even today in most villages there is always a *Choudhury*, head of the *Panchayat*,[202] an elderly person, much esteemed among the villages, who is elected by the people to represent their village, to solve the local desputes. Although Muslims also followed and adapted to this system, this has its orgin in the ancient period. There is no religious barrier while nominating or selecting such person. When any dispute arises between families, whether due to problems over the division of property or the separation of couples, a *Choudhury*, who may not have been formally invited but who has knowledge of the situation, may go with his advisers, on his own initiative, to mediate and call upon the good sense of the parties. The aggrieved party would have to listen to his suggestions and frequently problems are solved in this way. Neglecting the suggestions of a *Chaudhury* is taken badly and such persons can be heavily penalised, including expulsion from the village community. Slowly, as a result of the modernisation of the villages and of modern education, this practice is diminishing and newer forms of justice are taking over most of the cases which were dealt with formerly by these *Panchayats*.

All these explanations suggest that, in India, for centuries before the arrival of the Portuguese, people had been accustomed to the role of religious leaders and used to look at them with a sense of trust and respect. This the Portuguese had understood from the beginning, and that is why they initially sent a friar, Luís de Salvador, to the court of Vijayanagar, to learn more about this Empire and to mediate terms of friendship between the two states as well as to convert people to Christianity. He not only performed these tasks, but also sent reports about the affairs of the Vijayanagar to the Portuguese viceroy.[203]

d) Early Indian Diplomatic Realtions with the Neighbouring Countries

Records show that in India ambassadors of peace were being exchanged as early as the fourth and fifth centuries BC. Chandragupta, the first ruler of the Mauryan Empire, received the Greek ambassador, Megasthenes, sent by Seleucas Nikator, a general of Alexander the Great.[204] Megasthenes has left a vivid account of the Mauryan rule. He was much impressed by Chanakya, a minister and counsellor of the Mauryan Empire who wrote the *Arthshastra* (the science of polity), which outlines the basic rules for the conduct of relations with other nations.[205] He was a shrewd observer of the art and craft of diplomacy. To him, all means employed in the management of statecraft and the conduct of relations with the outside world, were fair as long as they advanced the interest of the Mauryan kingdom.

India and China regularly exchanged scholars, who became the unofficial ambassadors of their respective countries. Scholars like Kashyap Matanga and others were sent from India to China, and *Fa hian*[206] and *Hsiun-Tsang*[207] from China visited India for the purpose of education and increasing knowledge. They left a considerable amount of written information which throws a light on statecraft of the period. An exchange of embassies took place between Harshvardhana, the ruler of northern India and the T´ang Empire, during the sixth and the seventh centuries. Later in the fourteenth century, an Arab traveller, Ibn Battuta, was appointed by Mohammad Bin Tughlak (1326-51), the Sultan of Delhi, as ambassador to the court of Chinese Emperor.[208] In the south, the Zamorin of Calicut, and his predecessors of the Chera dynasty, exchanged messengers and ambassadors with various courts such as Egypt, Syria, Persia, Gujarat, and the South-East Asian states. These embassies maintained political, cultural and commercial contacts on a reciprocal basis.[209]

In the sixteenth century the South Indian rulers, especially the Zamorin of Calicut[210] and the Sultans of Bijapur, followed very precise diplomatic rules in their courts based on the scriptures as well as the experiences they had through the foreign visitors in their kingdoms. On the other hand, the rulers of Kanara, the Nayakas of Ikkeri, followed the systems used by the Emperors of Vijayanagar, a purely Hindu system. Details about the diplomatic procedure followed by each state are given in the respective chapters.

e) The Signing of the Treaties

The treaties, signed between the various states in the sixteenth and seventeenth centuries, were intended to achieve the lasting settlement of disputes. However, with a few exceptions, the treaties signed between the Portuguese and the major Indian powers of the south-western Coast (the Zamorins of Calicut, the Nayakas of Ikkeri and the Sultans of Bijapur) had no lasting effect over any considerable period of time. The reason was, as is mentioned elsewhere and quite known fact, that the Portuguese wanted to control all maritinme traffic and commerce, and the Indian rulers obviously had no intention of allowing them to do so. Therefore, most of the treaties provided only temporary settlements until each side was ready for further military action. Nevertheless, however, short lived as these settlements were, the most sophisticated forms of diplomacy were followed - the giving of grand receptions to the ambassadors, sending expensive presents and swearing everlasting peace with the utmost zeal. The positive sides of these interactions were that they gave time to develop a pattern of diplomatic relations.

In the early years of their contacts with the Portuguese, the rulers of Malabar, especially the Zamorin of Calicut, used to inscribe the terms of treaties on a copper or silver plate with a gold stamp. One such occasion was in 1500 when the Zamorin signed a peace treaty with Pedro Álvares Cabral, the Portuguese commander of the second naval expedition to India.[211] According to K.S. Mathew, they made two copies of the treaty, "one on silver plate with a gold stamp and the other on copper plate with his brass stamp. The former was to be taken to the King of Portugal and the latter to be kept in the factory at Calicut".[212] The ruler of Quilon also followed this tradition when signing a treaty with any governing state. The Portuguese governor, Afonso de Albuquerque and the Queen of Quilon inscribed their pact of friendship on a silver plate.[213] Signing treaties on a copper or silver plate was something peculiar to the Malabar states and was intended to symbolise the preservation of 'an everlasting peace'. However, peace between the Zamorin and the Portuguese was hardly ever 'everlasting'.

Normally, the terms of the treaties were written in two languages, in Portuguese and in Persian, in the case of the Muslim rulers; in Portuguese and Malayalam when a treaty had to be signed with the rulers of Malabar; and in Portuguese and Kannada when it was signed between the Nayakas of Ikkeri, even though both belligerents had their interpreters.[214] The signatures had to be certified by two witnesses from each side, and later had to be taken to the courts of both belligerents to obtain the signatures and oaths from the supreme authorities: the Viceroy in the case of the Portuguese and the kings of the Indian states with whom the treaties were being concluded.

It was customary, at the time of the signature of a treaty, for the Portuguese to require that their ambassadors should take a solemn oath, putting their hands on a Missal or the Holy Bible that they would obey the treaty signed by them in the name of their kings.[215] On the Indian side it was customary for Muslim or Hindu emissaries to observe their own way of taking oaths. The practice was also followed when the ambassadors of the Bijapuri Sultan or the Nayaka of Ikkeri came on diplomatic missions to the Portuguese at Goa.

Reference

189 The *Vedas* are the ancient scriptures or revelation (Shruti) of the Hindu teachings. They manifest the Divine Word in human speech. They reflect into human language the language of the Gods, the Divine powers that have created us and which rule over us. There are four Vedas; *Rig Veda, Sama Veda, Yajur Veda* and *Atharva Veda*, each consisting of four parts. The Vedas were compiled around the time of Krishna (c. 3500 B.C.),

190 (Also spelt as *Arthasastra*). *Arthashastra* is most simply translated as *Economics*. Literally, it is variously translated from the *Sanskrit* as *Science of Wealth, Science of Material Gain* or *Science of Polity* (i.e. of civil government or state). For the date of its compilation see the discussion in S.R. Goyal, *Kautilya and Megasthenese*, pp. 6-20.

191 K.V. Krishna Ayyar, *The Zamorins of Calicut*, Calicut, (see first two chapters).

192 N. Lakhminarayan Rao, *The Nayakas of Keladi, in Vijayanagar Sixcentenary Comm.* Volume. Dharwar, 1936; Nilakanta Sastri, *A History of South India from Prehistoric Times to the Fall of Vijayanagar*, Oxford University Press, Delhi, 1966.; D.C. Varma *History of Bijapur*, New Delhi, 1974; M.H. Rama Sharma, *The History of the Vijayanagar Empire: Beginning and Expansion*, 2 volumes, Popular Prakashan, Bombay, 1978, (Passim).

193 Burton Stein, *Vijayangara*, in the *The New Cambridge History of India*, (passim); Rama Sharma, *History of Vijayanagar Empire, (Passim).*

194 A *Rishi* can be regarded as a combination of a patriarch, a priest, a preceptor, an author of Vedic hymns, a sage, a saint, an ascetic, a prophet and a hermit into a single person.

195 Learned and highly respected persons of the Indian society. This was another way of referring to a *Rishi*. They, too, had very deep knowledge of Hindu scriptures but were not religious authorities.

196 Court Priest.

197 Professor/Teacher of the kingdom.

198 King of Kings.

199 Professor of the Universe.

200 Here Brahmins are strictly meant about the preasts and not the entire whole of Brahmins class. Nevertheless, we are mindful of dynasties which belonged to Brahmins.

201 *The Laws of Manu*, p. 226.

202 A group of five persons or five respected persons. The leader is known as Choudhury or who is head of four persons and including him are five. This is why the whole structure of the unity is called *Panchayat*. *Panch Prameshwar* (meaning, the Leader of *Panchayat* could be regarded as God, or the Five Councellors of the Punchayat could be respected as one respects God) is quite known dictum in the Indian society.

203 Castanheda, *História do Descobrimento...*, livro I, pp. 519-20; Joan-Pau Rubiés, *Travel and Ethnology in the Renaissance: South India through European Eyes*, 1250-1625, p. 190.

204 Sir George Dunbar, *History of India from the Earliest Times to the Present Day*, (first ed. 1936), Reprinted, DK Publishers, New Delhi, 1990, pp.37-42.

205 D.D. Kosambi, *The Culture and Civilisation of Ancient India in Historical Outline*, Vikas Publishing House, New Delhi (Fifth Ed.), 1977, pp. 121-125.

206 Kosambi, *The Culture and Civilisation of Ancient India...*, pp. 155, 193.

207 *Ibid.* pp. 180, 182-183.

208 Ibn Battuta (Trans.), H.A.R. Gibb, *Travels in Asia and Africa, 1325-1354*, D.K. Publishers, (Reprinted), New Delhi, 1999. pp. 214-215.

209 Ibn Battuta, *Travels in Asia and Africa, 1325-1354*, pp. 231-233. Also See K.S. Mathew, 'The First Mercantile Battle in the Indian Ocean: ... pp. 179-180.

210 João de Barros, *Da Ásia..., Décadas Primeira a Duodécima* 24 vols, I, Liv. IV. Cap. VIII, pp. 328-340.

211 Albuquerque, *Crónica do descobrimento e conquista ...*, p. 53.

212 K.C. Mathew, *Portuguese Trade with India in the Sixteenth Century*, pp. 44.

213 *Ibid.*, p. 55.

214 *Tarikh-i- Farishtah, vol.* II, pp 26-27, Muhammad Ibrahim Zubairi, *Basatin al-Salatin, pp* 48-49; Biker, *Tratados e Concertos de Pazes...*, tomo. I, pp. 192-96: *Assento e Contrato de Paz e amisade com El-Rey Nizamoxá, por intervenção de El-Rey Idalxá, sendo Viso-Rey D. Jeronymo de Azevedo*; Copied from *O Cronista de Tissuary*, vol. 4°, p. 6, (Ed. Cunha Rivara): Biker, *Collecção dos Tratados e Concertos de pazes*, tomo I, pp. 160-170: *Contrato de pazes feito com El-Rey Idalxá no anno de 1571;* And *Assento de paz com o Idalxá no anno de 1575.*

215 Biker, (ed.) *Collecção de tratados e concertos de pazes...*, tomo I, pp. 192-95: *Assento e contrato de paz e amisade com El-Rey Nizamoxá por intervenção de El-Rey Idalxá, sendo Viso-Rey D. Jeronymo de Azevedo, 16 de Outubro de 1615.*

Part III

Indo-Portuguese diplomacy, Information and spying services

1. Indo-Portuguese Diplomatic Interactions

One assumption of early Portuguese diplomacy was that it would be possible to exploit the divisions between the Muslim and Hindu states. Once the decision to establish a permanent commercial base and government on Indian soil was taken, and Dom Francisco de Almeida was chosen to be the first Viceroy of the *Estado da Índia,* the instructions given to him were very clear in relation to Hindus, Muslims and Christians. The very essence of this *Regimento* (instruction, guidelines) was the necessity of eliminating the Muslims while dealing in a prudent way with the Hindus and the Christians.[216]

From the time of their arrival, the Portuguese tried to exploit Indian divisions in every possible way, whether it was religious tensions between Hindus and Muslims, or the political conflicts between kingdoms of the same religion. Their aim was to derive the maximum benefit from these conflicts to strengthen their position. However, when they tried to exploit the Hindus against the Muslims, thinking that the Hindus hated the Muslims to the point of joining with the Portuguese to expel them from India, they misunderstood the nature of their relationship. Since the Portuguese themselves hated the Muslims due to the crusades which they had during the medieval period and the commercial hegemony they possessed in the Indian Ocean, they thought they could make use of the Hindus against them. However, this they were not able to do. The Zamorin never joined hands with the Emperors of the Vijayanagar Empire against the Muslim rulers of the North. Instead he allied with the latter against the Portuguese.

There are many other examples of friendship and cooperation between Hindu and Muslim rulers of India, of which a few will be sufficed to denote here. Although the ruler of the Vijayanagar Empire disliked the imperialistic habits of the Sultans of Bijapur, and the two rulers had differences on religious issues, they continued to support one another whenever it was necessary.

Religion was of minor importance when the political interest of the empire was in question. This relationship reached its height when the Queen of Vijayanagar, wife of Rama Raya, nominally adopted Ali Adil Shah as her son in the year 1558.[217] It may appear strange and even ridiculous to a person from a different cultural background, that a Hindu Empress should adopt a Muslim ruler, as her son. However, in India such symbolic acts had always existed. They were meant either to remove any suspicion that might exist between the two families or to strengthen the relationships they already had. They were intended to express the very deep sense of respect and affection that existed between the two. Such bonds are considered much stronger than those of birth alone. Ironincally, in this case it did not bear much fruit. One must note here that this practice also shows the deep influence that Hindu culture had over Muslim tradition.

Another example is provided by the queen of Amber, Karnawati, who in 1539 accepted Humayun, father of Akbar, as her brother and sent a symbolic *Rakhi,*[218] at the time when her kingdom was invaded by the ruler of Gujarat, Bahadur Shah. In this case Humayun did send a military expedition against the Sultan Bahadur of Gurjarat in support of Karnawati. All such examples are, simply to show that, in India, when the first European ships arrived on the western coast, there existed, altogether, a completely different socio-religious understanding than the Portuguese had expected.

From the early sixteenth century, on the contrary to the Indian socio-economica and political atmosphere, the Portuguese were engaged with Indian merchants and rulers in a complex web of diplomacy, intrigue, conflict and reprisal, which had an adverse impact on local trade. However, either the Portuguese did not understand the protocols of how to present their embassies to Indian rulers or they deliberately refused to observe them, though they were accustomed to follow similar protocols in their dealings with European countries. Vasco da Gama, for example, was not equipped for diplomacy[219] and was sent to India in 1497 with only insignificant presents,[220] which were inappropriate gifts from such a "great King",[221] who claimed to be "Lord of the seas", to a King like the Zamorin of Calicut.[222] In fact there is doubt whether Vasco da Gama had ever been appointed to be an ambassador at all. As one can see in the words of Gaspar Correia, Vasco da Gama was not sure how to present himself before the sovereign of Calicut.

"And because the ships arrived almost at sunset, in the night Vasco da Gama went to see his brother, Nicolao Coelho, and discussed the way they should present themselves to this king, because this was the place they had been looking forward to reach. Finally they decided that it should better be he (Vasco da Gama) who should present himself as ambassador and arranged some presents. However, they would say to the king they had been separated from the other ships in which the Captain-major was coming to fetch them and was bringing a royal letter with him".[223]

On the other hand, when the Zamorin, according to the custom of his court, wanted to communicate through his nobles, Vasco da Gama refused to comply, as mentioned above, giving as a reason that he had orders only to discuss political matters directly with the King. These incidents suggest that Vasco da Gama, acted according to what he thought best without observing or respecting the local customs, which, naturally, deeply affected the diplomatic relations with the states he visited.[224] The same lack of suitable presents, and shortcomings in the organization of the embassy, bedevilled the embassy to Ethiopia in 1520.[225]

When things did not go as he expected in Calicut, due to the intrigues of the local merchants, Vasco da Gama resorted to bombarding the town and burning the ships, which could certainly have been avoided by using peaceful methods, which would have demonstrated that he had been sent by the King of a civilised nation.

Vasco da Gama was followed in 1500 by Pedro Álvares Cabral who had the same mission, namely to establish diplomatic relations with the Zamorin. Cabral left Portugal for India with a fleet of 13 ships and over 1000 soldiers, a clear sign that he was not just leading a diplomatic mission. Moreover the instructions given to Cabral show that he intended, and was prepared for, hostilities with those who refused to accept Portuguese demands.[226] These instructions demonstrate that the use of violence was pre-meditated and that there was no intention of using diplomatic mediation to establish peaceful commercial relations. Cabral had already behaved in an undiplomatic way on his arrival at Kilwa on his way to India. When, after the initial exchange of courtesies and gestures of friendship, the King asked him to land to be received,[227] 'he replied that he would only step out of the ship to fight if someone refused to accept his friendship for which he had been instructed by his king'.[228] On the other hand the Zamorin, upon Cabral's arrival at Calicut, observed proper diplomatic protocol. He gave a grand reception and, according to his custom, came down, a few steps, from his throne of gold and precious stones, to receive Cabral, who with solemnity and calmness, handed over the letter of the King, written in Arab.[229] However, events that occurred soon after their meeting were not so pleasant for Cabral due to the intrigues of the Arab merchants in the market. As a consequence he lost his temper and resorted to the use of force, instead of seeking the support of the king.[230]

António Vasconcelos de Saldanha has tried to justify the arrogant behaviour of the Portuguese towards the Indian rulers at the beginning of the sixteenth century by saying that it was "*justificáveis*" (justifiable) and was the only way they could promote their political objectives.[231] To support his views he quotes Diogo do Couto, who compiled his work in the late sixteenth and early seventeenth centuries when the Portuguese had already formed strong opinions about the conduct of the Indian rulers, whereas the period to which Saldanha is referring was the early sixteenth century when the Portuguese had no knowledge of what was going to happen and the Indian merchants and rulers were not aware what to expect from the newcomers. It is completely inappropriate to quote Diogo de Couto to reveal the state of mind of the early Portuguese in the Indian Ocean. After decades of experience, during which the Asian merchants realised that the main intention of the Portuguese was to trade on their own terms, to the detriment of all others, it was natural that few of them would have tried to remain on friendly terms, while the Portuguese, for their part, would have understood fully the nature of the relationship that had developed. Saldanha has given the example of Africa and Brazil where, he claims, the Portuguese did not commit any atrocity or violence against the locals as they did not resist, in any way, the arrival of the Portuguese, or at least he does not consider the Portuguese use of force against them as violence. For Saldanha, all the wars that the Portuguese waged against the Indian merchants and rulers could be justified as "natural and lawful deeds", no matter under what circumstances.[232] It appears that Saldanha has followed the opinion of Alexandre Lobato, who also denied that the Portuguese had any intention of fighting with anyone except when they were obliged to. Lobato wrote, "Portuguese interest was peace, and if they followed the path of hostility, it was specifically only to protect the allies of Portugal against their enemies. The Portuguese felt their moral obligation to help their loyal friends".[233] Here, too, Alexandre Lobato, as well as Saldanha, has ignored the fact that the states they are referring to as Portuguese allies, especially on the Malabar Coast, were once part of other political systems, like that of the Zamorin and Travancore, and naturally the sovereign overlords were not happy to lose them. Just as these authors have claimed that the Portuguese had a moral obligation to protect those states, so the kings of Malabar, too, had a natural right to try to bring them back under their control. Lobato has further justified the action of Afonso de Albuquerque as, "his military policy, therefore, was to attack in order to defend, destroy in order to survive, and in this sense he was to destroy all the alliances which would threaten the Portuguese existence".[234] When the Indian rulers became aware of the Portuguese attitude and of their way of conducting diplomacy, it is not surprising that they tried to get rid of them in any way possible.[235]

The reason for this brief discussion here is to show that, from the first contacts with the Indian states, Portuguese conduct was based on erroneous assumptions and the use of force, which could, by and large, have been avoided by using diplomacy.

In general terms one can understand the sentiments of the historians who look favourably on the violence used by the Portuguese to attain their goals as rapidly as possible, but what cannot be understood is why they expected indifference from the Indian merchants and rulers towards such behaviour. The inhuman brutality employed to create fear in the minds of local merchants in order to establish a commercial monopoly, which most of the Portuguese historians have, in one way or another, called diplomacy, was certainly not acceptable to any of the rulers then and would not be accepted by any civilised human being today. D. Manuel's self-proclaimed title of the *Senhor da Conquista, Navegação e Comércio da Etíopia, Arábia, Pérsia e Índia,*[236] ("Lord of Conquest, navigation and commerce of Ethiopia, Arabia, Persia and India") which he adopted in 1499 on the return of da Gama, shows his ambitions and laid the foundation for the subsequent 'violent diplomacy'. Even Luís Adão de Fonseca has agreed in his paper, published in 1999, that "the selection of words [title] is not innocent".[237] Once Dom Manuel had assumed the title, he had to uphold his claims at no matter what cost, even if this meant employing measures of extreme violence. Moreover, there was a risk that Portugal might be challenged by other European powers. Therefore, it was, essential to establish Portugal's position as rapidly as possible.

Portuguese diplomatic relations with any state in Asia depended on how powerful that state was and how easily they could exploit its political weaknesses.[238] They could not exploit the Chinese kingdom as there were hardly any internal rivalries or conflicts and, therefore, after the fiasco of their initial visit, the preparation of their embassies to China was done with great care. However, in India the Portuguese found a different situation. There were many rival states whose ambitious rulers were seeking powerful allies. The Zamorin received the Portuguese embassy with full court honours but made it clear that he did not want any interference in his local affairs. Nevertheless, the Portuguese discovered that he had two weak points; firstly, he had many ambitious vassal kings and chiefs who wanted political independence, and secondly, he protected Muslims and their trading activities, on whom depended most of his state's economy.

Portuguese diplomatic relations with the Indian states of the south-western coast differed from state to state but, in general, they depended more on their naval strength and on pursuing a policy of divide and rule than on diplomacy and negotiations. Moreover, the fact that they considered Indians as heathen and lower in social status than themselves greatly influenced their conduct.[239] As a consequence of their extreme and radical policies, the Portuguese never enjoyed uninterrupted peace for any substantial period. Even when, at the outset of their activity in the Indian Ocean, they used diplomacy, as they were eventually forced to do in the case of Calicut, they always tried to make it clear that they were the superior power. Moreover, the Portuguese habit of interfering in local politics through supplying arms to weaken the rival forces and to guarantee their own security was more than evident to those rulers. This proved to be very harmful to Portuguese interests later in the seventeenth century when the Dutch and the English reached the Indian Ocean, as the same policy of creating alliances to fight against the Portuguese, while at the same time ostensibly seeking peace by sending diplomatic missions, was adopted by the Indian states. There is a Portuguese proverb for this and it says, "*o feitiço virou-se contra o feiticeiro*" (the magic spell turned against the magician).

Portuguese relations with the kings of Quilon, Cochin, Cranganore and Cannanore were like those of a sovereign with his vassals, whereby the Portuguese exploited their weak political and economic situation. Although these states continued to be friendly throughout the period, they remained as vassals of the

Portuguese and were, by and large, dissatisfied with this relationship, as their ambitions of becoming powerful and independent states never saw the light of success. As a result they proved to be of no substantial help when the Portuguese needed it most.

The *Estado da Índia*, in short, was based almost entirely on naval power and the exploitation of the political conflicts between rival states, which only brought them the support of a few weak Indian allies. Moreover, from the early sixteenth century, the Portuguese tried to use the same policy, the 'diplomacy of subordination', with all the Indian states, such as Calicut,[240] Kanara, Bijapur and Ahmadnagar. These states did not initially accept Portuguese military supremacy and, if occasionally they were forced to do so, it was due to the political situation: wars with neighbouring kingdoms in which they were involved. In order to gain the upper hand, the Portuguese helped one state against the other, while maintaining cordial relations with both. However, this turned out to be a very costly strategy as most of these states understood the intentions of Portuguese diplomacy. Had the Portuguese used diplomacy without involving themselves in local politics, they might have saved the considerable sums, which they spent on warfare, and their commerce would have flourished. This would have placed them in a much more favourable position than the one in which they found themselves in the seventeenth century.

As a consequence of the *Estado da Índia's* weakened position in the seventeenth century, with no prospect of help from any quarter, and with the income of the state severely diminished, the Portuguese found it necessary to treat ambassadors from the Indian states with greater respect than had been the case in the previous century. An example of this new concern for observing diplomatic courtesies is the reception given to Malik Yaqút, the ambassador sent by the Sultan of Bijapur in Goa towards the end of 1654. He was received with great pomp in the royal hall of the Viceroy's palace in Goa, on 3rd of January 1655.[241] In fact the two embassies of 1633 and 1638, respectively, are other examples of the Portuguese changing mentality.[242] Normally the Portuguese authorities would hardly have bothered to show so much courtesy and ceremonial to an ambassador from a Muslim state, had the situation being like that of the sixteenth century.

Manucci has given a good description of this hall where ambassadors were received and given audiences.[243] During the reception of the ambassador there were more than twenty high-ranking officers present including the governor, the captain of the city, Dom Pedro Henriques, one of the noblemen and officials of the Viceroy's Council, Dom Gil Eanes de Noronha, and Dom Fernando Manoel, the *capitão-mor* and the captain in charge for providing help to ports and forts whenever it was needed. In order to assist the governor and the ambassador, Krishna Sinai and Rama Sinai Cothari were present as interpreters. Malik Yáqút was accompanied by the Jesuit Father Gonçalo Martins and, in addition, Hani Haji Saiyad Raza, Narsingha Rao, Rao Naikwadi and Ricco Shah Gujarati, some of the nobles from the Bijapuri court, who had been on several missions to conduct peace negotiations.[244] Malik Yáqút carried with him messages of good will and friendship from the Sultan and also a robe of honour and many other valuable presents for the governor of Portuguese India. It might seem strange that a Jesuit priest of Portuguese origin, who was initially representing the Portuguese at the court of the Bijapuri Sultan, was now accompanying an ambassador from a Muslim court, but Father Martins was sent both as a companion and assistant to the ambassador, and as a sign of trust.

In the seventeenth century the Portuguese assumption of superiority had to adapt to the prevailing conditions. Now, in most cases, the terms of treaties were discussed between the representatives of the states before they were actually signed[245] and it was the rulers of India who sent the terms which, for the most part, were not negotiable. An example of this is provided by the Nayakas of Ikkeri who, dating from the time of the Venkatappa Nayaka, by and large, were in a position to dictate their terms to the Portuguese. Since they were aware of the Portuguese dependence on the purchase of food-grains, and as the general political situation was not favourable to the *Estado da Índia,* these Nayakas pressed hard to demand that their terms be accepted by the Portuguese, and to a certain extent they were successful. On several occasions the Portuguese authorities had to wait to receive terms and conditions from the Nayakas in order to settle a dispute over pepper prices and the cutting of timber. In the past it had been the Portuguese who sent the terms and conditions of the pepper contracts and decided the prices.

a) Permanent Diplomatic Missions in India

In the course of almost three quarters of a century of fighting in India, both the Portuguese and the Indian kings realised the need for some stable relationships, and after each conflict diplomacy was found to be the only means to resolve their differences and to bring their disputes to any conclusion. However, although there had been frequent exchanges of ambassadors between the Indian states and the Portuguese, the first permanent diplomatic missions started only in 1576 at the suggestion of the Sultan of Bijapur. He proposed to the Portuguese Viceroy in Goa that both sides should keep ambassadors at the other's court in order to avoid conflict and maintain friendly relations.[246] Towards the end of the sixteenth century the political situation of the northern Indian kingdoms was becoming precarious, particularly following the Mughal subjugation of Gujarat, Malwa, Bider and Barar, and the attempt to incorporate the empires of Golconda, Ahmadnagar and Bijapur. It became increasingly necessary for frequent exchanges of embassies. In addition, as the rivalries between the European companies for a share in the trade of Asia intensified in the seventeenth century, their diplomatic approaches to the Indian states to obtain greater privileges also increased. Therefore, as mentioned above, the Bijapuri Sultan proposed to maintain a resident ambassador at the Portuguese viceregal court at Goa and the Portuguese reciprocated by sending permanent ambassadors to the Bijapur court, who were mostly Jesuits.

The English and the Dutch also tried to maintain permanent ambassadors at the Indian courts to obtain prompt consideration of their requests. Sir Thomas Roe, for example, stayed at Jahangir's court in Delhi from 1615-18 to deal with the East India Company's affairs in the name of his country, and embassies of this kind became a common practice.

2. Spies and Diplomacy: the inflow of strategic information

a) Beginning of the Spying activities

It is well known that, before sending a large scale expedition to India, the king of Portugal, Dom João II, had tried to obtain detailed information about the places in India with which the Portuguese could establish commercial contact. For this purpose, in 1487, he sent Pêro da Covilhã and Afonso de Paiva overland, and Bartolomeu Dias by sea, to search for the places where pepper, spices and other merchandise were produced, to discover the types of money that were required and whether any Christians could be located. The most important part of the journey overland passed through the Arabian lands and Covilhã and Paiva, who travelled disguised as Arabs, were well trained in the Arabic language and the customs of the people. Covilhã somehow reached Calicut and only on his return was detained in life-long captivity in Ethiopia, while Afonso da Paiva died. Nevertheless it is probable that Covilhã, somehow, managed to send the report of his findings to the king of Portugal. The same year Bartolemeu Dias was sent to find the sea route to India. He rounded the Cape of Good Hope and returned with the news that the route to India was open. In this way the first the Portuguese information service between India and Portugal had its beginning.

Vasco da Gama, no matter how ruthlessly he behaved and how unfit he was for a diplomatic post, also took note of each detail worthy of reporting, and brought back information related to the cultural, linguistic, geographical, socio-economical and military aspects of each country he visited. Besides, he returned with four natives of Calicut, who were visiting his ship at the time of his departure, as hostages to Portugal. Naturally, they knew more about their land than the Portuguese and might have provided with the first hand knowledge about their political, economical and social condition. When these men returned to India, they served as interpreters and were among the first Indian converts.

In India, the Portuguese officials tried to establish alliances with persons who could provide information and any other kind of support which could damage their interests of the Muslim merchants and rulers. Although, as has been mentioned elsewhere, the Portuguese were not successful in forming an anti-Muslim alliance in India with any Hindu kingdom, including Vijayanagar Empire, they did recruit many dissatisfied elements who proved to be more effective than any military alliance.[247] Among such persons were some leading Hindu groups, especially Brahmins, who lived in the Muslim territories and hated to be governed by them. Their services as informants turned out to be among the most valuable help that the Portuguese received in India.

One such person was Timoja or Timmaya, who was a Brahmin by caste.[248] He has been referred to by many historians as a pirate and a rebel with whom the Portuguese had very close contact, as he was the one who informed Afonso de Albuquerque about the Bijapuri Sultan's involvement in war against the ruler of Vijayanagar and thus facilitated the conquest of Goa. Timmaya had also served the ruler of Gersoppa as its envoy to the Portuguese Viceroy, Dom Francisco de Almeida, seeking friendship,[249] in 1505. Later he had been sent to negotiate peace in 1507, when trouble between the Portuguese and Gersoppa arose over the Portuguese confiscation of Muslim ships.[250] Therefore Timmaya played many parts in Indo-Portuguese relations. His information proved to be of great advantage to the Portuguese conquest of Goa.

Before Timmaya even met the Portuguese governor, there were rulers on the south Malabar coast, the kings of Cochin, Cranganore and Quilon among others, who contributed to realising their own and the Portuguese ambitions by providing different kinds of support (including vital information) against the Zamorin from whose over-lordship they wanted to escape. Once freed from the Zamorin, they became puppets of the Portuguese and one of their most reliable sources of information. Naturally, information was passed to the Portuguese through men who enjoyed their utmost confidence and no official records were kept, but there is some information about their activities in correspondence that deals with other matters.

In India the Portuguese were very dependent on a group of persons, which they termed *línguas* (interpreters), in whom they trusted and who received a lot of privileges in the Portuguese service. Most of these were Hindus from noble families and in many cases this profession became almost hereditary. *Línguas* might, on occasion, be sent as messengers or emissaries. Some were even sent as ambassadors, when the Portuguese had full trust in them. Nevertheless, it seems likely, although clear proof is lacking, that the Indians who were *línguas* in the Portuguese services, also worked as double agents, much in the same way as the Portuguese priests at the Indian courts.

Among those who, like Timmaya, were possible sources of information for the Portuguese were the Sinai and Kothari families. They were in Portuguese service as contractors and suppliers of all kinds of merchandise for more than two centuries, besides which many of their family members served as *línguas* and as emissaries and messengers both for the Portuguese and the Indian rulers (which raises the possibility that they may have acted as double agents). However, their activities were not limited to those of merchants and emissaries and they kept the Portuguese informed about any hostile developments.

There were two well-known individuals, Azu Nayak and Krishna Sinai, who were employed in Portuguese service in the seventeenth century and whose services as informants were highly appreciated. There were other families, such as that of the Santuji Sinai Kothari, who during the fifth and sixth decades of the seventeenth century rendered good service as diplomats when they were sent to the courts of Bijapur and Mughal as well as to the court of Shivaji.[251]

It is clear from the documents in the *Corpo Chronológico* collection of the *Torre do Tombo de Lisboa,* (and from the works of Pissurlenkar) that the Brahmins of Goa, from the early sixteenth century, offered help to the Portuguese. Krishna Chatim, from one of the elite Brahmin families of Goa, could be considered as the most important person during the early decades of the sixteenth century. He not only met Afonso de Albuquerque, but also lent him a book (I suppose it might have been a diary) with exhaustive information about the merchants who carried on trade not only with the ports of Goa but also with the areas of Malabar and other parts of Asia. That book also contained information about the origin of those merchants and their contacts, especially the Muslims and 'Rumes', who had trade contacts with the ports of Cochin, Calicut, Kanara, Cambay and so on in Asia.[252] In this way, one person alone was able to provide Albuquerque with a vast range of information, which would have taken decades for the Portuguese to gather by other means. Krishna was not only a member of one of the leading Brahmin families of Goa but also became the captain of the Indian soldiers in the Portuguese service, besides serving from time to time as emissary and ambassador.

During the same period, another Brahmin, called Rahul Chatim (who is also mentioned as Rahul Seth) entered Portuguese service not only to provide trading commodities but also to pass on any information he obtained through his agents from the regions of Goa, Bijapur and along the coast to Malabar. Frei António de Loureiro, who in addition to his religious preaching provided information services, reported to the King of Portugal that these two persons, Krishna and Rahul, were very friendly to the Portuguese in India and suggested that the King could invite them to visit Portugal.[253] In the middle of the sixteenth century Krishna was still active negotiating the terms of peace between the Sultan Ibrahim Adil Shah of Bijapur and the Portuguese, over the disputed succession to the throne of that kingdom during the governorship of Martim Afonso de Sousa (1542-1545). To assist him in the whole diplomatic process the Portuguese governor sought the help of two Indo-Portuguese *casados* resident in Bijapur, Galvão Viegas and his nephew António Viegas, respected men in the capital. After the death of Krishna, his son Dadaji took over from his father. About their life and service, the Bishop of Goa, Fr. João de Albuquerque, made many appreciative remarks in his letters to the King, in 1548.[254]

In this way a spying and information network was formed to assist the *Estado da Índia Portuguesa,* consisting of members of prestigious Indian families and Portuguese mission priests among others.[255]

b) Construction of observation fortresses

All the Portuguese, whether they were religious or military, traders or *casados e moradores* (married men and settlers), were convinced that their safety ultimately depended on their administrative and military capability. To maintain the security of their position they constructed a chain of fortresses along the western coast of India where they fixed their commercial, administrative, religious and military headquarters. These fortresses became important as a way of maintaining a watch over the movements of the warships of the Zamorin (in the early sixteenth century a fortress was built in the territory of Cranganore to check the advances of the Zamorin towards the kingdom of Cochin) and later the Nayakas of Ikkeri, in the Kanara region, (the fortress of Cambolim for example) who were a constant threat to their control of Indian commerce. Slowly, the Portuguese tried to tight their circle around the territory of the Zamorin by constructing a fortress and naval base at Chaliyam, in the territory of the king of Tanur, virtually at the gates of Calicut, which enabled them to observe the movement of the Zamorin's ships. This fortress became the cause of several wars and remained an eyesore for the Zamorin until it was destroyed in the1570s war by the forces of Marakkar. The destruction of this fortress made the Portuguese situation more difficult, but after a further series of wars and increased pressure on the Zamorin, the Portuguese were successful in obtaining permission for the construction of a new fort at Ponnani, this time closer to the headquarters of the Marakkars.[256] This fortress not only allowed the Portuguese to keep a close watch on the Kunjalis but could be considered a noose around their necks. However, the Kunjalis were also not sitting idle and obtained permission from the Zamorin to build fortresses and dockyards at Pudupattanam, which became known as the Marakkar Kotta.[257] The Portuguese were eventually able to destroy this fortress, which threatened their observation fortress of Ponnani, during the wars of 1599-1600.

The fall of the Marakkars coincided with the rise of the Venkatappa Nayaka, from a simple chief to a ruler, in the territory of Kanara, making use of the decaying power of Vijayanagar Empire. Although the Portuguese were, initially, quite careful and kept well informed of the successes of the Venkatappa Nayaka, it became necessary for them to be able to keep a close watch on the movement of the Kanara shipping when he attacked the Banghel king during the war of 1614-16. It was with this purpose that they planned to construct another fortress in the vicinity of Barcelore, on the island of Cambolim, with the intention of gathering first hand information about the movements of the Venkatappa Nayaka's army and seagoing vessels. The fortress was eventually built in 1629[258] and early in 1631 the island was ceded to them by one of the leading contestants for the throne, Virappa Nayaka, in return for the Portuguese help against the Veerabhadra Nayaka, his nephew.[259]

One could also give the example of the captain of the fortress of Cambolim, António da Azevedo Coutinho, who informed the Viceroy about the construction of a fortress on the same island, at a distance of a gunshot from the Portuguese fortress, by Veerabhadra Nayaka, against all the promises made by his uncle by Virappa Nayaka.[260] Captain Coutinho was also informed of the intentions of Veerabhadra Nayaka to violate all the treaties sighed by him regarding the price of pepper. The letters sent by the priests, captains and other responsible persons, informing the viceroy about the situation in which they were living during the wars of Shivappa Nayaka between 1652 and 1656, contained information which they had gathered through the local agents.[261] All of these contributed in keeping the Portuguese authorities at Goa well informed.

The Portuguese also had fortified posts on the borders of the Goan territories, in the interior of Salssete and Bardez, which served as observation posts. These fortresses were situated at convenient places so that the informants and spies could easily come and go in any guise, as businessmen, fortune tellers and so on, bringing information especially from the kingdom of Bijapur.

To summarise, most of the fortresses that the Portuguese constructed near the frontiers of any neighbouring state, besides serving as residential complexes and as security for the Portuguese, were to keep a watch over the movement of soldiers and to serve as bases for spying activities, while the other fortresses, constructed near the coast, were to watch the movement of both their own and their enemies' ships.

c) St Thomas Christians

It had been one of the objectives of the Portuguese to discover Christian communities in the East with which they could form alliances to support their commercial ambitions, and the fact that the Christian followers of the Apostle St Thomas were active in th e pepper trade promised to realise their expectations.[262] However, the Portuguese soon discovered that these Christians had only limited connections with the Roman Church. Their sect had been establisahed in India for centuries in the major pepper producing zones of Malabar, such as Calicut, Parur, Managate, Cochin, Travancore and Quilon[263] and they received their Bishops and religious rites from the Nestorian Church of Selêucia.[264]

Initially, these Christians of Malabar responded amicably to the Portuguese approaches but when they realised that they were expected to give up all of their religious traditions and adopt those of Europe, they started to resist.[265] In response, their religious congregations were declared to be heretical and the Bishops, Mar Jacob and Mar Abraham, were taken prisoners.[266] This was an extreme and very threatening situation for the local Christians. In consequence they not only kept away from the Portuguese dominated areas and avoided any commercial transactions with them but feared to have any contact with them at all.[267] According to Fr. Mundadan, "...the Indian Christians had been already living for centuries in a positive encounter with the high caste Hindus and had developed a theological vision of the Hindu religion which was more positive and liberal. Today in the light of the modern theological approach to other religions, one must admit that the vision of the Indian Christians was a more enlightened one than that of their European contemporaries".[268]

Nevertheless, during the early period when the Portuguese and the St Thomas Christians were trying to establish a workable relationship with each other, these Christians, probably with the expectation of prolonged friendship and cooperation with the new comers, rendered good service by providing information which the Portuguese required for their safety. However, when relations deteriorated the Portuguese lost, though never completely, very reliable friends and a regular source of information.[269]

d) Portuguese Convicts, Missionaries, and Ambassadors

The role of *degredados* (convicts) in information gathering for the *Estado da Índia* was also of great importance, particularly in the early days. In the early sixteenth century when the first Portuguese ships entered the Indian Ocean and established contacts with the coastal states of Africa and India, the commanders usually never went ashore themselves but instead sent *degredados* to obtain information about the people, their religion and customs and whether there was any danger to the Portuguese. Only after sufficient information had been gathered were any respectable Portuguese officials sent ashore. In other words, they were the *"carne para canhão"* (escape goat), since, as it was commonly believed, "if they lost their lives in the service, it was hardly a loss" *("perdendo-se a deles, não se perdia muito").*[270] A good number of these *degredados* were sent from Portugal every year and in exchange for their services their crimes were pardoned. They, for their part, not only served the Portuguese *Estado*, but also sought employment in the service of Indian merchants and rulers when their status changed to *renegados* (renegades).

Among the *renegados* were also to be found deserters from the fleets and fortresses.[271] Although these were never reconciled to the delays in the payment of their wages and to the way they were treated by their own countrymen, they did, from time to time, keep the Portuguese officials informed of Indian military and trading activities in the areas where they resided.[272] In other words they were, despite the fact that they were renegades, among the most reliable sources of information that the Portuguese had.

There is a very interesting paper on the service rendered by the *degredados* and *renegados* in the East by Lima Cruz,[273] who shows that some of them eventually became captains and even governors of territories within the *Estado da India.*[274] In 1999 Lima Cruz published another paper on the '*marginais*' in the history of Portuguese India in the sixteenth century.[275] In 1997 Dejanirah Couto had published an article in *Mare Liberum*, on the role of the renegades in the making of the *Estado da Índia.*[276] The article of István Rákóczi, which appeared in 2000, added yet more information on the role of European *marginais.*[277] George Winius had already introduced the concept of the 'Shadow Empire' to show how these renegades and private merchants had created an alternative 'Empire' beyond the jurisdiction of the *Estado da Índia* and had contributed to the prosperity of the Portuguese-Asian economy.[278]

The available official sources provide only fragmentary evidence about the development of Portuguese information gathering, as it was not properly organised by any department.

Apart from regular spies from whom the Portuguese authorities obtained their secret information, it was through missionary priests that they gained most intelligence of political and commercial interest, and the activity of missionary priests was highly co-ordinated. Frei Luís de Salvador was the first Portuguese priest who travelled to Vijayanagar and other areas around and kept the Portuguese officials at Cochin informed of the political and military affairs of that kingdom. After him most of the missionaries, who grew in number as time passed, created a network to support their activities.[279]

Among the most important features of their activities was their habit of communicating among themselves and with their mother houses in India and in Europe through letters, which not only carried information about their religious achievements, but about political, economic and social aspects of the societies within which they worked. Many of these missionaries conducted trade to help pay for their activities and since they were frequently received with considerable respect and were in close contact with most of the Indian courts, besides the business class, they had direct access to a great deal of secret and strategic information which they in turn communicated to the administrative authorities of the *Estado da Índia*. Further research is needed into the many thousands of missionary letters, in many different languages, to establish the full extent of their intelligence activities but it is clear that the missionary correspondence also included information, which today can be classified as secret intelligence. The missionary priest thus performed a dual role, serving God and nation (Portugal) - and at the same time betraying the trust that the Indian rulers and people had placed in them.

Among the published correspondence are the letters of Luís Fróis S.J.,[280] Sebastião Gonçalves, S.J.,[281] Frei Paulo da, Trindade,[282] edited by Georg, Schurhammer S.J.,[283] Joseph Wicki, S.J,[284] António da Silva Rego,[285] and John Correia-Afonso.[286] There are also the letters written by the Jesuits from the Mughal court.[287] In addition to the published collections there are still many unpublished letters in the *Biblioteca da Ajuda, Torre do Tombo, Arquivo Histórico Ultramarino* and various other libraries and archives, both private and public in Lisbon, Coimbra, Porto and Évora.

In India, as in Europe, Portuguese ambassadors did not just carry out negotiations but were supposed to supply up to date information and to exert what influence they could in the countries to which they were appointed. Ambassadors might seek to influence the courts to which they were appointed by bribery, the giving of gifts etc., and to maintain a permanent spying service, but this only became possible when they started to have permanent delegations at different courts in India. The role of the ambassador thereby became a complex one, conducting negotiations leading to treaties being only one of his functions. However, most of the Portuguese espionage activity in India was carried out through clerics, businessmen and mercenaries, who were often employed by the Indian kings and governors for different purposes. It took some time for the Indian states to understand that the Portuguese preachers, doctors and others who they employed for specific services were also serving as spies for the Portuguese.

e) The Casados and the local Converts in the Portuguese Spying networks

It was also largely because of the activities of the missionaries that a new social group came into being known as the Indo-Portuguese. Since the time of Afonso de Albuquerque in the early sixteenth century, a policy of mixed marriages had been introduced in order to increase the Indo-Portuguese population. Portuguese men were married to native Indian women, especially from the rich and politically influential families who could benefit them during the time of troubles as well as keeping them informed of the local customs and eventualities.[288] However, intermarriage never became as frequent as it did in the north Indian empires a century and a half later,[289] due to the Portuguese selective and intolerant nature on the one hand and conservative Indian mentality based on the caste system, on the other.

In the Portuguese dominated areas and their immediate neighbourhoods, there were settlements of Indo-Portuguese and of Indians converted to Christianity who provided a good information service for the Portuguese state. The low caste Christian Indians were able to move in and out of many areas around the Portuguese territories unnoticed and could mix easily with the local population. On the other hand, the higher caste Indians, Brahmins for example, enjoyed far more advantages than did the lower castes, especially if they happened to belong to the nobility or to a rich trading family, and rendered good service in both spying and negotiating terms with the Indian states. In the seventeenth century there are many references to these influential Indo-Portuguese providing the Portuguese authorities with information about the military concentrations in the regions of Malabar, Kanara and Bijapur. For example, António Borges, a *casado* settled at Barcelore, informed the Viceroy in 1632 about the good intentions of the Veerabhadra Nayaka in reaching a peaceful solution if the Portuguese accepted the Nayaka's conditions regarding the price of pepper and the withdrawal of support from his uncle, Virappa Nayaka.[290]

Besides António Borges, there were other respected persons like Frei Pero da Costa, a Jesuit priest, and Ramogi Sinai Kothari, Rama da Gama and Sancara (Shankara or Shankar) da Gama, business magnates, whose families had been in the Portuguese service for over a century, who were among those who kept the Portuguese authorities informed about any unfavourable development in the Kanara regions against the Portuguese and mediated, many times, to find a solution to some tedious problems between the two states. It was these people who informed the Portuguese authorities about the Dutch diplomatic activities at the Nayaka's court.[291]

f) Land Travellers and Information gathering

Apart from these local Indo-Portuguese, the *casados* and priests, the Portuguese also made use of the land travellers, who passed through the Indian territories and besides enhancing their knowledge of the local culture, kept the *Estado da Índia* well informed of the internal political conditions, the movement of armies and the wars which might be taking place. *India in the Portuguese Literature* by Ethel M. Pope and *A Visão do Oriente na Literatura Portuguesa de viagens: os viajantes portugueses e os itinerários terrestres,* by Luís Graça, are two significant works which reveal the importance of the Portuguese travellers and writers during this period. These supplement the well-known traveller's accounts like those of Duarte Barbosa, Ludovico di Varthema, Tomé Pires, Jan Huyghen van Linschoten, Pietro Della Valle, Niccolau Manucci and François Pyrard, among various others, whose works were either published in their own lifetimes or circulated in manuscript copies. Naturally the vision of travellers and writers always differed depending on the society and culture in which they had been brought up. Their reports, even before they were published, were made use of by the Portuguese governors as well as, in many cases, by the Indian rulers. If the chroniclers like João de Barros, Diogo de Couto, António Bocarro, Fernão Lopes de Castanheda could make use of the travel diaries and other private sources of information and incorporate them into their histories, the viceroys and fortress captains would certainly have had access to the same information.

The list of Portuguese travellers who supplied information on their journeys is a long one and includes men such as Sebestião Manrique who travelled overland route to Portugal in the 1640s and Manuel Godinho, who made the same journey twenty three years later. Both wrote lengthy reports on their travels. Of scarcely less importance are Fr. (Franciscan) Tristão da Cunha, Fr. António Tenereiro, António Sorares de Albergaria, Fr. Pantaleão de Aveiro, Mestre Afonso, Fr. Gaspar de S. Bernardino, Fr. Nicolau de Orta Rebelo, Pedro Teixeira, D. Álvaro da Costa, and António de Andrade among many more. A brief account of their journeys and the information they left has been provided by Luís da Graça, whose work has already been mentioned above. Another study presented to the Indo-Portuguese International Seminar in 1985[292] provides yet more names including Fr. Bento de Góis, Fr. António de Andrade, Fr. Jerónimo Xavier, Fr. Francisco Henriques, Fr. Nicolau Pimenta, Fr. Mateus Ricci, Fr. João Fernandes, and Brother Manuel Marques. In this category the letters of St. Francis Xavier are probably the outstanding example for the richness of their detail and their wide circulation.

Pietro Della Valle's account of his stay in Goa provides a comprehensive overview of Portuguese sources of information during the early seventeenth century. He always notes that such and such a person has arrived from such and such a place, either by land or by sea, and has brought this or that news.

g) Indian Spies

In India the Brahmins (especially the priests of the court and temple who were the most popular and respected) were sent to discuss state affairs, even during time of war as it was known that they would be trusted by both sides. The available sources make it clear that, during the war between the Zamorin and the Portuguese in 1509, the king of Cochin sent Brahmins across the territory of the Zamorin, carrying some strategic information for the allied kingdoms. Brahmins were employed for spying though these were simple Brahmins and not clerics. The question is why Brahmins? The answer is simple. According to the Hindu caste system, the Brahmins and the Shatriyas could go wherever they liked or meet any person without any hindrance or prejudice. They were the privileged classes of Indian society. On the other hand, *Vaixrava* or *Vaixnavas* and *Súdras* faced a lot of obstacles and could not go to places where only a Brahmin could, inside a temple for example. Irrespective of whether a Súdra was engaged in spying activities or not, if he was found in a place forbidden to him by the caste system, he could be severely punished, including the death penalty.

On the other hand, a Súdra or his wife had access to places where they could freely gather information they required for their master and where no Brahmin or Shatriya could ever go for fear of being polluted. For example women of low caste, or Súdras, might act as midwives at any house from the lower to the higher strata of Hindu society and she could easily manipulate the women at her disposal. Ironically, according to the Indian tradition, she could be in contact with the women regularly for over forty days, for massaging the lady and taking care of the newly born baby but, although they had been able to touch their clients over a period of forty days, immediately after the ritual baths of the baby and the mother, they could never touch her deliberately again unless she was called back on some health care ground which would again be followed by a complete ritual bath. The access, which these women had to knowledge of the households were later to be manipulated by the British in the eighteenth and the nineteenth centuries.[293] However, there is no direct evidence that the Portuguese ever made use of this system for gathering information.

After the Brahmins, the group who were most commonly used as sources of information were members of the business class who used to travel between the kingdoms. In the guise of merchants they collected information and could move freely on the pretext of meeting someone who required his goods. However, during time of war it was far too dangerous for a trader to cross the border where he might lose his merchandise and even his life. The idea of sending the Brahmins was to guarantee the safe arrival of the information as nobody would dare to harm them, even the enemy.

The Mughals, the Bijapuri and Ahmadnagar kingdoms maintained hundreds of spies who operated throughout their dominions to gather all sorts of information useful for the sound governance but there are not many details of who was posted where. The Mughals used to have a whole department called *Khufia Naweesi*[294] and the head of this department was called *Vazir-e-Khufia* (the minister of secret services). The Bijapur and Ahmadnagar states followed the same information and spying system of the Mughals. Most espionage operations were performed by local police and those working in the *Khufia* (secret) department, and not by ambassadors or their companions. This could possibly be because, until the arrival of the Portuguese in India, there had not been any system of permanent diplomatic missions.

During the seventeenth century the Indian rulers, especially the Bijapuri and Ahmanagar sultans, were more concerned about the Mughal armies advancing towards their kingdoms than with the Portuguese. The Portuguese were aware of the danger that the Mughal forces could pose for their own settlements, and they tried to manipulate this situation as far as they could to their advantage. They also wanted to gather information about all the diplomatic developments that were taking place between the Dutch, the English and the Indian states and a whole network of spies and informants was on the alert all the time. This explains why a Portuguese embassy would rapidly be sent to any Indian court, whenever there was an embassy either from the Dutch or the English.

Both the Portuguese and the Indian rulers kept spies in each others' dominions.[295] For the Portuguese keeping spies at the Mughal court and in the neighbouring states was a most expensive business. Normally, their function was to provide information well in advance[296] of any movement of forces or of political changes that were taking place, what the possible reasons might be and which side the Portuguese would take.[297]

There were times when such spies were discovered and the Conde de Linhares told the King of Portugal how risky it was to keep spies at the courts of Bijapur and the Mughal Emperor.[298] In fact, in 1632, one such spy, Fernão Lopes da Horta, was discovered at the court of Bijapur and, as a consequence, the Sultan had his nose and an ear cut off. This incident has been bitterly criticised by some modern historians on the grounds that this was a very inhuman act. However, the story they tell about the punishment of Fernão Lopes by the Bijapuri ruler is different from what really happened. According to them Fernão Lopes's nose and ears were cut down because he could not save the life of the previous Sultan who died in 1627. This account is, however, completely wrong as this was only said to defame the new Sultan.[299] The letter of Conde de Linhares narrates what really happened.[300] The cutting of nose and ears was a common punishment given to spies when the crime was minor. Normally a serious case such as that of Dr. Fernão Lopes, and had he been an Indian, would have been punished by death. However, since he had served the royal family for years, his punishment had been reduced in this way just to give him a lesson. People at that time, seeing someone without nose and ears, would easily understand the reason.

Adil Shah, for his part, besides having his local spies and informants, had hired Diogo Lopes Bayão, a Portuguese trader and a soldier, a clever man, as a spy to inform him of all the happenings around Balaghat. He was paid three thousand *cruzados* a year,[301] a very substantial amount in that period, and worked for this Sultan for many years till he was discovered and sent to Portugal by the Inquisition on the charge of being an infidel since he was working for an infidel.[302]

There were false or double spies too. In the year 1655, the Portuguese authorities at Goa were informed by one of their spies at Tuticorim, in south-east India, that the Dutch were about to attack the territories of Caliture and Negapattam, where the Portuguese had commercial interests. As will be shown later, the Portuguese were at this time fighting all over the western coast of India with the Bijapuri ruler, the Nayaka of Kanara, and in Ceylon, and they had to find five ships and almost eight hundred soldiers to secure the safety of these places at a time when they needed all their forces elsewhere.[303] When the Portuguese arrived no Dutch were to be found.

Spying activities between the states, took a more professional and modern form during the expansion of the British in India, especially during the period of the decadent Mughal Empire in the eighteenth and the nineteenth centuries, when the East India Company set up its network of intelligence services to gather information relating to politics and the economic and social situation of the various states under the same Empire. However, so far as our knowledge from the available sources is concerned, the Portuguese spying network and intelligence services were much more limited in comparison to those created by the English. The Portuguese were not able to have their intelligence network so widely spread inside the Indian territories on the same scale as the English for, though they controlled a wide range of ports until 1663, they had limited economic resources at their disposal and their activities, whether commercial or political, were more limited to the coastal regions than was the case with the British in the following century.

Detailed information regarding the British spying networks in northern India can be gathered from Bayly's book *Empire and Information.*[304] Bayly has ventured deeply into a totally virgin field and has shown historians an altogether different point of view about British empire-building though, unfortunately for this present work, his study starts only in 1770. The British could easily interact with the local population, living inside the land and employing whoever was ready to be in their service.[305] Besides, the British administrators before creating their empire on the ruins of the Mughal Empire first laid their foundation deeply by winning over the Indian economic agents, while simultaneously trying to grasp all the political and diplomatic benefits they could. British intervention in the social and economic life, at least during the eighteenth and the nineteenth centuries, was apparently not based on creating hatred between the Hindus and the Muslims states. Instead it exploited the political weaknesses and rivalries among the *Nawabs* of Muslim India. The British were better able to cultivate a class favourable to their mentality and way of government than was possible during the time when the Portuguese started building their commercial and social networks in India.

The Portuguese did not try to gain the sympathy of the local people and instead endeavoured to dominate them by force of arms. The worst part is that, from the very beginning, they attempted, ultimately without success, to create anti-Muslim feelings among the Hindu kings of South India in order to obtain their sympathy. This policy had the reverse effect. They never tried to integrate the local class, except through conversion, and instead boasted the superiority of their culture. In contrast the British initially tried to show their sympathy towards local social behaviour, and many of them integrated in a way that built alliances among the people. Probably, the British had learnt from the folly of the Portuguese.

Reference

216 A. da Silva Rego, *Documentação para a História das Missões do Padroado Português do Oriente, Índia* (1499-1522), vol. I, doc. 7, pp. 29-32; See K.N. Chaudhuri, *Trade and Civilisation in the Indian Ocean: An Economic History from the Rise of Islam to 1750,* Cambridge University Press, 1986, p. 64, who thinks that "the claim and view point were propagandist, a part of the make-believe world in which ideology justified deeds".

217 D.C. Varma, *History of Bijapur,* Kumar Brothers, pp. 23, 122: John Briggs, (Ed.) *History of the Rise of Mahomedan Power in India,* vol. III, pp. 72-74.

218 The chaste bond of love between a brother and a sister is one of the deepest and noblest of human emotions. *'Raksha Bandhan'* or *'Rakhi'* is a special occasion to celebrate this emotional bonding by tying a holy thread around the wrist. This thread, which pulsates with sisterly love and sublime sentiments, is rightly called the '*Rakhi*'. It means 'a bond of protection', and *Raksha Bandhan* signifies that the strong must protect the weak from all that's evil. Although, it is exclusively a Hindu ceremony, there are innumerable cases in India and worldwide when it is copied by persons from a non-Hindu community.

219 See Sanjay Subrahmanyam, *A Carreira e a Lenda de Vasco da Gama,* Capítulo II, a Herança de Santiago, pp. 45-99

220 The presents carried by Vasco da Gama for the Zamorin were "*doze lambéis e quarto capuzes de grão e seis chapéus e quarto ramais de coral e um fardo de bacias, em que havia sei peças e uma caixa de açúcar e quatro barris cheios, dois de azeite e dois de mel*". See António Dias Farinha, 'As Relações dos Portugueses com os Árabes e os Persas na Área do Índico', in Vasco da Gama, vol I, FCG, Lisboa, 1999, p. 169; The Zamorin's ministers contested to these presents and said that the Zamorin would prefer articles like gold or fine cloths, as presents. Also see Joaquim Romero Magalhães, 'Vasco da Gama e a Índia', in Mare Liberum, n° 16, p. 120; Boxer, The Portuguese Seaborne Empire, 1415-1825, London, 1969, pp. 34; Om Prakash in his recent work on the Portuguese in India, vol. 2, chapters, 2-3, 11-13, is also very critical of the contents of the Vasco da Gama's present to the king of Calicut.

221 Fernão Lopes de Castanheda and other contemporary writers have given in this form *História do Descobrimento...,* livro I & II, pp. 47.

222 In fact the Portuguese negative mentality in relation to the Indian rulers is revealed in a profound way in the Portuguese sources of the period especially in *ACE, Livro das Monções,* and even till the late twentieth century it hardly changed. See for example Alexandre Lobato, *Fundamentos da Presença de Portugal na Índia,* Lisboa, 1954, p. 15. "*É curioso, e até importante, notar que os Portugueses chamam sempre rei a qualquer boçal chefe negro por mais selvagem que seja. Tratam-no, e referem-se-lhe por escrito, sempre com respeito pela posição soberana no meio social que governa. Conhecedores imediatos da hierarquia social e, política*

dos regulados ou sobados negros, a que chamam reinos e impérios ao estilo europeu, equiparam as figuras do xadrez feudal cafre a duques, marqueses e condes ou conferem-lhes oficialmente tais títulos pelo padrão dos quadros políticos da Europa".

223 *"E Porque as naos chegarão já quasi sol posto, de noite deitarão os bateis fora, e logo Vasco da Gama se foy pera seu irmão e Nicolão Coelho, e entre si estiuerão praticando o modo que terião com este Rey, pois aqui era o cabo do que vinhão buscar, que lhe parecia que seria melhor ordernar-se como embaixador e lhe fazer seu presente, todauia dizendo que se perderão da outra armada que ali vinhão buscar, em que vinha o Capitão-mor que lhe trazia cartas d'ElRey"*, Gaspar *Correia, Lendas da Índia,* volume primeiro, Lello & Irmão-editores, Porto, 1955, p. 71.

224 Most of the chronicles of this period give minute detail of these facts. Latino Coelho, *Vasco da Gama,* Lello & Irmão, Porto, 1985, (Passim). Most of the details which Coelho has provided could be found in Subrahmanyam's work *The Career and Legend of Vasco da Gama,* Oxford, 1997, (passim); he has furnished us detailed accounts of Vasco da Gama's behaviour throughout his stay in Asia, making use of most of the contemporary sources which have been published.

225 Elaine Sanceau, *Os Portugueses na Etiópia,* Livraria Civilização, Porto, 1961, pp. 76-77. However, it is to be noticed that initially, D. Manuel had sent very sumptuous presents to the Preste John. See pages 21-25, for the list provided by the same author. But it was during the rule of the Portuguese governor, after Afonso de Albuquerque, Lopo Soares de Albergaria, whom Elaine Sanceau has called *"homenzinho invejoso e mesquinho"*, and has further added, *"cheio de raiva perante obra de seu antecessor, quis contrariar tudo quanto achou começado por Afonso de Albuquerque. Devido às delongas que meteu, a embaixada ficou sem efeito. O Embaixador Duarte Galvão morreu em 1517 no mar Vermelho, e o governador não se preocupou em dar-lhe substituo. O maravilhoso presente apodreceu nas húmidas arrecadações da Índia tropical, e o pobre Mateus, em vez de ser repatriado como esperava, ficou aguardando em Goa"*, (pp. 25-26) and that the Embassy failed to reach it's destination due to some personal intrigues of Albergaria..

226 Faria e Sousa, *A Ásia Portuguesa,* vol. I, p. 129.

227 João de Barros, *Da Ásia..., Década* Iª, Livº V, Cap. III. pp. 398-399.

228 João de Barros, *Da Ásia..., Década* Iª, Livº V, Cap. III. pp. 399: and Faria e Sousa has given the same instructions in the following lines, *"tinha instruções para sómente desembarcar para combater com quem não aceitasse a amizade portuguesa..."*: Faria e Sousa, *A Ásia Portuguesa,* vol. I, p. 131.

229 Faria e Sousa, *A Ásia Portuguesa,* vol. I, p. 133; These lines Faria e Sousa has resumed from the text of Castanheda, *História do Descobrimentos ...* livro I & II, pp. 76-77. The full text of the letter which Cabral presented to the Zamorim has been given by Castanheda on the pp. 78-81.

230 See Latino Coelho, *Figuras do Passado, Vasco da Gama.* pp. 278-79.

231 He has even used a term *'subtileza portuguesa'* instead of word "violence" while using firearms with the Indian merchants and rulers. If "violence" is *"subtileza"*, one fails to understand what would constitute violence. António Vasconcelos de Saldanha, 'Os Portugueses no Oriente. Um Exercício de Poder: Paz, Tratados e Conflito Contido', in *Vasco da Gama,* vol. I, pp. 335- 336.

232 *Ibid.*

233 Alexandre Lobato, *Fundamentos da Presença de Portugal na Índia,* p. 34.

234 *Ibid.*, p. 37.

235 More details regarding the political and diplomatical process between the Indian rulers (sovereign and vassal states) and the Portuguese have also been furnished in their respective chapters.

236 Lúis Adão da Fonseca has shown very clearly that D. Manuel through his boastfulness wanted to impress the Castilian king, his own father-in-law. See Luís Adão da Fonseca, "O significado Político em Portugal das Primeiras Viagens à Índia de Vasco da Gama', in *Vasco da Gama,* vol. I, FCG, Lisboa, 1999, p. 74.

237 "A escolha da palavra não é inocente": Luís Adão da Fonseca, 'O significado Político em Portugal das Primeiras Viagens à Índia de Vasco da Gama', in *Vasco da Gama,* p. 73.

238 Luís de Albuquerque, *Crónica do descobrimento e conquista...,* pp. 120-131.

239 It appears that the Portuguese had plans to use the policy of Justinian, Emperor of Byzantine through the use of three diplomatic strategies: (1) Weakening the barbarians by inciting rivalry between them, (2) securing the friendship of frontier tribes with money and flattery, and (3) conversion of heathens to Christianity. Calvet de Magalhães, *Diplomacia Pura,* has provided insight and details about this matter on, pp. 43-49.

240 Albuquerque, *Crónica do descobrimento e conquista ...,* pp. 129-130.

241 HAG, *Livro grande de Pazes,* fols. 44-45v°, *Assento, reteficação e juramento de pazes feitas com o Senhor Rey Sultão Mamede Idalxá por seu enviado Melique Acute, de sua presença, e o Padre Gonçalo Martins, da Companhia de Jesus, governando o Estado da Índia o Senhor Dom Braz de Castro do Conselho de Sua Magestade, 7 de Março de 1655;* The Portuguese initially hesitated to receive him due to his carrier history when he was first posted in 1649, as an ambassador. Malik Yaqút, was an Abyssinian slave at the court of Bijapur where he distinguished himself to the extent that he was sent to Goa as ambassador. Malik Yaqút initially known as Sidi Rehan, an Abyssinian slave had been first employed by Mohammad Adil Shah as Ruqqa-e-rasan (carrier of personal messages, news and information). Later, he was made an army general, when he was awarded the title of Ekhlas Khan when he was

made governor of Dabhol and was awarded with the title of Khan-i-Khanan Khan Mohammad. In the end, he was entitled Malik Yaqút. When he was sent as an ambassador, in 1649 the Portuguese created a great fuss in receiving his credentials. After a couple of months of waiting, when the *Conselho do Estado* finally met in December 1649, it was decided that, to prevent some dispute of a diplomatic nature, there was nothing wrong in accepting his credentials; *ACE*, vol. III, doc. 86: *Sobre se auer de Receber Melique acute por embaxador ou não.* 3 de Dezembro de 1649; Sir Jadunath Sarkar, *History of Aurangzeb*, vol. I, (1618-1659), M.S.C Sarkar & Sons, Calcutta, 1924, Chap. XI, Vol. 1. 2nd rev. Ed. 1925.

242 See Chapter V for more details.

243 Manucci, *Storia do Mogor*, vol. III, pp159-169. It is to note that according the Manucci's translated text the whole diplomatic process took place in 1666 and not in 1655.

244 See P.S.S.Pissurlencar, (doc. Coordenados, anotados e prefaciados), *Agentes da Diplomacia Portuguesa na Índia: Hindus, Muçulmanos, Judeus e Pareses*, Tip. Rangel, Goa, 1952, (passim).

245 HAG, *Livro dos Segredos*, cod. 1, fol. 27-v°: *Carta do vice-rei Pêro da Silva, ao rei Virabadranaique (do Canará). Informa-o que Rama Poi e António Borges, casado e morador em Barcelor, lhe comunicaram o negócio secreto que o rei Virabadranaique lhes confiou, e pede-lhe que mande os capítulos necessários, afirmando que jurará e prometerá, ele vice-rei, guardar o capitulado logo que o rei Virabadranaique o jure e prometa, para que assim seja perpétua a amizade dos portugueses e de toda a gente do Canará "enquanto durar o sol, e a lua"; promete que, feito isto, diligenciará que a Rainha de Banguel tenha relações amistosas com o dito rei e que o seu embaixador na corte de Idalxá seja auxiliado na consecução do seu desiderato pelo embaixador português na mesma corte.* Goa, 14 de Dezembro de 1638.

246 *Contrato das pazes feitas com o Idalxá por seu Embaixador Zaerbeque, que veio do Reino, governando este estao António Moniz Barreto, no anno de 1576*, Biker, (ed.) *Collecção de tratados e concertos de pazes...*, tomo I, pp.170-176; *APO-CR*, fascículo, 5, doc. 742.

247 Joan-Pau Rubiés, *Travel and Ethnology in the Renaissance...*, 189-190.

248 Correa, *Lendas da Índia*, Tomo. 1, Pte. II[a], p. 565; Joaquim Veríssimo Serrão, *Commentário do Afonso de Albuquerque*, vol. I, Parte II, cap. XII, pp. 66-67. Prof. Shastry has provided detailed accounts of the services rendered by Timmayya to the Portuguese: Shastry, *Studies in Indo-Portuguese*...pp. 92-121; Contrary to these authors and many more, Pissurlenkar does not agree that it was Timmaya, instead he has given other name Madd Poi, which he has found in the local Marathi songs in Goa. Pissurlenkar, *Agentes da diplomacia portuguesa na Índia: hindus, muçulmanos, judeus e parses.* pp. XXIX. He has further given justification that this name Timmaya was put in order to conceal the real identity of Madd Poi. See pp. XL, which he has based on João de Barros, was invented by the Portuguese.

249 Correa, *Lendas da Índia,* Tomo. 1, Pte. II, p. 565; Shastry, *Studies in Indo-Portuguese*...pp. 92-121.

250 Shastry, B.S., *Studies in Indo-Portuguese History,* pp. 92-121; Also see the discussion in the Joan-Pau Rubiés, *Travel and Ethnology in the Renaissance...,* pp. 191& fol.

251 Pissurlenkar, *Agentes da diplomacia portuguesa na Índia: ...,* pp. 23-24.

252 *Ibid.*, pp. 1-3.

253 ANTT, *C.C.* cód. 1, fols. 23-133, there are various letters written by Frei António to the king, Dom Manuel, requesting the permission of sending Krishna to Portugal.

254 Pissurlenkar, *Agentes da diplomacia portuguesa na Índia...,* pp. 23-30.

255 For details of those who served the Portuguese as soldiers, spies, informers and messengers, see the *Cartas de Afonso de Albuquerque.*

256 Nambiar *The Kunjali: Admirals of Calicut,* p. 113

257 *Ibid,* See pp. 113-114, for the detailed history of this progress.

258 *APO-BP,* vol. IV, fol. 311; Although its construction had started in 1629, but it was still under construction in 1631, see the letter of Conde de Linhares, *LML,* cod. 29, fols. 1-3v°, de Goa a 20 de Julho de 1631, appendix- 1-A

259 Biker (ed) *Collecção de tratados...,* tomo I, pp. 277, 12 de Maio de 1631.

260 *LML, cod. 38,* fols. 4-10, Goa 5 de Março de 1637.

261 See chapter Portuguese Kanara Diplomacy.

262 Pius, Malekandathil, *Portuguese Cochin and the Maritime Trade of 1500-1663,* (unpublished Ph.D. thesis), Pondicherry University, 1998. pp. 75-76.

263 *Ibid.*

264 From the Patriarch of Babylonia, see Joaquim O. Bragança, (Introdução de), *Acta do Sínodo de Diamper,* Didaskalia, Lisboa, 1987, pp. 7-20; Om Prakash, *Portuguese in India,* pp. 149-159.

265 Not all the St. Thomas Christians resided in the Portuguese dominated areas. Quite a large population lived beyond Portuguese influence though they all maintained contact among themselves: Bragança, (Introdução de), *Acta do Sínodo de Diamper,* pp. 10-13.

266 Bragança, (Introdução de), *Acta do Sínodo de Diamper,* pp. 9-16: For more details of the Portuguese response to the St. Thomas Christians Bishops, António Gouveia, *Jornada do Arcebispo de Goa Dom Frey Aleixo de Menezes Primas da India Orienta,* (first published, 1606), reprinted by Edições Didaskalia, Lisboa, 1988. (Passim)

267 Joan-Pau Rubiés, *Travel and Ethnology in the Renaissance...,* pp. 178-179.

268 A. Mathias Mundadan, 'The St. Thomas Christians and the Portuguese' in *Vasco da Gama,* vol. III, pp. 9-10; Om Prakash, *Portuguese in India,* vol. II, pp. 149-152.

269 Om Prakash, *Portuguese in India*, vol. II, pp. 149-159.

270 Maria Augusta Lima Cruz, 'Degredados e Arrenegados portugueses no espaço Índico nos primórdios do século XVI' in *Povos e Culturas, Portugal e o Oriente. Passado e Presente*, Lisboa, Centro de Estudos dos Povos e Culturas de Expressão Portuguesa, Universidade Católica Portuguesa, 1996. p. 51.

271 See Sanjay Subrahamanyam, *The Political Economy of Commerce*, pp. 157-59, 244.

272 *Ibid*. pp. 41-61.

273 *Ibid.*

274 *Ibid.*

275 Lima Cruz, 'Os Marginais na Índia Portuguesa do Século XVI' in *Vasco da Gama*, vol. II, pp. 165-170.

276 Dejanirah Couto, 'Quelques observations sur les renégats portugais en Asie au XVIe siècle, in *Mare Liberum*, 16, 1998, pp. 57-85.

277 István Rákóczi, Nação Barbada: «Alguns Marginais Europeus no Estado da Índia» in *Encontros sobre Portugal e a Índia*, Fundação Oriente, Lisboa, 2000, pp. 187-194.

278 George D, 'The Shadow Empire of Goa in the Bay of Bengal' in *Itinerario*, Vol. VII, 1983.

279 The Franciscans were the first religious order to come to Goa, followed by the Dominicans (1548), the Jesuits (1542), the Augustinians (1572), the Carmelites (1607), and the Theatines; See Charles J.Borges, 'Foreing Jesuits and Native Resistance in Goa, 1542-1759,' in *Essay in Goan History*, (Ed. T.R. D'Souza), pp. 69-80.

280 Luís Fróis, (edição anotada por José Wicki) *História do Japão*, 5 vols, Biblioteca Nacional, Lisboa, 1976-1984.

281 Pe. Sebastiam Gonçalves, (publ. por José Wicki.) *Primeira parte da história dos religiosos da Companhia de Jesus e do que fizeram com a divina graça...*, 3 vols. Atlântida, Coimbra 1957-1962.

282 Frei Paulo da Trindade, *Conquista espiritual do Oriente*, 3 v.ols. CEHU, Lisboa 1962.

283 Georg Schurhammer, *S. Francisco Xavier e a sua época*, (Sep. Studia, 12). Frei António (ed. lit. G. Schurhammer), *Carta inédita sobre a fundação do convento de S. Francisco de Goa,*; Fr. G. Schurhammer has published numerous works and documents related to S. Francisco Xavier and his correspondence.

284 Among the most valuable works of Padre Iosephus (Joseph, José) Wicki could be included his editions of the monumental collections of the Society of Jesus of the Vatican Library, *Documenta indica, Monumenta Historica Societatis Jesu*, Roma, 1948-1988, (and this is only a brief catalogue of the docuemtns); *'As relações de viagens dos Jesuítas na carreira das naus da Índia de 1541 a 1598,'* in *II Seminário Internacional de História Indo-Portuguesa* Lisboa, CEHU-CA, 1985.

285 António da Silva Rego (ed.) *Documentação para a história das missões ...* 12 vols.

286 John Correia-Afonso, *Jesuit Letters and Indian History,* 2nd edition, Bombay, 1969. (passim)

287 Sir Edward Maclagan, *Os Jesuitas e o Grão Mogol*; Fr. Pierre Du Jarric, *Akbar and the Jesuits: An Account of the Jesuit Missions to the Court of Akbar by Father Pierre du Jarrics.*; Father António Monsserate, *The Commentary of Father Monsserate, S.J., on his Journey to the Court of Akbar.*

288 Charles J. Borges & Helmut Feldmann, *Goa and Portugal: Their Cultural Links*, pp. 43-49.

289 C.A. Bayly, *Indian Society and the Making of the British Empire,* (Passim)

290 HAG, Livro dos Segredos, cod. 1, fol. 27-v°., Carta do vice-rei Pêro da Silva, ao rei Virabadranaique (do Canará). Informa-o que Rama Poi e António Borges, casado e morador em Barcelor, lhe comunicaram o negócio secreto que o rei Virabadranaique lhes confiou, e pede-lhe que mande os capítulos necessários, afirmando que jurará e prometerá, ele vice-rei, guardar o capitulado logo que o rei Virabadranaique o jure e prometa, para que assim seja perpétua a amizade dos portugueses e de toda a gente do Canará "enquanto durar o sol, e a lua"; promete que, feito isto, diligenciará que a Rainha de Banguel tenha relações amistosas com o dito rei e que o seu embaixador na corte de Idalxá seja auxiliado na consecução do seu desiderato pelo embaixador português na mesma corte. Goa, 14 de Dezembro de 1638.

291 *ACE*, vol. IV, doc. 5: *Conselho sobre as cartas que hauião recebido do Barcellor do Capitam mor da armada dos periches Luis da costa.* 5 de Outubro de 1659; Pissurlenkar, *Agentes da diplomacia portuguesa na Índia...* (passim)

292 Luís Graça, 'O Mundo Indiano de seiscentos e a literature portuguesa de viagens', in *II Seminário Internacional da História Indo-Portuguesa*, pp. 479-501.

293 C.A. Bayly, *Empire and Information: Intelligence gathering and social communication in India, 1780-1870,* pp. 19, 43, 69, 92 (passim).

294 The department for gathering secret information for the state. The head of each department was also called *Khufia* (or hidden man) and other field employees were called as *Jasoos* (or gatherers of secret information). Both can be translated as secret agents.

295 Tavernier, *Travels in India,* vol I, pp. 233-234; Nayeem, *External Relations...,* p. 37; Joan-Pau Rubiés, *Travel and Ethnology in the Renaissance...*, pp. 130, 358.

296 *LMG, cod. 3-A*, fols. 164-166: Carta régia para o vice-rei da Índia, Dom Duarte de Meneses, Dando instruções ... *"acha necessário que procure sempre saber as intenções dos reis vizinhos, e demonstra satisfação por ter posto espiões em Cambaia e Balagate, para se conhecerem as intenções do Mogor,* Lisboa, 22 de Janeiro de 1587.

297 *LML*, cod. 1, fols. fols. 4-17: *Carta Régia para o vice-rei, Dom Martim Affonso de Castro, respondendo a carta do mesmo vice-rei "...me avisa das discórdias em que ficava o Equebar com seus filho e elles entre si, de que se esperavam seguir per morte do dito Equebar grandes divisões em seu reino, que he o que mais se pode desejar e convem á conservação desse Estado; e assi deveis procurar, per meios occultos e sem suspeita, de fomentar esta divisão e discórdia..."* 6 de Março de 1605.

298 *LMG*, nº 14, 4-4vº: Carta do Conde de Linhares ao El-rei: *O vice-rei informa sobre as guerras entre o Idalcão e o Mogor e sobre os espias que existem nas cortes destes reinos e que ficam muito dispendiosos ao Estado. Pede que seja deferida uma consulta, que fez sobre Fernão Lopes da Horta, que numa destas missões perdeu uma orelha e o nariz; participa que escreveu ao Idalxá sobre uns navios que o capitão-mor da armada do Estreito aprisionara e levara para Mascate, em virtude de transportarem mercadorias defesas e que o Conselho decidira que se entregassem ao Idalcão. Por fim, relata as negociações que entabulou com o Idalcão, a fim de que este lhe entregasse um filho do dito Fernão Lopes, que estava debaixo do "seguro real", e de como por fim se assentou em que também lhe fossem entregues todas as pessoas que estavam presas naquele reino, há mais de 4 anos.*

299 *O Cronista de Tissuary*, nº 4, pp. 92-93.

300 *LMG*, nº 14, fls. 4-4vº, op.cit; *LMG*, cod. 15, fols. 92-94: *Carta do Vice-Rei da Índia D. Miguel de Noronha, Conde de Linhares, sobre o Idalcão informando sobre as guerras entre o Idalcão e o Mogor e sobre os espias que existem nas cortes destes reinos e que ficam muito dispendiosos ao Estado. Pede que seja deferida uma consulta, que fez sobre Fernão Lopes da Horta, que numa destas missões perdeu uma orelha e o nariz; participa que escreveu ao Idalxá sobre uns navios que o capitão-mor da armada do Estreito aprisionara e levara para Mascate, em virtude de transportarem mercadorias defesas e que o Conselho decidira que se entregassem ao Idalcão. Por fim, relata as negociações que entabulou com o Idalcão, a fim de que este lhe entregasse um filho do dito Fernão Lopes, que estava debaixo do "seguro real",...* Goa, 29 de Novembro de 1632; *O Cronista de Tissuary*, nº 4, Abril de 1866.

301 Boxer, *The Tragic History of the Sea, 1589-1622*, p. 64.

302 Zubairi, *Basatin al-Salatin*, pp. 131, 357.

303 *ACE*, vol. III, doc. 205, 26 de Novembro de 1655.

304 Bayly, *Empire and Information: Intelligence gathering... op.cit.*

305 *Ibid.*

Part IV

Portugal, Spain and the Netherlands

a) Portugal under Spanish rule (1580-1640)

The union of the two crowns of Portugal and Spain in 1580 created a new context for Portuguese trade and commerce. In the beginning, according to the terms of the agreement made at the Cortes of Tomar in 1581, the Spanish and the Portuguese colonial empires were to be kept separate and each was to be administered by its own officials.[306] The affairs of the *Estado da Índia* were left untouched under the administration of the *Casa da Índia* at Lisbon. However, by a decree of 20th of November 1591, the king finally abolished the old financial offices that had functioned within the *Casa da Índia* and created a new *Conselho da Fazenda,* (Council of Finance) consisting men of his own choice. The *Casa da Índia* and the spice trade were placed under its jurisdiction and it soon became the centre around which all the agencies of Portugal's metropolitan and overseas government had to revolve.[307] The *Casa da Índia,* which throughout the sixteenth century had been the supreme body to decide on Asian affairs, now, at the dawn of the seventeenth century, became subordinate to a higher authority.[308]

One might imagine that the passing of Portugal under the control of the Hapsburg dynasty would have-solved some of its financial troubles or, at the very least, that the kings of Spain would have helped to improve the financial condition of Portugal and its colonies. However, the most immediate effect of the Union was to involve Portugal in Spain's European quarrels. Spanish and English relations had been deteriorating since the early 1580s, and the Dutch in the Netherlands were in revolt against Philip II. The involvement of the Portuguese ships in his "Invincible Armada" against England and the Netherlands in 1588, led to a sharp deterioration in Portugal's relationship with both countries. The Dutch revolt against their Spanish ruler continued uninterrupted and the closure of the Portuguese ports in 1585 and the confiscation of numerous Dutch merchant ships in 1592, followed by the blockade of Portuguese ports in 1595 and 1597, caused more trouble to the Portuguese and threatened the Dutch economy in Europe.[309] This prompted the Dutch to search for the sources from which Asian goods came[310] and to try to make themselves masters of the lucrative trade of Asia.[311] As they were aware of the commercial profits of the Portuguese,[312] the idea of trading directly with Asia had been discussed by the Dutch for some time. However, they were only in a position to implement this towards the end of the sixteenth century. Their arrival created a new balance of power in Asia, which greatly weakened the position of the Portuguese.

The Dutch and the English Companies, being private and self supporting, needed no permission from their rulers, at least in the beginning, to take decisions in relation to their commercial contacts in Asia or their diplomatic contacts with the Portuguese. However, they had to obtain permission from the directors of their Companies before they could carry on any long term military campaigns. The commercial and administrative institutions of the Portuguese, on the other hand, were subject to a very hierarchical bureaucracy. A Portuguese viceroy or governor general was bound to seek permission from the king of Portugal before he could act. The problems this caused were apparent from the early days of Portuguese-Dutch contact but became glaringly obvious after 1640, when the Portuguese authorities in India respected the treaties between their country and the States General of the Netherlands, while the Dutch Admirals in Asia hardly gave any heed to them and pretended they were not effective until they were published in Asia. Even after the treaties were published and made known to Dutch subjects in Asia, they hardly bothered about them. The Portuguese viceroy, on the other hand was hesitant to take any military action before receiving orders from the king. By the time the decision came, the Portuguese had already lost many of their numerous commercial centres and much commercial shipping.

Since, after 1580, the Portuguese dominions became a Spanish responsibility, the Dutch stopped differentiating between them and the Spanish.[313] Worse was still to come when the Thirty Years War started in 1618. The Spanish crown had neither the time nor the resources to concern with the Portuguese colonial possessions and their troubles. Nevertheless, the Spanish ruler had his responsibilities towards Portugal and its colonies and in protecting the fragile Portuguese territories, the Spanish were protecting their own interests. As a result, there were some occasions, especially in Brazil in 1624, when Spanish soldiers and ships aided the Portuguese against the Dutch, and Spain also invested heavily in fortifying the Portuguese possessions, building massive new fortifications to protect Angra in the Azores and Santiago in Cape

Verde. On the other hand, when the Spanish fought the Dutch in the island of Ternate in the Moluccas in 1607, they were fighting to protect their own interests as the Spanish soldiers had already displaced the Portuguese from that region in 1606. Ternate was already a Spanish possession when they fought against the Dutch.

There is no evidence that Spanish forces ever reached the south-west coast of India or Ceylon to fight against the Dutch. Nor did the Spanish rulers send extra funds to help modernise the Portuguese navy or to pay for the Portuguese soldiers in the war-affected areas whose wages were not paid for months or years and who were forced to look for other ways to survive, for example by taking service with the Indian kings. Therefore, the survival of the Portuguese in the Indian sub-continent was solely at their own expense and was largely due to the political situation of the Indian rulers who kept asking them for military support, thus enabling them to prolong their existence for some decades.

There are continuous reports from the Portuguese viceroys where they mention the lack of commerce and the fact that the treasury was empty. They received no help from Spain and had to ask for loans from various sources, from local businessmen or from the Church authorities and it is known that these loans were not repaid in some cases for thirty to forty years.[314] Information regarding the finance which the Portuguese *Estado da Índia* received from the king of Portugal, both during the Spanish regime, especially the period between 1600-1640, and during the period of the Restoration 1640-1669, are exhaustively provided in my earlier work[315] in the tables 3.1-3.5, 4.1-4.2, and chapter eight which deals with the financiers of the Portuguese trade in India. The details provided show the money sent from Portugal, revenues of the *Estado da Índia,* which were derived from the local (coastal) trade, from customs dues levied on Asian merchant shipping as well as the land revenues collected from the territories under their control.

The question arises how the Portuguese were able to survive so long, as a dominant force on the Indian sub-continent where, for over a century they maintained colonial establishments and fortified bases. Whatever the explanation, it is not to be found in any help they received from Spain.

The answer to the above question could be provided in the following line. First, there were some able and energetic viceroys like the Conde de Linhares, who virtually rebuilt the whole Portuguese navy which, according to him, had hardly any seaworthy ships or cannon on them to fight a sea battle when he took office as Viceroy. How was he able to do this? The answer might be that suggested by Maria Manuela in her thesis where she gives at least one example of how the Conde de Linhares was able to obtain prompt help from the local Portuguese community in Goa and other states. I quote, "Initially, as soon as the Viceroy joined the Office, he appealed the lively supports from the Portuguese community and other residents of Goa as well as from different Portuguese states and obtained a generous sum of 100,000 Ahrafis, which could be paid within next six years".[316] He also used some of his own wealth beside what he was able to obtain on loan from the religous orders, and *Casa da Misericórdia* in Goa. And this is how he constructed new war ships and repaired many damaged fortresses.

Second, the Indian rulers, as has been discussed elsewhere, because of the political circumstances in which they found themselves, still feared the Portuguese on the open sea. Third, was the fact that, to dismantle the widely dispersed Portuguese bases, which ranged from the Persian Gulf to Macau, required a lot of military resources which the Dutch investors in the Netherlands were not prepared to find, as their most important aim was to benefit from Asian trade and not to fight wars. Therefore, the Dutch tried systematically to weaken the Portuguese navy over a period of almost sixty years (much in the same way that the Portuguese used to do against the Zamorin by engaging him constantly in warfare throughout the sixteenth century on different fronts) and when they knew the time was right, in alliance with the forces of Calicut, they gave a final blow to Portuguese hegemony in their south Indian port towns of Quilon, Cochin, Cranganore and Cannanore.[317] The Portuguese strongholds in Kanara had already been taken over by the Nayakas of Ikkeri during 1654-1656.

b) Organisation of Portuguese Trade in India

To control and exploit the trade of the Indian Ocean, the Portuguese created a network of outposts and settlements. The kingdom of Kotte was made tributary to the King of Portugal in 1507,[318] but no part of Ceylon was actually occupied until around 1519. The ruler of Hormuz in the Gulf had submitted himself to Portuguese suzerainty in 1508 paying 15,000 ashrafis annually as tribute and a fortress was established there.[319] which remained in Portuguese possession until 1622.[320] Another port of importance was Muscat, which the Portuguese occupied for the purpose of controlling the movements of commercial vessels.[321] After occupying these ports, the Portuguese were in more or less full control of the Persian Gulf and the Gulf of Oman.[322] Malacca was another port in South-East Asia that the Portuguese brought under their control in 1511 driving out its ruler. A Portuguese fortress along with a factory was quickly constructed there.[323] Thus in a short space of time the Portuguese occupied all the key points in the Indian Ocean save Aden, which they twice failed to capture.

The most important customs house on the western coast of India was, of course, Goa. The Portuguese attempted, with some success, to make it the focus for trade from all over Asia. The most important customs houses in the north were Diu, Daman and Chaul, and in the south, Cochin, all of which had considerable importance for Portuguese revenues.[324]

According to the regulations of the *Casa da Índia,* which were to be strictly followed by the *Estado da Índia* from the early sixteenth century, ships from Portugal along with the money and a list of goods required by the king (which was sent by the *Casa da Índia*) were received by the Portuguese Viceroy and after the merchandise was collected from the different parts of India and the rest of Asia it was brought to Goa. Then a schedule of the cargo was prepared for each ship according to what was loaded on it. After all these formalities were complete, two copies of the manifest were handed over to the captain of the ships and another was kept for records in Goa, before the ships left for Portugal.[325] For almost 150 years this form of carrying trade was rigorously observed except in 1643 when, due to the Dutch presence near Goa,[326] two ships sailed towards Mozambique directly from Diu loading 40,000 pieces of cloths, and in 1658 when three ships left the port of Diu carrying textiles of various kinds for Mozambique.[327] Throughout the sixteenth century the Portuguese carried on local trade with all the western Indian ports to collect the necessary items to be sent to Portugal. Whatever trade was conducted on the coastal areas of India by the Portuguese, either on the private or official levels, had to be reported to the *Estado da Índia's* authorities at Goa. In a way it might be said that the Portuguese *Estado da Índia* had become almost a vassal state of the King of Portugal, and the officials worried more about their own income than the income of the state. In reality the regulation of the *Casa da India* is to be blamed for this since the income of the state was always given priority over the wellbeing of its own employees who had to live in a far off land without adequate resources for themselves and the families.

Nevertheless, Portuguese organisation and carrying trade followed after 1663, was governed with different set of regulations than it did earlier.

c) Rice, Saltpetre, commodities for survival

Historian like Sanjaya Subrahamanayam, in his study, has tried to maintain that the coastal trade in rice and saltpetre were on a large scale in the seventeenth century and should be included among the profitable commodities of Portuguese trade.[328] Thus one may assume that the Portuguese made a considerable profit from this trade and used it in their fight with the Dutch as well as the Indian rulers. In this he is completely wrong, firstly because these were not general items of trade on which a profit might be earned, but were rather bought to be supplied to the war affected areas for the consumption of the soldiers and the Portuguese residing in those parts. Secondly, the profits of this trade were made by the local Indian producers and by the 'married and settled merchants'[329] and not by the Portuguese *Estado da Índia*. This extra expenditure was a burden to the Portuguese economy when their resources were urgently needed for other purposes.

The coastal trade in rice, saltpetre and other commodities of prime necessity, which reached a peak during the period between 1628 and 1663, was mostly to supply the Portuguese war-affected areas, including Muscat in the Persian Gulf, Malacca and the ports of India and Ceylon. They were never commodities which could yield the Portuguese treasury any extra income,[330] except for the taxes they could levy over their transactions. A partial exception is the case of saltpetre, which was acquired from various regions of India to produce gunpowder for both the Portuguese and the Indian rulers in exchange for diplomatic favours against the Dutch and the English.[331]

The increase in demand for both the items was due mainly to the prevailing circumstances during three decades of war. However, among these, rice, certainly turned out to be a very important commodity in shaping Portuguese diplomacy with the rulers of Kanara and Bijapur. At least in the case of the Kanara region, where rice was produced in abundance, it gave a very powerful instrument to the Nayakas who used to bargain the prices of pepper against the purchase of rice and to a lesser extent saltpetre. This often created quite a tense diplomatic situation and led to diplomatic exchanges between the two sides.

On the other hand. Although the saltpetre had to be purchased, the gunpowder gave the Portuguese a commanding position in local diplomacy, thanks to the perpetual rivalry between the Mughals and the states of Ahmadnagar and Bijapur. In return for its supply, the Portuguese were able to insist on the expulsion of the Dutch and the English from their territories. The Sultans of Bijapur and Ahmadnagar urgently needed gunpowder, when, as happened often during the wars with the Mughals, their factories were not able to produce sufficient to supply their forces. However, the largest part of the gunpowder was used by the Portuguese themselves during their wars against the Dutch and the local states such as Kanara and Bijapur. This was, therefore, an additional expenditure for an almost empty treasury.

During the early years of the seventeenth century, Portuguese officials obtained their supplies of saltpetre from the regions of Sindh, Balaghat, Cranganore and Tuticorin, but as the demand increased due to the heavy pressures of war, supplies were also obtained from other areas like Madurai, Jaffnapattam and Bengal.

To conclude, although a substantial quantity of these commodities was bought by the Portuguese and carried in shiploads to their various coastal towns, they were mainly for strategic purposes and the Crown earned almost nothing from it, in comparison with the income from the trade in spices, pepper, textiles and diamonds. On the contrary, expenditure on these two commodities was an extra burden on the Portuguese treasury.[332]

Reference

306 F. Mendes da Luz, *O Conselho da Índia*, pp. 69-79; Lach, *Asia in the Making of Europe*, Vol. I, Book I, p. 135; Boxer, *The Portuguese Seaborne Empire*, pp. 10-78; Veríssimo Serrão, *O Tempo dos Filipes em Portugal e no Brasil*, (1580-1668), pp.19-20.

307 Da Luz, *O Conselho da Índia* pp. 81-82.

308 *Ibid.*, pp. 27-28.

309 *The Dutch in Malabar...*, doc...N° 13, p. 67; Davies, *A Primer of Dutch Seventeenth Century Overseas Trade*, pp. 82-83; Leonard Blussé & George Winius, «The Origin and Rhythem of Dutch Agression against the *Estado da Índia*,», pp. 73-84.

310 Kail, *The Dutch in India...*, p. 11.

311 *The Dutch in Malabar...*, N° 13, pp. 57

312 B. W. Diffe and George Winius, *Foundation of the Portuguese Empire*, vol. I, pp. 427-29; Kail, *The Dutch in.*, p. 11.; Y. R. Bruijn, F. J. Gaastra, and J. Schoffer, *Dutch-Asiatic Shipping in the 17th and 18th centuries*, pp. 2-8.

313 Poonen, *Dutch Beginnings in India Proper (1580-1615*p. 4-6; Panikkar, *Asia and the Western Dominances*, pp. 55-56; Shirodkar, «Dutch-Portuguese Relations in the East», in *Stvdia*, vol. 48, pp. 123-144, and many others; Pieter C. Emmer, «The Struggle over Sugar, The abortive attack of the Dutch on Portugal in the South Atlantic» in *Mare Liberum*, n° 13, pp. 59-68.

314 More details with documentary evidence can be found in chapter VIII of, Afzal Ahmad, *Indo-Portuguese Trade in Seventeenth Century (1600-1663), op.cit.*

315 *Ibid.*

316 For further efforts made by the Conde de Linhares in building the whole structure of the Portuguese *Estado da Índia*, see Manuela, *O Estado Português da Índia...* pp. 498-500.

317 The forces of Kunjali Marakkar were also destroyed with the support of a foreing power, the Portuguese.

318 Faria e Sousa, *Asia Portuguesa*, vol. I, pp. 220-230; Mathew, *The Portuguese Trade with India...*, p. 59.

319 Barros, *Da Ásia..., Décadas*, IIª, parte Iª, pp. 109-120; Faria e Sousa, *Ásia Portuguesa*, vol. I, pp. 233-50; Whiteway, *The Rise of Portuguese Power..*, p. 119.

320 *LML*, cod. 11, fols. 42/83-84, 76/135-37; cod. 12, fols. 3/78; cod. 13, fol. 46/91; AHU, *Índia*, cx. 4, doc. 192.

321 Barros, *Da Ásia..., Décadas*, IIª, pp. 20-57, 119-20; Whiteway, *The Rise of Portuguese Power...* p. 119.

322 Barros, *Da Ásia..., Décadas,* II[a], pp. 20-57, 119-20.

323 *Ibid,* p. 40.

324 HAG, *Fortalezas,* cod. 4460, fols. 412; *APO-BP.,* tomo IV, vol. II, part I, pp. 279-80; Pearson, *Merchants and Rulers..,* pp. 43-44.

325 Damião Peres, (ed.) *Regimento das Cazas das Indias e Mina*: manuscrito inédito.

326 *ACF,* cod. 1167, fl. 197v.

327 *India,* cx. 17, doc. 49.

328 *The Political Economy of Commerce,* pp. 52-59,

329 Afzal Ahmad, *Indo-Portuguese Trade in Seventeenth Century*...see chapter 5, appendice 5.12.

330 See the documents used in the appendixes II, F-H.

331 See chapter 6, Afzal Ahmad *Indo-Portuguese Trade...,* pp. 128-135.

332 The tables given in Appendixes II, F-H show the quantities of Rice and Saltpetre bought during the period under review in this work.

Part V

Portuguese, Marathas, Mughals and the Deccan States

Although Mughal expansion towards the kingdoms of southern India, such as Ahmadnagar and Bijapur, and the rise of Marathas as a paramount power in the territories of Bijapur, leading ultimately to their integration in the Mughal Empire, is not the subject of this study, it is necessary briefly to consider what took place, because this expansion not only altered the geographical boundaries of South India but contributed to reshaping the balance of power. If, on the one hand, Mughal power created a dangerous situation for the southern states of Ahmadnagar and Bijapur as well as for the Portuguese, on the other it gave more bargaining power to the Portuguese and weakened the resolve of the Indian states in dealing with them. The rise of Marathas towards the beginning of the third decade also weaken the military and burdened the economy of the Bijapur with the effect of helping Portuguese diplomacy and facilititating the incorporation of this state into the Mughal empire.

a) Mughals-Portuguese-Ahmadnagar-Bijapur: Complex Political Situation

The state of Ahmadnagar was the first to fall prey to the ambitions of the Mughal Emperor Akbar soon after the fall of Gujarat in 1572. Although the Nizam Shah of Ahmadnagar had been part of the Indian confederation, which had attempted to expel the Portuguese from the Western Coast of India in 1570, it was now his turn to join hands with the Portuguese to oppose Mughal expansion. The Portuguese welcomed these approaches and tightened their noose around the neck of the Ahmadnagar rulers. Portuguese-Ahmadnagar relations took a new turn in the first half of the seventeenth century with the rise of Malik Amber, the Ethiopian minister who joined with the Portuguese to face the new threat posed by the Mughals and to save the northern ports of the Portuguese.[333]

In 1604, Malik Amber granted to the Portuguese the right to collect half of the land revenue in Chaul in return for help against the Mughals.[334] This new arrangement did not continue for long, as the relations of the Portuguese with the peasants were not cordial. Malik Amber tried to put an end to these problems but the Portuguese did not agree. This resulted in hostility between the two, which lasted for several years.[335] Soon after this, the Portuguese and Ahmadnagar once again united, through the mediation of Ibrahim Adil Shah, to face a Mughal attack in 1615.[336] Misfortune, however, stalked the Ahmadnagar kingdom. Malik Amber died in 1627 and was succeeded by his son, Fateh Muhammad Khan. In the north, the Mughal emperor, Shah Jahan, ascended the throne. Ahmadnagar and Bijapur were more divided than ever and this enabled Shah Jahan to subdue Ahmadnagar once and for all in 1637.[337] Thus, Ahmadnagar's problems became the problems of the Mughals.

b) Rise of Marathas and the Balance of power

The emergence of the Marathas in the early decades of the seventeenth century as a threat to the Sultans of Bijapur, Ahmadnagar and the Portuguese, also turned out to be a deciding factor in changing the balance of power. The rise of Maratha power had begun soon after 1624 under the leadership of Shahji, father of Shivaji. During his first thirty years Shivaji experienced many adventures and changes of fortune but his firm and determined character stood him in good stead. For a man of his mettle, no problem was insurmountable.

The early successes of Shivaji were not of great importance to the Portuguese as his attention was mainly focussed on the Muslim kingdoms. He adopted slogans like, 'protector and saviour of Hindus' and 'creator of Hindutva Swaraaj.'[338] However, no Hindu kingdom in India fell for such a ploy, as they all understood that Shivaji was merely creating his own kingdom. Initially the Portuguese remained cautious and watchful of the progress he made in the Bijapuri and Mughal territories. Sometimes they supported the ambitions of Shivaji when he was attacking the Mughal and the Bijapuri states, as it fitted with the general policy they had adopted of helping the rival princes. On the other hand, the rise of Shivaji was accepted as a good sign as his constant guerrilla wars kept the Bijapuri state busy and over a period of time weakened it. This prevented the Bijapuri becoming any threat to Goa. However, once Shivaji's ambitions turned towards the territories of Bassein and Chaul, the Portuguese began to become concerned. By 1658, when in the vicinity of Chaul, Shivaji prepared a navy to face any challenge from the sea. His navy was built-up under renegade Portuguese nationals, fugitives escaped from prison and fortune seekers.[339] In 1659, a fleet of twenty warships was ready to sail in three different ports; Bhivandi, Kalyan and Panvel. Luís Leitão Viegas, a Portuguese national, was commander of the fleet. Shivaji asked him to seek permission from the Portuguese authorities for their departure. However, the Portuguese had already made up their minds regarding Shivaji. They not only prohibited the fleet from sailing but also tried to scuttle Shivaji's effort to build a navy.[340] The reason behind this was that the Portuguese wanted to help Siddi Rajapuri, who commanded the northwest hinterlands of the Bijapuri kingdom and had always been on friendly terms with the Portuguese. Shivaji was at war with Siddi and was ready to send his fleet against him. Portuguese officers also feared a threat to their own sea power. Therefore, no permission was granted for the ships even to leave port. Moreover the Portuguese succeeded in persuading Viegas and three hundred other compatriots, who were assisting Shivaji in his navy, to desert him.[341] This was a severe blow to Shivaji's ambitions but he was not a man to be prevented from reaching his goal. Till the end of his life he continued to pose a threat to the Portuguese sea power.

The Portuguese followed a varying policy of friendship, hostility, or neutrality towards the Marathas, depending upon the circumstances and in accordance with who their enemies were at the time. In the context of Shivaji's relations with Bijapur and the Portuguese there was hardly any occasion when Shivaji got Portuguese support against Adil Shah. The Portuguese were always cautious about the balance of power in the Deccan since this was a time when the Dutch were very active on the western coast and the ships of the VOC presented a permanent threat to Portuguese colonies and trade. Therefore the Portuguese chose to behave very diplomatically towards the Marathas, and most of the time remained inactive.[342] By the end of 1664, Shivaji had occupied Kudal, Perne and Bicholim in the Adil Shah's territories. The original holders of these areas, mostly Desais, were given shelter in Goa, from where they made raids into the Maratha territory. The basis for the Portuguese policy was that the Desais' were vassals of the Bijapuri Sultan and should therefore be supported by the Portuguese.[343]

Maratha-Mughal-Portuguese relations were governed by a different set of factors and as such varied from those discussed above. Here the Portuguese were sympathetic and helpful to Shivaji. The Portuguese were then at war with the Dutch in the southern ports of Malabar and Kanara and needed help rather than an enemy, on both land and sea. Another consideration was to keep Mughal power at a distance for, if the Mughals were successful against Adil Shah and Shivaji, they would next be knocking at Goa's door. Thus in 1663, Shivaji sought and found shelter with the Portuguese authorities in Bassein and Chaul because of the fear of the Mughals. Besides these two places, shelter was provided for his forces in Goa, while arms and ammunition were also delivered to them. On the other hand, the Portuguese instructed their officers in Bassein and Chaul not to supply any provision to the Mughals and thereby oblige them to retreat.[344] It is intriguing that the Portuguese were able to provide support to the Marathas when they themselves required all their forces in their southern protectorates of Quilon, Cranganore, Cochin and Cannanore which were under heavy attack from the Dutch and the Zamorin. The explanation appears to be that the Portuguese gave Shivaji shelter in their fortress of Bassein and Chaul secretly, and as a last resort firstly because they wanted to gain the friendship of Shivaji at this time and, secondly because they would be protected from the Mughals if Shivaji survived in between their settlements. In other words, for the Portuguese, it was simply a diplomatic move to protect their northern possessions without expending very much effort. On the contrary, as Delduque da Costa has suggested, no ammunition or gunpowder was actually sent. All that was used was what was already stored in respective fortresses for their protection.

In January 1664, when Shivaji attacked and looted the city of Surat, the Portuguese authorities not only expressed their approval but are said actually to have helped his forces. In fact Portuguese soldiers were observed plundering Surat with the Marathas, and when the Mughals complained to the Viceroy at Goa, the later blandly replied that they were not his men but deserters.[345] In 1665, Jai Singh, the Mughal general, sought Portuguese aid against Shivaji, and in particular he asked for some artillery. Furthermore, he requested that they cease helping Shivaji, and also that they should not return his ships that they had captured. None of these demands were accepted. Although they promised not to give any assistance to Shivaji, the Portuguese accepted Shivaji's request for shelter. The Portuguese also provided him with ammunition and food.[346]

A change is noticeable in the policy of the Portuguese after 1665. Shivaji's surrender to the Mughals created suspicion and uneasiness in their mind. From then on, they hesitated to give him outright help. After his escape from Agra in 1666, Shivaji again inquired of them whether he could find refuge in Portuguese territory along with his treasure. The reply was discouraging and made clear that the Portuguese were powerless to face such a mighty ruler as Aurangzeb.[347] However, after the Mughal Xivaji treaty, the Portuguese were more cautious in their diplomacies with the both.

Such were the ups and downs of Portuguese policies towards Shivaji vis-à-vis the Mughals. It is clear from this that the conflicting interests against which they were called to maintain their own position, created considerable problems for the survival of their colonies and ports in India.

c) Portuguese-Mughal Relations

Portuguese-Mughal relations became estranged, after the death of Akbar (October, 1605), for various reasons, most important of which were the Mughal attacks on the Deccan states and the arrival of the English ambassador, Captain Hawkins, in 1608 on a diplomatic mission.[348] Hawkins' main aim was to get trading facilities in the Mughal lands including their ports. The Portuguese made no attempt to stop the development of ties between the English and the Mughals. The English were received with great honour and respect[349] and were granted concessions for their trade in Surat.

In 1609 the new Portuguese Viceroy, André Furtado Mendonça, called upon the Mughal ambassador at Goa for a renewal of cordial relations. However, the attempt to create friendly ties did not last long because of the Portuguese attack on the English ships in 1612.[350] The Mughal Governor was furious at this act. Further deterioration set in when Portuguese ships looted a Mughal vessel off Surat and burnt it. This operation was carried out under the command of Luís de Brito de Mello from the fortress of Diu.[351] All the booty and prisoners were brought to Goa after the burning of the ship.[352] In response, the Mughals confiscated Portuguese lands within their territories and burnt a large number of villages in Daman and its adjacent areas where Portuguese were to be found.[353]

Peace was restored in June 1615 between the two powers through an exchange of embassies and negotiation, and shipping was regularised from Surat to Mecca through the cartaz system.[354]

Mughal-Portuguese relations remained quiet till 1632 when Shah Jahan, the Mughal emperor, ordered an attack on the settlements at Hoogly in Bengal, where the Portuguese had been settled since 1579 on the strength of a *Farman* from Akbar.[355] Shah Jahan's dislike for the Portuguese went back to 1622 when he was a rebel and was not taken seriously by the Portuguese.[356] His opportunity came in 1632 when Portuguese settlers in Bengal were accused by the governor of Hoogly, Qasim Khan, of gross interference in the local matters. The Mughal governor thereupon attacked Hoogly with great force. The Portuguese settlements were destroyed and a number of Portuguese were made prisoners. Out of some 300 Portuguese and 600 local Christians, it is difficult to estimate how many survived.[357] Nevertheless, through the effort of Father João de Cruz, one of the prisoners of war, peace was restored at Hoogly. Shah Jahan issued a Farman releasing all prisoners and returning all booty captured during the war.[358]

In 1635, Shah Jahan launched another expedition to the south, resulting in the permanent subjugation of Ahmadnagar in 1637.[359] Bijapur was also obliged to pay tribute every year and to render help against the rising power of the Marathas under the leadership of Shahji, father of Shivaji. However, war against Bijapur had to be renewed in 1657 because of the negligence on the part of its ruler in the payment of tribute for many years. The expedition against Bijapur was disrupted by the war of succession to the Mughal throne in 1658.[360] It was not until 1686 that the Bijapur kingdom finally fell into the hands of Mughals.

This political turmoil forced the Portuguese to expend large amounts of money and other resources, damaged their trade and greatly weakened their power. Their expenditure on defence affected their overall financial position and their investments in commercial activities. However, it proved just as harmful for the Indian rulers and meant that they were unable to show a united front against the frequent atrocities committed by the Portuguese on Indian merchant shipping.

Reference

333 Boxer, *The Portuguese Seaborne...*, p. 136

334 *APO-BP*, Tomo IV, Vol. II, parte III, pp. 17-24, 48-77, 85-92, 106-12, 218-22, 250-59, 303-8; M. Joshi, *History of Mediaeval Deccan*, Vol. I, pp. 265-66.

335 *Ibid*

336 *Ibid*

337 Nayeem, *External Relations...*, pp. 95-96.

338 Creator of the Hindu Kingdom

339 Lobato, *Relações Luso-Marata...*, p. 19; Shastry, *A Note on Portuguese...*, pp. 110-112.

340 Delduque da Costa, *Os Portugueses e os...*, in *BIVG*, No. 20, p. 4; Shastry, '*A Note on Portuguese...*, pp. 110-112.

341 Shastry, '*A Note on Portuguese*'..., pp. 111.

342 *Ibid.*, pp. 112.

343 Pissurlenkar, 'Português e Marata', *BIVG*, N°. I, pp. 48-98; *No.* 2, pp. 66-92; No. 3, pp. 66-92;

No. 6, pp. 80-89.

344 Delduque da Costa, *Os Portugueses e os...*, in *BIVG*, No. 20, p. 48.

345 Pissurlenkar, 'Português e Marata', *BIVG* No. I, pp. 48-98; *No.* 2, pp. 66-92; No. 3, pp. 66-92;

No. 6, pp. 80-89.

346 Shastry, 'A Note on Portuguese'..., pp. 113

347 Biker (ed) *Collecção de tratados...* Vol. IV, pp. 131-132.

348 S. Purchas, *His Pilgrims...*, vol. I, p. 206; Henry Beveridge, *A Comprehensive History of India*, vol. I, pp. 308-310.

349 S. Purchas, *His Pilgrims...* , vol. I, p. 206

350 Bocarro, *Década 13...*, part I, pp. 200-204.

351 *Ibid*, pp. 189-192

352 *Ibid.*

353 *Ibid., pp.* 200-204.

354 Biker (ed) *Collecção de tratados...*, tomo. I, pp. 189-192: *Capitulos das pazes que se fizeram entre os vassallos de El-Rey Jahanguir e os Portuguezes, por Nauabo Mucarreb Xhan e Gonçalo Pinto da Fonseca,* 7 de Junho de 1615; Biker, tomo 1: *Contrato de Pazes que o Padre António de Andrade e D. Francisco Coutinho de Ocem fizeram com El-Rey Mogor por meio do Nababo de Surrate, em Damão,* a 13 de Setembro de 1630, pp.237-239.

355 Campos, *History of the Portuguese...*, pp. 45-46.

356 *Ibid.*, pp. 129.

357 *Ibid.*, pp. 143-46.

358 *Ibid.*, pp. 142-44.

359 Tripathi, *The Rise and Fall of Mughal Empire*, pp. 447-476; Majumdar, *The Mughal Empire*, pp. 205-212

360 *Ibid.*

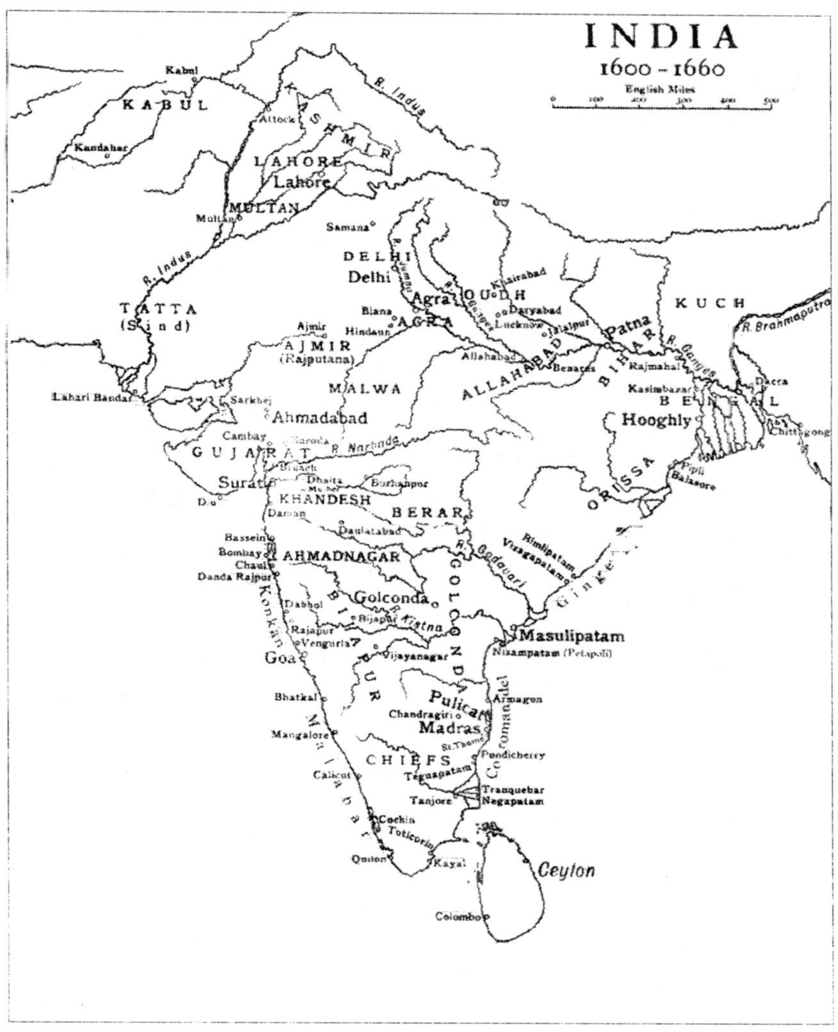

Map of India

Ref: W. H., *From Akbar to Aurangzeb: A Study in Indian Economic History*

Chapter- 3

Portuguese Diplomatic relations with the Malabar states in the Seventeenth Century

Certain factors need to be kept in mind while treating with the Portuguese Malabar diplomacy. Although all the states, especially Cochin, Quilon, Cranganore and Cannanore, irrespective of their size, produced spices, the only ruler who stood out against the Portuguese attempt to control the movement of commercial activities was the Zamorin. As we know, most of these small states were more inclined to fight for their political freedom from Calicut, even if this meant collaborating with a foreign power. Their dream of getting rid of the Zamorin's political sovereignty did indeed materialise but in the quest for political independence they lost all their other socio-conomical freedoms and remained effectively under Portuguese control till the Dutch conquered them in the 1660s. During this period of almost 163 years, these states were treated as part of the Portuguese *Estado da Índia* and political or economic matters were handled only through the Portuguese authorities. Therefore, since these kingdoms in effect became part of the *Estado da Índia,* Portuguese diplomatic relations in Malabar was confined to the state of Calicut.This chapter, for the sake of convenience, has been divided into two parts. Part first will deal with the Portuguese diplomatic relations with the Malabar states, especially with the kingdom of Calicut, together with its commercial importance in the world trade in the sixteenth century. It would also shed some light, in the early parts, on the poltical and diplomatical system of the Zamorins of Calicut, which was followed unabated and evolved over the space of time in the seventeenth century. Part second will be dealing with Portuguese Zamorin diplomacy in the seventeenth century, until the major Portuguese strongholds were lost to the Dutch.

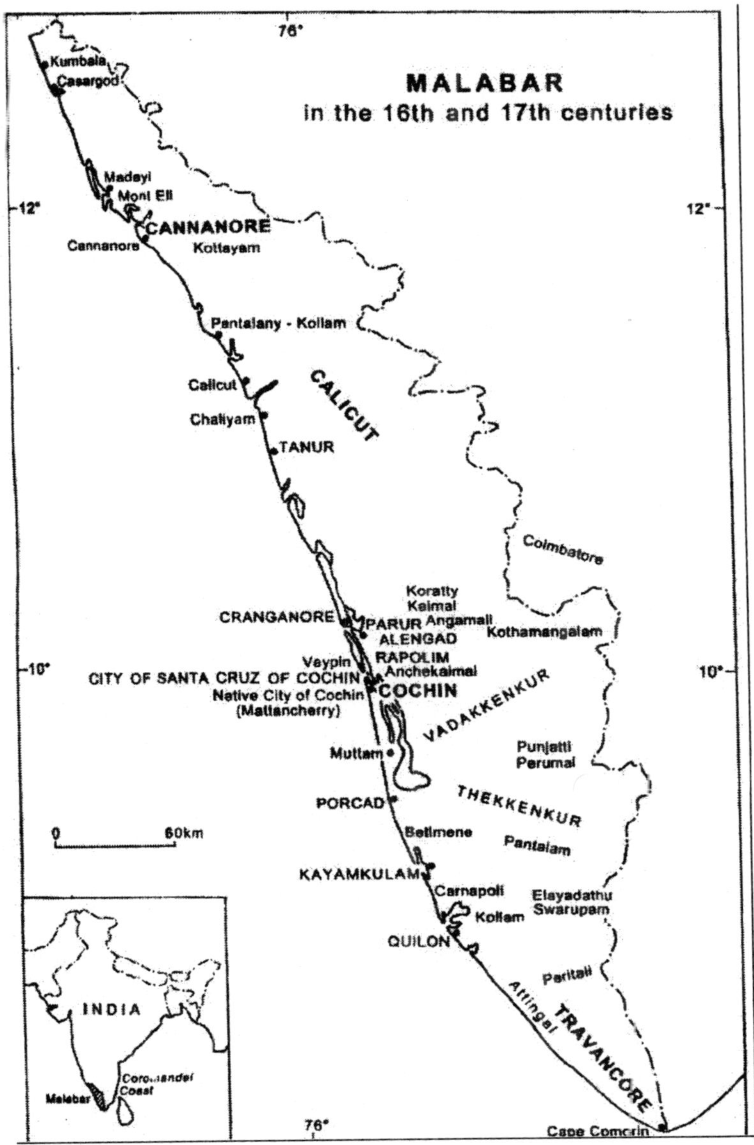

Map of South India, Malabar

Pius M.C. (Malekandathil), *Portuguese Cochin and the Maritime Trade of 1500-1663, Pondicherry,* 1998.

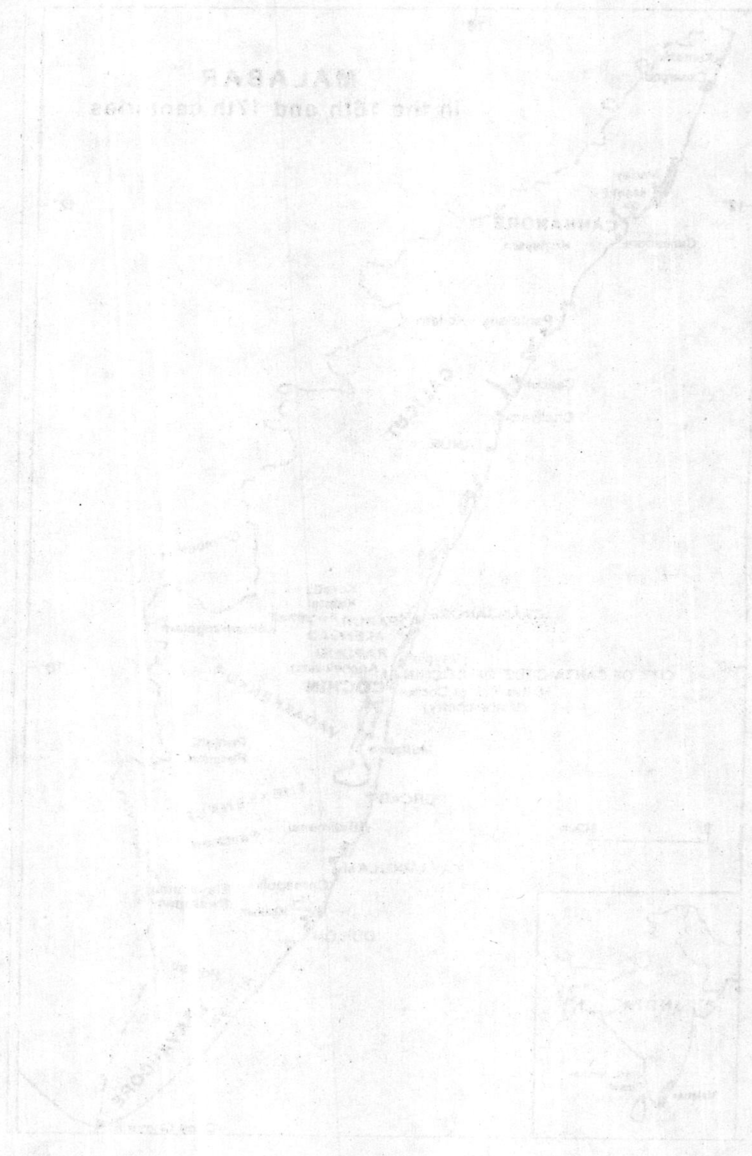

Map of South India, Malabar

Part I

The Portuguese Zamorin and the other Malabar states in the sixteenth century

Before studying the diplomacy between the Zamorin and the Portuguese in the seventeenth century, it is essential to look at their early contacts which shaped their relations and continued to haunt them into the seventeenth century. A brief account of the early Portuguese relations with the other states of Malabar will also be provided to better understand the circumstances that formed the Zamorin Portuguese relations.

a) Political and Diplomatic System of the Kingdom of Calicut

The ruler of Calicut and head of the Chera dynasty, Samutiri Tirumulpad, is generally called *Samuri* by the people, and it was transformed into Zamorin by the Europeans.[361] Whatever the name of the Zamorin, he is styled in all the formal correspondence as follows: *Srimatu Sakalaguna sampannarana Sakaladharma paripalakarana Mitrajana manoranjitarana Akhandita Lakshmi prasannanana Raja manya Raja Sri Manavikrama Zamorin Maharaja Bahadur Avargal"*.[362] The Chief Minister of the state of Calicut was called Mangat Acchan.

Before a Zamorin was sworn to be king of Calicut, very elaborate religious ceremonies used to take place which were performed by the head priest or the Brahmin of the Kingdom. This could take several days and a great number of people were always present on the occasion. Although Prof. Ayyar has given an exhaustive account of the coronation ceremonies,[363] it is only necessary to describe briefly the formal procedures that were followed at the installation of the Zamorin as ruler of the Chera Dynasty. According to Ayyar, after all the religious rituals were completed, which involved fourteen different ceremonies in different temples, the Zamorin used to return to the palace where he was dressed for *Ariyittuvalcha* or the coronation. He was helped by *Nandavanatti Nampi*, the keeper of the crown jewels.[364] These jewels, almost 35 in number were worn by the Zamorin on all important occasions, especially when he received ambassadors. As Ayyar says, "the absence of a crown is traditional. In its place, the Zamorin wore a gold band or fillet called *Tirumutippattam*. Although this ceremony marked the beginning of the reign of a Zamorin, in Malabar tradition, it is not known either as coronation or an enthronement; for neither the crown nor the thrones figures in it."[365] Instead of a throne "the Zamorin is throughout the ceremony seated on a white and a black carpet, spread one above the other. It is strange to note that in the Malabar area the wearing of a crown and coronation ceremonies were introduced by the Portuguese, "when, in A.D. 1505, Almeida placed a "golden crown brought from Portugal on the head of Unni Rama Verma, the Rajah of Cochin."[366] Nevertheless, it can't be assumed with this fact that the rulers of Calicut didn't wear crown or seated on a throne. Both these were used in day today's life of the Zamorin but not during the initial ceremony.

After having been blessed by the Brahmins, before whom the Zamorins customarily promised to protect Hinduism, ceremonies for the appointment of all the important ministers (such as ministers of finances and minting coins, minister of navy, minister of customs, minister of foreign affairs) took place and they were ordered to resume their duties. A lot of presents were given to the Zamorin by the ambassadors and the ministers of the states. On the other hand the Zamorin also gave offerings to the Brahmins, to the ambassadors and above all to the temples. It is noteworthy that when a Zamorin died all the functions of the state, temporarily, stopped and most of the ministers were removed from their posts. Very few could continue in their service, and that too, only after the new Zamorin had taken charge of the government. It was during this ceremony that the state governors were appointed, some being allowed to continue in their posts, depending upon the relationship they had with the new Zamorin when he was a prince.

At the end of all the ceremonies, the Zamorin took part in a public procession and returned to the palace where he would pass the night.

The court life of the Zamorins of Calicut was, in practice, simple but very precise. Upon his left side was always seated the Brahmin of the court and on his right the minister of state, followed by other important ministers. This arrangement carried symbolic meaning. The Brahmin used to be his principal adviser, although the Zamorin always consulted his ministers for their opinion, depending on the circumstances. However, except in religious matters, it was he who took the final decisions.

In most cases the rule of succession to the throne of a Hindu kingdom is clear. It was heredity and generally by patrilineal descent.[367] In the case of the Chera dynasty of Calicut, however, there is no direct evidence to show the rule of succession. It was certainly hereditary, but it has been convincingly argued that it was matrilineal in character, conforming to the system of succession prevalent among the non-Brahmin upper castes in Malabar.

The fact of hereditary succession made it necessary to ensure that there was an heir worthy enough to claim the throne. It is probable that for this reason, the Zamorins wanted to maintain the purity of lineage. The diplomatic and military considerations involved in the complex system of matrimonial alliances among the royal families, and between the royal families on the one side and the chiefly families on the other, may have been real enough; but the concern that there should be offspring of worthy ancestry on both sides would appear to be an equally important factor.

There is a marked difference to be noticed between the coronation ceremonies of a Muslim king and a Hindu king in India. When a Muslim ruler ascended the throne, his coronation took place in the court hall before all the ministers, guests and ambassadors who were present at the court and who had been invited for the purpose. However, when a Hindu king was crowned, this ceremony, usually, took place in the royal temple before the full public audience. In the case of Hindus, prolonged religious ceremonies took place, whereas in the case of Muslim rulers, there was only a brief reading of verses from the Qoran (*Khutbah*) and the name of the ruler to be was pronounced, after which presents were given to king.

b) Diplomatic Practice at the Court of the Zamorin

The Zamorin received ambassadors at his court following practices which were traditional in much of India, based on the Hindu scriptures and what was directed by the court Brahmin.[368] An ambassador representing a king was a highly respected person and had to be received with the greatest honour. The choice of an ambassador was made with great care. He had to be a refined, intelligent and respected member of the court. He was expected to bring peace and unite the two states or to discover ways of securing his country's interests.[369] To forward these ends, an ambassador took with him handsome presents, especially when the embassy was sent to a state of equal status. The same was done when sending a messenger to a vassal state but in this case the purpose was to impress and to maintain the supreme position of the sovereign state. The ambassadors for their part were supposed to respect court etiquette before and during the audiences with the ruler. According to Hindu custom the ambassador was honoured with presents for himself and highly expensive, though largely symbolic, gifts were given in return for his King, if it happened to be a state of equal status. In sending an ambassador to the court of his sovereign, the ruler of a vassal state sought to demonstrate the respect that he had for his overlord. In return his ambassador was given a good present and a present, usually, of double the value was sent to the vassal king to show emphatically that the sovereign ruler was much more powerful and prosperous.[370]

In Calicut, although in most cases ambassadors were given an audience by the Zamorin, they were only allowed to speak to him through his Minister of State or the Minister of Foreign Affairs,[371] as can be seen in the account of the first visit of Vasco da Gama - 'and while looking towards Vasco da Gama, the interpreter spoke that he should speak to those honourable persons who were present over there and they would communicate to the King. At this, Vasco da Gama did not feel content because he thought that he was despised and told the interpreter that 'he was ambassador of the King of Portugal, a very powerful king: and that the Christian kings used to speak to the ambassadors directly and not through the medium of any one and in the presence of a few persons of utmost confidence. 'This was the custom of his land,' as he continued speaking, 'and we speak to the king directly without the intervention of a third person. To this the king agreed and said that he would do the same.'[372] Exceptionally, relaxation of the diplomatic-protocol was permitted when communicating with certain foreign dignitaries and with an ambassador from a court of equal or superior status. Although the Zamorin accepted what Vasco da Gama requested, this incident reveals the arrogance of the navigator who was not even a properly accredited ambassador and the humility of an Oriental King. Most of the contacts between the Zamorin and his vassal states were made orally through emissaries and special envoys, the south Indian rulers usually sending as their ambassadors a highly respected Brahmin priest.

c) Commercial Contacts of Malabar in Asia

On account of the availability of pepper and various spices, the ports on the Malabar coasts were frequented by merchants from all over the world and, among the several ports of this region,

Calicut occupied the most important position in international trade. Muslim merchants from Ethiopia, Egypt Mecca, Aden, Persia and Turkey in the African and Central Asian sub-continent; Tenasserim,[373] Pegu, Ceylon and many other areas of Eastern Asia, were found in large numbers in Calicut prior to the arrival of the Portuguese. Even merchants from Tunis, speaking Castilian, were present in Calicut when Vasco da Gama reached there in 1498. Until the first half of the fifteenth century Chinese merchants also frequently visited Calicut and maintained a factory of their own there which was called Cinakotta.[374] The Gujarati merchants were the most prominent among the Indians and they also had settlements in Cannanore and Cochin. Copper, quicksilver, vermillion, coral, saffron, carpets, porcelain, tin, coloured velvets, gold, silver, raisins, opium, madder, horses and textiles were brought to the ports on the Malabar coast in exchange for pepper, ginger, cinnamon, cardamoms, myrabolans, tamarinds, canafistula, amber, rhubarb, aloes-wood, cloves, nutmeg, mace, sandalwood, brazilwood, betel, coconut, jaggery and areca-nuts.[375] Merchants from all over the world, especially the merchants from Arabia, considered it their entrepot and many of them settled there maintaining permanent business houses and residential complexes.

The kingdom of Gujarat, on the northwestern coast of India, had for centuries been known for its trade in textiles of various kinds and qualities, and held a pre-eminent position in trade before the arrival of the Portuguese. Many of the Gujarati merchants had settlements in Cannanore and Cochin and the most important Gujarati establishment on the Malabar Coast was in Calicut.[376] The Gujaratis, who were compared to the Italian merchants in the matter of trade in spices,[377] extended their commercial networks as far as Malacca, Arabia and Africa.

The Egyptian Sultan, Qansawh al-Ghawri, controlled almost all the important trade centres of the Middle East such as Cairo, Alexandria, Beirut, Damascus, Jidda, Mecca and Suez, dealing in Indian spices and textiles which were carried to the Italian coastal cities. The Arab merchants engaged in the trade had their main settlements in Jidda and Mecca, and kept their factors in Calicut. They sent gold, gold coins, silver, copper, lead, vermilion, quicksilver, alum-stone, saffron, rose water, silk clothes, velvets, coral to India to purchase spices, drugs, pearls, cotton cloths and other products which were taken to Mecca or Jidda in large ships built in Malabar. The commodities taken to Jidda were carried to

Suez in small ships and from there on camels to Cairo and Alexandria.[378] The sultan of Cairo drew large revenues by way of customs on these commodities in places like Jidda, Suez, Alexandria and Cairo.[379]

At the time of the arrival of the Portuguese there was another very busy commercial route, through which the merchants from India and Arabia carried heavy loads of Indian merchandise to Europe. This was via the Persian Gulf, using the ports of Muscat, Hormuz, Basra,[380] and many others, from where the goods were transported overland to the Mediterranean ports of Aleppo and Beirut and finally to the European continent.[381] This route was temporarily interrupted as the Portuguese started intercepting the shipping in the Persian Gulf in the early sixteenth century.[382]

The Venetians purchased the spices and other commodities at Alexandria, Beirut, Damascus, Aleppo, and from there they were taken to the various centres of Europe and sold at very high prices. The Venetians had their representatives in all these places and especially at Cairo. Though they had reasonably friendly relations with the Portuguese until the discovery of the sea-route to India,[383] the Portuguese enterprise in the East was described by contemporary Italian writers as the death-knell of the Venetian trade and consequently the ruin of Venetian prosperity.[384]

d) Zamorin -Portuguese diplomacy in the Sixteenth Century

The first ruler with whom the Portuguese came into contact on the south-western coast of India, as it is quite known, was the Zamorin of Calicut. Vasco da Gama, who reached Calicut on 20th of May 1498,[385] had to face, from the beginning, a reaction very different from the one he had expected[386] and it was not until 1513 that the Portuguese governor, Afonso de Albuquerque, was allowed to establish a fort and a factory in Calicut.[387] This agreement was ratified in 1515,[388] but did not last long as neither of the parties was ready to compromise and by 1525 they were again at war.[389] Here one should remember that most of the treaties between Calicut and the Portuguese were signed by the Zamorin because of the pressure of immediate circumstances and not because that is what the Zamorin wanted. Many of the clauses, such as who would or would not be allowed to trade in his dominion and what kinds of customs duties he would levy on merchandises, seemed outrageous to rulers who for centuries had been accustomed to do whatever they found to be in their own and their subjects' best interests. Therefore, the diplomatic

Vasco da Gama at the Court of Zamorin

facing page 144

understandings they reached were only to buy time and were not, as the Portuguese hoped, permanent solutions to the problems that they had created by trying to impose martial law in the Indian Ocean.

A further diplomatic rapprochement between Calicut and the Portuguese took place in 1531 during the time of the Viceroy Nuno da Cunha (1529-1538)[390] but the relations between the Portuguese and the Zamorin remained fundamentally unresolved throughout the sixteenth century. The Zamorin, with the help of the Kunjali Marakkars,[391] tried throughout almost the whole of the sixteenth century to oppose Portuguese control of Indian Ocean commerce, as it had caused severe damage to the trade and economy of his kingdom.[392] It was only in 1599 that the Zamorin and the Portuguese combined against the Kunjalis whose repeated successes towards the end of the century had made them arrogant. Or it could also be considered that the Marakkars successes and behaviour had made the Zamorin suspicious of their fidelity. Nevertheless, the jealousy in the mind of the Zamorin against his own captains, the Kunjalis, can't, altogether be left without consideration which took him to take drastic decision. Together they were successful in putting an end to Kunjali power in 1600, forcing the Kunjali himself to surrender to his erstwhile master, the Zamorin.[393]

e) Zamorin- Portuguese initial Troubles

Since the initial voyages of Vasco da Gama and Pedro Álvares Cabral, the Portuguese commanders were mindful of the Zamorin's resistance and the support they could get from rulers of states such as Cochin and Quilon. The wars of 1507 and 1508, although they had proved the weakness of the Indian forces, were hardly decisive. Besides, although constant Portuguese attacks on Indian shipping had been inflicting economic damage, the Portuguese understood that they had to do more than this before they could justify the title, assumed by their King, of being 'Lord of the seas…' etc. They knew that the most powerful ruler with whom they would have to deal would be the Zamorin. The new patent, brought by Marichal Dom Fernando Coutinho in 1509, released the Viceroy, Dom Francisco de Almeida from his services and replaced him as governor by D. Afonso de Albuquerque. However, Coutinho also brought an order from the King through which the Portuguese were instructed to destroy the ruler of Calicut once and for all. All the Portuguese officials now set to work on a strategy to achieve this outcome. The King of Cochin, besides sending some of his ships, also provided some secret information through his Brahmins and engineered a dispute between his own vassals and the Zamorin. This was intended to divert soldiers away from the Zamorin's capital so that the Portuguese would meet with no resistance at Calicut and could do as much damage as they could. Sure of their success, the Portuguese fleet anchored off Calicut on 3rd of January 1510. However, they failed to take the city and were completely routed losing some of the best men they had, including Fernando Countinho himself. Albuquerque himself was wounded and was carried to his ship. Had the Zamorin reached his captal in time, it is probable that none of the Portuguese would have been left alive. This was the most serious defeat that the Portuguese had experienced and it showed that they were really only able to fight effectively at sea.[394]

In the meantime, Albuquerque turned his attention towards Goa and the Arabian Sea, realising that the only way he could continue to trade in the Malabar regions was by establishing peace with the Zamorin. For this reason he sent Dom Garcia de Noronha, his nephew, to Cannanore, where the Zamorin was to be found to sign a peace treaty. The treaty was signed on 24th of December 1513.[395] Some of the clauses in the treaty were as follows:

1) That the Zamorin should sell to the King of Portugal all spices and drugs there may be in the land,
2) That the Portuguese would pay the usual dues to the Zamorin for the things bought,
3) That if the Portuguese brought horses or elephants they should pay the usual dues,
4) That the Portuguese would issue safe-conducts to the ships of Calicut.

The Portuguese also undertook to help the Zamorin in his wars as long as they were not against Cochin or Cannanore. This treaty, which was very beneficial to the Portuguese, brought peace to the region. However, it hurt the pride of the Zamorin who was forced to pay 1200 *Bahars*[396] of pepper to the Portuguese as compensation for the war.[397] The treaty allowed the Portuguese to build a fort near Calicut and to establish a permanent factory in the land of Zamorin from which to carry on trading activities. However, the ultimate ambition of the Portuguese authorities to monopolise the whole of Asian commerce was thwarted, since by this treaty the Portuguese had recognised the Zamorin as King of Calicut.

The treaty with the Zamorin also marked the decline in importance of Cochin and Cannanore. After the conquest of Goa in 1510, Cochin began to lose its importance as an administrative centre although it continued to be the commercial and naval headquarters. The treaty of 1513 with the Zamorin, naturally, was not welcomed by the Muslim merchants or by the kings of Cochin and Cannanore. The Muslims believed that the previous Zamorin had been poisoned at the instigation of the Portuguese, and the King of Cochin thought that, as a result of the treaty, he would lose his newly won independence and might be forced to return to his previous position and to abandon the "royal" privileges he had been enjoying under the Portuguese umbrella.[398] The Kings of Cochin and Cannanore had helped the Portuguese against the Zamorin on condition that they would always be treated as the friends and allies of the Portuguese. The peace treaty between the Zamorin and the Portuguese was not part of their plans. Therefore, they complained to the King of Portugal against Albuquerque.[399]

Peace between the Zamorin and the Portuguese was short. The Zamorin's dissatisfaction, which brought about a breach in their relations, was due to the increasing blockade by the Portuguese of Indian shipping and the collecting of taxes on mercantile transactions which had been his sole right for centuries. After the appointment of Duarte de Meneses as governor of the *Estado da Índia,* the rule of law began to deteriorate even among the Portuguese themselves. He preferred to engage in his own private trade rather than to bother about affairs of the state. The revenue of the government in India started to decrease. This was reported to the King, Dom João III, who proposed to set the matters right by immediately sending out as his successor, Vasco da Gama, this time as a Viceroy. Vasco da Gama reached Goa on 23rd of September 1524, and assumed office immediately without waiting for his predecessor who was still in the Moluccas. However, da Gama's death in Cochin on 24th of December of the same year left the whole matter unresolved.[400]

Portuguese ambitions to be the only commercial and naval power on the Indian Coast had been a constant cause of trouble. In 1524, the year of the arrival of Vasco da Gama on his third posting to India, some of the important Muslim merchants of Cochin, including the Kunjali Marakkars and their family associates, left Cochin because of the Portuguese control of their ships, and settled in Calicut.[401] This was humiliating to the

Portuguese authorities at Cochin because these merchants had been a great source of income for their treasury.

Moreover, the Portuguese fort that stood on the Zamorin's territory was a constant challenge to his authority. The treaty signed in 1513 had already been broken by hostilities from both the sides towards the end of 1525.[402] However, events took a more serious turn when Kutti Ali, the present Kunjali commander, tired of being controlled by the Portuguese, set out with a large fleet and did great damage to Portuguese trade. Now, as captain of the Zamorin's fleet he aimed to follow the same terror tactics as the Portuguese, and for over two years he practically cut off all communication between Cochin and Goa. Finally in 1528 the Portuguese governor, Lopo Vaz de Sampaio, was able to take Kutti Ali prisoner during a fight. This, however, was not sufficient to check the Kunjali's power at sea, as the son of Kutti Ali, Marakkar II, followed his father's footsteps with even greater enthusiasm.[403]

After 1535, the relations of the Portuguese and the Zamorin can be summarised in terms of the resistance to Portuguese pretensions by the forces of Zamorin under the command of the Kunjalis. The Portuguese tried different tactics to overpower the Zamorin and destroy his commercial supremacy while attempting to consolidate their own. To achieve this, they allied with the King of Tanur, who was an ambitious and unprincipled ruler. Ambitious, because he, like the King of Cochin, wanted to get rid of the Zamorin's suzerainty at no matter what cost, and unprincipled, because he had no political or religious ideology of his own. He was prepared to do anything in order to achieve his goals. In other words, he was acting only as politicians of today. He knew what would please the Portuguese authorities most and pretended to have a keen desire to embrace Christianity during the governorship of Garcia de Sá (1548-1549).[404] The Portuguese were only too happy to accept this proposal. Besides, he permitted the Portuguese to establish a fortress and naval headquarters at Chaliyam, virtually at the gates of Calicut, which enabled them to maintain a close watch over the movement of the Zamorin's ships. In return for this help he was to receive Portuguese military support against his sovereign and to become an independent ruler. In reality, he got nothing. He did not become a powerful ruler nor was he able to improve his commercial position in the region. He soon found that he had made a mistake, as the Portuguese were only interested in maintaining a powerful grip over the Zamorin.

Frustrated with his failure, he returned to the religion of his ancestors. The fortress of Chaliyam remained in Portuguese hands until the 1570s.

The other tactic that the Portuguese applied to destroy the Zamorin was to involve him in constant wars by attacking his small and less powerful vassals so that in this way he would exhaust his military and commercial resources. The King of Idappally was a close ally of the Zamorin, and his territories, which extended to the boundaries of Cochin, were thought to be a major obstacle to the Portuguese maintaining the safety of the King of Cochin since they allowed the Zamorin to march without much effort to the frontiers of Cochin with his army. Therefore, towards the end of 1539, on the pretext of some local dispute, the King of Cochin declared war on Iddapally. The ruler of Cochin knew this would bring the Zamorin to the aid of the chief, while the Portuguese would be there to resolve the matter in a way that was beneficial to both of them. After much bloodshed, a treaty was signed in 1540 between the Portuguese Viceroy, Dom Garcia de Noronha, and the Zamorin.[405] Among the various terms of a commercial nature, the Zamorin once again agreed to obtain Portuguese *Cartazes* for his commercial shipping and for the pilgrimage to Mecca.

The next victim of these political games was the King of Vadakkumkur, a Nayar chief who also happened to be a vassal of the Zamorin and controlled the market of pepper produced in the areas adjacent to the kingdom of Cochin. The cause of war, which broke out in 1550, was a dispute over the supply of pepper between the King of Vadakkumkur and the King of Cochin.[406] Here we must recall that the relation between the Portuguese and the King of Cochin depended on the availability of pepper and that the prices were fixed by the Portuguese and not by the producers or the suppliers. When the King was unable to provide sufficient pepper to the Portuguese from his territories, he tried to fetch it from the neighbouring states. When the King wanted some pepper to meet the Portuguese demand, and at a price which the Portuguese had fixed, the chief of Vadakkumkur had refused to cooperate. War was the only way found to resolve this problem.[407]

All these political and diplomatic manoeuvrings, provoked by the Portuguese to enable them to gain the upper hand, so infuriated the Zamorin that in 1569 he sought, once more, to create a united front against the Portuguese to expel them from the Indian Ocean.

He sought the help of the Sultans of Bijapur and Ahmadnagar who, during the recent alliance of 1565, against the Vijayanagar Empire, had proved their military capacity. The Zamorin and the Sultans were quite optimistic that a similar alliance would be victorious against the Portuguese. Although, the Portuguese and the allied forces did each other a great deal of damage, both understood that peace would be the best solution and that one way or another they would have to coexist.[408]

Though the Portuguese and the Zamorin signed a peace treaty in 1571[409] by which the latter agreed to accept *Cartazes* from the Portuguese, the Kunjalis were not happy with this decision and continued to fight. The Portuguese had not given up the idea of destroying once and for all the power of the Kunjalis who alone prevented the Portuguese from controlling the sea and inflicting final defeat on the Zamorin.

Soon after the treaty of 1571, the Portuguese started intercepting the import of rice into Calicut. The rice, on which the whole population of Calicut and its surroundings depended, was brought mostly from the Kanara states. This new situation caused much distress among the people and their rulers and continued until both sides reached a diplomatic understanding in 1578, though the Portuguese demand to be able to construct a fortress at Ponnani delayed the peace process. Eventually the Zamorin, who was a weak and less determined ruler than his predecessors, gave way to Portuguese persistence and allowed them to build a fortress at Ponnani.[410] Strategically, this was very favourably situated to enable the Portuguese to control the movements of the Zamorin as well as the Kunjali's shipping. The Portuguese imagined that in this way, they were creating a tight noose around the Zamorin's neck. On the other hand the Kunjalis, once again, did not like the treaty and hostilities between the Portuguese and the Kunjalis were resumed. This led to two naval battles in 1586 and 1589. The Kunjalis were successful in both of these and captured several Portuguese ships,[411] though the planned attack on their settlements at Colombo was a complete fiasco. A further treaty was signed in the year 1591 but the Zamorin's refusal to take *Cartazes* for his shipping led once again to a break down of this agreement.

The Kunjali's successes, and the services rendered by his famiy to the ruler of Calicut for almost a century, obliged the Zamorin to give them permission to build fortresses and dockyards at Pudupattanam for their own safety. The Portuguese authorities, however, protested at this and once again doubt was created in the minds of the Portuguese about whether the Zamorin was serious in his diplomacy.

The fortress of Kunjali, where he established himself as a feudatory of the Zamorin,[412] was known as the Marakkar Kotta.[413] In the year 1595 Kunjali IV succeeded his father as admiral of the Zamorin's fleet. He was even more successful against the Portuguese than his father had been and this made him proud and haughty so that he forgot his allegiance to the Zamorin. The incident that led to the final breakdown of relations has been described by Nambiar. "An elephant belonging to the royal stables was then in the neighbourhood of Kotta. Kunjali had its tail cut off in spite of the entreaties of the mahout, as an insult to the Zamorin".[414] This incident infuriated the Zamorin so much that in 1599 he entered into an alliance[415] with the Portuguese to teach Kunjali a lesson in obedience. At first the Portuguese were suspicious, but later they happily accepted the Zamorin's proposal as they saw in this a way of realising their objective of destroying the Kunjalis once and for all. And they also knew that the destruction of Kunjali was the destruction of the Zamorins' forces from the Indian Ocean, at the same. It is, however, difficult to understand why the Zamorin should have so eagerly joined with the Portuguese to destroy his own own navy commanders, whose family had served him so well for almost a century and made possible his resistance against the Portuguese. Nor is it clear why he should have been so offended by the cutting off of the tail of one of his favourite elephants? Was it considered an offense to his royal authority? This could be possible answer, but not only.

It seems that, although the incident of the elephant's tail was the immediate cause, the Zamorin's dissatisfaction dated from the time of the treaty of 1571. The Zamorin had signed the treaty that year, along with the Adil Shah and Nizam Shah, and had accepted Portuguese supremacy at sea. The Kunjalis had shown their displeasure over what had been decided between the belligerents. At the same time it should not be forgotten that, during fighting in 1571, the Zamorin, with the help of the navy of the Kunjalis had been able to get rid of the Portuguese fortress at Chaliyam, which was a constant humiliation to his authority. The Kunjalis wanted to continue the war against the decision of the Zamorin. Contradicting the authority of their sovereign in this way turned them into rebels. The Kunjalis had further objected to the Zamorin's decision to allow a Portuguese fortress at Ponnani in 1578, warning the Zamorin about the danger it represented to the integrity of his own state. Although the Zamorin took no notice of this advice, he recognised the concern that the Kunjalis had for their security and permitted them to build a fortress at Pudupattanam. This, in turn, created suspicions in the minds of the Portuguese.

The settlement of the Kunjalis as the Zamorin's feudatory at Kotta, and their success in the wars against the Portuguese, had made the Kunjalis proud and the Zamorin all the more dissatisfied and suspicious of them, all of which culminated in the incident of the cutting off of the tail of the royal elephant. This made the Zamorin so furious and humiliated that he did not give a second thought before allying with the Portuguese to destroy the Kunjali's sea-power.[416] This incident provided the final blow to the trust between the Zamorin and Kunjalis and, as Nambiar wrote, "that was the end of Kotta and the eclipse of an intrepid naval tradition as surely as that was the end of the prestige and glory of Calicut".[417] After the end of the Kunjalis, the Zamorin could never challenge the Portuguese at sea except when, from time to time, he could ally with the Dutch. Although the Dutch never helped him as the Kunjalis had done, they were a constant threat to Portuguese shipping and created a new balance of power in the region in the seventeenth century.

f) The Portuguese and the other Malabar States

Contrary to what happened in Calicut, the Portuguese were welcomed in the states of Cochin, Cannanore, and Quilon, which were looking for an ally who could help them get rid of the Zamorin's hegemony and improve their own position. These were the states which became major bases for Portuguese economic and political activity in the sixteenth century. Since the Portuguese knew about the rivalries between them and the Zamorin and understood that they did not have sufficient power of their own to be independent without Portuguese military help, the Portuguese were able to exploit them economically and control them politically. This situation made the small kingdoms extremely dissatisfied but there was hardly ever a time when they were able to shake off the dominance of their ally. The rulers of Cannanore and Cochin, long hostile to Calicut, in fact felt themselves menaced by the peace treaties signed between the Zamorin and the Portuguese in 1513,[418] 1515,[419] 1525,[420] 1531[421] and 1599,[422] and complained to the King[423] of Portugal that these treaties were in breach of the promises made to them earlier in the century.[424]

Inspired by ambitions of becoming rich and independent, the kingdoms of Cochin, Quilon, Cranganore and Cannanore offered the Portuguese all sorts of help including the supply of pepper in the quantities they required, in return for their military support to fight against the Zamorin. All of these states, except the state of Cannanore, as has been mentioned earlier, had been vassals of the Kings of Calicut. Therefore, when the dispute between the Portuguese and the Zamorin began in 1501 and the Portuguese proved their ability successfully to challenge the Calicut, through their firearms, which was had not yet been knon among the Asian countries, these states were happy to ally with them. The attitudes of these Malabari rulers, other than the Zamorin appears to be very strange as they had merely seen a few Portuguese ships armed with advanced artilleries and became so influenced that they offered to become vassals of a King about whom they had hardly any information. This only proves their greed and lust for power!

I. The Kingdom of Cochin

Although early in 1502, the Zamorin of Calicut had warned Trimumpara, the King of Cochin, through a letter, not to receive the Portuguese in his land,[425] he openly welcomed the Portuguese ships, commanded by Vasco da Gama. He further added to the anger of the Zamorin by giving the Portuguese captain a grand reception and entering into a diplomatic agreement to provide all kinds of support. The King intended to use the power of the Portuguese to free himself from the suzerainty of the Zamorin. He, therefore, extended full trading facilities to them and ceded a site to build a fort. In doing so, however, the King merely exchanged 'from one sovereign to another,' for he became a puppet in the hands of the Portuguese for another hundred and sixty years.[426]

The Cochin-Portuguese alliance proved to be a costly business for the King who was attacked by the Zamorin early in 1502 in revenge for his support of the Portuguese.[427] This situation provided the Portuguese with a good opportunity to put their diplomacy into practice by convincing the King of the necessity of constructing a fortress for the protection of the interests of both themselves and of the kingdom of Cochin.[428] The permission was granted immediately. However, matters did not stop there. By signing a pact with the Portuguese in 1505, and by accepting the crown from the Portuguese King, the ruler of Cochin not only changed his destiny and that of subsequent generations but he also changed the course of Indian history. The cost of his ambitions was so high that not only did he fail, in the end, to realize his dream but, by becoming a Portuguese ally against the will of his compatriots, he also lost in social status.[429] Eventually even the choice of a successor to the kingship came to be made by the Portuguese and not by the traditional means that had been followed until then. The King of Cochin and his successors were compelled to obey the Portuguese who even used to imprison him in his own palace when he refused to accept their demands. The King was forced to wear a crown sent from Portugal and, in the correspondence between the Portuguese authorities in India and Portugal, he was referred to as a 'faithful servant'.[430] After the King signed the pact with the Portuguese, his problems became the problems of the Portuguese. Whatever political troubles faced the Kings of Cochin, whether internal or external, it was the Portuguese who had to solve them.

In 1529 the Portuguese shifted their capital from Cochin to Goa. Goa was a nearer and more centrally located place than Cochin and thus better able to provide naval and military support to their expanding commercial operations. The fort at Cochin, however, was not abandoned, nor was the control over the King of Cochin relaxed, until the Dutch conquered the kingdom in the seventeenth century.

Although the Portuguese had freed him from the suzerainty of the Zamorin, their priorities were to look after their own economic and political interests and not to make him a powerful King as they had promised. Therefore, they pursued their own objectives in making peace or war with the local Indian kingdoms, often ignoring the terms they had agreed with the kingdom of Cochin. It was lucky for the King of Cochin that the Zamorin continued to fight for his own commercial empire and this kept him and the Portuguese constantly at war throughout the sixteenth century. Thus, the King of Cochin enjoyed freedom from the Zamorin's anger but not freedom from Portuguese domination.

The kings of Cochin, Quilon, Cranganore and Cannanore occasionally protested against the Portuguese authorities when these interfered in the social and economic aspects of the kingdoms; social, when they tried to impose Christianity on their Hindu or Muslim subjects; economic, when they tried to fix the prices of commodities without regard for the producers. This could lead to the disappearance of merchandise from the market, which naturally irritated the Portuguese, who would use force to make

ESTAMPA XXXIV *Ref. António Bocarro, O Livro das Fortalezas*

Fortaleza de Cochim

Portuguese Fortress of Cochin

facing page 154

the goods available. Apart from this kind of occasional protest nothing happened to make the kings withdraw from their loyalty to the Portuguese. Moreover, the relations between these states never became an obstacle to the maintenance of Portuguese power in the region. They always kept themselves allied with the Portuguese, in one way or another, till they were conquered by the Dutch during the years 1659-1663.

Cochin, one of the greatest pepper producing regions of Malabar and the most reliable ally of the Portuguese in India, was the major source of pepper next to Kanara. Cochin pepper was cheapest but of an inferior quality compared with that from Cannanore and Kanara.[431] During most of the sixteenth century, the Portuguese exploited their friendship with the King to obtain their pepper at a fixed price. It was in this context that the King of Cochin sometimes found he had to stand as guarantor for the purchase of pepper on occasions when the Portuguese lacked the ready cash for the payment. As the prices paid by the Portuguese were uneconomic for the producers, pepper would often disappear from the market and, in the seventeenth century, would be sold to the intermediaries who supplied the Dutch or English at a comparatively higher price.

II. The Kingdom of Cannanore

At the beginning of the sixteenth century the Kolattiri King of Cannanore was an enemy of the Zamorin, and sought to transform his country into one as rich and prosperous as Calicut. Alone he had no chance of confronting the Zamorin in war on land or at sea.[432] Therefore, he welcomed the Portuguese to his kingdom and entered into a diplomatic alliance with them against the Zamorin. The Kolattiri King was wiser than the King of Cochin, for he never allowed the Portuguese to interfere in his internal affairs. His capital, Chirekkal, was a few miles away from the shore and the Portuguese could not harm him there directly.

Cannanore was a flourishing port for the supply of pepper. The merchants dealing with the trade were mostly the Indianised descendants of Arab immigrants, locally known as Mopilahs. They dominated the trade not only in Cannanore but in all the other Malabar towns and were held in great respect by the local communities.[433] During the sixteenth and the seventeenth centuries, the Portuguese conducted most of their formal business in Cannanore with the family of Ali Rajah.[434] Ali Rajah himself became the hereditary leader of the Cannanore Mopilahs about 1625.[435] In fact, he became a kind of King of the merchants under the sovereignty of the King of Cannanore.

There was yet another Muslim family of very high standing with which the Portuguese maintained commercial contacts from the beginning of the sixteenth century. This was the family of Khoja Shamshuddin, who had business contacts all over Asia and was resident in Cannanore.[436] Apart from that, the Mammale Marakkar,[437] from Calicut, also enjoyed a prominent position in Cannanore. The Portuguese had to trade with these Muslim merchants, although, they were not willing wholeheartedly to maintain friendly relations with them and tried their best to subdue them. Besides the pepper trade, the port of Cannanore was, at this time, the major importer of horses for the Vijayanagar Empire.[438]

Pedro Álvares Cabral, when setting out for India, was given instructions that, in case he could not come to terms with the Zamorin, he should go to Cannanore and try to establish friendly relations with the Ali Raja (who is also called Ada Rajao in the Portuguese sources). He was to open a factory there in order to get sufficient cargo.[439] While he was loading his ships in Cochin he received an invitation from the Kolattiri King, whom he visited on his return journey from Cochin.[440] He arrived on 15th of January 1501 at Cannanore and was received with much courtesy by the King. The King also presented the Portuguese commander with more than a thousand *Bahars*[441] of cinnamon as a gesture of goodwill towards the Portuguese who had been ill-treated in Calicut.[442] In order to strengthen his diplomatic ties with the Portuguese, the King of Cannanore sent an ambassador to Portugal in the same fleet[443] with several presents for the King.[444] After this, regular commercial contacts were maintained[445] between the Portuguese and the states of Cannanore and Cochin[446] until the arrival of Vasco da Gama on his second posting in 1502.

Vasco da Gama was instructed by the King of Portugal to establish strong diplomatic relations with the King of Cannanore, who was evidently only too anxious to comply. However he was also instructed to try to fix the price of spices.[447] On 18th of October 1502 he was given a royal welcome by the King in a place specially designed for the purpose.[448] However, as far as fixing the price of spices was concerned, the King refused to interfere as it was the business of the merchants to deal with that. Vasco da Gama was not expecting such a reply from the King and, knowing that most of the merchants with whom he had to deal were Muslims, he took offence and left for Cochin.[449] However, the King of Cannanore later sent his emissary to Vasco da Gama inviting him to discuss terms.[450] Thus a treaty was concluded between King of Cannanore and Vasco da Gama who was allowed to establish a factory for the purchase of pepper.[451] Such insistence from the side of the Indian rulers was a clear indication to the Portuguese that these rulers had deep political grievances which the Portuguese could easily exploit.

The Portuguese way of controlling the commerce and maintaining friendly ties with the rival rulers were, somewhat, unorthodox. Their relations with Cannanore became estranged in 1507 when a ship belonging to one of the chief merchants of Cannanore, loaded with horses from Hormuz, was captured by the Portuguese although it had a *Cartaz* issued by them.[452] The conflict between the two had begun to take a serious turn when the King sued for peace.[453] Even when the Portuguese were the culprits, it was the Indian rulers who sued for peace. This situation encouraged the Portuguese to continue with the policies they had adopted in their dealings with the merchants and rulers of India. Later, in 1516, the King of Cannanore wrote to the King of Portugal to ensure that horses and ropes, from Gujarat (from the regions of Kutch) as well as from Hormuz, were supplied in sufficient quantity to Cannanore and that their ships would not be molested by the Portuguese in future.[454]

There were no further serious breaches of friendship between the two nations. With the exception of the trouble in 1507, relations remained fairly friendly and the fortress and factory at Cannanore functioned satisfactorily. In due course, one of the important Mopilah business families, to which Ali Raja belonged, became the major provider of pepper to the Portuguese official and unofficial trades.[455] There were exceptions like this when the Portuguese had to trust a Muslim business magnate to meet their requirements. Almost all the local producers of pepper in the interior of Cannanore, an area outside Portuguese control, had close links with Ali Raja, whose name is constantly encountered in the Portuguese sources from the very beginning of the sixteenth century[456] through to the seventeenth century.[457] His family was treated as a "state within a state" and that is why the Portuguese obliged him to acknowledge his vassalage to them. As will be seen later in Chapter III, the Viceroy, Conde de Linhares, burnt his market in Cannanore in 1629, when he failed to appear at the port to greet him.[458]

The quality of the Cannanore pepper was reputedly the best in Malabar. Throughout the sixteenth century the Portuguese purchased part of their supply of pepper from there at the prices they had agreed in the early sixteenth century, with the exception of some periods when they refused to buy due to the increased price demanded by Ali Raja.[459] In 1606, when supplies from Kanara and other regions of Malabar became scarce because of the wars of Venkatappa Nayaka, the Portuguese made an agreement on prices and resumed trade with Ali Raja.[460] Though purchases from Cannanore never rose to great volumes, they remained stable for the remainder of the first half of the seventeenth century.

III. The Kingdom of Quilon

To the south of Cochin lay the kingdom of Quilon. The ruler of this land too had ambitions to free himself from the sovereignty of the ruler of Travancore. Between 1501 and 1503 the King was able to persuade Cabral, and later Vasco da Gama, to establish trade relations with his kingdom[461] and a formal treaty on the pattern of those signed with the rulers of Cannanore and Cochin was concluded in 1503. From that time the King of Quilon agreed to become a vassal of the King of Portugal.[462] Later Afonso de Albuquerque was given a royal reception by the ruler of this kingdom and, according to K.S. Mathew, "secured permission to set up a factory and appointed a factor there. With some reluctance the Queen[463] gave in to the request to have a Portuguese judge appointed to look after the administration of justice for the Portuguese as well as for the local Christians who, according to the report of an eyewitness, numbered 3,000. The agreement was inscribed on a silver plate and in this way some sort of an extra-territorial jurisdiction on the Malabar Coast was granted to the Portuguese".[464]

However, the Portuguese ambition to control Indian trade soon started to produce a troublesome situation in this region also. In November 1505 António de Sá, the Portuguese factor, and the other Portuguese residents were killed and the church of St. Thomas was destroyed by the locals.[465] This was in response to the factor's attempt to prohibit four Muslim merchant ships from Calicut from loading pepper in the port of Quilon, forcing them, at the same time, to sell all the other spices they had in their ships. Peace was only restored after much damage had been done to the life and property of both Muslims and Portuguese.[466] Later, in 1516, the Portuguese governor and the King of Quilon further improved their relationships through a treaty signed on 25 September.[467] The ruler of Quilon and the Portuguese rebuilt the church of St. Thomas, destroyed during the fight of 1505. The King also paid

Portuguese Fortress of Cranganore

facing page 158

compensation for the deaths of the Portuguese in the form of pepper and agreed to sell the pepper from his land at the same price as the Portuguese paid in Cochin and not to levy any customs duties on the trade they conducted. The local merchants were to obtain *Cartazes* from the captain of Cochin or the *capitão-mor*.[468] Heytor Rodrigues started the construction of a factory and a fortress in September 1519, the fortress being named after St. Thomas.

However, such agreements between the Portuguese and the local rulers normally had little real effect as the Portuguese continued to resort to forcible means to obtain the merchandise they wanted. Their objective was to get the pepper and spices, no matter how. In the same year about 5,000 bullock-loads of pepper taken overland from Quilon via the Ariankavu Pass were captured by the Portuguese factor who maintained that all the pepper produced in the lands under the jurisdiction of a vassal king was the monopoly of the Portuguese and should be traded only with them, on pain of confiscation. In this case the ruler refused to intervene, saying that it was the wealth of the Brahmins.[469] The Portuguese never indicated any way in which they could purchase all the pepper produced and, since the prices were fixed by them, it became one of the causes of unrest among the business class which, consequently, led to numerous armed conflicts throughout the sixteenth century. A new agreement with the Portuguese was signed on 17 November 1520 which in effect renewed the conditions laid down earlier in 1519.[470] This treaty remained in force till 1543, when it was again renewed.[471] Since this kingdom, by virtue of its alliance with Portugal, was also considered as a vassal state, external affairs became the responsibility of the Portuguese.

Quilon was of lesser importance than Cochin. Although the pepper from this region was the same quality as that of Cochin, it was less intensively cultivated, and supplies were generally brought from Kayamkulam and other places to its factory and weighing house. However, in the seventeenth century the Portuguese bought most of their pepper from Quilon, especially during times of natural calamity or scarcity in the northern regions.

IV. The Kingdom of Cranganore

The King of Cranganore was a feudatory of the Zamorin who also endeavoured to become independent, taking advantage of the bitter hostilities between the Zamorin and the Portuguese. He allowed the latter to build a fortress at Cranganore in 1536 although this was never sufficient to protect the King against the Zamorin. However, the Portuguese fort at Cranganore did stand as a barrier between Calicut and Cochin and protected the latter from the vengeance of the Zamorin. For centuries Cranganore had been an important place for the royal family of the Zamorins. In this territory, in an area controlled by the Portuguese from the early sixteenth century, stood a Pagoda where all the Zamorins used to be crowned.[472] Cranganore's alliance with the Portuguese became an obstacle to maintaining this tradition. The Zamorins never forgot this humiliation and took every opportunity to attack this territory to take revenge. However, they could not carry out their objective until the early seventeenth century.

Reference

361 K.V. Krishna Ayyar, *Zamorins of Calicut,* Calicut, 1938, p. 11.

362 *Ibid.*, p. 7

363 *Ibid.* see pages 17- 29.

364 *Ibid.* p. 25: A detailed list of the jewel worn by the Zamorin when he first received Vasco da Gama is given by Prof. Ayyar.

365 Ayyar, *Zamorins of Calicut,* p. 25.

366 *Ibid.*

367 Kesavan Veluthat, *The Political Structure of Early Medieval South India,* pp.73-74.

368 He followed the Ancient Hindu system as depicted in *The Laws of Manu,* (Max Müller's edition), pp. 225-227; And to learn more about how the embassy of Vasco da Gama was received at the court of the Zamorin see Fernão Lopes de Castanheda, *História do Descobrimento ...* livro I & II, p. 47; João de Barros, *Da Ásia...*, *Década* I, Liv. IV. Cap. VIII, pp. 337-340.

369 Krishna Ayyar, *The Zamorins of Calicut,* pp. 73-74, 83-86, 142-149; *The Laws of Manu,* pp. 225-227;

370 *Ibid.*

371 Castanheda, *História do Descobrimento ...*, livro I & II, pp. 46-47; João de Barros, *Da Ásia...*, *Década* I, Liv. IV. Cap. VIII, pp. 337-340.

372 *"...& oulhando pera Vasco da Gama, disselhe por hu lingoa que falasse com aqueles homens honrados que ali estauam: & que dissesse o que quisesse que eles ho dirião. Do que ele não foy nada contente, porque lhe pareceo aquilo desprezo: & respondeo pelo lingoa, que ele era embaixador del Rey de Portugal, hu rey muyto poderoso: & que os reys Christãos costumauão de não receber as embaixadas por terceyras pessoas se não por si mesmos: & inda perante muyto poucas pessoas, & estas de muyta confiança. E por se isto assi costumar nas terras donde ele vinha, não auia de dar a exmbaixada a outrem se não a ele. O que el rey disse que era bem, & que assi se fizesse"* Castanheda, *História do Descobrimento ...*, livro I & II, p. 47.

373 In the present Burma, bordering Siam, (Thailand).

374 Zinadin, *Tuhfat-ul- Mujahedeen*, or *História dos Portugueses no Malabar,* pp. xxix-xxx, 36.

375 K.S. Mathew, 'The Trade in the Indian Ocean and the Portuguese System of Cartaz', in *The First Portuguese Colonial Empire,* (edited) Malyn Newitt, Exeter Studies in History, University of Exeter, 1986, pp. 69-83.

376 'Copia de uma carta de el-rei de Portugal enviada ao Rei de Castella acerca da Viagem de successo da India', in *Centenário do descobrimento da America: memorias da Comissão portugueza,* Typographia da Academia Real das Sciencias, Lisboa, 1892, pp. 29-30; Duarte Barbosa,

The Book of Duarte Barbosa vol. xi, p. 73; António Cruz, (ed.) (Ed. Facsimilada) *Diário da Viagem de Vasco da Gama,* Porto, 1970, vol. I, p. 78.

377 Tomé Pires, *Suma Oriental of Tomé Pires,* 2 vols., London, 1944, vol. I, p. 45; R.B. Serjeant, *The Portuguese Off the South Arabian Coast,* pp. 12-21; Mathew, *The Portuguese Trade with India...,* pp. 13-14.

378 Castanheda, *História do descobrimento e conquista da Índia pelos portugueses,* Livro II, pp. 381-83.

379 Álvaro Velho, *Roteiro da Primeira Viagem de Vasco do Gama,* Ag. Geral do Ultramar, Lisboa 1960, p. 69.

380 Tomé Pires, *Suma Oriental of Tomé Pires,* vol. I, pp. 17-30: For more details of the ports of the Persian Gulf and its trade; Duarte Barbosa, *The Book of Duarte Barbosa, An account of the countries bordering on the Indian Ocean,* vol. 1, pp. 74-107; Mathew, *The Portuguese Trade with India...,* pp. 22-24.

381 R.B. Serjeant, *The Portuguese Off the South Arabian Coast, Hadrami chronicles,* The Clarendon Press, Oxford, 1963, has studied the importance of the Arabian caravan trade before and during the Portuguese conquests to some of the important and strategic ports of the Persian Gulf and the Arabian sea, see pp. 19-20; Ten years later, Niels Steensgaard in his, *Carracks, Caravans and Companies: The Structural Crisis in the European-Asian Trade in the 17th Century,* Copenhagen, 1973, tried to emphasise the continuing importance of the Arabian caravan routes during the period of Portuguese dominance and after they lost their important strongholds in the Persian Gulf.

382 Boxer, *The Portuguese Seaborne Empire,* pp. 40-41; K.N. Chaudhuri, *Trade and Civilisation in the Indian Ocean: An Economic History from the Rise of Islam to 1750,* Cambridge University Press, 1986, see chapter 3, pp. 63-79; Serjeant, *The Portuguese Off the South Arabian Coast,* pp. 10-15.

383 Castanheda, *História do descobrimento e conquista da Índia pelos portugueses,* Livro II, pp. 381, 383.

384 Mathew, 'The First Mercantile Battle in the India Ocean', *op.cit,* pp. 181-184.

385 Barros, *Da Ásia..., Décadas,* I[a], parte, I[a], p. 328; Mathew, *The Portuguese Trade with India...,* pp. 42-43.

386 Alexander Herculano e Barão de Castello de Paiva, *Roteiro da viagem de Vasco da Gama em MCCCXCVII,* 2[a] ed., Imp. Nacional, Lisboa, 1861, pp. 42-51, 63-65; Mathew, *The Portuguese Trade with India...,* pp. 43-45; Panikkar, *A History of Kerala,* 1498-1801, pp. 38-40; R.S. Whiteway, *The Rise of Portuguese Power... op.cit.* pp. 90-103; F.C. Danvers, *The Portuguese in India...,* vol. I, pp. 100-105.

387 Afonso de Albuquerque, *Cartas de Afonso de Albuquerque*, tomo III, pp. 73-84; Biker, (ed.) *Collecção de tratados e concertos de pazes...*, tomo I, pp. 15-21: *Carta de Affonso de Albuquerque a El-Rey D. Manuel, sobre a paz com o Rey de Calicut, 24 de Dezembro de 1513;* pp. 21-23: *Concerto que a D. Garcia de Noronha fez com o Çamorim, Rey de Calecut, 24 de Dezembro de 1513.*

388 Biker, (ed.) *Collecção de tratados e concertos de pazes...*, tomo I, pp. 28-33; *Confirmação das pazes e contrato que Affonso de Albuquerque fez com o Rey de Calecut, 26 de Fevereiro de 1515.*

389 Barros, *Da Ásia..., Décadas,* tomo III, parte II[a], pp. 451-52.

390 *Ibid,* tomo IV, part I, pp. 470-75.

391 In the Portuguese documents they have been mentioned as '*Piratas*' (pirates). In fact they were the traditional captains and admirals of the Zamorin of Calicut. (As mentioned earlier) See Nambiar, *The Kunjali Admirals of Calicut,* (passim).

392 Nambiar, *The Kunjali Admirals of Calicut...* (passim); Panikkar, *A History of.* pp. 95-128, also see his *Asia and the Western Dominance, 1498-1945,* (Passim).

393 Faria e Sousa, *A Ásia Portuguesa,* vol. V, pp. 206-213; Nambiar, *The Kunjali Admirals of Calicut...*, pp. 132-34.

394 The whole history has been narrated by Barros, *Da Ásia..., Décadas,* II[a], parte I[a], pp. 350-375; Albuquerque, *Crónica do descobrimento e conquista da Índia pelos portugueses,* pp. 358-360: Capítulo 89, *Como depois de partido o Vizo-Rei, Afonso de Albuquerque e o Marechal se fizeram prestes com sua gente e deram em Calecute, e da morte do Marechal.*

395 Biker, (ed.) *Collecção de tratados e concertos de pazes...*, tomo. I, pp. 21-23: *Concerto que D. Garcia de Noronha fez com o Çamorim, Rey de Calecut.* Cananor, 24 de dezembro de 1513.

396 See the appendices on weights and measures.

397 Biker, (ed.) *Collecção de tratados e concertos de pazes...*, tomo I, pp. 21-23: *Concerto que D. Garcia de Noronha fez com o Çamorim, Rey de Calecut,* Cannanor, 24 de dezembro de 1513.

398 To see how the king of Cochin provoked a war between himself and the Zamorin and invoked the help of the Portuguese so that the treaty signed in 1513 should cease to exist, see Panikkar, *Malabar and the Portuguese,* pp. 97-98.

399 Albuquerque, *Cartas de Affonso de Albuquerque,* tomo III, pp. 73-84.

400 *Ibid.* P. 107

401 Nambiar, *The Kunjalis Admirals of Calicut,* pp. 76-77.

402 Barros, *Da Ásia..., Décadas,* III[a], parte II[a], pp. 451-52.

403 Nambiar, *The Kunjalis Admirals of Calicut,* pp. 76-80.

404 Paulo da Trindade, *Conquista Espiritual do Oriente*, CEHU, Lisboa 1962, *Parte* 1, pp. 96-97.

405 Biker, (ed.) *Collecção de tratados e concertos de pazes...*, tomo I, pp. 88-94; *Provisão e treslado do Contrato que o Viso-Rey D. Garcia fez com El-Rey de Calecut para as pazes com o Çamorim, feito no galeão S. Mattheus, na barra de Panane*, em o 10 de Janeiro de 1540.

406 Panikkar, *Malabar and the Portuguese*, pp. 125-126.

407 *Ibid*.

408 *Diogo de* Couto, *Década VIII, Caps. XXXIII-XXXVI*, pp. 283-340;Faria e Sousa, *Ásia Portuguesa*, vol. IV, Chapters VII-XI. He has provided an account of the events from the formation of the league till the capitulation. Danvers has translated the whole passages from Faria e Sousa in his *The Portuguese in India*, vol. I, pp. 551-572.

409 Biker, (ed.) *Collecção de tratados e concertos de pazes...*, tomo I, pp. 160-167:*Contrato de pazes feito com El-Rei Idalxá no anno de 1571*, 13-17 Dezembro, 1571.

410 Nambiar *The Kunjali: Admirals of Calicut*, p. 113

411 *Ibid*, p. 114.

412 *Ibid*.

413 *Ibid*, See pp. 113-114, for the detailed history of this progress.

414 Nambiar, *The Kunjals: Admirals of Calicut*, p. 118.

415 A detailed history of what happend between the Zamorin, the Portuguese and Kunjali has been provided by Diogo de Couto, *Década Duodécima, vol.* 23, pags 338-47: *De como André Furtado de Mendonça Chegou à barra de Cunhale, e se vio com o Çamorim: e das cousas em que se assentáram*, pp 348-357; *Das Capitulações que o Capitão Mór fez com o Çamorim: e dos reféns que lhe entregou: e dos socorros que lhe chegaram de Goa*, pp. 357-363; The same treaty has been reproduced by Biker in his *Collecção de tratados e concertos de pazes...*, tomo 1, p. 186, *Capitulações que o Capitão mor André Furtado de Mendonça fez com o Samorim*, Dezembro de 1599; Nambiar, *The Kunjals: Admirals of Calicut*, 117-134.

416 Nambiar, *The Kunjals: Admirals of Calicut*, pp. 118-134.

417 *Ibid*, p. 134, For the reaction of the Nayar chiefs of Calicut to the Zamorins' decision to ally with the Portuguese see Nambiar, *The Kunjals: Admirals of Calicut*, page 135.

418 Biker, (ed.) *Collecção de tratados e concertos de pazes...*, tomo I, pp. 10-14.

419 Biker, (ed.) *Collecção de tratados e concertos de pazes...*, tomo I, pp. 28-33; *Confirmação das pazes e contrato que Affonso de Albuquerque fez com o Rey de Calecut, 26 de Fevereiro de 1515*.

420 Barros, *Da Ásia...*, III[a], parte II[a], pp. 451-52.

421 *Ibid,* tomo IV, part I, pp. 470-75.

422 Biker, (ed.) Collecção de tratados e concertos de pazes..., tomo I, pp. 186-89.Faria e Sousa, A Ásia Portuguesa, vol. V, pp. 193-200.

423 *Cartas de Afonso de Albuquerque, tom.* III, Lisboa, 1903, pp. 73-84.

424 Faria e Sousa, *A Ásia Portuguesa,* vol. I, pp. 142-50; Mathew, *The Portuguese Trade with India...,* pp. 48-50.

425 Albuquerque, *Crónica de descobrimento e conquista da Índia pelos portugueses...,* pp. 159-165. There are series of correspondences between the two kings on these pages through which the Zamorin tried to dissuade the king of Cochin from entering into any alliance with the Portuguese, which the king categorically refused to accept.

426 Panikkar, *Malabar and the Portuguese,* pp. 98-99.

427 Albuquerque, *Crónica de descobrimento e conquista da Índia pelos portugueses...,* pp. 184-187.

428 *Ibid.* pp. 274-276.

429 According to the Xatriyas traditions, a man or a king entering into a pact or relationship with any non-Hindu or even low class Hindu, loses his social status. In other words he is no longer accepted by his group as he used to be. He transforms himself into a different person altogether. The same thing happened when one of the Rajputs or Xatriya ruler of Amber, Biharimal married his daughter, Jodha Bai, with Emperor Akbar in 1573, most of the other Rajputs discarded him socially and no longer even sat on the same table to dine as they used to honour him before.

430 Panikkar, *Malabar and the Portuguese,* pp. 164-166.

431 *LML,* cod. 12, fols. 285: *Carta régia ao conde vice-rei da Índia, D. João Coutinho. De Nuno Vaz Castelo Branco recebera informação muito circunstanciada relativa à pimenta importada do Canará, isto é, e de Onor, Barcelor e Mangalor, em comparação com a de Cochim, ficando esta muito mais económica, sendo ainda melhor do que aquela. Manda que se examine o caso em Conselho da Fazenda, presente também o dito Nuno Vaz de Castelo Branco.* 16 de Março de 1619; *Idem,* fols. 286, *O governador Fernão de Albuquerque responde à carta anterior. Cumprira-se a ordem régia. Verificar-se como de Mangalore não ia pimenta. A que se embarcava este ano (1620) era quase toda do Canará.* 12 de Fevereiro de 1620.

432 Geneviève Bouchon, *Regent of the Sea; Cannanore's Response to Portuguese Expansion,* p. 19.

433 About the family and commercial status of the Muslim merchants in Cannanore, see works by Geneviève Bouchon which mostly cover the early sixteenth century. See bibliography

434 Bouchon has given a very descriptive and interesting account of the origin and position of Ali Raja and his family: Geneviève Bouchon *Regent of the Sea; Cannanore's Response to Portuguese Expansion 1507-1528* pp. 22-26.

435 Baldaeus, '*A True and Exact Description...*, vol. III, p. 8.

436 Luís de Albuquerque & Inácio Guerreiro, 'Khoja Shams-ud-dín, comerciante de Cananor na Primeira metade do século XVI', in *Acta do II Seminário Internacional da História Indo-Portuguesa*, IICT-CEHCA, Lisboa, 1985, p. 231-239: This article provides us a very vivid and detailed account of this Muslim merchant's business set up in the whole Asia when the Portuguese reached at Calicut and later at Cannanore.

437 Whose family members are also known as Kunjali Marakkar.

438 Albuquerque, *Crónica do descobrimento e conquista da Índia pelos portugueses...*, pp. 297-302.

439 William Brooks Greenlee, *The Voyage of Pedro Alvares Cabral to Brazil and India*, London, 1938, p. 176.

440 'Letter of the King of Portugal to the King and Queen of Castile' in Greenlee, *The Voyage of Pedro Alvares Cabral*, p. 50.

441 For the exact weight in modern times, see Appendix – II-E.

442 *Cartas de Afonso de Albuquerque, tomo.* II, p. 400.

443 Albuquerque, *Crónica do descobrimento e conquista da Índia pelos portugueses...*, pp. 151-156.

444 Barros, *Da Ásia..., Décadas*, 1ª, Parte 1ª, pp. 455-58.

445 *Cartas de Afonso de Albuquerque, tom.* II, p. 400.

446 Barros, *Da Ásia..., Décadas*, 1ª, Parte 1ª, pp. 466-67.

447 António da Silva Rego, *Documentação para Historia das Missões do Padroado Português do Oriente, Vol.* 1, pp. 22-24.

448 Albuquerque, *Crónica do descobrimento e conquista da Índia pelos portugueses...*, pp. 151-156.

449 Thomé Lopes, *Collecção de noticias para a historia e geografia das nações ultramarinas que vivem nos domínios portuguezes ou lhes são visinhas*, Academia Real das Sciencias, Lisboa, 1812-1856, pp. 181-82.

450 *Ibid.*, p. 194

451 *Cartas de Afonso de Albuquerque*, tomo, IIº, p. 400.

452 *Cartas de Affonso de Albuquerque*, tomo. IIº, p. 401.

453 Barros, *Da Ásia..., Décadas*, IIª, parte 1, pp. 62-76; Albuquerque, *Crónica de descobrimento e conquista da Índia pelos portugueses...*, pp. 297-302.

454 Fr. João de Sousa, *Vestigios da lingoa arabica em Portugal ou lexicon etymológico das palavras,e nomes portuguezes que tem origem arabica composto....*(anot.) Fr. Joze de Santo Antonio Moura. Typ. da Academia Real das Sciências, Lisboa, 1830. p. 81.

455 George Winius, 'Private Trading in Portuguese Asia: a substantial will-o'-the-wisp' in *Vasco da Gama*, FCG, Lisboa, 1999, vol. II, pp. 91-100: In this article, Winius has studied in depth the meaning and differences of the private trade.

456 Geneviève Bouchon *Regent of the Sea: Cannanore's Response to Portuguese Expansion 1507-1528,* (Passim).

457 *AGS,* cod. 1571, pp. 306; Mendes da Luz, *Livro das Cidades...,* p. 45v; Disney, *Twilight of the Pepper...,* p. 8.

458 *ACE, vol. I, doc. 115: Sobre a relação que sua Excelência fez da sua jornada até Cochim que Conselho aprouou,* Goa, 22 de Abril de 1631.

459 Disney, *Twilight of the Pepper...,* p. 8.

460 *AGS,* cod. 1571, pp. 306; Mendes da Luz, *Livro das Cidades...,* fols. 45v.

461 *Cartas de Affonso de Albuquerque,* tomo, II, p. 268; Danvers, *The Portuguese in India...,* vol. 1, pp. 88-89.

462 Barros, *Da Ásia..., Décadas,* 1, parte 1, p. 448; Albuquerque, *Crónica de descobrimento e conquista da Índia pelos portugueses...,* pp. 57-63; Greenlee, *The Voyage of Pedro Álvares Cabral,* p. 50; For more details of how the Portuguese established their diplomatical and commercial contacts with the Malabari states in the sixteenth century, see José Manuel Correia, *Os Portugueses no Malabar* (1498-1580), Lisboa, 1997, pp. 114-115.

463 The king had died sometimes during 1503-1504.

464 Mathew, *The Portuguese Trade with India...,* p. 55.

465 Barros has given full details of the incident: Barros, *Da Ásia..., Décadas,* 1, Parte 2, pp. 345-46.

466 Barros, *Da Ásia..., Décadas,* 1, Parte 2, pp. 346-47; Albuquerque, *Crónica de descobrimento e conquista da Índia pelos portugueses,* pp. 144-45; Damião de Góis, *Crónica do felicíssimo Rei D. Manuel,* Parte II, pp. 24-27; *Cartas de Affonso de Albuquerque,* tom. II, p. 401.

467 Simão Botelho, 'Tombo do Estado da Índia' in *Subídios para a Historia da Índia Portugueza,* pp. 30-34.

468 *Ibid,* pp. 34-35

469 Danvers, *The Portuguese in India...,* Vol. 1, p. 346

470 Simão Botelho, 'Tombo do Estado da Índia' in *Subídios para a Historia de Índia Portugueza,* pp. 34-35; K.K. Kusuman, *A History of Trade and Commerce in Tavancore,* Mittal Publications, Delhi, 1987. pp. 18-20.

471 *Ibid.*

472 Regarding this, more information have bee provided in the later parts of this chapter.

Part II

Zamorin-Portuguese Diplomacy in the Seventeenth Century

Introduction

Although the destruction of the Kunjali's naval power at the end of the sixteenth century with the Zamorin of Calicut had brought peace for the Portuguese, this was, as usual, of short duration. Soon after the capture of the Kunjali Marakkar, the Zamorin realised his folly. By allying with the Portuguese he had cut off his own right arm. He had lost his ability to fight the Portuguese and regain the power and prestige of his ancestors. Even though he knew that what was done could not be undone, he realised that his ambition to get rid of the Portuguese had yet to be accomplished. Besides, neither the Portuguese nor the Zamorin had carried out what had been agreed in the treaty of 1599.[473] So, the arrival of the Dutch and the English East India Companies, at the very moment that the power of the Kunjalis had been eliminated, provided the Zamorin with new opportunities to realise his ambitions. In contrast to the situation in the previous century, the arrival of these companies initiated a period of more balanced diplomacy. In fact one could say that the period of forced and imposed diplomacy between the Portuguese and the Zamorin had virtually ended after the capture of Kunjali IV. This was replaced in the Zamorin's mind by a vacillation between his desire for continued support from the Portuguese to eliminated the remnants of Kunjali resistance,[474] which the Portuguese referred to as *ladroeiras*[475] and which was, at times, also directed against him, and his desire to ally with the Dutch to eliminate the Portuguese. The Kunjalis, for their part, after the war of 1599, had lost all faith in the Zamorin and organised their own independent guerrilla tactics against the Portuguese navy and commercial shipping.

Since the Portuguese now feared that the Dutch and the English, who were far better organised and more powerful at sea, might take over their position in the Indian Ocean, they tried to strengthen their relationship with the Malabari states through diplomacy. Although they continued to use their customary language, the Portuguese were now more prepared to accommodate themselves to the new situation rather than to try to dictate terms. The presence of the Dutch and the English had a profound effect not only in the Malabar region but on the whole Asian continent. As C.R. Boxer has rightly emphasised, "the Dutch expansion on the Seven Seas during the first half of the seventeenth century was in its way as remarkable as the overseas expansion of Portugal and Spain 100 years earlier".[476] Portuguese expansion in the Indian Ocean in the early sixteenth century, through their sea-laws and piracy, had played havoc with the Indian economic system, now a hundred years later Dutch expansion did the same to the Portuguese imperial economy. However, in approaching the Indian rulers, the Dutch and the English followed a policy which differed from that which the Portuguese had followed and this so alarmed the Portuguese that they were forced to become, relatively speaking, more subtle in their diplomacy with the Indian merchants and kings.

Quite apart from the arrival of the Dutch and the English, the political situation in the northern Indian sub-continent had already started to take on a new shape. In 1572, Akbar, the Mughal Emperor, conquered Gujarat and with it several trading ports, such as Diu, Daman, Cambay and Chaul, where the Portuguese had their commercial establishments and fortresses. These ports came under the jurisdiction of Akbar. This situation presented the Portuguese with an additional problem. However, fortune turned in their favour for, when they saw that Akbar did not stop his imperial adventures at the boundaries of Gujarat; the neighbouring states became alarmed, and started asking the Portuguese for military help. The territories that adjoined Gujarat were the Sultanates of Ahmadnagar and Bijapur and, under pressure from the Mughal army, the sultans of these states, which had combined against the Portuguese in 1571, were now, ironically, forced to seek their aid. This new alignment of forces was to continue for another hundred years and gave a different shape to Indo-Portuguese diplomacy. This new situation became the salvation of the Portuguese, after the arrival of the Dutch and the English in the region, as it provided them with some room for diplomatic manoeuvre.

The new political developments in the Indian sub-continent, and the arrival of the Dutch and the English, not only created a new balance of power but also a geographical shift in the area where diplomatic activity was most concentrated. Although the Zamorin of Calicut had signed a series of treaties with the Dutch in the early seventeenth century,[477] from the second decade onwards the Dutch and the English concentrated more on the textile producing areas of Gujarat, and on developing contacts with their rulers than on Malabar. They also approached all those rulers who might have been on bad terms with the Portuguese or who were looking for allies to fight them, just as the Portuguese had done against the Zamorin, when they arrived in that region a hundred years earlier. Embassies were sent to establish contacts with the Mughal emperors in the north and with the southern rulers of Ahmadnagar and Bijapur and with the Nayakas of Ikkeri. This persuaded the Portuguese to focus more of their attention on these states as well.

Therefore, Portuguese diplomatic contacts with the rulers of Malabar, although they were still necessary and turned out to be a decisive factor when they lost that region, lessened considerably during the first half of the seventeenth century. However, as the Zamorin of Calicut's capacity to resist Portuguese aggression in the Indian Ocean was reduced, there was now ample opportunity for the Portuguese to devote their resources to combating the new European companies, which were trying to infiltrate the commercial centres in the Malabar region. This does not mean that the Zamorin had ceased to present a threat or to cause concern to the Portuguese. On the contrary, the Portuguese always remained very preoccupied with him, even when, as mentioned earlier, the Zamorin allied with the Portuguese to try to end the resistance of the Kunjalis. This preoccupation can be seen in the numerous letters exchanged between the viceroys and the kings of Portugal, as well as between them and the Zamorin, during the period of this study. On the other hand, the Portuguese always underestimated the Zamorin's power, especially after the capture of Kunjali Marrakar in 1599, though in the end it was he who, allied with the Dutch, gave the final blow to the Portuguese presence in Malabar in 1663.

Besides their diplomatic contacts with Calicut, the Portuguese had to face occasional crisis in their relations with two other very important Malabar states, Cannanore and Cochin, which became a cause for concern to the viceroys. Although, these were Portuguese vassal states, their dissatisfaction arose from Portugal's cavalier treatment of them and the general lack of respect they showed. Especially serious was the capture of merchant ships and the violation of the basic clauses of the treaties signed between them, by which Portugal sought to protect its commerce and keep their territories free from the Zamorin's influence. Moreover, although there was a clause in the treaties, which had been signed in the sixteenth century, which obliged the Portuguese to buy a specific amount of pepper from the land of Cochin, in return for the King's alliance against the Zamorin,[478] it appears that frequently the Portuguese did not fulfil their side of the agreement. This was undoubtedly one of the reasons why the King of Cochin complained to the King of Portugal as he, for his part, always remained faithful to his promises. On the other hand there were several occasions when the Portuguese signed a peace treaty with the Zamorin and ignored the protests of the King of Cochin.[479] There were other times when the King's demands for help against the Zamorin had to be sent secretly so as not to stir up conflict with the Zamorin, whenever he was at peace with the Portuguese.[480] This situation offended the ruler of Cochin who became very dissatisfied and threatened to sever his relationship with the Portuguese, even to the point of joining hands with the Dutch who were ready to pay a higher price for the pepper from his kingdom.[481] However, since the beginning of the sixteenth century the rulers of Cochin had been mainly chosen by the Portuguese, their relationship with Portugal never became anything more than tense.

The ruler of Cannanore, on the other hand, who was a great patron of the Arab and local Muslim merchants, had frequently to mobilise his diplomatic resources when the Portuguese captured[482] a merchant ship belonging to any of these merchant communities. In this state, lived the well-known merchant-prince, Ali Raja,[483] who controlled the market in pepper throughout almost the whole of Cannanore. Although the King was able to meet the requirements of the Portuguese for Cannanore pepper from the neighbouring regions, he often had to face Portuguese reprisals. Many times his ships were captured, plundered or burnt by the Portuguese who were then forced to reach a settlement through diplomatic means to prevent the situation from deteriorating further. The Portuguese tolerated the Muslim merchants from this state because they depended on them commercially rather than because of any bond of friendship or affection.[484]

However, there were occasions when the states of Cannanore and Cochin, in order to bring the Portuguese to their senses, welcomed the Dutch, in this way bringing home to the Portuguese the fragility of their situation. Besides, after the Zamorin's pact with the Portuguese against his own Admirals, the Kunjalis, in

1599, all of the remaining members of the Kunjali family had moved to Cannanore, from where they directed their attacks against the Portuguese. Nevertheless, in 1631, although circumstances were highly unfavourable to the Portuguese, the Viceroy, Conde de Linhares, seized an opportunity to teach Ali Raja a severe lesson by burning part of his market (*Bazar*) in the main coastal city when he failed to appear at the port to greet him.[485] This naturally caused the King great offence. The Viceroy apparently forgot that this was the same King who in 1602 had refused to give any shelter and or sell any pepper to the Dutch commander, Van Der Hagen, when he tried to establish diplomatic contacts with Cannanore. On this occasion the King of Portugal had written a very pleasant and congratulatory letter to him in 1606, thanking him for his sincere loyalty to the Portuguese.[486]

Throughout this period the Portuguese attitude to their allies, although less aggressive than it used to be in the sixteenth century, was almost entirely negative. They treated the merchants of this state, and of the entire Malabar Coast, as pirates, if they had any commercial contacts with any merchants without Portuguese permission. In the case of Ali Raja, they accused him of protecting Malabari pirate ships,[487] especially when they were loaded with rich merchandise. On the other hand, whenever on such occasions the situation became tense, the Portuguese hurried to resolve the matter, fearing that Ali Raja might cause the merchandise needed for their annual fleet to disappear from the coastal markets, a thing he was quite capable of doing.[488] Each side blamed the other for the uneasy relationship that they maintained for over a century.[489]

Although there were times when the rulers of Cochin and Cannanore, received diplomatic missions sent by the Dutch and the English, they never entered into any offensive pact against the Portuguese. However, it was not only Portugal's vassal states which refused any offensive alliance with the Dutch and the English but also the rulers of Kanara and Bijapur.[490] These also refused on many occasions to enter into alliances, especially when they were at peace with the Portuguese, and for this they were gratefully thanked by the Portuguese authorities, either through the sending of an embassy with handsome presents or by means of a letter from the King himself.[491] Though this happened on only a few occasions, historians have failed to comment upon it. However, such friendly gestures from these states brought no change in the behaviour of the Portuguese, either on a political or personal level. They continued with their policy of commercial monopolies and on seizing the shipping of these states as reprisals, which eventually resulted in these Indian governments retaliating. In other words, the Portuguese authorities did not try hard enough to cultivate any long term diplomatic friendship with any of the Indian states.

a) The Portuguese and the Zamorin: Conflicts and Diplomacies

In the continuous conflicts between the Portuguese and the Zamorin, there was one constant factor, the kingdom of Cochin. The conflict between Calicut and Cochin continued without any conclusion even after the sack of Marakkar Kotta in 1599. As mentioned elsewhere, the King of Cranganore used to be a feudatory of the Zamorin before the arrival of the Portuguese. Cranganore had for centuries been a place of importance for the royal family of the Chera dynasty and contained a Pagoda where most of the religious ceremonies took place before the princes of Calicut were sworn to be kings. This practice had been stopped after the Portuguese occupied Cranganore and constructed a fort. Moreover, after the Portuguese had established themselves there, the King of Cranganore took advantage of the continued hostility between them and the Zamorin to declare his independence. The Zamorin had never forgiven this defection and in 1536 he had attacked and conquered Cranganore. However the King of Cranganore, with the help of the Portuguese, had soon been able to get rid of the Zamorin's yoke. After this, events took a new turn when the Portuguese established a fortress at Chaliyam with help of the King of Tanur,[492] and the Zamorin was not able to punish the King. Even after the fortress of Chaliyam was destroyed by the Zamorin's forces in 1571, he could not deal with the problem of Cranganore. He knew that, as long as the Portuguese fort at Cranganore remained between Calicut and the kingdom of Cochin, the conquest of the latter was next to impossible. When the new war with Cochin started in the early seventeenth century, the Zamorin asked the King of Cranganore to help him with soldiers, but he remained neutral as he did not want to offend the Portuguese nor did he want to see the Zamorin re-conquer the kingdom of Cochin and became powerful enough to subdue him as well.

As the quarrel between Calicut and the King of Cochin remained unresolved, the Zamorin, immediately after he was free from the troubles caused by the Marakkars, began, once more, to put pressure on Cranganore, which the Portuguese were not going to permit. In this way, the Portuguese were forced once more during 1614-1616 to become involved at military as well as diplomatic levels with the Zamorin.[493]

The alliance of 1599, between the Portuguese and the Zamorin, had already broken down in 1604, when the Zamorin entered into negotiations with the Dutch Admiral, Van der Hagen,[494] with conditions to oust the Portuguese from their settlements and factories not only in the region of Malabar but in the whole Indian subcontinent. This was seen by the Portuguese as a direct threat to their political and commercial survival. Besides, the Portuguese considered it a violation of the referred treaty. In response to this, the Portuguese avenged the Zamorin, in 1608, by cutting off the head of Kunjali Marrakkar in Goa, which was not what they had agreed to in the same treaty.

Through their diplomacy the Portuguese tried their best to keep the Dutch out of this area and sought to prevent them from concluding diplomatic agreements with any of the Malabar states. However, even after the Zamorin's treaty with the Dutch in 1604, as a matter of policy, the Portuguese did not break their ties, openly, with him and maintained formal diplomatic relations, except for the incident of 1508. They also kept their factory at Calicut until 1614 for the purpose of issuing *Cartazes* and to maintain a close watch over the movement of people and ships. However, mutual suspicion meant that neither side could continue friendly relations for long.[495] In 1614 the tensions between the Portuguese and Calicut reached a climax when the Zamorin, taking advantage of the Portuguese involvement with the Dutch, attacked Cranganore, annexing the northern part to his own kingdom.[496]

Attempts to negotiate peace did not bring any satisfactory results as the Zamorin was too angry with the King of Cranganore to make peace, even though the war had caused him to lose a lot of the income that he derived from trade. In 1616, the Zamorin renewed his attacks on the remaining parts of Cranganore[497] and these coincided with the arrival of three Dutch vessels which were supposed to help the Zamorin. Dom Bernardo de Noronha, the commander of the Portuguese fleets patrolling the Malabar seas, was successful in preventing the union of the Dutch and the Zamorin's forces and the Portuguese captured one of the heavily laden ships off the port of Calicut. Not surprisingly, the fighting continued and the dispute between the Zamorin and the King of Cranganore remained unresolved, once again.

During the years between 1618 and 1622, the king of Cochin was at war with the Zamorin over the issue of Cranganor where the Zamorin was constructing fortresses in the river of Cranganor as well as at Paliaporto, but the Portuguese had already signed a peace treaty with the ruler of Calicut and it would have been violation of the treaty had they openly sent any military support to the king of Cochin against the Zamorin. The Portuguese were not looking for any open war with him at this time when the port of Bombay was blockaded by the allied Dutch and the English forces, besides the English had been supporting the Shah of Persia against the Portuguese in the Persian Gulf.[498]

For a decade (1620-1630) the relations between the Portuguese and the Zamorin remained, relatively calm, even after the Zamorin's occupation of northern Cranganore, as the Portuguese had to concentrate their forces in the territories of Kanara and Bijapur where dangerously powerful rulers were fighting each other and frequently threatening the Portuguese settlements.[499] The Portuguese watched these events very carefully and tried to pacify the situation through diplomatic approaches, the envoys shuttling from one to the other. The Mughal military campaigns in the territory of Bijapur to collect the arrears of tribute also kept the Portuguese very watchful and busy.

These political upheavals in the northern states gave a respite to the Zamorin who was left almost entirely alone by the Portuguese to recoup his commercial losses and to consolidate political sovereignty over his vassal states. In fact the preoccupation of the Portuguese authorities during this period made them more cautious in their relations with Calicut and they tried hard to prevent any military involvement either with him or with the ruler of Cochin, which would have caused additional expenditure and would have become a burden on their exchequer.[500]

It was only in 1631, when the Conde de Linhares started rebuilding the Portuguese military and naval forces, that diplomats from both sides signed a truce in Cranganore. Some time before the Conde de Linhares's expedition[501] to impress the rulers of South India with his newly organised navy, the Zamorin had proposed a peace treaty to the Portuguese at Goa and the *Conselho do Estado* met on 6th of May 1630[502] to deliberate about this. As appears from the discussions at the *Conselho's* meeting, the Zamorin was offering the Portuguese authorities improved trading facilities and permission to construct a fortress, as well as allowing the building of churches and the propagation of Christianity in his kingdom. It was further proposed by him that he would give up protecting the Muslim merchants in his land and would favour the Christians instead. He went a step further offering to join with the King of Cannanore to attack the *ladroeiras*.[503] To obtain terms such as these had long been an object of Portuguese diplomacy. One can recall that it was the Zamorin's protection of his Muslim subjects that had started the whole trouble between him and the Portuguese in the early sixteenth century. In fact, as has been mentioned in the previous chapter, the Portuguese had tried to impose on the Zamorin, as one of the conditions of a settlement, that he should expel the Muslims from his dominions, a condition that the Zamorin had rejected outright. The Zamorin's refusal to accept this condition led to both parties fighting wars for over a century. Even when the Zamorin allied with the Portuguese against the Kunjali Marakkars, this ambition of the Portuguese was not fulfilled as the political rifts continued.[504] Now, after 130 years, it seemed that their dream was going to come true.

These terms were included in the treaty, which was finally signed on 28th of November 1631[505] at Ponnani, between the Zamorin and the *capitão-mor* (captain-in-chief) of the fort of Cranganore, António Moniz Barreto. The ambassadors from the King of Calicut were Mangat Achem, the Prime-minister of the Zamorin, and Trivim Chaledo, another courtier. What led the Zamorin to offer these terms now, at a time when the Portuguese were losing their military supremacy on all fronts? Among the possible answers to this question one thinks of the inability of the Zamorin to face the Portuguese on the open sea, as the Portuguese had already destroyed his naval capability in 1599, and the Dutch had not so far provided any reliable naval or military support, Therefore, after the naval demonstration of the Conde de Linhares, the Zamorin might have felt quite intimidated and, as a consequence, thought he might as well establish peace rather than see everything destroyed forever.

The new relationship between the Portuguese and the Zamorin reached its climax in the year 1636, when the Zamorin, as the Portuguese sources allege, conveyed to the Portuguese ecclesiastical authorities, especially to Dom Estevão de Brito, Archbishop[506] of Cranganore and Padre Francisco de Oliveira who used to be at his court, his intention of embracing Christianity.[507] This seemed like a triumph for both the Portuguese administrative and the ecclesiastical authorities in India. For the Portuguese administrative authorities, it meant they could now control the whole of the Malabar pepper trade undisturbed. The Zamorin of Caliçut had been the most powerful and determined of the rulers seeking to oust the Portuguese from Indian waters. His alliance, following his baptism, would mean that there would not be any Indian ruler or commercial group left to challenge the Portuguese in the Malabar region. For the ecclesiastics, this meant they could now convert the whole of Malabar to Christianity.

The letter of the Zamorin was received, as one might imagine, with much enthusiasm in Goa but at the same time with some reservation, as it appeared too good to be true. The Portuguese Viceroy, Pero da Silva, immediately called a meeting of the *Conselho do Estado* on 5th of September 1636, to decide about this matter which was of the utmost importance.[508] During the discussions more details emerged. Two nieces of the reigning Zamorin were also to be converted to Christianity on this occasion and married to Portuguese *fidalgos* while the two remaining princes, the fourth and the fifth in line, after conversion, were to be married to Portuguese ladies. However, the trouble was that the third prince, the heir apparent to the throne of Calicut, according to the sources, was going to revolt against this act of the Zamorin. Therefore, the Portuguese authorities had to find a way of neutralising his conspiracy in good time.

Naturally the Portuguese authorities expected that these marriages would bring with them big dowries in the form of land and money, besides commercial facilities in the lands of Calicut. It appeared that, after almost a century and a half, the Portuguese troubles were coming to an end and a new age was going to start, as the Zamorin also promised that the remaining members of the Kunjali family would be expelled from his kingdom, since they had been continuing their guerrilla tactics against Portuguese shipping and other interests ever since the Zamorin's treacherous pact in 1598-99.[509] Padre Álvaro Tavares was nominated by the provincial of Goa on 26th of September 1636 to perform the conversion of the Zamorin.[510]

Naturally the question arises why the Zamorin, whose family had consistently opposed the Portuguese since the latter's arrival in the early sixteenth century, should have wanted to become a Christian. The Portuguese had prevented Calicut from being the supreme commercial state in the Malabar region. They had lured away all the ruling princes who had once owed allegiance to the Zamorin and on whose loyalty the glory of Calicut had been based. The Zamorin for his part had become the inflexible enemy of the Portuguese and had constantly opposed them till the end of the sixteenth century. A heavy price had been paid on both sides in material and in lives, especially by the Zamorin. Tired of bloodshed, the Zamorin had eventually allied with the Portuguese against his own navy commanders who were not ready to obey the Zamorin and end the wars until they had obtained what they had been fighting for. However, even this did not bring peace. The Zamorin's dream of recovering the glories of his ancestors had not yet faded and he believed that, after the lesson taught to the Kunjalis, his alliance with the Portuguese would allow him to resume his dominant position in the Indian Ocean. This did not happen.

Although, after the peace, the Portuguese had left him free, probably rather unwillingly, to try to regain control over his former vassals and had allowed him to carry out most of his commercial activities in peace, still the Zamorin had not regained what had been lost in the previous century. What, then, could possibly have made him take the drastic decision to become a Christian? Was it because, through this, he wanted to become free to continue with his trading activities and to draw revenue from the movement of maritime trade? But why should he believe that the Portuguese would allow this when they had still not given up the idea of controlling the Indian Ocean and its commerce and were still fighting the Dutch throughout Asia? He had also promised no longer to protect his Muslim population, especially the merchant community which had contributed so strongly to the commercial strength of Calicut. The answer is open to speculation. Possibly he intended, in this way, to achieve some of the political aims, which his predecessors had been unable to achieve in a century of fighting, even though this meant abandoning the beliefs of his ancestors. However, he must have known that if he really put into practice what he had promised to the Portuguese, he would have had to face severe opposition from his own Nayer community.

In the end the Zamorin never embraced Christianity[511] or at least we do not have information, which could confirm that he ever did. Most probably it was a political trick he wanted to play on the Portuguese authorities in order to guarantee their help in ending the resistance of the Kunjali family on the Malabar Coast as well as the resistance of others who were opposed to the

Portuguese. Since he knew that the Portuguese had, for over a century, planned to achieve his conversion, they would see in this a realisation of their dream. Moreover, the Portuguese had promised to provide him with 5000 *Ashrafis* for his expenses.[512] With this proposal he was able to exploit Portuguese credulity and ignorance and earned himself a breathing space to prepare his own forces. Most probably, from the very beginning, he knew that the Portuguese would fall for his ruse. By convincing them of his plan to convert, he made fools of the Portuguese, but also of himself.

The negotiations for a treaty, during which the Zamorin revealed to the Portuguese his idea of becoming Christian, had an abrupt end when, in the year 1639, the Zamorin was approached by the Dutch to build a trading factory either at Chale or at Aicota, at the mouth of the river at Paliaporto.[513] The Dutch mission was well received and put forward a far-reaching plan for hostilities against the Portuguese. Moreover, this was the period of the complete blockade of Goa by the Dutch and there was no possibility of the Portuguese sending help to any of their fortresses or of their putting effective obstacles in the way of Dutch diplomacy anywhere on the Indian Coast. The Portuguese and the Zamorin only renewed diplomatic contacts in 1641[514] after which there were hardly any opportunities for the Portuguese to concern themselves with the Malabar region as they were fully occupied trying to preserve their fortresses and commercial interests in the north, especially in Kanara and Bijapur.

Zamorin-Portuguese diplomacy had always broken down through mutual mistrust[515] since neither side ever honoured the treaties signed between them for any considerable length of time. Over the decades there had been a constant trial of strength between the two: the Zamorin wanted to restore the commercial dominance of Calicut, while the Portuguese wanted to bring all Asian commerce under their control, which was of course a costly and impossible task. Resistance, wars and treachery were used by both sides to attain their objectives. As the Conde de Linhares, the Portuguese Viceroy, said in 1632 in reply to a letter from the King, the Portuguese attached very little credibility to what the Zamorin promised them. According to his letter it clearly appears that the viceroy was hardly convinced about the promises made by the Zamorin and in his own words, "it was a common thing for the Zamorins in Malabar to break promises and tell lies".[516]

Although the diplomatic relations between the kings of Malabar and the Portuguese were always kept on the agenda of the

Portuguese authorities in Goa, this diplomacy was less important in the seventeenth century than that with Bijapur or the emerging states of Kanara under the Nayakas of Ikkeri. Quite often, the Portuguese let the situation slip out of their grasp as their finances did not permit them to take the measures that were required. Troubles beset them on all sides. Their major concern, after the rise of Venkatappa Nayaka and the increase in the power of the Sultan of Bijapur, turned out to be the safety of their own capital and the *Provincia do Norte*. Here Mughal expansion at the expense of the southern Indian states gave the Portuguese, although weak, a bargaining position, but all these events meant that the Portuguese neglected their Malabar problems since these appeared of less importance than the maintenance of their sea-power as a whole, and this is where they did the biggest mistake. Moreover, the encroachments of the English, and the Dutch aggression against the Portuguese shipping and colonial settlements, together with the support these interlopers received from the Indian rulers, were weakening the Portuguese ability to dictate terms.

b) The loss of the Portuguese settlements in Malabar – Last Phase of Estranged Diplomacy

In 1650, the King of Cochin died, the queen of Cochin approached the Portuguese authorities to help her put her illegitimate son on the throne of Cochin, which most of the rulers of the Malabar kingdoms, including the Zamorin, tried to prevent. The Portuguese authorities tried to dissuade the Zamorin from interfering in the question of the Cochin succession,[517] as they wanted to help the queen in her efforts against the legitimate heir, even though they had clear orders from the King of Portugal not to become involved in this matter at that time.[518] According to Panikkar, it was the Portuguese authorities in Goa who favoured the idea of crowning a King of their choice,[519] although in reality it had been the queen of Cochin who had proposed it. As a matter of fact this illegitimate prince, too, was more favourable to the Portuguese than the heir apparent. Nevertheless, it could be said that this was the fatal mistake that the Portuguese authorities did. As the Zamorin was sure of Dutch naval support this time, he decided not to let slip such an opportunity to strike the long awaited blow to dislodge the Portuguese. Besides, he was also sure of the supports of many ruling chiefs and powers from his neighbouring state. The Portuguese had already sensed the danger and started reinforcing their fortresses in the territories of their allied states, Quilon, Cochin, Cranganore and Cannanore.[520]

While efforts to negotiate with the Dutch in Europe were still continuing, the Dutch in Asia, after the capture of Colombo in 1656,[521] had turned their attention towards Malabar Coast.[522] In December 1658, admiral Rijckloff van Goens attacked the fort of Quilon and captured it on 29th of December 1658,[523] but it was not until 10th of February 1661, that the Dutch, in alliance with the Zamorin, effectively occupied this kingdom.[524] Contrary to what might have been expected, the Dutch signed a treaty of peace with the Queen of Quilon[525] and not with the Portuguese, as they maintained that this state belonged to its rightful ruler. The Portuguese were ignored, altogether, in the negotiations.

After this the Dutch and the Zamorin waited for the right opportunity to attack the kingdom of Cochin.[526] Before they could invade the territory of Cochin, in favour of the exiled prince, they wanted to keep the situation under their control by expanding their diplomatic contacts in the surrounding territories.[527] They knew that it was necessary to improve relations with the kingdoms of Quilon and Travancore as they understood what might happen during the war with Cochin if these kingdoms decided to support the Portuguese. Therefore, they sent ambassadors to these states and a treaty between the Dutch and the kingdoms of Quilon and Travancore was jointly signed on 31st of March 1662. According to this treaty both the belligerents promised to help and protect the interests of the other and to honour the treaty at all costs.[528] Once sure of the neutrality of these two rulers, the Dutch and the Zamorin decided to remove another obstacle from their way before they attacked the kingdom of Cochin. It was the kingdom of Cranganore which the two forces wanted to subdue. Finally, after almost fifteen days fighting, on the morning of 15th of January 1662, the fortress of Cranganore was surrendered to the Dutch.[529] The northern part of the territory of Cranganore, according to this treaty, was given to the Zamorin and the southern part was ceded to the exiled King of Cochin.

After the capture of Cranganore, a new treaty was signed, between the Dutch Rijckloff[530] van Goens, and the Zamorin of Calicut in order to strengthen the friendship and cooperation between the two nations before the final blow was delivered to the Portuguese naval and territorial pride in India, the state of Cochin.[531] In fact, it was during the attack on Cranganore that the fate of Cochin was sealed, when a minister of Cochin, Paliyat Achan, secretly joined the Dutch and asked for help in restoring the Moottatavazhi prince, or the exiled prince, to the throne of

Cochin.[532] The Dutch made a treaty with the exiled prince to take joint military action against the territory of Cochin.[533]

Towards the end of October 1662 the Dutch offered terms to the Portuguese *capitão-mor*, Inácio Sarmento de Carvalho, to give up fighting and surrender the city and the King to them. However, Sarmento de Carvalho preferred to fight honourably than to experience the humiliation of surrender.[534] This left no choice to the Dutch but to take Cochin by force. This time they were more successful in their efforts and finally, on 7th of January 1663, Cochin fell into their hands and subsequently, a peace treaty was signed between the Portuguese and the Dutch.[535]

As used to be the case with the Portuguese in the past in their relations with the Asians, the Dutch, too, did not fulfil all the terms of the treaty. They maltreated the Portuguese returning to Goa after they had surrendered Cochin and seized all their belongings and brought them back as booty to Cochin.[536]

After the capture of Cochin, the Dutch still had another Portuguese stronghold, Cannanore, which they besieged for several days.[537] As the Portuguese commander had heard the news of the surrender of Cochin and had no hope of relief, he surrendered to the Dutch on 13th of February 1663,[538] and the Portuguese flag ceased to fly on the Malabar Coast. The Zamorin had achieved, though not in its entirety, what he and his ancestors had dreamt of for over a century and a half.[539]

Since, during the sixteenth century, the relations of Portugal with the Indian states were mainly based on Portuguese naval superiority, with little attention paid to diplomacy these relations fell apart when the Dutch appeared on the scene. The Indian allies of the Portuguese were mostly the weaker kings of Malabar, who proved to be little use in facing the challenge of the Dutch. The Portuguese commercial as well as the administrative organisation also militated against their survival. Had the Portuguese pursued peaceful diplomacy in which all parties, whether they were Asian merchants or Europeans, were treated with equality and respect, Portuguese commerce, and even the Portuguese empire, would have survived a great deal longer. However, by the third decade of the seventeenth century, it was more than obvious that the Dutch were not prepared to bargain if anything stood in the way of their Asian commerce, which they too aspired to monopolise, just as the Portuguese had done when they sought to oust the Arabs, Gujaratis and other Asian merchants. The difference was that the

Dutch, wherever possible, tried to work through diplomacy with the Indian rulers. They always kept their own commercial interest to the fore and they continued to fight the Portuguese, ignoring whatever diplomatic agreements the governing authorities in The Hague had made with the King of Portugal.

Naturally, the Dutch conquerors of the Portuguese colonial settlements also wanted to be king makers, but the nature of their relations as a dominant partner was different from that of the Portuguese. In the long history of Portuguese relations with the Indian rulers, one thing always emerged very clearly. The Indians resented Portuguese dominance in the field of commerce, less than they did their dominance in the social field. The Portuguese intervened not only in Indian Ocean commerce but in all walks of life. Above all, they gave priority to the conversion of all the Indians to Christianity, even those who were already Christians, the Syrian Catholic Christians, by whatever means was available. This was certainly one of the reasons why they became so hated. On the other hand the Dutch never showed any intention of interfering either in the social or religious affairs of the Indians. Probably they had learnt a lesson from the Portuguese experience.

Reference

473 *Ibid.* The Zamorin had agreed with the Kunjali Marakkar that he wouldn't hand him over to the Portuguese, but he did. On the other hand the Portuguese had promised the Zamorin that they wouldn't execute the Kunjali, but they did in 1608.

474 LML, cod. 47, fol. 89-89vº: *Carta do Vice-rei da Índia, João da Silva Tello de Menezes, Conde de Aveiras ao Rey,* 19 de Janeiro de 1641.

475 Until the end of the sixteenth century, while Kunjalis were in the service of the Zamorin, the Portuguese called them *Piratas*. However, after their defeat towards the end of the century when they had no patronage of their ruler and carried on their fight against the Portuguese on their own, the Portuguese termed them *Ladroeiras* (or the den of the thieves).

476 Boxer, *The Portuguese Seaborne Empire*, p. 109.

477 See more details in the later parts of this chapter.

478 LML, cod. 12, fol. 70: *Carta do Governador Geral, Fernão de Albuquerque para o Rei de Portugal, respondendo o seu inquérito sobre o rei de Cochin,* 26 de Fevereiro, 1619.

479 LML, cod. 12, fol. 71: *Carta do Governador Geral, Fernão de Albuquerque para o Rei de Portugal, "El-rei de Cochim viue desconfiado e descontente por ver se uão dilatando tantos annos e não hirem aquella cidade carregar as nãos do Reino, nem se mandar lá buscar a pimenta e de estar quebrado o contratto della de que elle tem algum proueito e não ser cousa de consideração o rendimento tem na alfandega para os gastos que tem com tão dilatada guerra com o Samorim...",* 7 de Feureiro, 1620.

480 LML, cod. 12, fols. 538: *Carta Régia ao conde vice-rei. O rei de Cochim e o Samorim de Calicut andavam em guerra. O de Cochim pretendia auxílio português, mas convinha emprega toda a prudência, para se não romper declaradamente com o Samorim. Fernão de Albuquerque havia escrito em 1620 que o rei de Cochim andava desgostoso, por não irem lá naus do Reino a carregar pimenta. Havia presunção que o rei de Cochim tinha pedido aos holandeses seguro para andar uma nau sua à China, levando por capitão um casado de Cochim chamada Ferreira. Convinha, portanto, empregar toda a prudência nas relações com Cochim.* 11 de Fevereiro de 1622. During the years between 1618 and 1622, the king of Cochin was at war with the Zamorin over the issue of Cranganor where the Zamorin was constructing fortresses in the river of Cranganor as well as at Paliaporto, but the Portuguese had already signed a peace treaty with the ruler of Calicut and it would have been violation of the treaty had they openly sent any military support to the king of Cochin against the Zamorin. The Portuguese were not looking for any open war with him at this time when the port of Bombay was blockaded by the Dutch and the English forces at the same time as well as the English had been supporting the Shah of Persia against the Portuguese in the

Persian Gulf; *LML*, cod. 16, fols. 534: *Carta Régia ao Conde vice-rei. Recomenda boas relações com este rei, e "que se lhe pague pontualmente o que lhe for devido de sua copa..." Menciona ele uma tentativa do Samorim de Calicut para construir uma fortaleza junto a Paliaporto. Era necessário evitar isso. O rei de Cochim recomendava também Manuel Vaz Pegando. Devia o vice-rei averiguar e satisfazer.* 4 de Março de 1622; *LML*, cod. 18, fol. 91: *Carta Régia a D. Francisco da Gama. O Rei de Cochim tinha-se queixado do Samorim de Calecut por andar este a construir uma fortaleza no rio de Cranganor. Queixa-se ainda de que os Portugueses lhe não compravam pimenta nem autorizavam os seus oficiais a entrarem na Alfândega. Recomenda el-rei bom entendimento com este rei.* 17 de Fevereiro de 1623.

481 *LML*, cod. 12, fols. 538: *Carta Régia ao conde vice-rei. O rei de Cochim e o Samorim de Calicut andavam em guerra. O de Cochim pretendia auxílio português, mas convinha emprega toda a prudência, para se não romper declaradamente com o Samorim. Fernão de Albuquerque havia escrito em 1620 que o rei de Cochim andava desgostoso, por não irem lá naus do Reino a carregar pimenta. Havia presunção que o rei de Cochim tinha pedido aos holandeses seguro para andar uma nau sua à China, levando por capitão um casado de Cochim chamada Ferreira. Convinha, portanto, empregar toda a prudência nas relações com Cochim.* 11 de Fevereiro de 1622..

482 *LML*, cod. 14, fols. 94: *Carta Régia para Vice-rei da Índia, D. João Coutinho. Recebera a informação do ano passado relativa à naveta que Francisco Henrique tomara ao Adarajao.* 7 de Março de 1620.

483 About this merchant prince, Geneviève Boucon, *Mamale de Cananor: un adversaire de l'Inde portugaise: 1507-1528*. Its English translation is *Regent of the Sea, Cannanore's Response to Portuguese Expansion*, 1507-1528; Ali Raja, or Ada Rajao as the Portuguese referred him in the documents, was one of the richest and most powerful businessmen of Arab origin. Although he was frequently in conflict with the local rulers for religious and economic reasons, the ruler of Cannanore never tried to expel him. On the contrary the Portuguese find in him a stern enemy. During the time of Viceroy, Conde de Linhares when he didn't go to receive the viceroy, his fortress and shipping had suffered severe attacks from the Portuguese navy and resulted in great loss of lives.

484 *LML*, cod. 14, fol. 93: *Carta régia para Vice-rei da Índia, D. João Coutinho, manifestando a sua satisfação pelo sucesso de Cananor. Recomenda exame dos serviços então prestado por Nicolau de Soveral, falecido. Envia uma carta dirigida ao Adarajao, a agredecer-lhe a colaboração.* 5 de Março de 1620.

485 *LML*, cod. 29, fols. 1-3v°: *Carta de Viso Rey da Índia, o Conde de Linhares para o Rey, dando conta da sua viagem ao sul.* Goa a 20 de Julho de 1631; *ACE*, vol. I, doc. 115: *Sobre a relação que sua Excelência fez da sua jornada até Cochim que Conselho aprouou, Goa, 22 de Abril de 1631: "E que chegando a Cananor, e vendo que o AdaRajao o não viera visitar ...polla qual causa lhe mandara dar hum castigo queimandolhe parte do bazar..".*

486 *LMG, cod. 6,* fols. 116, *Carta de El-rei Filipe II para o Rei de Cananor, agradecendo o auxílio prestado pelo referido rei à fortaleza de Cananor, atacada pelos Holandeses e recomenda-lhe que não permita o seu desembarque e comércio nos seus estados.* Lisboa, 23 de Dezembro de 1606; *The Cambridge History,* vol. V, p. 31.

487 LML, cod. I, fols. 157, *Carta régia para o Vice-rei Dom Martim Affonso de Castro, "Também vi o que me dizeis sobre o Ada Rajao, que com se dar por amigo d'esse Estado saem de suas terras os mais dos parós dos malavares, e hei por acertado o dissimulardes com elle, e assi vos encommendo o façaes até o Estado estar em melhor tempo, advertindo porem ao capitães das armadas trabalhem por acolher os parós e dar-lhes o castigo que merecerem". 16 de Janeiro de 1607; in reality they were merchants of this region:* LML, cod. 47, fol. 89-89vº: *Carta do Vice-rei da Índia, João da Silva Tello de Menezes, Conde de Aveiras,* 19 de Janeiro de 1641.

488 *LML,* cod. 1, fol. 157, *Carta Régia para o vice-rei D. Martim Affonso de Castro, sugerindo-lhe que conserve a boa harmonia com o Idalcão, o rei de Banguel, o Avantapanaique e o Ada Rajao...,* 16 de Janeiro, 1607.

489 *LML,* cod. IV, fols. 155, 165, *Carta régia para o Vice-rei Ruy Lourenço de Távora (he was governor but in this document the king of Portugal has referred him as "vice-rei") "Quanto ao que dizeis sobre o Adarajáo e rey de Cananor, tenho por acertado o aviso que lhe mandastes; porem, porque as insolencias do Adarajao vão em crescimento com grande descredito d'esse Estado, vos encarrego muito encarecidamente ordeneis se fortifique a fortaleza de Cananor o melhor que puder ser, e fortifacada, dando o tempo logar e havendo posses para isso, lhe dareis hum grande castgio, fazendo-se de maneira que, recebendo elle muito damno, o não tenham meus vassallos".* 11 de Março de 1611; *LML,* cod. 5, fol. 152: *"...e que o Adarrajao não he leal amigo d'esse Estado, e por manha e invenção lhe fazia todo o damno que podia".* 13 de Fevereiro de 1612.

490 *LML,* cod. 21, fols. 1, Lisboa ao primeiro de Março de 1625: *Carta Régia para o Vice Rei da Índia.*

491 *Ibid.*

492 Paulo da Trindade, *Conquista Espiritual do Oriente, Parte* 1, pp. 96-97.

493 *LMG,* cod. 12, fol. 216, 5 de Janeiro de 1616; *Carta do vice-rei para o rei sobre a guerra do Malabar, foi sempre de opinião que se deixassem "embaraçados" o rei de Cochim com o daquele reino, sem no entanto consentir que se oprimisse aquele, para não se arriscar a fortaleza de Cranganor. Neste sentido mandou ordens a Dom Diogo Coutinho. Finalmente diz que, segundo as ordens de el-rei, tem procedido cortêsmente com o rei de Tanor, a quem sempre envia uma cabaia pela armada do Malabar.* 5 de Janeiro de 1616; *LMG,* cod. 12, fols. 302-303: *Carta do vice-rei da Índia Dom Jerónimo de Azevedo para El-rei contando que em Cananor houve guerra durante uns dias, mas que tudo voltou à normalidade com a chegada do patacho que para ali enviara; em Cranganor está-se em contínua vigilância, por causa da vizinhança do Samorim, pois a diligência que fez o ano anterior não surtira

efeito; que o rei de Cochim lhe pediu auxílio contra o Samorim, e o tem ajudado com munições e alguma artilharia. Goa, 9 de Dezembro de 1616.

494 See the clauses of the treaty in Appendix III-B: Poonen, *A Survey of the Rise of the Dutch ...*, pp. 46-47; *The Dutch in Malabar-Selection from the Records of the Madras Government*, No. 13, pp. 68. (Henceforth cited as The Dutch in Malabar Records...) Pissurlenkar, 'Fragmentos Históricos' in *BIVG*, N° 47, p. 61; Kail, *The Dutch in India...*, pp. 30-31.

495 F.P. de Laval, *Viagem de Francisco Pyrard de Laval*, vol. I, pp. 405-406.

496 *LML*, cod. 7, fol. 170, *Carta Régia ao vice-rei da Índia D. Jeronymo de Azevedo. Approva o seu modo de proceder nas cousas do rei de Cochim, com quem procurará ultimar o negocio da alfandega. Recomenda-lhe que evite qualquer comprometimento para o Estado por occasião da guerra do mesmo rei com o Samorim. Ordena-lhe que se informe judicialmente das culpas de João Gomes Fayo, exonerado da capitania da fortaleza de Cranganor.* Lisboa, 17 de Janeiro de 1614; Danvers, *The Portuguese in India...*, vol. II, p. 168; Panikkar, *Asia and the Western...*, pp. 149-151.

497 *LML*, cod. 7, fol. 170, *Carta Régia ao vice-rei da Índia D. Jeronymo de Azevedo. Approva o seu modo de proceder nas cousas do rei de Cochim, com quem procurará ultimar o negocio da alfandega. Recomenda-lhe que evite qualquer comprometimento para o Estado por occasião da guerra do mesmo rei com o Samorim. Ordena-lhe que se informe judicialmente das culpas de João Gomes Fayo, exonerado da capitania da fortaleza de Cranganor.* Lisboa, 17 de Janeiro de 1614.

498 *LML*, cod. 16, fols. 534: *Carta Régia ao Conde vice-rei. Recomenda boas relações com este rei, e "que se lhe pague pontualmente o que lhe for devido de sua copa..." Menciona ele uma tentativa do Samorim de Calicut para construir uma fortaleza junto a Paliaporto. Era necessário evitar isso. O rei de Cochim recomendava também Manuel Vaz Pegando. Devia o vice-rei averiguar e satisfazer.* 4 de Março de 1622; *LML*, cod. 18, fol. 91: *Carta Régia a D. Francisco da Gama. O Rei de Cochim tinha-se queixado do Samorim de Calecut por andar este a construir uma fortaleza no rio de Cranganor. Queixa-se ainda de que os Portugueses lhe não compravam pimenta nem autorizavam os seus oficiais a entrarem na Alfândega. Recomenda el-rei bom entendimento com este rei.* 17 de Fevereiro de 1623..

499 See chapters 4 & 5.

500 *LMG*, cod. 16-A, fol. 4, *Carta Régia para o Conde de Linhares, recomendando ao vice-rei que procure por todos os meios manter a paz com o Mogor, embora secretamente ajude o sultão Bolanquin que lhe disputava o trono e trabalhe também por manter a paz com o Samorim, pois não convinha ao bem do Estado a hostilidade destes potentados.* Lisboa, 28 de Fevereiro de 1632; *LMG*, Cód. 18, fol. 110: *Carta Régia para o Vice-rei da Índia, mostrando a sua satisfação com a disposição em que está o vice-rei de tratar as pazes pedidas pelos Arioles e ainda de lhes conceder os cartazes que eles desejavam, decisão esta tomada em Conselho. Sua Majestade dá toda a sua aprovação a estas matérias, porque entende que deve existir a maior harmonia*

com os naturais, para melhor se poderem defender e empregar armas contra os inimigos da Europa. À margem, em carta datada de Goa, 10 de Outubro de 1633, o vice-rei informa que as pazes com os Arioles e tratadas em Cananor, durante muitos dias, estão quase concluídas, mas não resultarão, visto que estes povos são, de seu natural, ladrões e "vários". O Samorim mostra-se muito sentido por uns furtos que eles fizeram, enquanto ele e el-rei de Cananor se responsabilisavam por eles e o vice-rei "anima-o neste sentimento" oferecendo-lhe ajuda da armada para que o sustente no mar, enquanto os destroi por terra. O vice-rei mostra-se pouco confiante nas promessas do Samorim pois "em Malaca é honra dizer mentiras". Lisboa, 20 de Dezembro de 1632..

501 *LMG*, cod. 19-A, fol. 144: *Carta régia de D. Filipe III, para o vice-rei, conde de Linhares, pedindo explicações por lhe não ter comunicado os motivos por que empreendera a jornada do Malabar e a despesa que com a mesma fizera.* In the margin of the same letter, the viceroy has provided the reason why he had taken up the march of his navy to the south; Also see *LML*, cod. Fols. 1-3: *Carta de Viso Rey da Índia, o Conde de Linhares para o Rey dando conta da sua viagem.* De Goa a 20 de Julho de 1631.

502 *ACE*, vol. 1, doc. 98: *Conselho sobre as pazes do Samorim*, Cranganore, 6 de maio de 1630.

503 *ACE*, vol. II, doc. 36, *Copia do Conselho sobre a converção do Samorim e destruhição das ladroeiras*, 5 de Setembro de 1636; *LML*, cod. 47, fol. 89-89v°: *Carta do Vice-rei da Índia, João da Silva Tello de Menezes, Conde de Aveiras ao Rei*, 19 de Janeiro de 1641, Also see the letter of the Zamorin to the Portuguese Viceroy, fol. 90-90v°, *Copia da carta del Rey Samory escripta a S. Excelência*, Novembro de 1640..

504 *ACE*, vol. 1, doc. 98: *Conselho sobre as pazes do Samorim*, Cranganore, 6 de maio de 1630.

505 HAG, *Livro de pazes*, cod. 2 fols. 83-83v; Biker, (ed.) Collecção de tratados..., tomo I, pp. 281-292: *Pazes que fez o Capitão da fortaleza de Cranganore, António Moniz Barreto, com o Çamorim, Rey de Calecut*, em 28 de novembro de 1631. The same treaty is also published in detail in the *ACE*, vol. I, pp. 545-552; *Terlado das pazes que fes o Capitão e capitãomor da fortaleza de Cranganore António Monis Barreto com Samorim, Rey de Calecut*, 28 de Novembro de 1631..

506 Although it may appear that a place like Cranganor had an *Archbishop*, but the fact is that most of the Portuguese manuscripts referred Dom Estevão de Brito as *Arcebispo* quite frequently. Not only that there is a complete list of Bishops and Archbishops of Cranganor provided by José Manuel Correia, in his *Os Portugueses no Malabar*, Imprensa Nacional, Lisboa, 1997, pp. 260-261 which he has elaborated basing on BNL, *Fundo Geral*, Reservado, codices 464 e 536; Miguel de Oliveira, *Historia Eclesiástica de Portugal*, Lisboa, União Gráfica, 1968, pp. 454-455.

507 ACE, vol. I1, doc. 36: *Copia do Conselho sobre a converção do Samorim e destruhição das ladroeiras,* 5 de Setembro de 1636.

508 *Ibid.*

509 LML, cod. 47, fol. 89-89v°, 19 de Janeiro de 1641; ACE, vol. II, doc. 36: *Copia do Conselho sobre a converção do Samorim e destruhição das ladroeiras, 5 de Setembro de 1636: Aos sinco de setembro de 1656 estando o Illustrisimo* s^{or}*, viso-Rey Pero da silua com o conçelho que lhe assiste lhe propoz que hauia reçebido cartas do capitão de Cochim, Antonio de moura, Arçebispo de cranganor, e do* $p.^{e}$ *francisco de Oliueira que assiste na corte delRey samorim nas quaes dauão conta de como o dito Rey se queria fazer christão e padre olìueira propunha a materia com maes circunstancias como pessoa a que o dito Rey que de muito tempo a esta parte trazia diante dos olhos, o modo que seria de sua saluação, e tinha alcanssado não hauer outro, se não por meyo de nossa santa ley, e se declaraua com o dito padre para elle o poder fazer ao senhor visoRey, e que o dia em que elle se baptizaçe, se Bautizarião com elle o Principe quarto e quinto e porque o que suçederia era o terceiro erdeiro immediato Sabia de certo que lhe hauia de encontrar a esta sua resolução, e leuantarsse com parte do Reino e que estaua detreminado de o matar secretamente e juntamente a Mangate Achem seu Regedor mor, e pessoa principal de seu Reino, e que para isto ter bom suçesso lhe hera necessario tratar com alguma pessoa de confiança para com isso se lhe hauer de negoçear couza com que secretamente matasse as três pessoas nomeadas, e que juntamente fazião o dia de seu Baptismo huma irmã sua com duas Princezas suas sobrinhas christãs para poderem cazar com dous fidalgos Portuguezes, e elle com o Principe quarto e quinto com tres senhoras Portuguezas que o senhor visoRey lhe apontaçe para isso e que a todos daria terras, e comedias pera sustentação e fortalezas para deffenção do dito Reino em cazo que ouueçe algum leuantamento, e que para effeito de o não hauer em modo de conssideração, ja desde agora hauia adquirindo a sy os animos das cabeças de seus Pouos para não fazerem maes que o que elle quizeçe, e outras algumas particularidades...".*

510 ACE, vol. II, doc. 38, *Copia do Conçelho sobre a partida das Armadas do Cabo e sanguiceis, e Regimentos que hão de leuar seus capitães-mores, e hida do Padre Aluares Tauares ao samory.* 26 de Setembro de 1636.

511 Neither Faria e Sousa, nor Danvers nor any historian has mentioned this incident. Even the Portuguese *Conselho do Estado* never mentioned the outcome.

512 ACE, vol. II, doc. 38, *Copia do Conçelho sobre a partida das Armadas do Cabo e sanguiceis, e Regimentos que hão de leuar seus capitães-mores, e hida do Padre Aluares Tauares ao samory.* 26 de Setembro de 1636.

513 ACE, vol. II, doc. 38: *Copia do Conçelho sobre a partida das Armadas do Cabo e sanguiceis, e Regimentos que hão de leuar seus capitães-mores, e hida do Padre Aluares Tauares ao samory.* 26 de Setembro de 1636.

514 LML, cod. 48, fols. 86-v°: *Carta do Conde de Aveiras para El-rei, A Fidelidade intereseira do Samorim, que custava anualmente milhares de*

xerafins à Fazenda Real, permitiu manter os Holandeses arastados daquela costa, Goa, 17 de Dezembro de 1641.

515 *Ibid.*

516 LMG, cod. 18, fols. 110: *Carta del Rei, Filipe III, para of Vice-Rei da Índia,* Lisboa, 20 de Dezembro de 1632. This proverb reveals that telling lies in Malacca was a common thing. However, what the Portuguese are really trying to show is that, as in Malacca, it was a common thing for the Zamorins in Malabar to breal promises and tell lies.

517 LMG, cod. 23-B, fls. 371: *Carta de D. Brás de Castro para el-rei. Dando conta do pedido feito pela rainha velha de Cochim para ser reconhecido e coroado, segundo o antigo ritual português, um seu sobrinho em substituição do verdadeiro rei, e situação crítica que tal facto criava ao Estado, porque, acedendo ao pedido, comprometia-se com este que poderia vir a recuperar o trono, e não acedendo, privava a cidade de Cochim de alimentos.* Goa, 25 de Janeiro de 1654.

518 LMG, cod. 22-A, fol. 236: *Carta Régia ao Conde de vice-rei da Índia, ordenando que Cochim se conserve neutral em face da luta entre o rei de Cochim e o príncipe que lhe disputava o trono, e se não percão de vista as intenções do Samorim.* Lisboa, 27 de Fevereiro de 1652.

519 Panikkar, *Malabar and the Portuguese,* pp. 155-157.

520 LMG, cod. 22-B, fols. 375-375v: *Cópia de um capítulo das informações prestadas pela Câmara de Cochim aos governadores da Índia, dando conhecimento do estado decadente em que se encontrava a cidade de Cochim. E por não ter obtido resposta, vem novamente pedir socorro de munições e artilharia, tanto para Cochim como para Cranganor, sem o qual não têm defesa possível. Foram avisos para todas as fortalezas do Malabar para que estivessem prevenidas para qualquer ataque inimigo. Pede, finalmente que se mande ordem ao capitão de Cochim para que este faça um forte numa ilha que fica defronte da barra de Aicota, para defesa da barra e ilha de Paliporto.* Cochim, 8 de Agosto de 1652; LMG, cod. 23-B, fls. 372-374vº: *Carta de António da Silva de Meneses para D. Brás Informando sobre negociações com a rainha velha de Cochim sobre o juramento do novo rei. Ameaças dos reis vizinhos a Coulão e Travancor e socorros enviados a estas praças. Intervenção apaziguadora do rei de Changanate. Socorros a Cranganor ameaçada pelo Samorim. Mau estado desta fortaleza, incapacidade física de seu capitão, dívidas de ordenados a eclesiásticos e soldados, falta de armas e dinheiro. Alvitre para os direitos da pimenta e a renda do tabaco serem aplicados às despesas de Cranganor e Paliporto. Mantimentos enviados a Ceilão (arroz de Porcá). Galeota arribada a Santo André, toda desmantelada. Conclusão do baluarte de Nossa Senhora da Guia, em Cochim. Boa correspondência com os Reis Vizinhos.* Cochim, 8 de Dezembro de 1653; *LMG, Cod. 26-B, fols. 379: Carta dos Governadores da Índia Manuel Mascarenhas Homem, Francisco de Melo e Castro e António de Sousa Coutinho [3.º Conselho do Governo da Índia] para el-rei, informando sobre Ameaça holandesa a Cochim e a Cananor; Inácio Sarmento Rodrigues, capitão*

da armada do Norte, oferece-se para ir socorrer Cochim e Cananor. Goa, 5 de Fevereiro de 1659; *LMG*, Cod. 26-B, fols. fls. 533-533v: *Carta dos Governadores da Índia Manuel Mascarenhas Homem, Francisco de Melo e Castro e António de Sousa Coutinho para el-rei, Sobre a perda e recuperação de Coulão; desalojamento dos holandeses da feitoria de Calicoulão; tentativa de Ignácio Sarmento de Carvalho para ficar com 14 naus e pataxos na costa de Cochim; desembarque do capitão geral da frota disfarçado em Aicota, próximo das terras de Samorim para falar com o príncipe e aliar-se com este para guerrear o rei de Cochim; pedido de socorro do rei de Cochim aos aliados; bom sucesso das armas de Sua Majestade el-rei de Portugal; elogio de Ignácio Sarmento.* Goa, 22 de Março de 1660.

521 *LMG*, cod. 26-B, fols. 283-84v°: *Carta dos Governadores da Índia, Manuel Mascarenhas Homem, Francisco de Melo e Castro e António de Sousa Coutinho, para o Rei, Sobre a perda de Colombo e de toda a Ilha de Ceilão.* Goa, 29 de Agosto de 1658; *LMG*, cod. 26-B, fols. 348-349v°: *Carta dos Governadores da Índia Manuel Mascarenhas Homem, Francisco de Melo e Castro e António de Sousa Coutinho, para o Rei, A demora na viagem da embaixada ao rei Dialxá tem causado grandes despesas; Abdul Aquimo e sua política com os portugueses e holandeses; o ataque holandês à fortaleza de Ceilão e Cochim; resistência heróica de Cochim; pedido de socorro a Sua Majestade.* Goa, 12 de Janeiro de 1659; *Índia*, cx. 24, docs. 68, 138; *The Dutch in Malabar...*, No 13, pp. 89; Danvers, *The Portuguese in India...*, vol. II. pp. 323-325.

522 *Ibid.*

523 *LMG*, cod. 26-B, fls. 355-356: *Carta dos Governadores da Índia, Manuel Mascarenhas Homem, Francisco de Melo e Castro e António de Sousa Coutinho, para o Rei, Tentativas dos holandeses para se apoderarem de Coulão, Cochim, Cananor e Dio; resistência firme dos naturais de Coulão; tentativa dos holandeses para obter a neutralidade do Nayare e do adarragão; mudança repentina na política dos holandeses; incapacidade do capitão de Cochim*, Goa, 22 de Janeiro de 1659; *LMG*, cod. 26-B, fls. 379: *Carta dos Governadores da Índia Manuel Mascarenhas Homem, Francisco de Melo e Castro e António de Sousa Coutinho, para o Rei, dando conta da Ameaça holandesa a Cochim e a Cananor; Inácio Sarmento Rodrigues, capitão da armada do Norte, oferece-se para ir socorrer Cochim e Cananor*, Goa, 5 de Fevereiro de 1659; Poonen, *A Survey of the Rise of the Dutch Power in Malabar*, pp. 68-69.

524 *Índia*, cx. 25, doc. 45; Danvers, *The Portuguese in India...*, vol. II. pp. 325-26; Poonen, *A Survey of the Rise of the Dutch ...*, p. 71.

525 Poonen, *A Survey of the Rise of the Dutch ...*, 70-71: There is a full text of the treaty on these pages.

526 *LMG, cod. 28-A*, fols. 218*: Carta da Rainha, D. Luisa de Gusmão, para os Governadores da Índia. Sobre a informação obtida de que os holandeses estavam preparando uma esquadra de 30 naus e 8.000 homens para atacarem a Índia. Lisboa,* 26 de Abril de 1661.

527 *LMG, Cod. 26-B, fols. 355-356: Carta dos Governadores da Índia Manuel Mascarenhas Homem, Francisco de Melo e Castro e António de Sousa Coutinho, 3.º Conselho do Governo da Índia para el-rei, dando informações sobre o estado em que se encontrava o Estado da Índia, porque os holandeses já haviam tentado apoderarem Coulão, Cochim, Cananor e Dio; resistência firme dos naturais de Coulão; tentativa dos holandeses para obter a neutralidade do Nayare e do adarragão; mudança repentina na política dos holandeses.* Goa, 22 de Janeiro de 1659.

528 Full text of the treaty has been provided by Poonen, *A Survey of the Rise of the Dutch ...*, pp. 82-84.

529 AHU, *Índia*, cx. 25, doc. 148; Danvers, *The Portuguese in India...*, vol. II. pp. 15859; Panikkar, *Malabar and the Portuguese...*, pp. 150-70; Poonen, *A Survey of the Rise of the Dutch ...*, pp. 86-87.

530 Only Panikker has spelt as Ryklof.

531 Poonen, *A Survey of the Rise of the Dutch ...*, pp. 88-99.

532 Panikker, *Malabar and the Portuguese*, pp. 150-161, has given a detailed history of the problem of the succession in the kingdom of Cochin. Poonen, *A Survey of the Rise of the Dutch ...*, p. 86.

533 Poonen, *A Survey of the Rise of the Dutch ...*, pp. 75-76.

534 *LMG*, cod. 28-A, fols. 244: *Carta do Governador da Índia António de Melo de Castro para a Rainha, Informa sobre o socorro de Mombaça e pede socorros para acudir a Cochim*, Bombaim, 16 de Outubro de 166; *LMG*, cod. 28-B, fols. 331-331vº: *Carta do vice-rei da Índia, António de Melo de Castro, para o rei*, Sobre o envio de socorros para Cochim, Goa, 1 de Fevereiro de 1663; Danvers, *The Portuguese in India...*, vol. II., pp. 327-28.

535 *LMG*, cod. 28-B, fls. 333-333vº: *Carta do vice-rei da Índia, António de Melo de Castro, para o rei, sobre a perda de Cochim e o risco que corre Cananor se não for rápidamente socorrida*, Goa, 1 de Fevereiro de 1663; *LMG*, cod. 28-B, fls. 336: *Certificado do Provedor-mor dos contos sobre a tomada de Cochim pelos Holandeses*, Goa, 4 de Maio de 1663; *Índia*, cx. 25, docs. 147, 148, 183; cx. 26, docs. 13, 17, 41, 126, 151, 217; *The Dutch in Malabar...*, No 13, pp. 103-104; Danvers, *The Portuguese in India...*, vol. II. pp. 327-29: See Appendix III-C for the full text of the treaty.

536 Poonen, *A Survey of the Rise of the Dutch ...*, pp.109-110.

537 *LMG*, cod. 28-B, fls. 338-339vº: *Carta do capitão de Cananor ao vice-rei da Índia, António de Melo de Castro, sobre a situação na fortaleza e o perigo da sua tomada pelos holandeses*, Cananor, 20 de Janeiro de 1663.

538 *LMG*, cod. 29-30, fols. 22: *Carta do rei, D. Afonso VI, para o governador da Índia, António de Melo de Castro. Sobre as notícias recebidas acerca da tomada de Cochim e da fortaleza de Cananor pelos holandeses*, Lisboa, 13 de Abril de 1664; *The Dutch in Malabar...*, No 13, pp. 18, 103; Poonen, *A Survey of the Rise of the Dutch Power in Malabar*, 108-111; both the authors' versions ares supported by the Portuguese documents in AHU: *Índia*, cx. 26, doc. 224; cx. 27, doc. 96.

539 *Índia*, cx. 25, docs. 147, 148, 183; *Índia*, cx. 26, docs. 13, 17, 41, 126, 151, 217; *The Dutch in Malabar...*, No 13, pp. 103-104; Danvers, *The Portuguese in India...*, vol. II. pp. 327-29.

Chapter 4

Portuguese Diplomatic Relations with the States of Kanara During the Sixteenth and the Seventeenth Centuries

The states of Kanara, once integral parts of the Vijayanagar Empire, acquired commercial and political importance for the Portuguese only after the fourth decade of the sixteenth century, due to its extensive rice production and of high quality pepper. Here the role of diplomacy was, principally, played by using one commodity against the other, quite different from the one used either in Malabar or in Bijapur. If the Portuguese wanted to buy rice, they had to purchase pepper, which was of much superior quality than that of Malabar, hence more expensive. Therefore, the rulers of Kanara, initially, determined the terms for the sale of rice. The Portuguese who were accustomed to enforce their law in the sea, now in this region had to reckon with the local diplomacy. Initially, in the early sixteenth century, since the political condition of Kanara, which was under the rulers of Vijayangar Empire, almost at the zenith of their power, didn't provide the Portuguese the same oportunity as it did in the regions of Malabar, they had to accept the conditions imposed by the merchants or else there could have been trouble. Nevertheless, there were times when the Emperor of Vijayanagar did try to approach the Portuguese for help, but the lack of farsightedness and imprudence of the Viceroy left the opportunity go. So, when they themselves required the support of the Vijayanagar ruler, it was already too late. Therefore, the Portuguese had to wait for the right opportunity to extend their influence and power in this region. It was a question of survival, in its proper sense. Thus, as soon soon as the chances rose, especially after the war of Talikota, in 1565, they seized the opportunity to establish fortress and factories at the ports of Mangalore, Barcelore and Onor, in order to get the control of the paddy lands and obtain rice as per their requirements. Not only that, they intended to control the supply of rice to other regions, such as Malabar, of the western and the eastern coasts of India. But this situation, once again, took a new turn after the rise of Venkatappa Nayaka to power, since the early seventeenth century, who tried to put the condition as favourable as possible, as he knew the Portuguese depedence. In the following passages, a brief account of the Portuguese Kanara relation in the sixteenth century has been furnished in order to understand the changes that took place in the seventeenth century. This chapter, too, has been devided into two parts; part one will deal with the Portuguese diplomatic relations with the Vijayanagar Emperors, the rightful rulers of Kanara and, part two will deal with the Portuguese diplomacy with the Nayakas of Ikkery, who, after the Talikota war, emerged as the independent rulers of this kingdom, away from the influence of the weak rulers of the Vijayanagar Empire.

Part I

The Portuguese Vijayanagar Diplomacy, the Empire and its fall

During the three hundred years of its existence, the Vijayanagar Empire was subject to constant wars against its Muslim neighbours, especially the Sultan of Bijapur, besides the occasional uprising of the feudal lords that forced the rulers to be prepared all the time for both war and diplomacy. In theory, hereditary monarchs, weak rulers might face serious consequences, if they were unable to handle affairs of state in accordance with the laws of the country, which were mainly religiously oriented, or to follow the traditions established by the ancestors and those suggested by the Head Brahmin. Weak Emperors often had to face rival factions within the kingdom and were prey to the ambitions of able ministers who on occasion used to imprison them and usurp the kingdom.

The Emperors sought to defend their Empire from such incidents by maintaining a permanent standing army consisting of an elephant corps, cavalry and infantry, made up of both Hindu and Muslim soldiers, who were paid their salaries every four months in cash, a system very modern for the age. Under the conditions of their vassalage, the feudal lords, commonly known as the Nayakas, were also supposed to maintain their own armies and to provide a specific number of soldiers, elephants, horses, and troops ready to join the imperial forces during time of war. The Emperor also had his own reserve force, which was often needed to bring his vassals and Nayakas to submission. As Nilakanta Sastri has said, Vijayangar was a "war-state ever made by a Hindu kingdom; and its political organisation was dominated by its military needs."[540]

The Emperor was considered as semi-divine,[541] the protector and saviour of the people through his army, the provider of the necessities of life and, through his Brahmins, of spiritual satisfaction. The Emperors had a council of ministers, headed mostly by the state Brahmin or *Raaj Pandit*, who was consulted whenever required on administrative or the military matters. It was the Emperor who took the final decisions, although, on religious matters, he usually deferred to his chief Brahmin. He could dismiss even the most powerful ministers and punish them if it suited to his interest. The minister, Saluva Timma, for example, was punished by Krishnadeva Raya (1503-1530) when he was suspected of being involved in the murder of the heir apparent.

Although the eldest son of the first queen was suppose to inherit the throne, frequently rival court factions had their own preferences for other princes which resulted in court conspiracies and sometimes in the death of the rightful heir to the throne, as happened in the case of Imadi Narsimha in 1505. Like other Hindu rulers, the Emperors of Vijayanagar, were first received in the temple with full religious ceremonial before they were presented to the court.

The state's main income was derived from land revenues and the tribute received from the feudatories and provincial governors. The Vijayanagar Emperors also gained a part of their income from the international trade of the local merchants, both Hindu and Muslim. There were other international traders such as Arabs and from the sixteenth century the Portuguese, who were followed by the Dutch and the English, all of whom contributed to the Empire's annual revenue both in cash and in kind.[542]

Although Vijayanagar was a Hindu Empire and many Hindu historians regard it as being hostile to Muslims and a rival to the Muslim states of South India, the Emperors were very tolerant and not only had close contacts with the neighbouring Muslim states, but had a substantial Muslim population in their kingdom all of whom enjoyed freedom of worship and many of whom were employed in civil and military service. It was this community that was principally involved in the commercial activities of the kingdom. As Sastri has written, "the Hindu-Muslim 'problem' was virtually unknown in the South".[543] On the other hand the struggle to extend the boundaries of their states continued between the Vijayanagar and the Bahmani Sultans, till the latter was annexed, in 1687, by the Mughal Emperor, Auranzeb.

A Map of South India C. XVI-XVII

Ref: Joan-Pau Rubiés, *Travel and Ethnology in the Renaissance*, p. 12)

As mentioned above, the Vijayanagar Empire had, out of necessity, to become a military state. It was divided into provinces, each ruled by a Nayaka or a governor who was supposed to have his own standing army to maintain peace and to protect the areas he governed. Some of these Nayakas were very ambitious and frequently revolted against their sovereign, but, until the battle of Talikota in 1565, all of these rebels Nayakas were crushed by the central military forces and either deposed or had their position substantially reduced both in the geographical areas they governed and the number of soldiers they maintained. However, when the Emperor of Vijayanagar faced the four allied Muslim rulers in 1565, the Emperor, Rama Raya himself, was killed and most of the northern and western parts of the Vijayanagar Empire were annexed by the Bijapur, Ahmadnagar and Golconda Sultans. Most of the Nayakas, who used to pay tribute to the Emperors of Vijayanagar, now became vassals of these Muslim states. Nevertheless, in the absence of the powerful centralising the force of the Vijayanagar Empire, several Nayakas established what were in effect autonomous states. Such was the case with the Nayakas of Ikkeri[544] and Tanjor. It was in the territory of the Nayakas of Ikkeri that the Portuguese had established some of their major strongholds, since they too had taken advantage of the chaotic political situation after the war of 1565.

The period between the war of Talikota and 1583, proved to be decisive for the future of the fragmented parts of the Vijayanagar Empire. There were constant wars between the Muslims rulers and the Hindu Nayakas to control the weaker parts of the Empire and it is during this period, in 1570-1571, that the Indian allied forces, once again tried to destroy Portuguese power on the western coast. Several treaties were signed in an attempt to define the limits of the political authority of the various powers. The constant wars waged by the Bijapuri Sultans against the Nayakas, so weakened their military forces that in 1580 there was a coup d'état and Sultan Ali Adil Shah was assassinated. The same year the Sultan had received the Mughal ambassador and subsequently, in 1595, Bijapur became tributary to the Mughal Empire.

After the death of Adil Shah, the new Sultan, a young boy of fourteen years ascended the throne, and there was a struggle for power between the powerful *Omerahs*.[545] The Nayaka of Ikkeri, Venkatappa Nayaka, challenged the authority of the Bijapuri Sultan. From the very beginning of his rule in Ikkeri in 1583,

Venkatappa Nayaka had revealed his intention of uniting the whole western and north-western areas of Kanara, most of which were in the hands of the Sultan of Bijapur. Therefore, a struggle for power started between the two states, which was prolonged for more than two decades. This struggle increased the power of the Venkatappa Nayaka but it weakened the Bijapuri Sultan, and paved the way for further Mughal expansion. The Portuguese watched this situation carefully and had kept their forces on high alert, as they knew that Venkatappa Nayaka was not merely fighting with the Sultan of Bijapur but had declared open war on all those who had any political, military or economic pretensions in the areas of Kanara that had formerly been part of the Vijayanagar Empire.

a) Initial Portuguese Contacts with the Vijayanagar Empire

Since their arrival in Malabar, the Portuguese had tried to establish diplomatic relations with the rulers of Vijayanagar with the aim of creating a united front against the Muslim merchants and rulers, a policy, which has already been mentioned. The new Emperor of Vijayanagar was aware of the naval power of the Portuguese, whose exploits were reported to him, most probably by the Franciscan friar, Luís de Salvador, who was in Vijayanagar for some time prior to 1505.[546] However, the initial diplomatic approach from the Emperor, Vira Narasimha, in the year 1505, did not have any positive results. The ambassador from Vijayanagar offered sites for the construction of fortresses, food supplies and various other benefits,[547] in return for Portuguese friendship and military support. The Portuguese Viceroy, though he received the ambassador courteously, did not reciprocate. He raised doubts about the legitimacy of the emperor, who had seized power following the death of his predecessor, Immadi Narasimha, in 1505,[548] and clearly trusted more on his military capabilities for the establishment of a commercial empire than on peaceful diplomatic relationships. The emperor, for his part, thought to make use of Portuguese military forces for the consolidation of his own rule against his enemies.[549] The embassy was a complete failure, since the Portuguese were not interested in committing themselves to supporting him in his imperialistic expansion nor did they themselves did require any help at this stage. In this way the Portuguese lost the opportunity of cementing a diplomatic relationship with a powerful neighbour.

Two years later the situation changed and Almeida required an alternative site in place of Anjediva for a fortress on the Kanara coast. Besides, his son, Dom Lourenço, had lost his life fighting against the Asian naval alliance at Chaul in January 1508.[550] It was now the Viceroy's turn to seek Narasimha's friendship. Accordingly, he sent an embassy under Pero Fernandes Tinoco and Friar Luís de Salvador to Vijayanagar in 1508, offering to conclude a treaty of friendship, similar to the one proposed by the emperor in 1505, in return for permission to erect a fortress in Bhatkal. The emperor received the embassy well, but merely talked to them in general terms about peace and friendship without committing himself to anything concrete.[551] By 1508 Narasimha had consolidated his position within his empire and, therefore, no longer needed Portuguese aid and friendship as badly as he had in 1505. He was not prepared to give up the valuable port of Bhatkal and the Portuguese ambassadors had to face the same treatment, which they had previously given to the ambassador of Vijayanagar. They returned empty handed.

Portuguese diplomatic relations with Vijayanagar did not have any major consequences for Portuguese maritime power on the western coasts of India as Vijayanagar did not have any pretensions to maritime activity of its own. Occasionally diplomats were sent to seek Portuguese help against their rivals and enemies and in return some favours were also provided to the Portuguese.

It was not until the time of the Talikota war in 1565 that the Portuguese felt the need to buy some of their pepper and rice supplies from the region of Kanara, instead of depending exclusively on Malabar and Goa.[552] The defeat of the Vijayanagar Empire in 1565 had the effect of accelerating Portuguese settlement in the region. Until 1565 the ruler of Vijayanagar had maintained a supreme position in the south, thus creating a political barrier against the expansion of the Bijapuri kingdom. However, after the war most of the territories of the Empire fell into the hands of the rulers of Bijapur and Ahmadnagar while various small princely states began to assert their independence, among them the state of Kanara under the Nayakas of Ikkeri. In 1568 the Portuguese took advantage of the chaotic situation to establish fortresses and factories at Onor, Mangalore and Barcelore.[553]

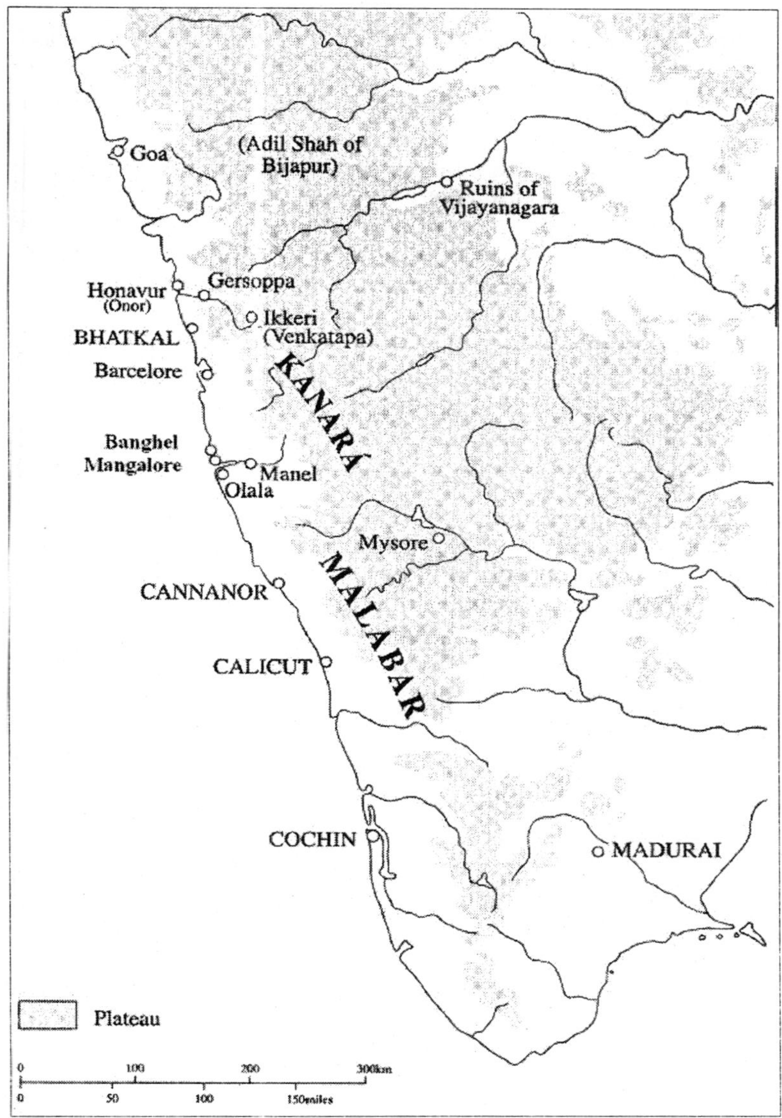

A Map of South-West India Showing States of Kanara/Ikkeri in the 17th Century

(Map adopted / Ref: Joan-Pau Rubiés, *Travel and Ethnology in the Renaissance,* p. 360)

Reference

[540] Nilakanta Sastri, *A History of South India ...*, p. 307; Joan-Pau Rubiés, *Travel and Ethnology in the Renaissance, 241-45;* Stein, *Vijayanagar*, 110.

[541] Joan-Pau Rubiés, *Travel and Ethnology in the Renaissance:* 241-242; Stein, *Vijayanagar*, pp. 23-26.

[542] For the commercial activities in the kingdom of the Vijayanagar ,Empire, one must consult the works of Sanjay *Improvising Empire:..; The Portuguese Empire in Asia,;* (edited) *Merchant Networks in the Early Modern World,;* Sanjay, *Political Economy...*, pp. 93-94; Jorge Flores, *Os portugueses e o mar de Ceilão...*

[543] Nilakanta Sastri, *A History of South India ...*, p. 309.

[544] Nayakas of Ikkeri are also known as Nayakas of Keladi, and as the rulers of Kanara from the second half of the sixteenth to the eighteenth centuries.

[545] The same as *Vezirs, Amirs* or ministers.

[546] Joan-Pau Rubiè, *Travel and Ethnology in the Renaissance...*, pp. 187-188.

[547] Castanheda, *História do descobrimento...*, Livro II, pp. 240-241.

[548] António da Silva Rego, *Documentação para a História das Missões ...*, vol. 1, pp. 33, 36.

[549] Nilakanta Sastri, *A History of South India*, p. 265.

[550] Albuquerque, *Crónica do descobrimento e conquista...*, pp. 323-339.

[551] Barros, *Da Ásia..., Décadas,* IIª, parte Iª, pp. 112-113.

[552] Simão Botelho, '*Tombo do Estado da Índia*', pp. 258-59; Disney, *Twilight of the Pepper..*, p. 35.

[553] HAG, Cod., *4460*, pp. 20-60; *BSGL, Res.* See Maço nº 8, *Livro de todas as receitas e despezas.*

Part II

Kanara under the Nayakas of Ikkeri: their Political and diplomatic System

a) Kanara Polity

From the beginning of his rise to power, Venkatappa Nayaka had proved to be an able soldier and a well-organised ruler. By some he was considered as a unifier and a just king, while others considered him a usurper - for instance, most of the small chiefs and Nayakas who dreamt of creating their independent states after the fall of Vijayanagar, as well as the Portuguese who did not welcome any powerful state near their fortresses or factories. Therefore, the rise of Venkatappa created a new critical political situation and disturbed the balance of power in the region. Under his sway, Ikkeri was to see unification of Kanara state.

Venkatappa Nayaka belonged to the *Lingayat* Sect.[554] The followers of this cult were devotees of Lord Shiva. In other words he too shared the same faith as the rulers of Vijayanagar. After the battle of Talikota and the defeat of the Emperor of the Vijayanara Empire, the Nayakas of Ikkeri continued to protect the interests of the Sringeri Temple. Sringeri flourished as a principal centre of education and as the propagator of Hindu religion and philosophy. In order to gain the sympathy of the principal Brahmins and the powerful communities of his kingdom, he wanted to show, as far as he could, that he followed the path of his ancestors. At the same time he kept religion separate from politics although he governed in accord with the advice of the Chief Brahmins of his court, observed all the religious ceremonies and religious traditions of his kingdom. As observed by many travellers of his period, Venkatappa Nayaka lived a simple life, very different from the luxurious life of the Mughal, Bijapuri or Persian courts.

Ikkeri, the capital from where the Keladi Nayakas ruled, is situated 76 kilometres to the north of the present Shimoga district and about 3 kilometres to the south of Sagar Taluk. The word Ikkeri means 'two streets'. The city was exquisitely planned with walls forming three concentric enclosures. The palace in the citadel was build of mud and timber and was adorned with carvings and false gilding. The stone temple of *Aghoreshvara* was the temple where most of the Nayakas were installed after the Venkatappa Nayaka had severed his relations with the weak Vijayanagar Emperor, sometime during the period 1605-1606, and had declared himself as *Dhokande Raya* and *Daneja*.[555]

Venkatappa Nayaka, like the Emperors of Vijayanagar, followed the policy of employing the Brahmins of his court and territories on diplomatic missions. Although, frequently, some powerful business magnates were also sent to negotiate terms of peace between his states and the Portuguese or the Sultan of Bijapur, they mostly belonged to the Sinai families, or to highly influential Brahmin families. Since they were known and respected by the Portuguese and by the Bijapuris, it was easy for the Nayakas to retain their diplomatic services even when one Nayaka died and another had taken the charge of the kingdom. Pietro Della Valle, the Italian traveller, was quite critical of the Venkatappa Nayaka and his increasing power and did not regard him as a legitimate king at all. Moreover, in his account, Della Valle simply ignored the military ascendancy of the Nayaka over the Portuguese who were no longer able to face him in the open field. According to him it was the Portuguese who had become weaker and it had nothing to do with the power of Nayaka. Della Valle also ignored the fact that the Nayaka had defied the Sultan of Bijapur in more than half a dozen battles and survived. Although he was a vassal of Bijapur he continually ignored the payment of annual tribute. Nevertheless, this was only possible because the Sultans of Bijapur became involved in a series of wars, which prevented them from absorbing the whole of Kanara. Therefore, the critical reflections of Della Valle must be attributed to his lack of a broader vision in this matter.

b) Diplomatic Etiquettes at the Court of the Nayakas of Ikkeri

Details of the etiquette of the court of the Nayakas of Ikkeri have been obtained from the direct testimony of Pietro Della Valle, who accompanied the Portuguese ambassador to the court of Venkatappa Nayaka in 1623. According to Della Valle's description of the Venkatappa Nayaka's citadel and the court, where the Nayaka received the Portuguese ambassador, it was decorated with exquisite but simple items, in comparison to the Mughal and the Bijapur courts.[556] Della Valle is very critical of the person of the Venkatappa Nayaka who, according to him, 'was little more than a usurper of the territory of the Vijayanagar Empire of which he used to be a vassal'.[557] He describes in minute detail how the Nayaka received the Portuguese ambassador who was also accompanied by a Jesuit father, Monteiro. One thing, which comes out very clearly from the meeting between the ambassador and the Nayaka, was the manner in which the credential ceremonies took place. The ambassador while giving the letter into the hands of the Nayaka first knelt before him and then put the letter in his hands without lifting his head. The Nayaka, without saying a word, gave that letter to Vitula Sinai who, in turn, gave it to the secretary of the court to read. However, Della Valle does not say if the letter was read before the court. Soon after the letter was given, the presents were displayed before the Nayaka. According to him, on the day that the credential ceremonies were performed, no other discussion usually took place. Normally, another audience was fixed to discuss the real business for which the embassy had come.[558] Ambassadors saluting a Hindu ruler of Southern India did not bow three times, as they did in the Bijapuri and the Mughal courts. Instead, they sat on the ground, which was lavishly covered with carpets, and there bowed the head. In the same position they placed the letter into the hands of the ruler without looking into his eyes. However, all ambassadors who visited the Bijapuri or the Mughal courts, whether they were from a Muslim or a Hindu kingdom followed the system of the court to which they were accredited and not the practice to which they were accustomed at home.

Pietro Della Valle's description of Venkatappa Nayaka was contemptuous of a man who was the ruler of a large kingdom, which he had succeeded in uniting. The Portuguese were careful enough not to come into conflict with him openly and immediately tried to establish friendly relations through embassies to his court. Pietro Della Valle forgot that he was in a palace different from any that he had seen in other countries in Europe or Asia. Venkatappa Nayaka tried to show that he was ruler of people and followed a very simple and old Hindu style of kingship. The sending of an embassy by the Portuguese and regular communication through the exchange of presents, were clear enough indications that the Portuguese accepted the sovereignty of the Venkatappa Nayaka of Ikkeri, even though they might not welcome it wholeheartedly.

c) The rise of Venkatappa Nayaka of Ikkeri

The early Portuguese governors had had a very clear vision of the need for diplomatic relationships with the non-Muslim states in India, but solely so that they could exploit the tense relationship between the various powers for their own benefit. Unfortunately, the Indian rulers were so ambitious and divided, on religious as well as territorial grounds, that at times they could not distinguish between their friends and their foes, and in this way they facilitated the intervention of a third state which wanted to exploit them to the maximum extent possible. The ambition for power of the Indian states constantly grew and they welcomed any support from whatever quarter it came as long as it served their purposes. It was not very difficult for the Portuguese to understand this, and they exploited such divisions with alacrity,[559] a situation, which has been brought into sharp focus in the writings of B. S. Shastry.[560] However, Portuguese policy in this region did not have the same success as it did in Malabar.

Although, some mention has already been made about Portuguese diplomatic relations with the Kanara states in the sixteenth century, in reality these begin in earnest with the rise of Venkatappa Nayaka as a paramount power, early in the seventeenth century. During the sixteenth century none of the Nayakas of that region, who were still under the sovereignty of the rulers of Vijayanagar, thought it necessary either to defend themselves against the Portuguese or to press their overlords for the protection of themselves and their commerce. It was the Venkatappa Nayaka and his successors, Veerabhadra and Shivappa Nayakas, who sought to make the Portuguese accept their terms, as they knew that the Portuguese were dependant on Kanara for rice and other necessary foodstuffs as well as pepper and saltpetre. With the rise of Venkatappa Nayaka, there started a trend toward equality in diplomacy between the state of Kanara (or Ikkeri) and the Portuguese, which ended when the Portuguese gave up trying to obtain terms from the Nayakas and lost all of their commercial and military settlements in that region, towards the end of the sixth decade of the seventeenth century.

The local princes and chiefs tried to protect their rights, but for the most part they were too weak to face Venkatappa Nayaka. Instead, they waited for the right opportunity to retaliate. The Portuguese hesitated to intervene in Kanara politics and tried to remain neutral even though they had several requests for aid from the weaker kings in this region. The only ruler to whom they offered outright support was the King of Banghel.[561] As a consequence of the unification of Kanara by Venkatappa, all the Portuguese

ESTAMPA XXXI *Ref. António Bocarro, O Livro das Fortalezas*

Fortaleza de Mangalor

Portuguese Fortress of Mangalore *facing page* 208

fortresses and ports in the region, including of Onor, Barcelore, Mangalore and Cambolim fell within his jurisdiction, or at least that is what he claimed. Although the Portuguese relations with Venkatappa suffered some set backs, Portuguese diplomacy meant that the fortresses remained in Portuguese hands for another half a century.

As a result of their early contacts, the Portuguese forced the states of Kanara to accept Portugal's exclusive right to buy pepper, and to refuse to sell to anyone but to them. By these treaties no Muslim merchant was allowed to buy any pepper while the Portuguese undertook to purchase 500 *Khandis* of pepper,[562] in particular from the ruler of Gersoppa, in whose territory the Portuguese port-town of Onor was situated. In the treaty of 1574, the price fixed was 25 *Pagodas* per *Khandi.*[563] All the sea-going ships were to adhere to the *Cartaz* system, on pain of facing the same fate as the ships belonging to the other states in the Indian Ocean region. Although the Portuguese imposed *Cartazes* on the sea-going ships and maintained their exclusive right to buy pepper, which one could see that it was a very limited amount, (never exceeded more than 500 Khandis), they did not indicate how the rest of the pepper produced in this region was to be sold and to whom. Therefore, in the lack of any proper orientation, the local merchants sold pepper to whom pleased to, and this was not agreeable to the Portuguese. This situation witnessed a complete change after the death of Venkatappa Nayaka, in 1629 when the Portuguese had to accept the terms from his successors who also determined how much pepper to be bought at what price in exchange for other supplies. It was a chaotic situation.

However, even though the contracts were signed between the Portuguese authorities and the merchants and rulers of Kanara, it is very unclear whether those contracts, initially established with the ruler of Gersoppa, were supposed to apply to the whole region of Kanara that included Barcelore and Mangalore or whether they had to buy the same quantity from each region? Nevertheless, when the Venkatappa Nayaka, through his expansionist wars, merged the whole region of Kanara into his own kingdom, the Portuguese found themselves under pressure and, so that they could continue to buy rice, agreed to the purchase of 1000 *Khandis* of pepper.[564]

In the late sixteenth century the price of pepper fixed with the ruler of Gersoppa had been 25 *Pagodas* per *Khandi*. In 1612 it had reached 28-29 *Pagodas* per *Khandi*[565] and during the time of the

Conde de Linhares, in 1629, when the Veerabhadra Nayaka proposed a price of 28 *Pagodas* and the condition to buy 500 *Khandis* of pepper, the Portuguese were extremely reluctant to agree. On the other hand, the pretender to the throne, Virappa Nayaka agreed to a much lower price. In the treaty of 1633, Veerabhadra Nayaka had at first accepted 22 *Pagodas* a *Khandi*, but soon raised this to 29 *Pagodas* and insisted that the Portuguese should buy 500 *Khandis* instead of 350 or else the supply of rice would be stopped. However, during this period, the prices changed according to the circumstances and not according to what had been agreed by the Kanara rulers and merchants, a policy that had for long been practised by the Portuguese. Above all, in whatever situation they were, the Portuguese insisted on the rulers of Kanara obtaining *Cartazes* for their ships, even for those which belonged to the King himself. These rulers, for the most part, complied with these demands to avoid conflict at sea and to enjoy the protection that the Portuguese promised in return. However, there were times when, even if they carried a *Cartazes*, the ships were confiscated without any proper justification which eventually lead to armed conflicts and reprisal from both the sides.

Venkatappa Nayaka had started his military adventures around 1583, when he openly opposed the Bijapuri authorities. The political situation of the Nayakas of Kanara was in a state of confusion. Both the Sultan Adil Shah and the Sri Ranga of Vijayanagar, although his state was in decline, disputed the sovereign rights over the Kanara region.[566] The early successes of the Venkatappa Nayaka could mostly be attributed to good luck as some misfortune always overtook the Sultan of Bijapur whenever he invaded the Kanara territories.[567] In 1583 the generals of the Bijapur army created some internal disputes and Venkatappa Nayaka was saved. In 1593, when Manjum Khan, the general of the Bijapur army, invaded the Kanara region to collect arrears of tribute, prince Ismail, brother of Ibrahim Adil Shah II, revolted and the whole campaign had to be called off.[568] After this the northern kingdom became more disorganised and divided which left Venkatappa free to increase his power and widen his ambitions. Although the Bijapuri army frequently invaded the Kanara region, sometimes to collect arrears of tribute and sometimes to remind the Nayaka who his sovereign was, the rulers of Vijayanagar remained indifferent and did not render any assistance as they were also aware of the ambitions of the Venkatappa Nayaka.[569] Moreover, the general situation in India favoured Venkatappa. He knew that

Akbar, the Mughal Emperor, was putting extreme pressure on the Bijapuri kingdom to accept his sovereignty, while the alliance, which the Adil Shah was seeking with the Vijayanagar ruler, was proving to be a failure.[570] This made Venkatappa even bolder and he started to act as though he was independent.

Between 1602 and 1607 he conquered many of the weaker states in the Kanara region, which owed allegiance either to the Sultan or to the ruler of Vijayanagar.[571] These early successes led Venkatappa Nayaka to attack the territory of Gersoppa, which belonged, at that time, to Adil Shah. In 1604 Queen Chenna Bhaira Dêvi, the ruler of Gersoppa, was forced by some internal dispute to ask for the help of Venkatappa Nayaka.[572] He was only too glad to assist but, after the internal dispute was over, he did not restore Chenna Barairava Dévi to her throne, but imprisoned her and took her to Kanara. Later, he installed a queen of his choice, Ira Devi Lakshmi Devi, on the throne.[573] Naturally, this created general dissatisfaction among the ruling classes as control of Gersoppa was disputed by the neighbouring states, including the Bijapuri Sultan, as mentioned above. The Portuguese did not intervene directly in this affair at that time.

Within a period of six years Venkatappa Nayaka had risen from being merely an insignificant chief to the position of a ruler of various small kingdoms, which included the district of Shimoga, South Kanara and parts of Kadur and North Kanara.[574] As soon as Adil Shah was free from Mughal pressure, he turned his attention towards the south. The aggression by Venkatappa Nayaka on the kingdom of Gersoppa, which was part of his dominions, was not going to go unpunished. In 1606 he sent his forces towards Gersoppa but the Venkatappa Nayaka was once again victorious, as the Bijapuri army had to return north to face another Mughal incursion. Gersoppa was not retaken and the Sultan was forced to accept a peace treaty. After this the Venkatappa Nayaka assumed the titles of *Dhokande Raya* and *Daneja*. Later, between 1615 and 1618 Venkatappa Nayaka incorporated almost all South Kanara's princely states into his kingdom.[575]

The initial Portuguese response to the expansionist wars of the Venkatappa Nayaka was very cautious as they knew that any small mistake could lead them to an open war with him and would create dangers for their own possessions, which were very vulnerable.[576] Therefore, special instructions were given to the captains of the forts to be on friendly terms with the neighbouring state.[577]

However, it is obvious that their policy was secretly to help the threatened princes, as they knew this would keep the Venkatappa Nayaka busy and at the same time weaken his position.[578]

Nevertheless, the Portuguese policy of remaining a neutral spectator of the Venkatappa Nayaka's expansion did not last long, as the Nayaka invaded the lands of Portugal's ally, the King of Banghel in 1618.[579] The principal reason behind the conflict between the King of Banghel and Venkatappa Nayaka appears to have been that the former did not pay the tribute and the elephants, which he owed to the Venkatappa Nayaka as his vassal. Making use of this conflict to check the rising power of Venkatappa Nayaka, the Portuguese started helping the King of Banghel with arms and ammunition, soldiers and artillery.[580] In the mean time, they also asked the King of Cannanore to help with soldiers. This Portuguese intervention infuriated the Nayaka and soon after he attacked Mangalore.

The war was already in progress in the land of Mangalore, when Dom Francisco de Miranda Henriques, the captain of Mangalore, added fuel to the fire by capturing a richly laden ship belonging to the queen of Olala who was in alliance with the Venkatappa Nayaka.[581] This incident brought the queen into the war in alliance with the Nayaka's forces. Together they laid siege to the fort of Banghel[582] and burned the town, thus weakening the Portuguese position. Venkatappa Nayaka now got more daring and without warning fell upon Luís de Brito de Melo, who was carrying relief to Dom Francisco de Miranda Henriques, and inflicted heavy losses, killing both of the commanders.[583]

The situation now became so serious that the Portuguese *Conselho do Estado* decided to put an end to this problem by handing over the fortress of the Banghel King, at that time under Portuguese protection, to the Venkatappa Nayaka through his emissary, Putappa, so that the Portuguese could concentrate on defending the fort of Mangalore.[584] A copy of the letter[585] that Putappa wrote to the Portuguese Viceroy, very clearly exposes the intentions of the Venkatappa Nayaka. According to this letter, Venkatappa Nayaka made it clear that the Portuguese had to give up interfering in the relations between him and the King of Banghel or else the friendly relations between the two states would come to an end. In fact, this emissary of Venkatappa Nayaka, in a very polite way, carried a message that if the Portuguese did not accept the conditions offered by the Nayaka, namely to withdraw all military support to Banghel, there would be war.[586] Putappa, on the other hand, knew that the Portuguese would not accept any conditions imposed by the Venkatappa Nayaka.

Through their support to the King of Banghel, the Portuguese wanted to keep the Venkatappa Nayaka at war and to exhaust his resources so that he could not threaten the Portuguese in any of their dependencies in the Kanara region, which seemed to be one of the Nayaka's plans.[587] However, the King of Banghel, weakened by the fighting, was more inclined to accept the terms offered by the Nayaka than to continue with the war. In response to the overbearing demands of the Nayaka, the Portuguese Viceroy, through the *Conselho do Estado*, wrote a letter to Venkatappa Nayaka suggesting that he should leave the King of Banghel in possession of his territory and his forts so that he could improve his financial situation.[588] Portuguese support to the King of Banghel appeared to have been insufficient to enable him to face the Nayaka of Kanara, and the whole strategy of weakening the Nayaka proved to be unsuccessful.

At this juncture, the King of Banghel wrote to the Portuguese Viceroy that he would accept whatever decision João Fernandes Leitão, *capitão-mor* of the Kanara region, would take in handing over the fort of Banghel to Venkatappa Nayaka.[589] Through a letter written by João Fernandes to the Viceroy from Onor,[590] it is quite evident that even the captains of the forts at Onor and Barcelore were anxious to reach a peaceful solution to the conflict with the Nayaka. He mentioned that Gaspar de Mello Sampaio, the captain in charge of the Banghel diplomatic mission, who was residing at Mangalore, needed ships to be sent as soon as possible, so that he could evacuate the place immediately because the more "we delay the more powerful the Nayaka will become". The negotiations had been going on for sometime and the situation had become uncontrollable. Furthermore, irritated by the reluctance of the Banghel King to continue the war, he even made use of very indiscreet language, writing "I would take steps to see that the negotiation is at last brought to an end, since I depend on the uncertain whims of this Negro, the so called Banghel who has decided never to speak the truth".[591]

Through this correspondence, it is evident that the Portuguese officers had no respect for the ruler with whom they had to maintain diplomatic and friendly relations, but it also shows how desperate and impatient the Portuguese authorities were during this period when, according to a letter that João Fernandes, the captain of the fortress, wrote to the viceroy, everything, from food to ammunition, was scarce.[592]

At the same time, Gaspar de Melo de Sampayo wrote from Mangalore reminding the Viceroy of the hardship that he and his companions were suffering in the fort because of the lack of food, which had not yet arrived, while the slow diplomacy took place between the Portuguese and the Nayaka of Kanara. He also pointed out that he owed more than 2,500 *Pardaos* to the local financiers, part of which he had spent in constructing a factory for producing gunpowder after demolishing a Pagoda.[593] The rest of the money he had spent on constructing a hospital where almost thirteen persons worked for the treatment of the patients. Besides, he had also spent some money on the maintenance of the fort, taking a part of it as a loan from the *casados*.[594]

Eventually, the situation reached the point where the King of Banghel thought that it would be much better to make peace with the Venkatappa Nayaka and accept his terms rather than to continue to fight with the limited support of the Portuguese,[595] whose only interest was to see war continue at whatever cost to him and his people. It should be noted that, in his reply, João Fernandes had suggested that the Portuguese would be better off being allies of the queen of Olala, as the King of Banghel had backed off from the Portuguese alliance and wanted to be friendly with the Venkatappa Nayaka. The Portuguese authorities at Goa, on the other hand, in order to ease the tension, wanted to give an impression to the Venkatappa Nayaka, through their ambassador, that they were merely trying to help their friend, the Banghel King, and their intention was never to wage war on the Nayaka.[596] The Portuguese did not want any more fighting because such "inconsistency in the behaviour of tne Indian rulers" cost them a lot, João Fernandes further added. Under such circumstances, he was ordered by the Viceroy to conclude a peace treaty between the King of Banghel and Venkatappa Nayaka soon,[597] as the political scene was changing rapidly. It was at this time that the Zamorin invaded Cranganore and peace talks were also in progress between him and the Portuguese.[598]

The Viceroy asked for the details of the proceedings, and Venkatappa Nayaka, as is obvious from the clauses of the treaty, did not lose the opportunity of making it clear that all the conditions had to be observed or else further war was unavoidable.[599]

The pressure was so great that the Portuguese officials had to accept the conditions proposed as they still had their fortresses of Onor and Barcelore in his territory and they wanted to maintain peace for fear of losing them as well as their trading posts in that region. It is clear that the Portuguese had lost numerous good men and a substantial amount of wealth during the conflict over Mangalore. Moreover, as Venkatappa had promised to support the King of Banghel and to honour the treaty of perpetual friendship,[600] peace was the best choice, especially since the provision of rice, and saltpetre for the manufacture of gunpowder, both of which were obtained from Kanara, were vitally necessary for the defence of Muscat now that the Shah of Persia, with the help of the English,[601] had started a war against the Portuguese in the Gulf region. Besides this, the Portuguese had other fortresses and towns which were constantly threatened by the Dutch and the English. All these factors explain why the Portuguese were forced to make peace and to persuade the King of Banghel to accept unfavourable terms from Venkatappa Nayaka and his ally, the queen of Olala.[602]

Among various conditions, Venkatappa Nayaka proposed in his letter to João Fernandez Leitão that the King of Banghel must destroy his fortress of Coddial and give him a special elephant, named Padmnabha. He emphasised that the ancestors of the King of Banghel had always been loyal to the service of Ikkeri. In return for his obedience, Venkatappa Nayaka promised to give the ruler of Banghel the villages of Nandavar, Sazapa, Turolguana Madaga, Belur and their adjacent lands, which would yield him a rent of 4275 *Pagodas*. Besides, in order to compensate him and to meet his expenses, the Nayaka promised him other rights, which would provide him with a total income of 7000 *Pagodas*.[603] Venkatappa also promised to destroy all the trenches he had constructed around Coddial along with the fortresses of Nandavar and Uparangui. However, he also made it clear in his letter to João Fernandes Leitão that if the King of Banghel did not accept all his conditions, there would be no further negotiastions. The Nayaka also wrote that the *capitão-mor* and the soldiers garrisoning Coddial might evacuate the fortress, which would help to maintain peace between the two powers.

The ambassador of the Banghel King at the court of Venkatappa Nayaka, Issar Sinai, Brahmin, also wrote a letter to João Fernandes Leitão[604] in which he said that, although he knew that his King was quite confident of the military support he would receive from the Portuguese Viceroy, João Fernandes Leitão should accept the conditions proposed by Venkatappa Nayaka, and further added that Gaspar de Mello might hand over the keys of the fortress to the King Banghel and take away all the artillery and men. The ambassador reminded João Fernandes Leitão that, in order to maintain peace between the kingdom of Ikkeri and the Portuguese, it would be better that the Portuguese would not become involved in any war, especially since they had fortresses at Onor and Barcelore from where most of their foodstuffs, especially rice, were obtained and sent to the fortresses of Hormuz and Muscat. He asked whether João Fernandes knew that, should he refuse to accept the proposal of the Nayaka, he, the King of Banghel, would be deprived of his land and all the properties he still owned. He suggested that, between the Portuguese and his King, peace would be the best solution in order to avoid further bloodshed.[605] Certainly, the ambassador of the Banghel King was under the influence of, and was being intimidated by, the court of Venkatappa Nayaka. In fact, during these negotiations a great shortage of rice had already been experienced as the men of Venkatappa Nayaka had started intercepting its flow to the regions of Mangalore and Barcelore.

After another couple of years of correspondence and after various efforts had been made to put an end to the prolonged hostilities between the two states, a peace mission was finally sent to the Venkatappa Nayaka in 1623. The conditions, proposed earlier by the Venkatappa Nayaka, were not agreeable to the Portuguese,[606] who still tried to maintain a show of power and were not prepared to accept the reality of their position.[607] However, the situation had now deteriorated to such an extent that it was considered wise to reach a permanent peaceful solution. Pietro della Valle, the Italian traveller who accompanied the embassy,[608] remarked on the growing weakness of the position of the Portuguese in India during this period. He had roundly criticised the Rani of Olala, when he met her while on the road, and described her as "rather a dirty kitchen wench, or laundress, than a delicate and noble queen".[609] This comment has been variously used by historians writing about the seventeenth century, as showing that the so called "Lord of the Seas", the Portuguese - were losing military supremacy and were in no condition to dictate any terms in this region of Kanara even to the insignificant queen of Olala, let alone her ally, Venkatappa. On the other hand, this comment of Della Valle has been sharply criticised by recent historians who have taken exception to his arrogance and lack of understanding in judging the Queen's political and military power by the simplicity of her demeanour.[610]

After this treaty had been signed, although Venkatappa Nayaka was not as true to his words as was expected, especially with regard to the payment of 7000 *Pagodas* to the King of Banghel,[611] he did abide by the promises he made in relation to the Portuguese fortresses of Onor, Barcelore and Mangalore. The Portuguese too did not interfere in the politics of Kanara any further. During the rest of his life, between 1623 and 1629, the relations between the Portuguese and Venkatappa remained peaceful.

d) Portuguese-Kanara Diplomacy - 1629-1635

Venkatappa Nayaka died on 10 November 1629, and civil war broke out between his grandson, Veerabhadra Nayaka and his brother, Virappa Nayaka. Virappa Nayaka had been imprisoned by Venkatappa Nayaka during his lifetime, and he was liberated after his death. After a couple of years of fighting between these two claimants for the kingdom of Kanara, Veerabhadra Nayaka successfully occupied the throne. During this period of turmoil several factions struggled for supremacy: one party, made up of the powerful small kingdoms which had been favourable to the Venkatappa Nayaka, supported Veerabhadra Nayaka, the other, made up of the princes of the annexed states, supported Virappa Nayaka, who was also secretly backed by the Portuguese. These princes were also supported by the Sultan of Bijapur.[612] The Portuguese acted cautiously and carefully during this 'war of succession' by secretly helping the cause of Virappa Nayaka, while at the same time trying to maintain cordial relations with Veerabhadra Nayaka. Later, however, after the death of Virappa Nayaka in 1631, the Portuguese started helping the Veerabhadra Nayaka, the man they had previously considered a usurper, as they did not want the Sultan of Bijapur, along with the dissatisfied chiefs and rulers, to become powerful in the region. One should not forget that during this time the Adil Shah of Bijapur still claimed sovereignty over more than half of Kanara, including the ruler of Ikkeri himself, who at times recognised his allegiance to him. As a result, the Portuguese provided support to Veerabhadra Nayaka secretly, as they did not want to offend the Sultan of Bijapur.

e) Portuguese Diplomacy during the viceroyalty of the Conde de Linhares

The arrival of Dom Miguel de Noronha, the Conde de Linhares, as Viceroy in 1629, coincided with the death of Venkatappa Nayaka, and both pieces of news were received with great pleasure in Goa; the arrival of the Conde de Linhares brought some hope for a revival of Portuguese fortunes, whereas the death of Venkatappa Nayaka, who during discussions in the *Concelho do Estado* at Goa was referred to as the "tyrant and enemy", relieved the pressure on the Portuguese in Kanara.[613]

On his arrival, the Conde de Linhares had found the *Estado da Índia* to be in a very weak condition and he developed a number of plans to restore its past glory. In Kanara, as in other areas, the fortresses and the areas adjacent to them, where the Portuguese used to hold effective sway, were in a very decadent state. In order to put into operation his project to strengthen the Portuguese occupied areas, it was decided during the meeting of the *Conselho do Estado* on 22 November 1629, that Francisco de Sousa Falcão would be sent as captain to the fortress of Onor with thirty soldiers, Miguel de Sousa Falcão, his brother, as captain with fifty soldiers to the fortress of Barcelore and António de Brito Pacheco as captain of another thirty soldiers to Mangalore. All of them were placed under Diogo de Sousa de Meneses, *capitão-mor* of Kanara.[614]

No sooner was the news of Venkatappa's death brought to Goa, through a letter of Francisco de Sousa Alcaforado, captain of the fort of Onor,[615] than the Viceroy called a meeting of the *Conselho do Estado* to decide what further steps should be taken in Portugal's relations with the Kanara states. The death of the Venkatappa Nayaka had led to revolt throughout his kingdom, as mentioned above, by the chiefs whose territories had either been annexed to his empire or been made feudatory. However, the biggest problem for the Veerabhadra Nayaka, who had been nominated heir to the throne by Venkatappa Nayaka, was Virappa Nayaka, Venkatappa's elder brother, who also claimed to be rightful heir, thus launching a civil war. Most of the chiefs who had been deprived of their land by Venkatappa Nayaka, joined the banner of Virappa Nayaka to recover their dominions and Veerabhadra Nayaka was under pressure from all sides and was attacked by several neighbouring princely states,[616] especially a group lead by Vira Odeyar, a brother-in-law of Veerabhadra Nayaka, and the chiefs of Sode and Biligi who in turn also sought help from the

Adil Shah of Bijapur.[617] Seeing no other way, Veerabhadra was obliged to send an embassy to the Sultan of Bijapur asking help against his enemies. Adil Shah accepted his proposal but suggested that he should return the territories conquered by his grandfather to their rightful owners.[618] In fact the Sultan of Bijapur, in his own way did not wish that any peace should reign in that region as he himself wanted to subdue most of the vassals, which had been subdued by the Venkatappa Nayaka. This he proceeded to do in 1638,[619] soon after he had rid himself of the problem of the Mughals in 1635-36.[620] However, although Veerabhadra Nayaka was in a very weak position, he still had sufficient power to face most of his rivals.

The Sultan of Bijapur, the moment he knew about the death of Venkatappa Nayaka, sent his ambassador, Mir Zaman, to the principal claimant of the throne, Veerabhadra Nayaka, to demand all the arrears of tribute that his grandfather owed him, amounting to nine million gold *mohurs,* five elephants, two hundred Arabian horses and 80,000 *Pagodas*.[621] The Sultan further insisted that all the lands and kingdoms that Venkatappa Nayaka had captured should be returned to their rightful owners,[622] as has been mentioned earlier. To this Veerabhadra Nayaka replied that he would pay three hundred thousand *Pagodas,* but only if the Sultan promised to help him against all those who had turned rebel. This was intended as a clear sign that he was ready for a war against the Sultan of Bijapur, and the ambassador, Mir Zaman, left his court very unhappy.

The political situation in Kanara now became completely chaotic and the Portuguese authorities, in order to protect their fortresses, proposed to strengthen the walls and the surrounding defences in case of opportunistic attacks by ambitious rulers who might try to take advantage of the confusion. As if this whole situation was not enough, the *Estado da Índia* had to face severe problems caused by the famine, which affected all of India from the north to south.[623] The Portuguese areas of Daman, Diu and Bassein were severely affected and this forced the Portuguese authorities, once more, to reconsider their position in the territories of Kanara.

The Portuguese Viceroy, the Conde de Linhares, who had already announced that he would provide military support to all those who wanted to help the Portuguese government in Asia,[624] proposed in a letter to the King of Portugal that this was the right time to attack and occupy one of the islands near Onor, which produced very good quality timber for shipbuilding and provided an income of over six thousand *Pagodas*.[625] He further added that, although the Portuguese had earlier tried to occupy this territory, it was a difficult enterprise and Venkatappa Nayaka had not permitted the Portuguese to cut down any tree for shipbuilding. The Viceroy also suggested that he intended to reinforce all the forts on the Kanara coast with strong and well-trained soldiers as well as, secretly, providing military support to all the kings, queens and landowners who had been made to surrender their territories to the Venkatappa Nayaka, especially to the King of Banghel whom he referred to as a "*grande amigo do Estado da Índia Portuguesa*". Linhares wanted to make a contract with the King of Barcelore by which he would surrender the island of Cambolim and the island of Onor to the Portuguese from where the Viceroy intended to get most of the timber for shipbuilding and rice to supply the other Portuguese dominions in Asia. He further added that "he promised to help the king of Coltar by attacking Virabhadra Nayaka in return for a certain quantity of pepper annually to be given to them".[626]

This letter of the Viceroy gives a very clear indication that he intended to continue with the policy of dual diplomacy, like other Portuguese viceroys, in the hope that he might find the right opportunity to strengthen the Portuguese position in the area.[627] However, it must be understood that the Portuguese authorities wanted to help all those dissatisfied chiefs only to weaken the position of Veerabhadra Nayaka as well as the Sultan of Bijapur and not because they were sympathetic to them. If this had been the case they would have provided some firm support when this was really required.

It is interesting to note that, while Conde de Linhares was planning to make contact with all the princes and dissatisfied factions of the Kanara region who might be looking for Portuguese support, by giving them presents and providing them with military aid, he was at the same time very concerned that none of their lands should fall into the hands of the Bijapuri Sultan. This difficult diplomatic task was entrusted to the captains of the fortresses. He also inquired what right the Bijapuri Sultan had to capture or recover the lands that had been conquered by the Venkatappa Nayaka, and he tried to investigate which would be the best party to be helped and what benefit the Portuguese might derive from this help.[628]

ESTAMPA XXX *Ref. António Bocarro. O Livro das Fortalezas* *Fortaleza de Barcelor*

Portuguese Fortress of Barcelore *facing page* 220

f) The Question of the Fortress of Cambolim

In 1629 the Conde de Linhares, in order to strengthen his position at Barcelore, constructed a new fortress at Cambolim,[629] for which a proposal had already been under study ever since 1621. It was named as *Fortaleza de São Miguel de Cambolim*.[630] Initially, it was intended that, after the fortress was constructed, the Portuguese would shift their residential and commercial activities to this place from Barcelore. Cambolim was indeed one of the most strategically located forts in the region and had many advantages over Barcelore as well as possessing a better water supply. It was favourably situated for controlling both the adjacent paddy lands and the arrival and departure of any sea-going ship.[631] However, the trouble was that the King of Banghel had kept the Portuguese quite busy and the Venkatappa Nayaka was not in a mood to allow such a development. For reasons that are not clear, the fortress at Cambolim had not been constructed but, now that the Venkatappa Nayaka had died and left two contestants for the throne, the right opportunity had arrived to put the plan into operation.[632]

Veerabhadra Nayaka naturally considered this fortress a threat to the harmonious relations between his state and the Portuguese. Linhares had originally intended to transfer the factory of Barcelore to the new site[633] according to the initial plan but, in the event, both places remained as a challenge to the authority of the rulers of Kanara until 1653-54, when Barcelore was surrendered to the Shivappa Nayaka, and the Cambolim fort was abandoned, after which there was never any opportunity for the Portuguese to reoccupy it.

On 6 January 1630[634] the Viceroy received a letter from Diogo de Sousa de Meneses, the *capitão-mor* of the Kanara region, who was in Barcelore, reporting that Veerabhadra Nayaka, in retaliation for the construction of the fortress at Cambolim, had strictly prohibited the supply of rice from the region of *Barcelor de Cima*. Diogo de Sousa de Meneses was notified about this change by Vitula Sinai,[635] ambassador of Veerabhadra Nayaka, who had been to Barcelore to regularise the contract of pepper with the Portuguese authorities. This prohibition came at a time when there was a great shortage of rice for consumption in that fort as well as the fort of Muscat.[636] To make the situation worse, Veerabhadra Nayaka's men had intercepted all the presents and the embassies that the Viceroy had sent to the rebel kings. There was now an imminent threat of war.

In May 1631 Portuguese-Kanara relations became even more complicated when Virappa Nayaka donated the land of Cambolim to the Portuguese in exchange for their help.[637] This donation strengthened the Portuguese position in Kanara[638] but it did not provide a permanent peaceful solution as Veerabhadra Nayaka, who was in reality exercising power in the kingdom, did not accept this donation as legal. Soon after the donation had been made, the Portuguese Viceroy appointed Diogo de Sousa de Meneses to take charge of all the Kanara forts with the assistance of Manuel da Câmara de Noronha and Claveiro Francisco da Silveira and their armadas. Immediately after taking up his command Sousa de Meneses fortified the area of Cambolim with trenches, at the same time starting to dig a canal to provide communications between the river and the sea. A lot of help was also sent for the fortifications and other necessary works.[639]

The Conde de Linhares, after rebuilding the Portuguese navy in 1631, commenced a series of military demonstrations, which took the form of expeditions to the kingdoms of the South to impose terms on all those who were avoiding the authority of the Portuguese on the western coast of India. In his relations with Kanara, the Viceroy played a double game.

Unlike Veerabhadra Nayaka, Virappa Nayaka was more favourable disposed towards the deposed princes who had been deprived of their rights during the reign of his brother, Venkatappa Nayaka, and wanted to restore them to their respective places. In order to fight his nephew and bring order to his domain, he sought Portuguese help through diplomatic channels. The revolt against Veerabhadra Nayaka for the most part involved all those who had been deprived of their kingdoms. These people considered Virappa Nayaka as the rightful heir to the throne.[640] At any rate this is how it appeared to the Portuguese. The Portuguese favoured Virappa Nayaka mainly because, as the Viceroy wrote to the King, "he was a man of principle and the rightful heir and, above all, because he kept open all the channels of food supplies, which used to come from the interior of Barcelore to the Portuguese settlements. He provided the Portuguese with more help than they could expect from Veerabhadra Nayaka".

The Viceroy received the ambassadors of the Virappa Nayaka, Vitula Sinai, along with Trimalia, one of the leading Brahmins of the Kanara state, and concluded a treaty very favourable to the Portuguese.[641] The treaty of peace and mutual understanding was signed on 7th of March 1631 at the port of Barcelore in the presence of many important dignitaries and the ambassadors.[642]

In order to put the terms into proper order, the Viceroy sent Baltasar Marinho with handsome presents in gold and some horses to the Virappa Nayaka. Virappa Nayaka agreed to remove all his military forces from Cambolim and leave the place for the Portuguese in perpetuity, at the same time offering an amount of 21,450 *Ashrafis* as compensation for the expenditure incurred on the Viceroy's journey.[643]

By the terms of this treaty, each side, the Portuguese representatives and the ambassador of Virappa Nayaka, agreed to help the other during periods of war and peace. On behalf of the King of Kanara, the ambassador also promised to cede the island of Cambolim to the Portuguese for their exclusive use and to be governed by Portuguese laws. The Portuguese were also allowed to cut the timber needed for the construction of their ships. The King of Kanara agreed to place an embargo on ships from Malabar or any other place, which did not have a Portuguese *Cartaz*. Barcelore and Onor were to be free from all the commercial and religious restrictions that the Venkatappa Nayaka had imposed. The Portuguese Viceroy was also freed from any obligation to buy pepper from the Kanara state. He could buy as much as suited his requirements and the prices would be negotiated between the Portuguese and the pepper contractors. The Portuguese promised to abide by the treaty and to allow the import of ten horses every year without any payment of customs. It was also decided that whichever party broke the terms of the treaty would pay a sum of ten thousand *Pagodas* or 35,000 *Ashrafis* before any new treaty would be signed.

This treaty shows the submissiveness of the Virappa Nayaka in relation to the Portuguese. The reasons are easy to understand. He wanted to have as much military support as possible against his rival, Veerabhadra Nayaka, and the Portuguese did not want to lose such a golden opportunity as this to gain some real advantage. They were able to guarantee the supply of food grains, pepper and saltpetre, as well as the other commodities they might require. Moreover, this treaty also demonstrates how advantageous such local disputes were for the Portuguese and how the Goan authorities sought to profit by them. While the two claimants fought for the throne of Kanara, the Portuguese were able to play an effective diplomatic role and the Viceroy lost no opportunity to remain on good terms with both of them. He wanted to make sure that whoever won power would maintain friendly relations with the *Estado da Índia*, because he knew that, as long as the Kanara state remained favourable to the Portuguese, the supply of food-grains to the other Portuguese settlements would not be a problem.

During the meeting of the *Conselho do Estado*[644] on 18th of November 1631, the issue of Cambolim had been raised. It had been a long-standing issue ever since the time of Venkatappa Nayaka and it was consuming a lot of Portuguese economic resources. A letter had been received by the Portuguese authorities from the captains of the King of Banghel, Mana Nayaka and Mala Sinai, in which they had asked for immediate help against the ruler of Kanara, Veerabhadra Nayaka. In the name of their ruler, the Banghel King, they offered "pepper in a great quantity, wood, iron and rice, carpenters and blacksmiths and many more persons to work in the construction of the fortress of Cambolim...,"[645] in return for Portuguese support. On the other hand, there was an imminent danger that Veerabhadra Nayaka was about to make an alliance with the Sultan of Bijapur in order to recover the whole of the kingdom of Kanara from Virappa Nayaka. Therefore, the Portuguese had to make a quick decision whether to provide military support to Virappa Nayaka, the King of Banghel, and other dissatisfied kings, against Veerabhadra Nayaka in order to make sure that the latter did not make a powerful alliance with the Sultan of Bijapur which could have been a disaster at a time when the Sultan of Bijapur himself was sometimes wavering in his diplomatic attitude towards the Portuguese.

Veerabhadra Nayaka had realised the dual nature of Portuguese diplomacy and therefore, when Portuguese emissaries had approached him, he had refused any diplomatic agreement regarding the supply of rice, saying that he would consider the matter as soon as the situation was under control.[646] In such circumstances, the Portuguese decided that they would continue supporting any king or queen who wanted a treaty of alliance with them against the Veerabhadra Nayaka. However, they would provide this support secretly and at the same time would maintain a good relationship with Veerabhadra and wait for the political turmoil in that region to die down.

In the meantime, towards the end of 1631,[647] Virappa Nayaka died[648] and the whole political scene changed once again. Since the internal conflict had suddenly come to an end, the Veerabhadra

Nayaka was now an undisputed ruler and was in a position to deal with all the problems relating to the Kanara state on his own. There was no one to play off against him. Therefore, the Portuguese Viceroy, after having obtained the approval of the *Conselho do Estado* on 25 May 1632, decided to send Balthazar Marinho, who had already been to the court of Virappa Nayaka, as ambassador to the court of Veerabhadra Nayaka to congratulate him on his accession to the throne of the Kanara kingdom, and also to discuss the matter of the island of Cambolim. At the same time he was to fix the prices of rice and pepper from Kanara.[649]

However, problems in the Kanara region continued for the Portuguese. In the middle of August, the captain of the fortress of Cambolim, António de Azevedo Coutinho, informed the Viceroy that, contrary to what had been promised earlier by Virappa Nayaka, Veerabhadra Nayaka had ordered the construction of a fortress on the same island at a distance of a gunshot from the Portuguese fortress.[650] The building of this fortress had begun and a substantial part was already constructed with the help of soldiers and other men. The construction was proceeding rapidly and the captain sought help to prevent its being completed. He also stated his opinion that, as soon as half of the fortress was built, the peace treaty would be at an end and he would consider that as a sign of war. The Portuguese fortress of Cambolim had been constructed with the permission of Virappa Nayaka in return for Portuguese support against the Veerabhadra Nayaka, as mentioned earlier. Now that Veerabhadra Nayaka was in full control of the Kanara kingdom, he considered the Portuguese fortress to be illegal and, in order to have a proper check on the Portuguese possessions he ordered a new fort to be built in front of the Portuguese fort. The Portuguese Viceroy, for his part, as soon as the information was brought to him, had sent an ultimatum that if the construction of the fortress did not stop immediately, and what had already been built was not destroyed, he would not hesitate to declare war on the Veerabhadra Nayaka.[651] At the same time, as a precaution, the Viceroy attempted diplomacy, as war did not seem to be a wise decision under the circumstances in which the treasury of the *Estado da Índia* found itself.

The new fort certainly posed a threat to the safety of the Portuguese. The Portuguese authorities had, for many years, intended to shift all their activities from the fortress of Barcelore to Cambolim. However, the King of Portugal, in response to the letter of Viceroy, had instructed him that he should not abandon the fortress of Barcelore, which would be seen as a humiliation for the Portuguese State. The King had suggested consulting the *Conselho do Estado* and, if possible, keeping control of both fortresses at the same time.[652] Naturally this proposal placed the Viceroy in a very difficult situation and did not help him in maintaining harmonious relations with his powerful neighbour.

The ambassador, Vitula Sinai, now in the service of Veerabhadra Nayaka, made it clear that the Nayaka would agree to stop the construction of the fort provided the Portuguese gave up the fortress of Barcelore. At the same time, Balthazar Marinho was sent by the Portuguese, with sumptuous presents, to the Veerabhadra Nayaka, to negotiate a reasonable solution. His mission was a failure. He could get no reply except that the ambassador, Vitula Sinai, would soon inform the Portuguese of the conditions proposed by the Nayaka. In the meantime, the construction of the fort continued.[653] By December 1632, the terms and conditions, on which the Veerabhadra Nayaka was prepared to sign a new treaty with the Portuguese, were sent through his ambassador. The conditions appeared to be more like dictating terms than the normal diplomatic agreement that the Portuguese were expecting. Some of the conditions were as follows: he wanted the Portuguese fortress of Barcelore to be demolished and he would then allow full control of the island of Cambolim to the Portuguese. He further added that the Portuguese must not build any more fortresses there, except what had already been constructed. For his part, the Nayaka would provide lands at Cambolim to the *casados* of Barcelore equivalent to what they used to have. The Portuguese were to buy 350 *Khandis* of Kanara pepper at the rate of 22 *Pagodas* per *Khandi*[654] and the rest was left to the choice of the Portuguese contractors and the local producers. Everlasting peace between both parties was to be sworn, based on a mutual guarantee of support. From the Portuguese, Veerabhadra Nayaka wanted a promise that every year the import of twelve horses should be allowed free of any duty. If the Viceroy wished, this could be increased to any higher number and it would be gratefully accepted. He also wanted three *Cartazes* for his ships. In return, he promised to provide all the timber and provisions required for the Portuguese ships, as used to be the case earlier.[655]

Although, initially, the *Conselho do Estado* had prepared a draft of the treaty to be celebrated between the two states, which included a condition prohibiting the ruler of Kanara from allowing any "*cossarios*"[656] (a term used during this period for the Dutch, English and Malabari ships) in his territories, this condition was removed at the instigation of the Veerabhadra Nayaka when the treaty was actually signed in 1633. In the meantime the Conde de Linhares wrote a letter to the King asking permission for the demolition of the fortress of Barcelore, a condition demanded by the Veerabhadra Nayaka, so that the Portuguese could concentrate their attention in strengthening their situation at the new fortress of Cambolim.[657]

The situation under which the diplomacy between the two states was carried on certainly shows the power and confidence of the ruler of the Kanara state. The Portuguese authorities complained that Indian rulers, especially the Nayakas of Kanara, did not honour the treaties signed by their own previous rulers. In this particular case, they pointed towards the treaties signed between them and the Virappa Nayaka, which were mostly favourable to their interests.[658] However, as this account has already shown, Virappa had not been the undisputed ruler of Kanara and had signed most of the treaties to obtain Portuguese help against his rival. Moreover, the honour of violating the terms of treaties rightfully belongs to the Portuguese who had introduced this practice from the time of their first contacts with the Indian states.[659] The Portuguese viceroys openly disregarded the terms and conditions signed by the previous holders of their office which turned out to be a great obstacle to maintaining long term cordial relationships between them and their Indian counterparts.

The Portuguese reaction to these terms was quite predictable. They refused to agree to give up the fort of Barcelore and its dependencies, but accepted the freedom to bargain for the best pepper prices and the proposal to supply food provisions and timber for shipbuilding.[660] In fact, most of the other councillors advised, not to accept the condition of dismantling the fortress of Barcelore, while accepting most of the other terms. The condition of dismantling the Barcelore fort, they agreed, should be accepted only as a last resort.

The Portuguese Viceroy's reaction to the proposed terms was that he was ready to defend the fortress of Barcelore until the last soldier, as was ordered by the King, though he, too, accepted all the other conditions. In order to deal with the matter, the Portuguese authorities sent the Bishop of Ernapolis, Dom Francisco de Moura and Gaspar de Mello de Sampaio as ambassadors to the court of Veerabhadra Nayaka.[661] This embassy was also accompanied by certain luck as the Mughal army had reached Bijapur to collect the arrears, in the early 1632. Veerabhadra Nayaka, fearing that if the Mughals were successful in eliminating the Sultan, the next step would be an attack on Kanara, proposed to help Ali Adil Shah. He also sought to bring the Portuguese to join a triple alliance to help Adil Shah against the common enemy.[662] Under the circumstances he relaxed his stand with regard to the demolition or evacuation of the fortress of Barcelore and sent his ambassador, Vitula Sinai, once again to find a way of resolving the dispute between his government and the Portuguese authorities at Goa. Great satisfaction was felt in Goa when the ambassador brought a letter with the new terms of peace,[663] especially as he came with credentials, which allowed him to sign the peace treaty. As far as the terms offered were concerned, the Nayaka of Kanara accepted the Portuguese proposal to maintain the fortresses belonging to both the belligerents at both Cambolim and Barcelore without any change. The King swore everlasting peace between the two states and agreed to provide all the provisions needed by the Portuguese, whether in the form of food, shipbuilding materials or pepper, without any hindrance. For their part the Portuguese would give three *Cartazes* for ships belonging to the ruler of Kanara. The Nayaka also sent a list of what he required, especially arms and ammunition and other things that his ambassador would explain in person.[664] It was his need for supplies of arms from the Portuguese, which probably explains why he, in effect, backed down the demand for the demolition of the fort at Barcelore.

Vitula Sinai was received in the royal hall by Portuguese officials of the *Estado da Índia* with great pomp.[665] The Nayaka of Kanara had sent some provisions, fruit and many other things as presents besides the promises he made to supply whatever the Viceroy required, as a gesture of friendship.

As well as signing the treaty, the Portuguese Viceroy tried to impress the ruler of Kanara through his new navy, which he had built after his arrival in Goa. As has been mentioned elsewhere, when the Conde de Linhares assumed office at Goa, the Portuguese navy was in a state of chaos and ruin. There were hardly any seaworthy ships and no vessel had proper cannon or arms capable of fighting a full-fledged war. In the past the Portuguese had tried to impress the Indian rulers of the coastal regions by demonstrations of their naval power and their firearms, and the Conde de Linhares wanted to maintain the tradition by showing off Portuguese maritime strength even though the extent of its decay had been exposed to all the Indian rulers as well to the Dutch and the English. In fact, what the Portuguese really needed to secure the *Estado da Índia* was a strong and stable economy, a capable administration and reliable diplomatic relations with the Indian kings.

The new treaty signed with Kanara did not prove to be as perpetual as the oaths taken had implied, and the impression made by the naval demonstration of the Conde de Linhares faded from the mind of the ruler of Kanara, as soon as he was free from the threats from the North. Veerabhadra Nayaka did not allow the shipment of pepper at the rate of 22 *Pagodas,* but only at the rate of 28 *Pagodas* as used to be the case before the treaty.[666] It was an alarming situation for the Portuguese as the Nayaka had prohibited the supply of any rice without the purchase of the pepper consignment.[667] To this the Portuguese Viceroy responded that, if the Nayaka did not honour the treaty signed by his ambassador, they would start war by blockading all his trading activities at sea, including the entry and departure of his ships. In this way they would bring disaster on his state.[668] The Portuguese authorities also asserted that, as had been agreed in the treaty, the Nayaka should pay all the expenditure incurred during the previous war. This resolution of the *Conselho do Estado* was in fact a declaration of war. The Viceroy reminded the Nayaka of his ill behaviour in relation to the Portuguese authorities and the lack of respect for the treaty that his ambassador, Vitula Sinai, had sworn to abide by, especially as most of the clauses of the treaty had been proposed by him.

In February 1635, the Conde de Linhares, while giving the details of the major incidents that had occurred, wrote in his letter to the King of Portugal that the Nayaka was not a person to be trusted as he was still at war with so many princes in his own kingdom. However, he also mentioned that he would do everything possible to get the food and other provisions supplied, as and when required, from any part of the northern territories and would try to maintain the prestige of the Portuguese arms. After all, as he wrote of the Indian rulers, "they depend more on us than we on them".[669] This remark was hardly justified, as we have seen earlier that he had written that without the supply of provisions from the territory of Kanara, things would be difficult for the Portuguese. Although he had been instructed, under the circumstances and contrary to what the King had suggested earlier, to hand over the fortress of Barcelore to the Veerabhadra Nayaka in exchange for the facilities provided by him and in this way to ease the tension, the Viceroy responded that, for the time being, he would not carry this out as the Nayaka was at war with several kings and the Portuguese might well be able to take advantage of this situation as soon as he required Portuguese help.[670] That situation soon occurred.

g) The Critical Period in Portuguese-Kanara Diplomacy

It was not only the Portuguese who kept themselves informed about political conditions in India. The Indian princes, too, were aware of the state of Portuguese military power. The Portuguese navy was in a very weak state, and the Portuguese needed all their military resources to defend themselves against both Indians and Dutch. The English, after the treaties of 1630 and 1635, became allies of the Portuguese and there was no threat of war from them, but they proved to be one of the chief competitors of the Portuguese in the purchase of Indian merchandise, especially pepper and rice. This led to an increase in prices.[671] Veerabhadra Nayaka knew the exact condition of the Portuguese navy and the trouble with the Dutch. He did not lose any opportunity to avail himself of the situation to force the Portuguese to accept his terms, as the Portuguese themselves had done to the Indian states in the past.[672] Nor did he hesitate to violate diplomatic ties though, as the Portuguese Viceroy wrote to the King in February 1635, "he has broken all that had been promised during the reign of his grandfather..."[673] However, the Viceroy added in his letter that he had informed the Veerabhadra Nayaka that "...he would be made to fulfil all the contracts or else he would be reduced to ashes. He soon obeyed".[674] This shows how the Portuguese authorities, in spite of their weak military and financial situation, still relied more on their sea-power when dealing with the Indian rulers than on diplomacy.

It was in these circumstances that Francisco Marques de Távora was sent to the Veerabhadra Nayaka as ambassador. He was well received and entertained by the Veerabhadra Nayaka at Onor[675] in the month of January 1636. He went there to fetch pepper from the Chattis and Belalis,[676] and the Nayaka informed him that he would send his ambassador to decide the price of pepper. Disregarding the earlier treaty, he also demanded that the fort of Barcelore be demolished once and for all and only then would he do something about the pepper supply.[677] He further stated that, until all these matters were decided, he had ordered all the ports to be closed for any transaction in rice or pepper, and had sent word to Martim Teixeira de Azevedo, the *capitão* of the fort of Barcelore, to inform the Viceroy at Goa not to send anyone for the purpose of buying pepper and rice. If the Portuguese Viceroy, even after this, decided to send any more emissaries, as he had done in sending Francisco Marques de Tavora, they would not be received.[678]

The response of the *Conselho do Estado* was that they would not accept any of the demands of the King, especially the price of the pepper. If they did, it would become a common practice and the price would always remain high. It was preferable that the ships should return empty rather than that the demands of the Nayaka be accepted. Besides, the members of the Council were very concerned about the prestige of the Portuguese *Estado da Índia*. They suggested that they should boycott the purchase of pepper, rice and other goods and that the money destined for the pepper should be invested in cinnamon instead.[679] They thought that would create havoc among the commercial classes in Kanara and that ultimately the King would back off from his demands.[680] This is what they wanted to show outwardly, but in reality the Portuguese were very much concerned that all the ships belonging to the local merchants carrying rice destined for Goa, should not be intercepted. In the meantime, they negotiated with Sancara da Gama,[681] a Luso-Indian and well-known business magnate in pepper, to get the annual supply of pepper.[682] In reality, it was he who kept the Portuguese informed about the changing behaviour of the Nayaka, especially in relation to the price of pepper.[683]

The anticipated political difficulties of Veerabhadra Nayaka duly occurred in 1636 when he was forced by the Bijapuri Sultan to pay the arrears of tribute. Now he approached the Portuguese for a peaceful diplomatic solution to the issues between them as he required some military help. Although he had been showing off his military strength to the Portuguese, he was becoming increasingly worried about the pressure from the ruler of Bijapur. Therefore, another ambassador, Deva Rasa Sinai, was sent to Goa who reached there in April 1636, with clear instructions and powers to negotiate.[684] The Portuguese authorities, too, were quite anxious to ease the tension without losing sight of their key interests, for they were well aware that the Dutch were waiting to seize any favourable opportunity to enter into a diplomatic pact with the Veerabhadra Nayaka. Although reluctant to do so, the Portuguese authorities were ready to demolish their fort at Barcelore, provided the Nayaka demolished his fort at Cambolim as well. Regarding the price of pepper, they wanted to negotiate directly with the Nayaka and not through the ambassador.[685] The Portuguese authorities were waiting for terms from the ambassador before deciding anything concrete.[686] It was now becoming a normal practice for the Nayakas of Ikkeri to send the terms of a treaty prior to its being signed, and the Portuguese authorities were forced to wait impatiently for terms and conditions in order to settle the dispute over pepper prices. In the past it had been the Portuguese who had sent the terms and the conditions of the pepper contracts.

The instructions from the Nayaka were brought by the ambassador, Deva Rasa Sinai, on 15th of April 1636 and were presented to the *Conselho do Estado* on 24 April. In the letter to the Portuguese Viceroy, Pêro da Silva, which accompanied the instructions and the terms of the treaty to be signed between the two belligerents, the Nayaka listed a series of complaints about the recent behaviour of the Portuguese viceroys. These mostly concerned the doubts that the Portuguese had raised about who was the rightful heir to the throne, for the Portuguese authorities had played an ambiguous and double game during the time of Virappa Nayaka and had questioned whether Veerabhadra Nayaka was the real heir. The ambassador, Deva Rasa Sinai, further added that the Portuguese had signed all the recent treaties with the Virappa Nayaka because they wanted to exploit the internal dispute over the throne. He wanted an explanation about their involvement. In fact, he added, Venkatappa Nayaka himself, in his testament, had declared who the heir to the throne of Kanara would be and it was not for the Portuguese to decide whether or not to accept the legitimacy of an heir to the throne.[687]

The Nayaka also complained about the underhand proceedings of the Portuguese government during the time of the Conde de Linhares whose only aim had been to help one claimant against the other, creating intrigues instead of following the path of friendship, as had been the practice during the reign of Venkatappa Nayaka.[688] Linhares, in fact, had weakened the diplomatic ties between the Indian states and the Portuguese by relying too heavily on demonstrations of naval power.[689] The Nayaka also expressed the hope that future Portuguese viceroys would do more to create harmonious, friendly and peaceful relations between the Indian states and themselves. He wished all the diplomatic ties that took place during the government of his grandfather, Venkatappa Nayaka, to be renewed and accepted thenceforward as binding. He assured the Viceroy that nothing would make him break any of the clauses of the previous treaties. The ambassador of the Veerabhadra Nayaka also suggested in his note that, in the name of friendship, the Portuguese should retain only one of the fortresses, either Cambolim or Barcelore.[690] He also sent his congratulations to Pêro da Silva on taking up his office as the new Viceroy of the *Estado da Índia.*[691]

Even in such difficult circumstances the *Conselho do Estado*, after considering the different strategic aspects of the two fortresses at Cambolim and Barcelore, did not reach any final conclusion about what to communicate to the Veerabhadra Nayaka. Instead they decided that the Nayaka should first demolish his fort at Cambolim, and only then would the Portuguese decide to dismantle the fortress of Barcelore but without evacuating the whole of the island, as they knew that the Nayaka had very little chance of forcing them to do so. The members of the Council were quite sceptical about giving up the fortress of Barcelore as they thought the Nayaka would make use of it for his own defensive purposes.[692] Regarding the pepper supply, the *Conselho do Estado* decided on 30 March 1637 that, instead of creating a tense diplomatic situation, it would be better to look for other ways of procuring pepper, probably from Cochin or some other place.[693] This decision was taken in order to avoid causing any offence as they were in no condition to risk a military confrontation with the Nayaka of Ikkeri,[694] as a Dutch embassy was already approaching the court of Adil Shah and other defensive measures had to be taken.

In the meantime, the political situation in Kanara started to change rapidly. The King of Banghel, along with other dissidents, had rebelled against their sovereign, Veerabhadra Nayaka.[695] As if this were not enough, the Sultan of Bijapur also, taking the side of the Banghel King, attacked the northern parts of Kanara, losing many men in the process.[696] Having received a letter from the Veerabhadra Nayaka requesting help against the King of Banghel,[697] the *Conselho do Estado* decided this time to remain neutral in this local conflict, as they were quite aware of what had happened on previous occasions, during the period of Venkatappa Nayaka, when they had taken the side of the King Banghel. Nevertheless, the Portuguese were eventually forced to take part in this conflict and to provide help to Veerabhadra Nayaka. Although the Portuguese had always taken the side of the King of Banghel in the past, they did not want the Sultan of Bijapur, who was taking the side of the Banghel King, to be successful against the Nayaka.

Here one should briefly recall that, during the years 1619-20, the kingdom of Banghel used to be one of Portugal's allies and had been conquered by Venkatappa Nayaka, even though the Portuguese had sent military aid for its protection. They had been warned by Venkatappa Nayaka to stop sending any help to the kingdom of Banghel or else they would face open war with him. The inadequate support of the Portuguese and the pressure of war made the then King of Banghel enter into an alliance with the Venkatappa Nayaka to protect his kingdom from any further destruction. The Portuguese backed off, as they had to deal other more important enemies. However, as soon as Banghel saw an opportunity of regaining its independence with the help of the Sultan of Bijapur, and had revolted against the Veerabhadra Nayaka along with all those who had suffered during the time of Venkatappa Nayaka, the Portuguese were prepared to help the man (Veerabhadra Nayaka) they had once called an "illegitimate king" against their own old ally (the Banghel King).

After the death of Venkatappa Nayaka, the kingdom of Banghel had been claimed as a feudatory of the Sultan of Bijapur, and he, as soon as Veerabhadra Nayaka ascended the throne, had demanded that the Nayaka should return to their rightful owners all the territories and lands forcibly taken by his grandfather. Since Veerabhadra did not do as was demanded, the small chiefs and landowners had revolted. This infuriated the Sultan who attacked Veerabhadra late in 1638, in order to teach him a lesson.[698] The kingdom of Banghel was now supporting all the dissatisfied chiefs. Furthermore, one cannot forget the Portuguese promise to the Sultan of Bijapur to provide military support against any attack on his territory. Indeed, the Sultan, through his ambassador, Mohammad Raza, had also asked for help against the Veerabhadra Nayaka which the Portuguese had very diplomatically refused.[699] Helping the Nayaka was an open violation of the treaty by the

Portuguese. The Portuguese now ran the risk of their relations with Bijapur deteriorating, which would certainly worsen their situation. The Portuguese authorities had already secretly sent military aid to Veerabhadra Nayaka, as they did not want to see the Sultan of Bijapur become a powerful neighbour who had won the favour of all the rebellious chiefs.[700] However, the councillors decided that, if the Bijapuri authorities discovered that the Portuguese had sent any help, they would claim that the aid had been sent to safeguard the Portuguese fortresses in Kanara.[701] Here it should be recalled that, during this period of turmoil, the Sultan of Bijapur had provided a site at Vengurla to the Dutch for their military and economic activities, although he had refused any military pact against the Portuguese. Possibly, this was retaliation for the secret help the Portuguese had given to the Nayaka!

Under the prevailing political conditions, the Portuguese were now on good terms with the Veerabhadra Nayaka and, the *Conselho do Estado* suggested providing help to any civilians who might come as refugees from the land of the Nayaka during the war. The Portuguese authorities, as usual, wanted to make the most of such opportunities by providing assistance to both sides.[702]

Veerabhadra Nayaka had sent his two emissaries, Deva Rasa Sinai and Rama Poi, to Barcelore with powers to decide matters relating to Cambolim and whatever might be needed to do this. In response to the help requested by the Veerabhadra Nayaka, Joseph Pinto Pereira, a member of the *Conselho do Estado,* suggested that they should, "send more support in the form of gunpowder, guns, cannons etc required by the Veerabhadra Nayaka"[703] It was decided to send the help with Martim Teixeira de Azevedo or, in his absence, Francisco de Sousa Alcoforado. The Portuguese intended to fulfil what had been promised during the recent treaty with the Nayaka with the aim of protecting not only Cambolim, but their interests in the whole of Kanara,[704] to prevent the kingdom falling into the hands of the Sultan of Bijapur. As has been mentioned earlier, the Portuguese required timber for shipbuilding, which was plentiful in this region. There had been times in the past when the rulers of Kanara had prohibited the cutting down of the timber forest, but now the right opportunity was at hand to get this decision reversed, as this time the Nayaka of Kanara was in need of Portuguese help. The Portuguese were largely indifferent as to who required help, for they needed to improve their own situation at all costs. Whatever served their purpose was right.

Since the Portuguese wanted to keep on good terms with the Nayaka of Ikkeri they had to risk sending help secretly. As the Nayaka, forced by the circumstances in which he found himself, was prepared to accept any condition regarding Cambolim, the Portuguese were now ready to propose terms to him. At the same time, they did not want to give the impression that they were exploiting the difficult political situation of the Nayaka, as is made clear in this extract from the Council's report: "Dom Fellipe Mascarenhas and Lourenço de Mello Deeça voted that the help should be sent but with much precautions so that nobody should know that we sent the help or there would be more complications with the Sultan of Bijapur."[705]

In the end, they suggested waiting until the end of the war for the conclusion of the treaty. This was a farsighted strategy to keep the power and the advantage in their own hands. They had in mind that, when a suitable time came, they would see that the fortification of the whole area of Cambolim, which was now in a deteriorating state, was carried out at the expense of the Nayaka in return for the help they had provided against the revolting princes and the Sultan of Bijapur.[706] Moreover they had let the Nayaka know that, he would be able to make use of the fortification of Cambolim for his own safety and could take refuge in it during the period of war, if he needed to.[707]

Normally, the Portuguese governors and viceroys were supposed to send annual reports on the state of affairs of the *Estado da Índia* in order to keep the King informed, and occasionally they were obliged to get his permission before taking any action on intricate religious, social, economic and diplomatic matters. The King, Philip IV, was fully aware of the political developments in the East. In a letter dated 18th of February 1640 he suggested that the Viceroy should handle all diplomatic negotiations with the Indian kings and that he should make use of the quarrels between the Indian rulers, helping one against another and sometimes helping both at the same time. In relation to Veerabhadra Nayaka, he suggested that the rise in the pepper price should not be accepted but that, at the same time, it was important to make sure that none of the European companies approached the Nayaka.[708] So far as the triangular political relationship between the Mughals, the Sultan of Bijapur and Veerabhadra Nayaka was concerned, the King suggested to the Viceroy that the Sultan and the Nayaka should both be helped so that neither of them would be defeated and disappear from the scene.[709]

In responding to the Veerabhadra Nayaka, through his ambassador, Rama Poi, the Portuguese Viceroy expressed great satisfaction at the friendship that the two states had had for a long time.[710] Rama Poi, who took António Borges, a *casado* settled at Barcelore, with him to Goa, also informed the Viceroy about the good intentions of the Veerabhadra Nayaka. The Viceroy promised, in his name and in that of those who would come in his place in future, that he would do everything to maintain a good and friendly relationship with the people of Kanara. Moreover, he promised that he would send messages to the ruler[711] of Banghel to persuade her to sign a peace treaty with Kanara and cease the hostility that had already taken numerous lives and destroyed property and commerce. The Viceroy also promised to write to the Portuguese ambassador at the court of the Bijapuri Sultan to do his best to reach a peaceful solution to the conflict between the kingdom of Bijapur and Kanara.[712]

Here it should be noted that between 1637 and 1640, there had been a total blockade of the ports of Goa by the Dutch and the entire military and economic power of the *Estado da Índia* was at risk. No homebound ships could leave Goa nor could ships from Portugal enter the port. Most of the ships that left Portugal either off-loaded at Diu or remained in Mozambique and only reached India after the blockade was over. Under such circumstances, priority was given to finding ways of continuing to trade rather than to maintaining fortresses or factories in places that were affected by continuous war. The King had expressed his concern about the state of commerce in Asia as he had been informed about the increasing price of Indian merchandise, especially pepper, on the Malabar and Kanara coasts, due to the Dutch contracts with the local merchants. He had also suggested that obstacles should be put in the way of the English trade in pepper and other merchandise, since they had been approaching the Nayaka of Kanara to establish diplomatic relations with him and had been responsible for the rise in the pepper prices in that region.[713] So at this juncture it was agreed unanimously by the members of the *Conselho do Estado* that, in order to maintain the supply of pepper from the region of Kanara, they would have to accept the demands of the Veerabhadra Nayaka.[714] Moreover, the fortress of Cambolim had become an additional expenditure for the Portuguese, costing over 14,000 *Pardaos* a year to maintain and producing no income for the state.

The English were not slow to understand this situation. The Portuguese Viceroy, in one of his letters, reported to the King that the Indian rulers were accustomed to maintain friendship with those who benefited them most or with whom they were forced to be friendly.[715] Lately they, especially the kings of Bijapur and Cannanore, had had quite close ties with the English who had been bringing a lot of merchandise to their ports. This had endangered Portuguese commerce. The Viceroy wanted to hinder these commercial ties between the English and the local kings, without creating any trouble of a diplomatic nature, as suggested by the King. It was not an easy task as the Portuguese did not have any way of pursuing their policy of interfering with the free commerce of the English.[716]

So far as the Indian kings were concerned, they followed the common practice in that their ports were always open for whoever wanted to be friendly and to do business, as mentioned elsewhere. The kings of Kanara, like other Indian rulers, welcomed all the Dutch and English merchants who wanted to trade in their possessions, while the Indian businessmen were willing to sell their goods to whoever paid the best price. The Portuguese, on the other hand, wanted to monopolise Indian commerce and therefore, decided to fight the merchants and rulers, whenever the latter did not accept their rule over the sea. In such circumstances it was not possible to maintain peace for any length of time.

h) New Ruler, New Diplomacy: the Last Phase of Portuguese Kanara Relations

In the year 1644 a civil war broke out in Kanara. Shivappa Nayaka,[717] one of the uncles of Veerabhadra Nayaka, who had been in royal service as ambassador to the court of the Bijapuri Sultan, during which time he helped in the process of mediation following the various wars between the two states,[718] and who had served also as a general in the army of the Nayakas of Kanara,[719] seeing that his nephew was showing less and less interest in the state's affairs, decided to take over control of the kingdom. It seems that Veerabhadra Nayaka was so tired of dealing with the affairs of the kingdom that, as Sharma has suggested, 'he took refuge in the hills where he pursued his devotions, leaving the conduct of political affairs to others'.[720] Shivappa Nayaka, who had been engaged in a number of battles against the Bijapuri Sultan and had, on several occasions, had to face serious situations due to the weakness of the Veerabhadra Nayaka, now found himself

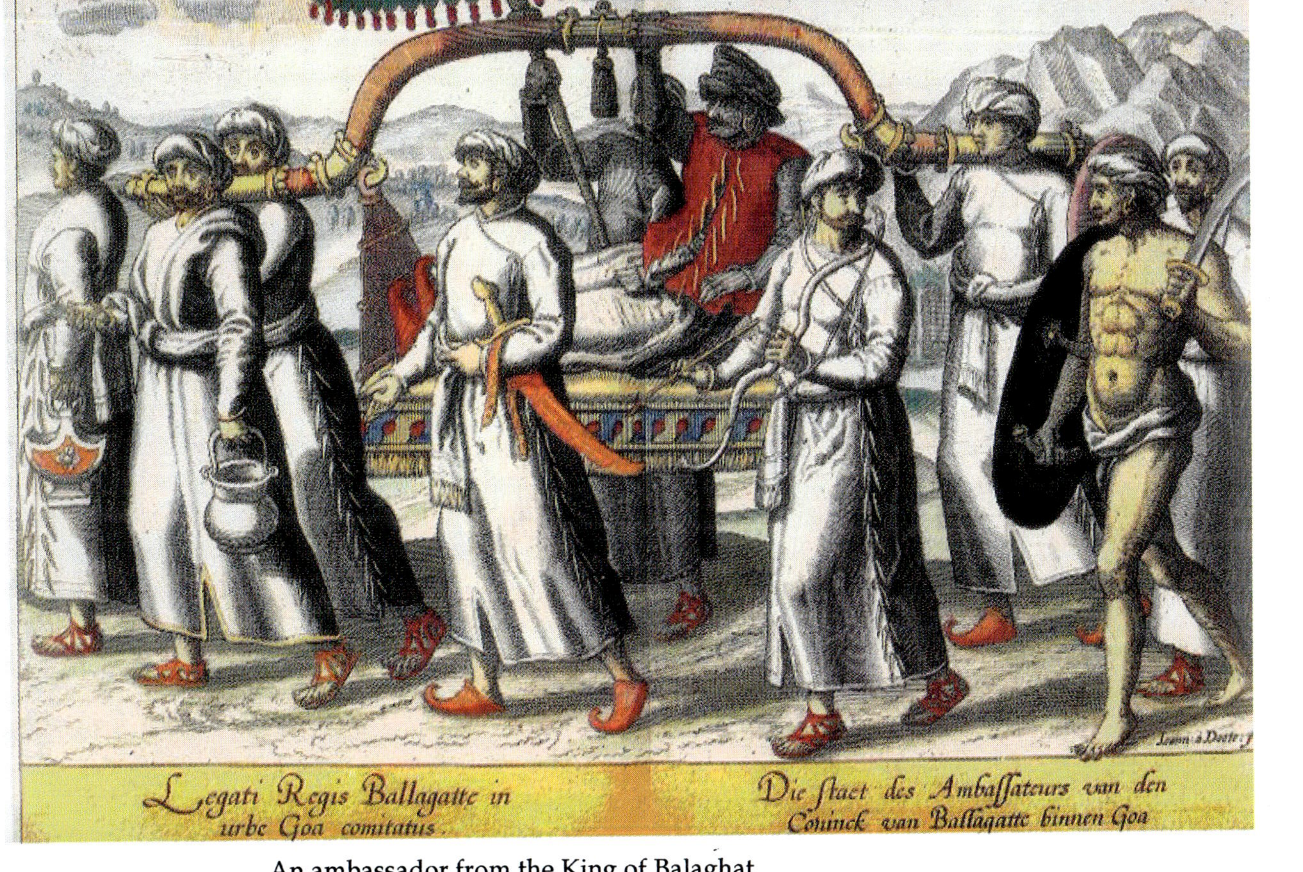

An ambassador from the King of Balaghat
(the Nayaka of Ikkeri?)

facing page 238

in command of a powerful army.[721] In 1644 he collected a large force and attacked Canarcota where Veerabhadra Nayaka had taken refuge and which was completely cut off both by land and sea. Finding himself in these circumstances, Veerabhadra Nayaka sought Portuguese help. The situation was also alarming for the Portuguese, as they felt this to be a threat to their own fortresses of Cambolim and Barcelore as well as to their commerce.[722] Help was immediately dispatched and it was decided to offer asylum to Veerabhadra Nayaka in case he wanted to take refuge in any of the Portuguese fortresses. In this way the Portuguese thought they would be doing a great favour to a neighbouring king and would be able to use him for their benefit in the future.[723]

Veerabhadra, however, was fighting a losing battle. The support from the Portuguese and his other allies did not bear any result and he was killed in the same year, 1644. Shivappa Nayaka, having seized the throne of Ikkeri, turned out to be a bad neighbour for the Portuguese and their settlements in Kanara. He was the most difficult ruler with whom the Portuguese ever had to deal, for he took maximum advantage of their precarious political, economic and military situation.

Trouble between the state of Ikkeri and the Portuguese started when Shivappa Nayaka (1644-1660) ordered the rebuilding of the fortress on the island of Cambolim which had been started by the Veerabhadra Nayaka.[724] The Portuguese authorities at Goa considered that the previous treaties were still effective and decided that António Borges da Costa, who was already at the court of Shivappa Nayaka, should insist that work on the construction of the fortress should stop and that there should be a reduction in the price of pepper below 23 *Pagodas*.[725] Regarding the future of the fortress of Cambolim, the Nayaka was to be informed in due course, as soon as the orders came from the King of Portugal.[726] However, one can presume that nothing concrete was decided at this time, as it was only in 1653-54 that this fortress and land were evacuated after a war which lasted for over two years.

After the accession to the throne of Shivappa Nayaka, the diplomatic relations between the Portuguese authorities and the Kanara states were never as peaceful as the Portuguese wished. Like Venkatappa Nayaka, Shivappa Nayaka initiated a policy of expanding his empire to the north and south. He sought to overcome every obstacle in his way and did not respect any of the diplomatic agreements made in the past. Taking advantage of the fact that the Portuguese were deeply involved in different parts of Asia, and that their financial and military situation was quite inadequate to face him, he declared open war on them, in order to occupy their settlements in Kanara.[727] The reason that Frei António da Conceição, one of the *comissários* of the *Estado da Índia* during this period, provided for the war declared by Shivappa Nayaka, was the price of pepper in his dominions. He wanted to increase the price, a move which the Portuguese resisted. In fact the Portuguese refused to buy any pepper at all, and this was not acceptable to the Shivappa Nayaka. Frei António also reported that the Dutch were behind his tough attitude against the Portuguese.[728]

However, the cause for the conflict, provided by Rama Sharma, is completely different. Though one cannot ignore the presence of the Dutch, who might possibly have provided the motive for the whole movement of Shivappa's forces, the explanation provided by Sharma seems to be more reasonable and factual than the supposition advanced by Frei António. According to Sharma the reason behind all the ventures of the Shivappa Nayaka was the serious illness and the rumours of the death of Muhammad Adil Shah of Bijapur.[729] This encouraged most of the feudatories of Adil Shah to make use of the opportunity to declare their independence and claim their rights, and first among them was Shivappa Nayaka. This provided the perfect opportunity to realise his dream of expanding his empire. He had been at war with several neighbouring chiefs since 1648 and by 1652 he had already gained several victories over states in the South. Now he turned his attention towards the Portuguese as well. The Portuguese had taken advantage of the disturbed state of the country to fortify their position in Kanara, activity that did not go unnoticed by Shivappa Nayaka whose army succeeded in capturing Kundapura, Ganguvalli, Onor and other areas adjacent to the Portuguese dominated territories from which they obtained their food supplies. Continuing the operations, he laid siege in the middle of 1652 to Cambolim, Barcelore and Mangalore.

The Portuguese fortresses of Cambolim and Barcelore were attacked on 14 June 1652, and fighting between the Portuguese and the Kanara ruler continued on both fronts till the 4 November, when the Portuguese surrendered Barcelore.[730] Only after the loss of Barcelore were the Portuguese authorities at Goa able to send reinforcements.[731] In the meantime the Cambolim fort stood firm. While the siege of Cambolim continued, a Portuguese fleet arrived on the 25 October and fought with the enemy, but it appears to have been repulsed with the loss of some vessels.[732] Thirty-five days later, another Portuguese fleet arrived, which, however, retired after doing some damage to the enemy. Later, the Portuguese sent more arms, ammunition and war material.[733] Meanwhile a regular siege of the fort of Cambolim commenced on 6 November and Onor and Mangalore were also invested by the Nayaka's army.[734]

On the 15th of January 1653 a third fleet arrived, but it appears to have caused little loss to the enemy, since two days later the garrison withdrew from Cambolim and went on board the fleet, taking with them all they could carry and leaving the fortress entirely dismantled.[735] During the siege seventy Portuguese were killed, but all the circumstances attending the abandonment of the place appeared so peculiar that an inquiry was made into the matter. This only resulted in the conclusion that the fortress had not been in a defensible state.[736] However, there appears to have been some difference of opinion on this point. One eyewitness went so far as to attribute the surrender to the action of the commander of the last relief expedition, and he expressed a strong opinion that the fortress could have been defended for some time longer. The Viceroy, in summing up the evidence, came to the conclusion that the fortress was not in a defensible state, and he added that most of the other Portuguese fortresses in India were in a similar condition.[737] It is, noticeable that, even when under such heavy pressure from all sides, the Portuguese authorities did not lose their arrogance, to the extent that they ignored the offer made by the King of Cannanore to support them against the Nayaka if they provided the gunpowder and ammunition, and some money for the payment for the Nayars (soldiers). Instead of accepting this offer, the Portuguese authorities merely sent orders to the fortress captains to fight to the last.[738]

Moreover no effort was made by the Portuguese authorities at Goa to find any diplomatic means to stop the war. The Portuguese were, undoubtedly, in a serious military situation and war was also continuing on the Island of Ceylon against the Dutch. Therefore, it would have been advisable to have reached a peaceful solution on the matter of the pepper price instead of fighting and losing all their settlements in that region. Indeed, at the Council's meeting, the opinion was expressed that the Nayaka should be approached for a peaceful diplomatic solution.[739] So, why did they not try to achieve this?

Surprisingly, the former ambassador of Shivappa Nayaka, Rama Poi, visited Goa, on the 19 December 1652 [740] and advised the Portuguese authorities that they should send Fr. Gonçalo Martins to the court of the Shivappa Nayaka to conclude a peace treaty based on the one concluded during the period of the Viceroys Conde de Linhares and Pêro da Silva. The Portuguese Viceroy suggested that, if Shivappa Nayaka returned the fortress of Barcelore, they would agree to buy over 500 *Khandis* of pepper at the rate of 28 *Pagodas* if this was the price they had to pay for peace.[741] However, the discussions between Rama Poi and the Portuguese authorities were not mentioned in the official letter to the Shivappa Nayaka which was sent through Fr. Gonçalo Martins and was dated 22nd of February 1653.

The ambassador of Shivappa Nayaka, Rama Poi, had made out that he was representing the people of Bedrur, who wanted to see the two governments make peace. This seems to have been the policy that Shivappa Nayaka wanted to apply, instead of sending the ambassador in his own name, which would have been according to accepted protocol since he was the one who had started the military campaign. On the other hand, the Portuguese were also not willing to sue for peace directly, as it would hurt their morale and prestige. Since Shivappa Nayaka was deeply committed elsewhere in the South and required his forces to counter the increasing pressure from the Bijapuri Sultan, he did not want to continue his war with the Portuguese on a different front. In this way Shivappa Nayaka, wanted to avoid showing his weakness. He hoped to be able to play a diplomatic game which would lead to a cessation of hostilities and would provide a way of salvaging his pride. Whatever the reason, it is clear that he intended to cease military intervention for the time being.[742]

It was decided unanimously during the meeting of the *Conselho do Estado* that took place on 19th of February 1653, that Fr. Gonçalo Martins should be sent to Onor with sufficient power to conclude a peace treaty with Shivappa Nayaka. The Viceroy, Dom Vasco Mascarenhas, the Conde de Obidos, however, opposed the idea as he alleged that, on a previous occasion, Fr. Martins had refused to perform any services for the state. The Council also decided that peace between the two governments was urgent as the treasury was not in a condition to bear any more expenditure since the war against the Dutch in Ceylon required more resources now than ever before.[743]

Eventually Fr. Gonçalo Martins and Ramogi Sinai Kothari were selected for this diplomatic mission to the Court of the Shivappa Nayaka.[744] Fr. Martins had previous experience in this region, whereas Ramogi Kothari was highly respected and had served the Portuguese government on several occasions at various courts.[745] Kothari acted as interpreter on this mission. However, the mission did not obtain the anticipated results, as Shivappa Nayaka was sick and was unable to meet the emissaries. Thus this mission was a failure.

In the meantime, the Viceroy thought it wise to send help to the fortresses of Onor and Mangalore as the Portuguese were not yet prepared to give up their resistance.[746] In the month of August 1653, the fort of Mangalore was again under attack by Kanara forces, which caused damage to property and life by burning the surrounding country.[747] The King of Cannanore again offered to send soldiers to fight if the Portuguese would agree to pay them. Nevertheless, although the Viceroy ordered some help to be sent to Mangalore, he considered that the five thousand Nayar soldiers offered by the King of Cannanore would be unreliable, "as they first need to be paid and are very superstitious. Before they really start to fight, they perform a lot rituals..."[748] As the King was still protecting the Ali Raja, the Viceroy once again refused his offer but thanked the King for his generosity.[749] The reason behind the Portuguese rejection of the Cannanore soldiers seems to have been, as the documents make clear, firstly, that the men were not trained and were fortune seekers, and secondly, that they had to undertake a lot of religious rituals before they actually started to fight. However, what seems to have weighed more with the Portuguese was that, at this time, they were experiencing marked financial difficulties, whereas these soldiers wanted their payment in advance. The Portuguese authorities were reluctant to spend their scarce resources under such circumstances. The King of Cannanore had his own interest in this matter. The boundary of his kingdom extended to the borders of the Kanara kingdom and he was worried that Shivappa Nayaka might attempt to expand his territories at Cannanore's expense. Moreover, since the early sixteenth century the Portuguese had a fortress and a factory in this kingdom and had complex commercial interests in the region from which they collected a considerable volume of pepper. Therefore, it was in the interest of both Cannanore and the Portuguese that Shivappa Nayaka should be checked. By helping the Portuguese, the King was trying to protect his own interests as well.

Early in 1654, the Viceroy received another offer to mediate peace between the Portuguese and the state of Ikkeri, this time from Vitoji Vishwas Rao,[750] the Nayaka Varimor of Ancola.[751] He suggested that he had enough influence with the Shivappa Nayaka and there was no reason why the two states should not live in peace. The Portuguese Viceroy accepted the offer with thanks but did not think it would help Portuguese prestige in the region. However, the councillors of the *Estado da Índia* advised that either Artur Desa or Manuel Ramos, an Indo-Portuguese and a business magnate of this region, should be sent to negotiate peace with the Shivappa Nayaka when they thought the time right for the purpose.[752]

All these efforts to end the hostilities between Portugal and Ikkeri proved to be total failures, on the one side because of Portuguese pride and the desire to preserve their prestige as rulers of the sea, and on the other because of the ambition of the Nayakas of Ikkeri to reunite their lost territories.

Meanwhile the only fortress still under Portuguese control was that of Onor, (all others, Barcelore, Cambolim and Mangalore[753] had been definitely lost between the July 1652 and February 1654)[754] and the conditions proposed by the Shivappa Nayaka to the Portuguese *capitão-mor de Canará*, Pero Pinto de Mello and the *capitão*, Francisco de Sousa Alcoforado, were that the Portuguese should now buy now 1000 *Khandis* of pepper at the rate of 28 *Pagodas*[755] per *Khandi*. Malappa Malό, son of Vitula Malό, who was the emissary of Shivappa Nayaka sent to sign the peace treaty, was another very influential business magnate of the Kanara region. The Portuguese authorities found this very humiliating and thought that the conditions imposed in the peace mission indicated that the Shivappa Nayaka was treating them as his tributaries. The Viceroy, the Conde de Obidos, thought it was advisable to ask the Sultan of Bijapur, whose feudatory the Nayaka of Ikkeri was, to mediate in this affair so that they could end the long war they had been having since 1652.[756] In the meantime, it was decided to send help, whenever possible, to the fortress of Onor until a peaceful solution was reached.[757]

The principal condition demanded by Shivappa Nayaka was very clear. Until an ambassador from the Portuguese government signed the treaty and accepted the condition proposed by him of buying 1000 *Khandis* of pepper in the first year, and 500 *Khandis* in the following year, he would not lift the siege of the fortress of Onor.[758] Frei António Nunes and Francisco de Sousa Alcoforado were sent as Portuguese ambassadors to the court of Ikkeri with clear instructions not to negotiate any quantity more than 500 *Khandis* in the first year and 250 the following year at the rate of 24-25 *Pagodas* per *Khandi*. They were to negotiate the terms with Malappa Malo, the intermediary proposed by Shivappa Nayaka. The Portuguese ambassador argued that now they had only one fort in Kanara, and that, when they had four fortresses in his land, his ancestors agreed to an annual purchase of only 250 *Khandis*. This condition demanded by Shivappa was excessive as the Nayaka was in effect forcing them to buy four times as much pepper as before. The Portuguese representatives also had to discuss the matter of the return of the three fortresses of Cambolim, Barcelore and Mangalore. The Viceroy further added in his instruction that, if no fortress was left under Portuguese control in his land, the Nayaka would be the greatest loser as he would have no way of forcing the Portuguese to buy his pepper at all.[759]

On 27th of April 1654, it was reported by the *capitão-mor* of the fortress of Onor, Pero Pinto de Mello that Malappa Maló, the representative of Shivappa Nayaka, had refused the Portuguese proposal and maintained the demand for a 1000 *Khandis* of pepper. This meant that the Portuguese in Goa had to send reinforcements immediately as the war would continue and the soldiers were outnumbered and were in no condition to resist the well-equipped army of Shivappa Nayaka.[760]

The situation appeared so serious that an urgent meeting of the *Conselho do Estado* was called to take a decision on the matter of the continuation of the war and to find a solution.[761] It was considered necessary, for the time being, to accept the terms offered by Shivappa Nayaka and to end the hostilities.[762] This insistence of Shivappa Nayaka that the Portuguese should buy 1000 *Khandis* of pepper from his dominion was a way of showing the Portuguese who really governed in the land of Kanara and was not simply pepper contract. The Portuguese, for their part, understood the point exactly and that is why they insisted on fighting instead of accepting the condition imposed by Shivappa Nayaka.

Meanwhile, as the proposed mediation of the Sultan of Bijapur had not yet begun,[763] reinforcements were sent to the fortress of Onor on 9th of September 1654.[764] However, the Council was also considering the possibility of dismantling the fortress of Onor as there was hardly any wall remaining and, instead of fighting a losing battle, abandoning the whole region. Eventually, after twenty-six months of continuous siege by the Shivappa Nayakas forces, it was decided to surrender the fortress and evacuate the garrison and the Portuguese property.[765] Towards the end of the same month, Onor was abandoned.

The Portuguese presence in Kanara had depended on the Euro-Asian population and their economic resources. However, there were never more than 30 or 40 *casados* living in any of their fortresses. In the fortresses of Onor and Barcelore, for example, although these were some of the most important commercial centres for the procurement of food-grains and pepper, there were 30 to 35 *casado* families towards the end of the third decade of the seventeenth century.[766] Otherwise the Portuguese depended for their manpower on the local population and the Indo-Portuguese *descendentes*. It would have been much more beneficial to have maintained friendly relations based on diplomacy than to have depended on the periodic demonstrations of power by their *armada*.[767]

As if this whole situation was not enough, in the month of October 1654, general Hakim of the Bijapuri army added more miseries to the already existing troubles of the Portuguese by invading the territories of Bardez and Salssette,[768] which is dealt with in the following chapter.

Strict orders were now issued to avoid any commercial or diplomatic ties with the Kanara kingdom. No support was to be provided to any Kanarese businessmen even if they were in difficulty or in danger of losing their ships near the Portuguese ports.[769] No correspondence was exchanged between the two states until the arrival in 1659 of a letter from the *capitão-mor* of Barcelore, Luís da Costa, who was a prisoner of the King of Kanara. It was proposed by the Portuguese *Conselho do Estado* to send the Jesuit father, Pero da Costa, who was well respected and had already been to the court of Ikkeri, to deal with the peace mission and to take some handsome presents for Shivappa Nayaka and his brother.[770] It was also reported in the same letter that the Dutch had, once more, established a diplomatic presence at the Kanara court. Through this mission, it was hoped that Pero da Costa would also try to place obstacles in the way of Dutch relations with this King.[771] This mission, however, did not bring any fruitful results. In the year 1661, another effort was made to release the Portuguese *capitão-mor* of Barcelore through the mediation of Ramogi Sinai Kothari, who had already been on such missions earlier to this court, and it was, through the mediation of Ramogi that the question of the prisoners was finally resolved.[772]

The Portuguese had been left with no choice but to abandon the Kanara region because of the continuous wars in Ceylon, which lasted till 1658, and in the southern Indian settlements of Quilon, Cannanore and Cochin, which continued till 1663 when they lost all of these colonies to the Dutch.

Though the period after 1663 falls beyond the scope of this work, but a brief history of what happened is provided here to sumup the history of the Portuguese Kanara diplomacy. After a gap of almost a decade, only in 1671 were the Portuguese able to conclude a peace treaty with the ruler of Kanara, Soma Shakar Nayaka, through his ambassador, Vitula Mallo, who visited the Portuguese capital on 20 April. The Portuguese were permitted to re-establish factories at Onor, Barcelore and Mangalore. They were allowed to make provision for their proper protection but not to fortify them. They were allowed to undertake missionary activities but they were not permitted forcibly to convert anyone or to violate the sentiments of other religious groups. The Kanara ruler on other hand agreed to pay compensation for all the damage done to the Portuguese armada captured during the period of Shivappa Nayaka. Although it may appear strange that the ruler of Kanara should now accept the Portuguese back in his dominions, the reason is quite obvious. The emergence of Shivaji as paramount military power in the territories of the Sultans of Bijapur and Ahmanagar, had taken all rulers of the North by surprise just as, in the early seventeenth century, the expansion of Venkatappa had done. The Sultans of Bijapur were no longer able to provide a buffer for the region of Kanara against the ambitions of either the Mughals or Shivaji. Therefore, in order to save some part of his kingdom, the ruler of Kanara, found it preferable to ally with the Portuguese than to lose all of his kingdoms to the Mughals who, after the fall of the Bijapur kingdom, now claimed to have sovereign rights in the region.

The ruler of Kanara agreed to respect the Portuguese *Cartaz* system for his own and his merchants' ships.[773] The Portuguese were not to capture Kanara ships without any proper reason and they should also see that the ships of Kanara were permitted to carry on their coastal trade with the neighbouring states, including Goa. Both the belligerents promised to maintain friendly relations henceforth and to respect each other's laws.[774]

With this came to an end the story of the Portuguese diplomatic relations with the rulers of Kanara during the period of our study.

Reference

554 Joan-Pau Rubiés, *Travel and Ethnology in the Renaissance...*, pp. 361.

555 Protector and saviour of the land and people.

556 Pietro Della Valle, *The Travel of Pietro della Valle in India*, pp. 251-252.

557 *Ibid.*, pp. 254-255.

558 *Ibid.*, pp. 251-252.

559 Shastry, *Studies in Indo-Portuguese History*, p. 84.

560 *Ibid*, 80-91.

561 In the Portuguese manuscripts and maps it is generally mentioned as Bangel, Banguel etc.

562 Diogo Velho, *Orçamento do Estado da Índia, 1574*, pp. 94-95.

563 *Ibid.*

564 *ACE*, vol. I, doc. 28, 7 de Março de 1620.

565 *LML*, cod. 5, fols. 89-vº: *Regimento para o Vice-rei da Índia, Ruy Loureço de Távora*, Lisboa, 19 de Março de 1612.

566 Rama Sharma, *History of the Vijayanagar*, vol. II, p. 211,

567 *Ibid.* and also see pp. 52-54.

568 *Ibid.*

569 Rama Sharma, *History of the Vijayanagar*, vol. II, pp. 77-79.

570 *Ibid.*

571 *Ibid.*

572 Della Valle, Della Valle, *The Travel of Pietro della Valle...*, vol. II, pp. 218-219.

573 *Ibid.*

574 Rama Sharma, *History of the Vijayanagar*... has provided a detailed history of his expansion. pp. 77-78.

575 Such as Nalavathu Nadu, Sankara Narayana, Bairdur and Halligere. After the capture of these states, Venkatappa sent his military expeditions to the Bangajala, (Banghel) Savanta, Chouta, Mula, Kumbale and Kasaragodu and overpowered their rulers. He then

marched to Mangalore and incorporated the whole kingdom into his, except the areas around the Portuguese fortresses. Porbabaly he was careful not to involve the Portuguese in his conflicts. But when he attacked Bangajala, and its ruler sought help from the Portuguese, it was unavoidable for them to interfere and land their soldiers in the territory of Mangalore. Confrotnation between the two was unavoidable. Venkatappa Nayaka next garrisoned and strengthened Mulki. Kodeyala, Muda Bidare, Ullala, Kumbala, Kasragodu, Puduvetta, Ballare, Kantamangala, Bandyadaka, Kundamkuli. Kothuru, Bachi, Sisita Chandragudi, Kidutar, Muda Kodayala and Phaniyala. The Queen of Olala also took part as allies of Venkatappa, especially when he attacked Mangalore and Banghel King. As retaliation the Portuguese attacked her capital but were repulsed and forced to retire. See Rama Sharma, *History of the Vijayanagar*, vol. II, pp. 142-143.

576 *LML*, cod. I, fols. 148-148v°: *Carta Régia para o vice-rei da Índia, dando instruções que tome providências para a seguranças de Onor, Barcelor, Mangalor e Cananore, em razação de andar Avantapanaique nas terras do Canará com um exercito.*10 de Dezembro de 1607; *LML*, cod. 2, fol. 15: *Carta Régia sobre o mesmo assunto*, 2 de Janeiro de 1608.; *LML*, cod. 13, fols. 157: *Carta Régia. Obras a efectuar nas fortalezas do Canará. Mudança da fortaleza de Barcelor para o Cambolim.* 5 de Março de 1620.

577 *LML*, 15, fol. 9: *Carta do governador, Fernão de Albuquerque, respondendo a carta régia relativa à necessidade de se manter política de boa vizinhança com os potentados vizinhos, afirma ter seguido sempre tal forma de proceder, havendo concluído, por exemplo, apaz com Vencatapa Naique.* 20 de Janeiro de 1621.

578 António Bocarro, *Década 13, da História da Índia...*pp. 40, 77, 182-83.

579 In fact the Banghel king had been on very friendly terms for long and he had sensed the trouble quite some time earlier. He had written several letters to the Portuguese authorities asking for help to fortify his land and equip his forces with the arms: *LML*, cod. 9, fol. 180-182: *Carta régia ao vice-rei D. Jeronymo de Azevedo, lembrando-lhe novamente que preste o auxilio possível ao rei Banguel contra o Eventecapa-naique, por assim convir ao Estado,* 14 de Março de 1616

580 *ACE*, vol. I, doc. 6, 19 de Janeiro de 1619; *Doc. 18*, 13 de Agosto de 1619; Faria e Sousa, *Ásia Portuguesa*, vol VI, pp. 170-171.

581 *LML*, cod. 11, fols. 558, 26 de Fevereiro de 1619.

582 The fight between the kingdom of Olala and Banghel king had its origin in the late sixteenth century when the ruler of Olala had started constructing a fortress in his territory. The king ordered that that fortress should be demolished at any cost as it was considered dangerous for the safety of their own fortress. *LMG*, cod. n° 3-B, fols. 406-425, 12 de Janeiro de 1591.

583 *ACE*, vol. I, doc. 6, 19 de Janeiro de 1619; Faria e Sousa, *Ásia Portuguesa*, vol VI, pp. 170-171.

584 *ACE*, vol. I, doc. 12, pp. 32-33; *Sobre o Rey Banguel e fortaleza de Mangalore*, Abril, 13, 1619.

585 *ACE*, vol. I, doc. 13, pp. 37-40; *Treslado da carta que Putapa Regedor do Vencatapanaiq escreveu a S.S.* 17 de Abril de 1619.

586 *Ibid.*

587 *Ibid*, fol. 45-46.

588 *Ibid.*

589 *Ibid.* pp. 65-66.

590 *ACE*, vol. I, 66-67: *Cópia da carta de João Fernandez Leitão escrita ao Sr. Conde V.R.*, 15 de Outubro de 1619.

591 *Ibid:*

592 *Ibid.*

593 One can imagine the wrath of Venkatappa Nayaka, who had recently taken the title of protector and saviour of land and people, after hearing that the Portuguese had demolished a Pagoda!

594 *LML*, cod. 16, fols. 46-46v°: *Carta Régia ao conde vice-rei. Receberá uma carta do rei Banguel a queixar-se das pazes feitas com o Vencatapa Naique, com prejuízo da sua fortaleza de Banguel. Recomenda el-rei que tal assunto seja estudado em Comselho, a fim de se resolver o que fosse de justiça*, 27 de Fevereiro, 1622. In this codex, on pages 48-48v°, 530-531v°; and 612, there are letters which give a detailed picture of diplomatic relations between the two states during 1620-623; *ACE*, vol. I: *Cópia da carta de João Fernandez Leitão escrita ao Sr. Conde* V.R., 15th of October, 1619, pp. 68-69.

595 *Ibid*, pp. 69-70; *Copia da resposta que se escreueo a João frz leitão (Reply to the letter of João Fernandez Leitão by the Portuguese Viceroy*, Goa, dated, 23 October, 1619)..

596 HAG, *Reis Vizinhos*- cod. 1, fols. 18-18v°, *Instrução do vice-rei para João Fernandes Leitão para fazer as pazes entre Vencatapa Naique e o Rei Banguel, procurando convencer o primeiro que, da parte de Portugal, nunca houvera intenção de lhe fazer guerra, mas apenas de defender o rei Banguel, por ser vizinho e amigo da rainha de Olala.* Goa, 19 de Abril de 1619.

597 HAG, *Reis Vizinhos*- cod. 1, fols. 18v°-19: *Carta do Vice-rei, Conde de Redondo para Gaspar do Melo de Sampaio, capitão-mor do Gente da Guerra de Mangalor: O vice-rei informa que dera instruções a João Fernandes Leitão para ir avistar-se com Putapaya, regedor de Vencatapa Naique e com o rei Banguel, trabalhando para assentar as pazes entre os dois reinos.* Goa, 19 de Abril de 1619; *Idem*, fol. 64: *Carta do Conde Vice-rei para João Fernandes, acusando a recepção da sua carta, ordena que procurasse assentar a paz entre o Banguel e o Vencatapa Naique com a maior brevidade e do que*

nesta matéria fizer avise imediatamente o capitão Gaspar de Melo de Sampaio, Goa, 28 de Junho de 1619.

598 See chapter III.

599 *ACE*, vol. I, doc. 18, pp. 63-64: *Cópia de treslado de huã lembrança que vencatapa deu ao lingua sobre o que concede ao Banguel;* and also see the letter of Venkatappa Nayaka and the conditions of the treaty on the pp. 98-99.

600 *Ibid.* 100-110; See the copies of the original letter from all the belligerents.

601 *ACE*, vol. I, doc. 31, 20 de Outubro, 1621.

602 *LML*, 15, fol. 9: *Carta do governador, Fernão de Albuquerque, respondendo a carta régia relativa à necessidade de se manter política de boa vizinhança com os potentados vizinhos, afirma ter seguido sempre tal forma de proceder, havendo concluído, por exemplo, a paz com Vencatapa Naique. 20 de Janeiro de 1621; LML*, cod. 15, fol. 14v: *Carta Régia para o governador, ordenando particular cuidado com a disciplina. O rei Banguel tinha ido para Canharoto, porto dos Mouros e abrigo de muitos paraus ladrões, não fazendo caso do que devia ao Estado. Pedia ele agora que o governador instasse com Vencatapa Naique para lhe dar as terras prometidas no tratado de paz, o que convinha se fizesse, a fim de deixar de viver em terras de inimigos do Estado.* 10 de Janeiro de 1621; *ACE*, vol. I, doc. 18, pp. 63-64: *Treslado de huã lembrança que vencatapa deu ao lingua sobre o que concede ao Banguel,* and see the letter of Venkatappa Nayaka and the conditions of the treaty, pp. 98-99..

603 *ACE*, vol. 1, doc. 26: *Copia dos appontamentos que Vencatapa naique por João Fernandez Leitão ao Sr. Fernão d'Albuquerque do Conselho de S. Magestade Seu capitão-mor e Governador da India,* 3 de Dezembro de 1619: This was the final report that João Fernandez made after the various correspondecs he had from the ambassador of Banghel king, Issar Sinai, on 18th of Novembro, 1619.

604 *ACE, vol. 1,* doc. 25: *Cópia do treslado da carta que Escrueo Issar Sinay Bramene embaxador do Rey Banguel (que está com Vencatapa naique, a João Fernandez Leitão*, 18 de Novembro de 1619.

605 It is strange to note that the letter written by an ambassador of the Banghel king to mediate the peace between his ruler and the Portuguese carried such language. Naturally, he was completely under the influence of the Venkatappa Nayaka and had sensed the power that the ruler of Kanara possessed..

606 *ACE*, vol. I, docs. 13: *Sobre a mesma guerra de Mangalor e se fazerem pazes com Vencatappa Naiaque*, 17 de Abril de 1619.

607 *LML*, cod. 21, fols. 55: *Carta Régia para o Vice Rey da Índia,* Lisboa a 16 de Feuereiro de 1625.

608 Della Valle, *The Travel of Pietro della Valle...*, vol. II, pp. 314-15: it is strange that there is no reference of this treaty or mission in any Portuguese document.

609 Della Valle, *The Travel of Pietro della Valle...*, vol. II, pp. 253-54, 307.

610 Joan-Pau Rubiés, *Travel and Ethnology in the Renaissance..., see his comments on* pp. 353-368.

611 *LML*, cod. 24, fols. 183/43: *Carta Régia para o Vice Rey da Índia,* Lisboa a 6 de Março de 1627.

612 Such as Nalavathu Nadu, Sankara Narayana, Bairdur and Halligere. After the capture of these states, Venkatappa followed his military expeditions to the Bangajala, (Banghel) Savanta, Chouta, Mula, Kumbale and Kasaragodu and overpowered their rulers. He then marched to Mangalore and incorporated the whole kindom into his, except the areas around the Portuguese fortresses. Porbabaly he was carefully to not to involve the Portuguese in his conflicts. But when he attacked Bangajala and its ruler sought help from the Portuguese, it was unavoidable for them to interfere and land their soldiers in the territory of Mangalore. Confrontation between the two was inevitable. Venkatappa Nayaka next garrisoned and strengthened Mulki. Kodeyala, Muda Bidare, Ullala, Kumbala, Kasragodu, Puduvetta, Ballare, Kantamangala, Bandyadaka, Kundamkuli. Kothuru, Bachi, Sisita Chandragudi, Kidutar, Muda Kodayala and Phaniyala. The Queen of Olala also took part as an ally of Venkatappa, especially when he attacked Mangalore and Banghel. As retaliation the Portuguese attacked her capital but were repulsed and forced to retire. See Rama Sharma, *History of the Vijayanagar*, vol. II, pp. 142-143.

613 *ACE*, cod.1, doc. 77: *Conselho que o senhor Conde de Linhars visoRey e capitam geral da India fez em 22 de nouembro sobre a morte de Vencatapa Naique de que avisou Francisco de Sousa Alcoforado por sua carta de 18 de nouembro de 1629*, 22 de Novembro de 1629; *LMG*, cod. 13 B-fls. fols. 447-454: *Emformação da couzas socedidas neste* Canara *Para ver o Sr. Conde de Linhares, Visorei da India, feita por Manuel de Sousa de Meneses, Barcelor,* 15 de Janeiro de 1630; No matter what the Portuguese documents speak about Venkatappa Nayaka, Indian historians like Rama Sharma refers him as "old (in terms of experienced) and able chief", *The History of the Viayanagar Empire,* vol. II, pp. 159.

614 *ACE*, cod.1, doc. 77: *Conselho que o senhor Conde de Linhares visoRey e capitam geral da India fez em 22 de nouembro sobre a morte de Vencatapa Naique de que avisou Francisco de Sousa Alcoforado por sua carta de 18 de nouembro* de 1629, 22 de Novembro de 1629.

615 ACE, vol. I, doc. 77: *Conselho que o senhor conde de Linhares, visorei e capitam geral da Índia fez em 22 de Nouembro sobre a morte de Venctappa Naique de que avisou Francisco de Sousa Alcaforado por sua carta de 18 de Nouembro de 1629,* 22 de Nouembro de 1629. A letter, addressed to the Viceroy from Barcelor, written by Diogo de Sousa Meneses on the 16th of January 1630, summarises these events: *"A vinte e sete annos que o Rey Vencatapa Naique comquistou todos os reinos e terras desta costa do Canara e de seu gonção sogeitando a todos os reis e rainhas e balalas*

a quemtomou todos seu tizouros fazendolhe em todos estes annos muita tiranias, athé que falecey na sua Cidade de aquery em des dias de Novembro de 629, em que logo foy aleuantado por Rey neto Virabadaranaique mançebo de vinte annos muito dado a delicias e maos custumes..".

616 Such as Sunda, Beleguim, Bassapatão, Belur, Serra, Rangel, Maizur, Gumbia, Nerenqui, and Umazar.

617 Rama Sharma, *The History of the Viayanagar Empire*, vol. II, pp. 159-60.

618 *Ibid.*

619 *LML*, cod. 42, fols. 59-59v°: *Carta do Vice-rey da Índia, Pero da Silva ao Rey dando conta dos acontecimentos na India*, 27 de Feverreiro de 1638.

620 *Ibid*; for complete details of the Bijapuri-Kanara wars of 1638-39, and how the Sultan of Bijapur took advantage of alliances of some dissatisfied fractions of that region see Rama Sharma *The History of the Vijayanagar Empire*, pp. 210-211, 213-223.

621 *Ibid; LML*, cod. 13-A, fol. 479v-482v: *Relatório anual preparado por Manuel de Sousa de Meneses, por ordem do Vice-rei, O conde de Linhares, começa por se referir ao falecimento de Vencatapa Naique, a 10 de Novembro de 1629 na cidade de Aquery, o qual havia muitos anos exercia forte tirania sobre os potentados vizinhos, tendo-lhes conquistado suas terras e roubado seus tesouros. O rei que lhe sucedera, Virabadar Naique, logo que tomara posse do governo, recebera um embaixador do Idalcão exigindo-lhe as páreas atrasadas e ameaçando-o de guerra, caso não entregasse aos seus legítimos possuidores as terras anexadas pelo avô, e vira-se atacado pelos reis de Sunda, Beleguim, Bassapatão, Belur, Serra, Rangel, Maizur, Gumbia, Nerenqui, Umazar, e muitas "balalas" e rainhas vizinhas. Barcelor*, 15 de Janeiro de 1630.

622 *Ibid.*

623 BNL, *FG*. Cod. 939, part. 2, fols. 4, 7; *LML*, cod. 30, fols. 249-51; Bib, Ajud. Cod. 51-VII-12, fols. 90-91, 98-99; ACF, cod. 1161, fols. 122v-123v.

624 *Ibid.*

625 *LMG*, Cod. 13-A, fls. 261-66: *Carta de Vice-rei da Índia para El-Rei*. Goa, 20 de Fevereiro de 1630. *Carta do Vice-rei, D. Miguel de Noronha, o Conde de Linhares, para o Rei, Informando ter exposto ao Conselho a carta de Francisco de Sousa Alcoforado, capitão de Onor, e ter sido decidido pelo mesmo seguir-se o conselho expresso na dita carta, e mandar-se para o Reino de Vencatapa Naique um homem experiente e capaz de executar, sendo escolhido para isso, Diogo de Sousa de Meneses. A este oficial competiria construir uma fortaleza na Ilha de Cambolim, tal como fora proposto. Em seguida diz ter assentado com o embaixador de Virabadar Naique o comércio da pimenta, em troca da madeira de Onor, mas sòmente por um ano, e ter mandado a Mascate um carregamento de arroz. Participa ter também enviado ao capitao Diogo de Sousa de Meneses mais três navios carregados de armas e outras mercadorias que lhe tinha pedido para poder auxiliar os inimigos de*

Virabadar Naique, e aproveitar a ocasião para levar o rei de Barcelor a ceder-lhe a referida Ilha de Cambolim. Refere-se também à recomendação que fizera ao dito capitão para obter do mesmo potentado o comércio do arroz e da pimenta e permissão para abrir um canal que ligasse o rio ao mar, indispensável para esse mesmo comércio, devendo ser esse canal defendido por um baluarte construído no local mais apropriado; todo este projecto estava bem encaminhado e o canal já estava em construção. Acrescenta que prometera também ajudar o rei de Coltor a atacar Virabadar Naique, a troco de o dito rei entregar anualmente uma certa quantidade de pimenta. Finalmente refere-se à falta de saúde de Diogo Sousa de Meneses, e à tenção que formava de o substituir por seu filho D. Fernando. Goa, 20 de Fevereiro de 1630.

626 *Ibid.*

627 *Ibid.*

628 *Ibid.*

629 *ABO-BP*, vol. IV, fol. 311; Although its construction had started in 1629, it was still under construction in 1631, see the letter of Conde de Linhares, *LML*, cod. 29, fols. 1-3v°, de Goa a 20 de Julho de 1631, appendix- 1-A

630 *LML*, cod. 38, fol. 4, *Carta do Vice-rei da Índia, Pêro da Silva, dando conta do estado geral das coisas no Estado da Índia,* Goa 5 de Março de 1637.

631 *ACE*, vol. II, pp. 79-83: *Copia do conçelho sobre os proes que Reçeberia o estado havendo fortaleza na ilha do Cambolim e quaes das duas fortalezas de Barçellor, ou do dito Cambolim seria conueniente ao estado,* 25 de Abril de 1636. *APO-BP*, Tomo IV, vol. II, parte I^a, pp. 311-318..

632 *LMG*, Cod. 13-A: *Carta de Vice-rei da Índia para El-Rei*, Goa, 20 de Fevereiro de 1630, fls. 261-66; *ACE*, vol. I, doc. 77.

633 *Ibid.*

634 *ACE*, vol. I, doc. 85: *Conselho que o Senhor Conde de Linhares fez em 7 de Janeiro de 1630*, 7 de Janeiro de 1630.

635 He is also known as Vitula Nayaka. He was one of the richest business magnates of this region and commanded high respect among the Kanara as well the Portuguese authorities.

636 *ACE*, vol. I, doc. 85: *Conselho que o Senhor Conde de Linhares fez em 7 de Janeiro de 1630*, 7 de Janeiro de 1630.

637 *LMG*, cod. 13-A, fol. 261: *Carta do Vice-rei, D. Miguel de Noronha, o Conde de Linhares, para o Rei, em que participa ter também enviado ao capitão Diogo de Sousa de Meneses mais três navios carregados de armas e outras mercadorias que lhe tinha pedido para poder auxiliar os inimigos de Virabadar Naique, e aproveitar a ocasião para levar o rei de Barcelor a ceder-lhe a referida Ilha de Cambolim.* Goa, 20 de Fevereiro de 1630.

638 Biker (ed.) *Collecção de tratados e concertos de pazes*, tomo I, pp. 277: *Auto de posse real e autual que Vitulá Sinay, Embaixador de El-Rey Virappá Naique, deo da ilha do Cambolim ao Embaixador do Senhor Conde de*

Linhares, V. Rey da India, Baltazar Mainho. 12 de Maio de 1631: This island of Cambolim was ceded to the Portuguese by the Virappa Nayaka, on 12 May 1631 during the civil war that followed after the death of Venkatappa Nayaka. However, Veerabhadra Nayaka, the grandson of Venkatappa Nayaka became the next ruler. But Vira Odeyar, (Virappa Nayaka) a son of Rama Raja Nayaka, the elder brother of the late Nayaka, set up a rival claim and began ruling at Kanara. Veerabhadra therefore, fixed his headquarters at Anandapura. In this dispute a lot of damage was done to the integrity of the State and there was considerable loss of life. In the end, Veerabhadra succeeded in establishing his power in Kanara and remained undisputed Nayaka of Kanara till 1644 when he was defeated by Shivappa Nayaka during a civil war.

639 *LMG*, cod. 13-A, fol. 261, Goa, 20 de Fevereiro de 1630.

640 *LMG*, cod. 14, fls. 212v-213.

641 Biker, (ed.) *Collecção de tratados...*, tomo I, pp. 270-72: *Contrato de Pazes celebradas entre o Vice-Rey, Conde de Linhares e os Embaixadores de Virapá Naiquee do Canará em* 7 de Março de 1631.

642 *Ibid.*

643 *Ibid; ACE*, vol. I, doc. 115: *Sobre a Relação que Sua Excelência fez da sua Jornada ate Cochim que o Conselho approvou,* 22 de Abril de 1631.

644 *ACE*, vol. I, doc. 126: *Conselho de 18 de nouembro de 1631 sobre não querer Virabadranaique jurar as pazes..,* 18 de Novembro de 1631, pp. 391.

645 *Ibid.*

646 *Ibid.*

647 No exact date has been found in the available sources.

648 *LML*, cod. 29, fols. 163: *Carta de Viso Rey da Índia, o Conde de Linhares para o Rey dando conta da morte do Virapa Naique e como o Virabadra naique negou todos acordos feito por ele.* De Goa a 18 de Dezembro de 1631.

649 *Ibid; ACE*, vol. I, doc. 138: *Conselho de 25 de mayo de 632 sobre o que escreueo Baltazar marinho que foi por embaxador a ElRey Virabdranaique,* 25 de Maio de 1632.

650 *LML, cod. 38, fols. 4-10: Carta do Vice-rei da Índia, Pêro da Silva, dando conta do estado geral das coisas no Estado da Índia,* Goa 5 de Março de 1637.

651 *LMG, cod. 15, fol. 27: Carta do Vice-rei, D. Miguel de Noronha, o Conde de Linhares, para o Rei, O vice-rei informa que Virabadar Naique se resolveu a fazer uma fortaleza na ilha de Cambolim, pertencente a el-rei; participa as providências que tomou quanto a este assunto, avisando o dito Virabadar que lhe declararia guerra se não destruísse tudo o que já estava feito e afirmando que nesta guerra favoreceria os seus inimigos de Banguel e Serra Grande, com os quais se aliaria. Informa ainda que nesta conformidade,*

mandou para aquelas partes uma armada, comandada por Domingos Ferreira Beliago. Goa, 22 de Novembro de 1632; *LMG*, cod. 15, fol. 96: *Carta do Vice-rei, D. Miguel de Noronha, o Conde de Linhares, informando o rei da maneira como tem provido e fortificado as fortalezas do Canará e de toda a assistência e cuidado que elas lhe têm merecido, como nunca mereceram a outro vice-rei. E, em virtude das guerras que os reis daquelas partes têm tido uns com os outros, foi também necessário "dobrar" as armadas do Canará, para que houvesse ali sempre grande assistência, além da protecção a dar às cáfilas.* Goa, 9 de Outubro de 1632.

652 *LMG, cod. 16-A, fol. 8: Carta régia para o Vice-rei, o Conde de Linhares, ordenando ao vice-rei que não aceite a proposta feita por Visapara Naique sobre a entrega da fortaleza de Barcelor, porque não era honroso aceitá-la e criaria maus precedentes entre os reis vizinhos. Em seguida aprova as medidas tomadas para se assentarem as pazes com o Canará e manda consultar o Conselho sobre se conservar ou a fortaleza de Cambolim ou a de Barcelor ou ambas, e enviar para o Reino os pareceres escritos dos conselheiros e demais pessoas experientes ouvidas sobre esta matéria, acompanhados do seu próprio parecer. Ordena ainda que intervenha nas desordens do Canará como lhe parecer ser de mais justiça.* Madrid, 3 de Março de 1632.

653 *ACE*, vol. I, doc. 147: *Conselho sobre a fortaleza que fazem os Canaras na Ylha do Cambolim*, 13 de Novembro de 1632.

654 Each *Khandi* used to weigh around 220 kgs: see Appendices on Coins-Weights & Measures.

655 *ACE, vol. I, pp. 569-571: Contrato de pazes com ElRey Virabhadra Naique do Canará. O anno de 1633.*

656 Or corsarios, means pirates, *ACE*, vol. I, doc. 150: *Conselho de 21 de Dezembro de 1632 sobre a chegada de vitula sinay embaixador delRey virabadranaique.*

657 *LMG*, cod. 15, fol. 110: *Carta do Vice-rei, D. Miguel de Noronha, o Conde de Linhares, para o Rei, participando que a ilha de Cambolim está debaixo da obediência do Estado, mas que ainda se não cobra dela o rendimento desejado. Já há uma fortaleza construída na dita ilha, mas há toda a conveniência em se levantar outra para sua maior segurança. Fala a seguir de assuntos de paz referentes ao Nirabocada Naique, dizendo que sem ordem expressa do rei não desmantelará a fortaleza de Barcelor, se bem que o ache muito necessário.* Goa, 11 de Outubro de 1632.

658 *LML*, cod. 29, fols. 163: *Carta de Viso Rey da Índia, o Conde de Linhares para o Rey dando conta como o rei de Canará queria facilitar tudo através do seu embaixador*, de Goa a 18 de Dezembro de 1631. See the same letter in the appendix.

659 *ACE*, vol. I, doc. 150: *Conselho de 21 de Dezembro de 1632 sobre a chegada de vitula sinay embaixador delRey virabadranaique.*

660 *Ibid.*

661 *LMG*, cod. 15, fls. 26: *Carta do Vice-Rei da Índia D. Miguel de Noronha, Conde de Linhares*, Goa, 22 de Novembro de 1632; HAG, *Livro das Ordens régias, cod. 2, fls. 20-20v°; Carta do Vice-rei Conde de Linhares para El-Rei*, Goa, 2 de Fevereiro de 1633.

662 *ACE*, vol. I, doc. 132, 22 de Março de 1632.

663 Biker (ed.) *Collecção de tratados e concertos de pazes...*, tomo I, pp. 299-304: *Contrato de pazes com ElRey Virabadra Naique do Canará. O anno de* 1633, Abril 5: Copied from *Livro de Pazes*, n° 2, fls. 17; *ACE*, vol. I, pp. 569-571.

664 *Ibid.*

665 *Ibid;* For the terms of the peace treaty and the letter of the Veerabhadra Nayaka, see, Biker (ed) *Collecção de tratados ...*, tomo I, pp. 299-305, 1633.

666 *ACE*, vol. II, doc. 5: *Sobre a pimenta que ElRey Virabadarnaique não quis dar pello preço do contrato da paz.*, 18 de Novembro de 1634.

667 *Ibid.*

668 *Ibid.*

669 *LMG*, cod. 19-B, fol. 563: *Carta do Vice-Rei Conde de Linhares a El-Rei*, Goa 6 de Feuereiro de 1635.

670 *Ibid.*

671 See Afzal Ahmad, *The Portuguese Trade in the Seventeenth century*...Chapters 3 & 4.

672 *LMG*, cod. 19-B, fol. 563: *Carta do Vice-Rei Conde de Linhares a El-Rei*, Goa 6 de Feuereiro de 1635.

673 *Ibid.*

674 *Ibid.*

675 *ACE*, vol. II, pp. 54-56 , 17 de Janeiro de 1636; *LML*, cod. 40, fols 16-16v°, 28 de Fevereiro de 1636.

676 Chatins *e* Balals, were contractors of pepper from Kanara. The present terminology of Chatim either could be Shethi and or Baneas; Belalas or Belalis were the cultivators or farmers of pepper in the seventeenth century. *ACE*, vol. II, p. 75, 15 de Abril de 1636: See Dalgado, *Glossário Luso-Aziático*, vol. 1.

677 *ACE*, vol. II, pp. 54-56: *Copia do conçelho sobre a Alteração dElRey virabadranaiq*, 17 de Janeiro de 1636.

678 *Ibid.*

679 *LML*, Cod. 40, fol. 225-226: *Carta do Vice-rey da Índia, sugerindo, perante ameaças olandesas e falta das verbas adequadas da pimenta, para comprar a canela para que o barco não fosse vazio para Portugal*. De Goa a 25 de Novembro de 1637.

680 *Ibid.*

681 LML, cod. 40, fols. 239-240v°: *Carta do Vice-rei e as cópias, em conjunto, das cartas do Govenrador geral das fortalezas do Canará e do contratador Sancara da Gama,* 29 de Outubro de 1637.

682 HAG, *Livro dos Segredos* cod. 1, fols. 15-16: *Regimento dado pelo vice-rei, Pêro da Silva, ao capitão-mor da Costa do Canará, Martim Teixeira de Azevedo, quando foi invernar a Cananor. Ordena-lhe que trate com a urgência possível, por intermédio de Sancara da Gama, "gentio", experimentado, o negócio de pimenta, visto que o rei Virabadranaique deseja aumentar o preço do mesmo género e que é necessário haver pimenta para várias naus do Reino, recomendando que admita o aumento no preço, sòmente em caso de extrema necessidade.* Goa 1 de Setembro de 1637.

683 LML, Cod. 40, fols. 138-138v°: *Carta do Vicerei da India para o rei participando das mudanças de atitudes de Virabadar Naique em relação à pimenta e sobre a fortaleza do Cambolim,* De Goa a 20 de Novembro de 1637: See the whole text of the correspondence in the appendix. IV-C.

684 ACE, vol. II, doc. 25: *Copia do conçelho sobre a partida da armada de Mallaca, e huns appontamentos que deo o embaxador delRey Virabadranaique,* 12 de Abril 1636.

685 *Ibid.*

686 HAG, *Livro dos Segredos*, cod. 1, fol. 27, v., *Carta do vice-rei Pêro da Silva, ao rei Virabadranaique (do Canará). Informa-o que Rama Poi e António Borges, casado e morador em Barcelor, lhe comunicaram o negócio secreto que o rei Virabadranaique lhes confiou, e pede-lhe que mande os capítulos necessários, afirmando que jurará e prometerá, ele vice-rei, guardar o capitulado logo que o rei Virabadranaique o jure e prometa, para que assim seja perpétua a amizade dos portugueses e de toda a gente do Canará "enquanto durar o sol, e a lua"; promete que, feito isto, diligenciará que a Rainha de Banguel tenha relações amistosas com o dito rei e que o seu embaixador na corte de Idalxá seja auxiliado na consecução do seu desiderato pelo embaixador português na mesma corte.* Goa, 14 de Dezembro de 1638.

687 ACE, vol. I, p. 75-78: *Apontamentos que apresentou ao Sr. Visorrey Deuarassa Sinay embaxador delRey virbadranaique,* 15 de Abril de 1636.

688 *Ibid.*

689 *Ibid.*

690 *Ibid.*, p. 78

691 *Ibid.*

692 ACE, vol. II, doc. 27: *Copia do Conçelho sobre os proes que Reçeberia o estado havendo fortaleza na Ilha do Cambolim e quaes das duas fortalezas de Barcelor, ou do dito Cambolim seria conveniente ao estado,* 25 de Abril de 1636; *LML*, cod. 39, fol. 17: *Carta Régia para o vice-rei da Índia dando instução para evitar demolir a fortaleza de Barcelor e tentar negociar paz com Virabadranaique a todo custo,* Lisboa 3 de Dezembro de 1637. (assinada pela D. Margarida, Duquesa de Mantua).

693 *ACE*, vol. II, doc. 49: *Copia do Conçelho sobre as cuazas delRey Virabadranaique, e se buscar Pimenta por todas as vias possiueis,* 30 de março de 1637.

694 *LML*, Cod. 40, fols. 138-138v°: *Carta do Vicerei da India para o rei participando das mudanças de atitudes de Virabadar Naique em relação à pimenta e sobre a fortaleza do Cambolim,* De Goa a 20 de Novembro de 1637: See the whole text of the correspondence in the appendix..

695 *ACE, vol. II,* doc. 52: *Copia do Concelho sobre os capitães de moçambique não fazerem auzençia daquella fortaleza e sobre o virabadranaique estar apertado do Banguel e mais Reis da Junta.* 29 de Julho de 1637.

696 *LML*, cod. 44, fols. 421-420v°: *Carta do Vice-rei, Pêro da Silva ao Rei, Sobre os problemas em que o Virabadra naique se achaua,* 1639.

697 *LML*, cod. 44, fols. 422, 6 de Maio de 1939. See Appendix- IV-D

698 *LMG*, cod. 21-A, fols. 50, Lisboa, 18 de Fevereiro de 1640; Rama Sharma *The History of the Vijayanagar Empire*, pp. 209-211.

699 See chapter five.

700 *Ibid.*

701 *ACE*, vol. II, doc. 62: *Sobre o Socorro que se deve mandar a Virabadranaique e segredo E sobre a Ilha de Cambolim e outras particulares,* 2, Março de 1638.

702 *LML*, cod. 45, fols. 348-49v°.

703 *ACE*, vol. II, doc. 62: *Sobre o Socorro que se deve mandar a Virabadranaique e segredo E sobre a Ilha de Cambolim e outras particulares,* 2, Março de 1638.

704 *Ibid.*

705 *Ibid.*

706 *ACE*, vol. II, doc. 62: *Sobre o Socorro que se deve mandar a Virabadranaique e segredo. E sobre a Ilha de Cambolim e outras particulares,* 2, Março de 1638. *"...E assentou que visto não ser possiuel ajuntarmos tanta gente (dous mil homens de armas dos naturais desta de Goa e alguns trabalhadores para que fizecem as fortificações necessárias) polla não hauer nem fazer as tais fortificações com a pressa que conuem allem de outras muitas difficuldades se encomendaçe este negoçeo ao capitão de Barçelor mandandolhe para isso as ordens necessarias para que quando virabadranaique quizeçe dar a Ilha do Cambolim procurasse que elle mesmo fizeçe a fortaleza".*

707 *Ibid.*

708 *LMG*, cod. 21-A, fols. 52: *Carta delRei para o Vice-rei da India, respondendo sobre as informações que recebeu das dissidências do Canará, entre o Idalcão, Mogor e Virabradanaique, e das queixas que a Rainha de Olala e Rei de Banguel fizeram ao Idalcão, contra o Virabradanaique. Recomenda ao vice-rei que empregue toda a diplomacia na sua convivência com estes reis, entretendo-os com esperanças e enviando-lhes socorros e munições*

secretamente. Pede-lhe relação dos nomes das pessoas que ficaram servindo nas fortalezas do Canará, assim como as mercês que lhes foram feitas. Acha que toda a atenção do vice-rei deve ser, em primeiro lugar, dirigida para que as coisas do Canará não sofram alteração, pois isso resultaria em grande prejuízo do comércio da pimenta, que se não deve pôr à mercê dos estrangeiros, tão cubiçosos dela. Quanto ao assunto da fortaleza de Cambolim, Sua Majestade propõe que seja apresentado em Conselho, e os votos sejam secretos e enviados para o Reino, a fim de que se possa deliberar sobre o assunto. Lisboa, 18 de Fevereiro de 1640.

709 *Ibid.*

710 HAG, *Livro do Segredo nº 1, fol. 27vº,* 14 de Dezembro de 1638.

711 This is the first reference in a Portuguese document to the ruler of the Kingdom of Banghel as a Queen. The previous king had died sometime toward the end of 1630s.

712 HAG, *Livro do Segredo nº 1, fol. 27vº, Carta para El Rey Virabadranaique,* 14 de Dezembro de 1638..

713 *Ibid,* fol. 22: *Carta de El-Rey Filipe para o Vice-Rei da Índia,* 7 de Março de 1640; *Ibid,* fol. 38, *Carta de El-Rey Filipe para o Vice-Rei da Índia,* 16 de Março de 1640.

714 *Ibid.*

715 *LMG,* cod. 21-B, fol. 514: *Carta do vice-rei da Índia, D. João da Silva Telo, Conde de Aveiras, para Sua Magestade.* Goa, 2 de Agosto de 1641.

716 *Ibid.*

717 He is also called Sivappa by many historians.

718 In order to understand the political structure of the Indian rulers of the South, see the second chapter where all the information has been provided in detail. For an exhaustive political history of south India, see vol. II, of Rama Sharma *The History of the Vijayanagar Empire,* pp. 209-224.

719 *Ibid.,* pp. 223-231.

720 *Ibid.*

721 *Ibid.*

722 ACE ACE, *vol.* III, doc. 15*: Conselho sobre o çerco que Sivapanaique poz a fortaleza de Canarcota, e receos que havia de vir sobre à do Cambolim, e o provimento que se deue mandar para ellas...,* 20 de Junho de 1644.

723 *Ibid.*

724 *ACE, vol. III, doc. 64, Conselho de 12 de Fevereiro de 1646.*

725 *Ibid.*

726 *ACE,* vol. III, doc. 71: *António Borges da Costa que era enuiado ao Canará a tratar de preço da pimenta...,* 1 de Abril de 1647.

727 Bib. Aj. Cod. 51-VII-29: *Carta que escreueo da India o Padre Frey António da Conceição comissário geral.* Goa, 1 de Janeiro de 1654. He has depicted

very minutely the political and economical situation of the Portuguese *Estado da Índia* in general and in the Kanara State in particular.

728 *Ibid.*

729 Rama Sharma, *History of the Vijayanagar*, vol. II, p. 288-89.

730 ACE, vol. III, doc. 121: *Sobre ser chamado ao concelho Dom Francisco de Castelo Branco para dar informação da perda de Barcelor e o estado em que ficaua Camboly*, 5 de Novembro de 1652; *LMG*, cod. 23-B, fls. 395-395v°: *Carta do Governador, D. Brás de Castro para el-rei, informando da Conquista da fortaleza de Mangalor pelo rei do Canará. Morte de Sebastião de Carvalho, seu capitão. Cerco posto pelo mesmo rei a Onor e perigo em que ficava. Negociações de paz propostas pelo tanadar de Ancolá e auxílio oferecido pelo rei de Sunda. Socorro enviado a Onor*, Goa, 20 de Janeiro de 1654.

731 ACE, vol. III, doc. 115: *Sobre se haver de socorrer as fortalesas do Canará com mais navios da armada do Canará os aprestos nesseçarios, 23 de Setembro de 1652;* doc. 116; *10 de Outubro de 1652;* Doc. 117, *Sobre auer de hir ao canara a armada do norte de que he capitam geral Tristão da Silveira*, 10 de Outubro de 1652.

732 ACE, vol. III, doc. 119: *Sobre se socorrer Canara depois de largado Barcelor.* 28 Outubro de 1652.

733 ACE, vol. III, doc. 121: *Sobre ser chamado ao concelho Dom Francisco de Castelo Branco para dar informação da perda de Barcelor e o estado em que ficaua Camboly.*, 5 de Novembro de 1652.

734 *Ibid.*

735 Rama Sharma, *The History of Vijajyanagar*, pp. 288-289.Danvers, *The Portuguese in India*, vol. II, pp. 303-304.

736 Bib. Aj. Cod. 51-VII-29, *Carta que escreueo da India o Padre Frey António da Conceição comissário geral*. Goa, 1 de Janeiro de 1654.

737 ACE, vol. III, doc. 12*: Sobre ser chamado ao concelho Dom Francisco de Castel Branco para dar informação da perda de Barcelor e o estado em que ficaua Camboly*. 5 de Novembro de 1652.

738 ACE, vol. III, doc. 120, *Sobre se haver vindo carta do capitam de Cananor e a guerra que o Rey daquella terra quer fazer ao Canara dando lhe poluora e moniçōes*. 30 de Outubro de 1652; *LMG*, cod. 24, fls. 127: *Carta Del-rei, D. João IV, para o governador da Índia, D. Brás de Castro, dando ordem para conservar as fortalezas do Canará, enquanto durar a guerra com aquele rei, principalmente a de Mangalor. Mas se a paz se fizer, com os votos dos Conselheiros, poder-se-á desmantelar a de Onor, etc*, Lisboa, 20 de Março de 1654.

739 *Ibid.*

740 ACE, vol. III, doc. 124*: Sobre a vinda de Ramapoi emviado dos pouuos do Canara com cartas para a cidade e ao Rverendo Padre Provincial da companhia de Jesvs*, 19 de Dezembro de 1652.

741 HAG, *Livro de Regimento e Instruções*, cod. 5, fols. 66-66v°, 22 de Fevereiro de 1653.

742 *Idem*, doc. 125, *Conselho Sobre a hida do mesmo Ramapoy*, 26 de Dezembro de 1652.

743 *ACE*, vol. III, doc. 129: *Sobre a nomeação que se fizerão do Padre Gonçalo Martins para hir ao Canara a tratar das pazes*. 19 de Fevereiro de 1653.

744 *ACE*, vol. III, doc. 130, *Sobre a hida do Padre Gonçalo Martins para o Canara e João Rodrigues Viegas para Onor*. 21 de Fevereiro de 1653.

745 Pissurlenkar, *Agentes Hindus da Diplomacia...*, pp. 32-34; Pissurlenkar has given exhaustive detail about the services rendered by Ramogi Kothari and his family to the Portuguese.

746 *ACE*, vol. III; doc. 135: *Sobre se mandar vir o padre Gonçalo Martins do Canara e ficar em Onor João Rodrigues Viegas*. 7 de Abril de 1653.

747 *ACE*, vol. III; doc. 146: *Sobre a entrada que fizerão os Canaras em Mangalor[e] hauerse de socorrer aquela praça com poluora pellouros repairos e algumas carnes*, 27 de agosto de 1653.

748 *Ibid; LMG*, cod. 23 – B, fols. 395-395v°: *Carta do Vice-Rei da Índia, D. Brás de Castro para el-rei Conquista da fortaleza de Mangalor pelo rei do Canará. Morte de Sebastião de Carvalho, seu capitão. Cerco posto pelo mesmo rei a Onor e perigo em que ficava. Negociações de paz propostas pelo tanadar de Ancolá e auxílio oferecido pelo rei de Sunda. Socorro enviado a Onor.* Goa, 20 de Janeiro de 1654.

749 *ACE*. doc. 146: *Sobre a entrada que fizerão os Canaras em Mangalore e hauerse de socorrer aquella praça com poluora pellouros repairos e algumas carnes*. 27 de Agosto de 1653.

750 Vithoji or Vithalji.

751 Ancola lies in the territory of Mangalore.

752 *ACE*, vol. III, doc. 163, *Sobre a carta que escreueo o naique Varymor de Ancola querer medianeiro e em effeituar a paz entre o estado, e El Rey Siuapanaique*. 19 de Fevereiro de 1654..

753 Mangalore was lost in August 1653.

754 In fact, no exact date for the losses of Portuguese fortress of Mangalore, Barcelore, Onor and Cambolim to the Shivappa Nayaka, has been provided by any Indian or European authors. Rama Sharma, whose work, *The History of Vijayanagar* has been quoted earlier, and who has used most of the Kannada (the language spoken in Kanara) sources, refers to this fact. See pp. 288-289. The process by which these fortresses were lost was prolonged over a considerable period of time while military and diplomatic measures were taken to try to save them. Also see Shastry, *Studies in Indo-Portuguese History*, p. 59.

755 *Ibid*.

756 *ACE*, vol. III, doc. 169: *Que visto não se concluir a paz com o enuiado del Rey Siuapanaique se socorresse Onor com o mais que pudesseser para se hir defendendo*. 27 de Fevereiro de 1654.

757 *Ibid.*

758 *ACE*, vol. III doc. 170: *Copia dos assentos feitos em Onor*...22 de Fevereiro de 1654.

759 *ACE*, vol. III, doc. 171: Sobr*e se ajustar com Malopa Mallo enviado del Rey Siuappanaique os contratos da paz na forma da ordem que se remeteo ao Capitam de onor, e a Pero pinto de Mello, e Padre António Nunes porquanto dantes hauia tratado não pode ter efeito por lhe faltar poder, 5 de Março 1654*; HAG, *Livro de Regimentos e Instruções*, cod. 5, fols. 82-82v°, *Regimento que se deu ao Padre António Nunes da Companhia de Jesus, a Francisco de Sousa Alcaforado e a Pero Pinto de Mello pera tratarem a paz com el Rey Siuappanaique*, 6 de Março de 1654..

760 *ACE, vol. III*, doc. 175: *Que havia vindo Pero Pinto de mello com auizo de que não esteue o enuiado de Siuapanaique pelas condições que o estado offerecia, e que se hia continuando com grande aperto e necessitaua de socorro.* 28 de Abril de 1654.

761 *ACE, vol. III*, doc. 176: *Sobre se tratar de nouo do conceguimento da paz com o Canara por via de Francisco de Souza pela maneira que neste assento se difere*. 4 de Maio de 1654..

762 *Ibid:* doc. 177, *Sobre se dar a execução o que se havia assentado no Concelho antecendente dese socorrer Onor,* 9 de Maio de 1654.

763 *Ibid;* It is important to note that this is the year when the Adil Shah of Bijapur became seriously ill and died. Therefore, the immediate task of sending someone to mediate between the Portuguese and the Shivappa Nayaka would not have been the priority of the nobles at his court.

764 *Idem.*

765 *ACE*, vol. III, doc. 185, 9 de Agosto de 1654; Doc. 186, 5 de Setembro de 1654.

766 *APO-BP*, vol. IV, fol. 311, 313.

767 *LML*, cod. 29, fols. 74: *Carta de Viso Rey da Índia, o Conde de Linhares para o Rey: Virapa Naique Rey do Equery e Canara com quem selebrey as pazes que nesta mesma via envio a V. Magestade he morto, suçedeo lhe no Reino Virabadranaique a quem elle havia despojado, athe esta hora me não tem o dito Virabadranaique mandado confirmar as pazes, mas persuadome o fará porque estão as armas de V. Magestade naqueles seus Reinos muy respeitads das guerras que tem este Rey, e os mais da Índia dou em carta particular conta a V. Magestade cuja Catholia e Real pessoa Deus guarde como a Christandade e Seus Vassalos havemos mister* de Goa a XI de Agosto de 1631.

768 *LMG*, cod. 23-B, fol. 375: *Carta do* Governador *D. Brás de Castro ao Rei sobre mau procedimento do bispo D. Mateus que não só exortou os naturais de Bardês à revolta mas ainda lhe escreveu cartas insolentes, motivo porque tentava apoderar-se dele para o fazer embarcar para o Reino.* Goa, 25 de Janeiro de 1654; Cod. 23-B, fols. 506; *Carta do Governador D. Bras de*

Castro ao Rei, 27 de Janeiro de 1654. *LMG,* cod. 24 fol. 142: *Treslado de outro capitulo da Carta do Conselho Geral escrita a Meza do Santo Officio desta Inquisição do anno* de 1654. Lisboa, 17 de Março de 1654; *LMG,* cod. 24, fol. 247: *Carta do governador da Índia, D. Brás de Castro, para o rei. Sobre o lavatório que os gentios costumam fazer em Chaúl, o editar que se publicou por parte do Santo Ofício e a alteração que daí resultou.* (Goa, 3 de Fevereiro de 1655; *Sobre a passagem dos cristãos e gentios ao Lavatório.* Também ver a carta do Vice Rey, Conde de Sarzedas ao Rei, 3 de Fevereiro de 1655: *ACE,* vol. III, p. 578: Note: This document doesn't exist in the original as cited in this edition. Therefore, I have used it as it is published in this edition. It might have been taken from elsewhere by the editor.

769 *ACE,* vol. III, doc. 199.

770 *LMG,* cod. 26-B, fol. 540: *Carta de Francisco de Melo de Castro para el-rei, sobre o envio dum mensageiro ao rei Sivapa Naique e as razões que levaram a isso; como o rei andava em guerra, o enviado falou com o irmão a quem chamam o rei Pequeno; boa recepção da parte do dito rei; as razões que apontou em como não podia dar resposta alguma na ausência do rei; pedido de entrega dos navios ali entrados, obrigados pelo tempo; os reis da Índia nos respeitam consoante o nosso poderio; o rei Sivapa Naique tem-se portado como nosso inimigo.* Goa, 21 de Março de 1660.

771 *ACE,* vol. IV, doc. 5: *Conselho sobre as cartas que hauião recebido do Barcellor do Capitam mor da armada dos periches Luis da costa.* 5 de Outubro de 1659.

772 *ACE,* vol. IV, doc. 13, 4 de Março de 1661.

773 Rama Sharma, *History of the Vijayanagar,* vol. II, pp. 291-322.

774 Biker (ed) *Collecção de tratados...,* tomo VI, *Contrato ds Pazes feitas entre os Governadores da India António de Mello de Castro, e Manuel Côrte-real de Sampaio com El-Rey do Canará Somaxacar Naique, por sey Embaixador Vitula Malló,* 20 de Abril de 1671, pp. 189-190.

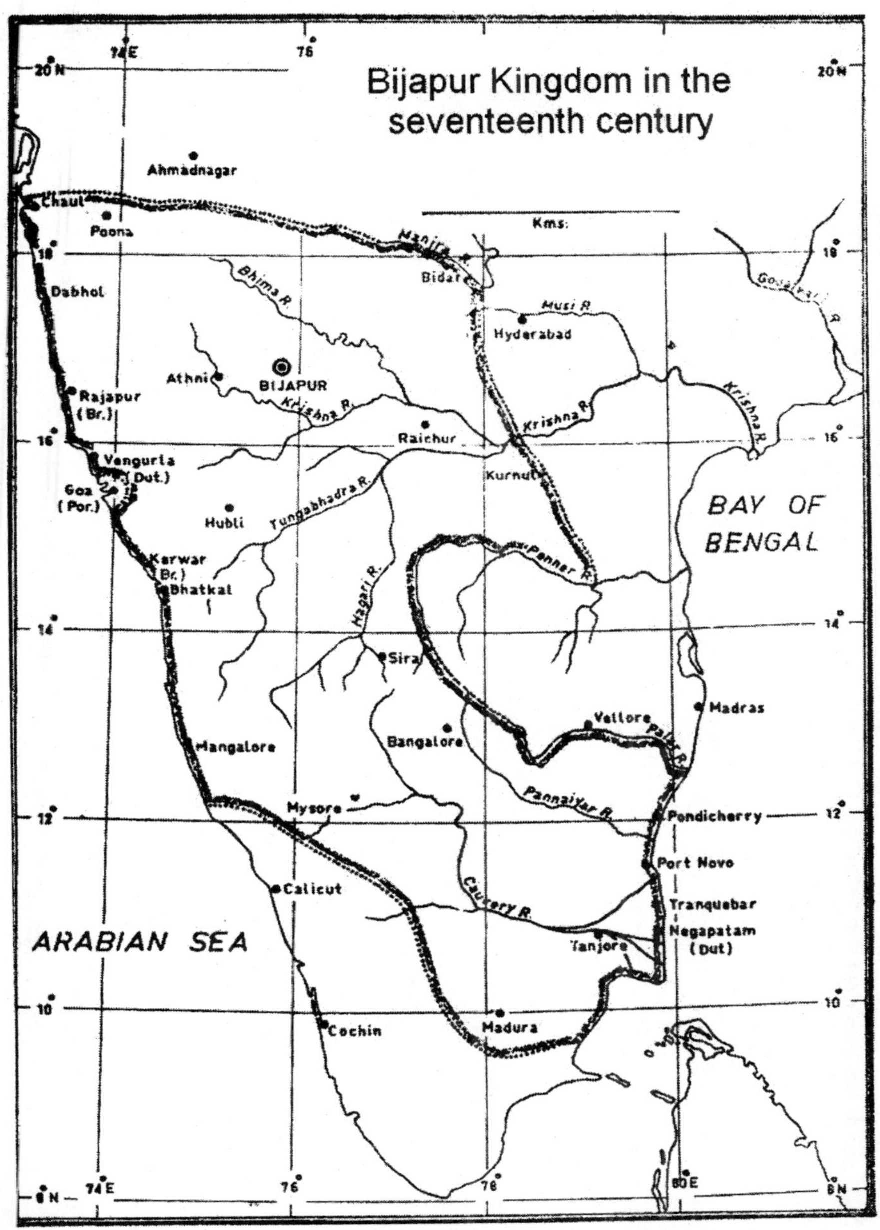

Bijapur Kingdom in the Seventeenth Century
Ref: Nayeem, *External Relations of the Bijapur Kingdom.*

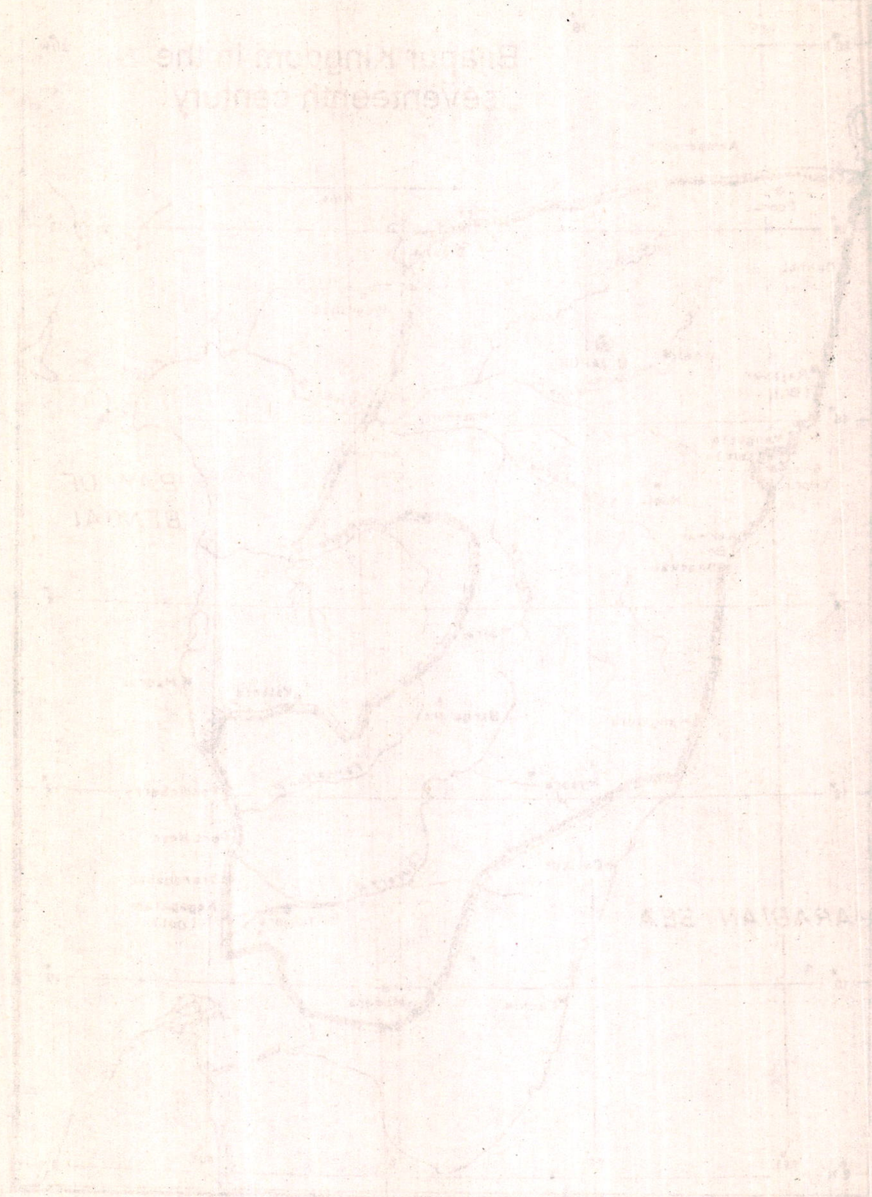

Chapter 5

Portuguese-Bijapur Diplomacy during the sixteenth and the seventeenth Centuries

Bijapur Portuguese relations, on the contrary to the Malabar and Kanara rulers, were governed by a different set of factors. If the rulers of Malabar, the Zamorin, The ruler of Cannanor and Travancore had difficulties in maitianing their vassal states under their powers, the Sultan of Bijapur was surrounded by several rival independent and powerful states, such as Vijayanagar Empire, Golconda, Ahmadnagar and Berar, which had expanding and rival tendencies and this kept, most of the times, the rulers of Bijapur very occupied in wars. As if this was not sufficient, the Brahmins and other powerful Hindu forces who did not like to be ruled by a Muslim ruler, had also invested in damaging the internal law and order situation to the point of even turning themselves spies and informers of the Portuguese who they thought could eliminate the Muslim rulers of Bijapur and provide them governing powers. Although the ambitions of such spies and Portuguese supporters were for their own personal interest of increasing their power, but they seriously damaged the integrity of the state, since the beginning of the sixteenth century when Goa was lost. The wars which the rulers of Bijapur, too, carried on in order to increase the boundaries of their Empire as well as to punish the revolted eliments of their states, on the other hand, weakended the forces of the government and contributed, heavily, in providing ample occasions to the Portuguese to fortify their position in this state. Much later the same will contribute to the fall this kingdom and be merged into the Mughal Empire.

Contrary to what they had been up to, they were brought to their senses towards the middle of the sisteenth century when Portuguese introduced the Inquisition and started demolishing temples and mosques and forcible conversion. It didn't stop here. Later, even the most loyal Hindu business magnates and influential diplomats like Ramogi Sinai Kothari,[775] among others, from Salssete, whose family had served the Portuguese government for more than a century and a half, both as providers of trading commodities from the neighbouring regions and as the Portuguese emissaries and ambassadors in resolving intricate diplomatic issues between the Portuguese, Bjiapur and the Kanara states, was forced to move with his family to Bicholim in the Bijapuri kingdom, since Ramogi didn't accede to be converted to Christianty and giver up his priviledges long given by the Portugueuse authorities.

It is keeping these outlines, that the Portuguese Bijapuri reltions have been studied. This chapter too has been divided into two parts. Part I will focus on the Bijapuri Poltical and diplomatic systems as well as the Portuguese Bijapuri diplomacy during the sixteenth century. Whereas the part II will study the diplomacy between the two states, amidst all around expansion of powerful Indian empires and European companies.

Reference

775 Pissurlencar, *Agentes da diplomacia portuguesa na Índia (Hindus, Muçulmanos, Judeus e Parses...*, p. 23.

Part I

A) Bijapur Polity: Administrative and Diplomatic Organisation

i) Bijapur Polity and Administration

Bijapur, in theory, like the Vijayanagar Empire, was a dynastic state. According to the prevailing Muslim ideas, sovereignty was hypothetical to reside in the entire Muslim population of the kingdom and the Sultan was, in theory, supposed to be elected by them. In practice, however, it was a few nobles who decided the future Sultan and in most cases the Sultan himself nominated his successor before he died.[776] However, there was no specific rule for the inheritance of the crown neither for the eldest son to become the next Sultan.[777] It was considered, according to Islamic philosophy, that 'the most able and apt person' should rule the state. This is why it was usually the most ambitious princes who thought they were the most apt for the position of Sultan and they in their turn were helped by the most ambitious nobility of the court. The difference between this state and the other Hindu kingdoms was that it had nobles of many different origins. Besides the ruling Perso-Turkish elements, its nobility had their origin in families from Central Asia and Arabia. However, the group which predominated, especially in the civil and military services, were the *Afaqi*. As a result there were always those who tried to conspire against the nobility of this group which, in reality, controlled the Sultan. This led to constant court conspiracies and assassinations which damaged the integrity of the state and which provided the neighbouring kingdoms with opportunities to exploit. The *Afaqis,* in pursuit of their own group interest, were, of course, with a few exceptions, loyal to the ruler and contributed much to the making of external policy and to the survival of the dynasty.

The Sultan was the supreme power as a sovereign head of the state. He was the ruler, judge, administrator, military general, sometimes even a preacher and leader of public worship. In short, he virtually held the position of the Imam of the Faithful. The basis of his power was military and religious. In strict Islamic theory the true king of a Muslim state is God. The Sultan is His agent on earth to enforce the divine law as expressed in the Quraan.[778] Some Sultans of Bijapur defied Qur'anic law and yet no one dared to remove them because they had the support of a powerful army and there was no constitutional device to remove such rulers peacefully from the throne. Thus, the Sultan was a military autocrat and the government of Bijapur was a centralised despotism. In case of a weak or infant ruler the sovereignty devolved upon the chief minister, which had a profound impact on foreign policy. Though the Sultan was a despot whose authority was unlimited, in practice he took the advice of his ministers on all matters especially when it was related to external affairs. Nevertheless, final decisions were always those of the Sultan, except when he was a minor.

Next to the Sultan, the highest officer of the kingdom was *Vakil-us-Saltanat* or simply *Vakíl,* as the Sultans of Bijapur followed the Persian system. In the Mughal Empire the same post was known was *Wazir* or *Wazir-i-Saltanat,* a title which the Bijapuri rulers adopted in the seventeenth century. During the sixteenth century the *Vakíl* was in charge of practically the entire administration of the kingdom. The *Vakíl* was also the head of the financial and general administration. Sometimes he acted as a regent for the infant Sultan and thus controlled all the affairs of the State both internal and external. The *Vakíl* could declare war or make peace at his discretion and he was also an army commander. Even during the reign of powerful Sultans the advice of the *Vakíl* in external affairs carried weight. All *Firmans* issued by the ruler bore his seal at the bottom. In the discharge of all these duties the *Vakíl* was assisted by several other officers of the central government at the capital, and by the provincial governors.[779]

The income of the Bijapuri state was derived primarily from the land revenue, which was sufficiently large for the Sultan not to have to concern himself with the small part of his income derived from levying customs dues on external trade. Most of the maritime concerns were left to the provincial governors and the powerful business elite.

ii) The Religious Policy of the Adil Shahi Rulers[780]

The religious policy of the Adil Shahi rulers needs to be examined from two points of view: their change of sect from Shia to Sunni, and their attitudes towards their non-Muslim subjects. So far as the change of sect is concerned, the rulers were swayed more by political considerations than religious ones, which brought serious internal troubles for the Sultans. However, in their relations with the Hindus, the Adil Shahs were consistently cordial until the reign of Muhammad Adil Shah in the seventeenth century. There was never any systematic or large-scale attempt to convert the Hindus in the Bijapur kingdom. Various factors were responsible for this. The Hindus constituted the vast majority of the population and their persecution would have created serious trouble for the infant kingdom of Bijapur, which was perpetually at war with the neighbouring Muslim states and with Vijayanagar. It was with great difficulty that the Bijapur kingdom was able to survive the attacks of its neighbours, and any internal uprising would certainly have brought the kingdom to an end. Secondly, the territory of Bijapur included many hilly and mountainous regions covered with forests in which there were many easily defensible fortified positions. People could quickly flee to these forts for refuge and from there they could offer tenacious resistance. These regions could not be conquered by the Muslims with a single cavalry charge or even by one year of campaigning. Here the native Hindus had an opportunity to maintain a long struggle against superior numbers. Fighting with them in these regions was, therefore, very difficult. Only the local Hindus had the necessary skill and experience of fighting in these regions and it was mainly this advantage which enabled Shivaji to defy the Deccan sultanates and the Mughals in the mid-seventeenth century. The Adil Shahs, therefore, could not afford to alienate the support of the Hindus by adopting a bigoted religious policy. Yusuf Adil Shah had a shrewd appreciation of this situation and knew that the strength of his kingdom lay in the support of the people, the majority of whom were Hindus. He, therefore, married a Maratha lady, sister of Mukund Rao, and nominated her son, Ismail, as his successor.

Ismail and Ibrahim Adil Shah continued the enlightened policy of Yusuf Adil Shah. Ismail arranged the marriage of his sisters with Burhan Nizam Shah, and Ala-ud-Din Imad Shah, both of whose fathers were originally Hindus. Further extending the scope of this policy, Ibrahim Adil Shah I replaced the Persian language with Hindi,[781] which not only satisfied the native inhabitants but also increased their numbers at the Adil Shahi court and in the state service, particularly in the revenue and record departments. Ali Adil Shah subordinated religion to politics. He did not mind becoming the adopted son of the wife of Ramaraya, the ruler of Vijayanagar, when it suited his interest and on one occasion, when

Ramaraya was his ally, he allowed the Vijayanagar army to commit great outrages in Ahmadnagar and even to worship in the mosques. However, later this very King united all the Muslim powers of the Deccan for the destruction of the Hindu kingdom of Vijayanagar during which campaign every type of excess was committed in the city of Vijayanagar by men who claimed Ali as their leader.

Ibrahim Adil Shah II was the most enlightened King of Bijapur in this respect. He was very liberal in his religious views and treated his Hindu subjects with consideration in grateful recognition of which he was called by them[782] *Jagat-guru*.[783] Muhammad Adil Shah, under the influence of some devout Muslims from his court, deviated from this line and adopted a policy of intolerance towards the Hindus. He imposed the much hated *Jaziya*[784] upon his Hindu subjects and gave the colour of *Jihad* to the conquests of Kanara and Mainad. He followed a systematic policy of weakening the Hindus. Hindus were not given positions of power and responsibility in the state and only low-paid clerical jobs were generally reserved for them. Of course there were exceptions, but they were few. He interfered even in matters of religion, decreeing that Hindus could perform their religious rites in private but not in public. The gist of his policy was not to allow the Hindus to grow too powerful. Muhammad Adil Shah's anti-Hindu measures spread widespread discontent among the majority of his subjects who chose Shivaji as their ruler and rose against his authority. Ali Adil Shah II and Sikandar Adil Shah were too busy with the Mughals and the Marathas to follow the policy of intolerance towards the Hindus. In fact, they tried to enlist the maximum support of the Hindu population to fight against the Mughals, until the kingdom of Bijapur was absorbed by the Mughals.

iii) Diplomatic Practice at the Bijapuri Court

The Sultans of Bijapur ostensibly followed the diplomatic pattern of their predecessors, the Bahmani rulers, but in practice they evolved their own system based on a grand mixture of Persian, Arab, Ottoman, and Mughal customs.[785] However, it was Persian diplomatic practice that was principally followed because five out of the nine sultans followed the Shiah sect and received insignia of royalty from the Shas of Persia.[786] Even in their correspondence the Sultans of Bijapur addressed the Shahs as if they were the vassals of the Persian rulers.[787] Although, after 1598, the Bijapuri Sultans were forced to become vassals of the Mughal Emperors,[788] each ruler addressed the other in the same way in their correspondence.

Recent historians have maintained that the Sultans of Bijapur adhered closely to the court etiquette of the Shahs of Persia and of the Mughals, so examples from these courts of the manner in which ambassadors from different kingdoms were received would give some idea how the Bijapuri Sultans might have conducted affairs in their own court. Most of the documents whether Indian or foreign, and travel accounts of the sixteenth and the seventeenth centuries, all refer to one thing very frequently, that all the Asian rulers insisted on giving and receiving substantial gifts, a practice that had been followed for centuries. In the Mughal period, even at the time of the posting of a *Vizir*, presents were offered by the *Vizir* to the emperors as a goodwill gesture which was commonly known as *Peshkash*[789] and later, in the time of Aurangzeb, as *Nazrana.*[790]

The first example is derived from the account given by Manucci of the reception of the English ambassador Lord Belmont at the court of the Shah of Persia. Another such narration has been given by Abbé Carré who witnessed the reception of four ambassadors, from France, England, Turkey and Poland, at the same time, in the 1670s. Although this falls beyond the period of this study, it is relevant because generation after generation this practice was followed unaltered. The second example would be from the Mughal court when Aurangzeb received various ambassadors from different countries of Asia on his accession to the throne.

Persian Shahs maintained special court etiquette, especially in receiving ambassadors, which was a way for them to demonstrate their importance and to impress their guests by revealing the power and grandeur of the court. A meticulous state protocol was followed by the court officers of Shah Abbas II, when the Persian governor at Erivan was notified of the arrival of the embassy of Lord Belmont from England on his way to meet the Shah.[791] The governor received the ambassador with all the pomp that the Shah would have used. Belmont was honoured by a banquet and was presented with four horses and several pieces of silk. The governor instructed his servants to take proper care of the ambassador and his companions. At the time of their departure to Qazwin, where the Shah was residing at that moment, the ambassador's party was escorted by horsemen and several soldiers for the rest of their journey that lasted almost a month. Before they were presented to Shah Abbas II, they were dressed in the Persian fashion, as the clothes they carried with them were not fit for the occasion. All their local expenses were met by the state. After arriving at Qazwin they were first received with great honour by the chief minister, Azmat-ud-daulah or Etamad-ud-daulah. Through their recorded dialogue with the chief minister, it is clear that the local authorities wanted to know what present the ambassador was carrying for the Shah and the rank of the ambassador in his own country, so that he could be treated according to his status. After all the enquiries had been made, the Shah received them almost a week later. On the day of his audience with the Shah, all the ministers of the court took their places and the ambassador was taken to the place that had been reserved for him according to his rank. After the formal introduction and salutations, which according to the Persian custom consisted of placing the right hand on the forehead three times and bowing the head at the same time, the ambassador offered the presents he had with him. Among the list of the presents were a breastplate, a head-piece (morion), and sword-mountings - all of fine workmanship, made in Paris.[792] He also presented the king's letter to the Shah, which was translated and read. Later, the Shah gave a sumptuous banquet where most of the state dignitaries were present.[793]

Though the content of the letter is not known, it is apparent through the conversation that took place between the ambassador and the Shah that Lord Belmont wanted the help of the Shah in the form of money in return for the assistance the English had provided in liberating Hormuz from the Portuguese in 1622. He also reminded him of the friendly ties that existed between the two countries. It was only after three months that the final discussions with the Shah and with the chief minister took place, and they were able to get a proper reply. The result of the meeting is not of much concern here. According to the tradition, the Shah presented the ambassador with fifty pieces of gold and silver brocade, velvet, and silk of various colours, four pairs of handsome carpets, and 2,000 *patacas*. In fact the ambassador had demanded a bigger amount as a recompense for the help the English had rendered the Shah in 1622. This was politely declined. The ambassador was very annoyed and turned aggressive to the point of losing his temper, forgetting his position as ambassador and behaving like a common man. He was given a sealed letter for the English (deposed) king, whose content is also not known.[794]

The Shah treated other ambassadors in a similar way, according to Abbé Carré almost three decades later. Carré has focused specifically on the importance that Shah Abbas II, attached to giving and receiving presents. The ambassador who brought a sumptuous present was received sooner than the one who brought less. But at the same time, he records that the Shah considered an experienced and wise ambassador to be of greater importance than one newly appointed.[795]

The Mughal Emperors were also accustomed to exchange presents with the royal envoys and ambassadors. They used to confer very lavish receptions on the ambassadors, naturally depending on the country or states they were representing, with a view to impressing the latter. When receiving ambassadors like those from Persia or the Ottoman sultan,[796] the Mughal Emperor usually sent provincial governors to greet them at the port of landing or at the frontier of the kingdom so that they might be escorted to the court wherever the Emperor might be, following the same practice as the Persians. Very elaborate arrangements were made for their reception in the court and all their expenditure was met by the royal treasury. It was only the ambassadors from these two countries who could approach the throne of the Mughal Emperor directly and hand over their credentials and the letters they might be carrying from their sovereign. After receiving the letters from their hands the Emperor used to give them to the *Vizir*, who might have been appointed for the reading of the letters before the court. Apart from the ambassadors of Persia and the Ottoman Empire, all other ambassadors entrusted their credentials and letters to a noble of at least the rank of foreign minister (*Vizir-e-Kharja*) who in turn first gave it to the Emperor, a formality which had to be followed. The Emperor would then hand it back to the minister who asked the person appointed to read the letter in a loud voice before the court.

Although soon after their arrival, they had been given sumptuous presents, these ambassador while displaying their presents would also receive an expensive robe of honour and much more valuable presents for themselves and their rulers. Quite often, for the reception of the ambassadors, an open space was specially built where the Emperor would sit along with his nobles to receive the ambassadors. After the formal greetings in the Mughal fashion (bowing three times half way down and simultaneously placing the right hand on the forehead),[797] the ambassadors or emissaries would only then display the presents before the Emperor which were quite often horses, camels and other exotic animals, besides expensive dresses, ornamented daggers and so on. This practice was followed, almost until the early nineteenth century.[798]

François Bernier had depicted the Mughal court etiquette on the occasion of the reception of the ambassador of the Uzbek Tartars by the Emperor Aurangzeb soon after his accession to the throne.[799] When the ambassador wanted to place the letter he had brought from his ruler, in the hands of the Emperor, one of the *Omrahs* took the letter and opened it and handed it over to the Emperor who in turn gave it to another *Omrah* who read it before the court. Later, the presents were shown of which Bernier has provided an exhaustive description.[800] The ambassador and the other delegates were given money for their maintenance, according to tradition, and were to live in the capital till they were allowed to return.[801] Most of the other ambassadors, including those from the Dutch and Ethiopians, according to Bernier, received similar receptions and presents. However, as mentioned above, the type of reception given to ambassadors differed from country to country. Bernier noticed that the reception given to the Persian ambassador was especially magnificent,[802] and was quite different from those given to the ambassadors of Uzbekistan, Ethiopia and the Dutch. According to one eyewitness,[803] "soldiers were posted on both sides of the street, a league in length, through which the ambassador would pass. The principal streets were decorated with rich stuffs, both in the shops and also at the windows, and the ambassador was brought through them, escorted by a number of officers, with music, drums, pipes and trumpets. On his entering the fort or royal palace, he was saluted by all the artillery...It was a fine sight to see the ambassador followed by his 500 horsemen, large-limbed and handsome men with huge moustaches, riding excellent and well-equipped horses."[804]

Emperor Aurangzeb displayed great pleasure in receiving the ambassador.[805] The ambassador saluted the Emperor in the Persian fashion but had this been done, even by mistake, by an ambassador from any other country, he would have had to face the anger of the Emperor resulting in expulsion and other sorts of punishments. The ambassadors from the Ottoman Sultans were given a reception similar to that of the Persian ambassador.[806]

When the Mughal court assembled to receive an ambassador, the nobles of the court had to be present in their proper court dress and were either seated, according to their status, or were to remain standing in the same order. The noble highest in status was placed closest to the Emperor and the others followed in sequence. To ignore any of the rules would threaten their careers and even their lives.

Diplomacy in India presumed the right of a number of independent kingdoms to exist and to pursue their own interests. In order to manage their increasingly complex external relations, the Sultans of Bijapur had developed a system of diplomatic etiquette, which accorded with the nature of the embassies, and was generally in accord with the customs of the other states. In order to pursue their diplomatic aims, the sultans adopted various means such as diplomatic correspondence, treaties, contracts and agreements, the use of diplomatic pressure, mediation, espionage and negotiations. All of these were exercised through permanent or extraordinary diplomatic missions, made up of messengers, envoys or ambassadors.[807]

Diplomatic correspondence was carried on between the states not only by the sultans but also by their ministers and by nobles, so that some preliminary problems might be resolved or terms of treaties be concluded before they were officially signed between the representatives of two or more states. Diplomatic communications adopted different styles of address; letters sent to the Deccan states were as between equals; those addressed to the Shah of Iran were couched in the terms of a subordinate official writing to a Sovereign; those addressed to the Mughal Emperors were written as though from a provincial governor[808] writing to an Emperor and were in the form of *Arzi* or requests; those addressed to petty kings, or Nayakas, were in the style of a sovereign writing to vassals; and to the European officials on the western coast, a *Farmán* was sent.[809] Diplomatic correspondence was sent through special envoys. The envoys had to pass on the letters to the resident ambassadors who in turn presented them before the king of the receiving state. In the absence of a resident envoy or ambassador, the special envoy himself presented the letter before the court of the receiving state. Secret matters were not mentioned in the letter but were communicated verbally.[810]

The formal manner in which diplomatic correspondence was phrased differed according to the relationship between writer and recipient. The different forms of address confirmed the underlying assumptions about interstate relations and were part of an elaborate structure, which included the giving of presents, as outlined above. For instance when the Mughal Emperors sent a letter to the Sultans of Bijapur they addressed the Sultan directly by name, "Adil Khan should know that..."[811] On the other hand, when the Sultans wrote a letter either to the Mughal or the Shah of Persia, it was addressed in the following manner: "This letter is from the humblest slave Ibrahim to the exalted Emperor Shah Abbas".[812]

On appearing at court, an ambassador was required to offer salutations to the Sultan by bowing to the ground three times.[813] After the greeting formalities were over, the next step was the delivery of the credential letter or royal letter to the Sultan.[814] The letter of credentials was handed over to a noble in attendance, who would then place it in the Sultan's hands. The Mughal, Persian, Portuguese and Vijayanagar ambassadors were exceptionally allowed to place the letter directly in the hands of the Sultan themselves – a fact which serves to demonstrate the status that the *Estado da Índia* had come to acquire in Indian diplomacy. The letter was then read in a loud voice by an official of the court. The credential ceremonies ended with the Sultan presenting a robe of honour and a reward in cash and kind, according to the status of the ambassador and of the state that he represented. The ambassador received this with ceremonial salutations and retired. No ambassador was allowed to turn his back while leaving the court. During subsequent ceremonies the ambassadors were seated in a place reserved according to the origin and status of their states. These ambassadors were invited to attend most of the ceremonies of the court, especially those related to foreign affairs. Bijapuri Sultans maintained permanent *Safirs* at the Mughal court, at the courts of Ahmadnagar, Golconda, Berar and Goa, and had regular correspondence with them on various matters.[815]

Safirs, or *Raajdoots* as they are known in Hindi, had different types of postings. According to the requirements, they were sent on a permanent, visiting, ordinary, or extraordinary basis. Usually, the resident ambassadors, although they had no fixed period of stay, remained on their mission between two and four years. However, the period of stay at, and departure from the court, was decided by the rulers to whom the ambassadors were accredited, and not by the rulers they represented.[816] It was customary that, before entering or leaving a kingdom, the ambassadors should ask permission either from the ruler of the state to which they were accredited. Arriving or leaving without permission was considered a great offence that could lead to the arrest of the envoy, and ultimately to some serious complications between the states.[817]

Besides the special envoys, visiting ambassadors were sent regularly on the occasion of feasts, birthdays or simply to send the presents and annual arrears of tribute to the sovereign ruler or to their provincial governors. Ordinary missions were sent with the political aim of the maintenance of peace between the two states, but special embassies were deputed on the sickness or death of a monarch and to congratulate the new sovereign on his accession. Ambassadors on political missions were chosen from among the most experienced members of the court, who were able to negotiate peace or war, to sign or ratify a treaty, or to form an alliance or counter alliance. However, there were also secret missions to form secret alliances against one or more states. On all these missions, irrespective of their nature, the envoys or ambassadors were obliged to carry a letter of credence, which included not only their identity but also the type of mission they were deputed to and the power of bargaining they were entrusted with. Normally, such letters of credence were called *Farmáns*. A *Farmán* acted as a safe conduct for the ambassadors. It allowed them free access to or from any court, violation of which could result in the severe punishment of those responsible, or even in war.[818]

A great deal of importance was attached to the arrival of an embassy from a foreign country.[819] It was a matter of the recognition of the position and status of a state. The arrival of embassies from Persia or from the Mughal Emperors, as well as from the Portuguese, English and the Dutch, especially on the occasion of the accession to the throne, was considered prestigious and meant the recognition of their succession. Those embassies were received with great pomp and respect and banquets were given to all the dignitaries lasting several days. Moreover, ambassadors were warmly welcomed at several different places within the state on their way to the court. A special officer was appointed by the Sultan to meet the ambassador well in advance and conduct him to the capital. *Farmáns* were issued to guarantee the safe arrival of ambassadors in the capital. In certain cases, when information was received that the ambassadors from Persia, the Mughal Court or Vijayanagar Empire were approaching the Bijapuri kingdom, the Sultan used to go to receive them in person at the frontiers of his state.[820] However, this practice was observed only with these states and only by the Sultans of Bijapur. On the other hand the Portuguese, the Dutch and the English ambassadors were given no such protocols. They were received respectfully in the usual manner.[821]

The Sultans of Bijapur rarely granted audiences to any ambassador immediately on his arrival at the capital. A date was fixed for the audience according to the will of the Adil Shah. During the period of waiting, all the envoys were treated as royal guests and their expenses were met by the state.[822] They were lodged in a house fit for the ambassador or sometimes at the residence of a leading court official. On the day of the audience, the ambassador was introduced to the Sultan by his protocol officer, who had already gathered knowledge about the ambassador and the purpose of the embassy. The letter of credence was then presented to the Sultan through his court officer and ambassadors were supposed to speak through these mediators even when they were in the presence of the Sultan, except for the ambassadors from Persia, the Mughal Court, and the court of the Vijayanagar empire. The Sultans of Bijapur were very fond of conferring rich presents on the ambassadors of different states with a view to enhancing their reputation and to please the ambassadors so that they would carry away a good impression to their monarchs.[823] The same practice, giving rich presents and attribution of credentials, was followed while sending an ambassador to other courts for political or commercial purposes. In all cases, the failure to give presents was considered an insult to the prestige of the court and empire and a severe violation of etiquette resulting in the punishment of the ambassador and a complaint sent to their rulers.[824]

iv) Changing Political Situation

At the end of the sixteenth century the Bijapuri Sultanate started paying annual tribute to the Mughal Emperor as his vassal. This relationship did not change in the seventeenth century, although the Sultans of Bijapur frequently defied the authority of the Mughals during the time of Jahangir, Shah Jahan and Aurangzeb, by not paying the tribute or purposely delaying it. This resulted in frequent punitive campaigns, resulting in the loss of lives and financial resources, which so weakened Bijapuri military capabilities that the sultans were, from time to time, obliged to seek Portuguese support. The Portuguese were able to exploit this situation to the maximum extent, until the whole Bijapur state was annexed to the Mughal Empire by Aurangzeb in 1686. Had the Sultans of Bijapur obeyed the Mughal emperors, they would have been able to face the military challenge posed by the Portuguese more successfully and would have obtained Mughal support in doing so.

For their part, the Nayakas of Ikkeri, from the early 1570s, owed formal allegiance to the Sultans of Bijapur and throughout the seventeenth century, till the fall of Bijapuri kingdom, they intermittently paid tribute, as their sovereign himself did to the Mughals. As far as relations between Bijapur, the Portuguese and Calicut were concerned, each treated the other as an equal as none of them owed any allegiance to another state.

Prior to the arrival of the Portuguese no ruler of coastal India ever bothered to maintain soldiers aboard the ships to fight at sea, except some fighting men to avoid being taken over by the pirates. As has been pointed out, the Zamorin of Calicut was the only ruler of coastal Western India who had a regular navy strong enough to fight the sea-pirates. By the time the need for a fleet powerful enough to fight with some nation like the Portuguese was realised, it was too late. It has been suggested that the Sultans of Bijapur, Ahmadnagar, the Nayakas of Ikkeri and even the Mughal Emperors lacked the resources for building a navy as powerful as their army. As this was clearly not the case why did they not build navies to defend their states? The answer must lie in the mentality of the rulers. It seems that most of the rulers of coastal Western India, except for the Mughal Emperors, were too busy with their wars on land, which were necessary to maintain the security of their states, and which were of much greater importance to them than the loss of maritime trade. By not maintaining a navy they lost no territory and only risked the loss of a small part of their income. Moreover, there was no serious threat ever felt to their controlled areas from the sea as it did after the arrival of the Portuguese. By the time the rulers of India realised, it was almost too late. However, in future it would be naval power that mattered most as the Europeans knew how to fight at sea with more sophisticated firearms than the Indians possessed. It would be by sea that invaders would come, not by land. Nevertheless, the appearance of the Dutch and the English on the scene turned the political situation against the Portuguese and gave the Indian powers more bargaining position.

Reference

776 Varma, *History of Bijapur*, pp. 216-217.

777 *Ibid.*

778 Zubairi, *Basatin al-Salatin*, p. 348.

779 Zubairi, *Basatin al-Salatin*, pp. 46-47; Farishtah, *Tarikh-i- Farishtah,* vol. II, p. 25.

780 For the Bijapuri rulers and the period of their reigns see appendix V.

781 *Tarikh-i- Farishtah, vol.* 11, *pp* 26-27; Muhammad Ibrahim Zubairi, *Basatin al-Salatin*, pp. 48-49.

782 Muhammad Ibrahim Zubairi, *Basatin al-Salatin*, pp. 279-280.

783 It literally means the 'Teacher of the world'.

784 A tax levied in the medieval period by the Muslim rulers on their Hindu subjects as a compensation of not being converted to Islam.

785 N. R. Farooqi, *Moghal Ottoman Relations*, pp. 12-13; Farooqui has provided a profoundly analytical work on the diplomatic system of two powerful empires. See also see Irfan Habib, (edited) *State and Diplomacy under Tipu Sultan, (Documents and Essays,)* (Passim).

786 Nayeem, *External Relations...*, pp. 58-59, 275-276.

787 *Ibid.*

788 See a transcription and translation of a *Farman* from the Mughal Emperor Shah *Jahan* to the Sultan of Bijapur in Nayeem, *External Relations...*, pp. 277-278.

789 Even now this terminology still exists but it is now used in pejorative terms and considered as Bribery.

790 M. Athar Ali, *The Mughal Nobility under Aurangzeb*, p. 143.

791 In fact, he was not sent as an ambassador though he did carry a letter from the king. He was escaping from the government of Oliver Cromwell, see Niccolao Manucci, *Mogul India or Storia do Mogol*, vol I, p. 13, and after reaching Persia he turned himself into an English ambassador, pp. 17-18. Niccolao Manucci was one of the companions.

792 *Ibid*, p. 22 As per Manucci, all these presents were bought on the way to Persia.

793 For details see, Manucci, Vol. I, p. 23

794 Manucci, vol., I, p. 34; In normal circumstances, the attitude of the English ambassador would have resulted in severe punishment not only in Asian but even European countries. The humble nature of the Shah, probably allowed him to remember the immunity of an ambassador.

795 Abbé Carré, *The Travels of the Abbé Carré in India and the Near East*, 1672 to 1674, vol. III, pp. 808-810.

796 N. R. Farooqi, *Mughal Ottoman Relations*, pp. 32-33.

797 J.F. Richards, "The Formulation of Imperial Authority under Akbar and Jahangir," in Muzaffar Alam and Sanjay Subrahmanyam (edited), *The Mughal State 1526-1750*, pp. 126-167.

798 Irfan Habib, (edited) *State and Diplomacy under Tipu Sultan, Documents and Essays*, (Passim)

799 Francois Bernier, *Travels in the Mogul Empire: AD 1656-1668*, pp. 116-120.

800 *Ibid*.

801 *Ibid*.

802 *Ibid*. pp. 144-146.

803 This was certainly Bernier but the author has omitted his name.

804 H.G. Rawlinson, *India: A short Cultural History*, pp. 342-343. Though the author has not given the origin of his information, it is most certainly taken from Francois Bernier's *Travels in the Mogul Empire*, see pp. 146-147.

805 *Ibid*, pp. 145-148.

806 Farooqi, *Mughal Ottoman Relations*, pp. 32-33.

807 Nayeem, *External Relations...*, pp. 34-35.

808 Only after 1595.

809 Nayeem, *External Relations...*, pp. 34-35.

810 *Ibid*.

811 *Ibid*. pp. 277.

812 *Ibid*. 275.

813 See J.F. Richards, "The Formulation of Imperial Authority under Akbar and Jahangir," in Alam and Sanjay (edited), *The Mughal State 1526-1750*, pp. 126-167. Francois Bernier, *Travels in the Mogul Empire: AD 1656-1668*, pp. 116-120.

814 *Ibid*., p. 42.

815 Nayeem, *External Relations...*, pp. 42-43.

816 Maclagan, Os *Jesuitas e o Grão Mogol*, (Passim).

817 *ACE*, vol. I, doc. 154: See for example, *Conselho sobre o embaxador delRey Idalxa, Mamede Zaman e licença qye pedio para hir a outra banda*, 17 de Julho de 1633; vol. II, pp. 84; *Copia do Conçelho sobre a licença que pedia o embaxador delRey virabadranaique para se hir,..*; *LML*, cod. 50, fols. 93v°-94: *Carta do Vise-rei da Índia, Tello da Silva Menezes, em que dá conta como o embaixador de Idalxá, Mirza Mamaede Raza, pedia autorização para ir outra banda*, 4 de Dezembro de 1643. Also see Maclagan, *Os Jesuitas e o Grão Mogol*, Jesuits could not leave or enter into the Mughal Empire without the prior permission, (Passim).

818 HAG, *Livro de Pazes I*, fls. 13-14; Biker (ed.) *Collecção de tratados e concertos de pazes...*, tomo I, pp. 296-97; *ACE*, vol. I, pp. 565: *Assento do juramento e retificação das pazes feitas com o Sultão Mamede Idalxá por seu Embaixador Mamede Zaman no anno de* 1633.

819 John Briggs, *History of the Rise of Mahomedan Power in India*, vol. III, pp. 27-29.

820 *O Cronista de Tissuary*, nº 2, Fevereiro de 1866, p. 39.

821 Nayeem, *External Relations...*, pp. 212-260.

822 *Ibid.*, pp. 41-43.

823 John Briggs, (Ed.) *History of the Rise of Mahomedan Power in India*, vol. III, pp. 27-29.

824 Nayeem, *External Relations...*, pp. 40-43.

STAMPA XXVIII Ref. António Bocarro, O Livro das Fortalezas

Fortalezas de Mormugão, Rachol e Salse

Portuguese Fortress of Rachol, Salsette

facing page 284

B- A Brief Sketch of the Bijapur Portuguese Diplomacy in the Sixteenth Century

In order to understand the intricate and fickle diplomatic relations that existed between the Portuguese *Estado da Índia* and the sultans of Bijapur during the seventeenth century, it is essential to trace the underlying issues that affected the two states and why the sultans tried so persistently to regain the lost territories of Goa, Salssete and Bardez. First the Portuguese used all sorts of political upheavals, that overshadowed the Bijapuri kingdom, in establishing their political and military supremacy, in the sixteenth century, and later, in the seventeenth century, the same policy was applied by the Bijapuri rulers against the Portuguese, making use of the presence of the English and the Dutch. A brief sketch of the political development of this dynasty, since its foundation until its downfall, has been provided in the following pages.

a) Conflicts and Diplomacies from 1510 to 1571

The loss of the port town of Goa in 1510 had hardly been forgotten when, in 1545, the Portuguese authorities tricked the sultan into ceding the areas of Salssete and Bardez and caused a renewed conflict. Although, this story has already been narrated in detail by several historians,[825] it is necessary to try to understand these events from a different perspective. Moreover an understanding of the detail of the treaties that were concluded in the late sixteenth century, especially those concluded between 1571 and 1582,[826] is essential as these treaties became the main points of reference for diplomats in the seventeenth century.

For thirty-five years after the loss of Goa, diplomatic relations between the Adil Shahs and the Portuguese continued to be, relatively, peaceful. Except for some occasional grievances over the detention of ships and merchandise by the Portuguese and the build ups of the military pressure from the side of the Bijapuri forces in the vicinity of Goa, and subsequent exchanges of embassies, nothing of any serious nature took place until the fourth decade.

Portuguese-Bijapuri diplomacy took a new turn when a court conspiracy drove the ruler's brother, Abdullah,[827] into revolt in 1542. It created a lot of diplomatic complications, including the loss of Salssete and Bardez, the Bijapuri territories, to the Portuguese and ended only in 1549.[828]

After an unsuccessful attempt to usurp the throne, Abdullah took refuge with the Portuguese in Goa in 1545.[829] There he proved to be a very valuable instrument in the hands of Portuguese diplomats for, as mentioned earlier, Portuguese power was invariably based on successfully exploiting the local political situation.[830]

Ibrahim Adil Shah demanded the surrender of Abdullah and, in return, offered to cede to the Portuguese the districts of Salssete and Bardez, which adjoined Goa. Martim Afonso de Sousa, the Portuguese governor, refused to surrender the prince but agreed to dispatch him to Malacca if the two districts were surrendered.[831] Although he had the prince taken to Cannanore, he did not send him on to Malacca and eventually brought him back to Goa with the intention of extorting further concessions from the Adil Shah. To add insult to injury, the Portuguese proceeded to occupy the districts of Salssete and Bardez by force. In this way Ibrahim Adil Shah had been deceived but he could not take any decisive action against the Portuguese as the disloyalty of his nobles and his involvement in the politics of the Vijayanagar Empire, as well as with the states of Golconda, Berar and Ahmadnagar,[832] made his own position too insecure. He, therefore, initiated fresh negotiations with Dom João de Castro, the new Portuguese governor, from whom he got an assurance that prince Abdullah would not be kept at Goa and would not be allowed to communicate with powers hostile to Bijapur. In return Ibrahim Adil Shah had to relinquish his claim to the districts already seized and to confirm the Portuguese in possession of them.[833]

Shortly after these events, however, Ibrahim Adil Shah, taking advantage of Portuguese involvement on the coast of Gujarat, marched his forces into the disputed districts and reoccupied them. The Portuguese soon returned from Gujarat. They attacked the Bijapuri port of Dabhol, plundered it and hastened towards Goa. Despite strong resistance offered by the Bijapuris, the districts of Salssete and Bardez were again taken by the Portuguese and Dom João de Castro despatched a fleet which sacked and burnt the Adil Shah's ports and coastal towns to the north of Goa.[834] As Ibrahim Adil Shah's position was so weak, he again opened negotiations for peace and by the treaty, which was signed on 22nd of August 1548, he confirmed the Portuguese in possession of the two districts.[835] It was also agreed that all the inhabitants of the two territories, whether they were Hindus or Muslims, would have freedom to practice their religion, and would also be free to trade and to move with their belongings. The Bijapuri sultan's ambassador, Mutabbir Khan, a noble from the court of Adil Shah, who had powers to negotiate during this diplomatic mission, also agreed, among other promises made on the Sultan's behalf, to provide political and military help to the Portuguese if required to do so.

However, the Portuguese went a step further and entered directly into an agreement with Abdullah Khan, promising to make him sultan and have him crowned at Ponda.[836] This agreement with Abdullah Khan clearly shows how the Portuguese tried to intervene in local affairs in order to derive full advantage from them. At the same time, it also reveals that they took little notice of the peace treaty signed with the Adil Shah for, no matter how just the cause of Abdullah Khan might be, this act of the Portuguese, of entering into diplomatic agreements with him, was deemed a hostile act by Sultan Adil Shah and cast a shadow over their future relationships.

b) Tribulation & Diplomacy between 1570 and 1582

Meanwhile the political landscape of southern India had started to change. Ali Adil Shah formed an alliance with the Muslim kings of south India - Murtuza Nizam Shah of Ahmadnagar, and the sultans of Golconda and Berar - against the expanding empire and increasing pretensions of the ruler of Vijayanagar.[837] The allies defeated him in the battle of Talikota on 2nd of January 1565,[838] which brought about the rapid downfall of his kingdom.[839] This success made Adil Shah overconfident and encouraged him to form a league between Bijapur, Ahmadnagar and the Zamorin of Calicut to recover their lost territories and their commerce from the Portuguese, and to expel them from the Indian sub-continent once and for all.[840] This resulted in the war of 1570-1571.[841] However, this adventure was a complete fiasco and ended in humiliation because Bijapur became sidetracked into undertaking an expedition to the south against what remained of the power of the Vijayanagar Empire.[842] Seeing no hope of success against the Portuguese, the ruler of Bijapur, Mohammed Adil Shah, sent two ambassadors, Malik Shah Mir and Shah Murad,[843] two of the highest dignitaries of the court, with the necessary powers to negotiate a peace treaty with the recently arrived Portuguese Viceroy, Dom António de Noronha, and to seek the renewal of the treaty of friendship.[844]

After the war of 1571 Portuguese-Bijapuri relations took a new turn. Although it might have seemed that the Sultan of Bijapur was the party most anxious to make peace, when one looks at the military and financial state of the Portuguese it can be seen that the desire was mutual. By the terms of the treaty that was negotiated between 13th and 17th of December 1571,[845] it was decided by the ambassadors of Bijapur that they would stop claiming their rights to the territories of Salssete and Bardez and that they would accept Portuguese jurisdiction over them forever. In addition to this the merchants from both sides would have freedom to carry on their business without hindrance from any belligerent. Apart from other decisions taken during these negotiations, both parties took an oath that they would always be friends and would help each other against their enemies, and that ships belonging to the Sultan of Bijapur would not be molested or captured even if they were found without a *Cartaz*. If this occurred, the matter would be dealt with amicably and any taxes due would be paid. Moreover, the Bijapuri authorities would not allow any ship belonging to other nations[846] to enter their ports without a *Cartaz* and, if any ship did so, it would be captured and the booty would be shared between the two nations. The Bijapuri ambassadors and the Portuguese Viceroy signed this treaty, along with other high dignitaries of the respective courts, such as the governor and *capitão-mor* of Goa.

The treaty of 1571 was renewed in 1575 through an embassy of Khorasan Khan, the ambassador of Sultan Adil Shah,[847] but the following year, in 1576, it was changed and some more clauses were added during an embassy sent to Goa under Zaheer Beg. By these new clauses it was agreed that the Sultan of Bijapur and the Portuguese Viceroy would each maintain an ambassador at the other's court so that no untoward incident could take place. If such an incident occurred they would inform their respective governments and do what was necessary to avoid hostilities.[848] Although it had been the practice to keep resident ambassadors or emissaries at various courts, and there is plenty of information before this period of Jesuits and members of the other religious orders being sent to various courts to settle diplomatic and political questions, this was the first time that the establishment of a permanent embassy was made an official policy.

Neither the question of Salssete and Bardez nor the humiliation of the 1571 war was ever forgotten by the Adil Shahs, although at the time they had accepted a peaceful diplomatic solution. On the Portuguese side, if they accepted some of the terms of the Sultan of Bijapur, it was only because of the tightness of their financial position, which placed limitations on their military strength. Both states were dissatisfied with the treaty.

In 1578, in spite of the terms of the treaty, Sultan Adil Khan allowed Malik Tucan, governor of Dabhol,[849] to build a fleet at the port town of Dabhol with the intention of sending it to Mecca.[850] The Portuguese authorities soon took notice of this and sent Dom Paulo de Lima Pereira to check on its progress as they feared it could strengthen the naval power of Bijapur. Moreover, the Portuguese considered that, by the terms of the treaties signed earlier in 1571 and 1575, the safety of the ships of the Bijapuri sultan was the responsibility of the Portuguese armada. Therefore, the sultan should not require any navy at all. This again strained the relationship between the two states. However, this did not lead to any untoward incident because of the deaths of Adil Shah of Bijapur and of Cardinal Henrique, the King of Portugal, at approximately the same time in 1580. Bijapur fell into political disarray as a result of the assassination of the Adil Khan in 1580,[851] since he left no heir. After some confusion and court conspiracies, his nephew, Ibrahim Adil Khan, then aged nine years, was recognised as Sultan.[852] Moreover, the arrival of a new Viceroy appointed by the Spanish regime in Portugal[853] with instructions to avoid hostilities with the neighbouring kings and political conditions at the Bijapuri Court, obliged both parties to avoid any further hostilities.

The Portuguese usually took advantage of such periods of disorder, but this time they merely followed what was happening closely and did not interfere, as the position of Portugal in India, at that time, was not a strong one.

After a gap of almost two years in official communications, another treaty was signed on 29th of January 1582. Abdul Malik and Khwaja Farhat-ud-Din were sent as ambassadors to Goa from the Bijapuri court to carry out this diplomatic mission. This mission was to decide the future of the fortress and arsenals at the port of Dabhol, a question which had been pending for some time and had become an obstacle to maintaining peace and friendship with the Portuguese. It was agreed that the fortress should be demolished and the cannon handed over to the Portuguese, as had been decided during the embassy of Zaheer Beg and Mustafa Khan in 1576.[854] After this, until the beginning of the seventeenth century, both sides, facing trouble elsewhere in their territories, abstained from any confrontation.

Still worst was to come for the Bijapuri kingdom when the Mughal Emperor Akbar invested the territories of Ahmadnagar and found his way into the kingdom of Bijapur, in 1595-98. After this, the Bijapuri rulers never experienced uninterrupted peace. There position in relation to the Portuguese became much more fragile and submissive than it used to be. Every time they failed to pay tribute to the Mughals, an army arrived to collect it by force and the Sultans of Bijapur had to look for Portuguese support. However, the Bijapuri had better luck when they were approached by the English and the Dutch who, although they never provided any effective military support against the Portuguese, served to keep the balance of power. It is in these circumstances that Portuguese-Bijapuri diplomacy took shape during the seventeenth century.

Reference

825 For example see João de Barros, *Da Ásia de João de Barros*; Manuel de Faria e Sousa, *Ásia Portugesa;* Castanheda, *História do descobrimento e conquista da Índia pelos Portugueses;* A. Lopes Mendes, *A Índia Portugueza,* 2 vols., Imp. Nac., Lisboa, 1886; Whiteway, *The Rise of Portuguese Power in India;* Danvers, *The Portuguese in India...;* Nayeem, *External Relations of the Bijapur Kingdom (1489-1686);* Boxer, *The Portuguese Seaborne Empire;* Gribble, *History of the Deccan;* D.C.Varma, *History of Bijapur,* and many more.

826 *APO-CR,* Fasc. 5°, doc. n° 742, *Contrato de pazes feito com El-Rey Idalxá no anno de 1571;* The same is also found in Biker, (ed.) *Collecção de tratados e concertos de pazes...,* tomo I, pp. 160-167; *APO-CR,* Fasc. 5°, doc. n° 779, *Assento de paz com o Idalxá no anno de 1575* (30 de Maio); Also published in Biker, (ed.) *Collecção de tratados e concertos de pazes...,* tomo I, pp. 167-170; *APO-CR,* Fasc. 5°, doc. n° 786; *Contrato das Pazes feitas com Idalxá por seu Embaixador Zaerbeque, que veio do Reino, governando este Estado António Moniz Barreto, no anno de 1576.*

827 He is also known as Mallu Khan and the Portuguese has mentioned as Meale (also as Meale Cão). Pissurlenkar, *Tentativas dos portugueses para a ocupação do Concão,* separata dos *Anais* II série, vol. 6, Lisboa, 1955, pp. 425-435.

828 The whole conspiracy to dethrone the Ibrahim Adil Shah and to put his brother Abdullah Khan in his place was organised by Assad Khan, the prime minister who had been a victim of the court politics (see *Tarikh-i-Ferishta,* vol. III, pp. 53-55) with the help of Rama Raya of Vijayanagar and Burhan Nizam Shah of Ahmadnagar. Eventually he also sought help from the Portuguese who were eager to join the pact. This made Adil Shah furious and he marched against the Portuguese who had become the major ringleaders. This problem of succession only ended in 1555 after the capture of prince Abdullah. In this campaign Ibrahim Adil Shah was also assisted by the forces of Rama Raya, contrary to what was expected. Ferishta in his *Tarikh* has provided a good detail of the whole plot. Diogo de Couto, *Década Quinta, parte segunda, Cap. VIII, pp.* 352-359, has also provided sufficient details about the revolts and its after-moths; also see Varma, *History of Bijapur,* pp. 120-121.

829 *Ibid,* Elaine Sanceau (ed.) *Collecção São Lourenço,* IICT, Lisboa, 1983, vol. II, *Traslado de uma Carta de Coje Xemaçadim para D. João de Castro.* Cananor. S.D., pp. 314-319; *Auto referente ao dinheiro de Coje Xemçadim, Cananor, 27 de Janeiro de 1546,* pp. 319; Pissurlenkar, *Tentativas dos portugueses para a ocupação do Concão,* pp. 425-427.

830 Pissurlenkar, *Tentativas dos portugueses para a ocupação do Concão,* pp. 425-427.

831 *Ibid.*

832 For wars and disputes during this period, see Sharma, *History of Vijayanagar Empire*, pp. 185-195.

833 Biker, (ed.) *Collecção de tratados e concertos de pazes...*, tomo I, pp. 116-117, *Treslado do contrato que governador D. João de Castro fez com o Idalxá, que dantes se chamava Idalcão, em 26 de fevereiro de 1546.*

834 Biker, (ed.) *Collecção de tratados e concertos de pazes...*, tomo I, pp. 122-27, *Treslado do outro Contrato que o Governador Garcia de Sá fez com o Idalxá,* em Goa, a 22 de Agosto de 1658; Danvers, *The Portuguese in India...*, vol. 1, pp. 474-77.

835 *Ibid.*

836 Biker, (ed.) *Collecção de tratados e concertos de pazes...*, tomo I, pp. 131-140; *Contrato das pazes, que se fizeram na cidade de Goa com o Mealecão em tempo do Viso Rey D. Pedro Mascarenhas, confirmadas em tempo do Governador Francisco Barreto*, 24-30 de Abril de 1555; Ponda is situated about 20-22 kms from present day Panjim. During the sixteenth century, when the Portuguese occupied Salssete and Bardez, Ponda turned out to be a place of great strategic importance and the Sultan made it a check point from which to keep a watch on Portuguese military activities and further encroachments in his own territories by them. It was put under a governor. Since Ponda had become a door into the Portuguese territories, a lot of commercial activities took place through this point and much customs revenue was derived from the movement of goods. However, local transactions and the movement of people from the Bijapuri territory to the Portuguese and vice versa were kept free, as mentioned in the treaty already referred to on the previous page. During the periods when there was a war or the threat of war or during the period of Goa's Inquisition, thousands of Hindus and Muslims fled from the Portuguese controlled areas to the territories of Bijapur. Ponda provided support to all of them.

837 For the details of the incidences that led to this the battle of Talikota, see Varma, *History of Bijapur*, pp. 123-127; R. Sewell, *A Forgotten Empire..*, (passim).

838 For details, Gribble, *History of the Deccan*, vol. I, pp. 186-197.

839 For details, see Ferishta, *Tarikh-i-Ferishta*, vols. II & III; Gribble, *History of the Deccan*, vol. I, pp. 186-197; Sharma, *History of Vijayanagar Empire*, pp. 220-221.

840 Partially, it was the Zamorin's idea too.

841 *Diogo de* Couto's *Década VIII, Caps. XXXIII-XXXVI*, pp. 283-340; Faria e Sousa, *Ásia Portuguesa*, vol. IV, *Caps.* VII-XI.

842 M.H. Rama Sharma, *The History of the Vijayanagar Empire*, vol. 2, pp. 5-6.

843 Diogo de Couto, *Década* IX, cap. III, pp.15-16.

844 Couto, *Década* IX, caps. IV-V, pp. 17-20.

845 Couto, *Década* IX, caps. IV-V, pp. 17-20; *APO-CR*, Vol V, doc. 742, *Contrato de pazes feito com El-Rey Idalxá no anno de 1571;* The same is also found in Biker, (ed.) *Collecção de tratados e concertos de pazes...*, tomo I, pp. 160-167.

846 This meant ships from the Malabar Coast especially those which came under the jurisdiction of the Zamorin and his admirals, the Kunjali Marakkars. Later in the seventeenth century, when the English and the Dutch arrived, the Portuguese presumed that they too were included.

847 *APO-CR, Fasc.* 5°-n° 779, *Assento de paz com o Idalxá no anno de 1575,* 30 de Maio; Also published in Biker, (ed.) *Collecção de tratados e concertos de pazes...*, tomo I, pp. 167-170.

848 *APO-CR*, Fasc. 5°-n° 786; *Contrato das Pazes feitas com Idalxá por seu Embaixador Zaerbeque, que veio do Reino, governando este Estado António Moniz Barreto, no anno de 1576.*

849 Faria e Sousa calls him Tojar, Faria e Sousa, *Ásia Portuguesa,* vol. IV, p. 193.

850 *Ibid*, pp. 193-199.

851 Ferishta, *Muntakhab-u-Twarikh*, vol. III, pp. 86-87; Abul-Fazal, *Akbarnama,* vol. I pp. 440-41; *Ain-i-Akbari,* vol I, p. 466; Burhani, *Ma'athir-ul-Umra,* vol. I, p. 569.

852 Gribble, *History of the Deccan, vol.* I, pp. 208; Danvers, *The Portuguese in India...*, vol. II, p. 25.

853 Spanish king Philip II took over the government of Portugal as king in 1580 and this continued until 1640, when king John IV, overthrown the Spanish regime.

854 Biker, *Collecção dos Tratados e Concertos...*, tomo I, pp. 184-186; *Assento que se fez com os Embaixadores do Idalxá por mandado do Conde de Villa d'Orta, Viso-Rey da Índia, sobre o comprimento das Pazes, feitas anteriormente pelo Conde de Atouguia com Mostafacão*, em 29 de Janeiro de 1582.

Coutinho [illegible] pp. [illegible]

Coutinho [illegible] pp. 1270-[illegible] [illegible] [illegible] Coutinho [illegible] [illegible] de 1648. The same is also found in [illegible] [illegible] [illegible] pp. [illegible]

The Spanish ships from the Manila galleons, especially those which came under the armada [illegible] and his admiral, the Council [illegible] [illegible] [illegible] [illegible] when the English and the Dutch [illegible] Portuguese [illegible] that [illegible] [illegible] [illegible].

[illegible] 1575-80 [illegible] [illegible]

[illegible]

[illegible]

[illegible]

[illegible] pp. 84-87 [illegible] [illegible]

[illegible] Portuguese [illegible]

[illegible] the Government of Portugal as long [illegible] 1580 and this continued until 1640, when King John IV overthrew the Spanish regime.

[illegible] pp. 184-186 [illegible] [illegible] [illegible] de 1512.

STAMPA XXVII *Ref. António Bocarro. O Livro das Fortalezas* *Fortalezas de Aguada, Bardês, Divar e Chorão*

Portuguese Fortress of Aguada, Bardês

facing page 294

Part II

Portuguese Bijapur Diplomacy in the Seventeenth Century

a) Introduction

Towards the end of the sixteenth century the Portuguese-Bijapuri relationship took a new turn. On the one hand the Portuguese experienced a change of regime and began to face new challenges from the English and the Dutch, while on the other the Bijapuri sultans now lived in constant fear of the Mughal army. Keeping the Mughals away from the territories of Bijapur and Ahmadnagar was beneficial for both the Portuguese and the rulers of the two states; for the Portuguese, because the kingdoms of Bijapur and Ahmadnagar stood as a barrier between them and the Mughals; for the rulers of Bijapur and Ahmadnagar because it was a question of the survival of their empires. Nevertheless, the Portuguese, although they were not very keen to see these neighbouring rulers become too powerful, understood, at the same time, that the conquest of these kingdoms by the Mughals would bring a worse situation to themselves.[855] With these considerations in mind, they applied two strategies. The first was to keep the Mughal Emperors, Akbar and later Jahangir, busy with their own internal political troubles (such as the revolt of prince Salim[856] in 1602,[857] and later prince Khusroo's revolt in 1607) by maintaining spies at the court and providing support to the rebel princes. The second policy was to support the rulers of Ahmadnagar and Bijapur with arms and ammunition, so that they would be able to oppose the Mughals effectively, naturally in exchange for their promises not to give any facilities either to the English or the Dutch in their dominions. For Bijapur and Ahmadnagar the situation resulting from Mughal pressure was so alarming that they could seldom afford to involve themselves against the Portuguese. The Portuguese for their part left no stone unturned to keep these states weak and dependent. However, when the Portuguese overstepped the mark, for example by capturing ships belonging to these states, they did not hesitate to open talks with the English and the Dutch with a view to challenging Portuguese pretensions. Therefore Portuguese-Bijapuri diplomacy had more than a touch of opportunism and deceit about it.

b) Appearance of the Dutch and the English in Asia: a New Balance of power Created

Between the years 1581 and 1616 the Sultan of Bijapur and the Portuguese enjoyed relatively peaceful relations, at least, there are no hostile incidents reported. This can be explained by the fact that both powers were engaged elsewhere in dealing with political and diplomatic problems. At the same time, it cannot be assumed that Bijapur had abandoned its ambitions to recover its lost lands or to expand its territorial possessions. A brief survey of the political developments affecting both powers would help to explain the reason why they were interested in maintaining a peaceful relationship during this period. The acquisition of Portugal by the Spanish King, Philip II, in 1580, as part of his inheritance from his mother's (Dona Isabela de Portual) side, coincided with the assassination of Sultan Ali Adil Shah of Bijapur. He was succeeded by his son, Ismail Adil Shah II, then a boy of nine years, who had to remain under the tutelage of four regents. This period was marked by internal disturbances and rivalry for the position of regent among the nobles. On the other hand, it had been the ambition of the Adil Shahs to bring the Kanara region under their control, while the Nayakas of Kanara, for their part, were determined to preserve their independence. The fighting between them for supremacy and independence, dominated the next twenty years, and the Bijapuri sultans became preoccupied with exercising their sovereignty over the Nayakas of Ikkeri, especially when the Venkatappa Nayaka determined to unite the whole Kanara region under his rule. At times the Bijapuris were successful in taming the Nayakas, who agreed to pay tribute, but frequently they sought to reassert their independence by refusing payment, and then expeditions had to be sent to extract the tribute. This absorbed a lot of the sultan's resources and prevented him from strengthening his position against the Mughals or even against the Portuguese. On the other hand the Portuguese had their own troubles in the Malabar region. The problem of Kunjali Marakkar, the approach of the Dutch embassies to the courts of Calicut, Cannanore and Cochin as well as the rising power of Venkatapa Nayaka are among the problems that occupied Portuguese attention.

During the period that followed the Spanish union with Portugal, a new phase in the history of European contacts with

Ambassadors from Badakhshan and Bijapur
Paying Tribute at the Mughal Court *facing page* 296

Asia began. On one side the English merchants, though careful not to interfere in the Portuguese dominions, started to take an active part in eastern commerce, while the Dutch merchants, after the Portuguese ports had been closed to their trade by Philip II, had also started to search for new trading opportunities. Though the Dutch were at war against their Spanish sovereign, they wanted to continue to trade with the Portuguese in the East. The Portuguese, however, had no intention of sharing their Asian commerce with anyone except those who agreed to carry a Portuguese *Cartaz* and to pay duties on the movement of their ships and merchandises under the regime of *Mare Clausum*. Whether the Portuguese had the right to demand this is a question that has been discussed by numerous historians, but here our objective is to provide a brief description of the diplomatic relations that the English and the Dutch sought to develop with the Indian states, and especially with Bijapur, towards the end of the sixteenth century and how these transformed the diplomacy of the existing powers in the region.

It is notable that in the sixteenth century, when the sultans of Bijapur and the rulers of Ahmadnagar, Berar and Golconda were fighting against one another and finally all together against the Vijayanagar Empire, the Portuguese availed themselves of the opportunity to strengthen their own power by helping one ruler against another, though in some cases they followed a policy of neutrality. This confusing state of affairs certainly weakened the Bijapuri state politically and resulted in its naval dependence on the Portuguese who manipulated the situation according to their own interests. Although the rulers of Calicut and the sultans of Bijapur and Ahmadnagar allied themselves on various occasions to expel the Portuguese from the Indian coast, notably in 1571, these efforts achieved no success. However, they did prove to the Portuguese that they had to be alert and that their presence was not accepted by the Indian rulers. The appearance of the Dutch and the English towards the end of the century offered the Indian states a new diplomatic opportunity. With the help of these newcomers, most of the states of coastal Western India tried, in the early seventeenth century, to regain their commercial independence. This can be seen especially when the Zamorin of Calicut, the Nayakas of Ikkeri, and the sultans of Bijapur and Ahmadnagar extended the hand of friendship to the northern Europeans thereby hoping to be able to end Portuguese dominance in Indian waters, which they had not been able to do by themselves.[858]

Unfortunately, during the early decades of the seventeenth century, the dreams of these south Indian rulers were more often overshadowed by the expansion southward of the Mughal Empire and in the second half of the seventeenth century, the Marathas also contributed to ruining their hopes.

When the Mughals started encroaching on the southern kingdoms of Berar, Ahmadnagar and Bijapur, which had commercial interests on the western coast of India, these states were obliged to approach the Portuguese for help. The Portuguese, for their part, were prepared to support these states against the Mughals so that they would remain a barrier to protect their own territories in western India. Although the Portuguese had signed a peace treaty with the Mughals, on 7 June 1615,[859] by which they agreed not to help any states which were at war with them, in order to safeguard their own interests, the viceroys secretly continued to provide help to the surrounding states.[860] The Portuguese were able to make use of this new opportunity to oblige these states to withdraw any support from the Dutch and the English. Temporarily this succeeded, but the Dutch persisted until they achieved their goal. So, from the late sixteenth till the early seventeenth centuries, the Portuguese had to be vigilant and considered carefully the diplomatic steps they needed to take in relation to the Indian states. This was a serious situation for them, for they risked losing all the political and commercial establishments that they had created in the sixteenth century.

As can be seen from the surviving documents, throughout the sixteenth and the seventeenth centuries the Portuguese had always prevented the construction of any fortification near any of their fortresses or territories, and had tried, by one means or another, to remove any that already existed.[861] Moreover, they also resented the construction and possession of any warship by either the Nizam Shahs of Ahmadnagar or the Adil Shahs of Bijapur. In addition the Portuguese continued their efforts to create divisions between the Bijapuri officials and the Sultan, and to spy on the Sultan's movements.[862] For example in 1605, although the Portuguese authorities had no complaint about the Bijapuri ruler, they had a grievance against the governor of Ponda, Sharif Malik, whom the Portuguese disliked and who had built trenches around Ponda. Therefore, they wanted to create some misunderstanding between him and the Sultan, and eventually bring about his removal from that territory.[863]

It is noteworthy that the Portuguese authorities, for one reason or another, resented most of the governors of Ponda district, which was the territory immediately adjacent to the Portuguese possession of Goa, and frequently complained about them to the Sultan or intrigued against them. The reason is obvious. The Portuguese, quite naturally, did not like anyone who held strong feelings against them and the officers in charge at the headquarters of Ponda were not too friendly with the Portuguese authorities. It is possible that the Sultans of Bijapur always intentionally posted such persons, and suspicions to this effect can be found throughout Portuguese and Bijapuri diplomacy. Most of the time the Portuguese authorities had grievances against the governors of Ponda either because they carried on some commercial activities or because they made frequent journeys between Goa and their own districts, all of which annoyed the Portuguese very much.

In the second decade of the century, when the governors of Ponda were given extra powers and were sent as ambassadors to the Portuguese viceregal court, the situation further deteriorated. The reason given by the Portuguese authorities to the Bijapuri court was that, since 1617, when a residential complex was constructed for the governors and the ambassadors in that area, the governors and ambassadors to the Portuguese court at Goa, crossed the borders regularly and carried on illegal trading activities, taking advantage of their diplomatic immunities.[864]

The dawn of the seventeenth century saw generally peaceful relations between the Portuguese and the sultans of Bijapur, as has been mentioned above, and it was through the mediation of the latter that the Portuguese were able to negotiate a treaty with the Sultan Nizam Shah of Ahmadnagar and to create an alliance together with the Sultan Adil Shah of Bijapur, on 9th October 1615,[865] against the Mughals, which was of mutual interest as none of the belligerents wanted to see the establishment of a superpower in their neighbourhood.[866] The Sultans of Ahmadnagar and Bijapur jointly signed the treaty in the city of Nauras Poor with the Portuguese Viceroy, Dom Jerónimo de Azevedo, to safeguard their political interests against the Mughals.[867] Alongside their mutual interests, the Portuguese and Bijapuri states also had a continuing dispute, supposedly created by the governor of Ponda, Sheikh Malik, who had received the Dutch and the English and had provided them with support. Since the help they had hoped for from the European companies had not materialised, the Bijapur authorities, as a matter of prudence, acceded to the Portuguese demands for the time being, and the Portuguese too signed the treaty, as they had already sensed the danger of the Bijapuri state joining hands with either the Dutch or the English.

Nevertheless, the Bijapuri authorities had already attained their objective of increasing Portuguese anxiety. At the same time, the Bijapuri were also aware of the support they might need at any time from the Portuguese against the Mughals. This alliance between the Bijapuri state and Ahmadnagar was considered desirable by the Portuguese as they thought that, as long as these two were united, the Mughals would be kept at a distance from their boundaries, while by the terms of the treaty of friendship neither the Dutch nor the English would be given any shelter in their dominions, a condition that stood them in good stead later in 1623 and 1638. Therefore, friendship and peace between the three states was, under the circumstances, most beneficial for all parties, which was a view that had been constantly put forward by the King of Portugal.[868]

In the year 1620 the Sultan of Bijapur ordered his ambassador, instead of living within Portuguese territory, to reside outside the boundaries of Goa in Ponda from where he would have to travel to the city in order to discharge his functions as ambassador.[869] This measure was probably taken because the ambassadors sent to the *Estado da Índia* were also usually governors (*hawaldars*) of the district of Ponda, and they could discharge both their functions from Ponda, which was close to the Portuguese capital. However, if they resided in Goa, it would certainly not be possible for them to serve also as governors. According to the Portuguese authorities, this created considerable difficulties as the ambassador wanted to come and go to suit his own convenience without respecting the protocols established between the two states. Moreover, it also created problems for the security of the ambassador himself and the Portuguese authorities were unable to take any official action if anything happened to the ambassador, as he was living outside their jurisdiction.[870]

Meanwhile, it was alleged that the ambassadors from Bijapur had started abusing their diplomatic immunities. Instead of carrying out their duties as diplomats, they indulged in private trade between Goa and the neighbouring areas without paying any customs duties since, as ambassadors, they were not liable to pay any. A letter written by the Portuguese governor on 8 May

1620, addressed to the Adil Shah,[871] accused the Bijapuri ambassador, Khwaja Noor, of abusing his diplomatic immunity by carrying on private business between Goa and some neighbouring states. It was alleged that Khwaja Noor had a house in the vicinity of Goa where, through the pretext of visiting his family, he carried on some of his business, in this way depriving the *Estado da Índia* of the customs dues that would normally have been levied. The ambassador, who was posted on a permanent mission, spent less time in the Portuguese capital than was necessary for the work he had been assigned to carry out. He made use of Ari Sinai, Vitula Nayaka and Norna Sinai for his personal commercial activities although they were supposed to be helping him in his official duties. This behaviour, according to the Portuguese governor, Fernão de Albuquerque, was extremely prejudicial to good diplomatic relations between the two states, and the Adil Shah was requested to recall the ambassador who would otherwise be imprisoned by the Portuguese. As soon as the Sultan was informed about these malpractices, he sent orders to the ambassador prohibiting him and other officials posted on diplomatic missions at the Portuguese capital from continuing with such illegal activities.[872] Officials at Goa were, nevertheless, directed to take precautions to prevent any diplomatic incident.

According to the Portuguese documents, many incidents arose in subsequent years between the state of Bijapur and the Portuguese as a result of the governor of Ponda's commercial activities, but they were minor in comparison to what took place in 1623. In that year the Sultan of Bijapur, the Sultan of Ahmadnagar and the Sultan of Golconda formed an alliance to expel the Dutch and the English from their territories in favour of the Portuguese. The King urged the Portuguese authorities in India to use all the means in their power to see that this actually materialised.[873] It seems probable that the sultans formed the alliance primarily with the intent of fighting the Mughals and, in order to secure Portuguese aid, they gave it a diplomatic flavour by declaring that, if the Portuguese joined with them, they would refuse any support to the English or the Dutch in their territories. Such an alliance would naturally be beneficial to all the belligerents and the refusal of their support to the other Europeans was not going to affect them in any way.

However, the Portuguese did not stop their protests against the commercial activities of the Bijapuri governors and retaliated by capturing a ship belonging to the Sultan at the port of Daman and confiscating all the goods and persons travelling in it, even though the ship carried a Portuguese *Cartaz*. In addition, some horses were also seized at the port of Chaul.[874] In fact, this was Portuguese retaliation for the detention by the port authorities of Dabhol a year before of one of their own ships, which was still being held by the Bijapuri Sultan.[875] The Portuguese ship had been in the jurisdiction of the Bijapuri kingdom without authorisation and had assumed that it had a right to be there and that nothing would happen to it.[876] However, the officials of the port had detained the vessel as it did not obey the jurisdiction of the local authorities. The Portuguese, for their part, instead of pursuing the matter with the higher authorities of Bijapur responded by capturing the ships belonging to the Sultan. Relations deteriorated still further when the Portuguese seized two more vessels belonging to Bijapur in the Persian Gulf in 1629, and killed all the passengers on them.[877] One incident led to another and the Sultan Adil Shah responded to the Portuguese action by withdrawing his ambassador from Goa, closing all his ports to the Portuguese and threatening to attack the provinces of Bardez and Salssette.[878] The Portuguese were quickly made to feel the consequence of this hostile atmosphere when the Sultan offered his support to the Dutch and interrupted Portugal's trade in textiles from the territory of Balaghat. This was now an alarming situation and Dom Jerónimo de Azevedo, the Portuguese Viceroy, immediately sent António Monteiro Corte-Real as ambassador to Bijapur to renew diplomatic contacts and to offer terms. The Portuguese demanded that, in order for friendly relations to be restored, the Malik of Ponda[879] should be imprisoned and the Dutch, who were trying to establish a factory in the Sultan's dominions, should be expelled. Vicente Ribeiro, who resided in Bijapur as an informer, played a vital role in securing the Viceroy's demands both of which were met.[880]

Adil Shah, for his part sent an ambassador, Mir Mohammad Raza, ordering him to respect the existing treaties concluded between their respective states, at the same time conveying to the Portuguese Viceroy a demand that all those responsible for the confiscation of the ship and the goods, including Paulo Rebelo, who captured the Bijapuri ship without consulting his superiors, should be punished.[881] The ambassador was to remind the Portuguese Viceroy about the good Bijapuri-Portuguese relations that had existed for more than a hundred years. Nevertheless, in a subtle way, he also warned the Portuguese that the English and Dutch were keen to establish friendly relations with him and that he could see no reason not to accept their request. The Sultan demanded a speedy and satisfactory reply.[882] In a subsequent letter the Sultan very clearly stated that, if Portuguese officials in Goa did not follow the path of friendship by returning all the goods, horses and passengers they had captured, as described above, he would be forced to invade Salssette and Bardez and might subsequently proceed to other neighbouring Portuguese areas.[883]

The problem persisted for a number of years and in the end the Bijapuri authorities pressed their charges with the new Portuguese Viceroy, the Conde de Linhares. In replying to the Adil Shah's ambassador, Conde de Linhares stated that he could not be held responsible for what had happened during the time of previous viceroys that he would abide by the treaties but that, if necessary, he was ready to defend his territory against any military invasion.[884]

Judging by the situation in which the Portuguese found themselves at that time, this was an irresponsible reply from a Viceroy who had yet to establish a firm foothold, whose treasury was reported to be empty and who needed to reorganise the navy, which was in a state of dilapidation. Moreover, the Dutch and the English were strengthening their relations with the Indian states. However, it is interesting to note that in his letter he says nothing about the capture of the Bijapuri ships at Daman or the seizure of the horses at Chaul. On the other hand, in one of his letters addressed to the King of Portugal on 18 February 1630,[885] he expressed concern at the state of affairs he found in the relations with the Bijapuri Sultan and he wrote that the Muslims (whom he called mouros) were "happy with the miserable condition in which the Portuguese state was found". He was very critical of the current ambassador, Khwaja Mohammad Raza, whom he refered to as "by nature a thief and dishonest",[886] certainly not language to be used publicly about a diplomat at a time when he was seeking to maintain harmonious relations with a neighbouring power. In this letter he also complained that, on his arrival as Portuguese Viceroy, this ambassador had not come to Goa to pay him a courtesy visit as had been the custom for over a century. Mohammad Raza had acknowledged that this was the custom in his letter of welcome to the Viceroy and had excused himself on the ground of sickness.[887] He had even requested the Viceroy to send a physician to cure him[888] and this had been considered.[889]

As a matter of protocol, the Viceroy proposed that Manuel Vicente, a person experienced and capable in dealing with delicate matters, should be sent to the Adil Shah to avoid hostilities and conclude a peace, which the Portuguese also urgently required.[890] While the Conde de Linhares was still very unhappy with what was going on, he received a letter from Balthazar de Azeredo, the Portuguese resident ambassador at the court of Ali Adil Shah, saying that he was not being well received at the Sultan's court,[891] to which the Viceroy replied, in a letter dated 27 March 1630, that the ambassador should maintain friendly relations at all costs.[892] It was considered that this was the price that would have to be paid to keep the Dutch and the English away from the courts of Portugal's allies.[893] However, it was also suggested that he should return to Goa with or without the Sultan's permission, if he found it necessary. If the Sultan should ask the reason for his leaving the court, he was to say that it was because he was not accorded the proper protocols as an ambassador.[894] In the meantime, the Carmelite, Frei Leandro, an assistant and interpreter to the ambassador at the court of the Adil Shah, had died and it was suggested that Fr. João da Rocha of the Augustinian Order should be sent to assist the ambassador, Balthazar de Azeredo, in his diplomatic tasks.[895] Azeredo was finally successful in obtaining a farmán[896] from the Sultan of Bijapur which confirmed the peace and friendship between the two governments, in return for the restoration by the Portuguese of the captured ships to their rightful owners.[897]

No sooner had the negotiations over the capture of the ships ended than another problem arose between the two neighbours. On 1 of November 1630, the Conselho do Estado met to take a decision on the information sent by the governor of Onor, Balthazar Marinho,[898] who had been informed, while on his way from Barcelore, about a large movement of armaments and preparations for war by the Bijapuri army.[899] These preparations were underway in the region of Ancola close to Goa. He was also told that the Bijapuri officials in the vicinity of Goa were in contact with Dutch and English ships[900] and, probably, had a secret plan to invade Bardez and Salssette to realize the long-standing Bijapuri objective of recovering those territories. As soon as the news was made public, the Portuguese Viceroy sent a letter to the Sultan demanding that he either act immediately to end the preparations for hostilities or the Portuguese would also prepare for war. He reminded the Sultan of the clause in the last treaty signed between the two governments, that the Sultan would pay a hundred thousand

Pagodas as compensation, if he was responsible for any hostilities.[901] In the letter, he also demanded that the ban on the movement of all people (merchants, travellers and ordinary people) must be lifted in order to relieve the tension. It is not very clear when this ban had started since only a couple of months before both states had signed a pact of friendship. So far as the preparations for hostilities in the neighbouring Kanara region are concerned, this was the time when the Sultan of Bijapur had ordered Veerabhadra Nayaka to restore to power all the princes who had been deprived of their lands by his grandfather on pain of facing the wrath of the Bijapuri army. The reason why the Sultan's army had started to gather around Ancola in the vicinity of Goa was to put a pressure on Kanara rather than to prepare for a war against the Portuguese.

It appears that the Portuguese were paranoid about the visits of the Dutch and the English to the court of Bijapur, which was contrary to the promises made in the treaties. It is also worth mentioning that in the year 1629, according to the Portuguese sources, the Dutch were given permission to build a factory at Ancola, in the territory of Bijapur, which the Portuguese authorities greatly resented.[902] Nevertheless, as mentioned earlier in this chapter, the Sultans of Bijapur most probably used such threats or bluffs of collaboration with the Dutch to create fear in the minds of the Portuguese authorities. In any case, we cannot ignore the response of the Portuguese Viceroy, the Conde de Linhares that "he was not responsible for what his predecessors had promised and had done" - meaning that what had been done during the period of one governor would not necessarily be adhered to by any subsequent head of state. Perhaps the Sultan of Bijapur was following the same policy. On the other hand, it should also be remembered that most of the Bijapuri Sultans ascended the throne at a very young age and had to remain under tutelage for many years. The Sultan's court was full of diverse nobility quite a substantial number of whom disliked the Portuguese presence. Therefore, many incidents took place without the consent of the ruler nor was he able to understand the consequences of agreements that he signed during his minority. By the time he took power into his own hands most of the damage had already been done and it became his responsibility to provide a remedy and to put the things right.

In the letter sent to the Sultan dated 4th of November 1630,[903] the Portuguese Viceroy complained about what had been said in the presence of Mustafa Khan and Ekhlas Khan[904], two of the most powerful nobles from the Bijapuri court, about the threat to occupy Salssette and Bardez with the help of the Malabaris, the English[905] and the Dutch. Of course, such threats from the side of the Bijapuri Sultans had occasionally been put into practice but, as has been mentioned elsewhere, on such occasions the Portuguese were usually fortunate as the Sultan of Bijapur had to withdraw his forces either to fight his Mughal enemies or the rulers of Vijayanagar. The Viceroy also complained about the insolent behaviour of the ambassador, Khwaja Mohammad Raza, who had shown disrespect to the good name of the King of Portugal and had almost brought the two nations to the verge of war. Knowing what was going on between the Sultan of Bijapur and the Mughal Emperor, Shah Jahan,[906] the Portuguese Viceroy proposed to provide military aid as and when it was required in order to maintain friendly relations between the two states. At the same time, he reminded the Sultan that, although any person or official of the Bijapuri state was allowed to travel by river in and around the Portuguese possessions, the river and the sea belonged to the King of Portugal who always maintained a close control over both with his fleets. He went on to propose either that the Sultan clearly bring hostilities to an end or that he should formally declare war, though the Viceroy stated that he preferred friendly relations that were always beneficial to both states.[907]

These heated exchanges of correspondence and threats between the two states, were concluded by the Portuguese agreeing to provide help to the Sultan of Bijapur against the common enemy, the Mughals, who had marched into Bijapur in 1632 to collect arrears of tribute. In return the Bijapuri sultan once again promised to provide no support to the Dutch and the English in his territories. After all, in these circumstances both the Portuguese and the Bijapuri Sultan needed friends.

Apart from these events, early in 1631 an angry diplomatic exchange took place between the two states because the Sultan had ordered that Fernão Lopes, a doctor who, in 1627, had been posted as a royal physician to the court of Sultan Ali Adil Shah to treat the father of the present Sultan who had eventually died, should have his ears and nose cut off.[908] According to Portuguese authors this "barbarous act of cutting off of nose and ears of doctor Fernão Lopes was done because, he could not save the life of the ailing Sultan" However, the real reason for cutting off his ears and nose was not that he had failed to cure the then ruling Sultan but that, in the guise of a physician, he had been a spy at the Bijapuri court.[909] When this was discovered he had received this punishment.[910] In fact, in one of his letters the Viceroy makes it clear that Fernão Lopes was a spy and that keeping spies at the court of rulers in India was becoming a very expensive business, especially now that the financial situation of the *Estado da Índia* was quite weak.[911]

However, there was another aspect to this story, which led to the withdrawal of the Bijapuri ambassador from Goa. It was reported that the Sultan's officers at Rajapur had seized a galleon belonging to the captain of Daman. This was done at the instigation of the ambassador of the Sultan who, as the Portuguese Viceroy alleged, instead of fulfilling his duties in Goa had given the excuse of his being ill for not having paid a courtesy visit to the Viceroy, a practice followed since 1576. The Viceroy sent various letters to the Sultan demanding an explanation for this matter and the removal of the ambassador.[912] However, before this could become a serious diplomatic issue, both sides decided to resolve the matter through an exchange of diplomats. In order to show that the Portuguese wished to maintain friendly relations, the Viceroy sent Balthazar de Azeredo as ambassador to the court of the Sultan to deal with the problem.[913]

It was a common practice of the Portuguese that they constantly attacked and plundered Indian shipping even when they needed Indian support. On 26 September 1631, a ship belonging to the Sultan of Bijapur was captured off the Persian coast at Tamaran.[914] It was reported that the *Cartaz,* which the captain showed, did not belong to that ship. The Sultan was informed about this incident and that the owner of the ship did not carry a valid *Cartaz.* In order to avoid a diplomatic problem the Sultan was asked to punish those responsible in this case. All such incidents, however, were overshadowed by the arrival of the Mughal forces in Bijapur and ended with a friendly exchange of diplomats, as mentioned earlier.

Meanwhile in 1632, once again confronted by a Mughal invasion, the Bijapuri Sultan wrote to the Conde de Linhares for immediate military aid and pleaded that all recent incidents should be set to one side.[915] As it was for the common interest, his request was agreed. The following text reveals that the Portuguese knew that the Mughals could be problem for them too if they did not send help soon, but secretly.[916] Here one should note that, Shah

Jahan, before he invaded the kingdom of Bijapur, also asked for help from the Portuguese with whom he was at peace, offering as compensation all the areas surrounding Goa. However, the Portuguese not only avoided giving help to the Mughals but secretly sent all the assistance that the Bijapuri Sultan had requested.[917]

The Sultan's request was unanimously approved by all the members of the *Conselho do Estado* but with the proviso that the arms and ammunition should be provided with the utmost secrecy as the Portuguese had also promised the Mughals not to aid any of their enemies on pain of causing a military confrontation, which was not what the Portuguese were looking for at that time.[918] The Sultan's request was followed by the arrival, in July 1633, of the ambassador, Mohammad Zaman, in person carrying a letter designed to strengthen diplomatic ties. Apart from an exchange of courtesies and the settling of some mutual grievances over the return of ships and the exemption from duties of non-commercial goods, it appears from the minutes of the Council that both parties, the ambassador of the Sultan and the Portuguese Viceroy, were anxious to secure a lasting end to hostilities.[919]

In fact this is the first occasion when the Conde de Linhares indicated that he was happy to receive the letter of the Sultan Adil Shah and that he regretted the insensibilities and lack of diplomatic tact of his predecessor in not sending a message of condolence on the death of Sultan Ibrahim Adil Shah II,[920] father of the present sultan, or a message of congratulations on the Sultan's accession to the throne. The Viceroy went on to say that he had immediately sent an ambassador[921] with presents, which even Mohammad Raza, the ambassador of the Bijapuri Sultan, thought was "beyond any obligation or custom".[922] The Viceroy also complained that the present ambassador, Khwaja Mohammad Raza, did not follow royal orders and did not behave as an ambassador and indulged in certain malpractices, which were prejudicial to both governments.[923] The Portuguese had kept him and his movements under surveillance and they had requested the Bijapuri authorities to recall him.[924]

As a matter of fact, having received several complaints from the Portuguese authorities, the Sultan had sent Mohammad Zaman to deal with the matter.[925] A new treaty was finally signed on 3 April 1633, by the ambassador and the Portuguese Viceroy, Conde de Linhares.[926] The letters of credential that the ambassador carried provided a guarantee from the Sultan that he would punish all the officers of his empire who had indulged in any malpractice or caused any alarm to the *Estado da Índia* or damage to Portuguese property, thereby injuring the good name of the Sultan.[927]

The ambassador was received with great pomp at the Viceroy's palace. The banquet was magnificent and, as the need for the treaty was mutual, the Viceroy felt able to say that "he felt the expenditure incurred on the banquet was nothing in comparison to the outcome of the mission".[928] Help was sent immediately in the form of gunpowder and cannon in order to keep the two empires occupied in the war with each other.[929] A sense of the Viceroy's diplomatic intentions can be gleaned from the words he used in a letter to the King: "for the safety of our State there is nothing better than war and disintegration among these [indigenous] people".[930]

The ostensible reason for the Mughal invasion of Bijapuri territory was to collect arrears of tribute, which the Adil Shah purposely held back in order to demonstrate his military strength. Although he was forced to pay the tribute, the hostilities brought heavy loss of life and property to both parties. The famine, which affected the Mughal military camp and the whole region of Gujarat and the surrounding states of western India, was another disaster experienced during this military campaign. Moreover, the Sultan of Bijapur was lucky, as in 1633 the Mughal Queen, Mumtaz Mahal, died and the Emperor, Shah Jahan, cancelled all military campaigns in the south for several years.[931]

However, nothing seemed to work out for the Portuguese, and the Dutch continued to intrude themselves into the Sultan's court, offering him sumptuous presents and holding out to him the prospect of the reconquest of Goa and of the surrounding districts occupied by the Portuguese and of sharing their revenues with him.[932]

In their relationship with each other the Portuguese and the Bijapuri had one thing in common. Each tried to solve immediate issues instead of dealing, once and for all, with the root cause of their problems. Neither one trusted the other. Although for this the Sultans could hardly be blamed, as most of them ascended the throne as minors who could not be responsible for policies pursued during their minorities. As for the Portuguese, most of the governors and viceroys adopted policies, which seemed to fit the immediate circumstances. This became the principal problem in maintaining harmonious relations with the neighbouring states during the short tenure of their governorships, which was for a maximum period of three years. Besides, the Portuguese continued to seize and burn Bijapuri ships, whenever they considered it necessary to enforce their maritime policies. The Bijapuri officials, for their part, used the presence of the Dutch and the English to put diplomatic pressure on the Portuguese. However, the ruler of Bijapur felt bound to observe the terms demanded by the Portuguese whenever he had to face bigger threats in the form of an invasion by the Mughals. The Portuguese, on the other hand, even when they had financial and military problems, tried to show off their naval might and superiority, whereas the Bijapuris dissimulated and tried to ignore their presence. The Portuguese never recognised that Bijapur and the other coastal states had the right to invite whosoever they wanted into their territories. The fundamental problems, therefore, persisted and were never resolved.

c) The Conde de Linhares: Efforts to Restore the Prestige and Power of the Estado da Índia

After his arrival in India in December 1629, the Conde de Linhares had many difficult problems to cope with. First and most important of all, he had to make the Portuguese navy operational as it was in a very bad state and, at the same time, he had to mobilise diplomatic support through the customary means of demonstrating Portuguese naval power. Like previous viceroys and governors, he also tried to make use of the political upheavals within the Indian states. His prime task was to bring the Sultan of Bijapur under Portuguese influence since, being young and inexperienced, he was dominated by his Persian nobles who were mostly hostile to the Portuguese,[933] and because the English and Dutch were constantly at his court seeking favours by tempting him with the offer of help to recover the districts of Salssette and Bardez.[934] The Viceroy in his letters appears furious with the Sultan because of his support given to the English and the Dutch and he even expressed his sentiments in this regard saying that "his desire was to go personally with a heavy force and give him a lesson, if he doesn't act, because it was not wise for the State, if the King wanted him to do so, he would fulfil his desire..."[935] In this letter, written in 1635, the Conde de Linhares mentions that he was in possession of an original correspondence, which took place between the Sultan of Bijapur and the English and the Dutch, that showed that the Sultan had asked for support from these two European nations against the Portuguese and had already gathered around 12,000 soldiers in the neighbouring areas of Goa. This was the reason why he appears to be so angry with the Sultan.

In these letters of the Portuguese Viceroy, two things appear very intriguing; first, how did he come by this correspondence? Was it a report from a Bijapur-based spy? Second, was it likely that the Sultan of Bijapur would be so ungrateful since a couple of years before he had sought help from the Portuguese against the Mughals and might require it again at any time in the future if the Mughals returned? On various occasions in the past he had knocked at the door of the Portuguese for help and Portuguese officials had many times referred to the Sultan of Bijapur as a "good friend and neighbour"? Perhaps the Conde de Linhares was seeking some excuse for further attacks on Bijapuri ships, which indeed took place a year later! The original correspondence that he mentioned did not accompany his own letter to the King. Such extreme oscillations in the relations between the two states are typical and quite difficult to explain.

The viceroys had clear instructions from the King of Portugal that, whenever there was a war between two states in India, it was better to let them fight, while occasionally helping one against the other.[936] This had been the case when Shah Jahan invaded Ahmadnagar and Bijapur early in 1632.[937] The Portuguese did not break off relations with the Mughal but at the same time secretly helped the Sultan of Bijapur, so that the Mughals would not defeat him and eventually become a problem for the Portuguese themselves.[938] On the other hand, when the Sultan of Bijapur was fighting against the Sultan of Ahmadnagar and the Mughals, it was in the interest of the *Estado da Índia* to profit as much as it could from these quarrels between the states.[939] The weaker they became during their wars, the better for the Portuguese. So, during such periods, both parties were helped secretly.

On the other hand, when the states of Ahmadnagar and Bijapur were invaded by the Mughals in 1632, the Conde de Linhares succeeded in uniting Ahmadnagar and Bijapur against them, and provided moral and military support.[940] While the allied Bijapuri and Ahmadnagar forces were fighting the Mughals, the Viceroy was organising his own forces against the Dutch.[941] The Portuguese spies, on such occasions, played a very important role by providing progress reports on the military campaigns. During early 1632, there was such a person, named Manuel da Silva, a resident in Surat, who provided information about what the Mughals thought of the Portuguese and where they were going to attack.[942]

However, the diplomatic game that the Conde de Linhares had dreamt of playing had a short duration. As has been mentioned earlier, controlling the sea was not a policy pursued by Indian rulers, nor did they care who sailed the seas as long as they obeyed the laws of the state whose ports they used. Portuguese ambitions to control the sea were not acceptable to any of the Indian kings, and certainly not to the sultans of Bijapur. They had agreed not to allow the Dutch or English a base for their commercial activity only because they could not face the Portuguese navy at sea and the military support from the other two Protestant nations never materialised in physical form. Therefore, unsure of any naval support, the Indian rulers, from time to time, had to accept conditions imposed by the Portuguese, because they feared losses to their commercial shipping and invasions from neighbouring states.

It is worth mentioning here that the Sultan of Bijapur, and other rulers in India, were quite aware of the opportunistic nature of Portuguese diplomacy, and they too played the game according to circumstances in the same way that the Portuguese did. In the year 1636, the Portuguese authorities captured a ship belonging to the Sultan of Bijapur, although it had a *Cartaz* given by the Conde de Linhares, as retaliation for their acceptance of the English and the Dutch embassies.[943] However, when the Sultan complained, the Portuguese authorities in Goa responded that the ship was carrying some illegal items, such as pepper, that were strictly prohibited from being carried on a non-Portuguese ship. Since the captain of the Bijapuri ship had tried to defend himself with firearms, the Portuguese authorities had had to take defensive measures and seize the ship.[944] This incident is typical of the actions taken by the Portuguese whenever Bijapur or other Indian states received any emissary or ambassadors from the Dutch or the English. The Portuguese tried to exert their authority in this way and put forward different kinds of reasons for the detention of the ships and persons.

However, the diplomatic efforts of the Portuguese authorities were not all in vain as can be seen from the contents of the letter sent in 1637 to the Portuguese Viceroy at Goa by the Portuguese ambassador, Balthazar Marinho, and the informer, António de Vite, who were both residents at the court of Bijapur. This letter revealed the true friendship (or diplomacy?) of the Sultan who had dismissed the Dutch ambassador, Van Twist, who had wanted to negotiate with the Sultan to expel the Portuguese from his dominions in exchange for permission to establish a factory in the Sultan's territory.[945] Balthazar Marinho suggested that goodwill presents should be sent to the Sultan thanking him for this recent development, but that it should be sent with much prudence and secrecy as Portugal's enemy, Mustafa Khan,[946] was always at the court and would do anything to dissuade the Sultan from continuing his good relations with the Portuguese.[947] This resulted in the preparation of an embassy with a sumptuous present, to be led by António Moniz Barreto, who was chosen as suitable for the mission. Here it is worth noting that the assumption of Manuela Blanco in her thesis[948] that the present was sent because "those, false, faithless and dishonest Moors" were "greedy",[949] is inappropriate as the said presents were sent to thank the Sultan for the services he had rendered to the Portuguese state.[950] Subsequently the Portuguese Viceroy, Pêro da Silva, did not forget to send António de Vite with a message of condolence to the Sultan Adil Shah on the demise of his wife.[951]

Portuguese diplomacy did not always have positive results. In 1637 the Dutch ambassador had been successful in obtaining permission for the construction of a factory and fortress at Vengurla, although this permission was withdrawn shortly afterwards. Finally, in 1638, he was able to obtain a permanent base at Vengurla but without any military pact against the Portuguese. The ambassador, António Moniz Barreto, who presented his credentials on 9 July 1638 at the court of the Adil Khan, tried to persuade the Sultan not to allow the Dutch settlements at Vengurla and Karwar[952] and to discourage the English mission at his court from pursuing the same purpose.[953] The failure of the embassy of António Moniz Barreto is mentioned in his own letter to the Viceroy, written early in 1639.[954] It is interesting to note in this letter that he had contacts with the Dutch ambassador who had informed him that "the Dutch emissary here is not dealing about the help, more than requesting for the port [Vengurla]. He has confirmed to me that within a couple of days he would be leaving from here".[955]

However, the permission to allow the Dutch to construct a factory at Vengurla was, according to Portuguese historians, an unfriendly act, which later proved to be very damaging to their

Goan settlements. We do not know whether the permission granted to the Dutch for a settlement so near to Goa was a farsighted plan by the Sultan? As mentioned earlier, the reigning Sultan was still very young. He had little knowledge of foreign affairs and was surrounded by numerous shrewd and experienced politicians, many of whom hated the Portuguese presence.[956] So, although António Moniz Barreto was happy with the overall treatment he received in Bijapur, it is not surprising that the results of his embassy were not as fruitful as he wished.

The permission for the construction of a Dutch commercial and military settlement at Vengurla proved to be a major obstacle to the safe arrival and departure of Portuguese shipping bound for Goa in the years to come. However, at the same time, the Sultan had refused any military campaign against the Portuguese. The Sultan was playing an ambiguous game. He did not want to give a clear "no" to the Dutch but neither did he say "yes". In brief, the Sultan applied the same policy in relation to the Dutch and the English as the Portuguese had been applying to him, of using one neighbouring state against the other. The Sultan wanted to make new friends but at the same time he did not want the enmity of the Portuguese.[957] There are many Portuguese documents, which show that the Sultan did not enter into any treaty against the Portuguese, as has been widely presumed, and the embassy of António Moniz Barreto to the court of Bijapur in 1638 was to thank the Sultan for not entering into any military alliance against them.

In 1639 the Sultan of Bijapur was at war with the Nayaka of Ikkeri, Veerabhadra Nayaka. His army plundered most of the northern lands of the Nayaka in alliance with the queen of Olala, the queen of Banghel and the king of Gersoppa who all wanted to recover their lands from the ruler of Kanara. The Sultan, being one of the vassal states of the Mughals since 1598, sought help from them against any offensive that might come from the Nayakas of Ikkeri in the south.[958] Adil Shah had by this time learned to play politics. Confident of the military support from his 'sovereign', the Mughal Emperor, against the Nayakas of Ikkeri, the Sultan tried to play a double game in his relations with the Portuguese and the other Europeans. The failure of Portuguese diplomacy under such circumstances can be understood. The Sultan was sure that the Portuguese this time would not retaliate while, for their part, the Dutch were happy to obtain a place so near to Goa even though they had failed to obtain an offensive alliance to dislodge the Portuguese.

In 1638, after constructing a strong base at Vengurla, the Dutch had started their blockade of Goa. The Portuguese put a lot of effort into the defence of the settlements around Goa. The *Conselho do Estado* tried to get their ships out of the port and had several meetings throughout the year to consider the matter but came up with no concrete solution.[959] The Viceroy did not consider it to be worthwhile to try to obtain any help from the Sultan of Bijapur against Portugal's European enemy but, after a continuous blockade of Goa by the Dutch, the Portuguese authorities planned to try to bribe the Sultan Adil Shah by paying him three hundred thousand *Ashrafis,* (one hundred thousand in cash and the rest in merchandise - cinnamon, elephants, horses and other necessary items) provided he expelled the Dutch from his ports.[960] This step was ostensibly taken in order to compensate the Sultan's subjects for losses suffered in the Indian Ocean and Persian Gulf during decades of plundering of their shipping. The Portuguese were now taking seriously the idea that the unfriendly behaviour of the Sultan was largely, though not entirely, due to their own bad conduct and that this was having an effect on the diplomatic as well as the commercial relations between them.[961] The Viceroy now offered to extend a friendly hand to the Sultan and to put an end to these controversies by paying for the damage done to the Sultan's shipping and to Bijapur's economy. The following passage shows how the Portuguese felt about their own past deeds against the Sultans of Bijapur: "we should have much consideration for this king, Adil Shah who had, if received the Dutch in his kingdom but didn't enter into any defensive alliance, it is we who had to be blamed for, as we have damaged a lot his ships, merchandises and killed his numerous person in cold blood, in the past. It would be worth while if we paid him fifty thousand *Ashrafis* in the name of friendship..."[962] As a matter of urgency they needed to earn the goodwill of the Sultan.[963] On the other hand one can understand why the Bijapuri authorities had been so indecisive in maintaining a continuous cordial relationship.

d) Tense Diplomatic Exchanges

The political situation soon took another turn in 1641, when the governor of Ponda wrote to the Portuguese Viceroy asking for military support[964] to attack[965] the fort of Danda, in the territory of Ahmadnagar since both Sultans (the Sultan of Bijapur and Ahmadnagar) were at war during this period.[966] If this failed, the governor, Mirza Mohammad Raza, told the Portuguese that he would be forced to ask for help from the Dutch.[967]

This was a critical situation for the Portuguese as can be seen from the discussions in the minutes of the *Conselho do Estado*. During the meeting, it was decided that they would not give any help to the Sultan as he had not complied with the earlier treaty of 1615 by which he had agreed to expel the Dutch from his territory.[968] However, Francisco de Mello e Castro, one of the councillors, favoured sending help as he thought it would be a good opportunity to demonstrate Portuguese military power in comparison with the Dutch. Other members of the Council, such as Dom Manuel Pereira, stated that, under such circumstances, as a matter of prestige and protocol, the request for help should have been sent by a higher dignitary, like Mustafa Khan, and not by an officer of inferior rank. The overseer of the treasury (*vedor da fazenda*), André Salema, the Inquisitor, António de Faria Machado, and António Moniz Barreto, the captain of the city and former Portuguese ambassador to the court of Bijapur in 1638, gave their opinion that help should be sent to the Sultan even though he did not deserve it, but with much prudence.[969] The Archbishop and João da Silva, the first Viceroy to be appointed after the Restoration of independence from Spanish rule, said that the Sultan should be helped to capture the Danda fort as the governor of this fort was an enemy of the Portuguese, and in this way, by helping the Sultan against the common enemy, they would solve their own problems too.[970] It is in this context, when the governor of Ponda wrote a letter threatening that he would ask for help from the Dutch, if the Portuguese failed to act, that the Viceroy after the meeting of the *Conselho do Estado* decided to send support to the Sultan.[971] But in reality, it was never sent.

The Portuguese attitude with regard to the Indian rulers never changed, and with respect to sending help to the Sultan against the Danda fort, they were in no hurry to do so as this was a fight of "Muslim against Muslim",[972] and, in fact, the Indian rulers were already aware of this.

There was no consistency in the policy of the Portuguese towards Indian rulers as they felt superior to them and only agreed to comply with terms that had been signed when they were forced to, due to some critical circumstances. At times even this did not work. In 1642, though they were in deep trouble all over Asia, the Portuguese did not lose the opportunity to show their power by burning and looting Indian ships even though, as already mentioned, the previous year they sent a large sum of money to the Sultan Adil Shah as compensation for the damage they had inflicted on his vessels. Now the same scenario was repeated. Though in the middle of negotiations to provide help to the Sultan, a ship belonging to Assad Khan[973] was captured and burnt by Francisco Pereira da Cunha off the Rajapur coast.[974] In his letter, Assad Khan complained about this fact and asked for the restitution of what he, his crew members, and the passengers travelling in it, had lost. The *Conselho do Estado* unanimously agreed to meet his demands,[975] perhaps because they had recently lost the territory and ports of Malacca to the Dutch. Moreover, the treaty signed in Europe between Portugal and the Netherlands had not been made public in the East and was not so far effective.[976]

A similar event occurred two years later when, on 18 July 1644, a ship belonging to Ekhlas Khan[977] was captured in the Straits of Hormuz with all his merchandise and personal belongings. The Sultan and Ekhlas Khan both demanded that this ship should at once be returned to him with all its cargo. It was, once again, decided unanimously by the *Conselho do Estado,* that the ship in question should be returned or compensation should be paid as the Sultan of Bijapur had been a good friend of the *Estado da Índia.*[978]

Discussions in the Council reveal the thinking behind Portuguese policy making. Francisco de Mello e Castro, *procurador da coroa e fazenda do Estado da Índia,* and Dr Lopo de Lagares Paçanha, *ouvidor geral do Ciuel,* suggested that "seeing the miserable condition in which we are, our king's suggestion that there should be good relations with this king, Adil Shah, sounds justifiable and the ship should be returned to him".[979] Francisco de Mello e Castro and the Viceroy, João da Silva Tello de Meneses, the Conde de Aveiras, were of the same opinion. It is not clear why the Portuguese made such difficulties about maintaining peaceful and friendly relations with the neighbouring states when they needed friends so badly. Whenever they did approach the Indian states for peace accords, it was only because they could no longer afford to continue with their traditional way of dealing with them. One can only conclude that, had the Portuguese been in a better situation financially and in terms of naval power, they would have continued confiscating ships and destroying property and men.

The question of the jurisdiction of the Inquisition was also discussed during the meeting of the *Conselho do Estado,*[980] on 20 July 1654, as to whether it extended to the territories of the Bijapur kingdom. This was due to a ban that the Inquisition wished to place on marriage ceremonies of an Indian origin within the jurisdiction of *Estado da Índia.* It was stated by the Inquisition authorities that those Indians, especially Hindus (*gentios*), practised 'diabolical rituals' during their marriage ceremonies and that they, the authorities, wanted to put an end to them once and for all. Naturally the Hindu priests and people protested against this and the matter was put to the Sultan of Bijapur.[981] This issue had been pending since 1634[982] and only now, in 1644, after a period of over a decade, had the Portuguese civil authorities tried to put an end to the dispute. However, it was far from a complete resolution. During this meeting it was also decreed that all the matters in dispute between the kingdom of Bijapur and the Portuguese government, which had also been pending for some time, should be dealt with only in Goa even though they might originate in other parts of the Portuguese dominions in Asia.[983] The dispute over the marriage and religious ceremonies continued till 1654 and led to a three days war and many more complications, as the Inquistion authorities did not accept or respect the jurisdiction of the *Conselho do Estado* over them and the Portuguese civil and military authorities were too weak to exercise any authority. This is dealt with in detail in a later part of this chapter.

The period from 1649 till October 1655 was full of incidents as the Portuguese were more preoccupied with the new political situation in Kanara where Shivappa Nayaka had declared war against them and their fortresses were in serious danger.[984] The port-towns of Ceylon – Jaffna, Galle and Colombo - were also under constant Dutch attack from 1650[985] and the Portuguese had to send regular help to assist the governor, António de Souza Coutinho.[986] The fortress and the port of Muscat was also facing the same fate.[987] Therefore, the Portuguese had very little chance of sending any courtesy mission to the Sultan of Bijapur to minimise the tension. On the contrary, friendly relations once more deteriorated towards the end of 1654. During the same period, the Sultan of Bijapur also had problems with Shivappa Nayaka which involved him more than once in armed conflict to safeguard his own position.

e) Hostilities and Compromises: Last Phase of Portuguese Bijapuri Diplomacy

In October 1654, the territory of Salssette was attacked by Abdullah Hakim, the commander of the army of the Sultan of Bijapur. This is the way that many recent historians have started their paragraph dealing with the troubles of 1654.[988] After a three days' skirmish the Bijapuri forces took Dom Manuel Lobo da

Silveira, the Portuguese military commander, prisoner without much resistance. Two priests, António Botelho and Gonçalo Martins, acted as mediators to get him released.

The story behind this incursion, as narrated by Niccolao Manucci, appears ridiculous if we consider it at face value. Apparently, a precious stone from the treasury of the Sultan Adil Shah[989] was taken by his treasurer prior to a visit to Goa for medical treatment. During the course of his treatment, the treasurer borrowed about twenty thousand *Ashrafis* from Father Gonçalo Martins, a Jesuit priest and a known moneylender, leaving the stone as security. When, after some time, the treasurer wanted it back, Father Gonçalo Martins refused to return it and pretended that he did not know anything about the jewel. According to a letter sent by the Conde de Sarzedas to the King, it appears that it was Malik Yaqut who wanted to buy the stone as a present to the Sultan,[990] although this took place after the war had already been over between the Bijapuri forces and the Portuguese. However, continuing with the story of Manucci: this case was taken to the Sultan and, after a proper inquiry, the Jesuit priest and some of his companions were invited to Bijapur on the pretext that the Sultan and his entire family might become converts to Christianity.[991] When the Jesuits reached Bijapur and found out the true situation, they flatly refused to give back the stone. Even the Portuguese Viceroy was unable to get any satisfactory reply from the Provincial of the Jesuits at Goa. This whole situation led to the invasion of Salssette and Bardez. After much loss of life and property, the Viceroy was able to get hold of the stone and hand it over to the Sultan.[992]

Though Manucci claims to have witnessed all these matters, he omitted to put the real state of affairs into his diary. In reality, there was another serious matter creating tension between the two states.[993] Moreover his statements are not supported by any Portuguese source, though a letter of the Sultan of Bijapur shows that he did request that Father Martins should be sent to Bijapur to deal with some diplomatic affairs.[994]

Teodoro de Matos has given another account of this invasion. According to him it was "Dutch influence and the weakness of the Portuguese military forces" that motivated the invasion.[995] P.P. Shirodkar,[996] on the other hand, has recently concluded that the Bijapuri Sultan invaded Salssette and Bardez, in order to force the Portuguese to abandon the defence of Onor.[997] Either of these could have been the reasons why Goa was attacked. However, the supposition that the Dutch wanted to keep the Portuguese forces busy near Goa while they invaded the territories of Ceylon and the Portuguese dominated areas of South India, also seems unrealistic if we accept that the pretext was just a matter of prestige and the acquisition of a stone. However, we cannot ignore this supposition entirely as the Dutch were constantly trying to get a better foothold in the Bijapuri territories, promising help to the Sultan against the Portuguese. If the Portuguese exercised a free hand in capturing and looting the Sultan's ships, the Bijapuri Sultan seized every chance that came his way to harass the Portuguese by land and to extend his support to the Dutch and the English. These prevented the Portuguese from showing off their naval power, but we do not find any instance when, in practice, these two powers ever fought in favour of the Sultan of Bijapur against the Portuguese. However, there was already a Dutch representative at the Sultan's court who was seeking to obtain privileges in return for Dutch military support to the Sultan to fulfil his longstanding desire to regain the port of Goa, and the Dutch planned to seize the opportunity to attack Ceylon whenever the Portuguese would be preoccupied with a Bijapuri attack on Goa. Matos supposition is mainly based on the evidence of the Conde de Sarzedas[998] who mentions that in November 1653 two Dutch emissaries were sent from Vengurla to Bijapur, after the end of the ten years Portuguese-Dutch truce, to plan an attack on Goa. It was supposed that the Dutch would blockade Goa by sea and the Sultan would invade by land. In reality, as he says, an attack on Goa was not the real intention of the Dutch. Instead they wanted to keep the Portuguese occupied at Goa while they concentrated on the conquest of an undefended Ceylon.[999] The Dutch presence in the court was certainly contrary to what had been agreed between the Portuguese and the Sultan, but during the three days' skirmish, we have no evidence of any Dutch forces present either on land or at sea around Goa to support the expedition.

So what did the Sultan gain from this exercise? In his letter to the Portuguese governor when he asked for Father Gonçalo Martins, he clearly mentions his interest in maintaining friendship with the Portuguese state as well as his intention of forcing the Kanara ruler, Shivappa Nayaka, to withdraw his forces from the Portuguese territories of Onor.[1000] Therefore, the argument of

Shirodkar that Bijapuri soldiers wanted to force the Portuguese withdrawal from the Onor seems to be a conclusion without any foundation. On the other hand the Sultan of Bijapur, still a sovereign overlord, although only in a shadowy sense, of the Nayakas of Ikkeri, did exercise some powerful influence over him and could have forced him to submit had he chosen to do so. In fact, his *fárman* sent to the Portuguese authorities at Goa, shows his intention of doing so.[1001]

The Dutch were everywhere threatening the Portuguese commercial posts in Asia and during the whole of this period the fort of Onor was under constant attack by Shivappa Nayaka of Ikkeri, one of the vassals of the Sultan of Bijapur.[1002] In such circumstances the Portuguese had to come to an agreement with the Sultan. According to a letter, and the instructions given to Father Gonçalo Martins for his journey to the court of Bijapur, Martins was to ask for the Sultan's mediation in the matter of Onor (which was still controlled by the Portuguese) as the Sultan himself had promised in his previous letter of 13 March 1654.[1003]

On 12 August 1654, the general of Adil Shah, Abdullah Hakim, did indeed, march against Bardez with 5000 men. In October he reinforced his army with 7000 foot soldiers and 800 horsemen and invaded the territory of Salssette. However, according to Danvers, as the Adil Shah knew that the Portuguese were preparing to defend more seriously than they did before, he withdrew his army to Bijapur.[1004] It is quite possible that the Sultan of Bijapur, given the precarious situation of the Portuguese in Asia, without declaring open war wanted to recover his territories from the Portuguese, but he was also aware that he had very ambitious and difficult nobles at his court, as well as the Mughal army on the borders of his kingdom. Therefore, such a venture on his part would be a serious mistake.

Though various reasons have been given by historians for the Hakim's attack on Goa the real reason that triggered the invasion has so far not been mentioned (or the historians never thought it worth mentioning). What is difficult to explain is why Manucci has given prominence to the whole story of the jewel when it was religious and cultural issues which were really at stake.

It is well known that the Portuguese presence in Asia was backed by the religious Orders, which were frequently able to dominate the Portuguese governing institutions. Whenever possible they tried to ban local religious ceremonies and to impose their own Christian practices.[1005] This is what happened in 1654[1006] when the Inquisition authorities tried to put a ban on Hindu bathing ceremonies in Chaul and in the regions of Bardez,[1007] as if the trouble over the prohibition of the religious ceremonies of the Hindus in 1634 had not been enough. The inhabitants of these areas, mostly Brahmins but some New Christians[1008] as well, rebelled and fled from their hometowns. They met the Bijapuri army general, Abdullah Hakim, who happened to be in the vicinity of Goa. He immediately invaded the territories of Salssette and Bardez, in order to punish those responsible, without any consultation with his superiors,[1009] and imposed a blockade on all Portuguese commercial activity in the surrounding regions subject to the Bijapuri sultan. The capture of a ship belonging to the Sultan by the Portuguese off Hormuz also added fuel to the fire.[1010] In India religious ceremonies have great impact in society and any ban or prohibition on any religious group has always ended in conflict and even in war. Moreover, the Sultan of Bijapur, being a Muslim ruler, as a matter of justice to the majority of his subjects who were Hindus, had as a top priority to safeguard their interests. If he did not, he would jeopardise their loyalty to him as he belonged to a different religion. Therefore, General Hakim might have considered this, inevitably, as a pretext for his exercise of military force.

In fact, Dom Braz de Castro, who had been acting as head of the *Estado da Índia* on his own and is sometimes considered as a usurper, in his reply to Dom João IV, had very clearly written that, if the prohibition of this religious ceremony was enforced, even though it was pagan, it would bring about confusion and revolt.[1011] This action of the Inquisition was a flagrant violation of the treaties of 1571, which had been renewed in 1575 and amplified in 1576 and later in 1582. These treaties between the Sultan of Bijapur and the Portuguese had guaranteed the maintenance of local civil rights. It is also necessary here to mention that, although quite a number of Hindus lived in the Portuguese dominated areas of Chaul, Bassein, Goa, they depended for their rituals and religious ceremonies on the neighbouring areas, still under the Ahmadnagar and Bijapuri regimes. The Portuguese officials, even though they opposed such actions by the Inquisition, tried to minimize their importance, probably because they were aimed against a non-Christian faith or because of the king's support for the Inquisition. Most historians have entirely ignored this reason for the attack.[1012]

It is known, through one of the letters of the Adil Shah, that at this time the Sultan proposed peace negotiations as he had been misled by some of his officers about the invasion. Either the Sultan had not been informed about this invasion or he pretended he did not know – though neither supposition is supported by any source. In a letter dated 3 October 1654[1013] the Sultan, after having been informed of the new developments around Goa, wrote to the Viceroy that he was sending an urgent message to recall Abdullah Hakim and that he would be sending Father Gonçalo Martins as his representative to seek peace between the two countries along with his ambassador Malik Yáqút,[1014] who had special instructions for strengthening the peace process[1015] and renewing the earlier treaties. He accepted that it was an unjustified invasion and wanted to compensate the Portuguese for their losses. Moreover, at the same time, news had reached Bijapur that the Mughal army, under Aurangzeb, was marching south and the Sultan, aged and sick, could not face a war on more than one front. He needed Portuguese support for the safety of his state.

In 1649 Malik Yáqút had been posted as ambassador to Goa. He remained there until 1654 when he was recalled by the Sultan when the trouble between the Portuguese and the Bijapuri State started, a period, when diplomatic relations were cut off between the two states.[1016] Malik Yáqut was now sent back to Goa as ambassador along with Fr. Gonçalo Martins, with plenary powers to settle the dispute through a peace treaty. The ambassador was received in the royal hall of the Viceroy's palace in Goa. Manucci has given a good description of this hall where ambassadors were received and given audiences.[1017] As well as describing the decoration of this hall, he mentions that, while the ambassador walked slowly into the hall observing the portraits of the previous viceroys, he made curious comments about these pictures. "I see none with their heads off; it is impossible they all ruled well, and a king who decapitates no one secures neither good decisions nor quiet government". He further mentioned that, "his own king beheaded anyone who governed badly".[1018]

The letter brought by Malik was dated 3 November 1654, and the ambassador himself reached Goa on 3 December the same year. He had total authority from the Adil Shah to conduct the peace mission and to sign in the name of the Sultan.[1019] Some time before his arrival, a letter from the Sultan of Bijapur had already been sent to the Portuguese headquarters declaring the cessation of all hostilities, thereby lifting all the embargoes on Portuguese trade in the Sultan's territories with immediate effect and allowing free movement of people and merchandise as used to be the case before the Bijapuri army invaded Goa.[1020] The Portuguese authorities were also eager to conclude a peace treaty because, as they said, "the Sultan is very inconsistent in his temperament and, before he changes his mind, we must conclude a peace treaty with him".[1021] The Portuguese authorities were in no position at that time to take any risks, as they feared that the Sultan would not hesitate to make a new treaty with the Dutch, so it was decided that, even with the very tight economic circumstances prevailing, some handsome presents should be sent to dissuade the Sultan from any more warlike adventures.[1022] Finally, the treaty was signed on the 3 January[1023] and ratified on 7 March 1655.[1024]

The new treaty followed the pattern of the earlier treaties of 1576,[1025] 1582[1026] and 1633[1027] and was intended to confirm them.[1028] Malik Yáqút brought with him messages of good will and friendship from the Sultan and also a robe of honour and a lot of other valuable presents for the governor of Portuguese India. Father Gonçalo Martins accompanied the ambassador both as companion and assistant, and as a sign of trust. As mentioned earlier in chapter one, it was a common practice for the Portuguese, as well as the Indian rulers, to send on diplomatic missions Jesuit or Catholic priests who were thought to be more trustworthy and capable of negotiating delicate matters because they had developed a greater degree of intimacy and trust among the Indians while conducting their missions. Since these rulers believed that the priests would be more trustworthy than any diplomat, they employed them as their own ambassadors to deal with the Portuguese, though often these priests were more interested in conversions and the preaching of Christianity than the diplomatic missions with which they were entrusted, whether they were in the services of the Portuguese or the Indian rulers. Gonçalo Martins and António Botelho, who were "spiritual guides" to the Sultan, were in reality serving as informers for the Portuguese state.[1029]

In the month of August 1655, Malik Yáqút was again sent back to Goa to strengthen the relationship, with greater diplomatic powers than he had earlier possessed although a treaty had already been signed, as mentioned in earlier paragraphs. Before entering Portuguese territory, he sent a personal letter, dated 13 August, containing reasons for his visit, to the Portuguese governor[1030] and seeking permission for an audience to present his credentials.[1031] On 17 August 1655, the *Conselho do Estado* met to decide whether or not to allow the request of Malik Yáqút to present himself at the palace of the Portuguese Viceroy.[1032] He was carrier of a letter from the Sultan Adil Shah, which contained some important information for the Portuguese State.[1033] The reason behind this hesitation was a letter from Father António Botelho. In his letter[1034] Father Botelho had warned the Portuguese authorities to be careful, as he did not trust Malik Yáqút. The letter of Malik Yáqút, on the other hand, shows that the Adil Shah found him most trustworthy and had given him increased powers to solve the problems between the two states. Malik Yáqút in his letter[1035] provided an explanation for the invasion of 1654, saying that "Nagoji Nayaka Pratap Rau Sardesai and Abdullah Hakim had together prepared the whole treason against the Portuguese state and people and, as a result, they will be punished severely so that it can serve as a lesson for those who want to disturb the peace and friendship between us in the future.[1036]" He went on, "as for Quissoa Nayaka and Calu Sinai, other traitors, who joined Hakim in organising the revolt and who committed crimes against the people of Bardez, I personally asked reinforcements from my king in order to finish them off. Only Prabhu, the Dessai of Pernem, helped me discover all those responsible for the trouble".

The Council decided to receive Malik Yáqút as ambassador against all the warnings of Father Botelho, whom they considered to be little more than a person of self-conceit and intrigue.[1037] However, they agreed to place guards at all the entrances to the city and to inquire about any persons who might be entering in disguise. The attitude of Father Botelho, and the reason why he was so sceptical of the embassy of Malik Yáqút, is difficult to understand. He himself was a spy and it was he who suggested that the Portuguese should watch out for soldiers entering the city in disguise. His letter also shows the kind of person he was. He was critical of the very people who were allowing him to live in the Bijapuri kingdom and to enjoy considerable respect and privilege. His opinion of the inhabitants of the Bijapuri kingdom was clear when he used phrases such as, "all of them are pernicious".[1038] It is difficult to know what he thought about himself – apparently a religious man, trusted and appreciated as a friend by the Sultan, but in reality, a spy! Although he might have meant to serve his country and faith well, he was about to spoil the whole diplomatic process between the two states.

Though the *Conselho do Estado* had decided on 17 August 1655 to permit the ambassador to enter Goa, the decision to grant him an audience was not communicated to him immediately. The Portuguese authorities failed to inform him of the decision, probably because of the handover of power from Dom Braz de Castro to Dom Rodrigo da Silveira, Conde de Sarzedas, who only took the oath of office on 24 August. The next meeting of the Council took place on 1f September and it was unanimously agreed that there should not be any more delays in receiving the ambassador who claimed that he was the bearer of very useful and important information for both the states.[1039] On the 10 September it was again decided that there should not be any further delays in receiving the ambassador, Malik Yáqút, or else some trouble night arise.[1040] Nevertheless, this decision was once more not communicated to the ambassador. Probably, the Portuguese authorities were waiting for an appropriate moment, such as an invasion by the Mughal forces, before they received the ambassador.

Before the Viceroy could receive the ambassador, another dispute arose between the Portuguese authorities and the Bijapuri state. It so happened that Quissoa Nayaka, earlier mentioned as one of the rebels during the Hakim's invasion of Salssette and Bardez, had built a fort in Colva, the region in Margão, and it was now reported that some more fortifications were in progress right in front of a Portuguese church. It was also notified by the Portuguese informant to the authorities that the fort was going to be occupied by Malik Yáqút by force, as Quissoa Nayaka was a rebel against the Bijapuri regime. This matter appeared to be very sensitive from the point of view of the defence of the Portuguese state, even though the fort referred to was not in Portuguese territory.[1041]

Even in such circumstances, the reply to the letter was ambiguous as they did not want to give support to the ambassador, Malik Yáqút. The Portuguese *Conselho do Estado* decided not to send the 500 soldiers, gunpowder and ammunition, a need which the ambassador had communicated to the Portuguese Viceroy through his letter dated 13f August,[1042] as it was going to be used against the revolted Dessais and Nayakas of Ancola, Mirizeo[1043] and Karwar who had always been good neighbours and who the Portuguese had always supported against the Sultan of Bijapur and whoever else were their enemies.[1044] The only difference at this time was that the revolt of the Dessais was against both the Portuguese and the Sultan of Bijapur.[1045] In reality the economic and military power of the Portuguese did not allow them to provide help to anyone who required it.[1046] The Viceroy, in his letter to the King of Portugal of 19th of October 1655, made it very clear, that "one can't trust this moor because of the friendships he has with the Dutch."[1047] Therefore, the Sultan would be kept waiting for the support which was never going to be sent. Though they had signed the peace treaty earlier which contained clauses about helping one another, Malik Yáqút had to return without his mission fulfilled, in retaliation, as the Portuguese thought, for the fact that the Dutch were still being given support by the Sultan of Bijapuri against the Portuguese.

The idea of the *Conselho do Estado* had been to make the Sultan more submissive to the Portuguese. However, as a matter of courtesy, they thanked the Sultan for his letter greeting the arrival of the new Viceroy, the Conde de Sarzedas.[1048]

In his diary, the Portuguese Viceroy revealed his doubts about the seriousness of Malik Yáqút and the "Muslims"[1049] in exercising their duties. He thought that "...That these moors have no consistency in anything, and I have information that they have been asking the Dutch for two years to throw us out of the port of Goa and they (the Muslims and the Bijapuri Sultan) should throw us out of the land.."[1050] In the letter that the Viceroy wrote to the King of Portugal on 4 September 1655, giving information about developments in India, he made it very clear that even if these "Muslims" were coming to meet him with the intention of negotiating peace and other diplomatic issues, he would, nevertheless, be ready for war.[1051] These suspicions seem to have been mutual as can be seen throughout all their contacts with each other.[1052]

Finally, after a couple of months of Council meetings, the Portuguese Viceroy agreed to give the ambassador, Malik Yáqút, an audience on 3 December and received the letter from the Sultan Adil Shah[1053] to which he said he would reply after the meeting of the Council.

With the question of a permanent peace with the Sultan of Bijapur still uncertain, the Conde de Sarzedas had to divert his attention toward Ceylon which was under attack from the Dutch.[1054] However, he died in Goa on 13 January 1656,[1055] leaving everything in confusion and about four months later, on 10 May 1656, Colombo was surrendered to the Dutch.[1056]

Upon the untimely death of the Conde de Sarzedas, since the letters patent for the succession were still on their way, the officials present elected Manuel Mascarenhas Homem, who took office on 14 January 1656. The following May patents of succession arrived, according to which, those designated to assume the government in the event of the death of Sarzedas, were Manuel Mascarenhas Homem, Francisco de Mello e Castro and António de Sousa Coutinho. While this commission was administering the government, the King appointed the Conde de Vila Pouca de Aguiar as Viceroy of the Portuguese *Estado da Índia.* However, it seemed that the viceregal office was cursed, for he died on the way to Goa and upon opening the letters patent in case of the death of the Viceroy, coincidently, the same names as before were found to form the commission to govern. Thus this commission continued in office till June 1661 when a new patent arrived which nominated another commission consisting of Dom Manuel Mascarenhas, Luís de Mendonça Furtado and Dom Pedro de Lancastre. This commission governed till 1662 when in the month of June António de Mello e Castro[1057] arrived as new governor of the *Estado da Índia.*

Meanwhile the Bijapuri state was also thrown into chaos. In the month of November 1656, Muhammad Adil Shah died, leaving his only son, Ali II, at that time only 15 years of age, to govern the whole of his empire. Ultimately, Bari Sahiba and Khan Muhammad, the prime minister, were appointed as regents to the Sultan while he was a minor. The following year, the kingdoms of Bidar, Ahmadnagar and Bijapur were invaded by the Mughal general, prince Aurangzeb, to collect the tribute.[1058] In the meantime, the Marathas under Shivaji had also emerged as a powerful contestant for control of the kingdoms of the South. They kept the Bijapuri forces occupied though at times they formed an alliance with the Sultan, when both were threatened by the Mughals.[1059]

In the year 1659, it is claimed that the Bijapur army under general Hakim, again invaded the Portuguese territories, whereupon Luís de Mendonça Furtado led an expedition against him, and inflicted a severe defeat upon his forces at Margão and obliged them to retire.[1060] According to the Portuguese sources, before this could happen, in March 1659, the Portuguese Commission, headed by Manuel Mascarenhas Homem, sent an ambassador, Dom Pedro Henriques to confirm the peace treaty concluded in 1655 with the Sultan.[1061] The reason for this agression, one can assume, was the failure to fulfil the treaty in which both states had promised mutual help against their respective enemies. For instance, Shivaji had attacked various fortresses of the Bijapuri kingdom and the Mughals were on the march to force the Bijapuri Sultan to pay tribute, and the Sultan had asked for military support and the Portuguese kept postponing it.[1062] However, the Portuguese, as usual, wanted the conflict between the two to continue. In addition the Dessais and Nayakas of Ancola and Karwar had revolted against the Bijapuri Sultan and the Portuguese had not sent any military support, although they had decided to do so in the meeting of the *Conselho do Estado*.[1063] Moreover, it is reported that the Portuguese had given shelter all these revolted elements in their territories.[1064] The Portuguese dissatisfaction was due to information that the Queen Mother of Bijapur had received a Dutch ambassador who had bribed her and encouraged her to send soldiers against Goa.[1065] The Dutch, for their part certainly wanted their conquest of Ceylon to be successful and if the Portuguese were involved in saving their capital, they would not be in a position to try to send any succour to their other settlements of Malabar or to attempt to re-conquer Ceylon. If this is true, the efforts of the Dutch met with success. Nevertheless, it was a very difficult period for both the states: the Bijapuri state had to face the Mughals and Shivaji, and the Portuguese had to cope with the Dutch in Ceylon and Malabar.

The Portuguese authorities decided to send Dom Pedro Henriques with a sum of 100,000 *Ashrafis* in order to dissuade the Queen Mother from sending these soldiers to attack Goa.[1066] In the letter of instructions given to Henriques, it is quite obvious that the Portuguese were incapable of raising this amount of money, but the situation would have been far more difficult if they had not tried to carry out this extraordinary mission to dissuade the Sultan or the regent Queen Mother from giving support to the Dutch that could damage still further the Portuguese politico-economic situation in India. However, this cannot be connected with the Bijapuri attack on the Portuguese settlements of Goa for the embassy of Dom Pedro Henrique had already left before the incursion of general Hakim. At the same time we are not sure if the embassy of Dom Pedro Henriques ever reached to its destination. Nevertheless, according to Glenn Ames, due to the financial troubles, the mission was delayed.[1067]

Although the Bijapuri general was forced to retire with some losses, as mentioned above, the Dutch plans to keep the Portuguese busy in Goa had met with success in Ceylon and now they were planning their attack on Quilon and Cochin.

Muhammad Adil Shah's death in 1656 had opened the floodgates of trouble for his Empire. He was succeeded by his only son, Ali II, then fifteen years of age. His legitimacy was questioned by Prince Aurangzeb, the Mughal governor of Deccan[1068] and the Mughals started their campaign in 1657 by reducing the forts of Bidar and Kalyani. Ali Adil Shah's government faced further threats for, by this time, Shivaji was powerful enough to become a constant menace. Although the Mughal military campaign against the Deccan states, including Bijapur, had been called off early in 1658, due to the war of succession among the pretenders to the throne of the Mughal Empire, Shivaji had made use of this opportunity well and become a danger to Bijapuri kingdom as well as to the Portuguese territories. The history of the Bijapuri kingdom, between 1659 and 1666, is a tale of the rise of Shivaji and the decline of Bijapuri military power. The effect of this was to pave the way for further Mughal expansion. The Portuguese themselves were in no condition to play any decisive role nor to provide any help to their immediate neighbour, as they had to fight hard, if unsuccessfully, to save their own Malabar settlements Quilon, Cochin, Cranganore and Cannanore, against the allied forces of the Dutch and the Zamorin. The Bijapuri Sultan lent his support to the Mughals, which resulted in Shivaji's imprisonment in 1665. However, later Shivaji supported the Mughals against him. The Sultan acted vigorously till 1666, but a sense of failure had taken possession of his mind. He desired to forget the miseries of his situation by embracing the pleasures of the harem rather than by devoting himself to the administration of his tottering state. Besides, his kingdom was so damaged due to wars on many fronts and treacheries among his own officials, that he was hardly in a position to remedy them. He was surrounded by powerful and ambitious nobles who thought of benefiting from the weakness of the Sultan instead of uniting the forces of the kingdom against the common enemy. Even the Portuguese who, off and on, had provided some help were in such a weakened state that they were in no position to assist the Bijapuri State. The Sultan died in 1672.

The last ruler of the dynasty, Sikandar Adil Shah, was only four years of age when he ascended the throne in 1672. Bijapur now did not possess sufficient means to resist the march of Mughal imperialism or the mounting Maratha aggression under Shivaji. For a short time, the Bijapuri and Marathas united against the Mughals but the untimely death of Shivaji in 1680 left the Sultan friendless and the kingdom of Bijapur was finally incorporated into the Mughal Empire in 1686.

The Portuguese for their part, because of their indecisive diplomacy, or rather it would be better to say diplomacy of mistrust towards the Bijapuri kingdom, sank in their own boat for it had left them in no condition to save Malacca, Kanara or Ceylon. Now while the Bijapuri kingdom was still waiting for its final collapse, the Portuguese were expelled from the entire Malabar Coast, leaving them only with Goa, Chaul, Bassein, Daman and Diu.

Reference

855 *LMG, cod. n.° 2-B, fols. 488-490: Carta Régia de Filipe II, 15 de Janeiro de 1598, para o Conde Almirante dom Francisco da Gama, Vice-Rei da Índia, dando instrução de que procurasse por todos os meios obter notícias certas dos desígnios do Mogor, e conserve a amizade de Chande Beby e moradores do reino de Iza Malucoe que seguisse a política de Matias de Albuquerque para com o Idalcão, tendente a unir os principais potentados da Índia contra o Mogor*; In this letter the king instructs the viceroy to watch the movements of the Mughal's military expeditions and orders him to maintain friendship with the sultans of Ahmadnagar and Bijapur with the aim of creating a front against the Mughals at their expense.

856 Salim, mostly known as Jahangir, ruled India as Mughal Emperor between 1606 and 1627.

857 *LML*, cod. 1, fols. 4-17: *Carta Régia de Filipe II, Dom Martim Affonso, vice-rei da Índia, Recommendan-do-lhe que aproveite e alimente a discórdia do Equebar com seu filhos. Pede informação das razões que teve Ayres de Saldanha para demolir a fortaleza do Morro de Chaul, e faz algumas advertências a respeito de Xarifão Maluco, capitão de Ponda e governador das terras do Hidalcão,* 6 de Março de 1605.

858 This was the intention of the Zamorin and later, such clauses were copied by other rulers of western coast of India: Poonen, *A Survey of the Rise of the Dutch Power in Malabar*, (1603-78), pp. 46-47; Davies, *A Primer of Dutch Seventeenth Century Overseas Trade.*

859 Biker (ed.) *Collecção de tratados e concertos de pazes...*, tomo I, pp. 189-192: *Capitulos das pazes que se fizeram entre os vassallos de El-Rey Jahanguir e os Portuguezes, por Nauabo Mucarreb Xhan e Gonçalo Pinto da Fonseca,* 7 de Junho de 1615; Biker, Tomo 1: *Contrato de Pazes que o Padre António de Andrade e D. Francisco Coutinho de Ocem fizeram com El-Rey Mogor por meio do Nababo de Surrate, em Damão,* a 13 de Setembro de 1630, pp.237-239.

860 *LMG*, cod. 19-A, fols. 55-55vº: *Carta Régia para o Vice-rei Conde de Linhares, aprovando a resolução que o vice-rei tomou de não declarar guerra aberta ao Mogor, e recomenda mais uma vez que mantenha boa amizade com os reis da Índia.* À margem, a resposta do vice-rei, de Goa, 29 de Novembro de 1634, *em que este diz ter procedido nas "materias do Mogor com grande estudo e industria" não se comprometendo com rei algum, e dando esperanças a todos para evitar inimizades; e, embora deseje a derrota do Mogor, não lhe convém pôr-se abertamente contra ele a fim de reservar todas as suas forças para ocasiões de grande necessidade.* Lisboa, 24 de Dezembro de 1633; Pissurlenkar, 'Tentativas dos portugueses para a ocupação do Concão', separata dos *Anais II* série, vol. 6, Lisboa, 1955, pp. 430-431.

861 *LMG, cod.° 3-B*, fols. 406-425, 529-535: *Carta Régia para Matias de Albuquerque, vice-rei da Índia*, Lisboa, 12 de Janeiro de 1591.

862 *LML*, cod. 1, fols. 4-17: *Carta Régia de Filipe II, 6 de Março de 1605, Dom Martim Affonso, vice-rei da Índia, Recommendando-lhe que aproveite e alimente a discórdia do Equebar com seu filhos. Pede informação das razões que teve Ayres de Saldanha para demolir a fortaleza do Morro de Chaul, e faz algumas advertências a respeito de Xarifão Maluco, capitão de Ponda e governador das terras do Hidalcão.*

863 *Ibid*. It reads, *"O anno passado vos escrevi o que tinha entendido do ruim procedimento de Xarifão Maluco capitão da ilha, e vos disse que procurásseis, per alguns meios convenientes e em muito segredo, ter intelligencia na corte do Idalcão com alguns seu validos, que procurem desacreditar com elle o dito Xarifão, e pol-o em disconfiança, para que com isso se mova a tiral-o d'quelle governo; isto mesmo vos torno agora de novo a encommendar, e assi que mandeis ver as tranqueiras de pedra e cal que o dito Xarifão fez junto d'essa ilha, e se note assi pelo engenheiro mor d'esse Estado, como por pessoas de experiência, o damno que d'ellas se pode seguir; e conforme e ao que entenderdes convem a meu serviço assi procedes, segundo estado presente das cousas derlogar, procurando ter muta advertencia que se não façam similhantes obras, sem vós as atalhardes e impedirdes no no principio"*; One should note that he had built these unexplainable trenches in the kingdom of Bijapur, and had nothing to do with the Portuguese territories. The Portuguese habit of interfering in local defence matters was highly irritating to the ruling authorities. On the other hand, they themselves kept building their fortresses anywhere and whenever they wanted. I personally find no reason for their unhappiness in this regard except to create an intrigue in the Bijapuri court.

864 *LML*, cod. 12, fol. 128: *Carta Régia para o vice-rei da Índia, D. João Coutinho, Conde de Redondo*. 7 de Março de 1619; *LML*, cod. 12, fol. 117: Carta Régia. *Acerca das casas que o embaixador do Idalcão tinha em Dicholim.*

865 *LMG*, cod.°12, fols. Fls. 161-167: *Carta do Vice-rei da Índia D. Jerónimo de Azevedo*, 31 de Dezembro de 1614; Biker (ed.) *Collecção de tratados e*

concertos de pazes..., tomo I, pp. 192-96: *Assento e Contrato de Paz e amisade com El-Rey Nizamoxá, por intervenção de El-Rey Idalxá, sendo Viso-Rey D. Jeronymo de Azevedo,* 9 de Outubro de 1615.

866 LMG, cod.° 4, fols. 780-787: *Carta Régia para D. Francisco da Gama, vice-rei da Índia,* Lisboa, 5 de Fevereiro de 1599; In fact this effort to create a united front against the Mughals continued during the next three decades. Most of the *Monções* series following this codex are full of correspondences that present this fact.

867 The Portuguese were represented by António Monteiro Corte-Real. Accompanying António Monteiro there were two other dignitaries, Nicolau Pais Bulhões and Bartolomeu Cardoso, as well as Duabbasi Rao as interpreter. Nawab Shah Nawaz Khan represented Adil Shah as ambassador while Kashi Pundit and Shamsher Khan represented Sultan Nizam Shah of Ahmadnagar. They were also accompanied by Khwaja Noor-Ain, (later he was sent on permanent mission to Goa) and Musa Ali Khan, nobles from the courts of Bijapur and Ahmadnagar respectively; Biker (ed.) *Collecção de tratados ...*, tomo I, pp. 192-96: *Assento e Contrato de Paz e amisade com El-Rey Nizamoxá, por intervenção de El-Rey Idalxá, sendo Viso-Rey D. Jeronymo de Azevedo,* 9 de Outubro de 1615..

868 *LMG*, cod. 2-B, fols. 488-490: *Carta Régia de Filipe II, 15 de Janeiro de 1598, para o Conde Almirante dom Francisco da Gama, Vice-Rei da Índia, dando instrução de que procurasse por todos os meios obter notícias certas dos desígnios do Mogor, e conserve a amizade de Chande Beby e moradores do reino de Iza Malucoe que seguisse a política de Matias de Albuquerque para com o Idalcão, tendente a unir os principais potentados da Índia contra o Mogor; LML*, cod.1, fols. 4-17: *Carta Régia para o Vice-rei da India,* 8 de Março de 1605.

869 *LML*, Cod. 15, fol. 17v°-18: *Carta do Vice-rei ao Rei de Portugal informando "O Idalcão havia substituido o seu embaixador em Goa, ordenando-lhe que residisse em casas situadas na outra banda, o que não convinha ao Estado. O governador esforçar-se por lhe difcultar apassadem nos "passos" mas sem resultado,* 10 de Fevereiro de 1621.

870 *Ibid.*

871 HAG, *Livros dos reis vizinhos,* n° 1, fols. 116-v°*: Carta do Governador, Fernão de Albuquerque ao Idalcão,* 8 de Maio de 1620; Also see *ACE*, vol. I, docs. 29 & 76.

872 *ACE*, Vol. I, p. 240: *Treslado do formão dElRey Idalxa meu S°r passado ao seu embaixador Mir Mahamede Raza.*

873 *LML*, cod. 21, fols. 1: *Carta Régia para o Vice Rey da Índia,* Lisboa, primeiro de Março de 1625.

874 *ACE*, Vol. I, p. 238-239: *Carta que mandou o embaixador do Idalxa para o Vicerei;* de *Dicholim,* 8 de Novembro de 1629.

875 B.S. Shastry, 'The Portuguese Commercial Relations with Bijapur in the Seventeenth century', in *Essays in Goan History,* Teotonio D'Souza,

(ed.), pp. 39-47: Shastry has studied in depth the commercial aspects of the Bijapuri trading ports, especially Dabhol and other commercial centres of the kingdom.

876 *ACE*, vol. I, Doc. 76: *Conselho que Senhor Conde de Linhares V. Rey ffez em 20 de Novembro de 629 sobre duas cartas que escreueo Dom Pedro Mascarenhas capitam de Dio, e sobre outras duas cartas que escreueo o Arçebispo de Cranganor e sobre as cartas que escreueo o embaixador do dialcão que mandou mostrar e cartas que Sua ex° em Resposta lhe escreueo e Recado que pelo seu lingoa lhe mandou*, 20 de Novembro de 1629.

877 *Ibid.*

878 *Ibid*

879 *LML*, cod. 1, fols. 4-17. This Malik of Ponda was also the governor of Dabhol at that time.

880 *O Cronista de Tissuary*, n° 2, Fevereiro de 1866, p. 41; N° 4, pp. 92-93.

881 One of the persons for this incident was the-son-in-law of Azu Nayaka who was one of the leading business magnates of Bassein and Chaul, dealing in rice and saltpetre. In addition he happened to be one of the contractors of the Tobacco *Rendas* in the service of the Portuguese *Estado da Índia. ACF*, cod.1163, *Rendas de Tabacco*, fls. 120-120v.

882 *ACE*, Vol. I, p. 240: *Treslado do formão, dElRey Idalxa meu S. passado ao seu embaixador Mir Mamede Raza.* 20 de Nouembro de 1629. (And there are other letters on the subsequent pages related to the subject).

883 *ACE*, vol. I, Doc. 76: *Conselho que Senhor Conde de Linhares V. Rey ffez em 20 de Novembro de 629 sobre duas cartas que escreueo Dom Pedro Mascarenhas capitam de Dio, e sobre outras duas cartas que escreueo o Arçebispo de Cranganor e sobre as cartas que escreueo o embaixador do dialcão que mandou mostrar e cartas que Sua ex° em Resposta lhe escreueo e Recado que pelo seu lingoa lhe mandou*, 20 de Novembro de 1629..

884 *ACE*, vol. I, fols. 243-44: *Conselho que Senhor Conde de Linhares V. Rey fez em 20 de Novembro de 629.*

885 *LMG*, cod. 13-B, fls. 274-75v°: *Carta do V. Rei para El-Rei de Portugal, Refere-se à atitude insolente tomada pelo embaixador do rei Idalxá e à sua animosidade para os portugueses e informa que, para evitar o rompimento de hostilidades com o referido potentado, enviara à sua corte, como embaixador, Manuel Ribeiro, encarregado de o inteirar sobre o procedimento do seu embaixador e trabalhar para que a paz não fosse quebrada.* 18 de Fevereiro de 1630.

886 *Ibid*; "by nature a thief and dishonest" see *ACE*, vol. I, doc. 154: *Conselho sobre o embaxador delRey Idalxa e Licença que pedio para hir a outra banda.*

887 *O Cronista de Tissuary*, n° 2, Fevereiro de 1866, p. 38-42.

888 *ACE, vol. I, pp. 238-239: Carta que mandou o embaixador do Idalxa,* Novembro 8 de 1629.

889 *LMG*, cod. 13-B, fls. 274-75v°, 18 de Fevereiro de 1630.

890 *Ibid.*

891 *ACE*, vol. 1, doc. 107: *Conselho sobre o movimento que há nas terras do Idalxá*, 1 de Novembro de 1630; *O Cronista de Tissuary*, n° 2, Fevereiro de 1866, p. 42.

892 *O Cronista de Tissuary*, n° 4, Abril de 1866, pp. 88-91.

893 *LMG*, cod. N° 13-B, fls. 274-75v°, 18 de Fevereiro de 1630; *ACE*, vol. I, doc. 90: *Conselho sobre o mogor intentar contra as fortalezas do Norte e auiso que se teve do embaixador Baltazar da Azaredo*, 27 de Março de 1630.

894 *Ibid.*

895 *ACE*, vol. I, doc. 92: *Assento sobre a hida de Fr. João da Rocha a Corte de Idalxa*, 15 de Abril de 1630.

896 A royal order issued by a Muslim ruler.

897 *ACE*, vol. I, doc. 101: *Conselho que o Sr. Conde VisoRey fez em 15 de Agosto de 630 com os fidalgos e ministros delle sobre a carta que escreve ElRey Mogor a S. Exª.*

898 *LMG*, cod. 12, fols. 116-116v°.

899 *ACE, vol. I,* doc. 107*: Conselho sobre o movimento que há nas terras do Idalxá,* 1 de Novembro de 1630; See chapter IV on *Portuguese Kanara Diplomatic Relations.*

900 *Ibid; O Cronista de Tissuary*, n° 2, Fevereiro de 1866, pp. 37-43.

901 *ACE*, vol. I, doc. 101, 15 de Agosto de 1630.

902 *Ibid.*

903 *Ibid.*

904 *O Cronista de Tissuary*, n° 2, Fevereiro de 1866, pp. 38-43.

905 It is worth mentioning here that on the 15 November 1630, a treaty of peace had been concluded between the Crowns of England and Spain in order to cease all the hostilities between the two nations in the East (Indian Ocean) and in the West (in the European Continent): Biker (ed.) *Collecção de tratados...*, tomo 1, pp. 239-245; *Capitulações das Pazes feitas entre El-Rei das Hispanhas, D. Filipe IV e El-Rey Carlos de Inglaterra que se concluiram pelos deputados n'ellas nomeados em Madrid., a* 15 de Novembro de 1630.

906 Bijapur was under the constant threat from the Mughals between 1630 and 1632 and the Sultan of Bijapur asked for help from the Portuguese. To this, the Portuguese viceroy, Conde de Linhares, actively responded as he foresaw that if the Mughals were successful in their conquest, there would be no barrier between the Portuguese and the Mughal territories and that could be a severe danger for their existence; Muhammad Ibrahim Zubairi, *Basatin-al-slatin*, pp. 293-294; for other related incidents of the period also see *LMG*, cod. 13-B: *Relação dos Reis visinhos do que por ora passa e contão,* fols. 447-454.

907 *ACE*, vol. I, doc. 107: *Conselho sobre o movimento que há nas terras do Idalxá*, 1 de Novembro de 1630; *Carte de Vice-Rei da India ao Rei, Refere-se à atitude insolente tomada pelo embaixador do rei Idalxá e à sua animosidade para os portugueses e informa que, para evitar o rompimento de hostilidades com o referido potentado, enviara à sua corte, como embaixador, Manuel Ribeiro, encarregado de o inteirar sobre o procedimento do seu embaixador e trabalhar para que a paz não fosse quebrada*. Goa, 18 de Fevereiro de 1630.

908 *O Cronista de Tissuary*, nº 4, Abril de 1866, pp. 92-93.

909 *LMG*, cod. 15, fols. 92-94: *Carta do Vice-Rei da Índia D. Miguel de Noronha, Conde de Linhares, sobre o Idalcão informando sobre as guerras entre o Idalcão e o Mogor e sobre os espias que existem nas cortes destes reinos e que ficam muito dispendiosos ao Estado. Pede que seja deferida uma consulta, que fez sobre Fernão Lopes da Horta, que numa destas missões perdeu uma orelha e o nariz; participa que escreveu ao Idalxá sobre uns navios que o capitão-mor da armada do Estreito aprisionara e levara para Mascate, em virtude de transportarem mercadorias defesas e que o Conselho decidira que se entregassem ao Idalcão. Por fim, relata as negociações que entabulou com o Idalcão, a fim de que este lhe entregasse um filho do dito Fernão Lopes, que estava debaixo do "seguro real",...* Goa, 29 de Novembro de 1632; *O Cronista de Tissuary*, nº 4, Abril de 1866.

910 *LMG, cod. 15*, fols. 24-26vº: *Carta do Vice-Rei da Índia D. Miguel de Noronha, Conde de Linhares sobre o Idalcão*, 29 de Novembro de 1632.

911 *LMG*, cod. 15, pp. 98-99: Carta do *Vice-Rei da Índia D. Miguel de Noronha, Conde de Linhares, sobre o Idalcão*, 29 de Novembro de 1632. Fols. 24-26vº; *O Cronista de Tissuary*, nº 2, Fevereiro de 1866, p. 38.

912 *Ibid. O Cronista de Tissuary*, nº 2, Fevereiro de 1866, p. 38; nº 4, pp. 98-99.

913 *Ibid.*

914 *Ibid.*

915 *LMG*, cod. 13-B, fols. 447-454: *Relação dos Reis visinhos do que por ora passa e contão; ACE*, Vol. I, doc. 134: *Conselho sobre o soccoro que se mandou ao Idalxá*, 3 de Abril de 1632.

916 *ACE*, vol. I, doc. 134: *Conselho sobre o soccoro que se mandou ao Idalxá*, 3 de Abril de 1632.

917 *LMG*, cod. 19-A, fols. 55-55vº: *Carta Régia para o Vice-rei Conde de Linhares, aprovando a resolução que o vice-rei tomou de não declarar guerra aberta ao Mogor, e recomenda mais uma vez que mantenha boa amizade com os reis da Índia*. À margem, a resposta do vice-rei, de Goa, 29 de Novembro de 1634, *em que este diz ter procedido nas "materias do Mogor com grande estudo e industria" não se comprometendo com rei algum, e dando esperanças a todos para evitar inimizades; e, embora deseje a derrota do Mogor, não lhe convém pôr-se abertamente contra ele a fim de reservar todas as suas forças para ocasiões de grande necessidade*. Lisboa, 24 de

Dezembro de 1633; Pissurlenkar, 'Tentativas dos portugueses para a ocupação do Concão', separata dos *Anais II* série, vol. 6, Lisboa, 1955, pp. 430-431.

918 *Ibid.*

919 *O Cronista de Tissuary*, nº 5, Maio de 1866, p. 117-121.

920 He died in 1627 and the Conde de Linhares reached Goa in 1629.

921 He was referring to the ambassador Balthazar de Azeredo who was sent in early 1631. *O Cronista de Tissuary*, nº 2, Fevereiro de 1866, p. 42.

922 *ACE, vol.* I, doc. 154: *Conselho sobre o embaxador delRey Idalxa e Licença que pediu para hir a outra banda*, 17 de Julho de 1633.

923 *O Cronista de Tissuary*, nº 2, Fevereiro de 1866, pp. 39-42.

924 *Ibid.*

925 HAG, *Livro grande de pazes*, cod. I fols. 13; Biker (ed) *Collecção de tratados ...*, tomo I, pp. 293-299: *Assento do Juramento e ratificação das pazes feitas com o Sultão Mamede Idalxá, por seu Embaixador Mamede Zaman em* 3 de abril de 1633; The same has been published in *ACE*, vol. 1, pp. 565-568.

926 *Ibid:* During these diplomatic proceedings, Vitula Sinai, acted as interpreter for the ambassador of Bijapur and Diogo Nunes Evangelo for the Portuguese.

927 *Livro de Pazes I*, fls. 13-14; Biker (ed) *Collecção de tratados...*, tomo I, pp. 296-97: *Assento do juramento e retificação das pazes feitas com o Sultão Mamede Idalxá por seu Embaixador Mamede Zaman no anno de* 1633; *ACE*, vol. I, pp. 565, 1633.; *O Cronista de Tissuary*, nº 2, Fevereiro de 1866, p. 40; nº 5, Maio de 1866, pp. 117-121.

928 *"sentia pouco estas despesas coando rezultauão dellas serviço de sua Magestade"*, LMG, cod. 13-B: *Carta do Vice-Rei da Índia, Dom Miguel de Noronha, Conde de Linhares, para o Rei, dando conta de atitude insolente tomada pelo embaixador do rei Idalxá e à sua animosidade para os portugueses e informa que, para evitar o rompimento de hostilidades com o referido potentado, enviara à sua corte, como embaixador, Manuel Ribeiro, encarregado de o inteirar sobre o procedimento do seu embaixador e trabalhar para que a paz não fosse quebrada.* Goa, 18 de Fevereiro de 1630; *ACE*, vol. I, doc. 90: *Conselho sobre o mogor intentar contra as fortalezas do Norte e auiso que se teve do embaixador Baltazar da Azaredo...*, 27 de Março de 1630; Bib. Ajuda, cod. 51-VII-12, *Discurso Diario do vicerei o Conde de Linhares*, fols. 64-v., 75 e 83; 25 de Julho 1630 and 19 de Augusto de 1630; About the treaties confirmed with the king Adil Shah and others see, BN, FG, cod. 7640; *Relação breue das principaes couzas que succederam em Índia o anno de* 1633, fols. 60-60vº; Biker (ed.) *Collecção de tratados e concertos de pazes...*, tomo I, pp. 293-299: *Assento do Juramento e ratificação das pazes feitas com o Sultão Mamede Idalxá, por seu Embaixador Mamede Zaman em 3 de Abril de 1633.*

929 *ACE, vol.* I, doc. 134: *Conselho sobre que se mandou ao Idalxá, 5 de abril de 1632; Diario do 3º Conde de Linhares,* vol. I, p. 60, *Cópia da carta para El Rey Idalxa,* 19 de Abril de 1634; also see pp. 118, 19 de abril de 1634.

930 *"para nós senhor na deste Estado nenhuma cousa pode ser milhor que tanta guerra e desunião entre esta gente". LMG,* cod. 15, fol. 5: *carta do conde de Linhares,* Goa, 6 de novembro de 1632.

931 Zubairi, *Basatin-us-Slatin,* pp. 342-43; 366-368; Varma, *History of Bijapur,* pp. 188-197.

932 HAG, *ACF,* cod. 1161, fols. 142vº-43; BNL, FG, cod. 7640, fols. 143-vº: *Carta do padre Xavier Manuel Severim de Faria 28 de novembro de 1637;* EF, 1637-41, p. 23, 18 of July 1637, & P. 231, *Letter from the President Fremlen,* Surat, 27 of January 1640.

933 *LMG, cod. 13-B, fols. 593-593v: Carta do vice-rei da Índia, D. Miguel de Noronha, Conde de Linhares, para El-Rei, Informando que o Idalcão é ainda criança, pelo que governam o seu reino uns persas que são inimigos declarados dos portugueses.* 7 de Fevereiro de 1635.

934 *Ibid.*

935 *Ibid.*

936 ANTT, *Manuscrito da Livraria,* cx. 3, tomo VI-F, *Regimento do conde da Vidigueira,* fol. 125; 30 de Março de 1622.

937 Zubairi, *Basatin-al-slatin,* pp. 293-294; for other related incidents of the period also see *LMG,* cod. 13-B, fols. 447-454: *Relação dos Reis visinhos do que por ora passa e contão.*

938 *LMG,* cod. 19-A: *Carta de Filipe III ao Vice-Rei da Índia, El-rei aprova a resolução que o vice-rei tomou de não declarar guerra aberta ao Mogor, e recomenda mais uma vez que mantenha boa amizade com os reis da Índia. À margem, a resposta do vice-rei, de Goa, 29 de Novembro de 1634, em que este diz ter procedido nas "materias do Mogor com grande estudo e industria" não se comprometendo com rei algum, e dando esperanças a todos para evitar inimizades; e, embora deseje a derrota do Mogor, não lhe convém pôr-se abertamente contra ele a fim de reservar todas as suas forças para ocasiões de grande ecessidade.* Lisboa, 24 de Dezembro de 1633. Fls. 55.

939 *LMG,* cod. 14-A, fls. 207: *Carta do Vie-rei Conde de Linhares a el-rei; ACE,* Vol. I, doc. 107: *Conselho sobre o movimento que há nas terras do Idalxá,* 1 de Novembro de 1630.

940 *Ibid.*

941 *LMG,* cod. 19-A, fol. 161, Lisboa, 12 de Novembro de 1633.

942 Bib. Ajud. Cod. 50-V-38, *Diário de Conde de Linhares,* fol. 146-v.

943 *LML,* cod. 45, fol. 193: *Carta do Vicerei da Índia, Pêro da Silva, dando conta dos aconteci-mentos no reino do Bijapur sobretudo em Ponda, e a morte do Mamede Raza, o Aualdar do concão,* Goa, 2 de Março 1639.

944 *ACE,* vol. II, doc. 32: *Copia do conselho sobre o navio dos vassalos delRey Idalxá que dous navios de nossa Armada tomarão no porto do sinde...,* 28 de Julho de 1626.

945 *ACE*, vol. II, doc. 48: *Conçelho sobre se mandar sagoate a Sidy Reane, e a ElRey Idalxa, e sobre haver despedido os embaxadores dos olandeses com ruim resposta*, 30 de Março de 1637.

946 Mustafa Khan belonged to the highest nobility of the Bijapuri Kingdom and had a great dislike for the Portuguese. He was one of the closest counsellors of the Sultan and had the final word in the foreign policy of the state. See *O Cronista de Tissuary*, n° 2, Fevereiro de 1866, pp. 38-40.

947 *ACE*, vol. II, doc. 48, 30 de Março de 1637.

948 See chapter I, for the details of this work.

949 Manuela, *O Estado Português da Índia...* p. 526: "*aquele mouros falços e fementidos de fee e de palaura eram cobiços*", Manuela has misquoted this document during the embassy of Balthazar de Azeredo in 1633, saying that a sumptuous present was sent to please the greedy Sultan. She has mistaken the embassy of 1633 with another of 1638 which was a courtesy embassy.

950 *ACE*, vol. II, doc. 48, *Goa*, 30 de Março de 1637.

951 *ACE*, vol. II, doc. 54: *Concelho sobre o pezame que sua Sehoria mandou dar a ElRey Idalxa da morte de sua molher por Antonio de Vite...*, 1 de Outubro de 1637.

952 HAG, *Ordens Régias*, cod. 4, fols. 199: *Regimento que levou António Monis Barreto quando foi por embaxador ao Idalcão*, 11 de Agosto de 1638;.Biker (ed) *Collecção de tratados ...*, tomo I1, pp. 88-100: *Nomeação de António Moniz Barreto para ir por Embaixador à corte do Idalxá, no anno de 1638; Also see Regimento que levou António Monis Barreto quando foi por embaxador Ao Idalcão*, 11 de Agosto de 1638. HAG, *Ordens Régias*, cod. 4, fols. 199.

953 *EF*, 1637-41, pp. 23, 35, 12 July, 1637*:* The English diplomatic mission was led by Leonard Woodman to the court of the Sultan of Bijapur. This mission was successful in obtaining trading facilities in the dominion of Bijapur in return of promises of help against the Portuguese, which never materialised. However, most of our knowledge regarding such anti-Portuguese pacts are based on the Portuguese sources; *LML*, cod. 37, fols. 505-v°, Goa, 5 de março de 1637; *Cod.* 40, fols. 130-v°.

954 *LML*, cod. 44, fols. 413: *Carta do embaixador António Moniz Barreto ao Vice-rei, Pêro da Silva*, Janeiro de 1639.

955 *Ibid*: See this letter in the appendix, V-F.

956 *LMG*, cod. 13-B, fols. 593-593v: *Carta do vice-rei da Índia, D. Miguel de Noronha, Conde de Linhares*, para El-Rei, *Informando que o Idalcão é ainda criança, pelo que governam o seu reino uns persas que são inimigos declarados dos portugueses*, 7 de Fevereiro de 1635.

957 *Ibid.*

958 LMG, cod. 21-A, fols. 52: *Carta delRei para o Vice-rei da India, respondendo sobre as informações que recebeu das dissidências do Canará, entre o Idalcão, Mogor e Virabradanaique, e das queixas que a Rainha de Olala e Rei de Banguel fizeram ao Idalcão, contra o Virabradanaique. Recomenda ao vice-rei que empregue toda a diplomacia na sua convivência com estes reis, entretendo-os com esperanças e enviando-lhes socorros e munições secretamente. Pede-lhe relação dos nomes das pessoas que ficaram servindo nas fortalezas do Canará, assim como as mercês que lhes foram feitas. Acha que toda a atenção do vice-rei deve ser, em primeiro lugar, dirigida para que as coisas do Canará não sofram alteração, pois isso resultaria em grande prejuízo do comércio da pimenta, que se não deve pôr à mercê dos estrangeiros, tão cubiçosos dela. Quanto ao assunto da fortaleza de Cambolim, Sua Majestade propõe que seja apresentado em Conselho, e os votos sejam secretos e enviados para o Reino, a fim de que se possa deliberar sobre o assunto.* Lisboa, 18 de Fevereiro de 1640.

959 *ACE*, vol. II, Doc. 44, pp. 117-159: *Copia do Conçelho sobre sairem os Galiões ao inimigo ou não*, 14 de Novembro de 1636. There is a detailed account of the Portuguese efforts to defend the *Estado da Índia* on the mentioned pages. The opinions of all the Counsellors have been given in detail.

960 *ACE*, vol. II; docs. 105: *Concelho sobre se dar a ElRey Idalxá trezentos mil xerafins e se botar fora de seus Portos os Olandeses, 26* de Agosto de 1641.

961 *ACE*, vol. II, doc. 106, Goa 11 de Julho de 1642.

962 *Ibid.*

963 *Ibid.*

964 As per the clauses of the treaties signed earlier, 1571, 1575, 1576, 1582, 1633, 1636, 1638; *LML*, cod. 47, fols. 31-32: *Carta do Vice-rei da Índia, João da Silva Tello de Menezes, Conde de Aveiras, dando conta dos acontecimentos e a ajuda que o governador de Ponda em nome do seu rei pediu ao embaixador Português e o socorro que se enviou*, Goa, 15 de Novembro de 1641.

965 The <u>Sidis</u> and Marathas of Dandas had revolted against the Sultan of Biajpur and had inflicted much damage on his commercial shipping.

966 The Bijapuri army was under the command of Assad Khan, son of Nawab Mustafa Khan

967 *ACE*, vol. II doc. 116*: Assento do Concelho de governo... sobre huma carta escrita ao senhor Conde V. Rey do Avaldar de Ponda, Mirza Mamede Raza, em que pede se lhe dee armada para tomar a fortaleza de danda Sobre a qual vay o cpitão geral do exercito DelRey Idalxa Assadeccão filho de Nababo Mostafacão*, 28 de fevereiro de 1642.

968 Biker (ed.) *Collecção de tratados...*, tomo I, pp. 192-96: *Assento e Contrato de Paz e amisade com El-Rey Nizamoxá, por intervenção de El-Rey Idalxá, sendo Viso-Rey D. Jeronymo de Azevedo*, 9 de Outubro de 1615: *"E Assentou Sua Alteza Ibraime Idalxá e o Nababo Xanavascan que as pazes*

ficassem feitas entre Sua Magestade e El-Rei Murtuzá Nizamsá, acrescentando mais que não agazalhará em seus portos nem terras Ingrezes nem Hollandezes, nem dará favor nenhum, as quaes pazes se feizerão o anno de 1571; e os ditos Embaixadores as aceitárão, e se obrigárão pollos poderes, que tinhão..".

969 *ACE*, vol. II doc. 116, 28 de fevereiro de 1642.

970 *Ibid*: The help they were asking for was in the form of gunpowder and ammunition; see the doc. 118, of *ACE*: *Assento sobre huma carta do Avaldaar doutra banda Mirza Mamede Raza em que pede que o capitão da fortaleza de Chaul dee Socorro de poluora e monições ao exercito DelRey Idalxa com que vay sobre a fortaleza de Danda,* 7 de Março de 1642.

971 *ACE*, vol. II, doc. 106, Goa 11 de Julho de 1642.

972 *ACE*, vol. II, doc. 122: *"...visto as guerras de chaul não serem de consideração por serem só entre os mouros sem em nada nos prejudicarem.."*. 23 de Abril de de 1642.

973 He was one of the important courtiers of the Bijapur regime. At that time he was prime minister of the state of Bijapur.

974 *ACE*, vol. II, doc. 133: *Concelho sobre Acedecão, filho de Mostafacão, mandar pedir que se lhe restituisse a embarcação que Francisco Pereira da Cunha tomou e queimou junto a Rajapur.*8 de Outubro de 1642.

975 *ACE*, vol. II, doc. 176: *Sobre o embaxador delrey Idalxa pedir seguro a S. Excelencia pera o Aualdar do concão se vir a esta cidade, e de como se lhe passou,* 1 de Outubro de 1643; Doc. 184, *Sobre a carta do geral das naos, e protesto que mandou fazer, e sobre largar a gente da não Pauão, e a carta delRey Idalxa para lhe ser entregue Mirza Mamede Raza Aualdar de Pondá.,* 16 de Novembro de 1643.

976 Portugal had proclaimed its independence on 1 December, 1640, and a ten years truce was signed between Dom João IV, through his ambassador Tristão de Mendonça Furtado and the representatives of States General on 12 June 1641, *LML*, cod. 48, fls. 253/205; *Cod.* 50, fls. 67/100v, 117v; cod. 51, fl. 49/107, 140/354, 141/356-57, 142/358-359; Biker (ed) *Collecção de tratados ...*, tomo II, pp. 108-135; However, the armistice was finally published on 10 November 1644: Borges de Castro, *Collecção de Tratados,* tomo I, p. 118.

977 Ekhlas Khan who is also known as Malik Yáqút, was a very trustworthy noble at the Bijapuri court.

978 *ACE*, vol. III, doc. 19: *Sobre duas cartas delRey Idalxa, e eclascan em que pede lhes largue hum navio seu que a ramada dos estreitos de Ormuz tomou, e o mais que sobre a matéria tratou,* 20 de julho de 1644.

979 *Ibid. "vistas as mizerias prezentes e o modo com que nos achavamos, e ElRey nosso senhor ter encomendado que aja boa correspondencia com este Rey Idalxa lhes pareceo justo, que o ditto navio se lhe desse".*

980 *ACE*, vol. III, doc. 19, 20 de Julho de 1644.

981 *LMG*, cod. 19-B, fols. 547-547v°:*Carta régia para o vice-rei da Índia, sobre os ritos e cerimónias usadas pelos gentios nos seus casamentos, o vice-rei respondera que dera ordem para se fazer uma Junta com os Inquisidores,* Lisboa, 7 de Janeiro de 1634.

982 *LML*, cod. 30, fols. 311-311v°: Relação aserca dos cazamentos dos gentios feita por juiz dos feitos de Sua Magestade, Pêro de Amaral Pimenta, Goa a 7 de Fevereiro de 1633.

983 *Ibid. ACE*, vol. III, doc. 19, 20 de Julho de 1644.

984 See chapter IV for more detail.

985 Fitzler, *O Cerco do Colombo*, p. 63; Botelho de Sousa, *O Subsídio para a História das Guerras*, pp. 268-269.

986 *ACE*, vol. III, Doc. 118: *Conselho sobre se hauer de vir a armada do estreito e soccorer Mombassa*, 25 de Outubro de 1652.

987 *ACE*, vol. III, Doc. 117: *Sobre se hauer de hir ao canara a armada do norte de que he o capitão geral Tristão de Silveira...*, 10 de Outubro de 1653.

988 Artur Teodoro de Matos, (edited), *Diário do Conde de Sarzedas, Vice-rey do Estado da Índia (1655-1656)*, see notes on the page 82.

989 Manucci, *Stória do Mogor*, vol. III, pp. 157-159; Though, the Portuguese viceroy, the Conde de Sarzedas, in his letter to the king of Portugal mentions about this stone "Balai", he doesn't narrate the same story as did Manucci, *LMG*, cod. 25, fols. 238-38v, fls. 238: *Carta do [vice-rei da Índia, D. Rodrigo da Silveira] Conde de Sarzedas. Sobre a jornada que fez de Lisboa para Goa; informações do estado em que achou a Índia; sobre a chegada de Malique Acute, embaixador do Idalxá; sucesso dos socorros enviados a Ceilão, sob o comando do capitão António de Sousa Coutinho; visita que fez ao forte de Tivy nas terras de Bardez; socorros enviados àquela ilha sob o comando do capitão-mor Manuel Salgado.* Goa, 15 de Dezembro de 1655.

990 *LMG*, cod. 25, fols. 241-241v°: *Carta do vice-rei da Índia, Conde de Sarzedas, para o rei, sobre o intento com que Melique Acute veiu a Goa; pedido insistente que fez para se lhe vender uma certa pedra (Balaes). Refere-se aos dois presentes que se mandaram, em tempo de D. Brás de Castro, ao Idalxá; sobre este rei não ter ainda ratificado as pazes.* Goa, 15 de Dezembro de 1655.

991 This is what Manucci says.

992 *Ibid.*

993 *LMG*, cod. 24, fols. 142-144: *Carta do rei, D. João IV, para o vice-rei da Índia, D. Brás de Castro. Sobre a proibição feita pelo Santo Ofício, à passagem de cristãos e gentios, para a festa do Lavatório, feita defronte do passo de Naroa. El-rei manda ao vice-rei que não se oponha a esta ordem.* 17 de Março de 1654; *LMG*, cod. 24, fols. 144v°: *Carta do governador da Índia, D. Brás de Castro, para o rei dando Informa pormenorizadamente das queixas que os gentios fizeram desta proibição antes e durante o governo do vice-rei Conde*

d'Óbidos. É de parecer que se levante esta proibição, pois é certo, que causará amotinações. Goa, 3 de Fevereiro de 1655.

994 *ACE*, doc. Vol. III, doc. 173: *Sobre a carta que escreueo el Rey Idalxa para haver de hir o Padre Gonçalo Martins a Vizapor*, 20 de Março de 1654; see on page 327 of the same volume, Cópia do Formão del Rey Idalxa, dated March 13 of April 1654, the letter mentions the sending of Gonçalo Martins to carry some present, (mimo) but there is no mention of the Stone (Balaí) nor the desire of the Conversion of the Sultan and his family to Christianity. If something of this nature would have been asked for, the Portuguese sources would have, undoubtedly, mentioned it, even if, later it didn't workout. On the other hand, the Jesuits had great influence all over India. Some of them always managed to become "favourites" of the Court because of their cultivated and diplomatic behaviour.

995 Artur Teodoro de Matos, (edited), *Diário do Conde de Sarzedas,* see notes on the page 82.

996 Shirdokar, 'Portuguese-Dutch Relations in the East (1580-1663) vis-à-vis Indian Peninsula', in *Stvdia, 48,* pp- 123-157.

997 *Ibid*, p. 138.

998 Conde de Sarzedas mentions in his diary about the two Dutch ambassadors at the court of the Sultan of Bijapur in 1653, but doesn't provide any evidence for this incident. However, Sarzedas only reached Goa in the month of September, 1654; Matos, (edited), *Diário do Conde de Sarzedas, Vice-rey do Estado da Índia (1655-1656),* pp. 90-91.

999 Matos, *Diário do Conde de Sarzedas,* see footnote no. 136 on the page 91.

1000 *LMG*, cod. 24, fol. 192: *Treslado da carta que escreve a Vossa Senhoria elrey sultão Mamede Idalxaa na qual se dis o seguinte. Afirma que será retirado o cerco da fortaleza de Onor, posto por Sinapa Naique, e serão restituídas as outras que foram tomadas. Assegura que este rei ficará tranquilo, ou então o terá por inimigo e o castigará, pois acima de tudo põe a sua amizade com o rei de Portugal que tem coroa de ouro. Espera a chegada do padre Gonçalo Moniz*, 13 de Março de 1654.

1001 *ACE*, Vol. III, pp. 327-328: See Appendix-V-G-a.

1002 *ACE*, Vol. III, docs. 169-171: *Que visto não se concluir a paz o enviado del Rey Siuapanaique se socrorresse Onor com o mais que pudesse ser para se hir defendendo.* 27 de Fevereiro de 1654.

1003 *ACE*, Vol. III, Doc. 173: *Sobre a carta que escreveo el Rey Idalxa para haver de ir o Padre Gonçalo Martins a Vizapor,* 20 de Março, 1654; HAG, *Regimentos e Instuções*, cod.5, fol. 84v, *Instrucção para o Reverendo Gonçalo Martins da companhia de Jesus que ora passa a corte del Rey Idalxá,* 16 de Abril de 1654.

1004 Danvers, *The Portuguese in India...*, vol. II, pp. 308; But Artur Teodoro de Matos, (edited), *Diário do Conde de Sarzedas,* page 82, has suggested that this invasion took place sometime before 11 October 1654.

1005 The Portuguese considered all the religious belief of the East to be Pagan. They didn't consider any religion worthy of being referred to as a religion. LMG, cod. 23-B, fol. 375: *Carta do Governador D. Brás de Castro ao Rei sobre mau procedimento do bispo D. Mateus que não só exortou os naturais de Bardês à revolta mas ainda lhe escreveu cartas insolentes, motivo porque tentava apoderar-se dele para o fazer embarcar para o Reino.* Goa, 25 de Janeiro de 1654.

1006 *LMG*, cod. 24, fol. 247: *Carta do governador da Índia, D. Brás de Castro, para o rei. Sobre o lavatório que os gentios costumam fazer em Chaúl, o editar que se publicou por parte do Santo Ofício e a alteração que daí resultou,* Goa, 3 de Fevereiro de 1655.

1007 *LMG*, cod. 23-B, fol. 375: *Carta do Governador D. Brás de Castro ao Rei sobre mau procedimento do bispo D. Mateus que não só exortou os naturais de Bardês à revolta mas ainda lhe escreveu cartas insolentes, motivo porque tentava apoderar-se dele para o fazer embarcar para o Reino.* Goa, 25 de Janeiro de 1654; Cod. 23-B, fols. 506; *Carta do Governador D. Bras de Castro ao* Rei de, 27 de Janeiro de 1654; *LMG*, cod. 24, fols. 142-144: *Carta do rei, D. João IV, para o vice-rei da Índia, D. Brás de Castro. Sobre a proibição feita pelo Santo Ofício, à passagem de cristãos e gentios, para a festa do Lavatório, feita defronte do passo de Naroa. El-rei manda ao vice-rei que não se oponha a esta ordem.* 17 de Março de 1654; *LMG*, cod. 24, fols. 144v°: *Carta do governador da Índia, D. Brás de Castro, para o rei dando Informa pormenorizadamente das queixas que os gentios fizeram desta proibição antes e durante o governo do vice-rei Conde d'Óbidos. É de parecer que se levante esta proibição, pois é certo, que causará amotinações.* Goa, 3 de Fevereiro de 1655.

1008 Mostly converted from Hinduism or Islamism to Christianity.

1009 *ACE*, cod. III, pp. 563-64: *Carta do Governador D. Brás de Castro ao Rey,* 27 Janeiro de 1654.

1010 *LMG*, cod. 24, fol. 142: *Treslado de outro capitulo da Carta do Conselho Geral escrita a Meza do Santo Officio desta Inquisição do* anno de 1654". *Sobre a passagem dos cristãos e gentios ao Lavatório,* Lisboa, 17 de Março de 1654; Idem, fol. 142v, Carta do rei, D. João IV, *para o vice-rei da Índia, D. Brás de Castro, sobre a proibição feita pelo Santo Ofício, à passagem de cristãos e gentios, para a festa do Lavatório, feita defronte do passo de Naroa. El-rei manda ao vice-rei que não se oponha a esta ordem. Lisboa, 21 de Março de 1654; Also see the letter of the Governador D. Brás de Castro a Er-Rei,* 3 de Fevereiro de 1655, LMG, cod. 24, fol. 194v.

1011 *LMG*, cod. 24, fols. 144v°: *Carta do governador da Índia, D. Brás de Castro, para o rei dando Informa pormenorizadamente das queixas que os gentios fizeram desta proibição antes e durante o governo do vice-rei Conde d'Óbidos. É de parecer que se levante esta proibição, pois é certo, que causará amotinações.* Goa, 3 de Fevereiro de 1655.

1012 *ACE*, cod. III, pp. 562: *see the foot note three on this page: "...os ditos gentios (gaoncares) [de Bardês por vezes intentarão motins e Rebeliões contra a Magestade dElRey meu Senhor, e ultimamente como no anno de 1654 entrando o exercito dElRey Idalxa nas ditas terras, sendo seu general Abdala Aquimo se rebelarão, e passarão aos mouros, e tomarão armas contra o estado seruindo lhe de espias leuandolhe mantimentos para o exercito.*

1013 LMG, cod. 24, fol. 190: Carta do rei sultão Mamede Idalxá: *Treslado da Carta que escreve a Vossa Senhoria el rey sultão Mamede Idalxa na qual dis o seguinte. Afirma ao governador a boa disposição em que está de manter amizade com os portugueses, referindo-se com carinho ao padre Gonçalo* Martins, 3 de Outubro de 1654.

1014 LMG, cod. 24, fol. 194: *Carta do rei sultão Mamede Idalxá, Treslado da carta que escreve a Vossa Senhoria el rey sultão Mamede Idalxaa...* 3 de Novembro de 1654.

1015 LMG, cod. 24, fol. 196: *Carta do rei sultão Mamede Idalxá, Treslado da* carta *que escreve a Vossa Senhoria sultão Mamede Idalxaa na qual dis o seguinte. Assegura a amizade que tem para com o rei de Portugal, sua obediência e desejo de paz. Refere-se com toda a admiração ao padre Gonçalo Martins,* 31 de Dezembro de 1654.

1016 In 1655 he was posted back again not only as ambassador but also as governor of Ponda and its surrounding areas. Not only that, the ambassadors posted to the Portuguese capital, normally lived in Ponda, outside the Portuguese dominated area, in Ponda.

1017 Manucci, *Storia do Mogor,* vol. III, pp. 159-169.

1018 *Ibid;* During the reception of the ambassador there were more than twenty high-ranking officers present including the governor, the captain of the city Dom Pedro Henriques, one of the noblemen and officials of the viceroy's Council. Dom Gil Eanes de Noronha and Dom Fernando Manoel, the capitão-mor (?) and the captain in charge for providing help to ports and forts whenever it was needed, were among those present. In order to assist the governor and the ambassador, Krishna Sinai and Rama Sinai Cothari were present as interpreters: these interpreters had been in the Portuguese panel lists and were, among the most reliable Portuguese officials. They had been on several missions to conduct the peace treaties; HAG, *Livro grande de Pazes,* fols. 44-45v°, *Assento, reteficação e juramento de pazes feitas com o Senhor Rey Sultão Mamede Idalxá por seu enviado Melique Acute, de sua presença, e o Padre Gonçalo Martins, da Companhia de Jesus, governando o Estado da Índia o Senhor Dom Braz de Castro do Conselho de Sua Magestade, 7 de Março de 1655;* See Pissurlencar, *Agentes da Diplomacia Portugesa na Índia (Hindus, Muçulmanos, Judeus e Parses*), (passim). [According to Manucci, this incident took place in the year 1666 and not 1655, probably a mistake by the translator!]

1019 *ACE,* vol. III, doc. 190: *Sobre o juramento e retificação de pazes com elRey Idalxa e prezente que se lhe ouesse de mandar, 3 de* Janeiro de 1655.

1020 *ACE,* vol. III, doc. 188: *Sobre a chegada da carta delRey Idalxa pela qual dizia ouuesse suspenção de armas,* 11 de Outubro de 1654.

1021 *Ibid.*

1022 *Idem*, doc. 190: *Sobre o juramento e retificação de pazes com elRey Idalxa e prezente que se lhe ouuesse de mandar*, 3 de Janeiro de 1655.

1023 *Ibid.*

1024 HAG, *Livro grande de Pazes*, fols. 44-45vº: *Assento, reteficação e juramento de pazes feitas com o Senhor Rey Sultão Mamede Idalxá por seu enviado Melique Acute, de sua presença, e o Padre Gonçalo Martins, da Companhia de Jesus, governando o Estado da Índia o Senhor Dom Braz de Castro do Conselho de Sua Magestade*, 7 de Março de 1655.

1025 *Livro grande das Pazes*, fol. 7; Biker (ed) *Collecção de tratados ...*, tomo I, pp. 170-180: *Contrato das pazes feitas com o Idalxá por seu Embaixador Zaerbeque, que veio do Reino, governando este Estado António Moniz Barreto, no anno de 1576*; *APO-CR*, Fasc. 5, doc. 786, pp. 921-930.

1026 *Livro grande Pazes*, fol. 12; Biker (ed) *Collecção de tratados ...*, tomo I, pp. 184-186; *APO-CR*, Fasc. 5, doc. 818, pp. 985-987: *Assento que fez com os Embaixadores do Idalxá por mandado do Conde de Villa d'Orta, Viso-Rey da India, sobre o comprimento das pazes, feitas anteriormente pelo Conde de Atouguia com Mostafacão*, em 29 de Janeiro de 1582.

1027 Biker (ed) *Collecção de tratados ...*, tomo II, pp. 232-239.

1028 HAG, *Livro grande de Pazes*, fols. 44-45vº; *Assento, reteficação e juramento de pazes feitas com o Senhor Rey Sultão Mamede Idalxá por seu enviado Melique Acute, de sua presença, e o Padre Gonçalo Martins, da Companhia de Jesus, governando o Estado da Índia o Senhor Dom Braz de Castro do Conselho de Sua Magestade, 7 de Março de 1655*; In addition to Father Gonçalo Martins, Malik Yáqút was accompanied by Hani Haji Saiyad Raza, Narsingha Rao, Rao Naikwadi and Ricco Shah Gujarati, some of the nobles from the Bijapuri court.

1029 HAG, *Livro de Regimentos e Instruções, nº 5*, fol. 94v-95, *Instruções para o reverendo Padre Francisco morando da Companhia de Jeus, 26 de Março de 1655; ACE*, vol. III, fol. 384-86: *Cópia da carta que o Padre António Botelho escreveo ao Senhor Governador*, 26 de Julho de 1655; The mission of Fr. António Botelho and Gonçalo Martins was more diplomatic than religious. However, being on a diplomatic posting and serving as informer was ethically wrong.

1030 Matos, (edited), *Diário do Conde de Sarzedas, Vice-rey do Estado da Índia (1655-1656)*, p.117: Cópia *da carta do Embaxador que veyo com a del Rey Idalxa; ACE*, vol. III, doc. 193: *Sobre a carta que escreueo Malique Acute ao Senhor Governador para vir a esta cidade como embaxador d'El Rey Idalxa e reposta que se lhe fez*, 17 de Agosto de 1655: It is worth mentioning here that Dom Rodrigo da Silveira, the Conde de Sarzedas, only took up his office as Viceroy on 24 August 1655, See *ACE*, vol. III, doc. 193: *Termo da Posse e entrega que toma o exmº Senhor Dom Rodrigo da Silueyra de Conde de Sarzedas do Concelho d'estado de S. Magestado da Gouernança de V. Rey e Capitão Geral da India de qye a my foi seruido encarregar*, 24 de

Agosto de 2, though he was already there during the government of Dom Braz de Castro who is known as "usurper", but in the diary of the Conde de Sarzedas, it has been put in a way that this letter was sent to him. In fact, during the meeting of the Council of State that took place on the 17th of the same month, Dom Braz de Castro chaired the session. Therefore, this letter must have been sent to the governor Dom Braz de Castro.

1031 Matos (edited), *Diário do Conde de Sarzedas,* pp. 117-118; the same letter had already been published earlier in the *Asssentos do Conselho do Estado, vol. III,* pp, 384-386.

1032 *ACE,* vol. III, doc. 193: *Sobre a carta que escreueo Malique Acute ao Senhor Governador para vir a esta cidade como embaxador d'El Rey Idalxa e reposta que se lhe fez,* 17 de Agosto de 1655.

1033 *Ibid.*

1034 HAG, *Livro de Regimentos e Instruções, nº 5, fol. 94v-95, 26 de Março de 1655; ACE,* vol. III, fol. 384-86, 26 de Julho de 1655.

1035 Matos, (edited), *Diário do Conde de Sarzedas,* p.117.

1036 *Ibid.*

1037 *ACE,* vol. III, doc. 193: *Sobre a carta que escreueo Malique Acute ao Senhor Governador para vir a esta cidade como embaxador d'El Rey Idalxa e reposta que se lhe fez,* 17 de Agosto de 1655.

1038 *Tenho feito auiso a V. S. Por varias vezes dos intentos com que o Malique Acute foi para o Concão os quais todos são malignos...* [all of them are pernicious], see *ACE,* vol. III, fol. 384-86: *Cópia da carta que o Padre António Botelho escreveo ao Senhor Governador,* 26 de Julho de 1655.

1039 *ACE,* vol. III, doc. 196, pp. 390-91, 1 de Setembro de 1655.

1040 *ACE,* vol. III, doc. 197, pp. 392-9, Goa, 10 de Setembro de 1655; *Doc.* 198, pp. 394-95, Goa 1 de Outubro de 1655.

1041 *ACE,* vol. III, doc. 201: *Conselho sobre a casa forte que Quessoua Naique fabricou defronte da Igreja do mesmo cítio da coloa...,* Goa, 15 de Outubro de 1655.

1042 Matos, (edited), *Diário do Conde de Sarzedas,* p.117: Cópia *da carta do Embaxador que veyo com a del Rey Idalxa.*

1043 This is Mirjan (or Mir Jaan).

1044 *ACE,* vol. III doc. 202, Goa, 19 de outubro de 1655; Also see the letter of Sultan Adil Shah, *LMG,* cod. 25, fol. fls. 242: *Treslado duma carta escrita pelo rei Idalxá, ao vice-rei da Índia, Conde de Sarzedas. dando notícias de algumas mercês que fez a Rustumuzamaa e pede auxílio de munições para poder tomar Ancola, Merizeo e Coroar onde há alterações. Pede para serem castigados os rebeldes (Dessais e Naiques) que envia ao vice-rei, e para atender bem ao seu enviado Malique Acute,* 29 de Agosto de 1655. Though in the Portuguese documents it is mentioned that they supported the Dessais quite often, I haven't come across any such occasion in any document so far.

1045 *Ibid.*, pp. 116-121.

1046 Bib. da Academia das Ciências de Lisboa, *Noticias dos Estado da Índia*, cod. 58, fols. 51v-55.

1047 *Ibid*, fol. 55: "*...deste Mouro ha se de fazer pouca confiança pelo trato, e amizades que tem com os olandezes...*".

1048 *Ibid.*

1049 He referred to the Sultan of Bijapur and the whole Muslim officials in general.

1050 *Estes mouros segundo tenho alcançado não tem firmeza em nada, e acho noticias que este tem trato com os olandezes e há dous annos que lhes pede se nos querião vir pôr na barra para elles nos sitiaresm por terra*": Matos, (edited), *Diário do Conde de Sarzedas,* p. 91, 1 de Setembro, 1655.

1051 Matos, *Diário do Conde de Sarzedas*, pp. 92-93. "*....e fui a Tivim que hé hum dos passos por donde entrou a gente do Idalxa (in 1654) o modo da fortificação...e se conseguir a obra será mais difficultozo aos mouros podem entrar nellas...e alem destas razoens também me aprecey em hir ver isto a respeito do Embaixador delRey Idalxa, lhe ter sinalado o dia de manhaã para uir falar que entendão os Mouros que ainda quando me dizem que vem fazer pazes comigo, e as trazem ajustadas que estou eu tam vigilante que vou tratando de me preuenir para a guerra*...4 de setembro de 1655.

1052 *ACE*, vol. III, 22 de Dezembro de 1655, p. 422.

1053 *LMG*, cod. 25: *Carta do vice-rei da Índia, D. Rodrigo da Silveira, Conde de Sarzedas. Sobre a jornada que fez de Lisboa para Goa; informações do estado em que achou a Índia; sobre a chegada de Malique Acute, embaixador do Idalxá*, Goa, 15 de Dezembro de 1655 fl. 238; Also see Danvers, *The Portuguese in Índia...*, vol II, p. 309. Danvers has mentioned that the ambassador presented the letter of the Sultan to D. Braz de Castro which is a mistake as he had been imprisoned by Sarzedas in August of the same year as he had assumed office on his own, without authorisation.

1054 *ACE*, vol. III, doc. 207: *Conselho sobre se deve enviar soccorro para Ceilão...*, 22 de Dezembro de 1655.

1055 He took office on 23 August of 1655 and governed almost six months.

1056 *LMG*, cod. 26-B, fls. 337-341: *Carta dos Governadores da Índia Manuel Mascarenhas Homem, Francisco de Melo e Castro e António de Sousa Coutinho, Carta do 3° Conselho do Governo da Índia para el-rei enviando relatório anual indica "...a perda de Ceilão, quanto à navegação e comércio da canela; inconstância do Samorim; na parte sul tudo está perdido, excepto Macau e Meliapor*; Goa, 13 de Dezembro de 1658; Fitzler, *O Cerco do Colombo*, p. 63; Botelho de Sousa, *O Subsídio para a História das Guerras*, p. 53; Winius, *The Fatal History of Portuguese Ceylon: Transition to Dutch Rule*, 1638-1658, Harvard University Press, 1971, see Chapter IV, Goa and Ceylon / The Debacle 1655-1656, pp. 141-166.

1057 In various letters from Portugal, he is also referred to as Viceroy.

1058 LMG, cod. 26-B, fols. 337-341: *Carta dos Governadores da Índia Manuel Mascarenhas Homem, Francisco de Melo e Castro e António de Sousa Coutinho, Carta do 3° Conselho do Governo da Índia para el-rei, dando conta de impossibilidade de conservar as terras de Salsete e Bardes, se Dialxá atacar; é infrutífero o envio de embaixadores ao Dialxá; tentativas para captar a amizade do Dialxá; a nomeação por votos, do fidalgo D. Pedro Henriques para presidir esta embaixada; divisão entre os vassalos de Dialxá por ele não ser rei legítimo,* Goa, 13 de Dezembro de 1658; Varma, *History of Bijapur*, pp. 165-182.

1059 *Ibid.*

1060 LMG, cod. 26-B, fols. 499-499v: *Carta dos Governadores da Índia Manuel Mascarenhas Homem, Francisco de Melo e Castro e António de Sousa Coutinho, Carta do 3.° Conselho do Governo da Índia para a Sua Majestade, sobre a vinda do capitão Abdoul Aquimo a Pondá; sua entrada nas aldeias de Cuculy, Ansolna e Margão, onde encontrou o capitão-geral Luís de Mendonça Furtado que o obrigou a retirar com algumas baixas; carta de Abdoul Aquimo a D. Francisco de Sousa, capitão de Daugim*, Goa, 16 de Dezembro de 1659; LMG, cod. 26-B, fols. 501: *Carta do 3° Conselho do Governo da Índia para a Sua Majestade, sobre a diligência feita para enviar notícias a Sua Majestade; chegada dos holandeses com forte poder; declaração de guerra feita pelo rei Dialxá por meio de seu capitão geral Abdoul Aquimo; os esforços feitos para se defender do inimigo*. Goa, 16 de Dezembro de 1659; Also see fols. 529-532, for more details.

1061 LMG, cod. 26-B, fols. 379: *Carta dos Governadores da Índia Manuel Mascarenhas Homem, Francisco de Melo e Castro e António de Sousa Coutinho, Carta do 3° Conselho do Governo da Índia para a Sua Majestade, enviando algumas informações sobre o Estado da Índia; referência às ameaças a Cochim e a Cananor; notícia de haver chegado a corte do rei Idalxá o embaixador D. Pedro Henriques*. Goa, 5 de Fevereiro de 1659; *ACE*, vol. IV, doc. I: *Em Conselho de Gouerno de seis de Março* de 1659; For the details of the political developments, see EF, 1655-1600, pp. 247-249, Letter written by Revington to the English Company, on the 10 of December, 1659; Glenn J. Ames,"The Salssette Campaign of 1658-1659...", p. 232.

1062 LMG, cod. 26-B, fols. 535: *Carta dos Governadores da Índia Manuel Mascarenhas Homem, Francisco de Melo e Castro e António de Sousa Coutinho, Carta do 3° Conselho do Governo da Índia para a Sua Majestade, sobre o sucesso na entrada em Salsete; perda de grande parte do reino do rei Dialxá; um capitão seu de nome Sivagi tem desbaratado alguns capitães do mesmo Dialxá; conquista do referido capitão e o modo como o rei pensa em fazer-lhe frente; guerra entre os filhos do Mogor; Auranzebo, um deles, é tirano e parece ser inimigo dos cristãos*. Goa, 22 de Março de 1660.

1063 LMG, cod. 25, fol. fls. 242: *Treslado duma carta escrita pelo rei Idalxá, ao vice-rei da Índia, Conde de Sarzedas, dando notícias de algumas mercês que fez a Rustumuzamaa e pede auxílio de munições para poder tomar Ancola, Merizeo e Coroar onde há alterações. Pede para serem castigados os rebeldes (Dessais e Naiques) que envia ao vice-rei, e para atender bem ao seu enviado Malique Acute,* 29 de Agosto de 1655.

1064 Glenn J. Ames,"The Salssette Campaign of 1658-1659: Issues of War and Peace in Bijapuri-Portuguese Relations during the mid-17th Century" *op.cit,* pp. 223-40.

1065 *Ibid.,* pp. 232-234.

1066 *LMG,* cod. 26-B, fols. 337-341: *Carta dos Governadores da Índia Manuel Mascarenhas Homem, Francisco de Melo e Castro e António de Sousa Coutinho, Carta do 3° Conselho do Governo da Índia para el-rei, dando conta de impossibilidade de conservar as terras de Salsete e Bardes, se Dialxá atacar; é infrutífero o envio de embaixadores ao Dialxá; tentativas para captar a amizade do Dialxá; a nomeação por votos, do fidalgo D. Pedro Henriques para presidir esta embaixada.* Goa, 13 de Dezembro de 1658; *EF,* 1655-1600, pp. 247-249, *Letter written by Revington to the English Company,* on the 10 of December, 1659; Glenn J. Ames,"The Salssette Campaign of 1658-1659..., p. 232.

1067 Glenn J. Ames,"The Salssette Campaign of 1658-1659...", p. 232.

1068 *EF., (1655-1660), Letter from Revington to the Company giving details of the political developments in the South India,* 10 Dec. 1659, pp. 247-251: This Sultan Ali Adil Shah II, was an illegitimate son of Mohammad Adil Shah Shah. His mother was Bari Saheba.

Chapter 6

Conclusion

Writing a conclusion is, sometimes, a more difficult task than writing the entire book. However, I should start by saying that the arrival of the Portuguese in the Indian Ocean certainly marked the beginning of a new era by introducing a new commercial system, new diplomatic policy, modern warfare, a new mode of thinking and above all a new religion. It brought about rapid change in all existing relationships from commerce and religion to warfare and diplomacy. On the one hand commercial relations were established with the aim of controlling not only the prices of the commodities but also the merchants who carried on maritime commerce, while religion served as a means to establish links between the Roman Catholic Portuguese and a mixed Indian society based on a complicated Hindu caste system surrounded by St. Thomas Christians, Muslims, Buddhists and Jains etc. On the other hand, the Portuguese were the first Europeans to use modern military technology such as explosives, cannon and firearms of different kinds. Portuguese methods of fighting revolutionised the way that war was conducted in the Indian subcontinent. The field of diplomacy was also not untouched. Both the Asian and European diplomatic norms were put on trial and a new but mixed system of international relations emerged.

This conclusion will focus on the development of Indo-Portuguese diplomacy, which has been discussed in the previous chapters, and the changes that resulted from this interaction.

Before the arrival of the Portuguese the Indian kings and people were accustomed to receiving all foreigners alike, irrespective of their religious or cultural background. We have the testimony of a traveller like Abdul Razzak, who visited India half a century prior to Vasco da Gama, who mentions that "...at Calicut every ships whatever place it might have come from or wherever it might be bound for, when it put into this port was treated like other vessels and had no trouble of any kind to put up with".[1069] There was a high degree of religious tolerance, security and freedom in mercantile transactions. Many travellers both Asians and Europeans bore witness to the religious tolerance in Malabar.[1070] It is hard to believe that, after the elapse of only half a century, the mentality of the Indian rulers had changed so much that they could not accommodate one more nation as they always had done and evidence shows that the Portuguese, when they arrived, were also treated with much dignity and respect.

It was the Portuguese who did not know how to respect the Indians and their customs. The immediate reason appears to be the lack of culture and education of those who came to India from Portugal, many of whom were *degredados* and *renegados*. A considerable number of these latter even attained high positions such as that of a *capitão*. The main aim of these *degredados* always remained to get a pardon from the king, which was only possible if they performed some heroic task. This could take any form from killing some important Muslim figure to destroying anything which belonged to the enemy of the Portuguese *Estado da Índia*. Such actions might be deemed heroic by the Portuguese but they severely damaged relationships with the Indian states.

The Portuguese, from the very beginning, employed force instead of diplomacy in all their contacts with local people from the east African coast to the western coast of India. A country like Portugal, which lacked adequate resources of its own to carry on such a huge worldwide trade, naturally had to look for some less traditional means which involved looting unarmed merchants ships and establishing a rule of terror across the whole of the Indian Ocean. Several recent Portuguese historians, such as Saldanha and Luís Adão de Fonseca,[1071] continuing in the tradition of an older generation, have tried to advance as justification that the reason why the Portuguese used violence against the Muslim merchants was due to the latter's opposition to Portuguese commercial activity.[1072] However, this could hardly justify the use of armed forces as there were other ways to solve the problems – for example by diplomacy or by seeking aid from the local authorities. Unfortunately this did not happen. Neither the Muslim merchants nor their rulers were able to prevent the Portuguese from continuing their brutalities because they did not have a navy as strong as that of the Portuguese. The Portuguese intentions were not only to displace the Muslims traders but, to eliminate their shipping from Asian waters replacing it with their own, and forming an alliance with the Hindus, who they thought were the hated enemies of the Muslims. This Portuguese obsession "to displace the Muslims from the trade of the Indian Ocean, substituting them with Christians and Gentiles"[1073] was to prove a costly business.

The Portuguese were unorthodox in their diplomatic policy. They preferred to exploit the internal political conflicts of the Indian states before seriously resorting to diplomacy. They employed missionaries for diplomatic purposes, which was nothing new in the Indian context as the Brahmins had been the soul of diplomacy for centuries and were an accepted part of the Indian (especially Hindu) political system. However, the Brahmins did not act as spies in the states to which they were sent, as the Catholic missionaries did, at least there is no specific evidence to prove that they did. However, before the arrival of the Portuguese in India, there had not been any system of permanent diplomatic missions. Although ambassadors in Asia, as in Europe, might stay at the courts for more than two years, this was due to the insistence of the rulers and the long distance they had to travel, and was not due to any system of permanent diplomatic representation as such. Through such lengthy stays the rulers used to demonstrate their importance to other visiting ambassadors. Even during the early stage of Portuguese diplomatic contacts, their ambassadors also were sent only to deal with urgent matters and were then expected to return. However, as conflicts between the states became more frequent, it was the Sultan of Bijapur, in 1575-76, who first proposed to the Portuguese that they should maintain permanent missions at each other's courts. In short one can say that the system of permanent missions was an outcome of two different political and cultural systems.

Permanent diplomatic missions gave birth to the activities of spying by emissaries and ambassadors, which had always been done by especialised personnel before. The diplomatic corps were also accompanied by missionaries, travellers and businessmen from the early sixteenth century who also contributed heavily in keeping their headquarters uptodate, through their knit information services. In addition the Portuguese received reports from dissatisfied and powerful Hindu Brahmins, Indian converts to Christianity, *degredados* and *renegados,* as well as the *casados.* Moreover, rulers of the states of Cochin, Cranganore, Tanur and Quilon, also discharged valuable services by keeping the Portuguese informed of the movements of the Zamorin's soldiers as well as by involving him in local disputes which eventually weakened his military power and gave the Portuguese free hands to establish and fortify their position. All of these contributed in keeping the Portuguese Estado da Índia successful and alive as martime power for over 160 years on the Indian coastal regions.

Since the nature of the Portuguese settlements and their government were new and completely different from those that had so far existed in India, the relationship had its peculiarities. For instance, before the arrival of the Portuguese, no group of merchants had tried to obtain political power. Instead they were content to follow the local customs. The Portuguese on the other hand did not respect local practice but tried to implant a maritime regime which was hitherto unheard of. They were able to obtain a few allies, such as the states of Cochin, Cranganore, Quilon, and conquered Goa and the surrounding provinces, but for the rest they had to depend on exploiting the weakness of one state against another. Often they provoked one weak state against its sovereign, for example Cochin against the Zamorin, by making promises of help. In short, they followed the policy of divide and rule to ensure their own survival. Their policy did not stop there. They also tried to exploit the religious differences between the Hindu and the Muslim states, but in this they had very little success. Although the Portuguese were able to obtain the backing of discontented elements among the Brahmins, who lived in the kingdoms like Bijapur and Ahmadnagar, but their dream of creating a united front allied with the Hindu kingdoms against the Muslims never materialised.

From the very beginning, the Portuguese idea of establishing a "commercial hegemony", was based in both theory and practice on weak foundations, The Portuguese King never thought it was necessary to train his *capitães-mores* and *fidalgos* in the art of diplomacy or to shape their mentality, so that they might appear to be representatives of a "civilised country" (a term frequently used by the Portuguese for themselves then and even now). In all their early contacts they first sent out *degradados* and *marginais* and these were only followed later by some educated men and even nobles. The Portuguese authorities might have thought those *degredados* were suitable for diplomatic missions at the Indian courts but in reality they were not fit for any civilised relationships. From the time of Vasco da Gama to that of the Conde de Linhares and later, the Portuguese, except for a few exceptions, were incapable of establishing sound diplomatic relationships without creating fear or relying on the might of their navy. In their approach to relations with the Indian states, the Portuguese understood that they had two advantages. First, they were advanced in their fighting technology and second, the Indian rulers were divided among themselves, some due to religious differences and others dissatisfied with their sovereign overlords. With these considerations in mind, and guided by their own superiority complex, they negotiated with rulers who had deep rooted political and social traditions. The results were disastrous both for themselves and for the Indian rulers.

Nevertheless, the Portuguese were able to utilise the services of some sensible men of religion, among whom the Jesuits were the most important throughout the period of our study. Though they supported Portuguese policies, they were educated and were trained to deal with different kinds of people. If the Portuguese success in the Indian Ocean could be attributed to anyone, it was to these missionaries who not only created a bridge between two societies but were also helpful in maintaining cordial relations between the two civilisations. Moreover, because of their local contacts and the trust they had created, they were frequently able to obtain local finance for the Portuguese annual pepper cargoes. Their contribution did not stop here. They became influential in diplomacy, a field which was supposed to be reserved for personnel trained for the task. However, since most of those who had any training or experience in diplomacy were solely concerned with their own commercial gain, the missionaries were often employed in this field as well. In order to make sure they were successful in both diplomacy and religious activities, the missionaries indulged in spying activity at the very heart of the states. As they were men of God, nobody suspected them, and their worldwide correspondence constitutes one of the most important archives for this period.

Besides their naval superiority, Portuguese success was also due to finding some important but dissatisfied groups of Hindus, mostly from the upper strata of the society in the regions of Goa who were ruled by a Muslim ruler from Bijapur. These groups, especially, the Timmaya, Krishna and others referred to in the previous chapters, were responsible for providing the Portuguese with very useful information relating to the military and other matters. In addition, the Portuguese constructed chains of fortresses along the western coast of India in order to keep a close watch over the movement of commercial as well as passenger ships, and to force them to carry a Portuguese passport, the *Cartaz,* without which those ships would be liable to confiscation.

The Portuguese were also successful because some Indian rulers such as the kings of Cochin, Quilon, Cranganore and Cannanore, welcomed the Portuguese with the intent of becoming independent from their sovereign. These rulers managed to free themselves from their overlords but instead enchained themselves to the Portuguese and became their vassals.

Among the Indian rulers, only the Zamorin of Calicut had a navy able to resist Portuguese domination and he fought the intruders for almost a century with the help of his Muslim admirals, the Kunjalis. However, towards the end of the sixteenth century, as a result of some insignificant quarrel, the Zamorin brought about the end of his own naval power by foolishly allying with his enemies, the Portuguese, to destroy the Kunjali Marakkars. The quarrel is symbolised in the story, repeated by many historians, that the Kunjali cut off the tail of a royal elephant.

Just when the Portuguese thought they were able to dominate the whole of coastal India, three new rival and very powerful empires threatened their supremacy. The Nayakas of Ikkeri, after the defeat of the Emperor of Vijayanagar at Talikota in 1565, had been trying to turn the entire Kanara region into an independent state, while the Sultan of Bijapur also started to expand his state and annexed a great portion of the former Vijayanagar Empire, obliging the Nayaka to accept his sovereignty. At the same time the Mughal Emperor, Akbar, mounted successive military expeditions against the southern states. To these three powers one should add the appearance of another very ambitious new force, the Marathas, who added another layer of complexity to the Indian political scene. While all the three great powers were trying to establish their power on the land, the Dutch and the English East India Companies, appeared to claim their share the lucrative trade of Asia. These companies came with armed ships better equipped than those of the Portuguese. This situation was a severe blow to Portugal's dream of controlling the whole of the Indian Ocean.

Now it was the Portuguese who had to adjust to new circumstances, which were far more threatening than those they had faced a hundred years earlier. Thus, at the beginning of the seventeenth century, the policy of divide and rule, once used so successfully by the Portuguese, was now going to be turned against them by Asian rulers making use of the Dutch and the English.

During the sixteenth century the Portuguese had largely neglected diplomacy, or rather they had not considered it as necessary and tended to ignore local customs in this respect. The diplomacy which the Portuguese had been accustomed to practice in the sixteenth century which had largely amounted to dictating terms to each of the coastal states now had to adjust to a new and threatening situation. The Portuguese realised that the presence of the Dutch and the English could do more harm to their century old hegemony, while the Indian rulers saw in them a new hope of getting rid of the Portuguese. Although this did not immediately happen, the arrival of the northern Europeans created a new balance of power, as the fear that the Indian states would ally with these new European companies, brought the Portuguese to their senses. However, even under these fast changing conditions they retained the illusion of their naval power and from time to time reverted to their old practices. The fact remained that in this threatening political atmosphere, the Portuguese had neither the resources nor the capacity to stand alone, and alone they were. For a century they had been content to exist without close allies but now they needed friends. As for the Dutch and the English, after their initial experiences at the hands of the Portuguese, they were in no mood to continue with peaceful relationships, even when they promised to abide by the treaties they had signed in the early seventeenth century. Therefore, with wars breaking out around them, the Portuguese and the Indian states had to develop a new diplomacy of opportunism.

The Portuguese now discovered that a strategy of divide and rule was being followed by the Indian states towards them and the northern Europeans. Whenever there was a Dutch or English embassy at the court of any Malabar ruler, the Portuguese would immediately send an embassy to curtail any progress made, as well as to try to remind the rulers of their former relationship with Portugal. Now, however, this was done with gestures of friendship and not by sending soldiers to teach them lessons. And when any of the northern kingdoms, such as that of Bijapur or Ahmadnagar were under Mughal attack, the Portuguese sided with the former so that there was always a barrier between the Mughals and their own territories. As a result, the kingdoms of Bijapur and Ahmadnagar accepted the Portuguese demands to expel the Dutch and the English emissaries. On the other hand, when the Portuguese destroyed or captured any property or ships belonging to these states, they immediately showed their eagerness to accept the northern European ambassadors at their court and to provide them with commercial and political privileges, all of which added to Portuguese anxieties.

A different policy was pursued when neighbouring states, such as the Kanara and Bijapur, were at war with each other. Then the Portuguese would often provide support to both of them or sometimes to only one, depending upon the situation, so that neither state became threat to their own settlements. The same diplomatic strategy can be found in the reactions of the Portuguese to the growing conflict between Bijapur and the Marathas. They sent military aid or offered asylum to Shivaji if he was fighting against the Mughals or even against the Sultans of Bijapur, but they also sent help to Bijapur if their own interest was threatened by the forces of Shivaji. Therefore, as mentioned above, if the Portuguese were in need of allies against the European companies, they would send ambassadors with sumptuous presents to the kings, whom they nevertheless still despised, while, when the Indian rulers needed Portuguese help, the Portuguese would delay to the point that the Indians would almost beg for assistance. Such strategies created great resentment against Portugal's opportunistic diplomacy and that is why the Indian states waited for the right opportunity to expel the Portuguese in spite of all the treaties they had signed.

Among the reasons for the deterioration of Portuguese relations with the Indian states, and for the failure to maintain their commerce in the second half of the sixteenth century, was the almost total abandonment of the *Estado da Índia* by the rulers of Portugal who concentrated on supporting their Brazilian settlements. Many historians such as Boxer, Poonen, Pearson and even Subrahmanyam are of the opinion, as the documents also reveal that the kings of Portugal, after the second half of the sixteenth century, gave priority to Brazil and almost abandoned India, failing to send supplies sufficient even for preserving what they already possessed. And Poonen has commented that, "had it not been for the missionaries, the Portuguese king would perhaps have abandoned India much earlier than the date of their eventual overthrow".[1074]

Portuguese relations with the St. Thomas Christians and even with Indians converted to Catholicism were full of caste and class prejudices. Teotonio de Souza[1075] and Charles Borges are of the opinion that the converted Christians were not treated with either respect or dignity.[1076] They were treated according to the caste to which they belonged before they were converted to Christianity. The hostility displayed by the Portuguese not only towards non-Christians but even towards their own Christian converts was one of the reasons that the Portuguese alienated even the local Christian community.

During the first encounter between Vasco da Gama and the Zamorin, da Gama had made it clear that Christian rulers were accustomed to receive ambassadors in private and in the presence of only a few courtiers who had the ruler's confidence, and not in front of whole court. However, in time the Portuguese learnt to follow the oriental pattern of diplomacy by receiving ambassadors in full court, which was how most of the Asian rulers, except the Chinese, used to receive them. Initially the Portuguese were reluctant to give sumptuous presents to the Indian rulers or to diplomats visiting the viceregal court and this was considered a lack of respect and even an insult to the rulers. Normally Indian rulers received ambassadors lavishly and sent back presents of the same or greater value than those they had received. Through this, they wanted to show both that they felt honoured with what they had received and that they possessed wealth and power superior to the country of the visiting ambassador. Eventually the Portuguese came to appreciate the problems their behaviour caused and in the seventeenth century were accustomed to send costly presents to the Indian rulers who reciprocated in kind. Nevertheless, although the Portuguese began to observe Indian diplomatic practice in the seventeenth century, this was only because they were forced to do so by circumstances and not because they wanted to, as is made quite obvious in the *Conselho do Estado's* reports.

In this world of increasing commercial and diplomatic competition, the Portuguese seldom respected the general norms of commerce. They themselves were in no position to buy all the Asian merchandise but they wanted to impose taxes on its circulation and refused to allow the Dutch and the English to trade without paying duties. They also wanted to force the rulers of India to restrict their diplomatic ties to states approved by Portugal. The idea that they were entitled to do this was not accepted by the Indian rulers nor even by sensible Portuguese of the seventeenth century who thought that, 'if the Indian rulers welcomed the Dutch at their courts, it was due to their [Portuguese's] own brutalities and excesses committed against those rulers for decades'.[1077] There are several occasions when rulers like the Zamorin of Calicut,[1078] the Sultans of Bijapur and Ahmadnagar, the king of Cannanore,[1079] and the Venkatappa Nayaka, tried to show their friendship by refusing any commercial facilities in their state to the northern Europeans as they were at peace with the Portuguese.[1080] In 1623, the Sultans of Ahmadnagar, Bijapur and Golconda even formed an alliance to expel the Dutch and the English from their territories.[1081] In 1638, the Sultan of Bijapur refused a pact with the Dutch against the Portuguese after which the Portuguese authorities thanked him by sending an important ambassador and rich presents. However, such deeds were forgotten by the Portuguese as soon as anything more lucrative, confiscating a rich ship for example, came to hand. Then the entire cycle of war and peace and diplomacy was repeated all over again.

The events of the 1620s and 1630s show how slowly and reluctantly the Portuguese changed the way they related to the neighbouring rulers - the *reis vizinhos*. In 1621, Fernão de Albuquerque, the Portuguese governor, while responding to the King's suggestion that it was important to maintain peaceful relations with the neighbouring kings,[1082] wrote, "we would only benefit if we were at peace with them so that we could divert all our forces against the enemies of Europe..."[1083] And he further added that "...maintaining good relations or friendships with these neighbouring kings is what we need most urgently."[1084] And there was no lack of sensible persons who understood the necessity of maintaining peace with the neighbouring kings and how that could be achieved. In the year 1625, a letter written from Goa, by someone whose identity is not revealed, further suggested that, "we should look for friendship and good rapport with the local Indian kings because having all of them against us is the sign of our total ruin and it will be like we never had anything at all".[1085]

However, in practice, diplomacy between the Portuguese and the Indian rulers continued to be based on suspicion and fear.

The Conde de Linhares, after his arrival to assume the office of Portuguese Viceroy in 1629, followed the policies of his predecessors, who believed in the use of force and in the policy of divide and rule, in order to maintain good relations with the neighbouring states of India, contrary to what had been stated by his recent fellow compatriot, Fernão de Albuquerque. In his efforts to renew diplomatic relations with the neighbouring states, Linhares first of all rebuilt the Portuguese navy which was in complete ruin, taking loans from the Indo-Portuguese community, *casados* and those who were in favour of the Portuguese presence, and followed this by a demonstration of naval power to make the Indian states realise that the Portuguese were still in command of the sea. In order to strengthen the Portuguese position, he made use of both force and diplomacy, to renew the old peace treaties with the various states, such as the Mughals, the sultans of Bijapur, the Nayakas of Ikkeri, the Zamorin of Calicut, and the rulers of Cannanore, Cranganore and Quilon. Though the Portuguese were losing their lucrative trade, their demonstration of maritime power could still be impressive, as could be observed during the expedition of the Conde de Linhares to the south to impose terms on the various kingdoms, which had repeatedly violated the treaties they had with Portugal, by allying with the English and the Dutch. The importance of this Portuguese diplomatic offensive can be imagined as even the Zamorin of Calicut, a century old enemy, extended his hand for friendship and offered to become a Christian[1086] as well as agreeing not to give any assistance to the other Europeans. This conversion does not seem ever to have materialized and was, probably, a trick that the Zamorin wanted to play with the Portuguese in order to gain some time, to reorganise his forces.

On the other hand, the Conde de Linhares was very careful, while dealing with Veerabhadra Nayaka of Ikkeri, who was in no mood to come to terms. However, his uncle Virappa Nayaka, who contested the succession to the throne, tried to obtain diplomatic and military support from all over southern India and this allowed the Portuguese Viceroy to play a double game, although very secretly, in order not to offend either claimant, as he was not sure which of them would establish himself as the ruler in future. His preference was for the Virappa Nayaka, who was more favourable to Portuguese interests.

In the 1632 the King wrote to the Conde de Linhares ordering him to adopt a policy of diplomacy towards the neighbouring kings, especially, he suggested, in relations with the Mughals, while at the same time he put forward the idea of secretly helping the rebel prince, Bolaqui, against the same Emperor.[1087] However, the Conde de Linhares suggested to the King that the only way the rulers of the East could be made to obey the western Christian powers was by force of arms.[1088] He further mentioned that "if we do not show off our power at sea more than what we have, I fear we may loose everything in an instant".[1089] He further added that "the recent violent confrontations, between the Portuguese Crown and the Dutch, have created terror in their minds and as a consequence they continue to obey us."[1090]

There is no doubt that the use of influential Indian families in diplomatic missions helped to strengthen the position of the *Estado da Índia* and enabled it to face the new challenges, thereby postponing its eventual downfall. Nevertheless, most of the measures, such as the use of diplomacy accompanied by sumptuous presents to the Indian kings, and the employment of Indians in the high diplomatic posts, were not as successful as they were intended to be. Too much wrong had already been done in the past. The weak and fractured relationships, coupled with a duplicitous diplomacy, undermined all their diplomatic efforts, as did the frequent capture of richly laden merchant ships in the Indian Ocean, a practice which the Portuguese foolishly continued during the seventeenth century and which frequently threatened to undermine their diplomacy.

Thus, in conclusion, it is clear from the early events in the Indian Ocean, that the Portuguese had something more in mind than simply conducting trade. Their diplomacy, based on creating rifts or taking advantage of already existing differences between the rulers and their subjects in India, was dangerous and irresponsible. In the long run it created suspicion and fragile relationships between those rulers and themselves. It was the Portuguese mentality that left them friendless, and led those who had any relations with them to favour the English and the Dutch.

The increasing expenditure on wars and expensive presents to the Sultans to retain their goodwill contributed to the serious deterioration in the military and financial situation of the Portuguese. Even under such circumstances, had they followed a consistent policy of diplomacy and friendship, instead of living in the shadow of their past maritime 'glory', they would probably have created some reliable allies to support them. However, their practice of providing military support to friends and foes at the same time destroyed the respect and trust of the Indian ruling class.

Instead, the contemptuous way they treated the people of the Bijapuri territories and the insulting words such, rascal, thief, greedy, faithless (*velhaco, ladrão, ganancioso, fementidos da fé*)[1091] etc. used to describe Indian diplomats and the governors of the surrounding territories of Ponda, Margão and Belgaon, even in their correspondence with the King, together with the treatment meted out to these authorities, from time to time, show their continuous hatred which led to a severe deterioration in their diplomatic relations with the Bijapuri sultans.

The religious policy of the Portuguese also alienated many potential supporters. Even though the Portuguese authorities knew well enough that the Indian kings and their subjects were not adherents of the same religion, they wanted to impose Christianity on them irrespective of the disastrous effects it had on their diplomatic relations. Frequently the Catholic Church spent more time worrying about converting the kings and their subjects or imposing bans on their marriage and religious ceremonies, than in trying to draw political and commercial benefits from their goodwill and friendship.

Given the bad relations that existed between the Portuguese and the *reis vizinhos* and the long term failure of their diplomacy, one may ask why it took so much time for the Dutch to dismantle the Portuguese "Empire"? The most important reason was the widely dispersed nature of the *Estado da Índia.* The Portuguese had numerous fortified towns from East Africa to China and it was difficult for the Dutch to concentrate enough military resources to attack them successfully. Had the Portuguese been concentrated at one point, it would have been easier for the Dutch to destroy them, but at the same time the Portuguese would have been able to unite their forces to face the Dutch. In either case the Dutch found they could not defeat the Portuguese except in alliance with the indigenous rulers in Asia.

Among the factors that enabled the Portuguese to survive were the major wars that erupted between the Sultans of Bijapur, the Nayakas of Ikkeri, the Maratha rulers Shahji and Shivaji and the Mughals to define and expand their territories. For this reason they required Portuguese arms and gunpowder, which the Portuguese were usually willing to provide in return for diplomatic and other concessions. However, eventually in the 1650s they had simultaneously to fight the Dutch and the Nayakas of Ikkeri they had insufficient resources and were forced to surrender all their positions in Ceylon and Kanara. When the Dutch found the time was right, they allied with the Zamorin whose ancestors had always dreamt of throwing the Portuguese out of Malabar and expelled the Portuguese from all their strongholds on the south-western coast.

Therefore, one might conclude by saying that the Portuguese prolonged their stay as "masters" of the sea and controllers of Indian seaborne commerce, due to the support of certain groups in India, mostly Hindu Brahmins and the Euro-Asian populations of Indian Christians, and the fact that that the Indian rulers fought among themselves for an extended period of time. This way they kept the Portuguese armament factory active, provided the Portuguese with a good income and enabled a balance of power to be maintained vis á vis Portugal's European enemies. But in the end it was the Indian rulers allied with the Dutch, who put an end to a hundred and fifty years of Portuguese maritime and commercial dominance. Nevertheless, a new era had already begun in the Indian history with a new system of warfare, diplomacy, espionage by the religious missionaries and above all a new controlled commercial policy which took root and obliged the Indians to change their mentality, assume it and survive.

Reference

1069 Quoted from Mathew, (edited) *Indian Ocean and Cultural Interaction*, p. XVI..

1070 Razzak, *Roteiro marítimo-geográfico da região do Índico*, (*Passim*); Varthema, *Travels of Ludoviço di Varthema in Egypt, Syria, …*, (*Passim*); see Mathew, (edited) *Indian Ocean and Cultural Interaction* .., pp. XVI.

1071 Luís Adão da Fonseca, 'Os commandos da Segunda armada de Vasco da Gama À Índia (1502-1503)', in *Mare Liberum*, vol. I6, pp. 12-13.

1072 Luís Adão de Fonseca, ' Vasco da Gama: uma Biografia Fantástica', in *Oceanos, Vasco da Gama*, n° 33, p. 77.

1073 ANTT, *As Gavetas da Torre do Tombo*, (ed.) Silva Rego, vol. IV (gav. XV, Maços 1-15), pp. 213-221; Sanjay 'Making India Gama, The Project of Dom Aires da Gama (1519) and its meaning' in *Mare Liberum*, vol. I6, pp. 33-55.

1074 Poonen, *A survey of the rise of the Dutch power in Malabar: 1603-78*, p. 5.

1075 Teontonio R. D'Souza, 'The Voiceless in Goan Historiography' in *Indo-Portuguese History: Sources & Problems*, (ed. John Correia-Affonso), pp. 114-131.

1076 Charles J. Borges, 'Foreign Jesuits and Native Resistance in Goa, 1542-1759,' in *Essay in Goan History*, (Ed. T.R. D'Souza), pp. 69-80

1077 See full ext in the last paragraph. *ACE*, vol. II, doc. 106, (p. 319): Goa 11 de Julho de 1642.

1078 *LMG*, cod. 12, fols. 21-24: *Carta do Vice-rei da Índia, D. Jerónimo de Azevedo, para El-rei..*

1079 *LMG*, cod. 6-A, fol. 116, Lisboa, 23 de Dezembro de 1606.

1080 *LML, cod.15*, fols. 42v°-43: 15 De Dezembro de 1620. It is held by several historians that the Indian rulers always violated the treaties signed with the Portuguese because they entertained the English and the Dutch into their territories. However, it is not true as the document below shows. Venkatappa Nayaka even when he had attacked the territories of the Banghel King refused the supply of pepper to the English Company providing the reason that he had signed a treaty of peace with the Portuguese and had a contract with them for the same purpose.

1081 *LML*, cod. 21, fols. 1: *Carta Régia para o Vice Rey da Índia*, Lisboa, primeiro de Março de 1625.

1082 *LML*, cod. 13, fols. 114v°-115v°: *Carta do Rey Filipe para o Conde viso rei da Índia*, 5 de Março de 620.

1083 *"so hauia vantagem em os ter quietos para poder virar as armas contra os inimigos da Europa"*; *LML*, cod. 15, fols. 17v°, 10 de Fevereiro de 1621.

1084 "a material da boa correspondencia com os Reis vizinhos lhe hera sobre todas as maes mui presente" LML, cod. 15, fols. 17v°: Carta do

Vise-rei, Fernão de Albuqeurque para a El-Rei, Recomendava el-rei boa amizade com os reis vizinhos. O governador assim procedia. 10 de Fevereiro de 1621.

1085 "*Deue-se procurar a amizade e correspondencia com os Reis naturais da India porque ter a todos por contrarios he sinal de grande ruina e de se não hauer feito como convuem.*" ANTT, *Colecção São Vicente*, cod. 19, fol. 388.

1086 *ACE*, vol. I1, doc. 36.

1087 Carta de Filipe III (IV of Spain) *para o Conde de Linhares*, 28 de Fevereiro de 1632, fol. 4; *LMG*, cod. 19-A, fols. 55-55v°: *Carta do Rei Filipe IV para o vise-rei, D. Miguel de Noronha*, 24 de Dezembro de 1633.

1088 *LMG*, cod. 19-A, fol. 31: *Carta do Vice-rei, o conde Linhares ao El-Rey*, Goa.

1089 "*se não fizera ostentações mostrando mais poder do que uerdadeiramente temos podera cair esta grão machina...*" *LML*, cod. 29, fls. 103 and 137: *Carta do Vice-rei, o conde Linhares ao El-Rey*, Goa 17 de Dezembro de 1631.

1090 "*os violentos confrontos entre as forças da Coróa portuguesa e os olandeses infundiam-lhes terror e contribuiam para os manter na sujeição ao rei de Portugal*" I have quoted from the summary of Maria Manuela Sobral Blanco, *O Estado Português da India: da Rendição de Ormuz a Perda de Cochin, 1622-1663*, (unpublished thesis) pp. 552, who has quoted from *LMG*, cod. 19-A, fol. 3: *Carta do conde de Linhares ao El-Rey*. Goa 29 de Nouembro de 1634.

1091 *ACE*, vol. I, doc. 154.

Glossary

Almirante : Admiral of a Portuguese fleet.

Armada: Armada or navy.

Arthshastra: The science of polity and economy. This word is derived from Sanskrit.

Arzi: a message, a request, information.

Ashrafis: Gold/silver coins, circulated between Arabia and China till the twentieth century. See appendixes II-C & D, for its counter values in Asia.

Bahar/Bhar: It was a weight used in the Kanara and Malabar regions. In today's terms, it was almost 117 kgs. See appendix II-E.

Bazar: Market place.

Cabedal: Money, wealth (It also means leather) which was destined to buy some Asian product. Well known use of this word is *Cabedal da Pimenta* (or the money to buy pepper).

Cáfila: It literally means the caravan, or a group of people, merchants or ships travelling together from one place to another or from one port to another.

Caixa: Box, especially to keep documents in the Archives.

Capitão-mor: Captain-major of a Portuguese ship or fortress.

Cartaz: A navicert or passport, issued by the Portuguese authorities for a non-Portuguese ship or ships to travel in the Indian Ocean.

Casado(s): It literally means a married man or men. This term was mostly used for the Portuguese bachelors who used to marry women of Indian (and or Asian) origin.

Casados e moradores: Men who married and settled in India or any part of Portuguese Asian settlements.

Comissão: Commission or a body of Portuguese officers selected to take charge of the government of Portuguese *Estado da Índia* in the interregnum between Viceroys.

Conde: Count, a member of the Portuguese nobility.

Conselho da Fazenda: The Council of Finance / Revenue Council. The body that used to decide financial matters.

Conselho do Estado: The Council of State/State Council. The body that used to decide all the administrative and commercial matters. It was this body that also used to take political and diplomatic decisions of the Portuguese *Estado da Índia*.

Cruzado: A Portuguese gold and silver coin which had been minted in the Portuguese mint-houses in Asia for the purchase of Asian goods. It was a Portuguese coin. For its counter value in the sixteenth and the seventeenth centuries, see appendix, II-B.

Degredados: Condemn, Degraded. Person(s) convicted on the charge of some serious crimes in Portugal.

Descendentes: Descendents. People of a Portuguese origin in Asia or in any continent other than Europe.

Desembargador: A Portuguese judge of the High court.

Dharma: Religion, Good deeds.

***Dhokande Raya* and *Daneja*.** Protector and saviour of the land and people (a title assumed by Venkatappa Nayaka)

Embaixador: Ambassador.

Estado da Índia: Portuguese colonial dominance in Asia and Eastern Africa is commonly known as the *Estado da Índia,* which denominated an area from Mozambique in the South-east African coast till Macao in China. Mozambique became a separate governorship in the eighteenth century and Macau in 1864.

Farmán: A royal order issued by a Muslim ruler.

Fidalgo: A Portuguese nobleman.

Gentios: Gentiles. A term used for the non-Christians, especially for the Hindus of India.

Governador: Governor.

Instruções: Instructions issued by the Portuguese kings or the Portuguese Viceroys to their subordinate officers when they were sent on some especial missions or to take charge of an office.

Jagat Guru: Professor of the Universe, or a spiritual guide in a Hindu kingdom.

Jaziya: A tax levied in the medieval period by the Muslim rulers on their Hindu subjects as a compensation of not being converted to Islam.

Khandi(s): It is also written as ***Candil,*** a weight used in the Kanara regions. In today's terms it would be around 220 kgs. See appendix II-E.

Khufia: It means secret.

Ladroeira: It literally means den of robbers or robbery, or even extortion. In India the Portuguese used this term to denote all those who resisted Portuguese control of Asian commerce or responded to the Portuguese detentions of Asian shipping. They also gave this name to the Marakkar families who resisted the Portuguese and even robbed the Portuguese commercial ships. When the Marakkar family fought as the Zamorins admirals, the Portuguese called them *Piratas* (or pirates) but after the war of 1599, they referred to them as robbers or *Ladroeiras*.

Laws of Manu: The law by which Indians, especially Hindus, were governed until British rule. This law-book is based on the old Hindu scriptures, such as Vedas.

Maharaaj: It lierally means King of Kings. But this was another way of calling a Hindu Priest and also to King.

Mare Clausvm: Closed Sea. The theory that the sea should be governed by Portuguese laws. This theory was presented by João de Barros who claimed that Portugal's rights were based on various Bulls issued by the Popes in the fifteenth century.

Mare Liberum: Free Sea. This theory was elaborated presented by Hugo Grotious, (Huig de Groot, **or** Hugo de Groot) the Dutch lawyer and philosopher to contest the Portuguese idea of Mare Clausum. He formulated a new principle, claiming that the sea was international territory and all nations were free to use it for seafaring and trade.

Mensageiro: Messenger or carrier of royal messages to another state.

Mouros: It was a general term used by the Portuguese to describe Muslims

Muni: Learned and highly respected persons of the Indian society. This was another way of calling to a **Rishi.**

Nayar/Nair: a race especially from Malabar. The Zamorin of Calicut belonged to this race. They were considered to be of a lower caste than the Xatriya or those who belonged to the ruling castes. It also meant the same as Nayaka.

Nayaka: Chief or ruler of a Kanara state.

Omerahs: (same as *Omrahs*) The same as nobles or ***Vizirs*** or ministers.

Pagoda: It was a gold coin of Malabar from very ancient times. It also means a Pagoda or a Hindu Temple. See appendix II-D, for its price.

Pardaos: This was another gold coin which circulated during the Portuguese period throughout Asia. See appendix II-B, for its counter value.

Procurador: Procurator. An attorney or person deputed by the Portuguese state to deal the official matters between two states.

Raaj Guru: Teacher/ Adviser of the kingdom.

Rajao/Rajá/Raja/: it means a king of a Hindu state. Sometimes Muslims also used the title, such as Ali Raja of Cannanore.

Rakhi: A sacred thread denoting a bond of love between brother and sister. It is also a Hindu festival.

Regimento: Set of rules drawn up by the king to regulate the conduct of officials or commanders.

Reino: Kingdom. In Portuguese sources it is often used by itself to refer to Portugal only.

Reis vizinhos: This term was used to refer the Indian kings and kingdom that had their geographical boundaries adjacent to Portuguese dominated areas.

Renegados: Renegated. A Portuguese, who had accepted to work for a non-Portuguese and especially, with a non-Chrisitian employer.

Rishi: A Rishi can be regarded as a combination of a patriarch, a priest, a preceptor, an author of Vedic hymns, a sage, a saint, an ascetic, a prophet and a hermit into a single person.

Ruqqa-i-Rasan: Bearer of personal message.

Sabha Pandit: Court Priest.

Safir: Ambassador. The origin of this word is Arabic. It could also mean messenger, depending upon the type of information an official from any Muslim state was carrying.

Sultão: Sultan.

Vakil-us-Saltanat: It explicitly means the Lawyer of the Kingdom. This post in the Mughal Empire was known as Amir-ul *Umerah*, or the Prime-Minister.

Varnasharam: Hindus caste system

Vassalo: Vassal.

Veda: The Vedas are the ancient scriptures or revelation (Shruti) of the Hindu teachings. There are four Vedas; Rig Veda, Sama Veda, Yajur Veda and Atharva Veda, each consisting of four parts.

Vedor da Fazenda: Inspector or overseer of the Portuguese treasury and or royal property.

Vizir/Wizir: Prime-minister or it could also used for a simple minister.

Vizir-e-Kharja: foreign minister.

Xerafim: It is a Portuguese name for ***Ashrafi.*** See Appendix II-C & D for its international market value.

Samorin/Samorim/Samudri/Zamorin: it means ruler, but the only state that had the right to use this title was the Zamorin of Calicut.

All the documents, especially in the appendices

I-A, I-B, I-C,

II-A,

III-A,

IV-A, IV-B, IV-C, IV-D,

V-A, V-B, V-C, V-D, V-E and V-F,

to the best of my knowledge,

have never been published and,

have been used in the present work.

Appendix I-A

Additional Information on the Available sources

Besides what has been discussed in chapter I, the present appendix has been created to provide some additional information about the sources dicrectly related to the Portuguese Asian history and remained pioneering for almost a century.

F.C.Danvers, a British imperial civil servant made a major contribution to the understanding of Portuguese-Indian relations through a compilation entitled *Report to the Secretary of State for India,* which provides information about the documents relating to Portuguese Asian history, preserved in the *Arquivo Nacional da Torre de Tombo, Biblioteca Nacional de Lisboa* and *Arquivo e Biblioteca Distrital de Évora.*[1092] In reality, this is a brief history of the Portuguese in Asia, totally based on the *Documentos Remettidos da Índia* and other series from the above mentioned archives and libraries. As a matter of fact, Danvers has simply translated letters of Viceroys into English which clearly narrates the Portuguese colonial history beginning from the sixteenth until the early nineteenth century that he later amplified and published in his *The Portuguese in India*. The *Letters Received by the East India Company,*[1093] in six volumes, is another documentary collection edited by Danvers of value to researchers, though it is only a calendar of papers. This is a collection of the correspondence preserved at the British Library, India Office collection.

Raymundo António de Bulhão Pato while directing the publication of one of the most renowned collections in the *Arquivo Nacional da Torre do Tombo, Documentos Remettidos da Índia,*[1094] was also editing Albuquerque's correspondence which he could not complete in his life time. Bulhão Pato, in addition, also wrote *Portuguezes na Índia* which concentrated on the Portuguese as conquerors and discoverers.

In Goa, the director of the archives, J.H. da Cunha Rivara, much earlier had started compiling some of the most notable and useful documents in a nine volume series entitled, *Arquivo Portuguêz Oriental*.[1095] This collection contains hundreds of documents pertaining to the Portuguese in Asia in general, and India in particular, especially dealing with the diplomatic, economic and cultural aspects of the areas under Portuguese control. These documents were selected from different collections in the Goa Archives, namely, *Os Reis Vizinhos, Tissuari, Livros Grandes de Pazes,* and *Livros de Pazes* which cover the period from the sixteenth till the early nineteenth centuries. It is worth noting here that a number of the documents relating to Portuguese diplomatic relations with the *Reis Vizinhos* were subsequently included by Biker in the fourteen volumes of his *Colleção de Tratados e Concertos de Pazes.* Therefore, it is no surprise if a researcher comes across a document in Biker, which he has already found in Cunha Rivara. Later Bragança Pereira followed the footsteps of Cunha Rivara in the same archives and published eleven volumes[1096] of documents dealing with the political and military history of the Portuguese in the sixteenth and seventeen centuries in India. In volume four of this series he reproduced the manuscript compiled by António Bocarro[1097] which contains a detailed account of the income and expenditure and of the resident Portuguese population in the fortresses in India, together with the maps of most of those fortresses.

Archival Sources:

Various scholars have referred to the importance of the inventories of the archival collections of the *Biblioteca Nacional* and the Archives of Goa. In 1928, the year when many of the most important studies on the Portuguese expansion appeared, the first ever *Inventário* was produced by M.A. Hedwig Fitzler and Ernesto Ennes.[1098] This is one of the best *Inventários* of the codices pertaining to India in the *Biblioteca Nacional* of Lisbon, of which a great part is now housed in the *Arquivo Histórico Ultramarino.* Much later, in 1952, Boxer picked up the idea of publishing another inventory pertaining to the documents of the Goa Archives.[1099] Although very brief, he gives an idea of the collection and of the period covered by those series of documents. This inventory of Boxer was more accessible to a wider range of scholars as it was in English. It was sufficient to inspire Panduronga Pissurlenkar, then director of the archives, to venture on the preparation of an exhaustive *Roteiro*[1100] (detailed catalogue) on the pattern of Fitzler and Ennes. This *Roteiro* is a complete picture of the Archives of Goa, although some of the series like, *Livros Pequenos* and *Livros Grandes de Pazes,* to which Cunha Rivara had so frequently referred, are not included. This very useful inventory of the archives is unfortunately now out of print. Much later, V.T. Gune, the director of the Goa Archives after Pissurlenkar, in order to make the *Roteiro* available in English, published a brief handbook, *A Guide to the Collections of Records from the Goa Archives,*[1101] similar to the one Boxer had published almost twenty years before, but including most of the new acquisitions of the Archives. However, by far the most complete guide to the archives of Goa, as well as to the various archives of Spain, England, Rome, France and various others, is undoubtedly the *Boletim da Filmoteca Ultramarina,* started by António da Silva Rego, and still continuing under the auspices of the *Junta da Investigação Científica Tropical,* which has now surpassed its fifty-fifth volume and is available on CD. This *Boletim* provides a brief summary of the documents of the various collections. In this series Silva Rego also published three of the five codices of the series of *Reis Vizinhos,* which pertain to the treaties, signed between the late seventeenth and the middle of the nineteenth centuries, between the *Estado da Índia* and the states surrounding Goa, especially the Maratha Empire.

Though a lot has been written about the *Livros das Monções,*[1102] pertaining to Goa Archives, it is difficult to describe their contents in detail. They are, basically, a collection of the official correspondence between the Portuguese Viceroys in India and the King of Portugal. However, besides the reports on official matters, this collection focuses on diplomatic and political questions. The instructions of the Kings to the Portuguese viceroys and governors in India about how they should handle diplomatic relations with the neighbouring Kings, as well as their responses, are all well documented in this series as are their impressions of the Indian rulers during the diplomatic meetings. It is through this series that one comes to know the real intentions of the Portuguese and what they thought of the Indian rulers. However, this correspondence does not contain the details of the treaties signed between the states. Besides describing Portuguese political and economic relations with the Asian merchants and rulers, the correspondence gives ample information about Portuguese relations with the English and Dutch from the early seventeenth century. There are about 450 volumes but only 48 volumes belong to the period of the present study. Moreover, there is a problem if one wants to depend totally on this series. There is a gap between 1617 and 1629, when there are hardly any documents.[1103] Therefore, a researcher is bound to depend on the Lisbon *códices* of this series. However, the information is scattered in different codices and a researcher has to look into each of them.

Documentos Remetidos da Índia or *Livros das Monções* from the *Torre do Tombo* in Lisbon is also a collection of considerable importance. Though some of the documents are the duplicates of those in the Goa *Monções*, there are a considerable number of documents which are not found in the Goa series and are very useful for Portuguese relations with the English and the Dutch in the East. This series consists of 62 bound volumes and all of them belong to the seventeenth century.

One of the most valuable manuscript collections used for this work are the *Livros dos Reis Vizinhos* from the Goa Archives where one can find a considerable amount of information regarding the treaties and the movement of embassies that took place during the seventeenth century.[1104] For those who cannot travel to Goa, this collection can be consulted at the Filmoteca Ultramarina Portuguesa in Lisbon. This collection consists of almost 22 bound volumes of manuscripts, but I have consulted only the first six, as the rest of them belong to the eighteenth and the nineteenth centuries. The collection *Os Regimentos* from the same Archives is another source of great value to the researcher. It furnishes information regarding the political conditions of the Portuguese as well as the Indian governments, besides the diplomatic understandings reached between the various states during the period from the sixteenth to the nineteenth centuries. Biker's *Colleção de Tratados e Concertos de Pazes*, as I have mentioned earlier, is a mine of information in fourteen volumes and alone stands as one of the major sources of information for the present study. As it covers a long period, only the first five volumes have been consulted in filling the gaps left by the other manuscripts. The *Archivo Português Oriental* of both Cunha Rivara and Bragança Pereira has also been used for the preparation of the present work. They fill gaps in the documents contained in the *Livros das Monções* and the *Livros dos Reis Vizinhos*. The collection of *Livros Grandes de Pazes,* although they do not provide a chronological series of documents on the treaties signed between the Portuguese and the various states of India, have been very useful for the present work and were published by Cunha Rivara in the *Boletim do Governo do Estado da Índia* between 1873 and 1875. Besides the above mentioned series, *Livros dos Regimentos e Instruções, Livros dos Assentos do Conselho do Estado* have also been consulted from the collection of Goa Archives. Even though these series have been made available by Pissurlenkar under the title, *Assentos do Conselho do Estado,* so far most scholars have overlooked its importance for the diplomatic relations of the Portuguese in India. I found this series one of the most important as it was through the *Conselho do Estado* that all the diplomatic and administrative decisions were taken. It was this *Conselho* that issued orders and instructions to the ambassadors going on any diplomatic missions and, before receiving any ambassadors from the neighbouring states, met to decide when to receive the incoming ambassador and what reception should be given to him. It is also, through the reports of this *Conselho do Estado* that we come to know the real intentions and feelings of the Portuguese authorities in relation to the Indian states. The correspondence between the Portuguese and the neighbouring Kings provides us with weaker picture of what the Portuguese had in mind than can be obtained from the reports of the *Conselho do Estado*. Quite often, the Portuguese decided to send an embassy to the various courts, sometimes just to convey greetings, but they could not be sent because of their financial situation. This would be discussed during the Council's meeting. Such information is rarely found in other collections. Even the information about the Portuguese maintaining spies at the various courts of India, has been known mainly through this series. Therefore this series has furnished information that was not to be found in any of the other records.

Various factory records and travel diaries have also been used in depicting the seventeenth century political and socio-economic situation. These have been listed in the bibliography at the end of this work.

Reference

1092 Frederick C. Danvers, (ed.) *Report to the Secretary of State for India in Council on the Portuguese records relating to the East Indies, contained in the Archivo da Torre do Tombo, and the public libraries at Lisbon and Evora,* Eyre and Spottiswoode, London 1892.

1093 Danvers, *Letters Received by the East India Company from it's Servants in the East, 1602-1615,* 6 vols. London, 1896.

1094 Raymundo A. Bulhão Pato, (ed.) *Documentos Remettidos da Índia ou Livro das Monções,* 1-V vols. 1880-95, which corresponds to the first 11 codex of the same from ANTT, and later during the years 1974-78, it was followed by António da Silva Rego. He edited from 12 till 18 codexes of the same Archives. In published form they are from Tomo VI to Tomo IX; *Cartas de Afonso de Albuquerque.* 7 vols., (ed.) Raymundo António de Bulhão Pato.; *Portuguezes na Índia,* Imp. Nac., Lisboa, 1883.

1095 J. H. da Cunha Rivara, (ed.) *Arquivo Português Oriental,* 6 vols. in 9 parts, Nova Goa, 1857-1876.

1096 A. B. de Bragança Pereira, (ed.) *Arquivo Português Oriental,* 11 vols., Tip. Rangel, Bastorá, Goa, 1936-1940.

1097 *O livro das plantas de todas as fortalezas, cidades e povoações do Estado da Índia Oriental.* This work has also been published separately by various authors.

1098 M.A. Hedwig Fitzler and Ernesto Ennes, *A Secção Ultramar da Biblioteca Nacional,* Sep. Anais Bibliotecas e Arquivos, n° 8, Biblioteca Nacional, Lisboa, 1928.

1099 Boxer, *A glimpse of the Goa archives* - Sep. de Bulletin of the School of Oriental and African Studies, XIV, June 1952, pp. 299-324.

1100 Pissurlenkar, *Roteiro dos Arquivos da Índia Portuguesa,* Tipografia Rangel, Bastorá, 1955.

1101 V. T. Gune, *A guide to the collections of records from the Goa archives,* Panaji, Historical Archives of Goa, 1973.

1102 *Monções,* literally means the Monsoon. This collection is called Monsoon series due to the fact that the ships from Portugal bound to India arrived just before the setting in of the Monsoons in the month of June and left for Portugal soon after it was over, by early September. Therefore, the correspondences that left from Portugal or India were named after the season. There is no other special explanation for the origin of the name of this collection.

1103 *Códice* 12 provides information for the years 1613-1617, and the codices 13-A passes right away to the years 1629-1630. Therefore, there is almost a 12 years gap in information.

1104 HAG, *Livros dos Reis Vizinhos,* 1-8.

Appendix I-B[1105]

This is a correspondence between the Conde Linhares and the King of Portugal, Philip IV of Spain, in which he reveals his intentions to create intrigues between the two contestants for the throne of Ikkeri, Veerabhadra Nayaka and his uncle Virappa Nayaka. The same behaviour is noticed between the ruling King and the heir to the throne of Cochin. This letter also gives a glimpse of the journey that the Conde de Linhares made to the South Indian States: starting from Goa, passing through the states of Kanara, Cannanore, Cranganore, Calicut and ending in Cochin, he tried to bring all the dissatisfied states to accept terms. In addition, he also tried to provision all the fortresses and factories which were in a bad condition.

Sr.

Em cinco de Março passado despachey de Barcelor a Ruy Lopes da Silva per terra leuasse a V. Magestade a carta de que com esta será a cópia a que me torno a Remetter, porque dou nella conta a V. Magestade de tudo o que obrey athe a particular das nãos the aquella hora.

Continnue em Barçelor com a pratica das pazes fazendo ciúmes a Virapanaique com as que auia de fazer a Virabadranaique, e a Virabadranaique com as que auia de fazer a Virapanaique e tanto pollo que me aconselhaua o Conselho que me assiste, como pollo alhar com mais poder, e mais justiça; com esta vay copia das pazesem que me parece fiz particular serviço a V. Magestade porque não só Vency partidos de authoridade, credito, e fazendas mas em mesmo deter ao primeiro acesso letiguey com as pessoas com que V. Magestade aqui me manda aconselhar, porque o medo, e respeito que aqui setinha aos Canaras, tomando se por exemplo o successo de Mangalor, e outros mais authorizados em que eu vi ouça ordem, fazia entender que tinhão elles grande superioridade armada de V. Magestade siruase V. Magestade por me fazer mercê de mandar se comuniquem estas pazes a alguns homens que estiuerão por estas partes por sabendo as declarar, conhecera V. Magestade que em hua mínima palaura dellas servey a V. Magestad com industria, actiuidade, e rezolução. Pareceo me cõveniente alem dos poderes com que os Embaixadores as celebrarão que o que o mesmo Rey as confirmasse, com título de Embaixador mandei Balthezar Marinho que serue de Procurador dos Contos que por andar com as couzas da pimenta os annos atrás estaua capaz da se tentar daquella partes, e como com as Reis da Índia se não negoçea nada sem se lhes darem prezentes primeiro, mandey pello Balthezar Marinho a aquelle Rey seis cavalos, e outras peças de menor porte, e com a pessoa de Balthezar Marinho, e dos que acompanharão entendo que faria despeza a V. Magestade de athe seis mil Xerafins, mais pudera ella valor senão sufrira minha fazenda com algumas couzas que não refiro, porque hé obrigação minha servir V. Magestade com a vida, com entendimento, e com a fazendas, foi bem recebido Balthezar Marinho, e com festas particulares e extraordinárias confirmarão se as pazes, e deu aquelle Rey porque o appontey eu assy para os Capitães da armada que leuarão navios a sua custa vinte e hum mil, quatro centos, e cincoenta Xerafins os quais se repartirão na forma que V. Magestade verá do Rol incluzo, e não foi a partida igual porque a sua despeza delles foi desigual.

Quando nestas pazes senão ganhara tanto, como vemos de prezente, e esperamos de facto /fols. 1v°/ por se segurar mantimentos para este Inverno a Goa, e a todas as mais fortalezas de V. Magestade forão ellas prezentemente necessárias, porque a esterilidade por falta dagoa foi de maneira que só no Reino de Cambaya se affirma são mortas de fome mais de quatrocentas mil almas.

No tempo que durou minha assistência em Barçelor, mandey continuar com a fortaleza de são Miguel de Cambolim, tem já feitos três baluartes, e os quatro passos de muro e por falta de pedra que não chegou de Goa, está indo informa aquella fortalezae acabar se há com o fauor de Deus brevemente, e fica já capaz para qualquer sucesso, e tirar lhe hey parte de guarnição que de prezente tem que há de cincoenta homens Portuguezes, e de cento e vinte espiguardeiros de salsete, por dentro do Rio e costa braua vy de toda a Ilha, e para se segurar convem tenha outra fortificação na parte por onde se faz península, e estreita aly tanto a terra ou hua restinga darea que com hua terra com doze soldados fica toda Ilha guardada, e com portas, cerco que dentro de breues annos renderá a V. Magestade muitos mil Xerafins e agora de prezente não só com o que paga se fará a despeza dos prezidios, mas ainda se hirá poupando para satisfazermos as despezas das obras, e das muitas gentes que aly assistio ategora em que se gastou muito.

No rio de Barçelor que tinha duas legoas de Barçelor se hauião recolhido doze parós de Malauares, mandey com hum toco darmada de que era Capitão Manoel da Câmara tomar lhe a barra, trattey com os capitães de fortalezas de Bacanor[1106] e de Calinia[?] por que estão naquelle rio que me entregassem os parós, e os Malavares, e porque Calinia por obedecia a Virabadranaique, e Bacanor a Virapanaique, as tinham sitiadas a gente delRey Banguel, do Rey da Serra, e a Rainha da Carnate cada hum dos Capitães das fortalezas estua com pensamento de que os Malavares o ajudassem. E assy se resolverão a mos não entregar, com o que me pareçeo conveniente mandar que a armada arremetesse com os parós, e os queimasse por estarem a bicados em terra trattarão de os defender, porem como mandey com rezolução e sahirão em terra quinhentos homens Portuguezes, fizerão retirar o enimigo, e sem sahir ninguém ferido fizerão em cinza os parós de que senão descontentou Virappanaique antes me deu satisfações offerçendo castigar ao Capitão de Bacanor porque os não entregou.

Passey a Mangalor vizitey aquella fortaleza, e provy a de neçessario. E posto que me detive aly dous dias não pode vir El Rey Banguel a vizitarme por estar desvio daly dez ou doze legoas, mandei lhe mostrar as capitulações das pazes porque respeito do que me pedio per carta sua de que com esta vay copia, e mettey nellas e aos Reys seus aliados, e do estado. Passey a Cananor vizitey a fortaleza que achey mal trattada e velha, e ainda desbaratada, e com falta de todos os provimentos sendo que inda /fol.2/ dos que mandey em meu tempo havia poucos porque está introduzido na Índia ser pajens dos Capitães tomarem tudo o que tem nome de V. Magestade e porque são muy continuadas as queixas, e aly me fizerão outras particulares do procedimento de Adarajao que hé quasi Rey de hua povoação de Mouros que aly esta que chamão Bazar, posto que tributário a El Rey de Cananor, o mandey chamar para que se visse comigo na galé Real duvidou o Mouro, ou posto berbo, ou por medrozo, e sendo que vão o Guazil de El Rey de Cananor vizitarme em come de seu Rey por estar como entrenado, e impedido, o qual Guazil he superior ao ditto Adarrajao, agenciou que elle viesse a Galé e tendo assentado por meio do dito Guazil fazelo o outro dia, não só se resolueo a não vir, mas ainda amanhecerão feitas alguas fortificações, e trincheiras, e acreçentou gente de guerra, sendo que como affirmão todos estão naquella Bazar quatro mil mouros de armas, e como em tempo de outros Viso Reis tinha experiençia o AdaRajao que lhes ofrião descortezias, pareçeo conveniente que não saísse com esta, porque do dito bazar se armão, E fomentão todos os parós que nos fazem guerra, mandey arrimar as gales a terra. E os navios de remo que abria sem os esporões na praya, com as gales baty a pouoção e da fortaleza se fez a mesma baterias, e comtão somente duzentos homens, que amparados dos navios das embarcações, se poz logo a pouoação, e posto que de terra com três pessoas, respondião os mouros a bateria, e toda fizerão a minha galé foi Deus seruido que não ficasse ninguém lastimado, e como o fogo se ateou maneira dey que agente se retirasse a fortaleza havendo se perdido della tão somente hum cafre, e desviey para o mar a armada para dar lugar que os mouros acudissem a matar o logo por que se de todo ponto se queimara hua pouoação, não auia com que fazer concerto de pois, e ainda com toda esta minha diligencia não deixarão de arder e pereçer de todo cento e quatro cazas, e alguns palmares, todas as embarcações que estauão Varadas, a perda se avaliam em mais de trinta mil Xerafins no ponto que desiuey a armada, me veo buscar o Guazil a pedirme Misericórdia da parte do Adarrajao, respondi lhe que senão mostrasse obediência que de todo, queimaria a pouvoação, com o que Veyo o Adarrajao ao limite da fortaleza de V. Magestade e affirmou que tinhão prohibição de sua ley os que fossem cabeças daquelle bazar de entrar em embarcações com appontamentos, mandey se fosse ver no sitio da fortaleza com o AdaRajao, dom Francisco de Moura, Diogo de souza Menezes, Ruy dias da Cunha, E o secretario Ambrozio de Freitas, e assentarão as capitulações que V. Magesade mandara ver da copia incluza.

/fol. 2v°/

Party me a Cochim onde mandey logo dizer aquelles Rey por António de Pinho da Costa que aly tem servido a V. Magestade muitos annos de Vedor da fazenda, e com grande satisfação porque he pessoa muito capaz que vinha só dar lhe satisfação, e gosto no que tiuesse razão, porem também a pedir lhe satisfação dos agrauos feitos às lojas, e Christãos vassalos de V. Magestade respondeo me El Rey cortezias, e sentimentos das possibilidades de paralítico, e entrenado lhe não permittirem vir me a vizitar e que daria satisfações neceçarias, no dia seguinte me andou vizitar por quatro

Regedores seus, e por hum Judeu lingoa, e valido seu, offerçendo satisfações e que me informasse em da razão dellas de António de Pinho, e de Arcebispo da terra que estuão presentes, respondy que tanto me conformaua com o que sua alteza queria que eu nomearia por Juizes louvados no que eu ou elle podiamos querer as pessoas que elle appontaria, para que como practicas, e experimentadas as assentassem de modo que a amizade dos Reis de Cochim, e o amor de V. Magestade se mostrasse milhor em conformidade desta minha resposta, forão ver se com El Rey de Cochim que acharão tão fora de caminho como constara da resposta que deu às propostas com que fiquey obrigado a escreuer a carta de que vai a copia, e de outra que me respondeu a que também dissery como se verá dos treslados por meo do Arcebispo me perguntou se lhe pagaria dez copas vinte e três que se lhes estavão devendo, e importão 8550 Xerafins disse que de muito boa vontade, e que não só faria isto, mas que deixaria assento com o Arcebispo que cobrasse duas copas, e ficando extinta a divida gozasse hua na forma que V. Magestade lha dá, e havendo debaixo deste meu offereçimento assentado com o Arcebispo que faria toda razão às Igrejas, Christão, e Vassalos de V. Magestade a que tem forsado, sem resoluer despois a que não queria, como que me pareçeo deuia passar a prouizão que vay com esta em razão de lhe não correr a alfandega, e ordeney que senão rompesse com o Rey porem que se lhe não sofressem forsas, porque quando elle as faça se acudir´a ellas como convem, tenho entendido que o animo deste Rey está muito danado para tudo o do nome Christão eu fomenta muito o seu Judeu que se chama Samuel Castiel, e ainda de quem suspeito que teue com elle ontem alguma pratica, ou inteligência com olandezes, mas não há disso nenhua prova, verdade he que a tenho, que quando o Dachem sitiou Malaca o soube El Rey de Cochim muitos mezes antes que aqui se tivesse notíçia, e que o calou por se não fazer o soccoro que depois se fez sem o qual se entende que passara aquella fortaleza grande trabalho, detreminado estou fazer ciúmes a este Rey com trauar amizade com o seu Príncipe herdeiro, E este Julgo o muito mais comveniente para o reduzir, mande me V. Magestade, o que deue fazer nesta matéria.

/fol. 3/

Aquella cidade achey inumerada, e posto por ruim modo grande ciremisto, poucas belluartes, nem hua artilharia para se defender qualquer mao animo daquele Rey he bastante, deixey prevenido e adeuirtido o neçessario.

Os Clérigos daquella cidade estão inda de pior umor que Rey porque vivem sem consideração da consciençia, e indo os males segundo dizem são mayores, procurey encaminhalos mas pude poucos arazão, comtudo, lhe assentey o pagamento que sempre se lhes faz, e tão infaliuel que prometterão senão fechavão mais a Sé, convem muito Senhor que V. Magestade proveja de Bispo, e tal pessoa que tenha rezolução e Valor para encaminhar os muitos dos serviços de Nosso Senhor que aly há, e todos são nascidos das provizões que V. Magestade tem andado passar aos Bispos e Arcebispos para que os Viso Reis nomeem para benefícios, e dignidades os clérigos que nos elles apontarem, e como os Bispos appontão os a que com isto pagão obrigações estão os cabidos cheos de moços mestiços, e mal acustumados.

Nas vias que leuarão as nãos dos annos passados auizey a V Magestade que mandaua a Cranganor a António Monis Barreto para ouvir a proposta das pazes do Samorim que António Moniz trabalhou galhardamente, e tinha capitulado o papel que será com esta que aprovey e por o Samorim estar ocupado em certo a levantamento de Vassalos seus, tardarão os Commissarios que hão dejimar as pazes para que as acabe de celebrar. Deixey ainda em Cranganor a António Muniz Barreto, e com ellas feitas tenho para me que com menos de cuidado posso estar daqui até o Cabo do Camorym, e julgo que com os reféns de suas embarcações cumprirá o Samorim a palaura, inda que a natureza do Malavar lho encontre.

Provy Cranganor das munições neçessarias, e para Coulão enviey as que se me pedirão.

Quando voltey a Mangalor se vio comigo na galé El Rey Banguel, pareçeo me homem de entendimento, se bem na pratica, colhi que era homem de fraco coração, e porque achey nouas, e ainda debaixo das capitulações que refiro que Gennte delRey da Serra, e Rainha de Carnate tinha sitiado hua fortaleza de Virapanaique fiz as Lembranças e aduertencias neçessarias a El Rey Nabguel pois em respeito do que me elle hauia pedido os hauia concertado, justificou muito com palauras El Rey Banguel que a faria tornar, mas reçeo que o não cumpra, porque os Rei uizinhos lhe conheçam falta de valor, porem satisfez se em me affirmar que em cazo que os outros Reis lhe não cumprissem a palaura, se poria elle da parte /3v°/ del Rey Virapanaique, quando party de Barçelor para Cochim a instancia dos Embaixadores dElrey Virapanaique deixey aly Domingos de Câmara com titulo de Capitão mor para que fauereçesse as couzas dElrey Virapanaique, Estando em

Mangalor já deuolta me chegou auizo de Domingos da Câmara que os Capitães de Virapanaique lhe pedião assistençia de Embarcações para passarem e socorrer Bacanor que estua çitiado, e apertado, despachey logo quinze navios, e por Capitão mor delles Dom Luís d'Ataide, e eu me vim a Bacanor depois de hauer feito em Mangalor o que era neçessario para mostrar a Virapanaique que lhe assistiria que fosse neçessario e porque chegando a Bacanor me veo avizo que já não podião socorrer me vim de Barçelor a prover e àcabar de compor as couzas que dependião de my. E Recolhendo as cáfilas de mantimentos neçessarios me vim a esta cidade tendo reconhecido toda a Costa que tenho também que muy importante aos serviços de Vossa Magestade.

Em 16 dAbril cheguei a esta cidade, e na mesma hora que puz os pés nella tratey das mais couzas de que por outras cartas desta mesma via dou conta a Vossa Magestade.

O gasto que se fés nesta jornada (que foi mui limitado) mandará V. Magestade ver da Relação da despeza e receita que também vay nesta via, e prezumo Senhor que com tão pouca fazendo ainda no tempo em que as couzas estauão quasi da balda senão fez nunca tamanha armada, os provistos que resultarão della refiro, Deus guarde a Catholica e Real pessoa de V. Magestade como a Christandade e seus vassalos he ve me mister. De Goa a 20 de Julho de 1631.

Reference

105 *LML*, cod. 29, fols. 1-3v°: *Carta de Viso Rey da Índia, o Conde de Linhares para o Rey,* de Goa a 20 de Julho de 1631.

1106 The real name in the local language is Bacanur (Buqqa-e-Noor).

Appendix I-C[1107]

At the request of the King, Padre Pero Amaral de Pimenta sends information about the way the Hindu Brahamins, local Christians (of St. Thomas) and other gentiles of India used to marry. According to him, during their marriages they used to sing many songs, carry out diabolical rituals and pray to their false Gods. In this way the Brahmin merchants, goldsmiths and all other high castes use Brahmins to perform their marriage ceremonies, using fire as a symbol of purification and making sacrifices. But, according to him low caste Hindus, such as Sudras, carriers of Palanquins and all other servants of society, do not require Brahmins for their marriages nor do they use fire or make any sacrifice to God. He suggested that these marriage rituals of the gentiles should be prohibited by the order of the King, as was decided during First Religious Council.

Relação aserca dos cazamentos dos gentios feita por juiz dos feitos de Sua Magestade.

Saney a informação que requere esta carta de S. Magestade de Clérigos que são de Casta Bragmanes, e de Christãos da terra e de gentios achey que os gentios casta Bragmanes e Bottos senão casar conforme a seus Ritos sem fazermos hua offerta ou sacrifício de fogo a quem chamão homu[1108] e que nos cazamentos cantão muitas cantigas em louvor dos seus falsos Deoses, e assy achey que os Bragmanes mercadores e ourives já por costumes uzão das mesmas serimonias e da dita offerta ou sacrifício de fogo leuando a seus casamentos aos Bragmanes que entre ellas são os sacerdotes e assy achey que os gentios da quartas e derradeira cabeça como são os sudras e da casta baixa como chaudorins alparqueiros e corrieyros pintores e farazes não uzão de Bragmanes e por conseguinte nem de cerimonias em seus cazamentos cem declaração que ainda destes gentios de quarta e derradeira cabeça os que são Ricos e não são macharicos levão o Bragmane sempre uza das ditas ceremonias e que só os baixos fazem seus cazamentos sem Bragmane /fol. 311v° E sem cerimonias nem offerta de fogo, como tudo mais largamente consta das informações que tomey que com esta me pareçeo, enviar a Sua Magestade, e ainda que os gentios Bragmanes na informação que lhe pedi que tão bem vai com esta quinta dos fraçar este sacrifício ou offerta de fogo que fazem em seus cazamentos, comdarem outros sentidos, comtudo a verdade he que levão, a elles Bragmanes como elles mesmo confessão e onde entrão Bragmanes tudo são superstições, ceremoniais offertas e sacrficios diabólicos e cantigas em louvor de seus falsos Deoses.

E no que toqua aos concílios Pronvinciães deste arcebispado que trata esta carta de sua Magestade achey que no primeiro concilio no decreto que se abomina grandemente o crime da idolatrão pelo qual rezão se pedia ao dito Senhor entre outras cousas que não consentisse aos Gentios fazer seus cazamentos na forma que costumavão que era com ritos diabólicos e invocações dos seus Deoses e no concilio 3° no decreto: 10. se trata a mesma matéria de que me pareceo enviar tão bem treslado, tirado de hu manuscripto que me veyo as mãos porque nelle se da arezão de senão consentirem semelhantes cazamentos, Goa a 7 de Fevereiro de 1633.

P° dÁmaral Pimenta.

Reference

[1107] LML, cod. 30, fols. 311-311v°: *Relação aserca dos cazamentos dos gentios feita por juiz dos feitos de Sua Magestade, Pêro de Amaral Pimenta,* Goa a 7 de Fevereiro de 1633.

[1108] Hawan. The religious ceremony.

Appendix II-A

Cartaz
Issued to Nizam Shah's Ships[1109]

Fernão de Albuquerque ettc faço saber aos que estevirem que tendo en repeito a amizade que Nizamoxa Ellrey do Decão tem com este estado, e pollo contrato das pazes que com elle este feito lhe serem concedidos sete cartazes para sete naos suas poderem navegar, cinco para Ormuz hum para Mecca, e outra para Malacca e da sua parte me ser ora pedido o presente, hey por bem desta dar licença e seguro a esta sua nao por nome Unexe[1110] que carrega seiscentos candis de que vay pela Nacoda[1111] Sidi Belela[1112] da hidade de trinta e seis annos e leva para defenção quatorze peças da artilharia de ferro, quarenta espinguardas, setenta e cinco lanças, com panelas de polvoura e cinquenta bombas de fogos para nesta monção do março seguinte possa partir de porto de Chaul pera Ormuz e tornar ao mesmo porto nao levando nem trazendo couza algua defeza a saber, rumes, turcos, abexins, aço, breu, cobre, chumbo, latao, ferro, pimenta, canela de ceilão nem de mato, bombas machos, salitre, emxofre, tudo mais contendo e declarando no regimento do S.M. nem levar Portugueses, nem trará cavalos sem minha licença e poder trazer escravos e escravas de sua nação (...) cartaz que valer por huma viagem somente a hida e vinda e ser sellado com o sinete das armas reaes da coroa de Portugal. Noteficoo assy ao capitão de Chaul, ao feitor e alcaide mor daquela fortaleza, para que assy o cumprão e quardão e fação inteiramente cumprir e guardar como se neste conthem sem dúvida nem embargo algum. Salvador Gonçalves o fez em Goa do 5 Janeiro de 1621. O secretario António Rodrigues de Guevaras o fez escrever.

Reference

[1109] HAG, *Consultas do serviço de partes*, cod. 1043, pp. 59-59v.

[1110] Probably INXA derived from an Arabic word, which means the will or it could even be Unni Shah.

[1111] Captain of the ship.

[1112] Sidi Belal.

Appendix II-B

Summary of the Cartaz

Fernão de Albuquerque, the Governor, taking into account the friendship between Nizam Shah the ruler of Deccan (Ahmadnagar) and the Portuguese and also in virtue of the terms of the treaty of peace and friendship, seven *Cartazes* for his ships were issued. Out of which five were destined to Hormuz, one to Mecca for pilgrimage, and the other to Malacca. These ships were due to leave the port of Chaul during the month of March 1621. There were certain items, specified in the *Cartaz,* forbidden to be carried on the ships. But a few pieces of arms and ammunitions for defence were allowed. The name of the captain of the ship is mentioned as Unexe[1113] and the name of Nakoda[1114] was Sidi Belela,[1115] who was thirty six year old. The *Cartaz* was issued in the month of January 1621 at Goa.

Reference

[1113] Probably INXA derived from an Arabic word, which means the will or it could even be Unni Shah.

[1114] Captain of the ship.

[1115] Sidi Belal.

Appendix II -C[1116]

Table of Equivalence of Coins in the sixteenth and seventeenth Centuries

The following coins were in circulation in the sixteenth and the seventeenth centuries. There were fluctuations in the value of coins during the seventeenth century due to some inflation and the import of bullion by other European companies. Besides, there were quite intense rivalries between the European merchants for Asian merchandise, which led to the rise in its value, consequently, resulting in the devaluation of the coins. This has been shown in Appendix – II-D.

All the coins: silver, gold or copper, have been reduced into Réis.

Name of the Coins	Reis
Ashrafi (xerafins)	380.00
Berganis	28.02
Cas (copper)	1.37
Cruzados	390.00
Dinheiro	4.88
Dobre (castillian coin)	400.00
Ducat	390.00
Horas (oras)	360.00
Livre (coin of frandos or Flanders)	1170.00
Madrafaxão (Muzaffar Shahi-of Gujarat)	1440.00
Metical (Chinese Coin)	420.00
Panam	20.53
Pardao	320.00
Raja (of Quilon)	40.00

Real (390 reis = 1 Ashrafi)	
Soldo	58.56
Sultani	420.00
Tanga (Tanka)	60.00
Tanka (silver)	72.00
Tanga Branca	115.02
Tare	1.37
Varel	160.00
Veneziano	420.00
Vintem	18.00

Reference

1116 SPHI, op. cit, pp. 61-64; A. C. Teixeira de Aragão, *Descrição geral e história das moedas cunhadas em nome dos reis, regentes e governadores de Portuga,* 2ª ed. Livraria Fernando Machado, Porto 1964-1966, pp. 464-471.

Appendix II -D

Indo-Portuguese Coins and their Relative Value in the World Market

Name of the Coins	**Value**	**Sources**
Ashrafi (Xs.)	300.00 Reis or 5 Tanka	*LMG*, 13a, pp. 164-79
Ashrafi	3.89 Fanaos	*Índia*, cx. 3, doc. 1
Bazarucos	25.00 Vintem or 450.00 reis	*ACF*, 1162, p. 21
Cruzado	400.00 reis	AHU, *Cod.* 39, p. 31v
Cruzado (Onor)	1.50 Xs.	*Índia*, cx. 3, doc. 185
Cruzado (Portugl)	2.00 Xs.	LMG, 13a, pp. 164-17 *Índia*, cx. 9, doc.177,18
9 Fanões (kayamkulam)	2.00 Xs.	*Índia*, Cx. 3, doc. 174
Marc (Gold in Goa)	197.00 Xs. and 28.00 reis	*ACF*, 1161, p. 5
Mahmudi (Diu). II, part 1	1.50 Xs	*APO-BP*, tomo IV, vo
Pagoda (Gold)	4.00 Cruzados	*ACF*, 1161, p. 41
Pagoda (Gold in Ceylon)	10.00 Xs.	*ACF*, 1164, p. 226v.
Pagoda (Onor)	16.00 Tankas	*ACF*, 1163, pp. 160-6
Pagoda (Onor)	12.00 Tankas	*Índia*, cx. 3, doc. 185
Pagoda (Onor)	2.00 Xs.	*Simancas*, 1571, p. 30
Pardao	6.00 Fanões	*Índia*, cx. 8, doc. 38
Pardao	1.55 Xs.	*Ibid.*
1.25	Pardao 1.00 Cruzado	*Ibid.*
Pardao (Quilon)	8.00 Tanka	*Índia*, cx. 3, doc. 174
Pataca (Onor)	8.00 Tanka	*ACF*, 1161, p. 42
Pataca	1.22 Xs.	*Ibid.*

Pataca (Cochin)	1.60 Tanka	*Índia,* cx. 9, doc. 26
Pataca	1.00 Pardao	*Índia,* cx. 8, doc. 38
Real	8.00 Tanka	AHU, *cod.* 33, p. 148
Sao Tomé	3.40 Xs.	*ACF,* 1161, p. 1
Sao Tomé	15.00 Tanka and1.00 Vintem	*ACF,* 1161, p. 82v.
Sao Tomé	16.00 Tanka	*ACF,* 1162, p. 182v.
Sao Tomé (Gold)	5.00 Xs.	*ACF,* 1168, pp. 51, 150
Sao Tomé (silver)	5.00 Xs.	*ACF,* 1161, p. 82v.
Sao Tomé	5.50 Xs.	*ACF,* 1166, p. 128
Tanka	60.00 Reis	*Ibid.*
Vintem	1.00 Xs.	*ACF,* 1162, p. 21

Appendix II- E

Table of Weights and Measures used in the Seventeenth Century

Weights (Kilograms)	Equivalent
Almeno	1.20
Arratel (Old weight)	0.36
Arratel (New weight)	0.41
Bhar	116.30
Candil / Khandi	220.32
Faraçola	6.31
Fardo	209.84
Mão	11.10
Mark	0.20
204 Mitkals	1.00
312.32 0itavas	1.00
39.04 Ounces	1.00
Quintal (old)	52.450
Quintal (New)	54.450
16	Ounces
32 Arratels	1 Arroba
4 Arrobas	1 quintal
1 Quintal=2048 Ounces	128 Arratels

Measures

Name	Measurements
Cori	20 Pcs

Covados	64 cms.
Pipa	27 Almudes
Bar	20 Cori

Appendix II- F

Rice Trade
1629 - 1652

Year	**From Various Parts to**	**Volume in Qunitals**
1629-1655	Ceylon	43,356
1629-1661	Goa	52,513
1628-1640	Malacca	22,319
1633-1657	Mozambique	16,620
1629-1652	Muscat	97,576
Over all total purchase and consumption -		**232,384**

Appendix II- G

Purchase of Rice with its Geographical Origin 1626-1661

Area	Purchase in Qunitals	Percentage
Goa	70,586	31.74 %
Kanara	110,974	50.00 %
Malabar	3,756	1.68 %
Northern ports	20,444	9.19 %
Unidentified	16,628	7.47 %

Appendix II- H

Saltpetre Purchases 1616-1663

Year	Volume in kgs.	Volume in Qunitals
1616	420	8
1621-1630	110,350	2,105
1631-1640	663,100	12,737
1641-1650	523,656	9,984
1651-1660	569,239	10,852
1661-1663	22,920	436
Over all total	1,894,693	36,124

Appendix III-A[1]

Letter from the Portuguese Viceroy, Pêro da Silva, to the King of Portugal, informing about the conditions in which the fortresses of Malabar: Cranganore, Quilon and Cochin, were found. He gave special attention to the situation of the kingdom of Cochin where the 'Rei Velho' had recently died. The King had been a great friend of a Jew, Samuel Castiel, to whom he had given the post of Regedor-mor (Prime-Minister). This was certainly not appreciated by the Portuguese as Samuel used to check over the prices of pepper and even control it as stockholder. Because of this the Viceroy decided to send António Mo[u]ra de Brito, Capitão de Cochim, to the new King with messages of condolence on the demise of the last King and to congratulate him for his succession to the throne. The Captain was also to intimidate the new King and remind him of their past relationship.

Sr.

No fim de Agosto me chegou nova de ser morto o Rey Velho de Cochim, e que sucedera no Reino o Príncipe o seu herdeiro e pella amisade que o estado tem com elle, me pareçeo mandalo logo Visitar, dando lhe o pezame da morte do Rey passado, e parabem de sua sucessão, e para que esta visita se fizesse com mais authoridade, ordeney que fosse a ella o capitão de Cochim António de Mora de Brito, mandando lhe para isso as cartas para elle as dar ao ditto Rey, e ordenando lhe que fosse com todo o acompanhamento qye lhe parecesse.

E porque em tempo do Rey passado privou com ele hum Judeo por nome Samuel Castiel seu Regedor mor, o qual he mal afecto ás nossas cousas e alteraua os preços da pimenta fazendose corrector della sendo também o contrattador que a vendia, ordeney a António de Moura que no tempo e occasião que lhe parecesse trattasse com o novo Rey que o lançasse de seu serviço apontando lhe as desordens que tem commettido e trazendo a memoria os beneficios que tem recebido dos Portugueses e os que inda hade receber com outras cousas a este propósito E espero que em tudo se faça o que convem, e que este Rey tome melhor termo nas cousas da Ilha de Bendurte que foi occasião de o estado ter algumas queixas do Rey morto.

Este António de Moura que como acima serve a capitania de Cochim, veyo provido della por. V. Magestade em minha Companhia (fol. 132v°) e tem procedido ategora bem, Aquella cidade e capitania [Palavra ilegível] posto que na miséria em que estão as mais da Índia por falta de comercio.

Na fortaleza de Cranganor está por Capitão Francisco de Faria Lobo provido também por V. Magestade alguas qeixas tive delle mas de pouca sustancia; A fortaleza esta quieta e provida pello cuidado com que tenho acudido a todas.

E coulão serve de capitão Miguel do Rego de Nigreiros em falta de providos por V. magestade não tenho della queixas nesta fortaleza. Sempre ouve bandos e desinquietações entre os moradores della, e hum dos cabessas chamado António Vieira o mattarão os do outro bando a espingarda e hum sobrinho seu de que se tirou devassa que remetti ao ouvirdor geral do Crime, e vendosse em Relação se assentou que se fizesse sequestro nos bens dos culpados e se citassem por edictos para assi se proceder contra elles as suas revelias como se vay fazendo com o que se escusa irem alçadas fora. Guarde Deus a Catholica e Real Pesoa de V. Magestade Como a Christandade e seus vassallo houvemos mister. De Goa a 25 de Novembro de 1637.

O Vice-Rey

Reference

1 *LML*, Cod. 40, fol. 132-132v°: *Carta do Vice-rey, Pêro da Silva,* de Goa a 25 de Novembro de 1637.

Appendix III-B

The Treaty Signed between the Zamorin of Calicut and the Dutch Admiral, Van der Hagen in 1604[2]

The treaty stipulated:

(1) a close alliance, eternal and unbreakable, for the oppression of the Portuguese, and for driving all their associates out of all the lands of His Majesty, and also out of the whole of India.

(2) That with the next opportunity ships and people should be sent to trade at Calicut, and that merchants might be stationed there for that purpose. To effect this on the best opportunity a fortress should be built which should remain' in the hands and dominion of the Dutch for all, time.

(3) No peace should be made by either side with the Portuguese without the other being informed, and, if the other side found it oppressive, then the treaty of peace should not be entered into.

(4) The inhabitants of the Coast of Malabar south of Goa to Cape Comorin should not be permitted to set out on any navigation enterprise without having first received a passport from the Zamorin for the same, and, if anything was caught without such permit, it should be declared confiscated to the king.

Reference

2 Poonen, *A Survey of the Rise of the Dutch ...*, pp. 46-47; *The Dutch in Malabar-Selection From the Records of the Madras Government*, No. 13, pp. 68; Pissurlenkar, 'Fragmentos Históricos' in *BIVG*, N° 47, p. 61; Kail, *The Dutch in India...*, pp. 30-31.

Appendix III-C

The Treaty[3] Signed between Inácio Sarmento de Carvalho, *capitão-mor* of the town of Cochin, along with the other representatives, on behalf of the King of Portugal, on the one side, and Jacob Hustaert, Councillor Extraordinary of India, representative of admiral Rijcklof van Goens, Ordinary Councillor of India, on the other.

"1. The town of Cochin shall be surrendered with all its jurisdictions, old privileges, revenues, lands, with the documents and papers relating thereto, and whatever else is held in the name of the King of Portugal, all rights and titles thereto being ceded to the Dutch General or His Worship's representative.

2. All artillery, ammunition, merchandise, victuals; movable and immovable property, slaves, and whatever else shall be handed over as above.

3. All free persons who have worn arms shall swear not to serve against the Netherlands in India for two years.

4. All the soldiers and others belonging to the army shall march out with flying colours, drums beating, fuses alight, bullets in their mouths, and two guns to a convenient place outside the town and lay down their arms beneath the standard of the General.

5. All true born unmarried Portuguese shall be conveyed to Europe.

6. All married Portuguese and *Mestiços* shall proceed to Goa and may take their beds, and such other articles as the General and his council may permit.

7. All free Topazes [semi-assimilated half castes and Indians] and Canarins [Konkanis] shall remain at the disposal and discretion of the General.

8. The clergy may take with them their images and church ornaments except those of gold and silver.
9. All free persons and all persons belonging to the church now wandering in the country shall, if they be subjects of the King of Portugal, be comprehended in this treaty".

Reference

3 These terms of the Capitulation have been mentioned by Danvers, *The Portuguese in India...*, vol. II. pp. 327-28; *The Dutch in Malabar...*, No 13, p. 14; Poonen, *A Survey of the Rise of the Dutch ...*, pp. 108-109, however, each has translated them in his own words. Therefore, there is some linguistic difference between the versions. So far I have not been able to find any original version of this treaty in Portuguese.

Appendix IV

Name of the Nayakas	Year of Accession to the Throne	Year of Death
Venkatappa Nayaka	1583?	1629
Virappa Nayaka	1629	1631
Veerabhadra Nayaka	1629	1644
Shivappa Nayaka	1644	1660
Chikkavenkatappa Nayaka	1660	1661
Bhadrappa Nayaka	1661	1664
Soma Shakar Nayaka	1664	

Appendix IV-A[1]

The King of Portugal wrote a letter to the Portuguese Viceroy at Goa, Dom Francisco de Mascarenhas, about the problem that existed between the ruler of Kanara, Venkatappa Nayaka and the Banghel King who, due to Portuguese interference, had to accept the demands of Venkatappa Nayaka and who had promised, as compensation, to pay 7,000 Pagodas to the King of Banghel. However, it appears that the earlier Viceroy, Conde de Vidigueira, had informed the King in his letter that Venkatappa Nayaka was not abiding by what he had promised. Not only that, he had not fulfilled his promises made with the rulers of Bhatkal and Gersoppa, either. There were a lot of pressure on the present Viceroy from the different corners of the Portuguese dominions, such as Cannanore and Cochin that the Portuguese Viceroy should see that Venkatappa Nayaka fulfilled his promises made earlier during the treaties.

Dom Francisco Mascarenhas, VisoRey da Índia amigo, Ev ElRey vos ínvio muito saudar; aquando tem o Rey de Banguel do prejuízo que recebeo, nas pazes que o estado fez com Vencatapanaique, e que nem lhe cumpre o capittulo do contrato dellas que trata dos sette mil pagodes que ficou de lhe dar cada anno pera sua sustentação, e a lembrança que me faz de sua restituição a seu Reino e da Rainha de Baticala, e Garsopa sua Irmã; e de outros seus particulares, sobre que me escreueo os annos passado o remetti ao Conde de Vidigueira sendoViso Rey desse Estado, para que propondo tudo no conselho que lhe assiste Respondesse ao Rey Banguel, como se julgasse que mais convinha a meu seruiço não o descontentando porque se acontecesse se restituísse a suas terras, o não tivéssemos desffeitto e pellas mais conçiderações que na meteria se podião ter e aquelle Rey mandey responder em carta minha que do dito conde Viso Rey entenderia a Resolução que mandara tomar em suas cousas e lhe tinha emcomendado a boa correspondência que deuia ter com elle, e que sempre lhe mandaria assistir com todo o fauor que fosse justo e esperaua também, viesse elle no que o ditto Viso Rey lhe aconselhasse, em suas cousas que seria o que mais lhe conveniesse.

E em resposta disso me escreueo o Viso Rey na via do anno passado que comonicando a matéria no Conselho se assentou que supostas as deligencias feitas com Vencatapanaique; sobre os sette mil pagodes de Renda promettidos ao Rey Banguel, e o pouco furto que dellas se tem tirado a resepeito do Vencatapanaique lhe não querendo dar a ditta Renda se não indo elle viuer em suas terras, e o Banguel os não querer, com esta condição por entender que estando em terras suas o há de mattar, nem também querer aceitar viuer na lhas de Goa ou em Salssette ou em Bardez, onde o Vencatapanaique lhe dizia dará a ditta renda, e suposto outro sy o estado das cousas não convinha por hora fazersse mais deligencia, nisso, e que ao Banguel se escrevesse assi mandoo e confiandoo com boas palauras mas não lhe mandando a carta que eu lhe escreuia per se conçiderarem nisso inconvenientes, e que pêra dita forma lhe escruera logo e auia se tomara nisso a resolução que conuinha.

E vendo eu hora o refferido, com outra carta que o Rey Banguel me escreueo em vinte de Janeiro do anno passado de 1626, sobre as mesmas cousas, e sobre hua diuida que diz lhe deue o estado de dinheiro que emprestou seu Avo de que pede paguamento. Em duas cartas dos Reys de Cochim e Cananor que me escreuem a fauor do mesmo Banguel significando estarem prestes pera em suas restituição o socorrerem dado lhe ou pera isso fauor e ajuda; me pareçeo dizer vos o que nesta matéria do Banguel he passado; e emcomendo vos a demonstração e boa correspondência com os Reys em tudo o que ouver lugar; e o Estado prezente das cousas o primittir, pera que entendão se faz algua cousa por elles; e pelo que convem conseruar a amizade dos Reys vesinhos e confederados, quando há tratos enemigos naturaes e Estrangeiros com que contender.

E Porque o Banguel aponta na sua carta que o contrato porque o Vencatapanaique prometeo cada anno os sette mil pagodes de Renda, o fez o estado a que será mais fácil arecadalos delle, deve o mesmo Estado tomar essa obrigação de os cobrar sobre sy é enteiralo da dita renda; me pareçeo remeter vos esta resposta, pera que nella se proceda como se julgar quam risco paguem; Escripto em Lisboa a 6 de Março de 1627.

Rey

Reference

1 *LML*, cod. 24, fols. 183/43: *Carta Régia para o Vice Rey da Índia, Dom Francisco da Gama,* Lisboa a 6 de Março de 1627.

Appendix IV-B[2]

Through this letter, the Portuguese Viceroy informed the King of Portugal about the death of Virappa Nayaka and that the Veerabhadra Nayaka was now an undisputed King. The Portuguese Viceroy also informed that Veerabhadra had now cancelled all the peace treaties that the Portuguese had earlier signed with the Virappa Nayaka and wanted to revise them according to his own ideals.

Morreo Como em outra carta o digo a V. Magestade Virapa naique Rey do Canara com quem tinha celebrado as pazes de que vay copia, suçedeo lhe a Virabadranaique que era o que estua desapossado, mandoume embaixador a propor nouas pazes, e que daquellas de Virapanaique que tirasse a condição de se vender a pimenta livremente e também que senão fechasse a pennisula do Cambolim pella parte que tem comonicação com a terra soberbo entrou com a proposta porque estaua Senhor de tudo sem oposição de ninguém porem Já se vay facilitando com a inteiresa com que respondy, e so tem duvida de presente na fortificação do Cambolim oreo[sic] se facilitará breuemente porque tem necessidade de nosso commerçio assy mo afirma seu embaixador porque Rey Banguel da Serra, e de Carnate o trazem ocupado com querras, e se tem restetuido nas fortalezas que Ventacapanaique [sic] havia tomado, e emquanto estes homens andarem em duvidas as quaes somento ficará o nosso partido milhor e mais autorizado para o que hauemos mister daquellas partes. Guarde Deus a Católica e Real Pessoa de V. Magestade como Christandade e Seus Vassalos havemos mister. De Goa a 18 de Dezembro de 1631.

Reference

2 *LML*, cod. 29, fols. 163, *Carta de Viso Rey da Índia, o Conde de Linhares para o Rey, De* Goa a 18 de Dezembro de 1631.

Appendix IV-C[3]

Through his ambassador Veerabhadra Nayaka, communicated to the Portuguese authorities his decision to increase six Pagodas more per Khandi in the price of pepper than it was stipulated in the treaty earlier signed. It was also communicated that he would sell the pepper to the English merchants. However, the Portuguese Council suggested to the pepper contractor, Sancara da Gama, who had also confirmed the decisions of the Veerabhadra Naya regarding the price of pepper, that he should look for the same commodity elsewhere, although, as the Portuguese governor suggested, that the Nayaka was not going benefit anymore by selling their pepper to the English merchants. Regarding the dismantling the fortress of Cambolim, it was communicated by the Council that they were going to wait till the decision over the pepper contract was taken.

Sr.

Larga Conta dei o ano passado a V. Magestade de tudo o tocante a Elrey Virabdarnaique, embaxador que mandou e propostas que fez sobre a pimenta e fortaleza do Cambolim, e nesta via o faça tambem da alteração que moveo sobre o contrato da dita pimenta polha querer vender aos Inglezes e assi nesta farey relação do que mais se offereçe.

Logo pouco dias depois da partida a Urca Bênção de Deus tive carta de Sancara da Gama que nas terras do dito Rey estava negoçeando a dita pimenta em que me avisava que este Rey queria inovar o contrato della, pedindo mais seis pagodes em cada candil allem do preço do contratto jurado e firmado por elle, fiz ver esta matteria no conselho que me assiste, onde se assentou que com bons modos se trattasse primeiro de conçertar estas cousas prevenindo ordens a todas as mais partes donde nos podesse vir esta droga, para que não dependêssemos toda delRey Virabadar naique, como mais largamente se contem no assento do ditto conselho cuja copia vay com esta, e conformidade do qual escrevi logo a ElRey Virabadar naique, representando lhe que não devia quebrantar o contratto que estaua jurado por elle, assi por faltar a sua palaura Real como pello que avançaua na nossa amizade e appontando lhe também a pouca utilidade que recebia do comercio dos Ingrezes e outras conveniências e no mesmo tempo escrevi a Cananor a Dom Phelipe Mascarenhas e a Cochim ao vedor da fazenda que lá está João de Sousa Pereira // fol. 138v°, que por todas as vias possíveis fossem ajuntando toda a quantidade da pimenta que pudesse ser encarregando lhes este negocio com grandes apertos por muitas e diferentes cartas duplicadas mandando juntamente o dinheiro que era necessário para a compra della para que assi se negoceasse com maior facilidade, posto que também a difficultava a pouca novidade que ouve de pimenta pella grande seca do anno passado.

Como El Rey Virabadar naique com todas estas diligencias não mandou o intento que levava, me pareçeo que assi para concluir com elle este negoçeo da pimenta como para fazer alcançar dally os Ingreses porquanto lhes tinha concedido feitoria em Batecalá para cujo effeito hião fazendo casas devia mandalo visitar por pessoa de authoridade e experiência, e assi pella muita que Martim Teixeira de Azevedo fidalago da casa de V. Magestade tem daquella gente e por cezudo e por ir autualmente por capitão mor da Costa do Canará a invernar em Cananor, me parçeo mandalo por embaxador ao ditto Rey Virabadar naique com os Regimentos de que com este vay cópia por entrar muito cedo o Inverno não pode o dito Martim Teixeira partir havendo estado alguns dias na barra esperando tempo, e assi porque se não faltasse em cousa tão necessária o mandei ir por terra nos primeiros dias do dito Inverno como foi e posto que a principio não pode concluir cousa alguma, com tudo na ultima carta que recebi sua·me avisa em resolução que El Rey Virabadar naique quer que se lhe tome a sua pimenta a razão de 350 Candiz para cada anno a metade por 22 pagodes e outra a metade por 26 que era o preço por que se havia contrattado com seu Avo, e assi vem a ser huma por outra a vinte quatro com que se fez grande negoçeo // fol. 139/ no tempo presente por a pimenta valer agora por dentro das terras do Canará muito dinheiro em razão da falta della pella grande secca que ouve e com isto se ficou atalhando dar se aos Ingrezes a poderem ficar com este comercio porque não tem por ora aquelle Rey outra que lhes possa dar conforme as informações que tenho e assi he forçado que fiquem descontentes delle e na licença que concede para comprar a mais pimenta a seus vassallos se fará sempre muito mais barato com que a fazenda de V. Magestade fica avançando muito.

Sobre a fortaleza de Cambolim escrevi mais o que V. Magestade mandará ver da copia da sua carta que vay e juntamente a da minha resposta para que se veja o que lhe tenho ordenado nestes particulares, e posto que entende Martim Teixeira que com assentarmos este preço na pimenta se aquietará Virabadar Naique na pretenção que tem de deșmantelarmos a fortaleza do Cambolim, e eu lhe tenho escrito que nas praticas que tiver se haja de maneira que elle não desespere até com effeito concluíssem com o negoçeo da pimenta, contudo pareçeo dizer a V. Magestade que deve ser servido mandar resolução nessa matéria com advertençia que este forte não he de nenhum effeito não sendo nos senhores da Ilha e que se tem por certo que o Rey a não há de largar pellos muitos pagodes que ally tem que lhe rendem grande soma de dinheiro e assim fica servindo somente de nos fazer ter guerra com Virabadar Naique sendo hum Rey de cujas terras se sustentão estas pella qual razão nos he muito necessário ter paz com elle allem de que também a pimenta nos obriga ao mesmo porque não temos outra parte donde nos venha como em outra carta desta via digo a V. Magestade cuja terra e Real Pessoa Deus Guarde como Christandade e seus Vassalos havemos mister. De Goa a 20 de Novembro de 1637.

Reference

[3] *LML*, Cod. 40, fols. 138-139v°: *Carta do Vice-rey, Pêro da Silva,* de Goa a 20 de Novembro de 1637; *LML*, cod. 42, fols. 26-27.

Appendix IV-D[4]

Letter of Veerabhadra Nayaka of Ikkeri to the Portuguese Viceroy in which he wanted to clarify some doubts, which the Portuguese authorities had about his involvement with the Dutch. The Nayaka clearly indicated in this letter that, although the Dutch had tried to establish contacts with him, he had refused on the ground that he had been in peace and friendship with the Portuguese.

Copia da carta que Virabadranaique Rey do Iquery escreveo a Senhor VisoRey

Ao bem aventurado estado de Goa a Visorey Pêro da Silva, escrevo esta o quellady Virabadranaique com muito amor e conformidade fazendo por ella a saber:

O embaixadores Martim Teixeira dazevedo, vindo do cá mandou dizer sobre o contrato da pimenta e no mesmo tempo tive aviso que os olandeses vierão por na barra de Goa empedirão o caminho e disto Vossa Senhoria me vão, mandou avisar, e emenso se tiver a entre vos e my algum arrufo sobre qualquer matéria della, se podia entender entre nos mesmo, também o consertara, mas não dera justo para que podemos dar noticia do caso a outros.

Os olandeses chegarão ao lugar de malapeo que he a enseada das galeas, [galcas?] donde mandarão ma dizer aos quaes não dey ouvido e lhes mandey responder na forma que havia de ser no mesmo tempo.

E Entre ElRey de Portugal e my há grande amizade pello respeito della escrevo esta a Vossa Senhoria e vejo querendo ajuda da minha parte, e mandando me V.S. auisar a mandarey a V.S. de boa vontade e nisto não tenho que encarecer V.S. esteja com boa vontade, na matéria dos meus negócios e na mesma conformidade estarey eu também com muita conformidade nos (nas) da parte de V.S:, e como corremos com esses bons termos que tem que depoes fazer nem escrever e considerando disto melhor me avize V.S. pró efeito.

E Eu Crisna Sinay lingoa do estado a trasladey da própria a que me reposto, Goa a 9 de Dezembro de 1637. (Singned Crisnasinay)

Reference

4 *LML*, Cod. 40, fols. 373-v°: *Copia da carta que Virabadranaique Rey do Iquery escreveo a Senhor VisoRey*, Goa a 9 de Dezembro de 1637.

p 422

Treslado da Carta que Escreveo a V. S.ª o Rey Virabadranaique na qual diz o seg.te

Do Bem aventurado Estado de Goa ao ViRey Pero da silva q sempre Esteja a bom salvamento, a Esta prezença Escreve Esta o que lady Virabadranaique com m.to amor, E fazendo por Ella a saber,

V. S.ª do Antonio borges E Rampoy tinha tratado o negocio do contrato das pazes a que lhes tinha mandado dizer que Entenderia por seus ditos E sobre isso V. S.ª me tinha Escrito carta conforme Ella fiz intentado, E os ditos Antonio borges E Rampoy me disserão o principio do intento do negocio que V. S.ª tinha mandado tratar com Elles, E em tempo [illegible] El Rey de portugal quando não veo correndo nova amizade sendo assi que tenho que Escrever mais largo per cartas,

Por V. S.ª me mandar dizer E se ha contentar E dar gosto a El Rey de portugal a cassa que Estava dos forasteiros na minha terra fica quebrada E desfeita, o que V. S.ª tinha tratado E dito sobre o canbolim de que lhe agora não tem avido comcluzão sobre a qual tinha mandado dizer a V. S.ª no tempo atrazado sobre o qual Respondeo V. S.ª que tinha Escrito a portugal de cuja Resposta se Espera, E que faria dar comcluzão conforme com a tal Resposta, E tendo V. S.ª Respondido nesta forma não deve de haver tal de[illegible] pelo que mande V. S.ª com brevidade o que se ha de dizer a isto,

Sobre todos os particulares de Sancara da garna mandarey per Escrito baltezar Ez.ª

Em Dadagisinay que ora serve de lingoa do Estado Em auzencia de meu pay Venacesinay o treslado da propria da letra Canarâ a que me Reporto, Goa, a 6 de Março de 1639,

Dadagisinay

Ref: LML, Cod. 44, fol. 422.

ಶ್ರೀಸದಾಶಿವ

॥೧॥ ಶ್ರೀಮದ್ದ್ರಾವವಿಜಯರಯರಾದ ಪರಿದಶ್ಶಿಲ ಅರಿಗೆ
ದೇವಿ ಅಪ್ಪ ಬದನಾಯಕರ ಗಂಗೆಯ ಉಂಡಾಯ
ನೈರ ಮಿದದ ಪನೆಂ ಗಾದಸ್ರ ಲ್ರಹಣ ನಿ ಬಾರ ಬಿರಾಮ
ವಯ ಬಂದು ಹೇಳಿದರು ದನಾವಿಕಾ ಯುದ್ಧೆಲ್ಲ ಲಾರು
ಗತ್ತಾ ಕಿರ್ತಿ ರುವ ಬದೆಲ ಲಾರು ಹೇಗ ಮಾನಿದಾರ
ಖಗೆ ಬಂದರೆಂದ ದರುವ ಬದ ನಾಗಪ ಯಿಂದಯಲ್ಲ
ಖಿರದ ನರನ ಸ್ವಗೆರಾಂದೆಲ ಲ್ರಹಣ ನಿ ಬಾಳರಾ
ಮಾವಯಾನಿಲ ರತ್ನ ರುವ ವನ ನಾಯದ ವಿರಾರಾ
ನೆಲ್ಲರ ಹೆ ದರನ ಮಗುಮಾಗಾ ಲಲರು ಖನರಾ
ಗನುಾನ ವಾನಿಬಂದಾ ಯುದ್ಧ ಸುತ್ತ ನಲ್ಲ ರಲಾ
ದಾದ ದ್ರಾನ ದಯ ಬದಲು ಪ್ರತಿ ಬರದ
ದಾನಾನ ರತ್ನ ರುವ ವನ ವರ ಸಮರಾ
ರಾಬನಾರ ಗೆ ಹ ಮಾರು ದ ಬೆರೆಂದು ನಂಯ
ನಮಸ್ಕಾರ ಮಾನೆಲ ಮಾಡದ ಉದಾ

ಶ್ರೀ ಸದಾಶಿವ

॥೬॥ ಶ್ರೀಮದ್ಭಾವವಿಚರಯರಾದ ಪೀಠದಶ್ಶಲಂಗಿ
ತ್ಕೆಯಪತ್ವದನಾಯಕರಾದಂಭೃಹಯಂಣಾಯ
ತ್ಕೆರುವಿದವನೆಂದಾದ್ದ ಲಂಶಿಗೆ ನಿಬಾರಚಿತಾಸ
ಎಯಬಂದುಹೆಂದರುದನಾಪಿತ। ಯತ್ನೆಲ್ಲ ಲಸರು
ಗನಸಾರಶಿತ್ಕೆರುವಿಬಧೆಂಉಲಸಾರುತ್ತೆನಾನಿವತವ
ಖಗೆಬಂಅರಿಂದಾದರುವಿದಶಾಗದಯಂದಯಲ್ಲ
ವಿಸರವಮಸಾನಸಿಗೆರಾಂದೆಉ। ಲಂಶಿಗೆನಿಬಾಳಿತಾ
ಮಾವಯಾನಿಸುತ್ತೆರುವಿನಿಶಾಯದ ವಿಸರ
ನೆಲ್ಲಾತ್ತೆದರಾನಮಸೂಮಾಗಾಲಲಸಬನಸರ
ಗಾನಗಾಾನವಾನಿಬಂದಾ। ಯತ್ನೆರುತ್ತುವಲ್ಲವಲ್ಲಾ।
ಹಾವಿದಶ್ಶಾಗದಾಮಯಬದಶ್ಚಶಿಕೆವಿಬರನುವದಿ
ಸಾರಾಸಾನರತ್ತೆರುವಿನಿವೆಲಸಮಶಗಾ
ಲಲರಬನಸಶಿಗೆಹರನಿರುಯಬೆಸಿಂದುನಂಮ
ತ್ಯದಯಂಗೆಜ್ಜರರವನಶಿತವಿನೆಉ। ಮೊದಲುನಿಉ
ಲಾಶಿಮಾಶಿದಶಿಗೆಗಂಡುವರ್ಗನಿವಾಸಾಗಶಿಕಾಯ್ಯ
ಯಲ್ಲಮಿಂದಿತ್ತೆರುವಿದಶ್ಶಮಾರ್ಗಾಶಿಗೆಬರ‍ಯ
ಧೆಉ। ಲತ್ತಂದಯಾರಬಂಥಮ। ಲನುಕಾಶಿವ
ಬಂದಿತ್ತೆಯಶಿನಿದಾಮಶ್ಶಲಾಶಿದಾಶಿಗೆ। ಮಿಗೆ
ಲಾಲನ್ಯಾಗಬಾರದು। ಎನೆಂಬದಶಾಶಿವಿದತ್ಯೆ
ರುವಿನುವಹಾಗೆವಾಯುವದುವಂಶಕಾರಾನವಿಬಾ

f.423 f.424

ರನ್ನೆಲ್ಲಾವಿಂದ ನಿಂದ ಬಾನೆ ನರುಯುದ್ಧಿ ಬಡ್ತಾರೆ

Appendix V

Adil Shahi Dynasty of Bijapur

Name of the Sultans	Year of Accession to the throne	Year of Death
YUSUF ADIL SHAH (KHAN) Founder	1496	1519
ISMAIL ADIL SHAH (KHAN)	1519	1534
MULLU ADIL SHAH (KHAN)	1534	1535
IBRAHIM ADIL SHAH (KHAN)	1535	1557
ALI ADIL SHAH (KHAN)	1558	1580
ISMAIL II ADIL SHAH (KHAN)	1580	1627
MOHAMMAD ADIL SHAH (KHAN)	1627	1656
ALI II ADIL SHAH (KHAN)	1656	1672
SIKANDAR ADIL SHAH (KHAN)	1672	1686 (imprisoned) (1700)

Appendix V-A[1]

The King of Portugal suggested to the Viceroy that he should participate in a confederation that Adil Khan, Malik and Qutub Shah were making in order to refuse to allow the English and the Dutch into their territories and into their ports. The King also recommended that the Viceroy should send help to the Shah (Adil) in his war against the Mughals.

Conde visoRey amigo, Ev ElRey vos ínvio muito saudar como aquele que amo. Per carta minha de seis de Março do anno de mil, e seis centos, e uinte e três, vos encomendey dardes calor à confederação que se dizia trattauão fazer o idalcão E o Melique, E o Catobaxá, sobre não darem entrada aos Ingreses, E Olandeses e nem os (a)dmittirem em seus portos, procurando que chegasse isso a effeito, E se declarasse a liga, busccando todos os outros meos de divirtir estes i[ni]migos de Europa, e os naturaes que os fauoreçesse e particularmente o Xá com a guerra do Mogor; e vendo que em reposta disso me Escrevestes na via do anno passado vos encommendo me auiseis do que em rasão desta matéria resultar da Embaixada; que me dizeis ficaueis para inviar ao Idalcão. Escripta em Lisboa ao primeiro de Março de 1625.

Rei

Reference

1. *LML*, cod. 21, fols. 1: *Carta Régia para o Vice Rey da Índia*, Lisboa ao primeiro de Março de 1625.

Appendix V - B[1]

The Portuguese Viceroy informs the King of Portugal about the internal situation of the Bijapuri court where the young Adil Shah, under the tutelage of the Persian nobility, was almost unable to decide any official matter on his own. Relations between the Bijapuri Sultan and Ahmadnagar's general, Malik Ambar, had been quite hostile. Under the circumstances, it was advisable to maintain peaceful a relationship with the state of Ahmanagar. However, the Viceroy further reports to the King about the overall political relations of the Mughals with these south Indian states.

O Idalcão esta muy quebrado e desaatorisado pelos mãos conselhos de huns Parsio[2] seo valido a que se entregou demasiadament. Sobre que lhe escreui muitas veses advertindo o que atentasse por suas cousas, e tiuesse boa correspondência com Melique Âmbar Capitão geral dos Reinos de Melique e que ser Abexim. E este conselheiro do Idalcao Parsio, E hauer entre os destas suas nações grandes ódios, forão em capelando as cousas de Maneira que o dito Capitão Geral trasendo ao seus Rey consigo, entrou pollas terras do Idalcao do mandado muita parte dellas e chegou quatro legoas de Visapor onde o Idalcao se tinha acolhido e lhe tomou hua sua cidade nova feita por elle em que residia chamada Nauraspor e lha destruyo sem deixar mais em pé que os seus paços de mais disto lhe matou e catiuou os melhores capitães que tinha E entre elles ao mesmo seu conselheiro fazedor deste ódios e desauenças e porto que tenho e se visto alguas veses ao Idalcão que sera bom comporem se e não dar lugar a se perder tudo, a nehua cousa differe, porque sobre [iligivel...] para pouco se me affirma que esta tão obstinado que diz que antes se entregar aos Mogores (os quaes procura trazer sua ajuda) que fazer nenhu concerto com o dito Melique Âmbar, que na verdade he grande capitão, E está tão cego da paxão que não monta dizer se lhe e emendar elle pollo procedimento que os Mogores costumão ter que entrados hua vez no seu Reino os não hão de poder botar fora, se há de perder, e como o embaxador que aqui tem he pessoa de pouca sustanciamente estes officiaes menos do que puderão fazer se fora homem de differente capacidade; E porque en ter ho alcansado que odito Melique Âmbar de seja que haja caso [iligível] por ser homem prudente do que ve a perdição notória e o que fez foi obrigado dos mãos officios que se lhe fazião tratando sua destruição e matallo como duas vezes se intentou ficando mui ferido de hua dellas, hey de apertar por hua e outra parte por lhe se os posso compor e pollo menos entretellos de maneira que sem que effectue a ajuda dos Mogores que o Idalcão solicita porque esta gente como está conforma logo, entra em Malícia, e não perdem occasião de nos inqueitar ao menos em quererem do estado cousa muy desordenadas com que dão trabalho. G.D. (Guarde Deus), De Goa a 20 de Fevereiro de 1625,

O Conde Almirante.

Reference

1 *LML*, cod. 22, fols. 42v-43: *Carta do Vice-rey, Dom Francisco da Gama*, de Goa a 20 de Fevereiro de 1625.

2 This refers to Persians.

Appendix V-C[1]

The Viceroy suggests in this letter that, as long as the two states remained one against the other, there will be no stability in the region and, above all the Mughals would have the opportunity to conquer both at once and thise would be in no way beneficial for themselves. Had it not been for the famine, and the alliance between the Sultans of Ahmadnagar, Bijapur and Golconda, the Mughals would have engulfed all of them long ago. The Portuguese Viceroy wanted to provide help to the Sultan of Ahmadnagar against the Sultan of Bijapur, which he had requested through his ambassador, because this Sultan had rendered great service to the Portuguese state by not allowing any English and the Dutch emissaries.

Em carta de se is de Dezembro passado dey conta a V. Magestade do estado das couzas do Rey Melique, e posto que na mesma carta, relataua outras matterias seguirey nesta tão somente as do Melique.

Em coformidade do que havia praticado mandou aqui o seu Embaixador que de Chaul para cá veo por conta e gasto da fazenda de V. Magestade porque assy pareçeo acertado. Propoz o dito embaixador em nome do seu Rey que conforme as capitulações das pazes que V. Magestade era obrigado a guerrear contra o Idalcão em seu fauor, pedio também se lhe prestasse dinheiro sobre penhores, offereçendo primeiro o de sua palaura. Ao dia seguinte respondy à proposta porque hauia para isso matteria excelente.

Dey conta a V. Magestade de como por parte do Idalcão hauia ameaças de guerra os quais para vão em ronca como em outras cartas desta via digo, e como para estas roncas a que de cà fizermos carrancas, respondy ao dito Embaixador que em virtude da obrigação em que V. Magestade estaua àquelle Rey tinhamos principiado a guerra hauia muitos dias e que respeito ao medo que fizermos ao Idalcão trattava elle de pazes com o dito Melique. E certo senhor que o entendo assy, porque a armada com que sahi a navegar fez baixar de todo a soberba que para nossas couzas tinhão todos os Reis vizinhos, muito trabalhey e instey para que a dita amizade do Melique e Idalcão se fizesse porque sem ella infalivelmente ganhará o Mogor os Reinos do Melique, Idalcão e Golconda juntos como hoje estão, mas não por amizade jurada, mas por tregoas capituladas tem feito rezistencia de maneira que o Mogor não só ganhou, mas ainda está retirado legoas atraz, e se Deus não permittira a peste e fome de que em outras cartas dou conta a V. Magestade tudo o da Índia ficará debaixo do poder deste Rey Mogor.

Há parte que toca a o dinheiro prestado, respondy que V Magestade o não tinha, porem que por accomodar ao Rey Melique o tomaria prestado como danno de dez porcento com correr na terra, porem que para segurança do principal se hauia de entregar nas mãos dos Ministros de V. Magestade a alfandega que El Rey Melique tem em Chaul a qual se auia de aualiar, e entregarse por ella o dinheiro que valesse a respeito do rendimento de dez porcento, pois do ditto rendimento se hauião de pagar os interesses das partes, satisfez muito o Embaixador da resposta que lhe dey que deu logo conta /fol. 17-v°/ a seu amo; neste meyo tempo se alterarão là as couzas em rezão de o Melique hauer nomeado para Capitão geral e Governador do seu Reino a Fratecan[2], filho de Melique âmbar,[3] que muitos annos hauia tinha prezo, com o gouerno deste homem que todos Gabão particularmente na guerra, mudou os Ministros, e tarda reposta ao Embaixador a quem aperto per ella, por que da fortaleza da V. Magestade se gasta cada mez cento e vinte e cinco Xerafins e posto que o negoçeo da alfandega se vier as mãos dos ministros de V. Magestade considero por couza de tanta importançia que para o effectuar aja de vender athe a prata das Igrejas, não convem todavia que façamos ao largo tanta despeza com este Embaixador, he bem verdade que na constançia que o Rey Melique tem tido no serviço de V. Magestade contra Ingrezes, e olandezes meerçe muito.

Com occazião das muitas morte que há neste Reino por razão da fome, tem havido alguns alevantados nelle, e de prezente chegou hum a Chaul de cima que o Capitão de Chaul Francisco da Sylveira pudera cuidar, se guardará a ordem que lhe dey para fauoreçer a parte do Melique, porem não tenho outra de consideração neste levantamento dos Mouros com facilidade se reduzem, porque não há defeito entre elles a traição de Sua Magestade. Continuo as diligençias pera que estejão conformes o

Rey Melique, Idalcão e Golconda sem embargo que custão as diligencias, e inteligências fazenda a V. Magestade cuja Catholica e Real Pessoa Deus guarde como a Christandade e seu vassalo averia mister. De Goa a 16 de Agosto de 1631.

Reference

1 *LML*, cod. 29, fols. 17: *Carta de Viso Rey da Índia, o Conde de Linhares para o Rey,* de Goa a 16 de Agosto de 1631.

2 Fateh Khan.

3 Malik Âmbar

Appendix V-D[1]

The King of Portugal wrote a letter to the Viceroy advising him to maintain good relationships with the neighbouring rulers especially the Niazam Shah of Ahmadnagar, Qutub Shah of Golconda and the Adil Shah of Bijapur who had formed an alliance recently to expel the English and the Dutch. He also suggested helping all these states in their wars against the Mughal and if they fought against each other to try to make peace between them so that they could remain united.

Conde sobrinho Viso Rey da Índia amigo, eu ElRey vos envio muito saudar como aquele que amo. Vi hua carta[2] Vossa de 8 de Novembro de 630 sobre o que vos mandei escrever acerca de terdes toda boa correspondência com os amigos desse estado e procurardes simentar a liga os que os annos passados se trattou entre o Idalcão e o Melique, e o Cotubxá contra os enemigos da Europa enviando embaixada ao Idalcã, e as que me escrevestes em 8 e 30 de Janeiro do anno passado que me dais conta do que passou na que levou Balthazar dazeredo e termos do rompimento de guerra em que ficáveis com aquelle Rey e havendo visto o que nellas se refere, me pareçeo dizervos que quanto a Índia estivera muito floreçente e livre das oppreções dos enemigos da Europa que a tem reduzido ao aperto que he notoreo, nem ainda então caminha chegarse a rompimento com os Reys naturais sem mayores cousas e empenhos do credito do estado, e muito menos com o Idalcão Príncipe vesinho de Goa cuja guerra sempre foi perigosa e trabalhosa e emquando se vay a ganhar pouco, e tudo isto se devera considera e se mais danado e de mayor risco nos tempos presente não somente pollo estado em que se acha a Índia acreçendo disso a alteração em mouvimento do Mogor, guerra do Canara e succçesso de Ceilão senão porque se aquelle Rey se entendesse com as nações estrangeiras (que tanto procuravão sua amizade e confederação, para seus fins e intentos) com ocasião desta guerra (sobre as outras) veria a porse em contingência a mesma cidade de Goa cabessa do estado donde envião os socorros, e provisões para todos os membros delle, os quaes todas ficarião desemparados, se com este rompimento visto ella apadeçer a mesma necessidade, e ainda mays sendo lhe forçado valerse de tudo e chegar apurar elles para sua própria defensão com o que as cousas acabarião de reduzirse aos aperto, nisto e impossibilidades que se dexão ver. Pello que vos encomendo muito e encarrego que tendo presentes estas razões (que com outras mais que nisso concorrem forão ordenadamentos porque ordeney sempre aos VReys de estado tiuessem toda boa correspondência com o Idalcão ainda que fosse dissimulando seus procedimentos na que isto se pudesse premitir sem perda de reputação procureis refiro com elle destes mesmo termos sem voss entendido dos que na forma sobre ditta separem tolerar quardando a emenda de tudo para certos tempos; Porque o que agora convem mais a meu serviço e ao bem e conservação da India he conveniente ter as forças do Estado sem diverção dos Reys naturaes contra os Rebeldes de Olanda, e mais nações da Europa que he o intento principal que haveis de leuantar nesse governos. & Sendo o Idalcão o menino, como dizeis e estando em poder de Xanavascam[3] e Mostafacam[4] que o governão, ainda parece que se divera reparar neste rompimento com mais causa acressendo as ficão appontadas poder se entender que não sahião de seu animo por sua pouca idade as occasiões, E havendo se de atrebuir aquelles dous mouros (como parece e se collige das vossas cartas) ter se por cousa fácil o poderem se lhe ganhar as vontades (sendo gente ambiciosa e Venal) e conseguirse disso não somente adiantaremse por aquella pare em muito intentos as cousas do estado, mas ainda do que se trattaua que era festarse a liga com o Melique e Cotubxa que /fols. 6/ tudo se pudera alcançar com muito (...) de meu serviço se as negoçeações disso se emprenderão por vias inteligências bem dispostas e com a sagacidade que pedem matterias semelhanes sem se chegar com aquelles mouros a desconveniençias em cousas que puderão desviar por muitos caminhos. E assi se os meyos de composição que avisaes se tinhão movido com o idalcão chegarão a ter effeitos estáveis aduertido docuidado com que haveis de trattar de aconservar escusando com prudência, e bom modo chegar outra vez a termos de rompimento dissimulando se com elle tudo o que se puder. Porquanto minha vontade he como fica ditto, que as armas e todas as forças desse Estado se occupe na expulção dos enemigos de Europa, e que para se poder conseguir se procure e conserve a paz com os Reys visisnhos, e em caso que durem ainda as desavenças com o Idalcão, trattereis de as compor e assentar a paz quanto antes ouver lugar entendendo que me auerey nisso por bem servido de vos. Escripto em Madrid a 14 de Março de 1632.

Rey

Reference

1 *LML*, cod. 30, fols. 5: *Carta de Viso Rey da Índia, o Conde de Linhares para o Rey,* Escripto em Madrid a 14 de Março de 1632.

2 Esta carta está na margem da presente carta do Rei.

3 Shah Nawas Khan.

4 Mustafa Khan.

Appendix V-E[1]

The Portuguese Viceroy, Conde de Linhares, informs the King of Portugal about the illegal action committed by António Borges, capitão-mor of a Portuguese ship, in issuing Cartazes, for which he had no authority, in the year 1631(?), to seventeen ships carrying pepper that left Adil Shahi ports, between Dabhol and Rajapur and were destined for Persia. However, the Portuguese Viceroy asked the King to punish for António Borges for his illegal act.

Sr.

Dos portos de Idalcão e Dabul até Rajapor sairão este anno dezasete navios pimenteiros para a Pérsia, estando no Comorão os sitiou tomando lhe a saída António Borges Capitão mor de hus navios que Ruy freire deixou no estreito o qual deo cartazes aos dittos pimenteiros na forma da copia que aqui vay não tenho sabido ategora o fundamento deste capitão, nem a quantidade dos direitos que pagarão com o que não será razão condenalo ou approvar o negoçio, he bem verdade que o tenho por de muita consideração, porque não he bastante a jurisdição de hu Capitão mor do estreito para o determinar!

Depois de me recolher de Malavar ordeney a 22 ou 23 navios que forão invernar ao norte, que esperassem por estes pimenteiros, e respeito aos cartazes que trazião me pezara deos haverem tomado, porque era sem duvida havermos de ter sobre a matteria contendas, mas sempre será muy conveniente que se dé hum pezado açoute aos pimenteiros seja verdade que o tenho por dificultoso, porque algu homem dos de quem com mais razão pollo officio que occupa pudermos confiar segundo o que me tem constado por certidões de compliçes he o que mais os fauoreçe e ampara, e trás dinheiro em suas mãos, mas não tenho eu Jurisdição, nem poder para castigar este homem solicito euitalo, E V. Magestade o poderá fazer pello que escreuy nas vias dos annos passados, e faça me V. Magestade merçe de me não mandar que eu diga mais no tocante ao ditto homem para què há para isso muitas razões justíssimas. Deus guarde a Catholica e Real pessoa de V. Magestade como a Christandade e Seus Vassalos havemos mister de Goa a 21 de Agosto de 1631.

Reference

1 LML, cod. 29, fols. 75: *Carta de Viso Rey da Índia, o Conde de Linhares para o Rey,* de Goa a 21 de Agosto de 1631.

Appendix V-F[1]

A Letter witten by António Moniz Barreto from Bijapur to the Viceroy, 28th of May, 1638, in his own handwriting.

1 *LML*, cod. 44, fols. 413.

Appendix V - G[1]

A <u>*Farman*</u> *Issued by Mohammad Adil Shah of Bijapur, in Persian, in which he confirms and provides guarantee that he would order Shivappa Nayaka to remove his siege from the Portuguese fortress and territories of Onor. (See it's translation below. Although this* <u>*Farman*</u> *has been published by Pissurlencar, as indicated in the footnote, but here it is found necessary to reproduce it again seeing its diplomatic importance in the present work.*

Reprodução duma carta de Mahamad Adilxá ao Governador da India

ACE, Vol. III, pp. 327-328.

Appendix V- G-a

Translation of the Farman

Ao assistente no alto estado, mando, poderes, gouerno, obra, animo, e Ventura, Sustentador da paz, e amizade, escolhido na ley do *Mixia* e liberal da condição, e lião do mar Dom Bras de Castro Gouernador e V. Rey do estado de Goa que sempre esteja a bom Saluamento, e cõ acressentamento do estado a que escreuo esta cõ amor, e cõ as letras emxeridas como aljofres, e fasendo por ell a saber.

Carta que ao prezente V. S. me escreueo por o estimado e honrado P.e António Botelho e o honrado, e de minha prezença Melique Acute, Vy a Sustançia della, e juntamente entendy tudo o que elles afirmarão de pa1aura a meu Seruiço real, em que tratava aserca de Siuapanaique pello trabalho, e oppreção que lhe daua, de tudo fui informado, a quem mando agora por meu real formão, cõ muita riguoridade que o leua meu maldar pell que esteja V. S. certo cõ elle o ficara muito quieto, e mandara tirar o serco que tem posto a fartaleza de onor, e restituira as mais que tem tomado, afora della, e estara cõ V. S. cõ muita paz e quietação, e se o não quizer, não tera bom fim, rezão, porq antre mim, e El Rey de Portugal que tem Coroa de ouro, ha, e corre antiga amizade, amor, e comformidade que pera tudo isto conuem que mande V. S. cõ muita preça, a minha real prezença ao honrado Vertuoso, e Reuerendissimo o Padre Gonçalo Martins e tanto que elle chegar quã, se siuapa naique não der comprimento ao que lhe tenho mandado e encontrar (sic) a minha ordem vera V. S. o castigo que para isso lho mandarey dar, e de palaura o que tenho falado cõ o Padre António Botelho, e cõ o dito Melique Acute, elles por suas cartas que escreuem a V. S. ficara inteirado milhor. Feita aos 25 do mes Rabilacar de 1064 mez e era de mouros que foi a 13 de Março de 1654.

Appendix V - H

Rulers of Portugal During the sixteenth and seventeenth Centuries

2nd Dynasty of Aviz

No.	Name of the kings[1148]	Title[1149]	Beginning of Reign	Year of Death
13	D. João II	O Perfeito	1481	1495
14	D. Manuel I	O Venturoso	1495	1521
15	D. João III	O Piedoso	1521	1557
16	D. Sebastião	O Desejado	1557	1578
17	Cardeal D. Henrique	O Casto	1578	1579
	Prior do Crato		1580	
	3rd Habsburg Dynasty (Philips of Spain)			
18	Philip II (1st of Portugal)	O Prudente	1580	1598
19	Philip III (2nd of Portugal)	O Pio	1598	1621
20	Philip IV (3rd of Portugal)	O Grande	1621	1640

4th Dynasty of Braganza

21	D. João IV	O Restaurador	1640	1656
22	D. Afonso VI	O Vitorioso	1656	1668
23	D. Pedro II	O Pacífico	1667	1707

Reference

1 Names of the kings have been maintained in Portuguese.

2 Title by which all the kings are known, too have been maintained in their original forms.

Appendix V - I

List of Viceroys and Governors of Portuguese in India 1505-1670

1	Dom Francisco de Almeida (Viceroy)	1505 - 1509
2	Afonso de Albuquerque (Governor)	1509 - 1515
3	Lopo Soares de Albergaria (Governor)	1515 - 1518
4	Diogo Lopes de Sequeira (Governor)	1518 - 1522
5	Dom Duarte de Meneses (Governor)	1522 - 1524
6	Dom Vasco da Gama (Viceroy)	1524
7	Dom Henrique de Meneses (Governor)	1524 - 1526
8	Lopo Vaz de Sampaio (Governor)	1526 - 1529
9	Nuno da Cunha (Governor)	1529 - 1538
10	Dom Garcia de Noronha (Viceroy)	1538 - 1540
11	Estêvão da Gama (Governor)	1540 - 1542
12	Martim Afonso de Sousa (Governor)	1542 - 1545
13	Dom João de Castro (Governor)	1545 - 1547
	Dom João de Castro (Viceroy)	1547 - 1548
14	Garcia de Sá (Governor)	1548 - 1549
15	Jorge Cabral	1549 - 1550
16	Dom Affonso de Noronha (Viceroy)	1550 - 1554
17	Dom Pedro Mascarenhas (Viceroy)	1554 - 1555
18	Francisco Barreto (Governor)	1555 - 1558
19	Dom Constantino de Bragança (Viceroy)	1558 - 1561
20	Dom Francisco Coutinho, Conde	

de Redondo (Viceroy)	1561 - 1564
21 João de Mendonça (Governor)	1564
22 Dom António de Noronha (Viceroy)	1564 - 1568
23 Dom Luís de Ataíde (Viceroy)	1568 - 1571
24 Dom António de Noronha (Viceroy)	1571- 1573
25 António Moniz Barreto (Governor)	1573 - 1576
26 Dom Diogo de Meneses (Governor)	1576 - 1578
27 Dom Luís de Ataíde (Viceroy)	1578 - 1581
28 Fernão Teles de Meneses (Governor)	1581
29 Dom Francisco Mascarenhas, Conde da Vila da Horta (Viceroy)	1581- 1584
30 Dom Duarte de Meneses (Viceroy)	1584 - 1588
31 Manuel de Sousa Coutinho (Governor)	1588 - 1591
32 Mathias de Albuquerque (Viceroy)	1591 - 1597
33 Dom Dom Francisco da Gama, Conde de Vidigueira (Viceroy)	1597 - 1600
34 Ayres de Saldanha (Viceroy)	1600 - 1605
35 Martim Affonso de Castro (Viceroy)	1605 - 1607
36 Dom Fr. Aleixo de Menezes, Archbishop of Goa (Governor)	1607 - 1609
37 André Furtado de Mendonça (Governor)	1609
38 Ruy Lourenço de Távora (Governor)	1609 - 1612
39 Dom Jeronymo de Azovedo (Viceroy)	1611 - 1617
40 Dom João Coutinho, Conde de Redondo (Viceroy)	1617 - 1619
41 Fernão de Albuquerque (Governor)	1619 - 1622
42 Dom Francisco da Gama, Conde de Vidigueira (Viceroy)	1622 - 1627
43 Dom Fr. Luís de Brito, Bishop of Meliapor (Governor)	1627 - 1628
44 Nuno Alvarez Botelho; Dom Lourenço da Cunha; Gonçalo Pinto da Fonseca (Commission)	1628 - 1629
45 Dom Miguel de Noronha, Conde de Linhares (Viceroy)	1629 - 1635
46 Pêro da Silva (Viceroy)	1635 - 1639

47	António Telles de Menezes (Governor)	1639 - 1640
48	João da Silva Tello de Menezes, Conde de Aveiras (Viceroy)	1640 - 1646
49	Dom Filippe Mascarenhas (Viceroy)	1646 - 1651
50	Dom Fr. Francisco dos Martyres; Francisco de Mello de Castro; António de Sousa Coutinho (Commission)	1651 - 1652
51	Dom Vasco Mascarenhas, Conde de Obidos (Viceroy)	1652 - 1653
52	Dom Braz de Castro (A usurper)	1653 - 1655
53	Dom Rodrigo Lobo da Silveira, Conde de Sarzedas (Viceroy)	1655 - 1656
54	Manual Mascarenhas Homem; Francisco de Mello de Castro; António de Sousa Coutinho (Commission)	1656 - 1661
55	Luís de Mendonça Furtado; Dom Pedro de Lancastre (Commission)	1661 - 1662
56	António de Mello e Castro (Governor)	1662 - 1663
57	João Nunes da Cunha, Conde de S. Vicente (Viceroy)	1666 - 1668
58	António de Mello e Castro (relative of the Viceroy of the same name); Luís de Miranda Henriques; Manoel Corte-Real de Sampaio (Commission)	1668 - 1671
59	Luís de Mendonça Furtado de Albuquerque Conde de Lavradio (Viceroy)	1671 - 677

Bibliography

The material for this work has been obtained mainly from the archival repositories in Europe and in India. The *Arquivo Histórico Ultramarino,* Lisbon; the *Arquivo Nacional da Torre do Tombo,* Lisbon; *Biblioteca Nacional,* Lisbon, *Biblioteca da Ajuda,* Lisbon, *Bilioteca João Paulo II da Universidade Católica,* Lisbon, *Biblioteca da Faculdade de Letras,* Lisbon, *Biblioteca Sociedade de Geografia de Lisboa,* all in Portugal; King's College Library, University of London Library, in England; Historical Archives of Goa at Panjim (of which most of the collection is microfilmed and is available at *Filmoteca Ultramarina Portuguesa,* in Lisbon), were some of the major sources of information for the present study from which I collected data not only in manuscript form but also books that each of these places host in their libraries. Some brief detail about the archives, libraries and the series utilised have been furnished below:

1. Manuscript Sources

a) Arquivo Histórico Ultramarino, (AHU), Lisbon

The *Arquivo Histórico Ultramarino* is the major source of information for reconstructing the history of Portuguese overseas trade and commerce. There are a vast number of documents pertaining to the Portuguese commercial diplomacy. Its only drawback is that these documents start mainly from the early seventeenth century. They are preserved in *caixas* (boxes), consisting of loose manuscript papers in files. Each file contains from 1 to 200 pages. If one wants to consult these documents, he would have to look into a separate hand made catalogue and under the heading *Documentos soltos relativos à Índia* (Loose documents pertaing to India). This is also known as *Caixas da Índia.* However, there are only forty *Caixas,* (boxes) organised accoding to dates which cover the period from 1509 to 1833, and a vast amount of documents still to be put into order. Although, rest of the documents, still kept in *Caixas,* almost over four hundreds are known as *Maços da Índia* (Bundles of India). They are housed in a hall called *Sala da Índia.* Other collections are still kept in *maços* (bundles of documents) and *códices* (bound volumes). The following are the series of documents which were consulted for the present work:

***Documentos soltos relativos a Índia* or *Caixas da Índia*:**

The years and other details of the each *Caixas da Índia* series consulted by me are as follows:

Section Sala da Índia	S. N. of Caixas	Period	No. of Documents (in files)
do	Caixa 1	1509-1611	109
do	Caixa 2	1612-1614	149
do	Caixa 3	1615	190
do	Caixa 4	1616-1617	208
do	Caixa 5	1618	201
do	Caixa 6	1619-1621	149
do	Caixa 7	1622-1623	171
do	Caixa 8	1624-1625	232
do	Caixa 9	1626-1629	233
do	Caixa 10	1630-1634	217
do	Caixa 11	1635	225
do	Caixa 12	1636-1637	153
do	Caixa 13	1638-1639	191
do	Caixa 14	1640-1643	184
do	Caixa 15	1643	132
do	Caixa 16	1644	173
do	Caixa 17	1644-1645	180
do	Caixa 18	1645-1646	200
do	Caixa 19	1646-1647	116
do	Caixa 20	1648-1650	199
do	Caixa 21	1650-1652	168
do	Caixa 22	1653-1654	145
do	Caixa 23	1655-1656	125

do	Caixa 24	1656-1660	173
do	Caixa 25	1661-1663	254
do	Caixa 26	1664-1665	229
do	Caixa 27	1668	192
do	Caixa 28	1669-1671	247

***Arquivo Nacional da Torre do Tombo*, (ANTT),** Lisbon

The second most important repository for the collection of valuable sources is the *Arquivo Nacional da Torre do Tombo* (National Archives of Lisbon). Here, the *Livro das Monções* or *Documentos Remettido da Índia* series, which are bound into *codices*, have been found the most important sources of information. Besides this, there were many other series which have been used in this present work.

Livro das Monções* or *Documentos Remettido da Índia:

This series has mainly the correspondence between the King of Portugal and the Viceroys and Governors of Portuguese India pertaining to, besides various other matters of the *Estado da Índia*, its diplomatic relations with the neighbouring kings, dealing with both the political and commercial aspects. However, the dates provided are only what each codex bears on its spine and not exactly the dates of the documents in it. This is to say that quite a number of codexes have documents that belong to a different period than that mentioned on the spine. Therefore, a document of a different period could be found in one volume where one does not expect to find it. All of these docuemtns can now only be consulted on microfilm as the originals are kept away for preservation. There are 62 volumes of this series consisting of between 200 and 800 pages in each *códice*. The following are the details of each series consulted.

No. of the Códice	Year	No. of the Códice	Year
Códice 1	1565	Códice 32	1635
Códice 2	1607-1608	Códice 33	1634-1636
Códice 3	1609-1610	Códice 34	1635-1636
Códice 4	1610-1611	Códice 35	1635-1636
Códice 5	1612	Códice 36	1636
Códice 6	1612-1613	Códice 37	1636-1637
Códice 7	1613-1614	Códice 38	1636-1637
Códice 8	1614-1615	Códice 39	1637
Códice 9	1616	Códice 40	1637-1638

Códice 10	1616-1617	Códice 41	1638
Códice 11	1618-1619	Códice 42	1637-1638
Códice 12	1619	Códice 43	1638
Códice 13	1620	Códice 44	1638-1639
Códice 14	16240	Códice 45	1638-1639
Códice 15	1620-1622	Códice 46	1639-1641
Códice 16	1622	Códice 47	1640-1641
Códice 17	1622-1645	Códice 48	1640-1644
Códice 18	1645-1623	Códice 49	1641-1642
Códice 19	1623-1624	Códice 50	1641-1644
Códice 20	1624	Códice 51	1642-1643
Códice 21	1624	Códice 52	1643
Códice 22	1625-1626	Códice 53	1643
Códice 23	1626	Códice 54	1644
Códice 24	1626-1627	Códice 55	1645-1646
Códice 25	1627-1628	Códice 56	1645-1653
Códice 26	1628-29	Códice 57	1645-1648
Códice 27	1630	Códice 58	1647-1649
Códice 28	1631	Códice 59	1648-1649
Códice 29	1631-1632	Códice 60	1649-1650
Códice 30	1632-33	Códice 61	1650-1651
Códice 31	1634-34	Códice 62	1651-1660

Corpo Cronológico

This mainly contains the correspondence between the Viceroys of India and the kings of Portugal, and the Papers of the Portuguese exchequer. The collection dates from 1611 to 1699 and is in 525 *Maços* consisting of 82,902 documents, but only one of this series is used in the present work.

Maço	1-3-20

Biblioteca da Ajuda, Lisbon

Although it is known as Biblioteca, but in reality it is an archive which host over hundreds of thousands of manuscript, almost all bound *codices*, related to Portuguese colonial dominions all over the world, but quite a vast amounts pertains to India. Like in other archives, here too, docuemtns are kept under various heads. The most important collection for my present study has been the *Jesuitas na Ásia*.

Jesuitas na Ásia :

The following are the series and documents consulted for the present work:

No. of Códice	Period	No. of Códice	Period
46-xiii-30	(1603-1664)	51-vii-13	(1603-1664)
49-v-8	do	51-vii-30	do
49-x-28	do	51-vii-32	do
49-xii-38	do	51-x-2	do
49-xiii-12	do	51-vii-13	do
50-v-37	do	51-vii-30	do
51-vi-2	do	51-vii-32	do
51-vii-12	do	51-x-2	do

Biblioteca da Sociedade de Geografia de Lisboa

Casa da Índia:

The *Reservado* section of this library host a very valuable series called ***Casa da Índia.*** Most of the documents in this section are still kept in the *Maços*. However, ***Maço nº 8*** is one of the most important set of manuscripts which is a *Livro de toda a Recita e despeza de todas as Fortalezas que S. Magestade tem no estado da Índia…, Feito por Barreto de Rezende, secretário do Conde de Linhares Vice-rei do Estado, e Contratador da Matricula Geral no anno de 1635,* has been consulted for the present work.

Historical Archives of Goa, *Panaji, Goa, India*

Livro das Monções ou Monções do Reino:

This is one of the biggest collections of the Goa Archives. It contains correspondence between the Portuguese Viceroys and the kings of Portugal regarding the political as well as the economic affairs. There are about 456 *códices* in this series, dating from the mid-sixteenth century to the early twentieth century (1560-1914). Only 28 *códices,* out of the total, of which many have been, due to their thickness, divided into sub-*códices,* a, b etc, have been found useful for the present work. The detail regarding the *códices* are as follows:

No. of the Códice	Year	No. of the Códice	Year
Códice 1	1605-1607	Códice 18	1633
Códice 2a	1583-1585	Códice 19-A	1633-1634
Códice 2b	1595-1601	Códice 19-B	1634-1635

Códice 3a	1585-1589	Códice 19-C	1634-1635
Códice 5	1595-1590	Códice 19-D	1634-1635
Códice 6-A	1604-1606	Códice 20	1634
Códice 6-B	1605	Códice 21-A	1640
Códice 7	1601-1603	Códice 21-B	1640-1641
Códice 8	1601-1602	Códice 22-B	1620-1653
Códice 9-11	1604-1609	Códice 23-A	1653-1654
Códice 12	1613-1617	Códice 23-B	1653-1654
Códice 13-A	1611-1630	Códice 24	1615-1654
Códice 13-B	1629-1630	Códice 25	1654-1656
Códice 14	1630-1631	Códice 26-A	1656-1658
Códice 15	1631-1632	Códice 26-B	1657-1660
Códice 16-A	1632	Códice 28-A	1661-1663
Códice 16-B	1632	Códice 28-B	1662-1663
Códice 17	1632-1633		

Regimentos e Instruções:

No. of the Códice	**Year**
Códice 1418	1564-1631
Códice 1419	1596-1640
Códice 1420	1616-1640

Other Séries:

Assento do Conselho da Fazenda	Códice 1161-64.
Livros dos Reis Vizinhos	Códice 1-4
Livro das Ordens régias	Códice 2
Livro dos Segredos	Códice 1
Livro de Pazes	Códices 1-13
Livros Grandes da Paz	Códice 1- 2

2. Printed Sources (Primary) and Travel Accounts

ABBÉ CARRÉ, *The Travels of the Abbé Carré in India and the Near East, 1672 to 1674*, Second series, no. XCVII, issued for The Hakluyt Society, 1948,

AHMAD, Afzal, & K.S. Mathew, (ed.) (*Privilégios da Sidade Samta Cruz de Cochim (l559-1614)*, (Mss. Códice de Biblioteca da Ajuda Lisboa) published as *Emergence of Cochin in the pre-industrial era: (A study of Portuguese Cochin)*, Pondicherry, University, 1990.

ALBUQUERQUE, Afonso de, *Cartas de Afonso de Albuquerque*. 7 vols., (ed. Raymundo António de Bulhão Pato), Acad. Ciên., Lisboa, 1884-1935.

ALBUQUERQUE, Luís de, (Introd. e notas de), *Crónica do descobrimento e conquista da Índia pelos portugueses:* códice anónimo, Museu Britânico, Egerton 20,901, Imprensa Nacional, Lisboa, 1984.

ALLAMI, Abu-L-Fazl, (Trans. H. Blochmann), *The A-in-i-Akbari, 3* vols, (Reprinted), D.K. Publishers, Delhi, 1989.

ALLAMI, Abu-L-Fazl, (Trans. Henry Beveridge), *Akbar Nama, 3* vols, (Reprinted), D.K. Publishers, Delhi, 1989.

ANTÓNIO, Frei (ed. lit. G. Schurhammer), *Carta inédita sobre a fundação do convento de S. Francisco de Goa*, Bastorá (Goa), 1957.

BALDAEUS, Philippus, 'A True and Exact Description of the Most Celebrated East India Coast of Malabar and Coromandel' in A *Collection of Voyages and Travels...*, (Comps. Awnsham Churchill and John Churchill), 4 vols., London, 1704.

BARBOSA, Duarte, (Transt. & ed Mansel Longworth Dames), *The Book of Duarte Barbosa, an Account of the Countries Bordering on the Indian Ocean and their Inhabitants*, 2 vols., Hakluyt Society, London, 1918-1921, (Reprinted) Asian Educational Services, New Delhi, 1989.

BARROS, João de, & Couto, Diogo do, *Da Ásia de...*, Décadas Primeira a Duodécima 24 vols., Livraria Sam Carlos, Lisboa, 1973.

BATTUTA, Ibn (Translated and Selected by), H.A.R. Gibb, *Travels in Asia and Africa, 1325-1354*, D.K. Publishers, (Reprinted), New Delhi, 1999.

BERNIER, Francois, *Travels in the Mogul Empire: AD 1656-1668*, (second edition revised by Vincent A. Smith), D.K. Publishers, New Delhi, 1999.

BÍBLIA SAGRADA, Versão dos textos originais, Difusora Bíblica, 7ª Edição, Lisboa, 1976.

BIKER, J.F.J., (ed.) Collecção *de tratados e concertos de pazes que o Estado da Índia Portuguesa fez com os reis e senhores em que teve relações nas partes da Ásia e África Oriental desde o princípio da conquista até aofim do Século XVIII*, vols. 1-13, Lisboa, 1881.

BOCARRO, António, *Década 13 da história da Índia,* 2 Vols. Public. Academia Real das Sciencias de Lisboa, dir. de Rodrigo José de Lima Felner. Typ. da Academia Real das Sciencias, Lisboa, 1876.

BOCARRO, António, *O livro das plantas de todas as fortalezas, cidades e povoações do Estado da Índia Oriental.* (Estampas) IN-CM, Lisboa, 1987.

BOTELHO, Simão, "Tombo do Estado da India" in *Subídios para a Historia de Índia Portugueza,* pp. 30-34. (ed. See in Felner).

BOTELHO, Simão, LEMOS, Jorge de, *Textos sobre o Estado da Índia,* (dir. e coment. Luís de Albuquerque, notícia biobibliográfica Justino Mendes de Almeida, transcrição em português actual, Maria da Graça Pericão, Luís Albuquerque)., Alfa, cop. Lisboa, 1989.

BOUCHON, Genevieve, (introd. éd.) *Caderno dos ofiçiaes da Índia da carreguaçam das naos que vieram o anno de 1518-bcxbiij,* Paris. 1977.

BOXER, Charles Ralph, *Descriptive list of the state papers Portugal: 1661-1780: in the Public Record Office London,* 3 vols. Acad. Das Ciências da Lisboa, 1979-1983

BRAGANÇA, Joaquim O., (Introdução de), *Acta do Sínodo de Diamper,* Edições Didaskalia, Lisboa, 1987.

BRASÃO, Eduardo, *The Embassy of Manuel de Saldanha to China in 1667-1670,* (*Notes on Sino-Portuguse Diplomatic Relations*), Imprensa Nacional, Macau, 1948.

BRASÃO, Eduardo, *Subsídios para a história das relações diplomáticas de Portugal com a China: a Embaixada de Alexandre Metelo de Sousa e Meneses: 1725-1728.*, Imprensa Nacional, Macau 1948.

BRÁSIO, António Duarte Pe, *Uma carta inédita de Valentim Fernandes,* Coimbra, 1959. (Sep. Bol. Bibl. Univ. Coimbra, 24)

BRIGGS, John, *History of the Rise of Mahomedan Power in India,* (Ed & Translated from the Original of *Tarikh-i-Ferishta*) (2nd Ed.) D.K. Publishers, 4 vols. New Delhi, 1990.

CAMPOS, J.J.A., *History of the Portuguese in Bengal*, Delhi, 1979.

CASTANHEDA, Fernão Lopes de, *História do descobrimento e conquista da Índia pelos portugueses*, 3ª ed., Imp. da Universidade, Coimbra 1924-1933.

CASTRO, José Ferreira Borges de, & Júlio Firmino Biker, *Suplemento à Collecção dos Tratados da Convenções, Contratos e Actos Públicos Celebrados entre A Corôa de Portugal e As mais potências, desde 1640 até ao presente,* Tomo I-X, Imprensa Nacional, Lisboa 1858.

CASTRO, José Ferreira Borges de, (2° Visconde de Santarém), *Collecção dos Tratados da Convenções, Contratos e Actos Públicos Celebrados entre A Corôa de Portugal e As mais potencias, desde 1640 até ao presente,* Tomos 1-VIII, Imprensa Nacional, Lisboa 1858.

CASTRO, José Ferreira Borges de, (2° Visconde de Santarém), Luiz Augusto Rebello da Silva e José da Silva Mendes Leal, *Quadro Elementar das Relações Políticas e Diplomáticas de Portugal com as Diversas Potências do Mundo desde o Princípio da Monarchias Portuguezas até aos nossos dias.* (This series belong to the ANTT), 18 vols., Paris, & Lisboa, 1842-1876.

COMMISSARIAT, M. S., ed., *Mandelslo's Travels in Western India,* 1638-39, London, 1931.

'COPIA DE UMA carta de el-rei de Portugal enviada ao Rei de Castella acerca da Viagem de succeso da India' in *Centenário do descobrimento da America: memorias da Comissão portugueza.* Typographia da Academia Real das Sciencias, Lisboa, 1892.

CORREIA, Gaspar, *Lendas da Índia,* (ed) Rodrigo José de Lima Felner, 4 vols., Coimbra, 1922.

CORREIA-AFONSO, John, *Jesuit Letters and Indian History,* 2nd edition, Bombay, 1969.

COSTA, Francisco da, 'Relatório sobre o trato da pimenta', feito por Francisco da Costa, escrivão da feitoria de Cochim, (cód. 1571, Sécretarias provinciales, Archivo General de Simancas, Espanha,) in *Documentação Ultramarina Portuguesa,* António da Silva Rego, (ed.) vol. 1, CEHU, Lisboa, 1963, pp. 295-379.

CRUZ, António, (ed.) (Ed. Facsimilada*) Diário da Viagem de Vasco da Gama,* Porto, 1970.

CUNHA-RIVARA, J.H. da, (ed.), *(Códice de HAG, Livros de Pazes) Boletim official do Governo do Estado da Índia,* Imprensa Nacional, Goa 1879-1938.

CUNHA-RIVARA, J.H. da, (ed.), *O chronista de Tissuary: periodico mensal*: Imprensa Nacional, Nova Goa, 1866-1869. (Mensal).

CUNHA-RIVARA, J. H. da, (ed.) *Arquivo Português Oriental*, 6 vols., em 9 partes, Nova Goa, 1857-1876.

DANVERS, Frederick. C., (ed.) *Letters Received by the East India Company from its Servants in the East*, 6 vols. London, 1896.

DELLA VALLE, Pietro, *The Travel of Pietro della Valle in India*, 2 vols., Hakluyt Society London, 1892.

FALCÃO , Luís de Figueiredo, *Livro em que se contém toda a fazenda e real património dos reinos de Portugal, Índia e ilhas adjacentes e outras particularidades*, Lisboa, 1859.

FARIA E SOUSA, Manuel de, *Ásia Portuguesa*, 6 vols., Livraria Civilização, Porto, 1947.

FELNER, José de Lima, *Subsídios para a História da Índia*, Lisboa, 1868.

FERGUSON, Donald, *Cartas de Raja Singa II, Rei de Candia, aos hollandeses: (1636-1660)*, Typ. Universal, Lisboa 1907. (Sep. *Boletim da Sociedade da Geographia de Lisboa*, n°s 2, 3 e 5).

FERISHTA, Abdul Qasim, *Tarikh-i-Ferishta*, (Ed. & Translated from the Original by John Briggs) and is known as *History of the Rise of Mahomedan Power in India*, (2nd Ed.) D.K. Publishers, 4 vols. New Delhi, 1990.

FOSTER, William and F. C. Danvers, (ed.), *Letters Received by the East India Company from its Servants in the East*, 1602-1617, 6 vols. London, 1896-1902.

FOSTER, William, (ed.) *The Embassy of Sir Thomas Roe to India*, 1615-19, Hakluyt Society, London, 1929.

FOSTER, William, (ed.) *The English Factories in India 1616-1669*, 13 vols. Clarendon Press, Oxford, 1906-1927.

FRÓIS, Luís, (edição anotada por José Wicki) *História do Japão*, 5 vols, Biblioteca Nacional, Lisboa, 1976-1984.

GALLETTI, A. (Tran.) *Selections from the Records of the Madras Government, Dutch Records Number 13: The Dutch in Malabar*, Government Press, Madras, 1911.

GÓIS, Damião de, *Crónica do felicíssimo Rei D. Manuel*. Ed. Nova, conforme a de 1566, Imprensa da Universidade, Coimbra, 1949-1955.

GONÇALVES, Pe. Sebastiam, (publ. por José Wicki.) Primeira parte da história dos religiosos da Companhia de Jesus e do que fizeram com a divina graça..., 3 vols. Atlântida, Coimbra 1957-1962.

GOUVEIA, António, *Jornada do Arcebispo de Goa Dom Frey Aleixo de Menezes Primas da Índia Oriental,* (first published, 1606), (Reprinted), Edições Didaskalia, Lisboa, 1988.

GRAÇA, Luís, *A Visão do Oriente na Literatura Portuguesa de viagens: os viajantes portugueses e os itinerários terrestres,* IN-CM, Lisboa, 1983.

GRAÇA, Luís, 'O Mundo Indiano de seiscentos e a literature portuguesa de viagens', in *II Seminário Internacional da História Indo-Portuguesa,* IICT-CEHCA, Lisboa, 1985, pp. 479-501.

GROTIUS, Hugo, *The Freedom of the Sea (Mare Liberum) or the Right which belongs to the Dutch to take part in the East Índia Trade,* Oxford University Press, New York, 1916.

HERCULANO, Alexandre, e Paiva, Barão de Castello, *Roteiro de Viagem de Vasco da Gama em MCCCCXCVIII,* Imprensa Nacional, Lisboa, 1861.

JARRIC, Fr. Pierre Du, (Edited Sir E. Denison Ross and Eileen Power) *Akbar and the Jesuits: An Account of the Jesuit Missions to the Court of Akbar by Father Pierre du Jarric,* George Routledge & Sons, Ltd. London, 1926, (Reprinted) by D.K. Publishers, New Delhi, 1999.

KAUTILYA, Vishnugupta, (ed.) R. P. Kangle, The *Kautilyas Arthashástra,* University of Bombay, 1965,

LINHARES, Conde de, *Diário do 3° Conde de Linhares, Vice-rei da Índia,* 2 vols. Biblioteca Nacional, Lisboa, 1937-1943.

LINSCHOTEN, Jan. H. Van, *The Voyages of John Huyghen Van Linschoten to the East Indies,* 2 vols. Hakluyt Society, London, 1895, (Reprinted) Asian Educational Services, New Delhi, 1990.

LUZ, Francisco P. Mendes da, 'Livro das cidades e fortalezas que a coroa de Portugal tem nas partes da Índia, e das capitanias e mais cargos que nelas ha, e da importância delles', in *Stvdia,* n° 6, CEHU, Lisboa, 1960.

LOPES, David, *Chrónica dos reis de Bisnaga: manuscrito inedito do seculo XVI,* publicado por Sociedade de Geografia de Lisboa, Lisboa, Impr. Nacional, 1897.

LOPES, Fernão, *Crónica do Senhor Rei Dom Fernando Nono Rei destes Regnos,* Civilização Editora, Porto, 1966.

MANUCCI, Niccolao, (trans. and edited by William Irvine), *Mugul India* or *Storia do Mogor, 1653-1708,* 4 vols. First printed, London, 1907-8, (Reprinted), D.K. Publishers, New Delhi, 1990.

MARQUES, João Martins da Silva, *Descobrimentos Portugueses: Documentos para a sua História.* (Publicada e prefaciada por) vol. I, (1147-1460) INIC., Lisboa, 1987. (Edição Facsimilada da 1ª Edição de Instituo de Alta Cultura, 1944).

MATOS, Artur Teodoro de, *Estado da Índia nos anos de 1581-1588: Estrutura Administrativa e económica, alguns elementos para o seu estudo,* Universidade dos Açores, Ponta Delgada, 1982.

MATOS, Artur Teodoro de, *Diário de Conde de Sarzedas, Viceroy do Estado Índia,* (1655-56), Lisboa, 2001.

MATOS, Luís de, (Introdução de) *Imagens do Oriente no Século XVI* (Reprodução do códice Português da Biblioteca Casanatense), INCM, Lisboa, 1985.

MONSSERATE, Father António, *The Commentary of Father Monsserate, S.J., on his Journey to the Court of Akbar,* (First published in 1922) reprinted by Asian Educationsal Services, New Delhi, 1992.

'MONUMENTA Historiae Índiae', in *Journal of Bombay Historical Society,* (JBHS) vol., Nºs. I & 2, Bombay, 1929 (March and September).

OVINGTON, John, *A Voyage to Surat in the Year 1689,* London, 1929.

ORTA, Garcia de, *Coloquios dos simples e Drogas da Índia,* 2 vols. IN-CM, Lisboa, 1987.

PEREIRA, A. B. de Bragança (ed.) *Arquivo Português Oriental,* 11 vols. Tip. Rangel, Bastorá, Goa, 1936-1940.

PERES, Damião, (ed.) *Regimento das Cazas das Indias e Mina,* manuscrito inédito, Coimbra, 1947.

PIRES, Tomé, (Trans. Armando Cortesão), *The Suma Oriental of Tomé Pires,* 2 vols. Hakluyt Society, London, 1944, (reprinted) Asian Educational Services, New Delhi, 1990.

PISSURLENCAR, Panduronga S. S., *Assentos do Conselho do Estado,* Governo-Geral do Estado da Índia, (Coord. e anot. Panduronga S. S. Pissurlencar). Tip. Rangel, Goa 1953-1957.

PISSURLENCAR, Panduronga S. S., (documentos coordenados, anotados e prefaciados por), *Agentes da diplomacia portuguesa na Índia: hindus, muçulmanos, judeus e parses.* Tip. Rangel, Goa 1952.

PURCHAS, Samuel, 1577?-1626, *Hakluytus posthumus or Purchas his pilgrimes: contayning a history of the world, in sea voyages and lande travells by Englishmen and others*., James MacLehose and Sons, Glasgow 1905-1907, 20v.

RAZAK, Abdallah ben Ahmad Ibn ar, *Roteiro marítimo-geográfico de Abdallah ben Ahmad Ibn ar-Razak*. Ms. *Roteiro marítimo-geográfico da região do Índico, ilustrado com vários gráficos e mapas do espaço marítimo do Oceano Índico, tendo na primeira folha o desenho da Rosa dos Ventos*. Lisboa, 1895.

REGO, António da Silva, *Documentação para a história das missões do padroado português do Oriente, Índia*, 12 vols, Agência Geral das Colónias, *Lisboa*. 1947-1958.

REGO, António da Silva, (ed.) ANTT, *As Gavetas da Torre do Tombo*, vol. IV (gav. XV, Maços 1-15). CEHU, Lisboa, 1964.

SANCEAU, Elaine (ed.) *Collecção São Lourenço*, IICT, Lisboa, 1983.

SANCEAU, Elaine, (ed.) *Documentação Ultramarina Portuguesa*, 3 vols, CEHU, Lisboa, 1962-1983.

SANCEAU, Elaine, *Os Portugueses na Etiópia*, Livraria Civilização, Porto, 1961.

SEN, Geeti, *Paintings from the Akbar Nama*, Lustres Press Pvt Ltd, Delhi, 1984.

SEN, Surender Nath, *The Indian Travels of Thevenot and Carreri*, vol. I. New Delhi, 1949.

SERRÃO, Joaquim Veríssimo, *Commentário do Afonso de Albuquerque*, 2 vols. IN-CM, Lisboa, 1973.

SCHURHAMMER, Georg, *S. Francisco Xavier e a sua época*, CEHU, Lisboa, 1964. (Sep. Studia, 12).

TAVERNIER, Jean-Baptiste, *Travels in Índia*, trad. Ed. V. Ball Crook, 2 vols. London, 1889, (Second edition), Munshirama Manhoarlal, New Delhi, 1995.

THOMAZ, Luís Filipe Ferreira R., *De Malaca a Pegu: viagens de um Feitor Português*, Lisboa, 1966.

TRINDADE, Frei Paulo da, *Conquista Espiritual do Oriente*, 3 Vols., CEHU, Lisboa 1962.

VARTHEMA, Ludovico di, *Travels of Ludovico di Varthema in Egypt, Syria, Arabia Deserta and Arabia Felix, in Persia, Índia, and Ethiopia*, Hakluyt Society, London, 1863.

VELHO, Álvaro, (notas e anexos por A. Fontoura da Costa), *Roteiro da primeira viagem de Vasco da Gama*, Ag. Geral do Ultramar, Lisboa 1960.

VELHO, Diogo, *Orçamento do Estado da Índia: 1574: feito por mandado de Diogo Velho, Vedor da Fazenda da Índia,* (*com um estudo de Guedo de Oliveira*). Bertrand Editora, Lisboa, 1960,

WEINSTEIN, Donald, *Ambassador from Venice Pietro Pasqualigo in Lisbon, 1501,* University of Minnesota Press, Minneapolis, 1960.

WELWOD, William, *An Abridgment of all Sea-Lawes.* It was first published in (*Oxford?*), 1613.

WICKI, Padre Iosephus '*As relações de viagens dos Jesuítas na carreira das naus da Índia de 1541 a 1598,*' in *II Seminário Internacional de História Indo-Portuguesa* Lisboa, CEHU-CA, 1985:

WICKI, Padre Iosephus (Joseph, José) could be included his editions of the monumental collections of the Society of Jesus of the Vatican Library, *Documenta indica, Monumenta Historica Societatis Jesu,* Roma 1948-1988.

ZINADIN, (Trad. David Lopes), *Tuhfat-ul-Mujahedeen,* or *História dos Portugueses no Malabar,* Imprensa Nacional, Lisboa, 1898.

ZUBAIRI, Muhammad Ibrahim, (Edited) *Basatin al-Salatin,* Hyderabad, 1824-25.

Secondary Works

A SHORT *Oxford English Dictionary,* vol. I, Oxford, 1947.

AHMAD, Afzal, *Indo-Portuguese Trade in Seventeenth Century (1600-1663),* Gian Publishing House, New Delhi, 1991.

ALAM, Muzaffar & Subrahmanyam Sanjay (edited), *The Mughal State 1526-1750,* Oxford University Press, New Delhi, (3rd ed.) 2003.

ALBUQUERQUE, Luís de & Costa, José Pereira da, *Cartas de "serviços" da Índia (1500-1550)* (Sep. de *Mare Liberum, nº 1*), 1990.

ALBUQUERQUE, Luís de, & GUERREIRO, Inácio, 'Khoja Shams-ud-dín, comerciante de Cananor na Primeira metade do século XVI' in *Acta do II Seminário Internacional da História Indo-Portuguesa,* IICT-CEHCA, Lisboa, 1985,

ALI, M. Athar, *The Mughal Nobility under Aurangzeb,* Asia Publishing House, New Delhi, 1970,

ARAGÃO, A. C. Teixeira de, *Descrição geral e história das moedas cunhadas em nome dos reis, regentes e governadores de Portuga,* [nota preambular Dr. Raúl Gonçalves, pref. Alexandre Ferreira Barros]. 2ª ed. Livraria Fernando Machado, Porto 1964-1966.

ARASARATNAM, Sinappa, *Maritime India in the Seventeenth Century,* Oxford University Press, New Delhi, 1994.

ARON, Raymond, *Paz e Guerra entre as nações,* Universidade de Brasília, 1986.

AYYAR, K.V. Krishna, *The Zamorins of Calicut,* Calicut, 1938.

AZEVEDO, João Lúcio de, *Historia dos Cristãos novos portugueses,* Livraria Clássica Editora, Lisboa, 1922.

AZEVEDO, João Lúcio de, *Épocas de Portugal Económico: Esboços de história,* Livraria Clássica Editora, Lisboa, 1928.

AZEVEDO, Pedro de, *Linhas gerais da história da diplomática em Portugal,* Imprensa da Universidade, Coimbra 1927.

BARENDSE, R. J., *The Arabian Seas, 1640-1700,* Leiden University, Leiden, 1998.

BAYLY C.A., *Empire and Information: Intelligence gathering and social communication in India, 1780-1870,* Cambridge University Press, 1996.

BAYLY C.A., *Indian Society and the Making of the British Empire,* Cambridge University Press, (First published in 1988) reprinted, 1999.

BEVERIDGE, Henry, *A Comprehensive History of India, vol. I,* (Reprinted) New Delhi, 1990.

BLANCO, Manuela Sobral, *O Estado Português da Índia: da rendição de Ormuz à perda de Cochim-1622-1663,* (Unpublished thesis) *Universidade Nova de Lisboa,* Lisboa, 1992.

BORGES, Charles J., 'Foreign Jesuits and Native Resistance in Goa, 1542-1759,' in *Essay in Goan History,* (Ed. T.R. D'Souza), Concept Publishing, N. Delhi, 1989, pp. 69-80.

BORGES, Charles J., & FELDMANN, Helmut, (Edited) *Goa and Portugal: Their Cultural Links,* Concept Publishhin Company, New Delhi, 1997.

BORGES, Charles J., 'Religious Orders in Portuguese India: 1622-1961', in *Vasco da Gama,* FCG, Lisboa, 1999, vol. III, pp. 85-97.

BOUCHON, Geneviève, *Bengal and Pegu at the Beginning of Sixteenth Century: According to an Anonymous Portuguese narrative,* Lisboa, IICT-CEHCA, 1985.

BOUCHON, Geneviève, *Afonso de Albuquerque leão dos mares da Ásia,* trad. Isabel de Faria e Albuquerque, Quetzal, Lisboa, 2000.

BOUCHON, Geneviève, *Mamale de Cananor: un adversaire de l'Inde portugaise: 1507-1528.* Genéve, Libr. Droz, 1975. Its English translation is *Regent of the Sea, Cannanore's Response to Portuguese Expansion,* 1507-1528, Oxford, 1988.

BOUCHON, Geneviève, *Portugal e o Oriente: 1° ciclo de conferências*, Lisboa, Fundação Oriente, Quetzal, 1994.

BOUCHON, Geneviève, *Vasco da Gama*, (trad.) Ana Santos Silva, Terramar, Lisboa, 1998.

BOXER, Charles Ralph, *Novas da Índia Oriental: ano de 1955, portugueses e holandeses*, Imprensa Ltd, (Sep. *Arqueologia e História*, 6), Lisboa, 1928.

BOXER, C. R., 'European rivalry in the Indian Seas, 1600-1700', in *The Mariner's Mirror*, vol. XIV, no. 1, January, 1928.

BOXER, C. R., 'The General of the Galleons and the Anglo-Portuguese Truce celebrated at Goa in January 1635', Sep. *Ethnos*, 1, Casa Portuguesa, Lisboa, 1935.

BOXER, C. R., 'O General do mar! António Telles, o seu combate naval contra os Hollandeses na barra de Goa em 1630', in *BIVG*, n° 37, Goa, 1938.

BOXER, C. R., *Breve relação da vida e feitos de Lopo e Inácio Sarmento de Carvalho: grandes capitães que no século XVII honraram Portugal no Oriente*, Imp. Nacional, Macau, 1940.

BOXER, C.R., 'A glimpse of the Goa Archives' - Sep. de *Bulletin of the School of Oriental and African Studies*, XIV, June 1952. pp. 299-324.

BOXER, C. R. *André Furtado de Mendonça, 1558-1610*, (por C. R. Boxer e Frazão de Vasconcelos), Agência Geral do Ultramar, Lisboa Divisão de Publicações e Biblioteca, 1955.

BOXER, C. R., 'António Bocarro and the "Livro do Estado da Índia Oriental": a bio-bibliographical note',. (Sep. *Garcia de Orta*, n° especial), 1956.

BOXER, C. R., 'Vicissitudes of the Anglo-Portuguese Alliance, 1660-1700', (Sep. *Rev. Fac. Letras de Lisboa*) 3, Lisboa, 1958.

BOXER, C.R., (ed. and trans.) *Tragic History of the Sea, 1589-1622*, Hakluyt Society, Cambridge, 1959.

BOXER, C. R., *Francisco Vieira de Figueiredo: A Portuguese Mercant-Adventurer in South East Asia, 1624-1667*, Martinus Nijhoff, Gravenhage, 1967.

BOXER, C. R., *The Anglo-Dutch wars of the 17th century*, 1652-1674, H.M.S.O., 1974.

BOXER, Charles R., *The Portuguese Seaborne Empire*, London, 1969.

BOXER, C. R., *Portuguese India in the Mid-seventeenth century*, Oxford University Press, Delhi 1980.

BOYAJIAN, James C., *Portuguese Bankers at the Court of Spain, 1626-1650*, New Jersey, U.S.A., 1983.

BOYAJIAN, James C., *Goa Inquisition- A New Light on the First 100 Years, (1561-1660)*, Fresno. CA, 1987.

BOYAJIAN, James C., *Portuguese Trade in Asia under the Hapsburgs, 1580-1640*, John Hopkins, 1993.

BRASÃO, Eduardo, *A diplomacia da Restauração*, Lisboa, 1934.

BRASÃO, Eduardo, *A participação portuguesa nas conferências pacifistas da Haia*,Tip. da Casa Portuguesa Lisboa, 1936.

BRASÃO, Eduardo, *A Restauração: relações diplomáticas de Portugal de 1640 a 1668*, Lisboa, Bertrand, 1939.

BRASÃO, Eduardo, *Apontamentos para a história das relações diplomáticas de Portugal com a China 1516-1753*, Ag. Geral das Colónias, Lisboa, 1949.

BRASÃO, Eduardo, *História diplomática de Portugal*, com um pref. Moses Bensabat Amzalak, Livr. Rodrigues, Lisboa, 1932.

BRASÃO, Eduardo, *The Anglo-Portuguese Alliance*, Sylvan Press, London, 1957.

BRAZÃO, Eduardo, *A Diplomacia Portuguesa nos séculos XVII e XVIII*, vol. I, 1640-1700, Editorial Resistência, Lisboa, 1979.

BRUIJN, Y. R., GAASTRA, F. J., SCHÖFFER, J. *Dutch-Asiatic Shipping in the 17th and 18th centuries*, Martinus Nijhoff, The Hague 1987.

CARDIM, Pedro, 'Embaixadores e Representantes diplomáticos da Coroa Portuguesa no século XVII' in *Cultura: Revista de História e Teoria das Ideias*, (II Série) nº 15, Universidade Nova de Lisboa, 2000., pp. 47-86.

CARVALHO, António Viana da Silva, Introdução aos apontamentos para a história diplomática contemporânea, Livr. Ferin, Lisboa 1907.

CHAUDHURI, K.N., *Trade and Civilisation in the Indian Ocean: An Economic History from the Rise of Islam to 1750*, Cambridge University Press, 1986.

CHAUDHURI, K.N., & BETHENCOURT, Francisco, *História da expansão portuguesa*, 5 Vols, Lisboa, 1998.

CLUNY, Isabel, *D. Luís da Cunha e a ideia de diplomacia em Portugal*, Livros Horizontes, Lisboa, 1999.

COELHO, J.M. Latino, *Figuras do Passado, Vasco da Gama*, Lello & Irmão, Porto, 1985.

CORREIA-AFONSO, John, (Ed.) *Indo-Portuguese History: Sources and Problems*, Oxford University Press, Bombay, 1981.

CORREIA, Alberto C. Germano da Silva, *História da colonização portuguesa na Índia*, Ag. Geral das Colónias, Lisboa 1950.

CORREIA, Alberto C. Germano da Silva, *Os portugueses na Índia no século XVI*, Tip. Rangel, Bastorá, 1936.

CORREIA, José Manuel, *Os Portugueses no Malabar*, Imprensa Nacional, Lisboa, 1997.

CORTESÃO, Armando, *Primeira embaixada europeia à China: o boticário e embaixador Tomé Pires e a sua "Suma Oriental"* (actualiz. e rev. do texto João Carvalho, trad. Li Fei), Instituto Cultural, Macau, 1990.

COSTA, A. Delduque da, *Os portugueses e os reis da Índia*: Tip. Rangel, Bastorá 1933. (Sep. do Boletim do Instituto Vasco da Gama, (*BIVG)*, nºs. 18, e 20).

CRUZ, Maria Augusta Lima, "Degredados e Arrenegados portugueses no espaço Índico nos primórdios do século XVI" in *Povos e Culturas, Portugal e o Oriente. Passado e Presente*, Lisboa, Centro de Estudos dos Povos e Culturas de Expressão Portuguesa, Universidade Católica Portuguesa, 1996.

CRUZ, Maria Augusta Lima, "Os Marginais na Índia Portuguesa do Século XVI" in *Vasco da Gama,* vol. II, FCG, Lisboa, 1999, pp. 165-170.

CUNHA, Ana Cannas da, 'A Inquisição de Goa', in *Vasco da Gama,* FCG, Lisboa, 1999, vol. III, pp. 59-73.

COUTO, Dejanirah 'Quelques observations sur les renégats portugais en Asie au XVIe siècle, in *Mare Liberum*, 16, 1998, pp. 57-85.

DANVERS, Frederick Charles, *The Portuguese in India,* 2 vols., London, 1894.

DAVIES, D.W., *A Primer of Dutch Seventeenth Century Overseas Trade,* Martinus Nijhoff, The Hague, 1961, pp. 54-56;.

DIFFIE, Bailey W., and WINIUS, George D., *Foundation of the Portuguese Empire,* 1415-1580, Vol. 1: *Europe and the world in the age of expansion.* Oxford, 1977.

DISNEY, Anthony R., *Twilight of the Pepper Empire- Portuguese Trade in South-West India in the Early Seventeenth Century*, Harvard, 1978.

DISNEY, A.R., *A Decadência do Império da Pimenta, Comércio Português na Índia no Início do séc. XVII*, Edicções 70, Lisboa, 1981.

DUNBAR, Sir George, *History of India from the Earliest Times to the Present Day*, (First Ed. 1936), (Reprinted), DK Publishers, New Delhi, 1990.

ELLIOT, Sir H.M. and DOWSON, John, *The History of India as told by its own Historians*, Vols. 1-8. (first published, 1867-1877), (Reprint), 1990.

ELPHINISTONE, Mountstuart, *The Rise of the British Power in the East*, London, 1887.

ENCONTROS *sobre Portugal e a Índia*, Fundação Oriente, Lisboa, 2000.

FANSHAWE, Richard, *Original letters of his Excellency Sir Richard Fanshaw, during his Embassies in Spain and Portugal: Which, together with divers letters and answers from the Chief Ministers of State of England, Spain and Portugal....*, Printed for A. Roper, London, 1702.

FARINHA, António Dias, 'As Relações dos Portugueses com os Árabes e os Persas na Área do Índico', in *Vasco da Gama, vol I*, FCG, Lisboa, 1999, p. 169.

FARINHA, Maria do Carmo Jasmins Dias - *Os documentos dos Negócios Estrangeiros na Torre do Tombo*, Arquivo Nacional da Torre do Tombo, Lisboa 1990.

FAROOQI, N.R., *Mughal Ottoman Relations*, Idarah-i Adabiyat-i-Delhi, Delhi, 1989.

FERISHTA, A. Qasim, *Tarikh-i-Ferishta*, (Ed & Translated from the Original by) John Briggs, *History of the Rise of Mahomedan Power in India*, (2nd Ed.) D.K. Publishers, New Delhi, 1990,

FERRÃO, António, *Os estudos de história diplomática em Portugal e as publicações da Academia das Sciências sobre tal especialidade, o corpo diplomático português e o quadro elementar das relações políticas*, Coimbra: Impr. da Universidade, 1928.

FERROLI, D., *The Jesuits in Malabar*, Bangalore, 1939.

FITZLER, M.A. Hedwig and Ernesto Ennes, *A Secção Ultramar da Biblioteca Nacional*, Sep. Anais Bibliotecas e Arquivos, 8., Biblioteca Nacional, Lisboa, 1928.

FLORES, Jorge Manuel Costa da Silva, *Os portugueses e o mar de Ceilão: 1498-1543: Trato, diplomacia e guerra*, Lisboa, 1991. (Tese de mestrado em História dos Descobrimentos e da Expansão Portuguesa apresentada à Fac. de Ciências Sociais e Humanas da Univ. Nova de Lisboa).

FLORES, Jorge Manuel Costa da Silva, António Vasconcelos de Saldanha, *Os Firangis na Chancelaria Mogol: Cópias Portuguesas de Documentos de Akbar, (1572-1602)*, Fundação Calouse Gulbenkian, Lisboa, 2003.

FONSECA, Luís Adão da, 'O significado Político em Portugal das Primeiras Viagens à Índia de Vasco da Gama,' in *Vasco da Gama*, vol. I, FCG, Lisboa, 1999.

FOSTER, William, ed., *Early Travels in India, 1583-1619,* Oxford Univeristy Press, London, 1921.

FOSTER, William, *The East India Company*, vol. V, Cambridge, 1929.

FURBER, Holden, *Rival empires of Trade in the Orient, 1600-1800,* University of Minnesota Press, Minneapolis, 1976.

GALVÃO, António, *Tratado dos Descobrimentos*, Liv. Civilização, Porto, 1944.

GLAMANN, Kristof: *Dutch-Asiatic trade*: 1620-1740. Nijhoff, The Hague, 1958.

GLENN, J. Ames,"The Salssette Campaign of 1658-1659: Issues of War and Peace in Bijapuri-Portuguese Relations during the mid-17th Century" in *The Portuguese, Indian Ocean and European Bridgeheads: Festschrift in Honour of Prof. K.S. Mathew* edited by Pius Malekandathil and Jamal Mohammed, Tellicherry, 2001, pp. 223-40.

GODINHO, Vitorino Magalhães, *Os descobrimentos e a economia Mundial,* First published in 2 volumes, Arcádia, Lisboa, 1963-1971. 2ª Edição corrigida e editada em 4 vols., Presença, imp. 1981-1982 Lisboa, 1981.

GOYAL, S.R., *Kautilya and Megasthenese*, Kusumanjali Prakashan, Meerut, 1985.

GREENLEE, William Brooks, (transl. with introd. and notes), *The voyage of Pedro Álvares Cabral to Brazil and India: from Contemporary documents and narratives,* The Hakluyt Society, London 1938.

GREENLEE, William Brooks, *The Captaincy of the Second Portuguese Voyage to Brazil, 1501-1502,* Washington, The Americas, 1945.

GRIBBLE, J.D.E., *History of the Deccan, 2 Vols.* Mittal Publications, New Delhi, 1990.

GUERREIRO, Inácio (coordenação), *A Epopeia das especiarias*, IICT, edições Inapa, Lisboa, 1999.

GULBENKIAN, Roberto, *As embaixadas e as missões diplomáticas portuguesas na Pérsia*,Acad. Port. da Hist., Lisboa 1986 . (Sep. Anais, 2ª série, 31).

GUNE, V.T., *A guide to the collections of records from the Goa archives*, Panaji, Historical Archives of Goa, 1973.

HABIB, Irfan, (edited) *State and Diplomacy under Tipu Sultan, (Documents and Essays)* Tulika, New Delhi, 2001.

HAMILTON, C. J., *The Trade Relations Between England and India (1600-1896)*, Delhi, 1975.

HEATLEY, D. P., *Diplomacy and the Study of International Relations*, Oxford, 1919.

HERAS, Henry, *The Expansion wars of Venkatapa Nayaka of Ikeri*, Government of India Press, Calcutta, 1929.

JOSHI, P. M. (ed.), *History of Medieval Decan*, 2 vols. Hyderabad, 1943.

KAIL, O. C., *The Dutch in India*, New Delhi, 1981.

KOSAMBI, D.D., *The Culture and Civilisation of Ancient India in Historical Outline*, Vikas Publishing House, New Delhi, (Fifth Ed.) 1977.

KOSHY, M.O., *The Dutch Power in Kerala*, Mittal Publications, New Delhi, 1989.

KUSUMAN, K.K., *A History of Trade and Commerce in Travancore*, Mittal Publications, Delhi, 1987.

KYD, N. Alexander, *History of Konkan*, London, 1899.

LACH, F. D., *Asia in the Making of Europe*, 2 vols. in two parts, Chicago, 1971.

LANE, Fredric C., 'Venice and History, The Mediterranean spice trade:Its revival in the sixteenth century' in *American Historical Review*, XLV, 1940, (Foreword by Fernand Braudel), Baltimore, 1966.

LANE-POOLE, Stanley, *Mediaeval India under the Mohammedan Rule*, (Reprint), Delhi, 1994.

LEUR, J. C. Van, *Indonesian Trade and Society: essays in Asian social and Economic History*, The Hague. W. Van Hoeve, 1955.

LOBATO, Alexandre, *Fundamentos da Presença de Portugal na Índia*, Lisboa, 1954.

LOBATO, Alexandre, *Relações Luso-Maratha*, Lisboa, 1965.

LOBO, António Costa, *Memórias de um Soldado da Índia*, INCM, 1987.

LOBO, Francisco Miranda da Costa, *A acção diplomática dos portugueses nos séculos XV e XVI, destinada à realização de descobertas e conquistas*, Lisboa, 1937.

MACEDO, Jorge Borges de, *História diplomática Portuguesa*: constantes e linhas de força, Rev. Nação e Defesa, Lisboa, 1987.

MACLAGAN, Sir Edward, *Os Jesuitas e o Grão Mogol*, Porto, 1964.

MAGALHÃES, Joaquim Romero, 'Vasco da Gama e a Índia' in *Mare Liberum*, nº 16, 1998, pp. 113-132, Comissão Nacional para as Comemorações dos Descobrimentos Portugueses, Lisboa.

MAGALHÃES, José Calvet de, *A Diplomacia Pura*, Bertrand Editora, Lisboa, 1995.

MAGALHÃES, José Calvet de, *Breve história diplomática de Portugal*, 2ª Ed. Europa-América, Lisboa, 1991.

MAJUMDAR, R.C., (Ed) *The History and Culture of the Indian People, The Mughal Empire*, vol. VII, Bhartiya Vidya Bhavan, Bombay, 1974.

MALEKANDATHIL, PIUS, M.C., *Portuguese Cochin and the Maritime Trade of 1500-1663*, (Thesis submitted to the Pondicherry University for the Award of the degree of Doctor of Philisophy in 1998.

MALEKANDATHIL, PIUS, M.C., & MOHAMMED, Jamal, (edited) *The Portuguese, Indian Ocean and European Bridgeheads: Festschrift in Honour of Prof. K.S. Mathew*, Tellicherry, 2001.

MALEKANDATHIL, PIUS, M.C., From Merchant Capitalists to Corsairs: The Response of the Muslim Merchants of Malabar to the Portuguese Commercial Expansion (1498-1600), in *Portuguese Studies Review*, volume 12, no. 1, Winter-Spring, 2004-2005, pp. 75-96.

MANCKE, Elizabeth (Department of History, University of Akron), 'Power, Space, and the Making of Early Modern Empires' paper presented at Ohio State University, in February, 2003.

MANSO, Maria de Deus Beites 'As Ordens Religiosas na Índia Portuguesa de 1498 a 1622' in *Vasco da Gama*, FCG, Lisboa, 1999, vol. III, pp. 71-84.

MARESCA, Adolfo, *La Diplomazia Plurilaterale*, Giuffré, Milão, 1979.

MARTINEZ, Pedro Soares, *Coordenadas da história diplomática de Portugal,* Acad. das Ciências, Lisboa, 1981. (Sep. Memórias Acad. Ciências de Lisboa, Classe de Letras, 22).

MARTINEZ, Pedro Soares, *História diplomática de Portugal,* Verbo, imp. Lisboa 1986.

MARTINS, Armando, *Portugal e o Japão: subsídios para a história diplomática,* Ag. Geral do Ultramar, Lisboa, 1955.

MARTINS, Manuel Gonçalves, *O novo imperialismo e os direitos de Portugal: elementos de diplomacia portuguesa e política internacional,* Associação Académica da Universidade do Minho, Braga, 1985.

MATHEW, K. S., 'Indian Merchants and the Portuguese Trade on the Malabar Coast during the Sixteenth Century', in *Indo-Portuguese History: Old Issues, New Questions, (ed. T.R. de Souza),* Concept Publishing Company, New delhi, 1985.

MATHEW, K. S., 'The First Mercantile Battle in the India Ocean: The Afro-Asian Front Against the Portuguese, (1508-1509)', in *II Seminário Internacional da História Indo-Portuguesa,* IICT-CEHCA, Lisboa, 1985, pp. 185-189.

MATHEW, K. S., 'The Trade in the Indian Ocean and the Portuguese System of Cartaz', in *The First Portugese Colonial Empire,* Malyn Newitt, Exeter Studies in History, University of Exeter, 1986., pp. 69-83.

MATHEW, K. S., *The Portuguese Trade with India in the Sixteenth Century,* New Delhi, 1983.

MATHEW, K. S., *The Portuguese and the Malabar Society during the sixteenth century: a Study of Mutual Interaction,* Lisboa, 1989, (Sep. *Stvdia,* 49).

MATHEW, K.S., (edited) *Indian Ocean and Cultural Interaction (A.D. 1400-1800),* Pondicherry University, 1996.

MATHEW, K. S., *Indo-Portuguese Trade and the Fuggers of Germany,* Manohar, N. Delhi, 1997.

MATOS, Artur Teodoro de, THOMAZ, Luís Filipe F. Reis. (dir.) *A Carreira da Índia e as Rotas dos Estreitos: actas* do VIII Seminário Internacional de História Indo-Portuguesa, Angra do Heroísmo, 1998.

MATTINGLY, Garrett, *Renaissance Diplomacy,* Penguin Books, Baltimore, 1964.

MAX MÜLLER, F., (edited), *The Laws of Manu,* D.K. Publications, Delhi, (2nd ed.) 1996.

MEILINK-ROELOFSZ, Marie Antoinette Petronella, *Asian Trade and European Influence between 1500 and about 1630*. The Hague, 1962.

MENDES A. Lopes, *A Índia Portugueza,* 2 vols., Imp. Nac., Lisboa, 1886.

MENDONÇA, Maria Manuela R. C., *As Relações Externas de Portugal nos finais da Idade Média,* Edições Colibri, Lisboa 1994.

MENON, A. Sreedhara, *A Survey of Kerala History,* Kottayam, 1970.

MENON, K. P. Padmanabha, *A History of Kerala: written, in the form of notes on Visscher's letters from Malabar* (ed. by T. K. Krishna Menon), 4 vols. Cochin Government Press, Ernakulam, 1924-1937.

MORELAND, W. H., *From Akbar to Aurangzeb: A Study in Indian Economic History,* first published, 1923, (reprinted), New Delhi, 1994.

MORELAND, W. H., *India at the Death of Akbar,* First published, 1920, (reprinted), New Delhi 1990.

MORENO, Humberto Baquero, *O papel da diplomacia portuguesa no Tratado de Tordesilhas,* Faculdade de Letras, (Sep. de *Revista da Faculdade de Letras,* 2ª Série, vol. XII,) Porto, 1995.

MORGENTHAU, Hans J., *Politics Among Nations: The Struggle for Power and Peace,* Alfred A. Knoff, New York, 1978.

MORRIS, W., & Morris, M., *Morris Dictionary of Word and Phrase Origins,* Harper & Row, 1988.

MUIR, Ramasay, *Mare liberum the freedom of the seas London*: Hodder & Stoughton, London, 1917.

MUMELIN, Ragnar, *The Beginnings of Diplomacy,* Oxford University Press, London, 1950.

NAMBIAR, O. K., *The Kunjalis: Admirals of Calicut,* Delhi, 1963.

NAYEEM, M. A. *External Relations of the Bijapur Kingdom, 1489-1686,* Hyderabad, 1974.

NEWITT, Malyn, D.D., *The First Portugese Colonial Empire,* Exeter Studies in History, University of Exeter, 1986.

NICOLSON, Harold, *Diplomacy,* Oxford University Press, 1969.

NICOLSON, Harold, *The Evolution of Diplomatic Method,* Constable & Co. Ltd., 1954.

NUMELIN, Ragnar, *The Beginning of Diplomacy,* Oxford University Press, London, 1950.

OATEN, E.F., *European Travellers in India*, 2nd ed., New Delhi, 2000.

OGG, David, *Europe in the Seventeenth Century*, Adam and Charles Black, London, 1948.

OLIVEIRA, Julieta Teixeira Marques de, *Veneza e Portugal no século XVI subsídios para a sua história,* Comissão Nacional para as Comemorações dos Descobrimentos Portugueses, Lisboa imp. Lisboa, 2000.

OLIVEIRA, Luís Soares de, *História diplomática: o período europeu 1580-1917*, P.F. Pedro Ferreira, Lisboa, 1994.

OM PRAKASH, 'European Commercial Enterprise in pre-colonial India: The Portuguese in India, 1500-1640,' in *The New Cambridge History of India,* part. II, Cambridge University Press, 1998. pp. 23-71.

OM PRAKASH, 'The Portuguese Indian Economy in the first Half of the Seventeenth Century' in in *Vasco da Gama,* vol. I, FCG, Lisboa, 1999, pp.67-74.

OM PRAKASH, (Ed.) *Portuguese in India*, 2 vols., Anmol Publications Pvt. Ltd, New Delhi, 2002.

PANIKKAR, Kavalam Madhava, *Malabar and the Portuguese*, Bombay, 1929.

PANIKKAR, K. M., *Malabar and the Dutch: Being the History of the Fall of the Nayar Power in Malabar,* (Foreword by Evan Cotton), D. B. Taraporevala Sons, cop. Bombay,1931.

PANIKKAR, K. M., *India and the Indian Ocean.* 2nd Ed. George Allen & Unwin, London, 1946.

PANIKKAR, K. M., *India and the Indian history,* 2nd. ed., George Allen and Unwin, London, 1951.

PANIKKAR, K. M., *Asia and the Western Dominance, A Survey of the Vasco da Gama Epoch of Asian History*, 1498-1945, London, 1953.

PANIKKAR, K. M., *A History of Kerala 1498-1801,* Annamalainagar, 1960.

PEARSON, M. N., 'Indigenous Dominance in Colonial Economy-The Goa Rendas 1600-1670', in *Mare Luso-indicum,* Librarie Droz, Geneva, 1973, pp. 61-73.

PEARSON, M.N., *Merchants and Rulers in Gujarat: The Response to the Portuguese in the Sixteenth Century,* Munshi Ram Manoharlal, New Delhi, 1976,

PEARSON, M. N. and Blair B. Kling, (edited) *The Age of Partnership: Europeans in Asia before dominion,* University Press of Hawaii, 1979.

PEARSON, M.N., *Coastal Western India: Studies from the Portuguese Records,* Concept, New Delhi, 1981.

PEARSON, M.N., and DAS GUPTA, Ashin (edited by), *India and the Indian Ocean 1500-1800* , Oxford University Press, Calcutta, 1987.

PEARSON, M.N., *The Portuguese in India: The New Cambridge History of India,* Cambridge University Press, Delhi, 1987.

PERES, Damião, *História dos Descobrimentos Portugueses,* Porto, 1943.

PIERIS, P. E., *Ceylon: the Portuguese era: being a history of the island for the period 1505-1658* 2 vols .The Colombo Apothecaries Co., 1913-1914.

PINTO, Eduardo Augusto Vera-Cruz - *Comparar a diplomacia portuguesa no séc. XIV com a diplomacia do séc. XV,* Lisboa, 1984.

PINTO, Eduardo Vera-Cruz - *Comparar a diplomacia portuguesa no séc. XIV com a diplomacia do séc. XV* , Lisboa, 1984. - Relatório de mestrado em história diplomática.

PISSURLENKAR, P.S.S., 'Fragmentos Históricos' in *BIVG,* n° 47, Goa, 1940.

PISSURLENKAR, P.S.S., 'Portuguese e Maratha' in *BIVG,* n°s 1-6, Goa, 1926-1929.

PISSURLENKAR, P.S.S., 'Tentativas dos Portugueses para a ocupação do Concão', separata dos *Anais,* Lisboa, 1955.

PISSURLENKAR, Panduronga S.S., *Roteiro dos Arquivos da Índia Portuguesa,* Tipografia Rangel, Bastorá, 1955.

POONEN, T. I., *A Survey of the Rise of the Dutch Power in Malabar: 1603-78,* (with a foreword by K. Zachariah), St. Joseph's Industrial School Press, Trichinopoly, 1948.

POPE, Ethel M., *India in Portuguese Literature,* Tipografia Rangel, Bastorá, 1937.

PRESTAGE, Edgar, *A embaixada de Tristão de Mendonça Furtado à Holanda em 1641: primeiras embaixadas de el-rei D. João IV: com documentos elucidativos,* Imp. da Universidade, Coimbra, 1920. (Sep. *O Instituto,* 67)

PRESTAGE, Edgar, *Chapters in Anglo-Portuguese Relations,* Voss and Michael, Watford, 1935.

PRESTAGE, Edgar, *Duas cartas escritas de Inglaterra a el-rei D. João IV,* por António de Sousa de Macedo, Academia das Sciencias de Lisboa, Lisboa, 1916.

PRESTAGE, Edgar, *Primeiras embaixadas del-rei D. João IV, Relação da embaixada do Padre Mestre Inácio Mascarenhas à Catalunha em 1641,* Imp. da Universidade, Coimbra, 1926. (Sep. *O Instituto,* 73, 5)

RADWAN, A. B., *The Dutch in Western India,* 1601-1632, Calcutta, 1978.

RAJA, P K. S., *Medieval Kerala,* Calicut, 1966.

RÁKÓCZI, István, Nação Barbada: «Alguns Marginais Europeus no Estado da Índia» in *Encontros sobre Portugal e a Índia,* Fundação Oriente, Lisboa, 2000, pp. 187-194.

RAMOS, João de Deus (edited), *Estudos Luso-Orientais* (Séculos XIII-XIX) *Subsídios para a História Portuguesa,* volume 28, Academia Portuguesa da História, Lisboa, 1996.

RAMOS, João de Deus, *História das Relações Diplomáticas entre Portugal e a China,* (1721-1725), Instituto Cultural de Macau, 1991.

RAO, N. Lakhminarayan, *The Nayakas of Keladi, in Vijayanagar Sixcentenary Comm. Volume,* Dharwar, 1936.

RAWLINSON, H.G., *India: A Concise History of the Indian People,* (First Published, 1938) Rep. D.K. Publisheres, New Delhi, 1994.

REGO. António da Silva, *A Presença de Portugal em Macau,* AGC., Lisboa, 1946.

RIBEIRO, V., *Fatalidade Histórica da ilha de Ceilão,* Lisboa, 1971.

RUBIÉS, Joan-Pau 'Giovanni di Buongrazzia's letter to his father concerning his participation in the second expedition of Vasco da Gama (1502-1503), *Mare Liberum,* 16, 1998, pp. 87-112.

RUBIÈS, Joan-Pau, *Travel and Ethnology in the Renaissance: South India through European Eyes, 1250-1625,* Cambridge University Press, 2002.

SALDANHA, António Vasconcelos de, 'Os Portugueses no Oriente. Um Exercício de Poder: Paz, Tratados e Conflito Contido', in *Vasco da Gama,* vol. I, FCG, Lisboa, 1999, p. 335.

SAMPAIO, Luís Teixeira de, *Arquivo histórico do Ministério dos Negócios Estrangeiros: (subsídios para o estudo da história da diplomacia portuguesa)* Imp. da Universidade, Coimbra, 1925. (Sep. *Arquivo de História e Bibliogarfia*).

SAMPAIO, Luís Teixeira de, *Estudos históricos,* pref. e notas de Eduardo Brazão, palavras prévias José Calvet de Magalhães. M.N.E., Lisboa, 1984.

SARKAR, Sir Jadunath, *History of Aurangzeb,* vol. I, (1618-1659), M.S.C Sarkar & Sons, Calcutta, 1924. Chap. XI, Vol. 1., 2nd, rev. Ed. 1925.

SASTRI, K.A. Nilakanta, *A History of South India from Prehistoric Times to the Fall of Vijayanagar,* Oxford University Press, Bombay, 1966.

SCAMMELL, V., 'England, Portugal and the Estado da India C. 1500-1635', in *Actas II Seminário Internacional de História Indo-Portuguesa,* IICT, CEHCA, Lisboa, 1985.

SCHAMA Simon, *The Embarrassment of riches: an interpretation of Dutch culture in the golden age,* University of California Press, London 1988

SCHELLING, Thomas C. *The Strategy of Conflict.* 2nd ed. Harvard University Press. London, 1980.

SEN, Surendranath, ed., *Indian Travels of Thevenot and Careri,* New Delhi, 1949.

SERRÃO, Joaquim Veríssimo, *O Tempo dos Filipes em Portugal e no Brasil,* (1580-1668), Colibri, Lisboa, 1994.

SERRÃO, Joel (dirigido por), *Dicionário de História de Portugal,* volume 1/ A-D, Iniciativa Editoriais, 1971.

SERJEANT, Robert Bertram, *The Portuguese Off the South Arabian Coast, Hadrami chronicles,* The Clarendon Press, Oxford, 1963.

SEWEL, Robert, *A Forgotten Empire,* London, 1900.

SHARMA, M. H. Rama, *The History of the Vijayanagar Empire: Beginning and Expansion.* 2 volumes. Popular Prakashan, Bombay, 1978.

SHASTRY, Bhagamandala Seetharama, "The Portuguese Commercial Relations with Bijapur in the Seventeenth century", in *Essays in Goan History,* (ed.) Teotonio R. De Souza, (ed.), Concept Publishing Company, N. Delhi, 1989. pp. 39-47.

SHASTRI, B.S., «A Note on Portuguese Shivaji Relation» in *Chhatrapati Shivaji Coronation Tercentenary Commemoration Volume,* Bombay, 1974-1975.

SHASTRY, B.S., *Studies in indo-portuguese history,* 1st ed. I.B.H. Prakashana, Bangalore, 1981.

SHIRDOKAR, P.P., "Portuguese-Dutch Relations in the East (1580-1663) vis-à-vis Indian Peninsula", *Stvdia, 48,* pp- 123-157.

SHUKLA, Dinkar, 'Indian Diplomacy down the Ages', in *India Perspective,* July, 2002. New Delhi, 2002, pp. 17-19.

SILVA, Isabel Maria Botelho de Gusmão Dias Sarreira Cid da, *O livro das plantas de todas as fortalezas, cidades e povoações do Estado da India Oriental de António Bocarro:* Estudo histórico, codicológico e paleográfico, transcrição e índices, Lisboa 1988. (Contém bibliografia. Tese de mestrado em Paleografia e Diplomática apresentada a Fac. de Letras da Univ. de Lisboa).

SILVA, Richard Chandra da, *The Portuguese in Ceylon, 1617-1638,* Colombo, 1972.

SMITH, Ronald Bishop, *The first age of the Portuguese Embassies, Navigations and Peregrinations to the kingdoms and islands of Southeast Asia (1509-1521),* Decatur Press, Bethesda, 1968.

SMITH, Ronald Bishop, *The first age of the Portuguese embassies, navigations and Peregrinations to the Ancient kingdoms of Cambay and Bengal (1500-1521),* Decatur Press, Bethesda, 1969.

SMITH, Ronald Bishop, *The first age of the Portuguese Embassies, Navigations and Peregrinations in Persia (1507-1524),* Decatur Press, Bethesda, 1970.

SMITH, Vincent A., *The Oxford history of India: from the Earliest Times to the end of 1911,* 2nd ed., Clarendon Press, Oxford, 1923.

SOUSA, Alfredo Botelho de, *Subsídios para a História Militar Marítima da Índia,* vol. 1, (1585-1605), Lisboa, 1930.

SOUSA, Carlos Hermenegildo de, *A Aliança Anglo-Portuguesa,* Livraria Portugália, Lisboa, 1939.

SOUSA, Fr. João de, *Vestigios da lingoa arabica em Portugal ou lexicon etymológico das palavras, e nomes portuguezes que tem origem arabica composto....* João de Sousa, anot. Fr. Joze de Santo Antonio Moura. Typ. da Academia Real das Sciencias, Lisboa, 1830.

SOUSA, Francisco de, S.J., *Oriente conquistado a Jesus Cristo pelos Padres da Companhia de Jesus da Província de Goa,* Lello & Irmão, Porto, 1979.

SOUZA, George Bryan, *The Survival of Empire: Portuguese Trade and Society in China and the South China Sea, 1630-1754,* Cambridge University Press, 1986.

SOUZA, Teotonio R. de, *Medieval Goa, a Socio-economic History,* New Delhi, 1979.

SOUZA, Teotonio R. de, 'The Voiceless in Goan Historiography' in *Indo-Portuguese History: Sources & Problems,* (ed. John Correia-Affonso), Oxford University Press, Bombay, 1981, pp. 114-131.

SOUZA, Teotonio R. de, (ed.) *Indo-Portuguese History: Old Issues, New Questions,* Concept Publishing Company, New Delhi, 1985.

SOUZA, Teotonio R. de, 'Embassies and Surrogates: Case-Study of a Malacca Embassy to Siam in 1595', in the *Indica,* Journal of the Heras Institute of Indian History and Culture- (Separata) no. 49, pp. 39-45, Bombay, 1989.

SOUZA, Teotonio R. de, (ed.) *Essays in Goan History,* Concept Publishing Company, N. Delhi, 1989.

SOUZA, Teotonio R. de, & Garcia, José Manuel, (ed.) *Vasco da Gama, Índia,* (Acta de Seminário realizado em Paris) 3 vols, FCG, Lisboa, 1999.

STEENSGAARD, Niels, *Carracks, Caravans and Companies: The Structural Crisis in the European-Asian Trade in the 17th Century,* Copenhagen, 1973.

STEIN, Burton, *Vijayangara, - The New Cambridge History of India,* Cambridge University Press, Cambridge, 2005.

STEPHEN, Jayaseela, *Portuguese in the Tamil Coast: Historical Explorations in Commerce and Culture (1507-1749),* Navajothi Publishing House, Navajothi 1998.

SUBRAHMANYAM, Sanjay, (edited) *Merchant Networks in the Early Modern World,* Aldershot, Brookfield, Great Britain, 1996.

SUBRAHMANYAM, Sanjay, (edited) *Merchants, Markets and the State in Early Modern India.* Oxford University Press, Delhi, 1990.

SUBRAHMANYAM, Sanjay, *Improvising Empire: Portuguese Trade and Settlement in the Bay of Bengal 1500-1700,* Oxford University Press, Delhi 1990.

SUBRAHMANYAM, Sanjay, *The Career and Legend of Vasco da Gama*: Cambridge University Press, London, 1997.

SUBRAHMANYAM, Sanjay, *The Portuguese Empire in Asia, 1500-1700: A Political and Economic history,* Longman, London, 1993.

SUBRAHMANYAM, Sanjay, *The Political Economy of Commerce, Southern India 1500-1650,* Cambridge University Press, Cambridge, 1990.

SUBRAHMANYAM, Sanjay, 'Making India Gama, The Project of Dom Aires da Gama (1519) and its meaning' in *Mare Liberum,* vol. I6, pp. 33-55.

TRACY, James D., (Edited), *The Political Economy of Merchant Empires: State Power and World Trade, 1350-1750,* Cambridge University Press, 1991.

TRIPATHI, R.P., *The Rise and Fall of the Mughal Empire,* Allahabad, 1969.

THUCIDIDES, *History of the Peloponnesian War,* William Benton, Chicago. 1952.

VARMA, D.C., *History of Bijapur,* Kumar Brothers, New Delhi, 1974.

VEEN, Ernst van, *Decay or defeat?*: An inquiry into the Portuguese Decline in Asia, 1580-1645, Research School of Asian, African and Amerindian Studies, Universiteit Leiden, Leiden, 2000.

VILLIERS, J., "The Estado da India in the Southeast Asia, in *The Portuguese Colonial Empire,* (Ed) Malyn Newitt, Exeter, 1986, pp. 48-49.

VELUTHAT, Kesavan, *The Political Structure of Early Medieval South India,* Orient Longman, Delhi, 1993.

WEBSTER'S *Third New International Dictionary,* G&C, Meriam Co, USA, 1966.

WHEELER, Mortimer, *The Cambridge History of India,* Cambridge University Press, Cambridge, 1953.

WHITEWAY, R. S., *The Rise of Portuguese Power in India,* New Delhi, 1979.

WILLS, John E, *Embassies and Illusions:Dutch and Portuguese envoys* to K'ang-hsi, 1666-1687, Council on East Asian Studies, Harvard University, Harvard, 1984.

WINIUS, G. Davison, *The Fatal History of Portuguese Ceylon, Transition to Dutch Rule,* Harvard, 1971.

WINIUS, George D, 'The Shadow Empire of Goa in the Bay of Bengal' in *Itinerario,* Vol. VII, 1983.

WINIUS, George D., 'Jewels and Jewel Traders in Portuguese Asia', a Seminar paper presented in the IV International Seminar on Indo-Portuguese History, 1985, at *Junta de Investigação Científica Tropical,* Lisboa, 1985.

WINIUS, George D., *The Black Legend of Portuguese India: Diogo do Couto, his Contemporaries and the soldado prático: a contribution to the study of political corruption in the empires of early modern Europe,* Concept Publishing Company, New Delhi, 1985.

WINIUS, George D., & Blussé, Leonard, "The Origin and Rhythm of Dutch Aggression against the *Estado da Índia" in Indo-Portuguese History: Old Issues, New Questions,* (Edited Teotonio R. D'Souza), Concept, New Delhi, 1985, pp. 73-83.

WINIUS, George D., *Francisco Rodrigues da Silveira, the Forgotten soldado prático*, IICT-CEHCA, Lisboa, 1985.

WINIUS, George D. & VINK, Marcus P. M., *The Merchant-Warrior pacified: the VOC (the Dutch East India Company) and its changing political economy in India*, Oxford University Press, Delhi, 1994.

WINIUS, George D., 'Private Trading in Portuguese Asia: a substantial will-o'-the-wisp' in *Vasco da Gama*, FCG, Lisboa, 1999, vol. II, pp. 91-100.

WISE, Bernhard R. *The Freedom of the seas*, Darling & Son, London, 1915.

Seminar papers and Historical Magazines

A diplomacia na história de Portugal, Actas do Colóquio a Diplomacia na História. Academia Portuguesa da História. Lisboa, 1990.

Boletim da Sociedade de Geografia de Lisboa, Imprensa Nacional, 1882, and continued then after.

Boletim do Instituto Menezes Bragança, Panjim, Goa.

Boletim do Instituto Vasco da Gama. Imprensa Nacional, Nova Goa, 1926-1961. Trimestral.

Cultura: Revista de História e Teoria das Ideias, (II Série) nº 15, Universidade Nova de Lisboa, Lisboa, 2002.

India Perspective, July, 2002. New Delhi, 2002, pp. 17-19.

Mare Liberum, Revista de História dos Mares, Comissão Nacional para as Comemorações dos Descobrimentos Portugueuses, Lisboa, Nºs 1-20.

II SEMINÁRIO Internacional da História Indo-Portuguesa, (Estudos de História e Cartografia Antiga, IICT-CEHCA, Lisboa, 1985.

O ORIENTE português: Revista da Comissão Arqueológica da Índia Portuguesa, Imp. Nacional, Nova Goa, 1904-1911.

O ORIENTE portuguez: semanario dedicado aos interesses portuguezes da China e Oceania, Administração A. V. da Silva, Macau, 1892.

SEMINÁRIO diplomático A diplomacia portuguesa: perspectivas e prioridades, Ministério dos Negócios Estrangeiros. Instituto Diplomático. Instituto Diplomático, Lisboa, 2000.

STVDIA, Vols. 1-54. IICT-CEHCA, Lisboa, 1958-2000.